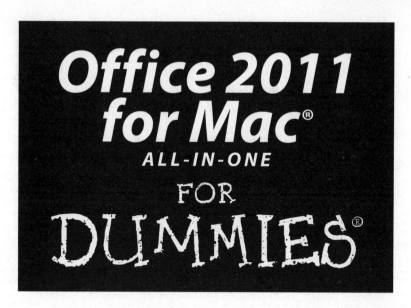

Office 2011 for Mac®
ALL-IN-ONE
FOR DUMMIES®

by Geetesh Bajaj and James Gordon
Microsoft MVPs

WILEY

John Wiley & Sons, Inc.

Office 2011 for Mac® All-in-One For Dummies®

Published by
John Wiley & Sons, Inc.
111 River Street
Hoboken, NJ 07030-5774

www.wiley.com

WILEY

About the Authors

Geetesh Bajaj has been creating Microsoft Office documents, presentations, and templates for over a decade now. His activities span three fronts:

✦ Running Indezine.com, a presentation related Web site.

✦ Authoring books on PowerPoint and other Microsoft Office programs.

✦ Training enterprise customers to create and deliver better presentations.

Geetesh has been a Microsoft-awarded Most Valuable Professional (MVP) for over ten years, and he is based out of Secunderabad, India.

James Gordon is a lead programmer/analyst at the University at Buffalo where he also teaches workshops on Microsoft Office and other technologies. For more than ten years, Microsoft has presented its Most Valuable Professional (MVP) award to James for his contributions to technical communities.

James has written several programs, including the popular InsertPicture add-in that runs in PowerPoint for Mac, and he's a member and past-president of ProMac Users Group, Inc. in Buffalo, NY.

Dedication

To Steve Jobs, Bill Gates, Mac loyalists, and switchers everywhere.

Authors' Acknowledgments

We thank the divine, and other mere mortals with divine abilities.

Special thanks to everyone at Wiley for helping us put this book together. Acquisitions editor Kyle Looper and project editor Jean Nelson kept everything on track. Thanks go to the editorial team, including copy editor Virginia Sanders and technical editor Echo Swinford. Like Geetesh and James, Echo is a Microsoft PowerPoint MVP.

Thanks also to SharePoint MVP Uday Ethirajulu and Microsoft Messenger MVP Jonathan Kay for graciously co-authoring files so we could get screen shots. Thanks go to our families and friends for allowing us to focus on our writing without deserting us. We express our appreciation to them all.

Geetesh wishes to thank his office staff who helped him take the time off to write this book as well as the amazing bunch of other Microsoft MVPs who are too numerous to be listed here.

Jim wishes to extend special thanks to the University at Buffalo Libraries for allowing leave to work on the book. The University at Buffalo is truly one of the best places to work or attend university.

We thank the Macintosh Business Unit of Microsoft, who created the subject matter of the book, and Microsoft Corporation for the awesome MVP program, without which it is unlikely the authors would been able to meet and collaborate. And we also thank Apple for creating an enriching OS platform.

Finally, both the authors thank each other!

Publisher's Acknowledgments

We're proud of this book; please send us your comments at http://dummies.custhelp.com. For other comments, please contact our Customer Care Department within the U.S. at 877-762-2974, outside the U.S. at 317-572-3993, or fax 317-572-4002.

Some of the people who helped bring this book to market include the following:

Acquisitions, Editorial, and Vertical Websites

Project Editor: Jean Nelson

Acquisitions Editor: Kyle Looper

Copy Editor: Virginia Sanders

Technical Editor: Echo Swinford

Editorial Manager: Kevin Kirschner

Vertical Websites Project Manager: Laura Moss-Hollister

Vertical Websites Assistant Project Manager: Jenny Swisher

Vertical Websites Associate Producers: Josh Frank, Marilyn Hummel, Douglas Kuhn, and Shawn Patrick

Editorial Assistant: Amanda Graham

Sr. Editorial Assistant: Cherie Case

Cartoons: Rich Tennant (www.the5thwave.com)

Composition Services

Project Coordinator: Patrick Redmond

Layout and Graphics: Samantha K. Cherolis, Timothy C. Detrick, Joyce Haughey

Proofreaders: John Greenough, Evelyn C. Wellborn

Indexer: Broccoli Information Management

Publishing and Editorial for Technology Dummies

Richard Swadley, Vice President and Executive Group Publisher

Andy Cummings, Vice President and Publisher

Mary Bednarek, Executive Acquisitions Director

Mary C. Corder, Editorial Director

Publishing for Consumer Dummies

Kathleen Nebenhaus, Vice President and Executive Publisher

Composition Services

Debbie Stailey, Director of Composition Services

Contents at a Glance

Table of Contents

Introduction

Welcome to *Office 2011 for Mac All-in-One For Dummies*. Long-time Mac aficionados as well as recent switchers and newbies alike will discover valuable tips, find advice, and learn from how-to-do-it instructions throughout the pages of this book.

Office 2011 has some dazzling new features. This book explains everything in plain English and is arranged so that you can easily find information about any Office topic. Use it to broaden your knowledge and make your documents, workbooks, e-mails, and presentations better than ever.

We understand that many people have been using Microsoft Office for years but may be new to the Mac. Most of the features in Microsoft Office applications are the same on both the Windows and Macintosh platforms, which makes switching easier.

How to Use This Book

Turn to the Table of Contents or use the Index to locate the page number for the topic you're interested in. You'll find basic information as well as in-depth information. Rather than reading this book from front to back, we make it easy for you to look up specific topics and jump right in.

Throughout this book are screen shots, step-by-step instructions, tips, and cautionary warnings to keep you out of trouble so that your experience using Microsoft Office will be pleasant, productive, and sometimes even delightful.

How This Book Is Organized

This book is organized in five self-contained minibooks. Each minibook is described in the following sections.

Book 1: Introducing Office 2011

We start by covering the many tools and features that are common to all or more than one of the Office applications. For example, pictures, text formatting, charts, and diagrams work in the same way across the applications. Rather than repeat these common features for each application, we save time and pages by covering these common features in depth in Book I.

Book II: Word 2011

In this minibook, we show you how you can use Word's amazing capabilities to do everything from writing letters to printing envelopes. Along the way, you discover how to mail merge from a database and format your fonts. We also show you how to create newsletters in Word and take notes of your meetings, including audio notes. Have fun!

Book III: Excel 2011

Excel is chock-full of interesting stuff you can do. This minibook covers the basics and then shows you how to do some advanced stuff with step-by-step instructions. We take you on the journey of understanding cells and data validation, and we help you with lists, forms, charts, tables, and the new solver.

Book IV: PowerPoint 2011

You can build presentations with pizazz and deliver them with confidence and professionalism with the help of the PowerPoint minibook. Not only do we show you how to effectively use PowerPoint, we've included some of the most powerful tips for helping you build and deliver great presentations.

Book V: Outlook 2011

Outlook is your one-stop shop for e-mail, contact management, calendars, notes, and tasks. This minibook helps you improve your office and home productivity with explanations on everything from setting up regular e-mail accounts to using Outlook with Microsoft Exchange and Messenger.

Conventions Used in This Book

The *For Dummies* books by Wiley are famous for their easy readability and wonderful consistency. This book follows the same *For Dummies* format. We try to make things as simple as possible. Sometimes we ask you to type commands and click the mouse in particular sequences. When we do that, we use the following conventions:

+ **When you need to type:** We use a **bold** font to tell you what to type. For example, if we say, "Type **22** and then press the Return key" we want you to type the number 22 and then press the Return key on the keyboard.

+ **When you need to choose a command from a menu:** When we give you a specific sequence of menu commands to use, it looks like this: Choose File➪Share➪Save to SkyDrive. In this example, click the File menu, choose the Share item, and then choose the Save to SkyDrive option.

✦ **When you need to choose a command from the Ribbon:** Sometimes, you need to use the Ribbon rather than the menu bar. When you choose a command on the Ribbon, we let you know what tab to click (if it isn't already selected), what group the command is in, and finally what command to click. For example, "Click the Ribbon's Home tab. In the Font group, click the Bold button to apply bold formatting."

✦ **When you need to press a key combination:** Keyboard commands involve pressing two or more keys at once. Then you let go of all of the keys. We use a hyphen (-) to chain together the keys to press. (*Note:* The Command key, ⌘, is the same as the Apple key.) An instruction to "Press ⌘-Shift-3" means to hold the ⌘ key down along with the Shift key and press the number 3 to activate the action, and then let go of all the keys after the action takes place. Incidentally, if you do press ⌘-Shift-3, a picture of your current screen will be saved to your computer's desktop.

✦ **When you need to press a key and click, or you need to right-click:** To show that you need to press a key when you click, we use a hyphen like in key combinations, such as "⌘-click" or "Shift-click." If your Mac has a single-button mouse, when we say right-click, you should Control-click.

If you're using a laptop, you may need to press the Fn key in addition to the keys we tell you to press.

If you're switching from Windows to a Mac, Apple has a wonderful table that shows what you used in Windows and the equivalent action on your Mac at `www.apple.com/support/switch101/switcher/2`.

Icons Used in This Book

The icons in this book are important visual cues for information you might not want to miss.

This icon indicates special timesaving advice and other helpful suggestions.

This icon alerts you to pay close attention because every once in a while we might discuss a topic that if not followed carefully might cause problems.

Of course, we expect you to remember absolutely everything you read in this book. You'll have to take part in an online exam that becomes part of your permanent record. Just kidding! We use this icon to point out important info for you to keep in mind.

Not everyone is a true geek, so we've identified some topics as a bit on the complex side or that most users might find daunting or uninteresting. Information with this icon isn't critical to your understanding of the topic.

 Several excellent features of Microsoft Office are available only in Macintosh versions. If you're new to the Mac and are already familiar with Office for Windows, look for this icon to alert you to features that may be new to you. If you work in a cross-platform environment, be alert to the fact that features marked with this icon work only on Macs.

 Although we could have put this icon on half of the topics covered in this book, we use the icon to alert you to major new features introduced in Office 2011.

Where to Go from Here

Turn to just about any page or flip through the book. We're sure you'll find a lot of useful stuff. The Table of Contents and Index are perfect places to get your feet wet finding specific topics.

The Help system in Office 2011 is another excellent resource. Sometimes we will point to specific topics in Help so that you can see just how good Office Help is. We also refer to resources that are created and maintained by Microsoft MVPs (Most Valuable Professionals).

Microsoft MVP

The MVP program was established by Microsoft to recognize "the best and brightest from technical communities around the world" according to the Microsoft MVP Web site at http://mvp.support.microsoft.com. MVPs are volunteers and don't receive compensation from Microsoft and are independent from Microsoft Corporation.

The authors and this book's Technical Editor have received MVP awards for many years. We encourage you to participate in user groups and online activities. People who regularly contribute high-quality information to the community at large may eventually become candidates to receive MVP distinction.

Book I

Introducing Office 2011

The 5th Wave   By Rich Tennant

"The odd thing is he always insists on using the latest version of Office."

Contents at a Glance

Chapter 1: Going Over the Preliminaries

In This Chapter

- Choosing an Office suite
- Migrating and upgrading Office
- Installing Office the right way
- Using AutoUpdate
- Removing Office properly
- Discovering additional tools
- Storing and sharing documents in the clouds

Mac users almost always expect to lay their hands on the best, fastest, easiest-to-use, and most reliable hardware and software that "just works." And because Office 2011 for Mac is clearly a product that has a huge following, we know that expectations from this large base of users is very high! Fortunately, there's plenty in this new release of Office to address those expectations and to be very happy about. So as we take you through the new features and the consistent, existing options, be prepared to go on a journey of discovery. If there's just one thing that we want to do through this book, it's to show you how you can work better with Office 2011 for Mac.

You may or may not have heard about the trend to collaborate, the Ribbon, sharing in "the cloud," and other new technologies. Don't worry if all that sounds vague. We do know that you simply want to know the best way to get your everyday work done. We help you overcome any fears you might have about upgrading and then show you around Office 2011.

Jumping into Office 2011

The first thing you need to know about software you're considering is the system requirements. Usually these are pretty technical, but for Office 2011, all you need is an Intel-based Mac with Mac OS X Leopard 10.5.9 (or later; this includes Mac OS X Snow Leopard 10.6). Simple!

Next comes the decision about which edition of Office is the right one for you. There's a free, online-only edition; a Home and Student Edition; and a Home and Business Edition from which to choose. For large organizations, a Volume License Edition is also available. We discuss all these editions in just a bit.

Deciding whether you should upgrade or switch

We think that if you have an Intel processor–based Mac, there's really no question at all about whether to upgrade or switch. Office 2011 is a must-have upgrade and is by far the best version of Office ever released for the Mac. If you're switching from a version of Office for Windows, Office 2011 will feel familiar to you regardless of which version of Office you are switching from. Office 2011 introduces the Ribbon to the Mac but doesn't do away with the older-style toolbars and menus. Speaking of older, if your Mac is PowerPC based, you have to stay with Office 2004 and/or Office 2008 or use the free, online, browser-based SkyDrive version of Microsoft Office.

Choosing the right edition

You can choose among several editions of Office 2011. Each version has a different set of applications and features, as well as a different price. The following list helps you pick the edition that's right for your purposes:

✦ **Home and Student Edition:** This version comes with complete editions of Microsoft Word, Excel, PowerPoint, Messenger, Microsoft Query, Visual Basic for Applications (VBA), and Silverlight. In addition, you get some nifty new fonts. Purchasers of Home and Student Edition are entitled to use the free templates, add-ins, sounds, backgrounds, clip art, and other materials from Microsoft's extensive online offerings. Home and Student Edition users can also store and share documents on Microsoft's SkyDrive Web site. Product validation is required.

✦ **Home and Business Edition:** In addition to everything included with Home and Student Edition, the Home and Business Edition comes with the Microsoft Outlook e-mail and organizer program and the ability to use the SharePoint portal server, a file server often used by large businesses.

✦ **Volume License Edition:** Purchasers of large quantities of Office 2011 may save considerable amounts of money by purchasing under the volume license program. Many universities, colleges, and schools take advantage of this program to offer free or low cost Office 2011 to employees, faculty, staff, and students.

✦ **Limited time trial:** This is not a separate version of the product, but a test version. After using this version for the trial period, you should know whether you plan to purchase Office 2011. To purchase, all you need is a product key, so you don't have to reinstall anything if you decide to keep Office 2011. If you decide not to keep the trial version, be sure to follow our instructions for removing Office in the "Using additional tools" sidebar in this chapter.

✦ **SkyDrive Edition (free):** SkyDrive is the name of a Microsoft Web site where you can upload, share, and edit documents. On SkyDrive, Microsoft offers lightweight editions of Word, Excel, PowerPoint, and OneNote for free online to compete head-to-head with other free applications such as Google Docs, OpenOffice, and Lotus Symphony. In addition, the SkyDrive versions of Office applications work as a seamless complement to the desktop versions of Office 2011 for Mac.

Being online, SkyDrive requires no installation. There's no software to download or install other than your Web browser, which may already be installed as part of your Mac OS X. SkyDrive editions of Office applications run equally well in Apple Safari or Mozilla Firefox. We discuss SkyDrive more in Chapter 4 of this minibook.

Choosing a language

The suite of Office for Mac applications is available in several languages. In the United States, you most likely will encounter the English and Spanish language versions. If you want the entire Office interface in French, for instance, you need to obtain the French localized version. Most major languages are supported, but not right-to-left languages such as Arabic and Hebrew. Microsoft is very aware that there's a large market for right-to-left language versions of Office for the Mac, and it's working with Apple on a solution.

Upgrading from Previous Versions of Office

For the most part, you can expect that upgrading from any previous version of Office will be trouble-free on your Mac. Your new Office suite is fully compatible with your old documents and file formats. However, the Home and Student Edition of Office 2011 doesn't come with Outlook or any other e-mail client. If you've been using Microsoft Entourage, the older e-mail client that has been part of previous Office suites on the Mac, you can continue to use Entourage along with Office 2011 by simply not removing Entourage during your install of Office 2011. (If you accidentally remove Entourage, you can do a custom install from your old Office installer and choose to install just Entourage, and then you can allow the updates to install.)

If you aren't upgrading to Outlook, you can still use the default Apple Mail program that's included as part of your Mac OS X.

Migrating from Office for Windows

Because the file formats for Word, Excel, and PowerPoint are identical on both Macs and PCs, no file conversions are needed. With very few exceptions, after you copy your files from your PC and move them to your Mac, you can simply open your documents and templates in Office 2011. In fact, with Office 2011 on the Mac, and with the newest Office 2010 on Windows, Microsoft has taken rapid strides to make sure that compatibility between Mac and Windows versions is more seamless than it has ever been.

Files that contain properly written add-ins and macros should also work. Macros and add-ins that use Windows platform-specific code don't work, but you usually can modify them to work in Office 2011.

Migrating Publisher files

Microsoft Publisher files cannot be opened directly in Office 2011 for Mac. You need to convert these files to Word (.docx) format using Microsoft Office on a PC. To convert a Publisher document in Office 2010 on Windows, do the following:

1. **Open the document you want to convert using Microsoft Publisher 2010 for Windows.**
2. **Press Ctrl-A to select all the content.**
3. **Press Ctrl-C to copy all the content to the Windows Clipboard.**
4. **Open a new, blank Microsoft Word 2010 document.**
5. **Press Ctrl-V to paste the Clipboard contents into Word.**
6. **Click the Save button on the Quick Access Toolbar.**

   The resulting Word (.docx) file can now be moved to your Mac.

When you open the Word file from Windows on your Mac, the result won't be perfect. You have to re-create the links between the text boxes (we cover how to do this in Book II, Chapter 8), and the layout may need tweaking, but this is the best way we found to migrate Publisher files.

Migrating OneNote files

Microsoft OneNote doesn't come with Office for Mac. In Office for Mac, similar functionality is provided within Microsoft Word using Notebook Layout view. If you don't need to modify your OneNote documents, move your files to your SkyDrive, where you can open and edit OneNote files.

Migrating Outlook PST files

If you're using Microsoft Outlook for Windows, Outlook typically saves all your e-mail and other content within a special file with the .pst extension.

We explain how to import your .pst file from Outlook for Windows into Outlook for Mac in Book V, Chapter 1.

Installing Office, Sweet!

Before you can start using Microsoft Office, you need to install it, of course. To take advantage of the new document collaboration features, you need either a free SkyDrive account and/or an account on a Microsoft SharePoint server. After we show you how to install Office, we explain how to activate a free SkyDrive account in the later section "Soaring with Cloud Computing."

Enterprise and higher education Information Technology (IT) departments typically support Microsoft SharePoint. Contact your IT department and ask whether SharePoint is available to you. If it is, ask your IT department to have a SharePoint account set up for you.

Preparing your system

As time passes, errors can creep into your computer's file system. You might also wind up with duplicate or corrupt fonts. We show you how to check your system for errors before installing and how to repair file permissions and check your fonts after installation. This may sound rather technical, but it's actually quite easy to do these tasks.

 If you have a good disk maintenance and repair utility (such as Alsoft DiskWarrior, TechTools Pro, Drive Genius, or a similar program), be sure to use it on your startup volume and other drives before installing a big product such as Microsoft Office. Even if you don't have any of these programs, every Mac includes the Disk Utility program — this program's icon appears in the margin. At a minimum, make sure your startup disk verifies as OK with Apple's Disk Utility program. Here's how to check your hard drive with Disk Utility:

1. **In Finder, choose Applications, choose Utilities, and then open Disk Utility Application (shown in Figure 1-1).**

2. **In the panel on the left side, select your startup disk.**

   Your startup disk is the one at the top of the list of volumes. Select either the first or second item in the list as shown in Figure 1-1.

3. **On the First Aid tab, click the Verify Disk button.**

   Progress update messages and a progress bar appear. The bigger your hard drive is and the more files you have, the longer Disk Utility will take.

4. **When the process is complete, quit the Disk Utility application.**

The message you hope to see when Disk Utility is finished is green and says, "The volume *[name]* appears to be OK." Most likely you will get this go-ahead, and you can proceed directly to installing Office and skip the next steps.

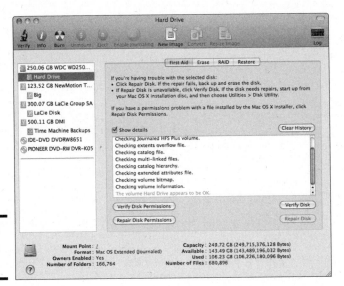

Figure 1-1:
Apple Disk
Utility.

If the Disk Utility indicates that your disk needs to be repaired, the Repair Disk button will remain grayed out, and you need to take additional actions. You can find additional instructions by doing the following:

1. **In Disk Utility, choose Help⇨Disk Utility Help.**

The Disk Utility Help window displays.

2. **Choose Repairing a Disk.**

Follow instructions for repairing your disk(s).

Sometimes Disk Utility can't repair a disk. If that happens to you, don't despair. Instead, try using another disk repair utility, such as Alsoft DiskWarrior, TechTools Pro, Drive Genius, or similar programs. They can find and repair more problems than Disk Utility can.

Do not install Office until Disk Utility or another reliable maintenance and repair utility tells you that your startup disk appears to be okay. If your startup disk is not okay, Office may not run properly.

Installing Microsoft Office

The installer for Microsoft Office is delivered using a disk image (.dmg) file. Unlike previous versions of Office, the same disk image is used for Home and Student Edition, Home and Office Edition, and the limited trial. The installer will know what features to make available to you based upon the product key that you enter. You can download the Office install file from the Microsoft Web site: www.microsoft.com/mac. This offers several advantages:

✦ **Purchase from any vendor.** The downloaded file needs to be activated. The product key is what you absolutely need. The download site provides a free trial key and suggests vendors. You purchase a product activation key for the edition you want to purchase from any authorized sales outlet. (You don't have to use a suggested vendor.) You can purchase the boxed physical media if you prefer, and that will have a conventional DVD along with your product key(s).

✦ **No waiting!** All you need is your product key and the download.

✦ **No worries about lost or damaged install discs.** As long as you have your product key, you can download a fresh installer anytime from Mactopia. In fact, if you get a copy of the installer from a friend without the product key, you won't be breaking any laws.

✦ **Media drive is not required.** MacBook Air users will love this because the MacBook Air typically doesn't have a disc drive!

✦ **No need to remove the trial version.** In previous versions of Office, you had to run the Remove Office utility to remove a trial version to avoid conflicts with the licensed copy. You don't do this with Office 2011. The trial version becomes the licensed version when you enter a product key.

Volume License Edition users need a special installer that is customized for them by their IT department. If your employer or school uses a volume license, contact your local support department to get the installer.

Running the installer

Microsoft Office uses the standard Apple installer. When you open the Office installer disk image (.dmg), just double-click the installer icon to start the installer. There are no surprises, and you should be able to accept all the defaults unless you're an advanced user and want to make a customized installation. The installer takes you through six stages:

1. **Introduction.** A friendly welcome screen is all you see here.

2. **License.** This is where you get to read (and if you want, print) the license agreement between you and Microsoft. You need to agree to that license in order to continue the installation.

3. **Destination select.** Normally, you install Office on your startup disk.

4. **Installation type.** Here you can customize the install options if you feel you must.

5. **Installation.** This is where the installer does the job of placing the Microsoft Office 2011 folder into your Applications folder. It installs the Office applications, fonts, templates, and the framework to make Office run.

6. **Summary.** Click the Finish button to quit the installer. You may be prompted about joining the Customer Experience Program (CEP), which lets Microsoft automatically obtain system information about your computer in the event of a software problem. Joining is optional and won't affect your ability to use Office in any way. It's possible for personal information from your computer to be transmitted to Microsoft if you join. If you choose to register your copy of Office, you will receive occasional newsletters from Microsoft about its products.

When you get to Step 6, the Microsoft AutoUpdate application (see Figure 1-2) opens to check whether there are updates from Microsoft available for your Office software. You should immediately install all updates that are available.

If you're pressed for time, make sure you install these updates as soon as you can. To access the Microsoft AutoUpdate application at any time, refer to the next section, "Keeping current with AutoUpdate."

It's very important to leave your installation of Office exactly as the installer generated it. Don't move or rename any of the applications, files, or folders of your Microsoft Office installation in the Applications folder, or Office or parts of it probably won't work. However, it's okay to make aliases that link to your Office applications.

Keeping current with AutoUpdate

Microsoft AutoUpdate (see Figure 1-2) is the application to use to keep your copy of Microsoft Office up-to-date. Your computer must be connected to the Internet to use AutoUpdate. To launch AutoUpdate from any Office application, do the following:

1. **Choose Help⇨Check for Updates.**

   Microsoft AutoUpdate opens, as shown in Figure 1-2.

2. **Set the frequency with which you want to have AutoUpdate check for updates.**

   Your options are Manual, Daily, Weekly, or Monthly.

3. **Click the Check for Updates button.**

   AutoUpdate checks for updates. If any are available, click the Install button and allow the installer to do its work.

4. **When you're done installing all updates, or if there are no updates to install, quit (⌘-Q) AutoUpdate.**

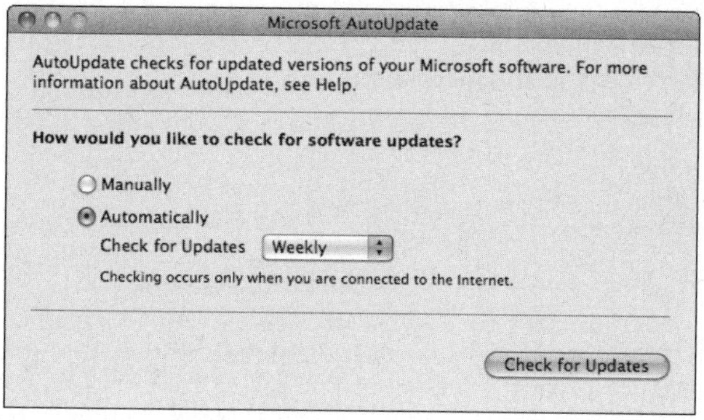

Figure 1-2:
Keeping
Office up-
to-date.

Keeping Office and Mac OS X up-to-date is a smart thing to do. Bug fixes, security patches, and feature enhancements are delivered with coordination between Apple and Microsoft. This helps both companies deliver the best possible experience for Mac users.

Fixing your fonts

We think everyone who installs Office should examine his or her font collection. Bad fonts can cause applications to crash. Font management is an art, but we're not artists. We give you a quick *For Dummies* way to manage your fonts.

Mac OS X comes with an application called Font Book, which should be in your Applications folder. We don't go deeply into Font Book. Instead, we show you only enough to avoid font problems by resolving duplicate fonts first and then dealing with defective fonts.

Resolving duplicate fonts

You can take the following steps to disable any duplicate fonts on your system. Remember, this procedure does not remove any fonts, and you just want to turn off these duplicates so they don't cause trouble.

1. **Double-click the icon for Font Book in the Applications folder.**

   Font Book opens, as shown in Figure 1-3.

2. **In the Collection column, click All Fonts.**

3. **Select any font listed under the Font column.**

4. **Press ⌘-A to select all your fonts.**

   The entire list of font names should be highlighted now.

5. **From the menu bar, choose Edit➪Resolve Duplicates.**

   If Resolve Duplicates is grayed out, good for you! That means your system doesn't have any duplicate fonts, and you can move on to checking for bad fonts in the next section.

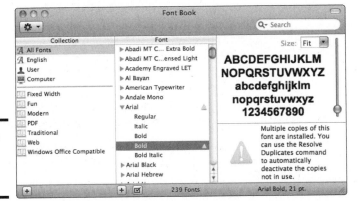

Figure 1-3: Resolving duplicate fonts.

Give Font Book a minute or two to process. You'll know when it's done when you no longer see the twirling wait indicator in the lower-right corner of the Font Book window. The more fonts you have and the more duplicates you have, the longer it takes. After completion, all duplicate fonts are disabled and won't be used by your system. The fonts remain on your hard drive, mostly just wasting space.

Font Book is great for adding new fonts and managing your fonts. For more information, while running Font Book choose Help➪Font Book Help and then browse the Help topics.

Checking for bad fonts

You can use Font Book to identify fonts that have problems and help you remove these fonts. Font Book classifies fonts into three categories:

✦ Passed (safe to use)

✦ Minor problems

✦ Major problems

The procedure is similar to resolving duplicates (described the preceding section):

1. **Double-click the Font Book application in the Applications folder.**

Font Book opens, as shown earlier in Figure 1-3.

2. **In the Collection column, click All Fonts.**

3. **Select any font listed in the Font column.**

4. **Press ⌘-A to select all your fonts.**

The entire list of font names is highlighted now.

5. **From the menu bar, choose File⇨Validate Fonts.**

The Font Validation window opens. (See Figure 1-4.) Allow the process to complete. It may take a while if you have a lot of fonts that have problems. Font Book puts a green badge next to fonts that are okay. The yellow badges with an exclamation mark and the red badges indicate fonts that have problems.

6. **Click the pop-up menu in the upper-left corner of the Font Validation window, and choose Warnings Or Errors, as shown in Figure 1-4.**

Font Book filters the list to show only fonts that have problems that need to be resolved. A yellow or red badge appears next to each font that has a problem.

7. **Select each check box next to fonts that appear in the list when you've turned on the Warnings Or Errors filter.**

Each font selected should have a yellow or red badge. Don't select fonts with green OK badges, which have check marks.

Be certain the Warnings Or Errors filter is applied before selecting the check boxes. Do not use Select All — that can select *all* your fonts. You don't want to remove your good fonts or system fonts!

8. **In the Font Validation window, click Remove Fonts.**

Any fonts you've selected are moved to the Trash. When you empty the Trash, they are completely removed from your system.

9. **Restart your computer.**

To put your fonts back, right-click them in the Trash and choose Put Back. You can drag your deleted fonts out of the Trash and copy them to a disc to make an archive copy. To get rid of the fonts forever, empty the Trash while the fonts are in the Trash.

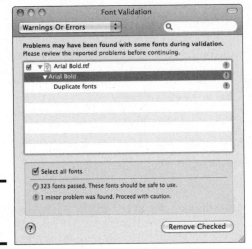

Figure 1-4:
Removing
bad fonts.

Soaring with Cloud Computing

Cloud computing is an exciting expression for a rather dusty-sounding concept. Cloud computing means that instead of running applications and storing files on your own computer, you use someone else's computer (typically a server) via your Internet connection. For Office 2011, it means you have new ways to distribute and share documents with co-workers, classmates, and friends.

Because the Internet is such a changeable place, by the time you read this, things could change. As we write, there are four main cloud computing platforms available to you:

✦ **Docs.com:** This option is a Facebook application that's owned and operated by Microsoft. It requires a Facebook account.

✦ **SkyDrive.com:** This Microsoft site has built-in integration with Office applications. It requires a Windows Live or Hotmail account.

✦ **SharePoint:** This option is used by large organizations to provide a *private cloud,* one that is not on the Internet. SharePoint offers the most privacy and security, but requires a dedicated server and network.

✦ **Google Docs:** This application is similar to Docs.com but is owned and operated by Google.

Each platform is a bit different. The following list describes the major comparison points, and Table 1-1 gives you the quick-and-dirty summary of the comparison:

✦ **Share files:** This refers to the ability to upload, store, download, and set permissions on files so that you and the people you choose can have a common access point for files.

✦ **Co-authoring:** Office 2011 lets you and another person make changes to a single document simultaneously in real time. SkyDrive and SharePoint allow this feature to work.

✦ **Web applications:** Web applications are lightweight word-processing, spreadsheet, and presentation software that runs in your Web browser. By no means are any of these even remotely as good as the applications in Office 2011.

✦ **File integration:** SkyDrive in all editions of Office and SharePoint (in Home and Business Edition) file systems are integrated into the Office 2011 interface.

✦ **Privacy:** With all services except SharePoint, you exchange your contact information, content, habits, and screen space for advertising in exchange for the privilege of using cloud services. Although you can specify who gets to share your files, you must let the cloud provider's computers analyze your content and contacts. SharePoint is the only cloud option we suggest that can be configured to work with information that must be kept private or confidential.

Table 1-1	Cloud Computing Services Comparison			
Cloud Share Files	*Co-authoring*	*Online Web Applications*	*Office Integration*	*Privacy*
Docs.com	Yes	Yes	No	Limited
SkyDrive. live.com	Yes	Yes	Yes	Limited
SharePoint	Yes	Yes	Yes	Private intranet
Google Docs	Yes	Yes	No	Limited

We discuss SkyDrive and SharePoint in this book because both are integrated into the Office interface.

Chapter 2: Interfacing with Office

In This Chapter

✔ **Meeting the menus**

✔ **Tooling around with toolbars**

✔ **Creating and customizing button icons**

✔ **Getting wrapped up in the Ribbon**

*W*ith all the changes in this new version, the Office 2011 interface is more flexible than ever. New to Office 2011 for Mac is the Ribbon, which is a blend of commands from menus, toolbars, palettes, the Elements Gallery, and more. If you're used to the older menus, it may take a while to get used to the Ribbon but we think that it's time well spent. If you aren't as enthusiastic as we are about the Ribbon, you'll be glad to hear that the new Ribbon with its tabs does not come at the expense of losing familiar interface features such as traditional menus and some toolbars. Put together, all these features provide many convenient ways for you to accomplish your goals within the programs that comprise Microsoft Office.

Within the Ribbon, you can find many commands that were on palettes in previous Office versions. And of course you can also find newer commands that were not available in previous versions!

The main reason to celebrate the existence of the Ribbon is that no longer will overcrowded palettes spill over past the bottom of the screen or obstruct your view of the document, spreadsheet, or the slide that you're working on. Like other Office interface features, the Ribbon is *context sensitive,* meaning that the choices that are available to you based upon where the cursor is and what's currently selected.

We come back to the Ribbon later in this chapter and show it to you. But before we do that, we take you on an exploration of other familiar interface options.

Musing about Menus

Menus are a staple of Mac applications. Even though they've been around since the first Mac, they continue to be popular and are still preferred by many. They're especially useful to people who need or want the keyboard control that menus typically provide to these applications.

In every Office application, at the top of your screen you can see the menu bar. (See Figure 2-1.) The menu bar continues to the right edge of the screen, but everything to the right of the Help menu belongs to Mac OS X or other open applications. Of course, you can activate individual menus by clicking corresponding menu items to expose their contents and submenus.

Another way to navigate menus is using arrow keys to navigate and then pressing Return to activate your menu choice. To get to the menu bar using the keyboard, press Fn-Control-F2 (or Control-F2 on keyboards without the Fn key).

Figure 2-1:
The
Application
menu.

The menu bar has certain default characteristics regardless of which Office application you're using. Starting from the upper-left corner of your entire screen (or feel free to refer to Figure 2-1) you can find:

✦ **Apple menu:** Mac OS X, rather than the current application, supplies this menu.

✦ **Application menu:** Located immediately to the right of the Apple menu, this menu offers access to these important options:

• *About [Application Name]:* Displays a message box that describes the current version of the open application and its installed updates. Include this information when making inquiries about this product, when contacting the manufacturer, or when using online community forums.

• *Online Registration:* Enter a product key that you've purchased to sign up for newsletters from Microsoft.

• *Preferences ⌘-, (Command-comma):* Displays the preferences for the current application. Notice the keyboard shortcut for this is displayed to the right of the command. Some preferences that you access here may influence more than one application. For example, if you make changes for Spelling or AutoCorrect in PowerPoint, then those changes will show up in Word and Excel too.

• *Services:* All sorts of additional features from Mac OS X and other applications can be found here. The right-pointing arrow indicates there's a submenu. It's worth exploring the Services Preferences option, which opens Mac OS X Services preference panel, where you can turn services on and off.

- *Hide [Application Name] ⌘-H:* This hides the application from view. Use ⌘-Tab or click the application's Dock icon to return to (unhide) the application.

- *Hide Others Option-⌘-H:* The Hide Others command hides all other open applications except the one you're working on within your Mac OS X desktop. (Yes, this may make former Windows users feel more at home.) Use ⌘-Tab or click another application's Dock icon to switch to a different application.

- *Show All:* This becomes available when you hide one or more applications. Choose Show All to make all hidden applications visible.

- *Quit [Application Name] ⌘-Q:* Closes all open windows of the active application and then completely quits the application itself. If you have files with unsaved changes, the application prompts you to save them before quitting.

✦ **File and other menus:** These menus offer the array of commands that are associated with your Office application. The options vary depending upon the Office application that you're using.

✦ **Application Script menu:** This menu has a small symbol icon rather than a menu name, as you can see in Figure 2-1. You will find Sample Automator workflows on this menu. Further to the right, you find an identical Script Menu icon that contains AppleScripts and Automator actions, including Automator actions that you create yourself.

Automator is a small program built within Mac OS X that lets you automate stuff that you do often, and Microsoft Office applications are compatible with Automator.

✦ **Help Menu:** Compared with the previous versions, the Help system in Office 2011 is revamped and interactive. Display the Help menu (see Figure 2-2) by clicking Help on the menu bar.

Figure 2-2:
The
Application
Help menu.

- *Search:* Within the Help menu, the Search box locates commands that match your search criteria. As you type commands, they are listed below. Move the mouse over a search result, and the command itself becomes highlighted in the menu, as shown in Figure 2-3. This is fun and can be addictive, so do it when you don't have a deadline to finish an important task!

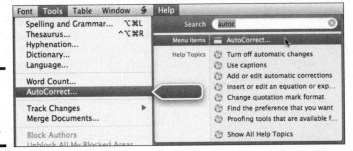

Figure 2-3: Searching for commands.

- *[Application Name] Help:* This is where you can find help for whatever application you are using. You can also access Help using the blue help icon on the standard menu bar and some application dialogs.

- *Check for Updates:* Launches Microsoft AutoUpdate. (See Chapter 1 of this minibook.)

- *Visit the Product Web Site:* Opens the Microsoft web site for the program in your default web browser.

- *Send Feedback about [Application Name]:* Your Web browser takes you to an online suggestion box where you can send comments and make suggestions to Microsoft. You won't receive a reply to these messages, but do know that folks at Microsoft read each one.

Talking about Toolbars

Standard toolbars in Office 2011 behave like some Web browser toolbars and are incorporated into the document window. By default, you encounter the Standard toolbar beneath the menu bar. Take a look at Figure 2-4 as we point out features of the Standard toolbar in Microsoft Office applications.

The first few controls aren't really part of the Standard toolbar because they show up even if you hide this toolbar. However, we still cover them here:

✦ **Window Controls:** The upper-left corner of each window contains the standard Close button (red), Minimize button (yellow), and the Zoom button (green).

◆ **Title:** The title is also the filename associated with the window.

◆ **Show/Hide button:** This button toggles the visibility of the toolbar on and off. Sooner or later, you may accidentally click this button and hide your toolbars. Click this button to restore your toolbars.

◆ **New, Templates, Open, and Save options:** These icons to the extreme left of the Standard toolbar allow you to make new files, display the Word Document Gallery, and open files in Finder. It also allows you to save your files.

◆ **Print:** This icon allows you to print some or all of your content to a connected physical printer, or in many cases a virtual printer driver that saves to PDF files.

◆ **Undo and Redo:** These icons allow you to return to how your file was a few clicks ago, or redo something you just did.

◆ **More controls:** If you resize the window to be smaller or customize a toolbar and put more controls onto it than can be easily displayed, a chevron appears at the right end of the toolbar. Click the chevron to display controls that don't fit in the toolbar.

Figure 2-4:
Using a
Standard
toolbar.

Standard
toolbar

Show/hide
toolbar

People who switch from Office 2007 or 2010 for Windows can think of the Standard toolbar as analogous to the Quick Access Toolbar (QAT) because it's always available and can be customized to your needs. Folks who switch from Office 2003 and earlier for Windows are already familiar with the Standard toolbar.

Where's Project Gallery?

If you've used a previous version of Office for the Mac, you'll notice that the Project Gallery doesn't launch when you run any of the Office applications. Project Gallery was a unified document, content, and template browser in previous versions of Office for the Mac. In Office 2011, a new customized gallery individualized for each application has replaced the Project Gallery. We discuss these new galleries for Word, Excel, and PowerPoint in their respective minibooks.

Customizing Menus and Toolbars in Word, Excel, and PowerPoint

Whenever you feel the need to tweak the interface of a Microsoft Office application, you need to summon the Customize Toolbars and Menus dialog. This is a super-powerful dialog in Word, Excel, and PowerPoint that lets you exert total control over all the toolbars and menus. You also have easy access to all kinds of wonderful hidden features — brilliant jewels in the form of off-the-beaten-path commands kept secret from others, but not from you! We show you how you can do any such customizations.

Just about everything we mention in these sections about customizing toolbars and menus can also be controlled via Visual Basic for Applications (VBA). VBA is a built-in programming language that's part of Microsoft Office. See Chapter 12 in this minibook to get more familiar with VBA.

Outlook's menus and toolbars are very different. We cover those in Book V, the minibook for Outlook.

Adding a jewel of a command

The Fit to Window command is a Word feature that's so handy you might wonder why it's not always on by default, or why it is not part of any toolbar. The Fit to Window command automatically keeps the document sized proportionally to the document window. After you try this command, you'll probably use Fit to Window a lot; it's a great example for discovering how easy it is to add commands to any toolbar.

To add the Fit to Window command to a Word toolbar, take these steps:

1. **In Word, choose View⇨Toolbars⇨Customize Toolbars and Menus.**

   The Customize Toolbars and Menus dialog appears, as shown in Figure 2-5.

2. **Click the Commands tab.**

3. **In the Categories list (on the left), select the View category.**

4. **In the Commands list (on the right), scroll down to find the Fit to Window command, and then select it.**

   Notice that when you select a command, its description appears in the Description area. This is very handy for finding out more about commands you may have never explored or seen before.

5. **Drag the Fit to Window command from the dialog to any toolbar and then release the mouse button when you see a shadowed insertion bar.**

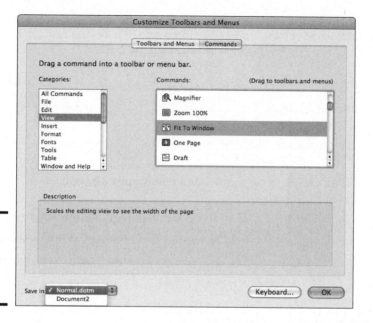

Figure 2-5:
Choosing
commands
custo-
mizations.

When the Customize Toolbars and Menus dialog is open, you can move any toolbar command or menu item by dragging it to any toolbar or menu. You can also rearrange the commands on any toolbar or menu by dragging the commands to new positions on the same or other toolbars.

6. **Click OK to close the Customize Toolbars and Menus dialog.**

   You can use these same general steps to add other commands in Word, Excel, and PowerPoint.

Of course, after you get into the magical Customize Toolbars and Menus dialog, you'll want to try hundreds of commands that you never knew about. This can be a nice thing to try when you have some spare time or when you're on an airplane with no Internet access!

Don't delete Customize Toolbars and Menus from the View menu. If you do, you can't go to the Customize Toolbars and Menus dialog. Well, we lied a bit! You can always right-click (or Control-click) an empty area within any visible toolbar and then choose the Customize Toolbars option from the contextual menu that appears.

Ditching a dud command

Believe it or not, you really can add too many commands to your toolbars. Soon, it might look like your toolbars are infested with more icons than mosquitoes in a jungle! Sometimes a command that sounds perfect turns out not to be at all what you'd hoped it'd be. You can easily get rid of an unwanted or little-used command. For Mac diehards, it's akin to removing a Dock icon without the *poof!*

Follow these steps to clean your toolbars:

1. **From the menu bar, choose View⇨Toolbars⇨Customize Toolbars and Menus.**

This brings up the Customize Toolbars and Menus dialog. (Refer to Figure 2-5.)

2. **Click and drag any unwanted commands off toolbars or menus and let go anywhere.**

You can drag it back to the open dialog or just into empty space.

3. **Click OK to close the Customize Toolbars and Menus dialog.**

Now you can get back to your non-infested jungle . . . er, program interface.

Making your own toolbars

You might think that you could design much better toolbars than the ones the Microsoft folks provided. Maybe you noticed that having the same toolbar repeat over and over again in each window is less of a convenience and more like a waste of valuable screen real estate. Not everyone has a gorgeous Apple 30-inch cinema display or two placed in a dual-screen setup. And even if you do, you paid good money for that and have every right to design your own toolbar!

You'll be pleased to know that you can make your own toolbars, fresh from scratch. They're healthier for your computing environment because they're homemade with only the finest commands that you select. While you're at it, you can make your own menu choices, too! If only growing organic vegetables were this easy.

Also keep in mind that your new customized toolbars aren't prisoners of the document window. Instead, they *float* — they can be moved by your mouse to any screen position. You can change their shape by clicking and dragging the lower-right corner of the toolbar. They're also *dockable* — they gently stick to the top, bottom, left, or right edge of the screen and out of your way.

To make a new toolbar in Word, Excel, or PowerPoint, here's what you do:

1. **From the menu bar, choose View⇨Toolbars⇨Customize Toolbars and Menus.**

The Customize Toolbars and Menus dialog appears. (See Figure 2-6.)

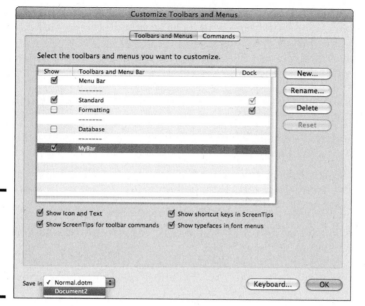

Figure 2-6:
The
Customize
Toolbars
and Menus
dialog.

2. **On the Toolbars and Menus tab, click the New button.**

   The Add a Toolbar dialog, as shown in Figure 2-7, opens.

Figure 2-7:
Naming a
new toolbar.

3. **Type a name for your new toolbar and click OK.**

   A very small box with an empty space on it appears onscreen. This small box is your new toolbar.

4. **Click the Commands tab of the Customize Menus and Toolbars dialog (refer to Figure 2-5), choose any of the categories from the list on the left, drag commands to the new toolbar, and click OK to close the Customize Toolbars and Menus dialog.**

   Your new toolbar appears in the toolbars list.

Renaming, deleting, or resetting toolbars and menus

Maybe you got a little carried away with all this moving and customizing of toolbars and menus, and now you're not so keen on some of the changes you made. Maybe you moved a command from the Standard toolbar and now you want the Standard toolbar restored to the way it was originally. No need to worry; resetting is easy. All these operations are done on the Toolbars and Menus tab of the Customize Menus and Toolbars dialog. (Refer to Figure 2-6.)

+ **Rename:** Click the Rename button and then type a new name for your toolbar or menu. You can't rename built-in menus and toolbars.

+ **Delete:** Click the Delete button to permanently delete a toolbar or menu. This can't be undone. You can't delete built-in menus and toolbars.

+ **Reset:** Click the Reset button to restore the selected menu or toolbar command. This resets the built-in menu or toolbar to how it appeared when you first installed Office.

You can always right-click on toolbars, toolbar buttons, and in blank spaces on toolbars for instant access to button and toolbar customization options. You can also choose View⇨Toolbars to find a submenu that lets you toggle your toolbars on and off.

Customizing button icons

Okay, your new toolbar looks nice, but not all commands have nice icons, or any icon for that matter. You can control whether to display a command's icon, text description, or both. You can even change a toolbar icon. To see the command controls, right-click a command button and choose Properties. The Command Properties dialog appears, as shown in Figure 2-8.

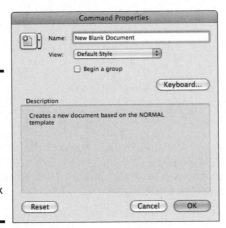

Figure 2-8:
With the Command Properties dialog, you can make toolbar buttons look just right.

Changing a command button icon

While the Command Properties dialog for any toolbar button (see Figure 2-8) is displayed, take these steps to change the button icon for this command:

1. **Click the Customize Icon downward-pointing arrow (next to the button icon in the upper-left corner of the dialog).**

The menu shown in Figure 2-9 appears.

Figure 2-9:
Choosing a
new button
icon.

2. **Choose from any of the available icons in this menu.**

Alternatively, if you copied a small picture from any application to the Mac OS X Clipboard, you can use the Paste Button Image option to replace the command button icon with the picture on the Clipboard.

Remember that the Paste Button Image option works only with pictures copied to the Mac OS X Clipboard. You can't copy text characters and paste them as a button/icon for any command.

Assigning a keyboard shortcut to a command button

As if that weren't enough customization, you can set or change the keyboard shortcut for any command. Remember that it's possible to do this customization in Word and Excel only, not PowerPoint. To proceed with assigning keyboard shortcuts, follow these steps:

1. **Make sure you followed steps in the preceding section to access the Command Properties dialog, as shown in Figure 2-8.**

The keyboard button is also available in the Customize Toolbars and Menus dialog, shown earlier in Figure 2-6.

2. Click the Keyboard button.

A dialog opens that shows you any existing keyboard shortcuts for the selected command. In addition, it lets you type a new shortcut for the command in the Press New Keyboard Shortcut text box. Also see the following chapters for more about keyboard shortcuts:

- Book II, Chapter 1 (Word)
- Book III, Chapter 1 (Excel)

3. Click OK when done to get back to the Command Properties dialog.

At this point, you can work with other Command Properties options or click OK to get back to your application's interface.

Fine-tuning toolbar and button properties

Using the Command Properties dialog shown earlier in Figure 2-8, you can do more to customize buttons:

✦ **Name:** View or change the name of a toolbar or menu command. Knowing a command's name can be helpful when you're programming in VBA or AppleScript.

✦ **View:** Choose whether to display an icon's name, icon, or both in custom toolbars. This doesn't affect the Standard toolbar or menus.

✦ **Begin a group:** When selected, this option adds a dividing line to the left of a button or above a menu item to help visually distinguish groups of commands.

✦ **Reset:** Restores the default toolbar icon for the command.

Using Customize Toolbars and Menus dialog shown earlier in Figure 2-6, you can do the following:

✦ **Show:** Select to show, or deselect to hide any toolbar.

✦ **Rename:** Change the name of a custom toolbar or menu.

✦ **Delete:** Permanently delete a custom toolbar or menu.

✦ **Reset:** Restore a built-in toolbar or menu's default commands.

✦ **Show Icon and Text:** When selected, this option shows a command's name under the command's icon on the Standard toolbar, as shown in Figure 2-10.

✦ **Show ScreenTips for toolbar commands:** When selected, this option displays the command name in a ScreenTip when the mouse cursor is positioned over a toolbar command, as shown in Figure 2-10.

Figure 2-10:
Viewing
icon
text and
ScreenTip.

✦ **Show shortcut keys in ScreenTips:** When selected, this option displays the keyboard shortcut for a command in the ScreenTip. See the example ScreenTip and keyboard shortcut in the left margin.

✦ **Show typefaces in font menus:** When checked, shows small preview examples of fonts in font selection pop-up menus.

Tearing off a toolbar

Some toolbar commands offer tear-off toolbars. This includes line drawing tools, shapes, and color palettes that you have added to a custom toolbar. (See Figure 2-11.) A special floating toolbar displays when you "tear off" a toolbar this way. These floating toolbars can be handy for repetitive tasks because they take up very little screen space.

Figure 2-11:
Choosing a
new button
icon.

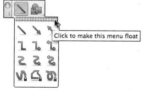

There's a secret to knowing which toolbars can float. When you click a command button on a toolbar, if you see a double row of dots at the top of a submenu, you can click that double row of dots to make the submenu into a floating toolbar. Sometimes commands that can't be made to float from the Ribbon can be made to float when accessed from a custom toolbar.

Sharing toolbars and menus

Customizing your toolbars and interface is really cool, but what's even cooler is that you can share these customizations with other folks. However, make sure that you advise people that you've done this before you share your documents with them; otherwise, they might be surprised when they open your document and see a different toolbar or menu arrangement than what they're used to.

Instead of saving your customizations just for your own computer, save them in the current document. Then, when your customized document is opened on another computer, your customized menus and toolbars will appear while that particular document is open.

To do this, follow these steps:

1. **From the menu bar, choose View⇨Toolbars⇨Customize Toolbars and Menus.**

   The Customize Toolbars and Menus dialog (refer to Figure 2-6) appears.

2. **In the lower-left corner of the dialog, click the Save In pop-up menu. Choose from the currently opened document, other open file, or the default application template.**

   - If you see the name of your file in this list, you can choose that option to save the customizations as part of this file.

   - If you see an option similar to Normal.dotm, that refers to the application default settings template in Microsoft Word.

   - If you see something like Document2, Presentation1, or similar, you haven't saved the file you're working on yet.

3. **Click OK.**

If you want to have a collection of templates, each with its own customized toolbar and menus, make several documents and customize each one differently. Before you start your toolbar and menu customizations, change the Save In setting (as described in the preceding steps) to keep the customizations within the current document. When you're done, choose File⇨Save As⇨Template. Save your document into the My Templates folder, and your customizations are available in the Templates Gallery. Remember that any documents you make from this sort of template carry your customized toolbars and menus with them wherever they go.

Riding the Ribbon

The Ribbon is a sophisticated, yet easy interface component that's new to Office 2011 for the Mac. It's like a large, thick toolbar that takes up a fixed area of screen real estate. Starting at the top of the Ribbon is a row of tabs, and each tab is almost an equivalent of a menu or toolbar. The Ribbon has large icons that are called buttons. When clicked, these buttons perform tasks with one click. However some buttons can spawn small menus or galleries or summon a dialog. Figure 2-12 shows the Ribbon in PowerPoint 2011.

Working in Ribbon groups

When you click a Ribbon tab, it displays buttons (or commands) arranged in *groups*. Many groups offer submenus with big, easy to see previews in galleries. Some groups have the dynamic content of the erstwhile Office 2008 Elements Gallery. Many commands that used to be in the Toolbox now live on the Ribbon tabs. Like menus and toolbars, the Ribbon tabs are context sensitive, displaying different commands depending upon what you selected and what you're doing.

Click any of the Ribbon tabs to reveal the commands available for that tab. Commands are grouped, with the group labels in a small band just under the top row of tabs. (See Figure 2-12.) Group dividers are perforated lines dividing the groups within the Ribbon tabs. Many commands offer submenus when clicked. Some submenus even have additional options at the bottom. If you already have Office 2011 installed, we encourage you to play around with the Ribbon tabs.

Ribbon tabs

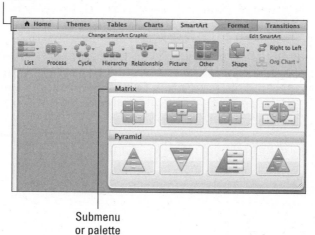

Figure 2-12:
Scoping out
the Ribbon.

Submenu
or palette

Beyond the default tabs, the Format tab displays whenever you select an object that can be formatted. For instance, you can see the Format tab if you select a picture, text box, shape, SmartArt, or another object. To format selected text, use options available on the Home tab.

When you select an object such as a picture, you'll only end up making the context-sensitive Format Picture tab visible, but to actually use the options within this tab, you may have to click the tab to display the commands available.

Some groups on the Ribbon tabs contain galleries of options. You can see more options by clicking the arrows at either end of the gallery, which works the way the Elements Gallery did in Office 2008. New in 2011 is the ability to display submenus for galleries. For example, see the Table Styles gallery shown in Figure 2-13.

Further, some galleries have a downward-pointing arrow below them. Clicking this arrow converts these galleries to a drop-down gallery.

Click for more options.

Figure 2-13:
Galleries give you visuals of options available to you.

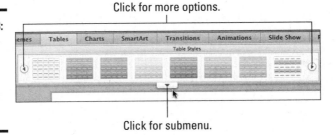

Click for submenu.

Customizing the Ribbon

This first iteration of the Ribbon in Office 2011 offers limited customization capabilities. You can customize the Ribbon by clicking the wheel at the right edge of the Ribbon, as shown in Figure 2-14. The Ribbon doesn't respond to XML, VBA, or other programmatic customizations.

Figure 2-14:
Accessing Ribbon preferences.

Ribbon Preferences...
Customize Ribbon Tab Order

When you choose Ribbon Preferences from the menu, a Ribbon dialog opens. Figure 2-15 shows Word's Ribbon preferences dialog, and the same dialog in other Office 2011 applications look similar. Another way to access the same dialog is through *[Application Name]*⇨Preferences; then click the Ribbon button.

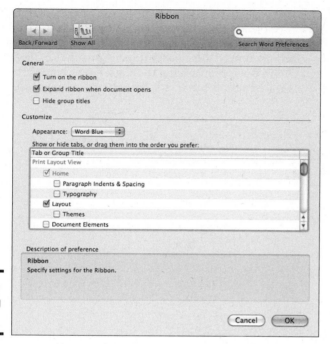

Figure 2-15:
Customizing
the Ribbon.

The Ribbon dialog has the following options:

✦ **Turn on the Ribbon:** When selecting, the Ribbon is on and this is the
default setting. To turn the Ribbon off, deselect this setting.

✦ **Expand Ribbon When Document Opens:** When selected, the entire
Ribbon is visible when opening a file. When deselected, only the Ribbon
tabs are displayed when a document opens. If you choose this option
and then want to see the entire expanded Ribbon, just click any of the
Ribbon tabs visible.

✦ **Hide Group Titles:** This turns off the display of group names in the
Ribbon tabs, which may give you a little more screen estate.

✦ **Appearance:** Choose between either the application theme or graphite.
The application theme is different for each Office 2011 application. In
Word 2011, it's called Word Blue.

✦ **Show or Hide Tabs, or Drag Them into the Order You Prefer:** Select or
deselect tabs and groups. Drag items in this box to re-order the Ribbon.

✦ **Description:** As you move your mouse over command buttons and controls, a description dynamically appears in the panel.

In addition to using the Ribbon preferences, you can choose the Customize Ribbon Tab Order option from the pop-up menu shown in Figure 2-14. This option temporarily changes the appearance of the tabs and allows you to drag Ribbon tabs to change their order. (See Figure 2-16.) Click the Done button when you're done rearranging the tabs. If you made changes that you don't like, click the Reset button to set the tab order to default.

Figure 2-16:
Reordering
Ribbon tabs.

Chapter 3: Traversing the Toolbox

In This Chapter

✔ **Turning on the Toolbox**

✔ **Sleuthing the Scrapbook**

✔ **Finding references quickly**

✔ **Using Office cross-platform**

*B*eyond the menu and the Ribbon, the Toolbox is another context-aware interface tool available to you in the Office 2011 suite. What exactly is the Toolbox? It's a floating palette that has tabs.

The Toolbox and its tabs are wonderfully consistent across all Office 2011 applications, but certain portions apply to specific applications, and we discuss them in the appropriate minibook for that particular application. In this chapter, we discuss three Toolbox tabs that work the same way across multiple applications:

✦ **Scrapbook:** This tab is the regular Clipboard on steroids.

✦ **Reference Tools:** A collection of reference materials, such as a dictionary, a thesaurus, and more.

✦ **Compatibility Report:** Find out how compatible your Word documents, Excel workbooks, and PowerPoint presentations are with older versions on both Mac and Windows.

Tinkering in the Toolbox

Of course, before you can use the Toolbox, it must be visible. You can turn on the Toolbox by either of these methods:

✦ **Click Toolbox on the Standard toolbar:** It's shown in the left margin.

✦ **Choose View⇨Toolbox ⇨*[Choose Toolbox tab]***

Although the tabs of the Toolbox contain super-useful tools, you may not need them all the time, and sometimes this large palette of tabs can get in the way. To dismiss it, click the red Close button in the upper-left corner just as you would with any other Mac window. Alternatively, you can click the Toolbox button on the application's Standard toolbar to close the Toolbox so that your tools don't fall out.

Scrapbook: The Clipboard Evolves

Whenever you select something, such as a picture on a PowerPoint slide, and then choose Edit⇨Copy, you end up sending that picture to the Clipboard. You can then go to your open Word document and choose Edit⇨Paste to bring a copy of that picture from the Clipboard to your Word document.

The Clipboard is an area in your computer's memory that stores the last thing you copied from any application. As long as you don't copy something else, that last thing copied normally stays in the computer's memory as part of the Clipboard unless you shut down the computer. Thus, every once in a while you might wonder why the Mac OS X Clipboard can't remember what was on it after you restart your computer. Someone in Microsoft obviously wondered the same thing and came up with *Scrapbook,* a great solution that essentially is a multiple-item Clipboard with a memory, as shown in Figure 3-1.

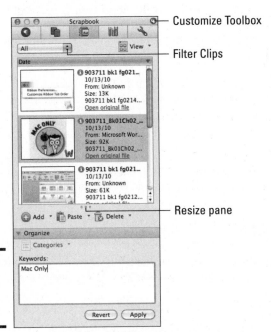

— Customize Toolbox

— Filter Clips

— Resize pane

Figure 3-1:
Scrapbook, the super Clipboard.

Adding clips to Scrapbook

The Scrapbook is one of the important tabs within the Toolbox interface. If for some reason it isn't visible to you, go ahead and summon it by choosing View⇨Toolbox⇨Scrapbook.

To put Scrapbook to work automatically, you have to do a little setup so that the Scrapbook works almost as seamlessly as the Mac OS X Clipboard. Here's how to toggle Scrapbook's automatic Add to Scrapbook setting:

1. **Make sure the Scrapbook tab is selected in your Toolbox.**

2. **Click the small down arrow next to the big, green Add button (see Figure 3-2) to summon a pop-up menu.**

   The Add button may be a slightly inconspicuous greyish green button unless you already have something selected.

3. **From the pop-up menu that appears, choose the Always Add Copy option.**

   That's all you need to do, and the Scrapbook setting is now set to automatic so that every time you copy something within your Office 2011 applications, it's added to your Scrapbook in addition to being added to the Mac OS X Clipboard, but only while the Scrapbook tab of the Toolbox is displayed.

Figure 3-2:
Automating
Scrapbook.

Although the default for the Add pop-up menu is the Add Selection option, you can choose to add entire files or the contents of the Mac OS X Clipboard.

That's all there is to it. Well, almost. The automatic Scrapbook setting can be changed individually in Word, Excel, PowerPoint, and Outlook. Changing the setting in one application doesn't take immediate effect in the other Office applications if they happen to be open at the time you toggle this setting. The setting change takes effect in other Office applications the next time the other applications have been closed and then re-opened. The clips you put into Scrapbook are available in all the Office applications. Pop a picture into Scrapbook in Word, for example, and it's also available to you in Excel, PowerPoint, and Outlook.

Now all you have to do is get some stuff into your Scrapbook. If you followed the preceding steps and made that small change to the Always Add Copy option, adding items to Scrapbook happens automatically every time you copy something in Office 2011 with the Copy command while the Scrapbook tab of the Toolbox is open.

Of course, if you prefer to add items one at a time on demand, there are other ways to add selections to the Scrapbook (refer to Figure 3-2):

✦ **Click the Add button (the button itself, not the arrow next to it).** Adds the current selection.

✦ **Click the small arrow to the right of the Add button and then choose Add File.** Opens a file browser so you can select items in Finder.

✦ **Click the small arrow to the right of the Add button and then choose Add from Clipboard.** Adds what's on the Mac OS X Clipboard.

✦ **Choose Edit⇨Copy to Scrapbook.** Adds the current selection.

✦ **Drag a clip from a document into the Scrapbook window.**

Getting clips from Scrapbook

Pasting clips from the Scrapbook into your documents, spreadsheets, presentations, and HTML mail is easy. Here's a quick rundown of the ways to get your selected clip out of Scrapbook:

✦ Right-click or Control-click on a scrapbook entry, and choose Paste in the resultant pop-up menu.

✦ Click the Paste button on the Scrapbook palette. (Refer to Figure 3-2.)

✦ Click the small down arrow found to the right of the Paste button for special paste options.

✦ Drag a clip from Scrapbook into a document.

⌘-click clips in the Scrapbook tab of the Toolbox to select more than one clip at a time.

Becoming a Scrapbook saver

Scrapbook has some interesting capabilities. All you need is a little guidance from us about what's going on, and then you'll be whizzing around Scrapbook.

✦ **Filter Clips:** After you have a bunch of clips assembled within your Scrapbook palette, you might find it difficult to locate that elusive clip you saved a few weeks ago. It's at a time like this that the pop-up menu buttons at the top of the Scrapbook palette become immensely useful. When you click the Filter Clips pop-up menu at the top left, the menu shown in Figure 3-3 is displayed. Choose which clips to display. If you choose the Title Contains option for example, you get a small box in which you can add some search terms.

The Filter Clips pop-up menu can also help you clean up by removing clips you no longer need. Use the Large Items option to reveal clips that take a lot of drive space, making them good candidates for deletion from Scrapbook. When using the List option from the Scrapbook's View button you can order your clips by title or date.

Figure 3-3:
Filtering
Scrapbook
clips.

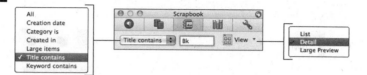

✦ **Date:** By default, clips are organized by date with the most recent at the top. Reverse the order by clicking the thin Date strip at the top of the pane. Refer to Figure 3-1 for Date and for the rest of these commands.

✦ **View:** The View pop-up button toward the top right changes the way clips are displayed in the Scrapbook. Choose from these views: List, Detail, and Large Preview.

✦ **Information:** Displays the filename of the source of the clip, the date it was added to Scrapbook, its source application, and its size.

✦ **Rename:** Double-click a clip's name to activate the Rename capability. Type a new name in the resulting input field.

✦ **Preview:** The preview is visible when Detail or Large Preview is chosen from the Scrapbook's View menu.

✦ **Delete:** Offers three options for deleting clips from Scrapbook:

  • *Delete:* Deletes the selected clip(s)

  • *Delete Visible:* This one is tricky! Clips that are displayed while using a filter with the Filter Clips feature will be deleted. But if you have Filter Clips set to show all clips, then *all* clips will be deleted.

  • *Delete All:* Deletes all clips from Scrapbook.

✦ **Resize pane:** Drag the three dots to adjust the size of the clippings pane.

✦ **Organize:** Click the disclosure triangle to expose the Organize pane.

✦ **Categories:** Choose a category from the pop-up menu. After you assign categories, you can filter by category using Filter Clips. At the top of the Categories' pop-up menu, you can choose the following:

  • *Assign Categories:* Displays a dialog that lets you assign more than one category to a clip.

  • *Edit Categories:* Displays a dialog that lets you add and remove categories. Click a category's color box to pick a new color.

✦ **Keywords:** You can tag selected clips with keywords. After you apply keywords, you can filter by keywords using Filter Clips.

✦ **Apply:** You must click Apply to apply keywords to clips.

✦ **Revert:** Revert is like Cancel. Type some keywords and then click Revert instead of Apply. Your keywords disappear.

Looking Things Up with Reference Tools

Going to the local library and exploring books is a great experience. Who doesn't love all the books and journals, the people, and even that book smell? Pleasures small and large are there to be discovered, and a librarian is there to help you. Now you can extend that experience to your workflow within Office 2011 by using Reference Tools. It's like having popular tools from your local library integrated into Office right on your Mac.

When you choose the Reference Tools on the Toolbox, you're presented with a pane that's divided into sections, as shown in Figure 3-4. You can expand or collapse each section by clicking the disclosure triangles to the left of the section labels.

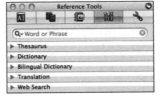

Figure 3-4:
Finding
references.

At the top of the References Tools is a versatile search field. To use it, follow these steps:

1. **Type a word or phrase into the search field at the top of the Reference Tools tab of the Toolbox.**

2. **Click the disclosure triangle to expose the desired reference tool(s).**

3. **Press Return to see the results.**

   Note that some tools access information that's continuously updated and require a live Internet connection to get results.

Although you can, you really don't have to type anything into the search field to use Reference Tools. Here's an easier alternative:

1. **Open a document, spreadsheet, presentation, or e-mail that you want to work with.**

2. **Select a word or phrase and then right-click to bring up a pop-up menu, and choose a reference option such as Look Up, Synonyms, or Translate.**

   Some of these options also have submenus with more options you can choose.

Reference Tools does the rest. In fact, if the desired result appears as a pop-up suggestion while you're editing, all you have to do is click that option to accept the suggestion.

Being Compatible

It's hard to believe, but a lot of people are still working in organizations that haven't switched from older versions of Office on both the Windows and Mac platforms to the shiny new versions. In fact, even if some of them have moved to newer versions, they might be working on the Windows version of Office and not the new Office 2011 for Mac like you. The end result is that here you are with your fancy new Office for Mac, making files that might not play well with older, but still serviceable hardware and software.

Office 2010 for Windows and Office 2011 for Mac are very compatible with each other. Still, there are advanced features in Office for Mac, such as Word's notebook and publishing layout views, which are not yet in Word for Windows and may not be in certain older versions of Office for Mac.

Checking for compatibility

This is where the Toolbox's Compatibility Report panel (shown in Figure 3-5) comes to the rescue. Compatibility Report knows almost every aspect of each Office version since Office 97 (that's the last 11 versions of Office collectively on Windows and Mac platforms!), and it can tell you whether things in your document might not play nice with an older version. Not only can Compatibility Report give you a report; it might be able to fix some aspects of your document so that what you see in Office 2011 is what your co-workers or friends see when they open your file in their older software.

Before you start using the Compatibility Report, it's a good idea to keep a backup copy of your original document:

1. **First save your document by choosing File➪Save.**

   Or just click the Save icon on the Standard toolbar.

2. **Now that all changes you last made are saved, choose File➪Save As to create a new copy of your file. Give the compatible document a new name.**

   This way, if you use the Fix feature in the Compatibility Report, you will still have an unchanged version of your original document.

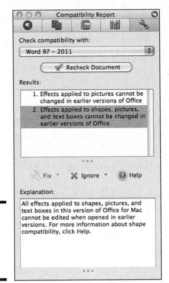

Figure 3-5:
Checking
for version
conflicts.

You use the Compatibility Report tool by starting at the top and working your way down:

✦ **Check Compatibility With:** Choose which version of Office you want your document to be compatible with.

You can opt to make your document compatible with a particular Windows or Mac version, or with all Windows and Mac versions.

✦ **Document:** Click to start checking your document, spreadsheet, or presentation.

✦ **Results:** Potential problems are displayed. Click a result to see an explanation.

✦ **Fix:** If Compatibility Report knows how, the potential problem may be fixed if you click this button. Alternatively, the Fix option might be grayed out.

Formatting or other changes needed to make your document compatible with the version you chose in Step 1 will be made. You may have to manually fix certain problems.

✦ **Ignore:** Tells Compatibility Report to ignore instances of the selected problem. If you click the small downward arrow, you can:

• Ignore Once

• Ignore All

• Don't Show Again

✦ **Help:** Opens Office Help.

Working with compatibility in mind

If you work in a cross-platform environment, you can do some things to make sharing documents easier with older versions of Office for Mac and Office for Windows. The following sections explain some guidelines you can follow to avoid compatibility issues.

Using compatible file formats

File formats for Word, Excel, and PowerPoint are identical for Office for Mac and Office for Windows. The default file format for Word, Excel, and PowerPoint in Office 2011 is standard open XML. It's also the default file format for Office 2007 (Windows), Office 2008 (Mac), and Office 2010 (Windows). It's sometimes referred to as the "new" format, but open XML is the standard format now.

Documents that are four or more years old may have been saved in the old '97 through 2004 formats. If you open one of these in an Office 2011 application, watch out for some info at the top of the application window, where you see the filename along with a "Compatibility Mode" suffix.

Compatibility Mode turns off certain new features like SmartArt so that you don't accidentally introduce these objects into your documents. This increases the chances of creating files that are compatible with older versions of Microsoft Office applications.

Updating from an older file format to standard open XML format

If your file is in Compatibility Mode but you want to use new Office features, choose File⇨Save As and from the Format pop-up menu choose Word Document (`.docx`), Excel Workbook (`.xlsx`), PowerPoint Presentation (`.pptx`), or other current file format such as a template or macro enabled file. This ends Compatibility Mode and converts your file to standard open XML file format.

Changing a file from standard format to 97–2004 format

When the file you are working on is in the standard open XML file format, you don't see `Compatibility Mode` at the top of the window. If you need to share this file with someone who has Office 2004 or older, you can save a copy in the old format. Choose File⇨Save As and from the Format pop-up menu choose 97–2004 file format. For example, if you're working on a file in standard Word (`.docx`) file format, save a copy to Word 97–2004 (`.doc`) format.

On the other hand, there are updates for Microsoft Office all the way back to Office 2000 (for Windows) and 2004 (for Mac) that enable old office applications to open and work with files saved in the current standard open XML file formats. You don't have to feel put out if you prefer to work in the standard open XML formats. People should install their updates. You can also inform them about these free updates!

If you know you need to share your file with someone who doesn't have Office 2007 or later, simply keep using the old format. Office won't update the format unless you specifically change it using File⇨Save as and choose a different format, or choose File⇨Convert Document in Word.

E-mailing attachments

If you and your recipient are both using Outlook for either Mac or Windows, you should have no problems with the e-mail software at either end. However, we have two scenarios and guidelines that you can follow to reduce problems, if you're willing to do some extra work:

✦ The first scenario is if your recipient is using an old e-mail program that hasn't been updated to know about the current (now at least four years old) Office file formats. Current standard Office file formats are typically suffixed with four-letter extensions such as DOCX, XLSX, and PPTX rather than the older three-letter extensions such as DOC, XLS, and PPT, respectively. If you use the current file formats, your recipient may have problems opening your attached documents. (You would think any up-to-date e-mail client ought to know the proper file associations by now.)

✦ The second scenario involves poorly designed and/or managed e-mail systems, including servers and faulty malware protection schemes. These bad boys alter the mail instead of delivering it as sent, damaging attachments in the process and making them unreadable by the recipient's computer.

Often, you're not in a position to tell the recipients to fix their own problems. So you may need to put yourself out a bit:

✦ **Zip before attaching.** After you close a document, you can right-click its file in Finder and choose either Compress or Archive to turn it into a zip file. Attach the zip file to your e-mail. Of course the recipient needs to know how to unzip the file on his or her computer. Usually, double-clicking a zip file is all it takes to unzip it.

✦ **Use something other than e-mail.** There are plenty of alternatives to e-mail these days. Consider using SkyDrive, Microsoft Messenger, or iChat to send your documents thereby completely bypassing e-mail altogether. You can also use a service like YouSendIt (www.yousend it.com) to send download links rather than attachments.

Using Windows-compatible fonts

Sticking with compatible fonts is easy. The default font for Office, Calibri, is Windows compatible. When choosing fonts from the Home tab on the Ribbon, choose Font Collections⇨Windows Office Compatible, as shown in Figure 3-6.

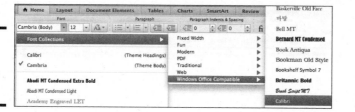

Figure 3-6:
Choosing
compatible
fonts.

Customizing the Toolbox

Click the Customize Toolbox button in the upper-right corner (refer to
Figure 3-1) to flip the Toolbox over and expose settings, as shown in Figure
3-7. The settings are in two groups:

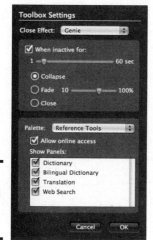

Figure 3-7:
Customizing
Toolbox
settings.

+ **Close Effect:** These settings adjust how the Toolbox behaves visually:

  • From the pop-up menu, choose Genie, Scale, or No Effect.

  • If you select the When Inactive For check box (optional), you can
    use the slider to determine how long a period of inactivity will pass
    before the Toolbox displays as collapsed (displays toolbar only),
    fades to the amount of fade you specify with the slider, or closes
    itself completely.

+ **Palette:** Choose which tools to display on the Toolbox palette.

  • *Allow Online Access:* Select the check box to allow reference tools to
    have online access (when it's available).

  • *Show Panels:* Choose which reference tools to display.

Chapter 4: Working with Files

In This Chapter

✔ Opening files

✔ Performing file and content searches

✔ Saving files

✔ Making templates

✔ Working with templates

✔ Saving to the cloud with SkyDrive

In April 2009, *MacWorld* magazine ran a feature titled "19 Ways to Open a File." Readers promptly came up with even more ways. If that makes you feel overwhelmed with possibilities, don't worry! We stick with the methods that we think are easiest and most common for opening and saving files. This chapter focuses on file dialogs that you encounter in all Office 2011 applications. And in case all those options in the dialogs make you dizzy, we help you wade through the myriad options so that you discover the coolest options related to working with Office files.

Opening Files

In this chapter, we assume you already have your application open and running. You encounter Open dialogs whenever you choose File⇨Open or when you insert content into existing files using a file browser, such as when choosing a picture to insert. Office 2011 applications tell the Mac operating system to display the familiar file browser dialog you encounter all the time while using Mac OS X.

Here, we dissect an example Open dialog accessed using the File⇨Open command in Microsoft Word. (See Figure 4-1.)

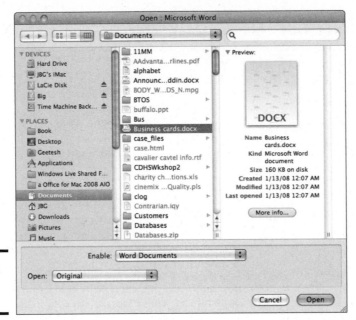

Figure 4-1:
Opening a
file.

As in a typical Open dialog, this one also has these features:

+ **Forward and Back buttons:** Help you navigate the folders in your directory.

+ **Icon view, List view, and Column view buttons:** Display files as icons (Icon view), in a list (List view), or with a mini preview and file details (Column view). In List view, you can click the column headers to reorder the list.

+ **Shortcuts pop-up menu:** Includes major directories and recent places.

+ **Search field:** Search is special. See the next heading.

+ **More Info button:** Displays Mac OS X Get Info for a selected file.

+ **Resize:** Drag to resize the pane. Double-click to resize all panes.

+ **Enable pop-up menu:** Enables you to choose which file type to open. Use this to choose a file type other than the application's default format.

+ **Open pop-up menu:** Choose from Original, Copy, and Read-Only. Original opens the selected file, Copy opens a copy of the selected file, and Read-Only opens the selected file as read-only.

+ **Open and Cancel buttons:** Open the selected file. (Double-clicking a file does the same thing.) The Cancel button closes the dialog without opening a file.

Want to peek inside an entire file without actually opening it? You can! This feature is great for those times when you have several similar files and you aren't sure which one you want to open. Just select an Office file in the file browser shown in Figure 4-1 and then press the spacebar. That small act lets you look at the entire document from start to finish. When previewing an Excel workbook, you even get to choose tabs. Amazing!

To open multiple files, hold ⌘ down to select individual files or hold Shift down to select a range of filenames in the file list. Then click the Open button.

Searching for Files and Locations

You can search files in both Open dialogs and Save dialogs. If you're a switcher from Windows, prepare to be amazed by this search experience. Mac OS X includes Spotlight, a search system that automatically indexes your files, their attributes, and the first 1,000 words of every file. When you use the Search field in an Open or Save dialog (look in the top-right area of Figures 4-1 or 4-2), you're using Spotlight.

Using search is easy and can be highly interactive. All you have to do is type a keyword, phrase, text string, filename, or any part of a filename in the Search field of an Open or Save dialog. See our example in Figure 4-2. The moment you start typing, the dialog instantly undergoes a transformation into a specialized search tool. It happens so fast that you might not even notice.

Search locations

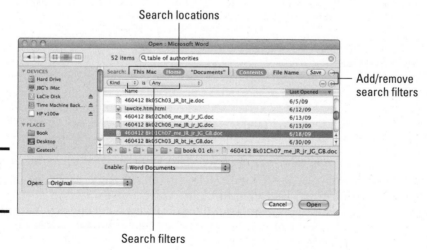

Add/remove search filters

Search filters

Figure 4-2: Searching for a file.

Before you've even finished typing your search, Spotlight finds your file or narrows the search down considerably. However, search provides a lot of filtering tools in case you need them, as shown in Figure 4-2. In this example, we show an Open dialog, which provides the functionality we discuss in the previous section, combined with the power of Spotlight searching.

These features become available when using Spotlight search in File dialogs:

✦ **Enter search terms:** Type keywords, phrases, or filenames in the Search field.

✦ **Clear search box:** Click the X in the Search field to clear the field.

✦ **Number of hits:** Displays how many items match your search criteria.

✦ **Search locations:** Click to limit your search to specific places.

✦ **Search filters:** These appear when you click the plus and minus signs (labeled as Add/remove search filters in Figure 4-2).

✦ **Search results:** Results appear almost instantly and can be ordered by clicking the column headers.

✦ **File path:** When using Open dialogs, if you click a search result item you can see its file path. This is not available in Save dialogs.

✦ **Contents or File Name:** Choose whether to include results by the contents contained within your files, or limit the search to just file names.

✦ **Add/remove search filters:** The plus and minus buttons turn on search filters, add more search filter options, or remove search filter options.

✦ **Sort:** When you click a column header, it sorts either ascending (alphabetically) or descending (reverse alphabetical) each time you click the header (List view only).

Saving Files

Save

Save dialogs look very similar to Open dialogs, which we discuss earlier in the chapter. Saving a file that you're working on is as easy as clicking the Save button on the Standard toolbar, pressing ⌘-S, or choosing File➪Save. If your file has been saved previously, saving the file replaces the existing copy of the file with your updated version.

If your file has *not* already been saved, the Save As dialog opens automatically when you save your file. Save As lets you name your file and choose a location for saving. You can call up the Save As dialog anytime you're working on a document to save it with a new name and/or location by choosing File➪Save As. An example Save As dialog is shown in Figure 4-3.

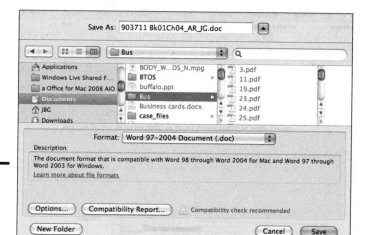

Figure 4-3:
Saving
files with
Save As.

A typical Save As dialog has the following options:

✦ **Icon view, List view, Column view:** Displays directory files as icons
   (Icon view), as directory filenames in a list (List view), or as directory
   filenames in columns (Column view).

✦ **Shortcuts:** Includes major directories and recent places.

✦ **Save As:** Type a name for your file here.

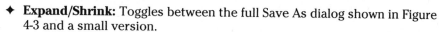

   You can click the name of an existing file to automatically populate the
   Save As field to save time typing. You can then edit that name if you
   don't want to overwrite the original file.

✦ **Expand/Shrink:** Toggles between the full Save As dialog shown in Figure
   4-3 and a small version.

✦ **Search:** Enter search criteria. We cover searching in more detail earlier
   in this chapter.

✦ **Resize:** Drag the dividers to resize the panes. Double-click the resize
   handle to automatically resize the pane to the longest file name.

✦ **Forward/Back:** For navigation within your directories.

✦ **Format:** Click this pop-up menu to change the resulting saved file to a
   format that's different from the default file format. We discuss alternative file formats in detail within the minibook for each application.

✦ **Description:** Gives details about the selected file format.

✦ **Learn More About File Formats:** Click this link to open Office Help.

✦ **Append File Extension:** When selected, this option appends the correct file extension for the selected format. You should always select this option.

✦ **Options:** Displays more options applicable to the selected format.

✦ **Compatibility Report:** Runs Compatibility report in the Toolbox.

✦ **New Folder:** Lets you create a new folder on the fly.

✦ **Save:** Saves the file using the settings you chose in the Save As dialog.

Saving and Using Templates

Templates are documents, workbooks, or presentations that are used as starting points to build new files upon. When you save a file as a template, it becomes available in the templates gallery of Word, Excel, or PowerPoint. A classic example of a template is a business letterhead that contains both formatting and content ready to be filled in. Each application has built-in templates that you see when you choose File➪New from Template. It's easy to make your own templates, too.

Saving as a template

To make a template, you start with something customized, ready to use as the basis of new files. All you have to do is to use Save As and change the Format pop-up menu to *[Application Name]* Template. (See the earlier "Saving Files" section and Figure 4-3.) The shortcut changes to My Templates, which is where you should save your template. Just give it a name, click Save, and you're all done! Your saved template will appear in the template gallery of Word, Excel, or PowerPoint as appropriate.

Opening a template

Choosing File➪New from Template opens the current application's template gallery. Your saved templates will appear in the gallery under My Templates. When you open a template from the gallery, a new document identical to the saved template will open and it will have a generic name, such as Document 1, Workbook 3, or Presentation 2.

If you want to edit a template, choose File➪Open. Change the Format to Template, and then navigate to the My Templates folder, select the template you want, and then click Open. When you open a template this way, it opens the template itself, as opposed to a new file based on the template. Choose File➪Save to overwrite the template or File➪Save As to create a new template.

Modifying template locations

When you save a template from within Word, Excel, or PowerPoint, the default file location is the My Templates folder. And you should be happy about saving to that location because it's easy to save and use templates from the default My Templates folder.

Perhaps for some reason you *do* need to change the default file location settings or add other locations for keeping templates. You might want to do this because you don't create templates just for your own use but need to share it within a group of users or across your entire organization. Unless you want to know more about this subject, please feel free to move on. If you need to use templates that are shared, the following sections were written with you in mind.

Finding the default My Templates folder

Here's the complete file path to the default My Templates folder:

```
Hard Drive:Users:UserName:Library:Application Support:Microsoft:Office:User
    Templates:My Templates
```

Unless you have a particular reason to change the default, we recommend that you park your templates using the default location.

User and workgroup templates

Office looks at two folders to populate the application template galleries and for saving templates:

✦ **User templates:** The My Templates folder described in the preceding section is also known as the user templates folder. You can choose a different folder in Word preferences. A how-to step-by-step is just ahead.

✦ **Workgroup templates:** In addition to a local templates location, you can set a second location for Office to use for templates. This setting lets you choose a shared location, usually on a shared network drive, for additional templates to appear in application template galleries.

In previous versions of Office, you used Project Gallery to set or change these locations. In Office 2011, these settings are made in Microsoft Word for Word, Excel, and PowerPoint, as shown in Figure 4-4. To set or change the local or workgroup templates, take these steps:

1. **With a document open in Microsoft Word, choose Word⇨Preferences⇨ File Locations.**

The File Locations preferences dialog opens, as shown in Figure 4-4.

2. **In the File locations section, in File Type column, choose either User Templates or Workgroup Templates.**

   The file path shown in the location column is the default storage location for each of the file types listed in the File Type column.

3. **Click the Modify button to display a Choose a Folder dialog.**

4. **Navigate to the desired folder and then click Choose.**

   The selected folder then appears in Word's preferences.

5. **Click OK to have your changes take effect and close the dialog.**

To see the complete file path in File locations preferences, hover your mouse cursor over the file path shown in the preferences dialog.

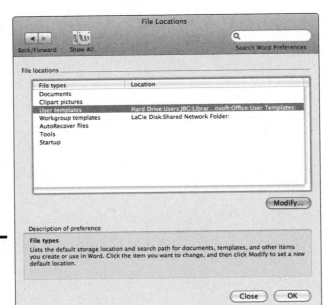

Figure 4-4:
Change template locations.

Sharing and Collaborating with SkyDrive

Collaboration is built into Office 2011. You can save your documents directly to the *cloud* (SkyDrive or a SharePoint server for our purposes) by choosing File⇨Share. Choose your public cloud using Save to SkyDrive. If your organization has SharePoint, then you can save to your organization's private cloud using Save to SharePoint. (See the later section, "Saving to SharePoint.")

SkyDrive offers the following in exchange for you being subjected to advertising and also to the terms of Windows Live (which may change from time to time, so we don't print them here):

✦ **You get 25GB of file storage (any kind of file is okay).** You can set file sharing permissions and set passwords on file folders.

✦ **You can save files directly to SkyDrive and open files directly from SkyDrive from Word, Excel, and PowerPoint.**

✦ **You can share a Word or PowerPoint document in real time with a collaborator.**

✦ **You get access to Office Web Applications.** More on this after the bullet list.

✦ **You can synchronize folders from one computer to another and your cloud.**

✦ **You get version control.** Keep track of who modified a document and when. On the SkyDrive Web site, select a filename in a folder list and choose More⇨Version History to access this feature.

✦ **You can co-author documents.** Within in the SkyDrive Web site, you can co-author documents with others.

SkyDrive has free, online limited feature versions of Word, Excel, PowerPoint, and OneNote. These rudimentary Web applications are designed to compete against other simplified free Office applications, particularly Google Docs and OpenOffice. Office Web applications give you access to your content from any computer that's connected to the Internet. Also, it's expected that Microsoft will continue to evolve these Web applications to make them more useful.

If you need to share a file with someone who doesn't have Office or you want to open a file on a computer without Office (either Mac or PC), Web applications (SkyDrive or Google docs) can sometimes suffice for displaying or making simple edits to Office files. For example, Web applications are useful as free PowerPoint players.

Signing up for SkyDrive

If you already have a Hotmail, Microsoft Messenger, or Windows Live account, you're already signed up and don't have to do anything more. If you need to sign up, follow these steps:

1. **Launch your favorite Office application and, with any file open (even a blank, new file will work), choose File⇨Share⇨Save to SkyDrive.**

   If you don't already have a Live ID, you're prompted to create one, as shown in Figure 4-5.

Figure 4-5:
Sign in
with your
Windows
Live ID or
get one.

> Windows Live Sign In
>
> Enter your Windows Live ID to sign in.
>
> Windows Live ID:
>
> Password:
>
> ☐ Save password in my Mac OS keychain
>
> (Get a Live ID...)   (Cancel) (Sign In)

2. **To create a new Live ID, click the Get a Live ID button.**

   Your Web browser (it must be Safari or Firefox) will take you to a page where you can sign up for a Windows Live ID, which lets you use SkyDrive. If your default browser is a different browser, then open Safari or Firefox and go to the SkyDrive site at `http://skydrive.live.com`.

Managing your SkyDrive

The SkyDrive Web site is where you perform SkyDrive file management tasks such as creating folders and setting permissions for who can access those folders. You must access SkyDrive through your Safari or Firefox Web browser at `http://skydrive.live.com`. You can create Personal and Shared folders. Take a look at Figure 4-6, which shows the screen you see as you enter SkyDrive. *Note:* Because SkyDrive is an evolving Web site rather than a desktop application, it's continuously being modified in appearance and function, so the site may not look exactly like what you see in Figure 4-6.

Here's an explanation of the options you can find in SkyDrive:

✦ **Folders:** Click a folder to see its contents. Contents can be files or other folders.

✦ **New:** Click to start a new, blank Word, Excel, PowerPoint, or OneNote file in an online Web application; you can also make a new folder.

✦ **Add Files:** Displays your folders. Choose a folder to display a File dialog that lets you choose files in your Mac's Finder to upload into SkyDrive. Also, because SkyDrive is platform agnostic, you can upload files to your SkyDrive account from a Windows computer. SkyDrive thus is a great way to exchange files if you're on a multi-OS environment.

Windows Live Sync.app

✦ **View synchronized folders:**

   • If you've already synchronized at least one folder, SkyDrive displays a list of your folders.

   • If you have not synchronized any folders, SkyDrive displays a dialog that lets you download the Windows Live Sync application.

Download the application (look for the Mac version) and then drag the application's icon into the Applications folder before running it. It will prompt you to specify a folder on your Mac as a shared folder. In Live Sync's preferences, select the check box to allow sharing with others.

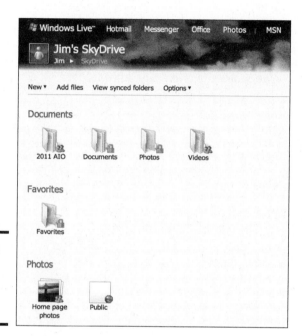

Figure 4-6:
Managing your SkyDrive cloud.

+ **Search documents:** Off to the right (not shown in Figure 4-6) is a search field that lets you search your SkyDrive documents.

+ **Space available:** Also off to the right is a space remaining indicator.

Saving to SkyDrive

After you've established your SkyDrive account, you have two ways to save to SkyDrive without your Web browser:

+ Saving directly from Office to SkyDrive.

+ Saving to a folder that's synced to SkyDrive.

Saving directly to SkyDrive

From Word, Excel, and PowerPoint, you can choose File➪Share➪Save to SkyDrive to display the Windows Live Sign In dialog, shown in Figure 4-7. If you select the Save Password in my Mac OS Keychain check box, you won't have to enter your username and password each time you sign in.

When you're signed into SkyDrive, you see a file browser that displays your SkyDrive file folders, as shown in Figure 4-8. Choose a folder and then click Save to save your file into the folder. You can save only to the first folder level of SkyDrive. You can't save to subfolders from within Office 2011 applications.

Saving to a folder synched to SkyDrive

If you've created one or more synced folders in Finder using the Windows Live Sync application, you can choose File⇨Save or choose File⇨Save As and treat the Live Sync folder just like any other folder.

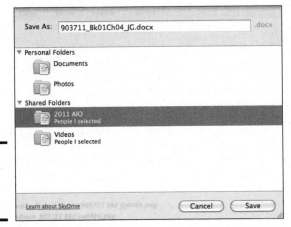

Figure 4-7:
Saving
directly to
the cloud.

Windows Sync automatically synchronizes your folders with SkyDrive for you. Files in synced folders in Finder work exactly the same as ordinary files saved anywhere in Finder, but they are synced to the corresponding folder in your SkyDrive.

Opening files on SkyDrive

Of course, after you put files into SkyDrive, you'll want to open them, and so will the people you share them with. Refer to Figure 4-8 or sign into your SkyDrive account with a Windows Live ID as we go through these options.

Opening directly within an application

By choosing File⇨Open URL in Word, Excel, or PowerPoint, you can display a dialog that lets you paste the URL of a SkyDrive file. You can obtain the URL from SkyDrive by visiting your SkyDrive cloud in a Web browser and choosing either Share⇨Get Link, which presents the URL immediately, or Share⇨Send a Link, which sends an e-mail containing the link to either yourself or someone with sharing permissions.

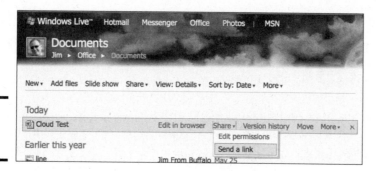

Figure 4-8:
Opening in
the cloud.

Opening in Office 2011 from SkyDrive

In your Web browser, when you select a saved office file, you can choose
Open in *[Application Name]*. This option causes the selected file to download to your Mac and to open in the appropriate application. This process
takes a bit of time, so be patient and allow it to complete.

Opening in a SkyDrive Web application

Another option is to open the document for editing or viewing right in the
Web browser by choosing Edit in Document. Figure 4-9 shows the Word Web
application in Editing View, with its minimalist Ribbon, displaying a portion
of this chapter.

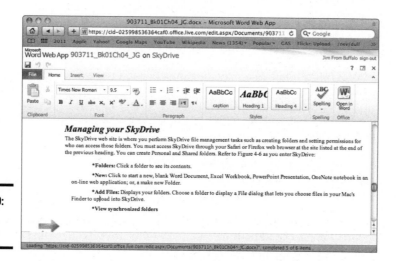

Figure 4-9:
Editing in
the cloud.

Your online editing options are as follows:

✦ **File:** Similar to the File menu in Office. When you choose Save, you are saving to your SkyDrive folder.

✦ **Home:** Displays the Ribbon in Editing View. You can edit the file in your web browser.

✦ **Open in *[Application Name]*:** Downloads a copy of the file and opens the file on your computer in Word, Excel, or PowerPoint on your Mac.

✦ **Spelling:** Check spelling on line.

✦ **Insert:** Choose Table, Picture, ClipArt, or Link.

✦ **View:** Choosing View⇨Reading View displays the document in what would normally be called Print Layout in Word. In the PowerPoint Web application, you can choose View⇨Slide Show, which runs your presentation as a show, or View⇨Notes to display what in PowerPoint 2011 is Normal view for editing (not Notes view).

✦ **Format:** Selecting picture objects displays the Picture Tools tab of Web application's Ribbon.

Opening as a regular file

You can always download a file from SkyDrive and save it in Finder on your computer. If you used the Live Sync application, you can open files in your synched folder as you would any other file.

Saving to SharePoint

Think of SharePoint as a private cloud. Typically, an organization purchases SharePoint and runs it on an in-house computer or pays a hosting company to run the server. SharePoint does not subject its patrons to advertising and is private and secure. Instead of signing up for SharePoint, your IT department would assign a connection, username, and password to you.

Similar to the public cloud, in SharePoint you may share files in managed folders, but of course these folders are accessible only to your organization. SharePoint is different from SkyDrive in these ways:

✦ **Check-in/check-out:** SharePoint can manage who has a document so that only one person at a time can make edits, thereby avoiding conflicts.

✦ **No advertising.**

✦ **Enhanced privacy and security:** Accessible only to your organization.

✦ **No synced folders:** SharePoint does not support synced folders. You can drive your IT department nuts and set up shared folders in Mac OS X.

The mechanics of SharePoint are analogous to working with SkyDrive (discussed in the preceding sections). You use a Web browser to manage your folders and set permissions. You choose File⇨Share⇨Save to SharePoint to display a file browser that looks similar to the SkyDrive browser shown in Figure 4-6, except it saves to SharePoint instead of SkyDrive.

Sharing via E-Mail

E-mail remains a popular way to share documents. Word, Excel, and PowerPoint offer several options for sending files:

✦ **E-mailing as attachment (File⇨Share⇨Email [as Attachment]):** When you want the recipient to get an exact copy of a Word document, Excel workbook, or a PowerPoint presentation, use this option to send the active file as an e-mail attachment.

✦ **E-mailing as HTML (File⇨Share⇨Email [as HTML]):** For Word and Excel, this method takes advantage of Office applications' ability to create HTML documents, and most modern e-mail programs do a decent job of interpreting HTML mail. Use this method when exact reproduction isn't critical and the recipient doesn't need to edit the document. However, remember that e-mail sizes can be considerably larger if you use this option. In Word, to get a better idea of how your document will look when received, choose View⇨Web Layout before sending.

✦ **E-mailing the link (File⇨Share⇨Email [as Link]):** If you opened a document from a SkyDrive link, you can e-mail that link to a collaborator. Be sure you've set permissions within SkyDrive for that person's e-mail address so they can open that link from SkyDrive.

✦ **Sending via Messenger or Communicator (File⇨Share⇨Instant Message⇨[Recipient's name or other]):** This option appears if Messenger or Communicator is open. Choose a contact, and your file will be sent to them. Choose Other to enter an e-mail address.

Chapter 5: Getting SmartArt

A picture is worth a thousand words, yet some pictures still need words to make them relevant. These types of pictures are actually graphics created using both visuals and words, and they're broadly called *info-graphics*. Info-graphics come in two flavors:

✦ **Diagrams** that take logic and relationships and present them in a visual form

✦ **Charts** that take data and present them in a visual form

We look at charts in Word and Excel in Book II, Chapter 6 and Book III, Chapter 6, respectively. Diagrams in Office are available as part of SmartArt, a component that lets you represent your ideas visually. SmartArt graphics are sophisticated design combinations of shapes and text that you can customize quickly. This chapter is about SmartArt and is organized around the options available in the SmartArt tab of the Ribbon, which is found in Word, Excel, and PowerPoint.

Smiling with SmartArt

A large variety of SmartArt graphics is available from the Ribbon. They're fun to use and easy to create. Their emotional power lies in their simple yet powerful visual appeal.

Inserting a SmartArt graphic

When you click the SmartArt tab on the Ribbon, the leftmost group is Insert SmartArt Graphic, shown in Figure 5-1. Here you find several buttons that represent various types of SmartArt graphics. Hold the cursor over any of these buttons to reveal a tooltip with suggestions about how you might use them.

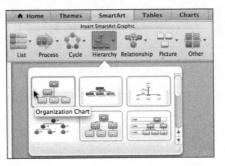

Figure 5-1:
The Insert
SmartArt
Graphic
group on the
SmartArt
tab.

To insert a SmartArt graphic in your document, follow these steps:

1. **Determine where the SmartArt will be inserted in the file.**

In Word, click in the document to make sure the insertion point is right where you want it. For Excel, select a cell. For PowerPoint, just make sure that the slide where you want to insert the SmartArt graphic is the active slide.

2. **Access the SmartArt tab of the Ribbon and click any of the buttons in the Insert SmartArt Graphic group to reveal a gallery. To insert your choice, just click it.**

You can use arrow keys to move the selection cursor around on Ribbon galleries. Press the spacebar to insert the selected SmartArt graphic. Hover the mouse over a SmartArt variant within a gallery to see its name.

Are all options in the SmartArt tab of the Ribbon grayed out and unavailable? This can happen if you're using any of the older Word document file formats such as .doc. To fix this problem, choose File⇨Convert Document to convert your document to the current XML file format. In PowerPoint and Excel, you'll need to choose File⇨Save As and choose the current format to preserve SmartArt.

Don't be shocked at how large some of the galleries are. They're designed so you can easily see the previews. Grab the resize handle at the lower-right corner and tame these monsters by dragging them down to size. As you do, scroll bars appear as needed.

All SmartArt graphic variants have similarities in the way you create, edit, and format them. Figure 5-2 shows an Organization Chart that we created from the Hierarchy category within the SmartArt tab of the Ribbon.

Show/Hide Text Pane

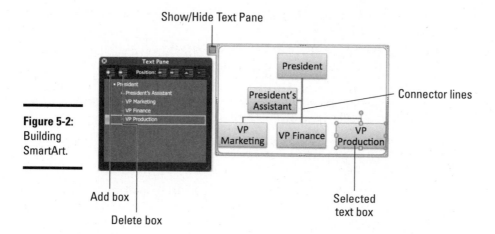

Connector lines

Figure 5-2:
Building
SmartArt.

Add box

Delete box

Selected
text box

Refer to Figure 5-2 or run your Office application alongside as we run down
the features of SmartArt graphics:

✦ **Text Pane:** The Text Pane contains all the text content of a SmartArt
graphic organized as an outline. Type in words within the Text Pane,
and you'll automatically find new shapes such as boxes that include the
same text added within your SmartArt graphic. Of course, you can type
straight into the Text Pane or directly inside the SmartArt shapes — mix
and match as you please. The handy icons in the Text Pane help you
manage your text:

• *Promote:* Move the selected position(s) up in the hierarchy.

• *Demote:* Move the selected position(s) down in the hierarchy.

• *Add:* Click to add a new position to the hierarchy relative to the
shape that was selected before clicking the Add icon.

• *Delete:* Click to remove selected position(s) from the hierarchy.

• *Resize:* Drag the resize handle to resize the text pane.

✦ **SmartArt shapes:** SmartArt objects contain text boxes and other elements, usually with connector lines, constrained by a border that displays whenever you have selected your SmartArt object. Here are things
to look for when working with SmartArt objects:

• *Show/hide text pane:* Click to show or hide the Text Pane.

• *Text boxes:* Click to select and then type in a text box. If the box
already contains some text, you can either edit it through the text

pane or you can select the text within the box itself and then over-type to edit or replace text.

Text boxes come in various shapes, which you can change if you like. (See the "Editing SmartArt" section later in this chapter.)

- *Picture boxes:* SmartArt shapes in the Picture group on the Ribbon have picture placeholders. Click a SmartArt picture placeholder to activate a file open dialog to choose a picture.

- *Connector lines:* The lines connecting shapes in SmartArt objects are usually attached to the shapes so that if you move a shape, the line moves, too.

- *Selection indicator:* When you click a shape, small circles at the corners and edges of the shape visually let you know the object is currently selected.

- *Resize:* You can resize SmartArt by dragging edges and corners of the frame surrounding the diagram.

Editing SmartArt

If you select a SmartArt graphic, you can use the Edit SmartArt group (see Figure 5-3) of the SmartArt tab of the Ribbon for three things:

- ✦ **Shape:** You select one or more boxes or shapes within a SmartArt object and then click the Shape button. A menu appears with several galleries that contain many different shapes. Click the shape you want to the selected boxes to have.

- ✦ **Right to Left:** Some SmartArt objects are asymmetrical. Click this button to change the arrangement of the shapes so that things grouped on the right are pushed to the left. Click a second time to put them back. Clicking this button with an Organization Chart selected, for example, flips all your listings horizontally.

- ✦ **Org:** This option is available only if you have selected a shape within your Organization Chart. Organization charts are discussed in detail in the "Making Organization Charts" section later this chapter.

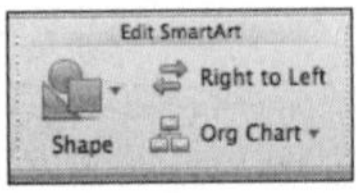

Figure 5-3:
Editing
SmartArt.

Applying graphic styles to SmartArt

When you've selected a SmartArt object, the SmartArt Graphic Styles gallery is activated on the SmartArt tab of the Ribbon. The gallery provides previews of styles that you can apply to your SmartArt as well as color variations, as shown in Figure 5-4.

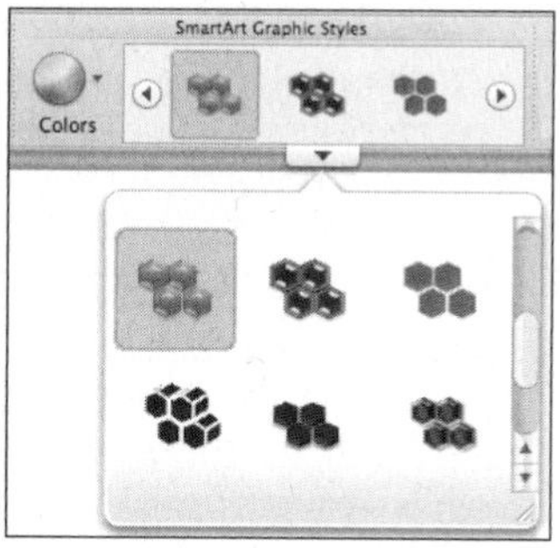

Figure 5-4:
Applying a
SmartArt
style.

SmartArt can take its color from your document's theme. Before using the color control of the styles grouping, change your theme:

✦ If you're using Word or Excel, visit the Home tab of the Ribbon and click the Themes button. Then make selections from the resultant Themes gallery.

✦ If you're using PowerPoint, visit the Themes tab of the Ribbon and select a new theme from the Themes gallery. You can also access the Theme Options group and just change your Theme Colors from the Colors button, which brings up a gallery of the same name.

After choosing a theme, return to the SmartArt tab of the Ribbon and access the SmartArt Graphic Styles group to explore these options:

✦ **Colors:** This button opens the Colors gallery. Choose from an assortment of tints and shades of the current color. If your SmartArt contains a picture, you can tint the picture by choosing the Match Picture to SmartArt Graphic Color option right at the bottom of the Colors gallery.

✦ **Styles gallery:** Click the arrows at each end of the gallery to scroll, or click near the center at the bottom of the gallery to expose the drop-down gallery. Click to apply a style.

Resetting SmartArt

The Reset group on the SmartArt tab has two functions:

✦ **Reset Graphic:** Click to remove the style you applied and restore the default look to the SmartArt graphic.

   This won't remove the tint from pictures. To do that, you have to access the Colors gallery again and choose the Reset Picture Color option.

✦ **Convert:** In Excel and PowerPoint, you have two options.

   • *Convert to Shapes:* Converts your SmartArt object to shape objects. Right-click the converted result and choose Grouping⇨Ungroup to ungroup into individual shapes.

   • *Convert to Text:* Converts your SmartArt object into a bulleted text box. This is particularly handy in PowerPoint if you converted text into a SmartArt graphic and you want to turn it back into text.

To convert bulleted text in PowerPoint to a SmartArt graphic, first select all the text, then right-click it and choose the Convert to SmartArt option in the resultant pop-up menu. This will activate the SmartArt tab of the Ribbon. Now choose any of the SmartArt categories to open relevant galleries and choose the SmartArt variant you want to apply. Your bulleted text will now metamorphose to a SmartArt graphic!

Making Organization Charts

Office offers two different approaches for making organization charts: The newer SmartArt method can produce visually appealing charts, and the application called Microsoft Organization Chart creates embedded charts.

SmartArt Organization charts

The SmartArt Hierarchy group has three different organization charts from which to choose:

✦ Organization Chart

✦ Name and Title Organization Chart

✦ Half Circle Organization Chart

If you refer to Figure 5-1, earlier in this chapter, you can see that these are the first three options available in the Hierarchy gallery. You can use all the features of SmartArt with these organization charts. But when you select an object in a SmartArt organization chart, notice that the Org option becomes available in the Edit SmartArt group.

To use these features, first select the position at the top of the organization chart's hierarchy and then select one of the following from the Org menu:

✦ **Horizontal:** Arranges the chart in horizontal style.

✦ **Vertical:** Arranges the chart in a vertical style.

✦ **Left hanging:** Arranges position boxes to the left of the centerline.

✦ **Right hanging:** Arranges position boxes to the right of the centerline.

✦ **Add Assistant:** To add an assistant to a position, first, select a position within the SmartArt organization chart's hierarchy. Then, choose Add Assistant from the Org menu in the Edit SmartArt grouping.

Chapter 6: Selecting and Formatting

However you may work within Office 2011, you will find that the applications are continuously providing visual feedback to you. Sometimes this feedback is subtle, as in dozens of cursor designs, and sometimes the feedback is obvious, as when the Format tab appears on the Ribbon because a picture is selected. In addition, formatting actions almost always work consistently across Office applications, but you should know the important subtleties so you can get the best use out of Office.

In this chapter, we refer to objects such as text and shapes that already exist in your document, workbook, or presentation. (If you want to know how to add media objects, see Chapter 8 of this minibook.)

Selecting Objects

You can find all kinds of objects in Office: lines, pictures, words, text boxes, charts, cells, paragraphs, and more. When you select an object, its appearance changes in some way to let you know that it's selected. The options available to you in the interface also change depending upon what's currently selected. You can usually copy, cut, delete, or apply formatting options to whatever is selected. Often, the mouse cursor changes from the default arrow to provide additional visual information.

Most people are so used to working with text they don't stop to think about what's going on. You click into a word, and the blinking insertion cursor appears. It works the same with typing text in a Word document, clicking in a bulleted list in PowerPoint, when using SmartArt, and so on. To select objects, click on them, within them, or on their borders. Table 6-1 shows the most common selection options.

Table 6-1	Selection Tips
Doing This	*Makes This Happen*
Click into text	Insertion cursor appears in text
Drag mouse over words	Selects words
Double-click in text	Select a word
Double-click elsewhere	Format object dialog may appear
Triple-click in text	Select entire paragraph
Click a shape	Selects the shape
Drag over shape(s)	May select the shape(s)
Click into shape	Sets text cursor position in shape
Click object border	Selects entire object
Right-click	A context-sensitive menu appears
⌘-A	Select all
⌘-C	Copy selection to Mac OS X Clipboard
⌘-X	Cut selection to Mac OS X Clipboard
⌘-V	Paste from Mac OS X Clipboard
⌘-Y	Repeat last operation
⌘-Z	Undo

You can modify certain selection behavior in each application's Preferences panel. For example, the default in Office is that when you drag the mouse over any part of a word, the entire word becomes selected. To change this selection behavior in Word or PowerPoint, do the following within each application:

1. **Choose the Word or PowerPoint menu and then Preferences.**

   The Preferences panel for Word or PowerPoint displays. (See Figure 6-1.)

2. **Choose Edit.**

   Preference options display.

3. **Choose When Selecting, Automatically Select Entire Word.**

   In the resulting Preferences dialog, deselect When Selecting, Automatically Select Entire Word.

Knowing what's selected is key to using Office. The entire Office interface constantly changes depending upon what's currently selected. Menus, the Format dialog, toolbars, and Ribbon options change based on what is currently selected. Even copy, cut, and paste options change based on what is being copied, cut, or pasted.

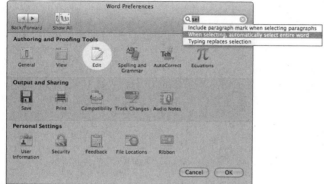

Figure 6-1: Setting selection preferences.

Understanding Formatting Basics

You can change the format of a selected object in two main ways:

✦ **The Ribbon:** Click the Home tab and, when displayed, click the purple Format tab. When you select objects, look for and then click purple tabs like Format Picture and Chart Layout.

✦ **The Format dialog:** Access the Format dialog by either of the following methods:

• *Format⇨[Object]:* Use the Format menu to open a Format dialog.

• *Right-click and choose Format:* From the contextual menu, choose the Format option to open a Format dialog.

There's no right or wrong way to go about this. Use whichever method you prefer. Of the methods, using Format dialogs is the most comprehensive, but using the Ribbon or right-clicking may be more intuitive and easier. When you want to see a list of the kinds of things that can be formatted at any given moment, head to the menu bar and click Format.

There are three Format dialogs: Shape, Text, and Picture. Many of the same controls are found in each of these three dialogs.

Formatting with the Ribbon

The Home tab of the Ribbon was engineered to display the formatting and other commands used most often. The formatting options on each application's Home tab are different for Word, Excel, and PowerPoint, so we cover the Home tab in each application's minibook.

In this minibook, we cover the portions of the Ribbon that are the same or almost the same throughout Office applications. Some additional formatting features are specific to individual applications, so we cover them within the respective minibook for each application.

The Ribbon's Format tabs become available when you select objects such as text boxes, pictures, graphs, and shapes that offer additional formatting opportunities. Note that each type of object has a different Format tab that is context sensitive to the object you have selected. These are covered in this chapter.

Formatting ordinary text

Head to the Font group on the Ribbon's Home tab when you want to format selected text. (Figure 6-2 shows PowerPoint's set of Font tools.) Although most of these controls may seem familiar, some of them work a little differently in Office 2011.

Figure 6-2:
Formatting
ordinary
text.

You may enjoy working with text a bit more after you go through the explanations of the Ribbon's Font group:

✦ **Font name:** Click to choose a font. Notice the first item in the list, Font Collections, which appears when you click this control (see Figure 6-3):

  • *Fixed Width:* Lists fonts where every character is exactly the same width instead of using a proportional amount of space. This is quite like the old typewriters where the characters *i* and *w* took the same amount of space.

  • *Fun:* Fonts that may add some zest. You may not want to use any of these in a corporate document unless you're in the entertainment business.

  • *Modern:* Modern from a 1960s perspective, perhaps. All fonts here though are clean and upright.

  • *PDF:* Fonts that look great when saving in PDF format.

- *Classic:* Not boring Times New Roman as the label implies. There are plenty of classical fonts here.

- *Web:* Fonts that play nicely with Web browsers. Use these if you're planning to use Save As Web Page.

- *Windows Office Compatible:* Stick with these fonts if you plan to share with Windows users. You'll avoid most font substitution problems. Office 2010 for Windows has these fonts.

Also note the Theme Headings and Theme Body selections right below the Font Collections (see Figure 6-3). These fonts change depending on the Theme you are working with. Themes are covered in Book IV, Chapter 5.

Figure 6-3: Choosing compatible fonts.

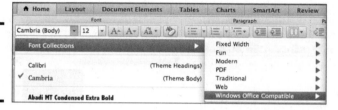

- ✦ **Font Size:** Type a size in the box, or click the arrow to select a size from the pop-up menu.

- ✦ **Larger:** Each click bumps the size up a notch.

- ✦ **Smaller:** Each click shrinks the size a notch.

- ✦ **Change Case:** (Word and PowerPoint only) Offers five options, formatted exactly as they look: Sentence case, lowercase, UPPERCASE, Title Case, tOGGLE cASE.

- ✦ **Clear Formatting:** Restores default properties to the selection.

- ✦ **Bold:** Makes font bold.

- ✦ **Italic:** Makes font italic.

- ✦ **Underline:** Makes font underlined. In Word only, there's a small downward arrow next to this button that reveals a pop-up menu with several underlining options.

- ✦ **Strikethrough:** Places a horizontal line right through your text.

- ✦ **Superscript:** Makes font go up and become smaller, like the 2 in $3^2=9$.

- ✦ **Subscript:** Makes font go down and become smaller, like the 2 in H_2O.

- ✦ **Character spacing** (PowerPoint only): Offers several options to manipulate spacing between individual characters:

  - *Very tight, Tight, Normal, Loose, and Very Loose*

- *Character Spacing Options:* If the five presets above don't give you ample control, choose this option to display the Format Text dialog, where you can control the spacing by the numbers.

✦ **Font Color:** Displays font color palette.

✦ **Text highlight color** (Word only, not illustrated): Click to add, change, or remove a highlight color.

✦ **Text effects:** Click to display a submenu of assorted text effects in Word and PowerPoint.

Formatting text boxes and shapes

Office has all kinds of shapes, including text boxes, shapes, SmartArt shapes, and content placeholders in PowerPoint. But that's just the beginning. In addition to using the Font tab offerings, you can apply an incredible amount of interesting text effects. In this chapter, we focus on the shape itself, the container, rather than on formatting the text within the container, which we save for Chapter 9 of this minibook.

The moment you click on or into a shape, the Format tab appears to the right of the Home tab on the Ribbon. Click the Format tab to display the formatting options in this tab of the Ribbon.

Selecting shapes and text

Knowing what's currently selected is very important when formatting text that's inside a shape of some sort. You can format the text inside a shape as well as format the shape containing the text independently.

Figure 6-4 (top) shows a shape that's selected, but the text inside is not currently selected. When the shape itself is selected, the resize handles are shaded with color.

Figure 6-4 (bottom) also shows the same shape, but this time we double-clicked the text within the box so that the word Text is selected, as indicated by shading.

Text within shapes responds nicely to the Font section of the Ribbon, regardless of whether the shape or the text within the shape is selected. Because you can apply formatting options such as reflection and shadow to both the entire containing shape as well as text inside the shape, it's important to pay attention to what you have selected, the shape or the text within a shape, before applying formatting.

Rotation   Resize
handle   handles

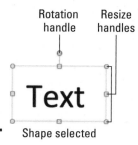

Shape selected

Figure 6-4:
Selecting
a shape
(top) and
text within
a shape
(bottom).

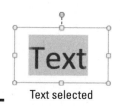

Text selected

Do you want to rotate a shape? Easy! Just drag the little green rotation
handle at the top of any selected shape. See Figure 6-4.

Applying shape styles

Like the Font group, when you use the Shape Styles tools in the Format tab
of the Ribbon (see Figure 6-5), the formatting changes are applied to the
shape itself, as well as the text inside the shape. Many of the tools have an
option that takes you to the Format Shape, Picture, or Text dialog. Format
dialogs are discussed later in this chapter. On the Ribbon's Shape Styles
group, you can find these interface options:

✦ **Arrow buttons:** Click the round arrow buttons at each end of the Shape
Styles group to display more of the available styles.

✦ **Submenu:** Click at the bottom of the group near the middle to display all
the styles on a submenu palette as a drop-down gallery.

✦ **More Options:** Click to display the Format Shape dialog.

✦ **Fill format:** Displays the color palette (shown in Figure 6-6) with a Fill
Effects option. Choosing Fill Effects displays the Format Shape dialog.

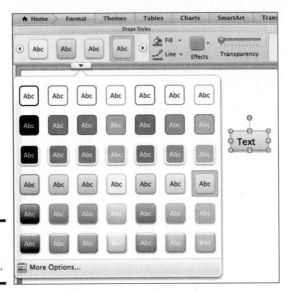

Figure 6-5:
Applying a
shape style.

✦ **Line format:** Formats the line that surrounds a shape. You have the following options (see Figure 6-5):

- *No Line:* Removes the line that surrounds a shape.

- *Theme Colors:* Displays theme color palette theme with gradations of the ten colors beneath.

- *Standard Colors:* Ten ordinary colors.

- *Recent Colors:* Ten of your last color choices, assuming you made those choices from the More Colors option we discuss next. If you made no recent choices, no Recent Colors option is available (as is the case with Figure 6-6).

- *More Colors:* Displays the Mac OS X color picker.

- *Line Effects:* Displays the Format Shape dialog.

- *Weights:* A submenu offers various line widths.

- *Dashed:* A submenu offers line styles from which to choose.

- *Arrows:* If the selected shape is a line with a beginning and end, you can choose arrow-shaped and rounded ends for your line. On the other hand, if your line is the perimeter of a circle that does not have an identified beginning and end, the Arrows option will be grayed out.

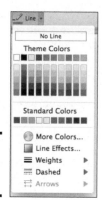

Figure 6-6:
Applying a
line format.

Clicking the Effects button (see left margin) produces a submenu divided into five categories, each of which has additional submenu palettes with a wide variety of formatting effects. A click on a palette is all it takes to apply an effect. The categories are:

✦ Shadow

✦ Reflection

✦ Glow

✦ Bevel

✦ 3-D Rotation

Transparency is a measure of how much you can see through something when it is on top of another object or the background. Something that is adjusted to 100% transparent is invisible. When adjusted to 0% transparency, it is completely opaque. The fun comes in when you adjust transparency somewhere in between and pile objects on top of one another.

The transparency slider (refer to Figure 6-5) is the final tool in the Shape Styles group of the Ribbon. Drag the slider control right and left to adjust how much see-through you want to give the selected shape.

Formatting with the Format Shapes Dialog

Many of the formatting options on the Ribbon lead you to the different tabs of the Format Shape dialog shown in Figure 6-7. You can get to this dialog directly by selecting a shape and then choosing Format⇨Shape from the menu bar or from the right-click contextual menu. While the Ribbon offers fast and visual formatting options that complement and follow the consistent theme of the document, the Format Shape dialog offers the complete set of options and fine tuning. These options may not be consistent and visually pleasing all the time, but remember that a host of formatting options await!

After formatting a shape as you want, right-click it and choose Set as Default Shape so that any future shapes you make in that document, workbook, or presentation will follow the same formatting by default.

We now start at the top and work our way down through the powerful Format Shapes dialog.

Applying a solid fill

You can apply a fill to almost any shape that is not a point-to-point line. This includes shapes from the Media palette and shapes in graphs such as those representing series.

The fill color is separate from the color of the line that surrounds a shape, which is formatted independently and discussed later in this chapter.

The term *solid fill* means that the fill color is uniform throughout the shape. In the Format Shape dialog, you access these options by choosing Fill in the left column and then clicking the Solid tab, as shown in Figure 6-7.

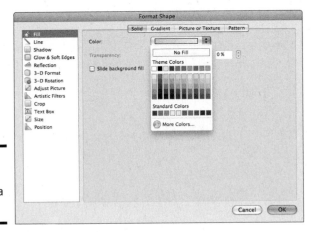

Figure 6-7:
Applying solid fill to a shape.

The controls work like this:

✦ **Color:** Click this area to bring up a pop-up menu that lets you choose a solid fill color.

  • *No fill:* Makes the fill area of the shape completely empty. You can see through this shape if you position it above another shape or text. If there's nothing behind this shape, you'll see the background. Such shapes continue to have a line attribute that remains visible unless you turn that off, too. If you do that, you just created an invisible object!

  • *Theme Colors and Standard Colors:* Click to apply.

  • *More Colors:* Opens the Mac OS X color picker.

✦ **Transparency:** Use the slider, enter a percentage, or use the increase/decrease control to adjust how much see-through you need for the selected shape.

✦ **Slide background fill** (PowerPoint only): Select this check box to have the shape's fill match the slide background.

Applying a gradient fill

The Gradient tab of the Fill panel in the Format Shape dialog, shown in Figure 6-8, is one of our favorite options. Although it looks complicated at first, after you play with it, you'll love its flexibility. This dialog is fun to use and can produce superb-looking gradient fills.

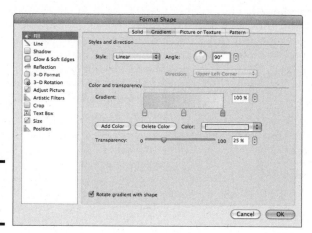

Figure 6-8:
Making a
gradient fill.

The Live Preview feature makes the selected shape reflect the adjustments you make to the controls in this dialog as you adjust the controls. If your selected shape is covered by the dialog, move the Format Shape dialog to uncover the shape.

The Styles and Direction section of the Gradient tab is where you begin making your gradient fill adjustments. The first thing you do is choose a style from the Style pop-up menu:

✦ **Style:** Choose from four different styles: Linear, Radial, Rectangular, and Path. There's also a None option, which can be helpful if you want to remove pre-applied gradients and change them to solid fills.

✦ **Angle direction:** There are three ways to set the angle direction of a gradient fill. Angle direction applies to linear style only:

• Click the dot on the round control and drag around the circle.

• Type a specific value into the spinner control.

• Click the spinner control's up- and down-arrow buttons.

✦ **Direction:** Click this pop-up menu to choose a gradient direction from several different positions within the shape. Use this control instead of Angle direction when working with Radial or Rectangular styles. This option is not available for the Linear and Path style gradients.

The Color and Transparency section lets you add multiple colors and shades of color to your shape's gradient fill:

✦ **Color handle:** Each color handle underneath the live preview rectangle in the Format Shape dialog represents a color in your gradient fill. You can drag the color handles left and right to control the gradient stop blending percentage within the gradient. The control affects one color within your gradient. When you click a color handle, it becomes darker, and the Color control will update to let you know which color you're controlling. To add a new handle, click the Add Color button.

✦ **Gradient Stop:** Adjusts the blending point of the selected color handle within the shape expressed as a percentage. You have three ways to adjust intensity:

• Drag the color handle left and right.

• Type a value in the gradient stop's spinner control.

• Click the gradient stop's spinner control buttons.

✦ **Add Color:** Each time you click the Add Color button, a new color handle is added beneath the Live Preview rectangle and becomes the selected handle.

✦ **Delete Color:** Deletes the currently selected color handle and its associated gradient color.

✦ **Color:** Displays the color palette so you can choose a color to apply to the currently selected color handle's gradient.

TIP

Gradients that are pleasing to the eye are easy to make by choosing colors that are within a single column of the Theme colors of the color palette.

✦ **Transparency:** Drag the slider or use the spinner control to adjust transparency of the selected color handle.

✦ **Rotate Gradient with Shape:** Select this check box if you want the gradient fill to rotate along with the shape when you rotate it.

Filling with a picture or texture

Shapes can be filled with a picture from a file or filled with one of several textures from a menu by way of the Picture or Texture tab of the Format Shape dialog, as shown in Figure 6-9.

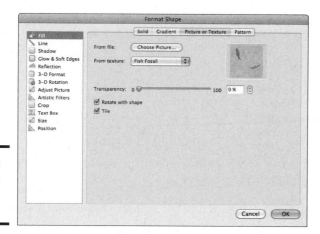

Figure 6-9:
Filling with picture or texture.

✦ **Choose Picture:** Click the Choose Picture button to display the Choose a Picture dialog. Browse or use Search to find a picture file and then click Insert, and your selection fills the shape.

✦ **From Texture:** Click the From Texture pop-up menu to look through some texture options. Unlike pictures, textures tile (most of the time, seamlessly) in the shape area.

✦ **Transparency:** Drag the slider or use the spinner control.

- ✦ **Rotate with shape:** When selected, the picture or texture rotates when the shape itself is rotated.

- ✦ **Tile:** When selected, the texture or picture is tiled within the shape. By using this option, you can make any picture behave like a texture.

Filling with a pattern

Patterns are geometric designs that use two colors. Here are four occasions when using the Pattern tab in the Fill panel of the Format Shape dialog (see Figure 6-10) might be your best choice. You may think of more uses.

- ✦ When filling shapes (especially in charts and graphs) that will be used for publication, especially when you are limited to two color prints as in black and white.

- ✦ When you want to make it easier for color-blind people to distinguish colored areas by adding visual cues.

- ✦ When you plan to print your output in black and white, or grayscale.

- ✦ Whenever you desire a high-contrast fill.

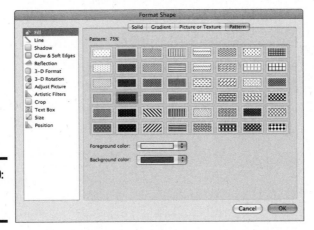

Figure 6-10:
Filling with
a pattern.

Using a pattern is a matter of clicking a pattern to choose it. The default is black and white, but you can adjust foreground and/or background color as you please by clicking the Foreground Color and Background Color swatches.

Formatting a line

You're offered line-formatting options when you choose to format a line and also when you format a solid shape. Solid shapes have lines around them, and those lines (outlines, really) can be formatted just like simple lines. In the Format Shape dialog, when you select Line in the left column, the first two tabs are Solid and Gradient. These two tabs work identically to the Solid and Gradient tabs of the Fill panel that we discussed in the preceding sections, "Applying a solid fill" and "Applying a gradient fill."

When you choose the Weights & Arrows tab (shown in Figure 6-11), the Line Style options are available for all shapes. Arrows are available when you have chosen a line that is freestanding and has ends.

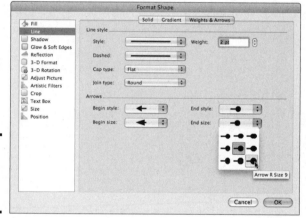

Figure 6-11:
Formatting
weights and
arrows.

Sometimes it's easier to work with fine adjustments to positioning lines if you use the zoom control to zoom in.

The Line Style section of the Weights & Arrows tab has several pop-up menus plus a spinner control that lets you adjust the weight, or thickness, of a line:

+ **Style:** Has several preset single-line weights, double lines, and a triple line from which to choose. You can adjust the weights further in the Weight option to its right.

+ **Weight:** Use this spinner control to adjust the line weight (thickness).

+ **Dashed:** Choose from preset dashes.

✦ **Cap type:** Choose from three end-cap types. You probably won't notice a difference in cap type unless the line is at least 6 points in weight or more. The elbow connector line in Figure 6-12 is formatted at 10 points and zoomed in to 400% so you can see the differences easily.

- *Square:* Adds a box-style cap to a line.

- *Round:* Adds a rounded cap on a line.

- *Flat:* Does not add a cap to a line. It looks square and appears shorter because nothing is added.

✦ **Join type:** When a line joins another line and at points within a line, you can make variations in join type styles. Like end-caps, these styles are easier to see on lines that have a weight of 6 points or more.

- *Round:* Rounded.

- *Bevel:* Cut off corner.

- *Miter:* Sharp angle.

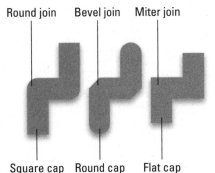

Figure 6-12:
Formatting
end-caps
and joins.

When you make a line, you drag from a beginning point, and when you let go after dragging, you have an end point. You can format these line beginning and end points by turning them into arrows using the Arrows controls on the Weights & Measures tab of the Format Shapes dialog. (Refer to Figure 6-11.)

✦ **Begin style and End style:** Choose from six different styles.

✦ **Begin size and End size:** Choose from nine proportional sizes.

Formatting a shape's shadow

When you use the Shadow formatting controls of the Format Shape dialog, you can choose from inner, outer, and perspective shadow styles, illustrated here in Figure 6-13.

Figure 6-13:
Choosing
a shadow
style.

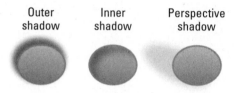

Outer
shadow

Inner
shadow

Perspective
shadow

After you choose a shadow style, you can control several aspects of the
shadow by using slider and spinner controls: angle, color, size, blur, distance from the shape, and transparency, as shown in Figure 6-14. To turn
shadows on or off, select or deselect the Shadow check box.

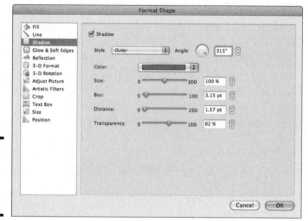

Figure 6-14:
Formatting
a shape's
shadow.

Adding a glow effect

Similar to the shadow effect is the glow effect. It's like a shadow, but it surrounds the entire shape like a halo instead of being directional. An example
of a rectangle with a glow effect is in the left margin. To add a glow effect, in
the Glow and Soft Edges tab of the Format Shape dialog, click the Color
pop-up menu and choose a color. Drag the sliders or use the spinner controls to adjust the size of the glow and how transparent it is.

The same dialog has an option for Soft Edges, which is like an inverse of a
glow because it eats into the shape area itself rather than growing it larger.
You can decide how big the optional soft edges should be. (See Figure 6-15.)
As with most special effects, limit using glow to specific purposes so you
don't overuse it.

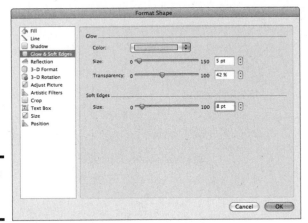

Adding reflection

Reflection is a popular feature, but be careful not to overuse it. If you've added reflection from the Ribbon and wondered whether you can fine-tune how the reflection looks, the Format Shape dialog is the place. You can control the following aspects of the reflection (see Figure 6-16):

✦ **Reflection:** When the check box is selected, the shape has reflection.

✦ **Transparency:** Use the slider or spinner to adjust see-through.

✦ **Size:** Use the slider or spinner to adjust the reflection's size.

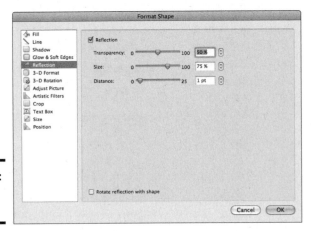

+ **Distance:** The slider and spinner determine how far away the reflection will be from the shape.

+ **Rotate Reflection with Shape:** When selected, the reflection will rotate when the shape is rotated.

Making a 3-D format

Using the 3-D format controls, you can easily take a simple shape and give it a three-dimensional appearance. The diamond in the left margin is just a shape that has 3-D formatting applied using the settings on the Bevel and Depth and Surface tabs we show in Figures 6-17 and 6-18. On the Bevel tab (see Figure 6-17) of 3-D Format option in the Format Shape dialog, you control the following:

+ **Bevel Top and Bottom:** Click either control to choose from several pre-formatted styles.

+ **Bevel Height and Width:** Use the spinner controls to make adjustments.

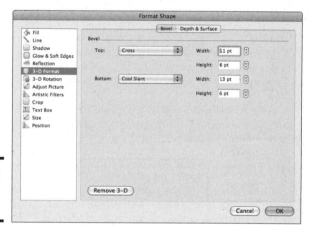

Figure 6-17:
Adjusting
the bevel.

The Depth & Surface tab offers two sections: Depth & Contour and Surface. Figure 6-18 shows these sections.

If nothing seems to be happening when you adjust these controls, first apply a 3-D rotation (discussed in the next section). After you rotate the shape, you can see what happens when you adjust the Depth & Contour controls.

+ **Depth Color and Contour Color:** Click to display the colors palette.

+ **Depth:** Use the spinner control to increase and decrease depth.

✦ **Size:** Use the spinner control to adjust size. Smaller is often better.

✦ **Surface Material:** Click to choose from a pop-up menu.

✦ **Lighting:** Click to choose from a list of fancifully named effects.

✦ **Angle:** Use spinner controls to change the angle of the light source.

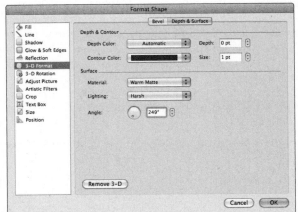

Figure 6-18:
Adjusting
depth,
contour, and
surface.

Rotating in 3-D

Not only do you have the ability to give 3-D appearance to a shape, but you can also give true 3-D rotation and perspective to a shape using the Format Shape dialog. As shown in Figure 6-19, you can control the following:

✦ **Rotation type:** Choose from several types, including oblique perspectives.

✦ **Axes X, Y, and Z:** These options refer to the axes about the center of the shape. Remember geometry class? We bet you never thought you would actually use that stuff! We put a reminder in the margin. The axes do not display on screen — you have to use your imagination. Use the rotation buttons or spinner controls to rotate the shape about the axes.

✦ **Perspective:** Increase and decrease perspective using the arrows or the spinner controls.

✦ **Distance from Center:** This is the distance from the center of the shape, which is where the axes cross.

✦ **Keep Text Flat:** When selected, keeps text in the shape in the same relative position.

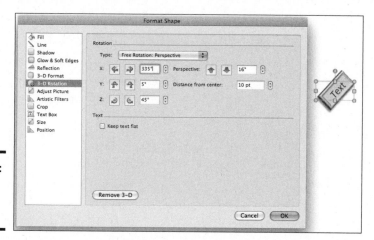

Figure 6-19:
Rotating
shapes
precisely.

Copying formats

Copying formats isn't an extensive topic, but it's important because it's so popular. To copy formatting in Word, Excel, or PowerPoint, take these steps:

1. **Select something — just about anything that has formatting associated with it.**

2. **Click the Format Painter button on the Standard toolbar.**

3. **Click an object you want to apply the formatting to.**

This step applies the formatting of the object from Step 1.

Be sure to copy formatting from similar objects. For example, you can copy the formatting of a table and apply that formatting to another table.

Tip: Double-clicking the Format Painter button tells the Format Painter to remember the copied format until you press the Escape key or click something that's not an object that accepts formatting.

Chapter 7: Formatting Pictures

In This Chapter

✔ **Formatting pictures with the Ribbon**

✔ **Changing brightness, contrast, and more**

✔ **Having fun with filters**

✔ **Removing backgrounds**

✔ **Cropping and compressing pictures**

✔ **Applying picture styles and effects**

✔ **Working with layers**

*I*n the preceding chapter, we explore formatting text and shapes. In the same way, Office 2011 provides several formatting options to make your pictures look more interesting. Styling your pictures consistently makes you look better to your audience. Something as simple as adding a thin border helps set your picture apart from its surroundings. Correcting pictures that are too dark, too light, or off color keeps people from being distracted or squint-eyed. And, of course, there are times when you want the extra attention a special effect can provide. Office makes it quick and easy to format your pictures.

The Ribbon's Format Picture tab shows up when you have a picture (or pictures) selected. The Format Picture tab has controls that let you make adjustments on the fly with easy-to-use, instant previews so you can work picture-enhancing magic in just a few clicks. We start this chapter by examining the Ribbon's picture formatting tools and then go even deeper with the Format Picture dialog that lets you use precise picture formatting controls.

In this chapter, we refer to objects that already exist in your document, workbook, or presentation. If you want to know how to add media objects, see Chapter 8 of this minibook.

Formatting Pictures Using the Ribbon

When you click a picture in a document, workbook, or presentation, Office lets you know your picture is selected by putting light blue resize handles around the edges, and the green rotate handle appears at the top. At the same time, the Ribbon spawns a Format Picture tab. Remember that you must click the purple Format Picture tab to display the entire set of formatting controls on the Ribbon. Figure 7-1 shows PowerPoint's Ribbon.

Figure 7-1:
The Format
Picture tab.

In Word and PowerPoint, you have to double-click a picture or click the Format Picture tab in the Ribbon to display the tab's controls. Excel displays the Format Picture controls automatically when you select a picture (we much prefer this behavior). If you click anything that's not a picture, the Format Picture tab disappears. To get the Format Picture tab back, all you have to do is select a picture and click the tab, or double-click a picture.

The Adjust group on the Format Picture tab, shown in Figure 7-1, has tools that let you make all sorts of adjustments to your pictures. Office isn't trying to be Adobe Photoshop, but you can do some quick touch-ups and apply some really nice effects in Office. We explain each tool in this chapter.

Making corrections

Not every picture is perfectly exposed, and some can look better with just a bit more or less contrast or sharpness. The Corrections button displays a preview of your picture within a gallery of adjustment increments, as shown in Figure 7-2. Hover the mouse cursor over a preview to see how much adjustment you would get if you chose it.

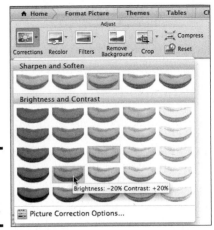

Figure 7-2:
Making
simple
corrections.

Choose Picture Correction Options at the bottom of the gallery to display the Adjust Picture tab of the Format Picture dialog, shown in Figure 7-3. Using sliders and spinner controls, you can fine-tune adjustments for the following:

✦ **Transparency:** Change how much you can see through the picture.

✦ **Corrections:** Adjust brightness, contrast, and sharpness.

- *Brightness:* The amount of light in the picture.

- *Contrast:* How much difference there is between light and dark areas of the picture.

- *Sharpness:* How fuzzy or "in focus" the picture looks.

✦ **Color**

- *Recolor:* Choose grayscale, black and white, sepia, gray, and color tones from this pop-up menu.

- *Saturation:* Adjusts how rich the colors will be.

- *Temperature:* Color temperature is pretty complicated to explain here. But you can still play around with this tool and experiment to see whether you can attain a visual effect you like.

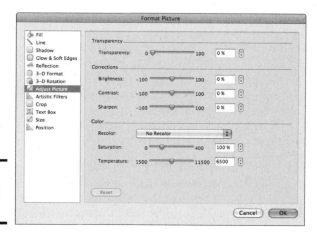

Figure 7-3:
Fine-tuning a picture.

Recoloring a picture

Tinting a picture changes it to a single (monochrome) color. This effect can change the mood and sometimes add more visual interest than was present in the original picture. Or you may just need to change your pictures to grayscale for a publication that needs to be printed without color. Office makes these accent colorations easy. Click the Recolor button to display the recolor palette, as shown in Figure 7-4.

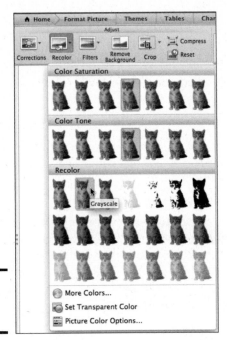

Figure 7-4:
Recoloring
a picture.

Hold the mouse cursor over each preview to see what changes it will make. The palette is divided into three sections:

✦ **Color Saturation:** Choose a level of color intensity.

✦ **Color Tone:** Various color "temperatures" are offered.

✦ **Recolor:** Accents, tints, grayscale, and black and white are offered. The top-left position is No-Recolor. Grayscale is immediately to the right of No-Recolor. The rest of the top row is Washout and various shades of black and white.

The second and third rows thereafter provide darker and lighter varia-tions of recolored pictures, this time with the Accent colors. These Accent colors are influenced by the theme. If you change the theme, the Accent colors change too. We cover themes in minibook Book IV, Chapter 5.

The following additional options are offered near the bottom of the recolor palette:

✦ **More Colors:** Displays the Mac OS X color picture. Choose a color from millions of colors.

✦ **Set Transparent Color:** When you choose this option, the mouse cursor becomes an eye-dropper. If you click a color in a picture, it becomes

100 percent transparent. Whatever is behind the picture shows through. Not all picture types support transparent colors, so this may not work on every picture. For pictures where this doesn't work the way you expect, you might want to explore the Remove Background option that we discuss later in this chapter in the "Removing the background" section.

✦ **Picture Color Options:** Displays the Adjust Picture tab of the Format Picture dialog (refer to Figure 7-3).

Take advantage of the fact that all objects are in layers in Office. To make a *mask* (an opaque shape or picture with transparent areas that you can see through), set a transparent color in a picture and then position it over another picture, or even a movie, graph, or SmartArt. In PowerPoint, you can even apply animation to the mask and/or objects behind the mask.

Applying filters

The Filters palette has a variety of special effects from which to choose.

Select a picture and click the Filters button on the Format Picture tab of the Ribbon to bring up the gallery shown in Figure 7-5.

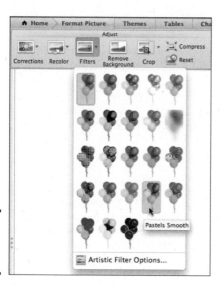

Figure 7-5:
Applying
a filter.

Each of the small thumbnail previews in this gallery actually shows previews of the various filters. Click any of these thumbnails to apply the filter on your selected picture.

If you choose the Artistic Filter Options at the bottom of the gallery, you display the Artistic Filters tab of the Format Picture dialog, as shown in

Figure 7-6. You can then choose a filter from the Artistic Filters pop-up menu. Each filter comes with slider and spinner controls. Depending on your computer's speed, some of the effects may take up to several minutes to process.

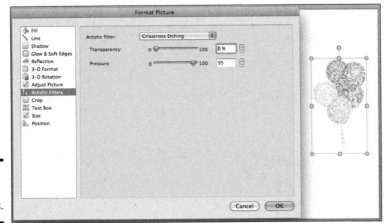

Figure 7-6:
Adjusting filter effects.

Removing the background

Remove Background is a new feature for Office 2011 that figures out a shape's boundaries automatically. In many ways, this tool is easier and more capable than Photoshop, and it works amazingly well on many pictures.

The Remove Background feature found the picture in Figure 7-7 easy to figure out. As you can see, it isn't easy to visually separate the rose from the background, but Remove Background still managed to make the separation. Here's how it works:

1. **Select a picture.**

2. **Click the Ribbon's Format Picture tab. In the Adjust group, click Remove Background.**

    Remove Background surrounds the area(s) of your picture it guesses that you want to keep with a selection box. Remove Background indicates what it interprets as the background with a pink overlay. Resize the selection box by dragging the handles so that the desired foreground is highlighted. In the example in Figure 7-7, we dragged the selection indicator down a little. As you drag, the size of the selection is indicated in a ScreenTip, also shown in Figure 7-7.

3. **Press Return to remove the background.**

    The perfect result, determined automatically, is shown in Figure 7-8.

Figure 7-7:
Defining the
background.

Figure 7-8:
Background
removed.

Manually selecting the background

After trying many examples, we discovered the Remove Background tool is
simply brilliant at picking out the subject from the background. But if you
have a picture that Remove Background did not interpret perfectly on its
own, you can help it out by specifying which portions of your image are foreground or background. See Figure 7-9 for this example.

Our objective is to keep the astronaut and remove the rest of the background. We repeat Steps 1 and 2 of the previous example, but this time Remove Background is able to determine only part of what we want to keep.

 To manually add to the selected area, take these steps:

1. **Notice that as you move the mouse cursor over the pink overlay, it becomes a green plus.**

2. **When the cursor is a plus, drag a line across a portion of the picture you want to add to the selection.**

3. **To manually remove portions of the selected area, hold ⌘ down to change the plus to a minus and then drag over the area you want to remove.**

If you make a mistake, click the small circle in the center of each line to undo that line. Note that you don't click on boundaries — you draw lines over the center of areas to select them.

Figure 7-9:
Manually removing a background.

Cropping a picture

 The Crop tool has new behavior in Office 2011. Instead of just one kind of crop, Office now has four kinds. To get at the additional crop tools, click the small triangle to the right of the Crop button, as shown in the margin.

Making a simple crop

Here's how to perform a simple crop, as shown in Figure 7-10:

1. **Select the picture you want to crop.**

2. **On the Format Picture tab, go to the Adjust group and click the Crop button.**

   Dark crop handles appear in addition to the selection handles.

3. **Drag the crop handles to select the area you want to keep.**

4. **Click away from the picture.**

   Everything except the selected area is subtracted from the picture.

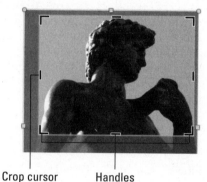

Figure 7-10:
Simple
cropping.

Crop cursor   Handles

Mask to Shape

With Mask to Shape, you start with a picture and finish with a shape that's filled with your picture. Here are the steps to take:

1. **Select a picture**

2. **Click the purple Format Picture button on the Ribbon.**

   Picture formatting tools display on the Ribbon.

3. **In the Adjust group of tools, click the small triangle on the Crop button and choose Mask to Shape.**

   You're presented with a submenu that takes you to the Shapes gallery, as shown in Figure 7-11.

4. **Choose a solid, fillable shape.**

   Your picture is cropped to the chosen shape. Figure 7-11 shows a picture that has been cropped using the trapezoid shape.

Some shapes have yellow diamonds, which you can drag to alter the shape's appearance.

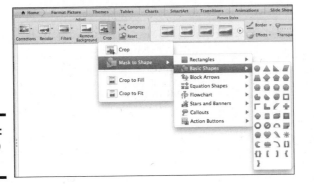

Figure 7-11:
Cropping to
a shape.

Crop to Fill

With Crop to Fill, you start with a shape. You move the shape in a see-through mode over a picture from a file. The result is shape filled with the see-through portion of your picture, as in Figure 7-12.

This example has fireworks. We think the Sun shape might give an interesting result. Here are the steps to take:

1. **From the Standard toolbar, choose Media Browser.**

    The Media Browser displays.

2. **Choose the Shapes button on the Media Browser.**

    All Shapes display in the Media Browser.

3. **Drag a solid shape to use as the cropping shape.**

    We chose the Sun shape for our screen shots.

4. **Right-click on the shape. From the pop-up menu, choose Format Shape.**

    The Format Shape dialog displays.

5. **In the Format Shape dialog, choose the Picture or Texture tab and then click the Choose Picture Button.**

    The Choose a Picture file browser appears.

6. **Choose the picture you want to crop and then click the Insert button to return to the Format Shape dialog.**

    For our example, we chose a picture of fireworks. You can select or deselect the Rotate with Shape check box. We suggest not using the Tile option with Crop to Fill.

7. **Click OK to close the Format Shape dialog.**

   Your picture is now inside the shape.

8. **On the Format Picture tab of the Ribbon, click the small triangle on the Crop button and choose Crop to Fill.**

   The shape is now in see-through mode. You can now adjust the crop shape and the picture size and position independently.

9. **Drag the shape's handles, as shown in Figure 7-12.**

   You can resize both the shape and the picture. Drag the handles on the shape to adjust the crop. Drag the picture handles and the picture itself to reposition it under the shape until you get just the crop you want.

10. **Click away from the picture to display the cropped area, as shown in Figure 7-12.**

    To add a finishing touch for Figure 7-12, we chose the Line tool on the Format tab of the Ribbon. From the pop-up menu, we chose No Line.

Figure 7-12:
Cropping to
a fill.

Crop to Fit

The Crop to Fit option lets you use a shape to crop a picture, and the shape can extend beyond the size of the picture. As with Crop to Fill, you start with a shape that is filled with a picture. But with Crop to Fit, you can make the crop constraint extend beyond the edges of the picture. The instructions are the same as for Crop to Fill in the previous heading, except you choose Crop to Fill in Step 8. Figure 7-13 compares the crop options.

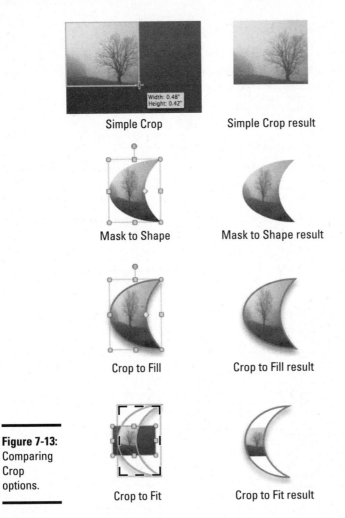

Simple Crop   Simple Crop result

Mask to Shape   Mask to Shape result

Crop to Fill   Crop to Fill result

Figure 7-13:
Comparing
Crop
options.

Crop to Fit   Crop to Fit result

Compressing pictures

The Compress feature is new to the Mac version of Office. By default, Office simply copies your inserted pictures into your document, workbook spreadsheet, or e-mail, leaving the size and file format unchanged. However big the picture is, your Office file grows by that much. Now in Word, Excel, and PowerPoint, you can reduce the size of the file using picture compression. To display the Reduce File Size dialog, in your Office document, select the picture. Then go to the Format Picture tab of the Ribbon and then Choose Compress. This brings up the dialog that you see in Figure 7-14.

Figure 7-14:
Reduce file
sizes by
compressing
pictures.

Choose from these compression and selection options:

✦ **Picture Quality:** You get four options:

  • Best for printing (220 ppi)

  • Best for viewing on screen (150 ppi)

  • Best for sending in e-mail (96 ppi)

  • Keep current resolution (no compression is applied)

✦ **Remove Cropped Picture Regions:** Normally, Office keeps the original
picture even after you've cropped it. If you select the Remove Cropped
Picture Region check box, the portions of the pictures that you cropped
off are permanently removed. You won't be able to reset the picture and
remove the crop after selecting this option.

✦ **Apply To:** You can choose All Pictures in This File or Selected Pictures
Only.

Resetting a picture

You can undo most picture formatting options by using the Undo command
on the Standard toolbar. In addition, you can often reset a picture as it
was when you inserted it. To reset a picture, select the picture. Then click
Format Picture on the Ribbon. In the Adjust group, click Reset.

Resetting may work even if you've saved your file and reopened it. However,
resetting doesn't work for all picture formatting options.

Applying Picture Styles

For a special picture that you want to set off from the rest, consider applying a picture style. The Picture Styles gallery is built into the Picture Styles group on the Format tab, as shown in Figure 7-15. Additionally, you can click near the middle-bottom of the gallery to expose the drop-down gallery. To apply a picture style, simply select a picture and choose a style from the gallery.

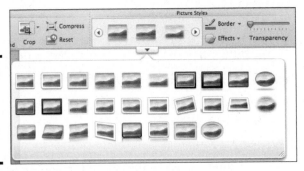

Figure 7-15: The Picture Styles gallery offers many options.

Formatting picture borders

Pictures are also shapes, so each picture has a line border around it. You can format the border outline using the Format Picture Ribbon's Border control. When you click this control, you see a menu that includes the Office theme-based color palette, as well as line formatting options that we discuss in Chapter 6 of this minibook.

Formatting picture effects

You can find some fun effects on the Format Picture tab by going to the Picture Styles group and clicking the Effects button. (These effects are separate from the filters in the Adjust group.) These picture effects, shown in Figure 7-16, are the same as the effects that you can apply to any shape and are discussed in Chapter 6 of this minibook, where we discussed applying these effects on shapes.

Adjusting picture transparency

Drag the Transparency slider (refer to Figure 7-15) left and right to adjust how much you can see through a selected picture.

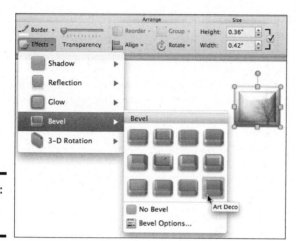

Figure 7-16:
Choosing
an effect.

Working in Layers

When you sit in a theater to watch a play, the experience is very three-dimensional. As you sit facing the stage, your depth perception tells you that the objects placed closer to you appear larger, and objects that are farther away generally appear smaller. Behind all these objects is the stage background. While you sit in front of your computer, Office documents offer the same sort of layered experience.

Everything you see in Office is on a layer. Some things are closer to you than others. Farthest away from you is the background layer. The next layer closest to you from the background is the text layer. Any additional objects, such as pictures, WordArt, shapes, or text boxes that are added, are placed in layers closer to you with each additional object. In the following sections, we explain how to format the background, group objects together into a single layer, control the order of the layers of selected objects, and even rotate or flip objects.

Formatting the background

The layer that's farthest to the back is the background layer. Whether it's Word, Excel, or PowerPoint, there's a background layer that's like the back wall of a stage. This background layer is a thing unto itself that can be formatted independently, and everything else is in front of it. You can access the background by the following three methods:

+ **Word:**

   1. Click the Ribbon's Layout Tab. In the Page Background group, click Color. In the pop-up menu, choose Fill Effect.

2. In the Resulting Fill Effects dialog, click the Picture option.

3. Click the Select Picture button to display the Choose a Picture dialog.

4. Choose a picture to use as the document background.

✦ **Excel:** Choose Format➪Sheet➪Background. In the resulting Choose a Picture dialog, choose a picture to use as the worksheet's background. The picture will be tiled. For a non-tiled picture, insert a picture into the worksheet's header. (See Book III, Chapter 11.)

✦ **PowerPoint:** Choose Format➪Slide Background to display the Format Background dialog, which has many of the same controls as the Format Shape dialog discussed in Chapter 6 of this minibook.

Arranging the layers

Until Office 2011, to arrange the order of objects in the layers above the text layer, you would right-click an object and choose one of four Arrange options:

✦ Bring to Front

✦ Send to Back

✦ Bring Forward (one layer)

✦ Send Backward (one layer)

Of course, you can still do this in Office 2011, and these options are now available on the Format tab of the Ribbon. Using these tools requires you to keep track of how many layers deep any particular object is.

Word's Publishing Layout view and PowerPoint's Normal view have the new Dynamic Reorder objects feature that relieves you of the burden of keeping track of the order of your objects. A simple, intuitive interface displays your objects in order, numbered beginning with the number 1 as the layer on top, the one that's closest to you. You can simply drag any layer to a new position in the order.

Here's a simple example: We have a text box, a picture of a dog, and a rectangle for visual appeal. Because we added the rectangle last, it's on top of the other objects, as shown in Figure 7-17. Yuck!

To fix this problem, we went to the Arrange group on the Format tab and clicked the Reorder Objects button to display the fancy, new Reorder Objects tool. (See Figure 7-18.) All we have to do is drag the rectangle from position 1 in front of the other objects to position 3 behind the other objects, as shown, and then click OK. Click Cancel or press Esc if you decide not to reorder the objects.

You can see the finished result in Figure 7-19. We're very pleased!

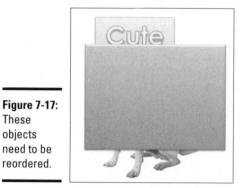

Figure 7-17:
These objects need to be reordered.

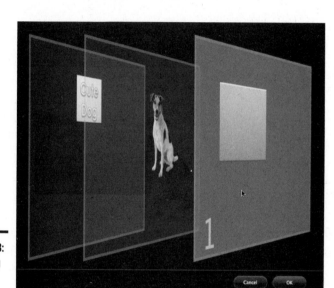

Figure 7-18:
Reordering objects.

Figure 7-19:
Reordered objects.

Reorder Objects has to be one of the coolest features you've ever used to manage layers! It certainly is fun to use. This feature should win awards for Microsoft.

If you want, you can restrict the objects being reordered to only those objects that overlap each other: In the Arrange group of the Format tab, click Reorder Overlapping Objects. The tool automatically determines which objects are overlapping — you don't have to do any work!

Rotating and flipping

The Rotate button (found in the Format tab's Arrange group) offers options that allow for rotation in specified increments:

✦ Rotate Right 90 Degrees

✦ Rotate Left 90 Degrees

✦ Flip Vertical

✦ Flip Horizontal

Grouped objects behave unpredictably with these controls. You may need to ungroup the objects, use the controls, and then regroup everything. For exacting rotation control, right-click an object and choose Format⇨Format Shape⇨3-D Rotation, which opens the Format Shape dialog, described in Chapter 6 of this minibook. You can drag the green handle of a selected picture or shape to rotate it, too!

Grouping multiple objects

When working with multiple objects above the text layer of a Word document, spreadsheet, or presentation, sometimes you may want to combine *(group)* several objects into a single object that you can move, order, and format together as a unit. Take a look at Figure 7-20 as you group several objects into one:

1. **Position and order all the objects you want to include in the group.**

2. **Select the objects.**

Hold the ⌘ key down and click individual objects to add to the selection. In PowerPoint, you can simply click and drag over the objects to select them.

3. **With everything you want grouped being selected (see the left side of Figure 7-20), click the Ribbon's Format tab. In the Format group, choose Arrange⇨Group.**

The Arrange group is on the Ribbon on both the Format and the Format Picture tabs. Alternatively, right-click any of the selected objects and choose Grouping⇨Group.

The selected objects become a single object on one layer, as shown on the right side of Figure 7-20.

Selected   Grouped

Figure 7-20:
Grouping
objects.

Ungrouping and regrouping

Office remembers that your group is composed of independent objects. You can ungroup a grouped object:

1. **Select a grouped object.**

2. **Click the Ribbon's Format tab, and in the Arrange group, click Ungroup. You can also right-click and choose Grouping⇨Ungroup.**

   You can regroup by reselecting the objects and then choosing Regroup in Step 2.

Flattening

You can permanently turn a grouped object into a picture object. This action is called *flattening*. Right-click a grouped object and choose Save As Picture from the pop-up menu. Choose a picture format and save the file in a location you want. You can then insert the resulting picture, which can't be ungrouped.

Chapter 8: Inserting Media

Media is a broad term that includes content of all sorts, and Microsoft Office 2011 literally takes that definition to extreme limits. Put photos, music, movies, Clip Art, symbols, and shapes to work for you by means of the Media browser.

The Media browser also includes a complete set of drawing tools as part of shapes that let you create everything from a simple line to an intricate piece of artwork. This chapter explains how to add all of these worthwhile objects.

This chapter's goal is to help you insert interesting media objects. After you've inserted objects, additional formatting options are available to you. We cover additional formatting options in other chapters in this minibook.

Activating the Media Browser

The Media browser is a floating palette available in Word, Excel, and PowerPoint. There's even an abridged Media browser in Outlook, so you can add media to e-mail. To activate the Media browser, click the Media browser button (shown in the left margin) on the Standard toolbar, or choose View⇨Media Browser. Note that the Media Browser button on the Standard toolbar is a toggle because if you click it a second time, it hides the Media browser.

The following sections discuss how to add content using each of the six tabs in the Media browser: Photos, Audio, Movies, Clip Art, Symbols, and Shapes.

Browsing Your Photos

Clicking the Photos button at the top of the Media browser provides a view of your iPhoto collection and your Photo Booth pictures, as shown in Figure 8-1. Your Media browser may look like one of the two instances in Figure 8-1. The difference between them is that although the window on the left has a pop-up menu showing locations of your media, the window on the right has the same locations within a scroll-equipped area. It's easy to change from one view to another: If you see the view on the left of Figure 8-1, click the *view splitter,* which is the small dot above where your content shows and drag that down so the pop-up menu no longer shows. Your Media browser now looks like what you see on the right of Figure 8-1.

Figure 8-1: Inserting media from iPhoto.

The Media browser is divided into two panes. The top pane lets you navigate your albums, and the lower pane shows you previews of your photos.

The Media browser works as you might expect. You drag the lower-right corner to resize the browser. You drag the view splitter up and down to adjust the sizes of the upper and lower panes. Drag the slider at the bottom left and right to adjust the size of the photos in the preview pane. If you type a filename in the Search field, the available photos instantly update. The number of photos available in your preview pane is also visible.

Inserting photos

To insert a photo, drag it from the lower panel of the Media browser into your open document, spreadsheet, presentation, or e-mail message. You can also drag a photo into the picture placeholder of an Outlook contact. You can even drag photos into Outlook notes.

Right-clicking Media browser

While the Media browser looks quite innocent, it has a few tricks up its sleeve. The first trick is that you can right-click any previewed picture and choose the Open in iPhoto option in the resulting contextual menu. Another trick is to double-click a photo to enlarge it in the preview pane. Click the picture again to restore its original preview size.

The next trick is that you can right-click in the picture preview area on the lower part of the Media browser and choose Display as List, as shown in Figure 8-2. This changes the preview into a table that you can sort by clicking the column headers. Also shown in Figure 8-2 is that if you right-click the list, you can add and remove headers by choosing them from the Show Columns submenu. Drag the column dividers to resize columns.

Figure 8-2:
Displaying photos in list view.

Browsing Audio

Music is powerful and personal. Sometimes it's the perfect thing to insert, and sometimes it's totally inappropriate for the audience. Always consider the tastes of your audience members. You can add music or other audio clips to Word, Excel, PowerPoint, and even to Outlook e-mail.

Audio and movie improvements

Office 2011 completely revamps how music and movies are treated. Music and movies are now embedded (not linked) by default. That means in Word, Excel, and PowerPoint, the muss and fuss of worrying about media file types and broken links is finally over! This benefit is a direct consequence of switching to the new XML file format. Movies no longer always have to play "on top" in PowerPoint: Now you can layer other objects, such as text boxes and pictures, on top of a movie. Objects on top of a movie can display while the movie plays. (These improvements were also made to Office 2010 for Windows.)

Having said that, you should not add audio just because it's possible — Excel isn't a media player! We think audio is best suited to PowerPoint presentations, and even in that case, moderation is best.

When you click the Audio button at the top of the Media browser, by default you can browse your GarageBand and iTunes music collections.

As with the Photo tab, the browser is divided into an upper pane and lower pane (as shown earlier in Figure 8-1). Click disclosure triangles to reveal or hide the contents of folders, subfolders, podcasts, and music playlists. In the preview pane, you can select music and then click the Play button (the large right-pointing arrow) at the lower-left corner of the Media browser to preview your selection.

When you drag a sound into your document, spreadsheet, or presentation a sound icon appears. To play the sound in Word or Excel, double-click the sound icon. In PowerPoint, click the Play button on the sound control. (See Figure 8-3.)

Figure 8-3:
Playing a
sound.

As you would expect from a presentation program, PowerPoint has more controls available. Select an inserted sound on a slide and you'll see the contextual Format Audio tab in the Ribbon.

As with pictures, you can right-click in the preview section and show previews in a sortable list. In list view, if you right-click you can add and remove columns from the pop-up menu.

Browsing Movies

Everyone loves movies, and you can insert them into Word, Excel, PowerPoint, and even Outlook mail. But be careful! No one wants to see movies of talking heads, especially movies of someone reading from a script. Ever! Only your closest relatives really want to see the latest antics of your baby on a spreadsheet. Okay, even they would prefer it on a PowerPoint slide instead!

In the Media browser, by default you see movies that are in iMovie, your Mac OS X Movies folder, Photo Booth, and iTunes. Insert your movies by dragging them. When the movie is added to your document, the movie's poster frame is displayed. Use the movie controller, as shown in Figure 8-4 with an iTunes podcast from Mr. Excel. We cover playing movies in PowerPoint presentations in the PowerPoint Book IV, Chapter 6.

Figure 8-4:
Playing a
movie.

Although it's easy to add movies to your files, movie files can be large. Whenever you add media to Word, Excel, PowerPoint, or Outlook, the file size after dragging will be larger by the size of whatever you dragged into your work. For smaller movies, that's probably not a problem in Word, Excel, and PowerPoint. It is a big problem for Outlook e-mail. Try to keep your total e-mail message size less than 5 MB if at all possible. Before inserting videos into e-mail, save them in 3GP format using QuickTime Pro, iMovie, or other conversion software on your Mac. Even in 3GP format, only short movies will fit into an e-mail.

As with pictures and music, you can right-click in the preview section in the Media browser and show previews in a sortable list. In list view, if you right-click, you can add and remove columns from the pop-up menu.

In the Media browser, click a movie preview and then click the Play button (the large right-pointing arrow) to play the movie in the preview pane. Click again to stop the movie and return to the preview list.

Browsing Clip Art

Office has two distinctly different ways of browsing your Clip Art collection. The quick, easy way is to use the Clip Art tab of the Media browser. A more robust way of working with your clips is provided by Clip Gallery.

Inserting from the Media browser

The Clip Art tab of the Media browser displays your Clip Art collection. (See Figure 8-5.) Click All Images at the top of the browser to display a pop-up menu that lets you filter results by pre-selected categories. Drag the slider at the bottom left and right to resize the clip previews.

Figure 8-5:
Browsing
Clip Art.

Size slider

Mastering the Clip Gallery

Another way to view your Clip Art collection is the Clip Gallery. You're probably wondering how to get clips from Clip Gallery into a document. That's easy. First open the Clip Gallery by choosing Insert⇨Clip Art⇨Clip Art Gallery. In the Clip Gallery, select the clip you want and do one of the following:

✦ **Double-click a piece of Clip Art.** You might think that nothing happened. Actually, every time you double-click a piece of Clip Art, it's placed behind the Clip Gallery window in your document. So don't double-click more than once!

✦ **Click the Insert button.** This option exits the Clip Gallery window and places the piece of Clip Art in your document. Hold the Shift key down to select more than one clip.

✦ **Drag the piece of Clip Art from the Clip Gallery to your document.** If the Clip Gallery is covering your document, you need to drag the Clip Gallery window a wee bit so that you can see both this window and your document at the same time.

Finding more Clip Art

The Media browser shows only a limited collection of pictures and drawings that belong to the larger Office Online Images and Media collection, which includes millions of pictures, drawings, sounds, and animations. Before you launch your browser and start looking for the Clip Art, we suggest you read the rest of this section.

As the proud owner of Microsoft Office, you're entitled to use the content available from Office Online at www.office.com. If you visit that site, you might find it entirely Windows-centric. But don't worry — all the pieces of Clip Art that you can download from this site work within Office for Mac applications.

Downloading new Clip Art

You can download as many clips as you want to your computer and use them however you want, even commercially, but you can't sell them. As long as you have a Web browser, grabbing Clip Art from Office Online is a breeze. You can get started from right within your Office application. Follow these steps:

1. **From the menu of any Office application, choose Insert⇨Clip Art⇨Clip Art Gallery.**

   This summons the Clip Gallery. (See Figure 8-6.)

2. **At the bottom of the Clip Gallery, click the Online button.**

   Your default Web browser opens and connects to the Office Online Images tab. If your Office application asks you for permission to launch your default browser, click Yes.

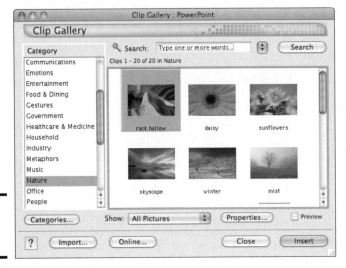

Figure 8-6:
The Clip
Gallery.

3. **Search or browse the collection by entering keywords in the Search text box.**

   We don't show you the actual interface because Microsoft updates this site fairly often, and the location of the Search text box may change.

4. **After the search is finished, select a clip you want to download. With each clip, you can choose from the pop-up menu:**

   • *Download:* Saves the clip as a file in Finder using your web browser.

   • *See Similar:* Displays pictures having the same keywords.

   • *Add to Basket:* Choose this option to get your clips into the Clip Gallery.

   Unless you searched for an exotic keyword that yields no results, you end up with some or many results. Each result is actually a thumbnail with a check box.

   As you select the check boxes in your browser, you'll see a Selection Basket that shows the number of clips you've opted to download.

5. **When you're ready to download your clips, click the Download link.**

6. **Agree to the Microsoft Service Agreement.**

   You have to agree to the service agreement to download any clips. If you have lots of time or if you love legal gobbledygook, go ahead and read each word, and then accept the agreement.

7. **Click the Download button.**

   Your browser downloads the clips as a single file.

8. **Select the Save option when you're prompted by a dialog.**

   The same dialog that provided the Save option also lets you choose an Open With option. Make sure you don't choose Open With.

9. **Make sure the saved filename has the `.cil` file extension.**

   Apple Safari does it right, but you have to manually append a `.cil` file extension in Mozilla Firefox and some other browsers that save the file without the `.cil` extension.

10. **Click the Save button and wait for the download to complete.**

11. **In the Web browser's Download window, double-click the CIL file.**

    This automatically loads your clips into the Clip Gallery.

If your Web browser's Download window is hidden or not turned on, use your Web browser's menus to open the Download window. Firefox users can choose Tools⇨Downloads, and Safari users should choose Window⇨Downloads.

Now that you have your clips in Clip Gallery, you can tag your clips so that they can be searched, and you can categorize them so they can be filtered.

Changing the categories and keyword tags of Clip Art

The clips you download from Office Online enter into Clip Gallery with default keyword tags already, and are also categorized by default into the Favorites category. However, you can change the categories and keyword tags to suit your own needs. To change the category of a clip, follow these steps:

1. **Select the clip in the Clip Gallery. (Refer to Figure 8-6.)**

2. **Click the Properties button to open the Properties window, as shown in Figure 8-7.**

3. **Click the Categories tab.**

4. **Select and deselect the check boxes beside the categories as desired.**

   You can also create a new category by clicking the New Category button. In the New Category dialog, type a name for your new category and click OK to return to the Properties window.

5. **Click OK to exit the Properties window and go back to the Clip Gallery with any changes you made.**

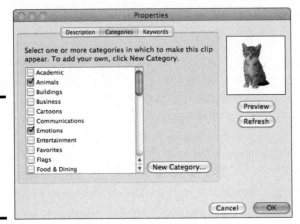

Figure 8-7: The Category tab in the Clip Art Properties window.

Follow almost the same steps if you want to set or change the keyword tags for a selected clip:

1. **Select a clip in the Clip Gallery.**

2. **Click the Properties button to open the Properties window.**

3. **Click the Keywords tab to edit keywords, as shown in Figure 8-8.**

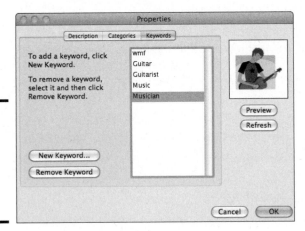

Figure 8-8: The Keywords tab in the Clip Art Properties window.

4. **Click the New Keyword button to add a new keyword; to remove a keyword, select it in the list and click the Remove Keyword button.**

   Any new keywords that you add with the New Keyword button are available in the keyword list that you see in this window.

5. **Click OK to exit the Properties window and go back to the Clip Gallery with your changes.**

Browsing Symbols

Symbols are elegant and oh, so simple! And they're useful, too, because you really need to insert things like symbols for keyboard characters, foreign languages, registered and copyright symbols, currency, and so on. Just position your insertion cursor (the blinking vertical bar) where you want the symbol inserted in your document and then use one of the following tools to browse the symbols in your Mac's font collections:

✦ The Symbols tab of the Media browser is a quick, easy way to get at the most popular symbols.

✦ In Microsoft Word, you can choose Insert⇨Symbol⇨Advanced Symbol to display a more advanced symbol browser.

We cover these tools in the following sections. For even more options on viewing symbols, see the sidebar "Browsing Character Viewer."

Inserting quickly with Media browser

The Symbols tab of the Media browser (shown in Figure 8-9) contains only popular symbols, fractions, mathematical signs, and even some music notations. This is a quick, easy-to-use tool. Simply click a symbol, and it's inserted as text into your document at the insertion cursor's position. A pop-up menu lets you filter the symbols. Drag the slider at the bottom to adjust the symbol preview size.

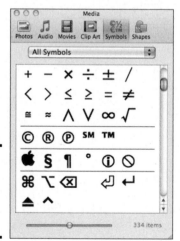

Figure 8-9:
Inserting symbols from Media browser.

Using the Advanced Symbol tool in Word

Within Microsoft Word is a feature that people switching from PC to Mac will find familiar. You display the Symbol dialog shown in Figures 8-10 and 8-11 by choosing Insert⇨Symbol⇨Advanced Symbol. The basic operation is simple: Choose a symbol and then either click the Insert button or double-click the symbol. You find two tabs: Symbols and Special Characters.

Inserting from the Symbols tab

The Symbols tab (see Figure 8-10) offers a grid-based preview of symbols contained in the font selected in the Font pop-up menu. When you click a symbol, the description area updates and displays the font's ASCII number and Unicode character number, which you can ignore if you don't know what that means. If you've assigned a keyboard shortcut to a particular symbol, the shortcut is displayed in the Description area. We discuss AutoCorrect and Word's keyboard shortcuts in the minibook about Word.

To insert a symbol, select it in the grid and click the Insert button.

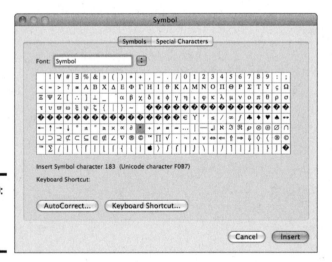

Figure 8-10:
Inserting a symbol in Word.

Inserting special characters in Word

The Special Characters tab of the Symbol dialog (see Figure 8-11) has a list of frequently used characters and displays the built-in keyboard shortcuts for those characters in Word. To insert a special character, select it from the list and click the Insert button.

Browsing Character Viewer

By far, the most versatile and fun-to-use tool for browsing your fonts is Character Viewer, which is included in Mac OS X. Character Viewer works with all applications that use text, not just Microsoft Office.

Before you can use the Character Viewer, you must turn it on, like this:

1. **Choose Apple⇨System Preferences⇨ Language & Text⇨Input Sources.**

2. **In the Select Input Methods to Use list box, scroll to the top of the list and select the On check box for Keyboard and Character Viewer.**

3. **Click the red Close button to quit System Preferences.**

Let the fun begin! Click the new little icon on your menu bar and choose Show Character Viewer from the menu. The Mac OS X Character Viewer displays. If your window appears smaller than the one you see in the following figure, change the View option to All Characters and then click the disclosure triangles next to Character Info and Font Variation. Then resize the window larger.

This is an amazing viewer that morphs constantly. Character Viewer lets you see and insert every variant of every glyph within all the fonts on your system. We could write an entire book about just this one feature, but it's rather intuitive, so just give it a try!

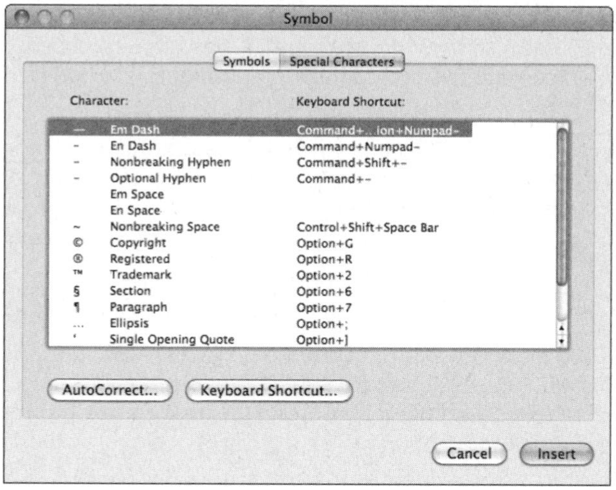

Figure 8-11: Displaying Word's special characters.

Browsing Shapes

The Media browser is where you can find an assortment of shapes to add to your documents, workbooks, and presentations. You'll also find the same shapes on various places in the Ribbon. Each shape can be customized and formatted in endless ways so that you can get just the right look. Shapes can be simple lines. Solid shapes can act as containers for text and even pictures.

Inserting Media browser shapes

Finding just the right shape is a breeze with the Shapes tab of the Media browser, shown in Figure 8-12. Click the Media browser's Shapes tab to display the built-in shapes available to you. You can filter shapes by category by clicking the All-Shapes pop-up menu at the top of the Media browser. At the bottom edge of the Media browser is a slider control, which you can drag left and right to zoom in on and out of the shapes in the palette. There are several distinct kinds of shapes:

- ✦ **Solid shapes:** A solid shape has an area that has a fill, such as a triangle or rectangle. Solid shapes can double as text boxes. To add text, you can simply start typing while a solid shape is selected. Every solid shape has a line that is the border of the shape. The fill area and the line are formatted independently.

- ✦ **Lines and Arrows:** These shapes have no fillable area. Lines can be formatted to have arrows at either end. Lines have thickness (weight) and style. You can make a solid shape by connecting a line to itself to form a fillable area.

- ✦ **Connectors:** Connectors are special lines that have *elbows*. You can adjust the elbows by dragging the yellow diamond associated with the elbow. Connectors are *sticky* in that if you connect the ends to other objects, when you move those objects the connector stays attached to the object.

- ✦ **Callouts:** These are boxes with connectors permanently attached.

- ✦ **Action Buttons:** These are available only in PowerPoint. Action Buttons have built-in properties that you can use for navigation, playing media, running macros, and more. We describe actions in Chapter 4 of Book IV on PowerPoint.

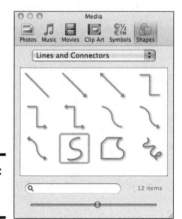

Figure 8-12:
Browsing
shapes.

You're probably itching to get your hands on one of these shapely shapes, but first, here's the procedure for inserting shapes:

1. **Click inside your document in the approximate place you want to insert the shape.**

2. **In the Media browser, select the Shapes tab. Click a shape in the Shapes palette.**

3. **Hold down the left mouse button and drag across the document to draw a shape the size you want.**

   Alternatively, click once on the shape in the Shapes palette and then once again in the document to place the selected shape. This creates a 1 x 1 inch shape. You can also drag a shape from the browser: Right-click a shape in the browser and choose copy to copy it to the Clipboard.

4. **Let go of the mouse button when you're done.**

If you hold the Shift key down while dragging a new shape, your shape's height and width will retain their current proportions. This method keeps your squares and circles perfect so they don't become rectangles and ovals.

Here's some more info on manipulating shapes (see Figure 8-13):

✦ **Rotating a shape:** You can rotate a shape by dragging the green dot at the top of the shape. Press the Shift key while rotating to constrain it to 15 degree rotations.

✦ **Shape controls:** Most shapes (but not all) have one or more yellow diamonds that act as shape controls. Drag a diamond to alter a shape's appearance.

✦ **Text controls:** If you see a purple diamond, drag the diamond to alter the appearance of the text contained within the shape.

✦ **Resizing handles:** Each shape has eight resizing handles. The corner handles resize the shape proportionately in the direction you drag, whereas the other handles resize the shape by altering only the width or only the height. You may have to hold the Shift key down to maintain proportional height and width at times.

✦ **Formatting text within a shape:** You can take several different approaches to formatting text within a shape. Drag over text within the shape to select text. Double-click to select a word or triple-click to select all the text before trying to format it. We discuss the formatting options in Chapter 6 of this minibook.

✦ **Formatting the shape itself:** When the shape itself is selected, you have your choice of formatting tools and methods. See Chapter 6 of this minibook.

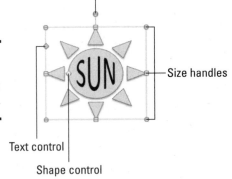

Figure 8-13:
Controlling a shape and added text.

Making a curvy line

Even with the plethora of prefabricated shapes to choose from in the Media browser, you may have a hankering for some good old-fashioned simple shapes, or maybe you want to try your hand at creating your own shapes. Mixed in with the shapes are three special tools that you can use to make your own lines and shapes: Curve, Freeform, and Scribble.

Follow the instructions in this section to modify motion path animation lines in PowerPoint as well, which we discuss in Chapter 6 of Book IV.

Try using the Curve tool first, and after you get the hang of that one, try Freeform and Scribble. For our examples, we focus on the Curve tool:

1. **Click the Media button on the Standard toolbar to display the Media browser, if it isn't already visible.**

2. **Click the Shapes tab and then choose Lines and Connectors from the pop-up menu.**

3. **Click the Curve tool.**

   The Curve tool is the one that looks like a handwritten S. (Refer to Figure 8-13.) When you select the Curve tool, the cursor changes into a plus sign (+) to signify it's ready to start drawing a line as soon as you drag in the document, spreadsheet, or presentation.

4. **Click into your document and click the cursor as you move it; then move the cursor in another direction and click again.**

   Your line continuously gets longer as you move the cursor around, until you double-click the mouse, which signifies the end of the line you're drawing. Each time you click while you move the cursor, you create a point, which behaves as an axis for your line's curves.

This sort of drawing creates Bézier curves, as shown on the left side of Figure 8-14. By doing a variation on the steps in the preceding section to create a curvy line, you can end at the same point you started and then double-click at the end of the line, which results in a closed path. When you create a closed path, you get a solid shape, as shown in the right side of Figure 8-14.

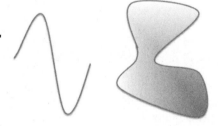

Figure 8-14:
A wavy line (left) and a solid shape (right).

Editing points on a line or shape

Now the fun begins. You can format lines and the borders of solid shapes with great precision. For the ultimate in precision control of your lines and shapes, right-click or Control-click your line or shape and then choose Edit Points from the pop-up menu. Each click you made when drawing the line displays as a point. Right-click a point to display the Edit Points menu, as shown in Figure 8-15. You get the same menu when working with a line or a shape.

Figure 8-15: Editing a point.

When Edit Points is active, you can drag, add, and delete points as well as control exactly how the line behaves while it passes through each point. There's still more! Right-click or Control-click right on top of a point. Notice the little handles that appear at the point, as shown in Figure 8-16. Drag the handles to control how the line passes through the point.

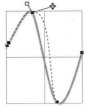

Figure 8-16: Working the handles of a point on a line.

It's often easier to work on small portions of a line by using the application's Zoom feature to zoom in and work closer.

Shapes you draw and shapes from the Media browser are classified as *vector* shapes. For a great article that explains the difference between vector shapes and pictures (also known as *bitmaps*), look at this site: `www.indezine.com/articles/bitmapvectors.html`.

Chapter 9: Fancy Text Boxes

In This Chapter

✔ **Making text boxes**

✔ **Formatting text boxes using the Ribbon**

✔ **Applying text styles**

✔ **Applying text effects**

✔ **Formatting using the Format Text dialog**

✔ **Controlling text layout**

*I*f you want to add drama or excitement, use a stunning text effect. Office 2011 lets you format text in ways that go beyond the basic font controls we discuss at the beginning of Chapter 6 in this minibook. In this chapter, we cover ways in which you can use text boxes and format them for special occasions when you want precise layout.

Making a Text Box

You need to start with a text box before you can apply any of the fancy text effects, so we begin with making a text box. In Word and PowerPoint, you can find the Text Box button here: On the Ribbon's Home tab, in the Insert group, click the Text Box button. Then drag over your work area to make a text box. If you prefer, you can choose Insert⇨Text Box from the main menu instead of using the Ribbon. In Excel, Insert⇨Text Box is the only way.

A text box is also a shape, so you can use all the shape formatting tools we discuss in Chapter 6 of this minibook on your text box. And because shapes have lines around them, and text boxes are also shapes, you can format the line around your text box using the formatting tools discussed in Chapter 6 of this minibook. And because a text box is a text box, you can use the special text formatting tools discussed here in this chapter. Whew! What that means is that in this chapter we discuss only the special formatting options available for text contained within text boxes. Please consult Chapter 6 of this minibook for tools that format the box itself and the line associated with the perimeter of the box.

Formatting Text Boxes with the Ribbon

When you select a text box, or text within a text box, the resize handles become visible, and the green rotation handle appears. Most importantly, the Format tab becomes visible on the Ribbon. Click the Format tab to display the Format controls on the Ribbon.

Applying quick styles and text styles

A *style* is a collection of formatting settings. If you select a text box or shape and then click the Ribbon's Format tab, in the Text Styles group you may see the icon shown in the left margin, or the gallery, as shown in Figure 9-1. You see the gallery if the window is sized wide enough to display it. Otherwise, you see the icon.

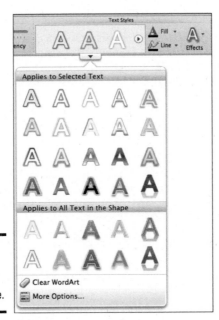

Figure 9-1:
Applying a
quick style
or text style.

The Text Styles gallery in the Text Styles group has these goodies for you:

✦ **Text Styles gallery:** Click a style in the gallery to apply a style (PowerPoint and Excel).

✦ **Scroll arrows:** At the left and right ends of the gallery, click the arrows to scroll (PowerPoint and Excel).

✦ **Submenu:** To display the full drop-down gallery, click the submenu near the bottom-center of the Text Styles gallery in PowerPoint and Excel, or click the Quick Styles button in Word. Click a style to apply its format to a selected text box or text.

- *Applies to Selected Text:* When you choose from this section, the format is applied only to the characters you have selected.

- *Applies to All Text in the Shape.*

- *Clear WordArt:* Removes applied text style formatting.

- *More Options:* Displays the Format Text dialog.

To the right of the Text Styles gallery are a couple more neat buttons:

✦ **Fill button:** Displays the colors palette. It offers a shortcut to the Format Text Effects dialog.

✦ **Line button:** Displays the colors palette, which has these submenus:

  - *Line Effects:* A shortcut to the Format Text dialog.

  - *Weights:* Choose line weights from a submenu.

  - *Dashed:* Choose line styles from a submenu.

✦ **Effects button:** A submenu with lots of fun options. (See the following section.)

These settings apply to the text inside the box, not to the box itself.

Applying Text Effects

When you click the Effects button on the Format Tab of the Ribbon, you can choose from the following effects, each of which has a submenu that displays preconfigured options. Most have a shortcut to the Text Effects dialog, which we discuss later in this chapter.

✦ Shadow

✦ Reflection

✦ Glow

✦ Bevel

✦ 3-D Rotation

✦ Transform

We refer you to Chapter 6 of this minibook, where we describe all of these effects (except Transform, which is discussed next). These effects work in the same way on text as they do on shapes.

REMEMBER

Keep in mind that when you apply text effects within a box or shape, there needs to be enough room around the text for the effect to show. Resizing the text box to be larger can make room for the text and its effect.

Making a Warp transform

The Transform effect is unique to the Effects button. At the top of Figure 9-2, we show two cylinders that are identical except that the Can Down effect has been applied to the text on the cylinder on the right. To get this effect, take these steps:

1. **Click into the text within a text box or shape.**

2. **Double-click the text, in this example *Drink,* to select it.**

3. **On the Ribbon, click the Format tab. In the Text Styles group, choose Effects⇨Transform. In the submenu's Warp group click the Can Down effect. (See Figure 9-2.)**

Drag diamond

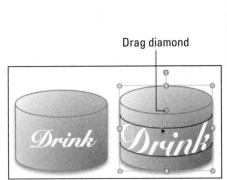

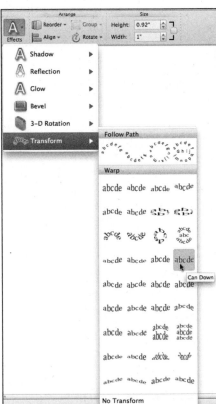

Figure 9-2:
Applying a warp transform.

4. **Drag the purple diamond downward deep into the shape to squish the text so that it fits better on the cylinder.**

Hold the mouse over a Transform button to see its name in a ScreenTip.

Making a Follow Path Transform

You have the ability to make text follow a curve, using the Follow Path transformation, as shown in Figure 9-3. We thought it would be nice to have text wrap above a picture of a front door, so we followed these steps to make the text follow a curve:

1. **Click the Ribbon's Home tab, and in the Insert group, click the Text Box button.**

2. **Drag a text box in your document.**

3. **Again from within the Home tab of the Ribbon, choose a font and apply some font format options like making the text bold.**

   Try making the text a little larger (at least 20 points) and use a phrase that has plenty of characters. We use the phrase "Welcome to Our Home."

4. **Click the text box border to select the box.**

5. **Click the Ribbon's Format tab. In the Text Styles group, choose Effects⇨ Transform. In the submenu's Follow Path group, click Arch Up. (Refer to Figure 9-2.)**

6. **Drag the purple diamond and resize the box until the text has a nice arch.**

As you drag the purple diamond, the ends of the curve grow or shrink. Let go of the diamond, and the text tries to fill-in to the end of the lines. In Figure 9-3 on the left side, you can see the curve as we dragged the purple dot. On the right side is our finished arch.

Figure 9-3:
Applying a
follow path
transform.

Formatting Text Boxes with the Format Text Dialog

You'll want to use the Format Text dialog for the precision control of text formatting it offers. You can get to the Format Text dialog in a bunch of ways. Rather than give you too many directions, though, we show the three easiest ways to get to the Format Text dialog after you select text and/or a text box:

✦ Right-click the text or text box and choose Format Text.

✦ Click the Ribbon's Format tab. In the Text Styles group, click Quick Styles. Click More Options at the bottom of the gallery.

✦ From the main menu, choose Format⇨Font.

Visiting the Format Text dialog

Figure 9-4 shows a Format Text dialog from PowerPoint. The list of command categories on the left pane of the dialog varies depending upon which application you're using and what path you took to get to the dialog. If you encounter categories not shown in Figure 9-4, they are specific to Word, Excel, or PowerPoint and are discussed in the respective minibooks. Additionally, the first four categories work differently in each application, so these topics are covered in the respective minibooks for each application:

✦ Font

✦ Paragraph

✦ Bullets and Numbering

✦ Columns

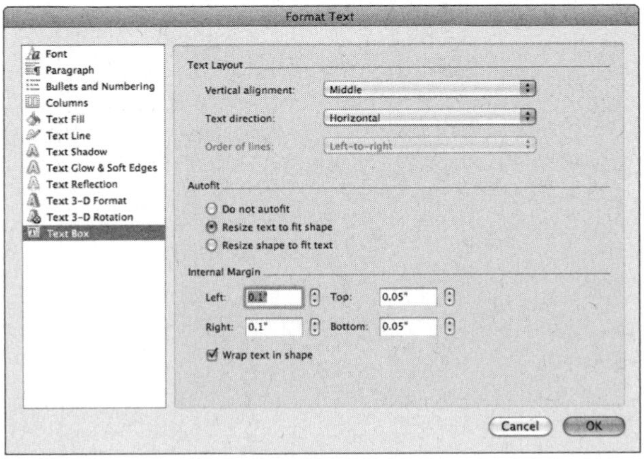

Figure 9-4:
The Format
Text dialog.

Also shown in the left pane of the Format Text dialog in Figure 9-4 are seven text effects that work the same on text as they do on shapes. The corresponding shape effects are discussed in Chapter 6 of this minibook.

Because these controls work the same way on text as they do on shapes, we refer you to Chapter 6 of this minibook for information about these topics:

✦ Text Fill

✦ Text Line

✦ Text Shadow

✦ Text Glow & Soft Edges

✦ Text Reflection

✦ Text 3-D Format

✦ Text 3-D Rotation

Formatting text layout

Three pop-up menus in the Text Layout section of the Format Text dialog affect how text is positioned within a selected text box. You can use many possible combinations. We show examples in Figure 9-5. Notice that we chose Do Not Autofit in the Autofit section. We resized the text boxes larger than their default sizes.

✦ **Horizontal Alignment:** Controls the positioning of the text within your text box. The default position is Top. Choose from the following:

  • *Top, Middle, or Bottom:* Available when text direction is horizontal.

  • *Right, Center, or Left:* Available when text direction is rotated or stacked.

  • *Top Centered, Middle Centered, or Bottom Centered:* Available for horizontal, rotated, or stacked text.

✦ **Text Direction:** Controls which direction the text is flowing within the text box. Horizontal is the default. See Figure 9-5. You can choose from these options:

Figure 9-5:
A few examples of text layout options.

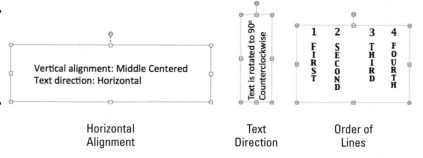

Vertical alignment: Middle Centered
Text direction: Horizontal

Text is rotated to 90° Counterclockwise

1 2 3 4
FIRST SECOND THIRD FOURTH

Horizontal
Alignment

Text
Direction

Order of
Lines

- Horizontal
- Rotate to 90 degrees counterclockwise
- Rotate to 90 degrees clockwise
- Stacked

✦ **Order of Lines:** This option is available only when Text Direction is formatted as Stacked. Figure 9-5 shows stacked text formatted Left-to-Right displaying a numbered list. You can choose from the following two options:

- Left-to-Right (Default)
- Right-to-Left

Chapter 10: Common Tools That Make Life Easier

In This Chapter

✔ Checking your spelling and grammar

✔ Working on your themes and templates

✔ Saving in different formats

✔ Making figures and formulas with Equation Editor

✔ Connecting with friends and colleagues

✔ Taking over a Windows computer

✔ Making hyperlinks

This chapter covers an eclectic collection of tools shared by Office 2011 applications, ranging from everyday features such as spell checking, themes, and styles to specialized tools such as Equation Editor, AppleScript, and Automator.

Proofing Your Spelling and Grammar

Fat fingers get a lot of the blame for spelling errors. Thankfully, Office can help you fix most spelling errors. Don't let that make you think you don't have to do any checking of your own, though. Good grammar is as much a good habit as it is a skill, and you need to review your work because even Word's advanced grammar checker can't tell when to use *there, they're,* or *their.* Clear communication with the right words, correct spelling, and a rich command over language is essential at home, office, and school.

Running spelling and grammar checks

A red squiggly line under the misspelled word indicates a spelling error. You can rectify such errors by right-clicking the word and then choosing the correct spelling from the resulting contextual menu. With the same procedure, you can also get help with grammar by Control-clicking or right-clicking words with green squiggly lines in Microsoft Word. Office also has *AutoCorrect,* which fixes spelling errors for you while you type.

Even with all the squiggles, you might accidently overlook an error. A good idea is to always run the spell and grammar checker before you share a document with someone. The most common way to fire up the spell and grammar checker differs depending upon the application you're using:

✦ In Word, use any of these methods:

   • Choose Tools⇨Spelling and Grammar.

   • Select some text or click a squiggle and then press Option+F7. Choose spelling or grammar from the contextual menu.

   • Click the book at the bottom of the window (shown in the margin).

   Notice that Word has both spell and grammar checking, but other Office applications have only spell checking.

✦ In Excel and PowerPoint, choose Tools⇨Spelling. (Figure 10-1 shows the Spelling dialog.)

✦ In Outlook, choose any of these methods:

   • Choose Edit⇨Spelling and Grammar⇨Show Spelling and Grammar, or press ⌘-Shift-; (Command-Shift-semicolon).

   • Choose Edit⇨Spelling and Grammar⇨Check Document Now, or press ⌘-; (Command-semicolon) to advance to the next flagged mistake without using the dialog.

   • In the Message Compose window, select the Options tab of the Ribbon, and click the Spelling button to display the Spelling and Grammar dialog.

Figure 10-1:
Spell
checking.

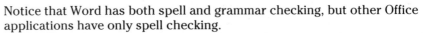

In this chapter, we focus on aspects of spell checking that all the Office applications have in common. Be sure to visit Book II, Chapter 5 for details about spell and grammar checking; AutoText details are in Book II, Chapter 7; AutoCorrect settings are explained in detail in Book II, Chapter 7; and dictionaries are covered in Book II, Chapter 5.

Controlling the AutoCorrect feature

Every word you type is compared with at least two lists of words. One list is Word's built-in dictionary, and the other is Word's built-in AutoCorrect list. Okay, although we call it Word's dictionary and AutoCorrect list, they actually are the same reference lists of words that PowerPoint and Excel refer to. Outlook refers to the Apple dictionary.

You have control over both dictionary and AutoCorrect lists. For example, you can customize your dictionary however you want, and you can add additional dictionaries. You can even make your own dictionary in Word. If you want to create your own dictionary, see Book II, Chapter 5. In addition to regular dictionaries, you can create a dictionary to exclude from spell check so that it doesn't flag misspelled words when more than one spelling is acceptable, such as *color* and *colour*.

The mysterious blue flash that briefly underlines a word for a second or two after you mistype is AutoCorrect at work. This flash is Office's way of alerting you that what you typed was changed automatically based on a rule in the AutoCorrect preferences. We cover those preferences in minibook Book II, Chapter 5.

Understanding Themes and Templates

Office has various ways that you can save formatting and document information so that it can be reused easily. Among the available file formats you can use to open new documents are templates and themes. Themes and templates are platform agnostic, and work on both Windows and Mac versions of Office. This means that you can use the large number of themes and templates designed on Office for Windows on the Mac, and your themes and templates will work in Office for Windows!

We discuss templates and themes throughout this book, but here we introduce you to these two concepts.

A *theme* contains formatting information. This includes the following:

✦ Twelve colors:

- Four background and text colors, two of which are invariably white and black
- Six accent colors
- Two hyperlink colors for link, and followed link

✦ A font family that comprises two fonts.

✦ An effects family that is used for shape styles that we cover in Chapter 6 of this minibook.

> The effects in Office 2011 for Mac change only when you change the whole theme (as we show you later in this chapter), unlike in Office for Windows, where you can individually alter just the effects family.

✦ PowerPoint specific features such as slide backgrounds, Master slides, and slide layouts.

A *template* is a boilerplate for an entire document, workbook, or presentation that can be used to open new, identical files. These files can be used as starting points for further customization. A template can contain everything that can be in a regular file including macros, charts, SmartArt, Word fields, tables, custom toolbars, and more.

Chart templates are different from document templates and contain chart-formatting information only. See Book III, Chapter 6.

Using themes for consistent colors and fonts

The idea behind using a theme is that you get consistent colors and fonts for the elements included within your Word documents, Excel spreadsheets, and PowerPoint presentations. Corporations and organizations seeking to brand their documents find themes very attractive. When you apply a theme and stick with the theme colors on the color palette, your graphs, charts, styled text, drawing objects, tables, and so on look professionally matched to the theme. You can choose from Office's built-in themes or make your own.

If you want everything consistent for Word, Excel, and PowerPoint, choose the same theme while working on documents in each application. Here's how to apply a theme from the Themes gallery:

✦ **In Word and Excel, click the Ribbon's Home tab. In the Themes group, click the Themes button.** When you click the Themes button, the themes gallery displays, as shown in Figure 10-2. Choose a theme. All elements in the document or workbook that respond to theme colors and fonts will be affected.

✦ **In PowerPoint, click the Ribbon's Themes tab.** This displays the Theme gallery. You can choose a theme from the gallery or click at the bottom-center of the gallery to display the Themes submenu as shown in Figure 10-2. To apply a theme to only selected slides:

   1. Before choosing a theme, select specific slides in Slide Sorter View or in the Slide Preview Pane.

   Reminder: Hold ⌘ to select more than one slide at a time.

2. Right-click a theme.

   A pop-up menu lets you choose to apply the theme to the selected slides or the entire presentation.

Alternatively, you can choose Browse Themes within the Themes gallery and navigate in the resulting dialog to a saved theme file. Choosing a saved theme applies the theme.

Themes are not supported in Compatibility Mode. When working on files that were saved in 2004 or earlier format, themes options are grayed out. Save the file in a current format to enable themes.

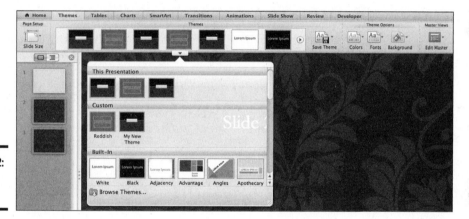

Figure 10-2: Applying a theme.

When you directly apply a color format in Word, Excel, or PowerPoint, you see the familiar color palette. The colors in the Theme Colors row of the color palette (see Figure 10-3) change to match the colors of the theme you applied. The color variations beneath the theme colors row provide shades (darker variations) and tints (lighter variations) of the theme colors. Each column has these shades and tints of the theme color at its top. The color palette does let you wander away from the theme colors by choosing the More Colors or Standard Colors options, but if you choose to do so, you defeat the purpose of using themes. In Book IV, Chapter 5, we explain how you can set precise colors for each of the color blocks of the theme colors row of the color palette in PowerPoint.

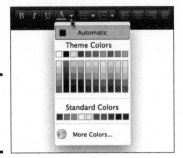

Figure 10-3: Choosing theme colors.

Saving everything as a template

When you open a template, a copy of the template is opened with a new filename so that the template file itself remains unchanged. That way, you can reuse the template whenever you need it. When you save a document as a template from Word, Excel, or PowerPoint, your document is saved with the entire contents intact as a Word, Excel, or PowerPoint template. A template includes everything, such as the document's words, formatting, objects, pictures, graphs, charts, and content. Typically, people save a document that has room for additional content, such as a business letterhead or a form, as a template.

Each application has its own built-in templates, which you can choose from by choosing File⇨New From Template, which we discuss at the beginning of each application's minibook.

The letter *t* in the file extensions `.dotx`, `.xltx`, and `.potx` alerts you that you're creating a template. Of course, PowerPoint's regular file format `.pptx` also has a *t* in the second to last position, but that's an exception!

You can easily save Word, Excel, or PowerPoint files as templates in the My Templates folder. Here's a step-by-step procedure to follow:

1. **Create a document that has all the basic formatting you want to reuse in other documents you create henceforth.**

   For example, you can make a letterhead document in Microsoft Word.

2. **Choose File⇨Save As.**

   The Save As dialog appears, as shown in Figure 10-4.

3. **Type a filename for your template in the Save As text box.**

4. **In the Format drop-down list, choose the appropriate template and then click the Save button.**

Depending upon which application you're using to create the template, the appropriate format is one of the following:

- Word Template (.dotx)
- Excel Template (.xltx)
- PowerPoint Template (.potx)

To make it easy for you, when you choose a template format, Office automatically saves your template in the My Templates folder by default, which is convenient for most users. If your Save As dialog looks a lot different from Figure 10-4, click the Show/Hide Full Dialog toggle button, which is the triangle to the right of the Save As field. That changes your screen's appearance to match ours.

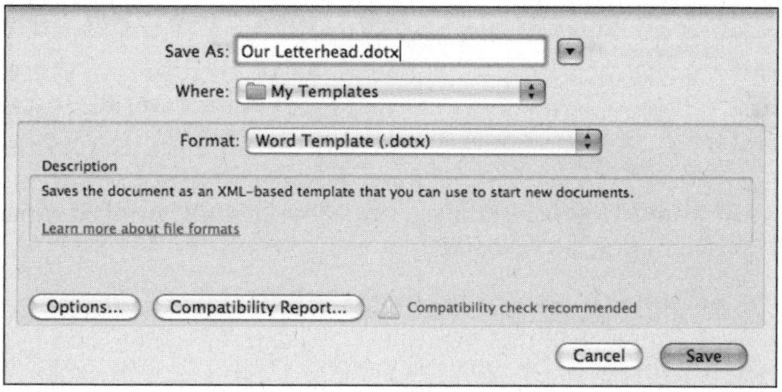

Figure 10-4:
Saving a file
as a Word
template.

Save As:	Our Letterhead.dotx
Where:	My Templates
Format:	Word Template (.dotx)

Description
Saves the document as an XML-based template that you can use to start new documents.

Learn more about file formats

(Options...)   (Compatibility Report...)   ⚠ Compatibility check recommended

(Cancel) (Save)

Sharing Files in Other Formats

Although Office 2011 and 2008 use the latest standard open XML file formats, not everyone has the latest version of Microsoft Office. Office programs offer various file formats; choose File⇨Save As⇨*[Format]* to accommodate various compatibility needs. We feature examples specific to each application in other minibooks. The following formats are common to all the Office applications.

Saving as an Adobe PDF

The Adobe *Portable Document Format* (PDF) has long been a popular way to distribute documents, especially to people who don't have Microsoft Office. PDF documents keep the look and feel of the original document even if the recipient doesn't have the needed fonts. You can also use PDFs to make it less convenient for others to edit a document. Simply choose File⇨Save As⇨PDF.

Saving as a Web page

A few years ago, this was a really hot feature. You can turn your Word documents and Excel workbooks into Web pages that can be uploaded to a Web server to be delivered via a network or on the Internet. Although you can still do this, SkyDrive, Docs.com, and other online office products made Web-saving capabilities in Office almost obsolete.

Saving with older formats

Use a format from '97 through 2004 if you know your recipient has an older version of Microsoft Office (for Mac or Windows) or other older software products that know `.doc`, `.xls`, and `.ppt` file extensions. Before saving in this format, be sure to run Compatibility Report, which is described in Chapter 3 of this minibook. Here's how to save in a format from '97 through 2004:

1. **Choose File⇨Save.**

   This saves your document in its current state with its current file name.

2. **Choose File⇨Save As.**

3. **In the resulting Save dialog, click the Format pop-up menu and choose a '97 through 2004 format.**

4. **Choose a file location and then click Save.**

This should not be necessary very often. Free software updates and service packs from Microsoft have updated older versions of Office to open, edit, and save with the current standard open XML file formats. These versions of Office can open, edit, and save in standard open XML file formats, although many objects and formatting won't be editable or display as expected when using an earlier version:

✦ Office Mac 2004, 2008

✦ Office for Windows 2003, 2007, and 2010

Getting Mathematical with Equations

Teachers, students, scientists, and other academicians need occasionally to represent numeric equations that ordinarily aren't possible to type from the keyboard. The solution to this dilemma is in two resolutions:

✦ The Equation option in Word 2011.

✦ The Equation Editor in Word, Excel, and PowerPoint within Office 2011.

We first explore Word's standalone Equation option and then look at
Equation Editor.

Equations from the Ribbon

Follow these steps to create a symbol or a formula in Word 2011 from within
the Ribbon:

1. **Position the cursor in your document where you want to place the
   symbol, formula, or equation.**

2. **Choose Insert⇨Equation from the menu.**

   This brings up the Equation Tools tab in the Ribbon, as shown in
   Figure 10-5.

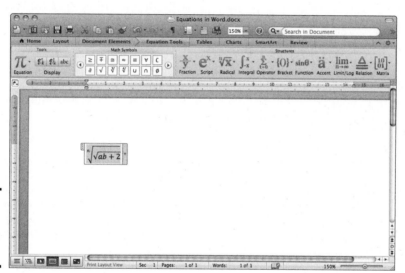

Figure 10-5:
Equation
Tools tab on
the Ribbon.

3. **Click a category from the Structures group on the Equation Tools tab.**

   Categories include Fractions, Scripts, Radical, and many more. All categories have a submenu that reveals galleries with several options, such
   as the one shown in Figure 10-6. Hover your cursor over each option in
   the gallery, and descriptions appear as a ScreenTip. When you click the
   option you want to insert, a placeholder for the equation is placed in the
   open document.

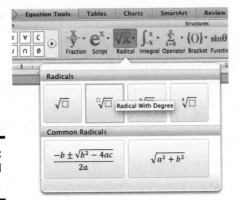

Figure 10-6:
The Radical
gallery.

4. **Click inside dotted boxes to type numbers or text.**

   You can add text by simply typing inside the doted boxes.

5. **Click outside the equation area when you're done.**

The result is an equation placed in your document. To make additional edits to your equation, just click to select it and bring up the Equation Tools tab of the Ribbon. Edit and make changes as required.

Using the Equation Editor

Equation Editor (see Figure 10-7) is included with Microsoft Office and lets you type mathematical symbols and equations. This feature is made by Design Science, and the company provides it as a *light* version of MathType, which has more symbols and fonts. For information about the complete MathType package, please visit the Design Science Web site at www.dessci.com/en/products/MathType_Mac.

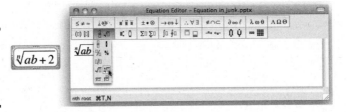

Figure 10-7:
Microsoft's
Equation
Editor.

Being savvy with AppleScript

Deep down inside your computer is a scripting language called *AppleScript* that's extremely powerful. Some applications on your computer support AppleScript just a little bit, but Office 2011 was designed to offer excellent AppleScript support. Great AppleScripts are waiting on the Internet for you to find, particularly for Outlook, so you don't have to become a scripter to take advantage of Office's AppleScript capabilities. Apple has a Web site devoted to helping people figure out AppleScript. The URL is `http://developer. apple.com/applescript`.

Although Equation Editor looks complicated, it's actually quite easy to use:

1. **Position the cursor in your document where you want to place the symbol, formula, or equation.**

2. **From the main menu, choose Insert⇨Object.**

This step brings up the Object dialog.

3. **Scroll up or down and choose the Microsoft Equation option, and then click OK.**

Equation Editor opens in its own window.

4. **Click a formula template from the symbols categories.**

Some categories have submenus from which to choose. Descriptions appear when you mouse over the various symbols.

5. **Click inside dotted boxes to type numbers or text.**

You can add text by simply typing in the Editing pane. For example, you can take a formula and turn it into an equation by typing **y=** in front of the formula.

6. **Click the red Close button when you're done.**

The result is an Equation Editor object in your document. To reopen Equation Editor to make additional edits to your object, just right-click the border of the Equation Editor object in the document and then choose Open Equation Object from the pop-up menu.

Connecting with Messenger and Communicator

Joining Microsoft Messenger is a new business counterpart in Office 2011, Microsoft Communicator. Both products offer similar features and interfaces, but each is designed for a different market:

✦ **Microsoft Messenger:** Uses your Windows Live ID (such as your Hotmail e-mail address) to communicate with contacts using public servers. Requires a Windows Live account to sign in.

✦ **Microsoft Communicator:** Designed to use fully updated Microsoft Exchange Server 2007 or later to communicate within a closed business environment. The corporate contact list has been moved from Messenger to Communicator. Communicator supports Microsoft Exchange Global Address List (GAL).

If all this talk about Communicator sounds complicated, you'll be glad to know that all this is normally set up by your company's IT team or system administrator.

Both Messenger and Communicator offer a variety of ways to communicate, collaborate, and share work. Logging in to either product involves a simple username and password sign-on. After you log in, you see an interface similar to the one shown in Figure 10-8.

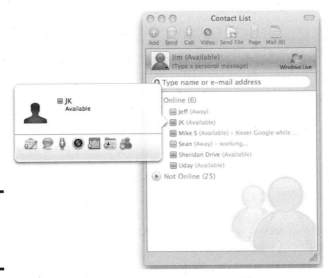

Figure 10-8: Communicating and messaging.

As you can see, a lot of functionality is crammed into a small interface. You can find access to features on the toolbar, menu bar, Presence Indicator, and right-click menus, which you use as you please.

Managing contacts

The Contact List, shown in Figure 10-8, displays when you open Messenger or Communicator. Starting at the top, you have access to a lot of tools:

✦ **Add:** Displays the Add a Contact dialog.

✦ **Send:** Click the Send button and then choose a contact from the pop-up menu to open a text instant message conversation window.

✦ **Call:** Click and then choose a contact from the pop-up menu to request initiation of a voice call. This feature requires speakers and microphones on both ends of the call. Communicator supports PC to phone dialing.

✦ **Video:** Click and then choose a contact from the pop-up menu to request initiation of a video call. This feature requires video camera, speaker, and microphones on both ends of the call.

✦ **Send File:** Click and then choose a contact from the pop-up menu. You see a file Open sheet, which you can use to choose a file or photo to send to the selected contact.

✦ **Page:** Click and then choose a contact from the pop-up menu. If you haven't set up your mobile message preferences, the Preferences dialog opens. Normally, Page displays the Page message input window. Type a text message to be sent to your contact's cellphone or mobile device.

✦ **Mail:** Opens your Web browser to view your mail account. Displays how many unread messages you have in your inbox.

Indicating Presence

The Presence Indicator is a new feature of Office 2011. You can display the Presence Indicator by clicking a status icon next to a contact's name in the Outlook Contact List, and when you mouse over an e-mail address in Outlook. (See Book V, Chapter 3 for details.) The Presence indicator has these buttons across the bottom:

✦ **Send Mail:** Opens a new browser window to a new, blank, pre-addressed e-mail message window.

✦ **Send Instant Message:** Opens a conversation window and requests the contact to engage in a text chat session.

✦ **Voice Call:** Sends a request to establish a voice call. This feature requires speakers and microphones on both ends of the call. Communicator supports PC to Phone dialing.

✦ **Video Call:** Sends a request to establish a video call. This feature requires video camera, speaker, and microphones on both ends of the call.

✦ **Schedule Meeting:** Opens a new Meeting dialog in Outlook. See the Calendar chapter of the Outlook minibook for details.

✦ **Open Outlook Contact:** Opens the Contact in Outlook.

✦ **Add to Contact List:** Adds this person to your Messenger or Communicator Contacts List.

✦ **Phone Number:** In Communicator, click to initiate a telephone call.

Instant messaging

When you choose to send an instant message, the Message Conversation dialog shown in Figure 10-9 opens. The dialog lets you chat using text. You can drag files and pictures into the input area to send them to your correspondent. Most of the functions are described in the previous sections. If you haven't already set your preferences, the first time you close a chat window when you're done chatting with a contact, you're prompted as to whether or not you want to automatically save your chat sessions. You can also use the following features in the Message Conversation dialog:

✦ **Save:** Saves the dialog of your chat. Messenger only.

✦ **History:** Displays the Conversation History window. Messenger only.

✦ **Open Drawer:** Opens the side drawer and displays Contact pictures.

✦ **Presence Indicator:** Click to display the contact's Presence Indicator.

✦ **Close Drawer:** Closes the side drawer.

✦ **Input area:** Type your message or drag a file into this section.

✦ **Font:** Click to change characteristics of the font you send.

Figure 10-9:
Instant
messaging.

Reviewing conversation history

When you click the History button (see Figure 10-9) or press ⌘-O in Messenger, the Conversation History dialog appears. You get the following options:

✦ **Save as Web Page:** Saves the selected conversation in HTML that can be opened in a Web browser.

✦ **Print:** Prints the conversation.

✦ **Delete:** Deletes selected conversation.

✦ **Search:** Find conversations using keyboards.

✦ **Show/Hide toolbar:** Click this little button when your toolbar disappears and you want it back.

Becoming Undone

The single most important feature in all of Office is the Undo button. The ability to easily back out of document changes makes it possible to be daring, but not reckless. Some things, such as file operations, can't be undone, but most of the changes you make in Office aren't set in stone.

Most people know that each time you click the Undo button or press ⌘-Z, the most recent change is undone. Some people even know that each successive click of the Undo button reverts the next most recent change, and you can keep clicking the Undo button until you've undone all the changes in the Undo history. But only a select few know that you can click the down arrow next the Undo button. (See Figure 10-10.) This action reveals the Undo history with the most recent action on top. And if you like, you can undo multiple actions all at once with one click.

Figure 10-10: Undoing multiple actions at once.

Hyperlinking

One of the most useful tools in all of Office is the ability to make hyperlinks to just about anywhere. You can link to the Internet; to files on your hard drive; and to places within documents, workbooks, and presentations. You can make a link work from selected text or from practically any object such as a picture or shape, so to begin you select text or an object.

In Word, Excel, and Outlook, you simply click a hyperlink to activate the link. In PowerPoint, the slide show must be running before you can click a hyperlink to activate it. In Outlook, you simply type or paste a hyperlink into the message body of an e-mail, or into the hyperlink field of a contact. The following sections explain how to insert a hyperlink in Word, Excel, and PowerPoint.

Hyperlinking to the Internet

You can link to almost any Internet Web page that has a URL starting with *http://*. Follow these steps:

1. **In a Web browser, navigate to the page you want to link to and then copy the URL in the address bar.**

2. **In Word, PowerPoint, or Excel, right-click selected text or an object and then choose Hyperlink from the pop-up menu, or press ⌘-K, or from the main menu choose Insert⇨Hyperlink.**

   This step displays the Insert Hyperlink dialog, shown in Figure 10-11.

3. **Select the Web Page tab.**

4. **Paste the URL of the Web page in the Link To field of the Insert Hyperlink dialog.**

   You must include the *http://* portion of the Web address.

5. **(Optional) Click the ScreenTip button to display a dialog where you can type a ScreenTip that appears when someone hovers a mouse pointer over the hyperlink.**

6. **(Optional) Click the Locate button.**

   If the Web page has anchors (bookmarks), the Select Place in Document dialog displays and lists the anchors. You can choose an anchor. Choose a bookmark from the list in the Select Place in Document dialog. Then click OK to close the dialog.

7. **Click OK in the Insert Hyperlink dialog.**

   The hyperlink displays.

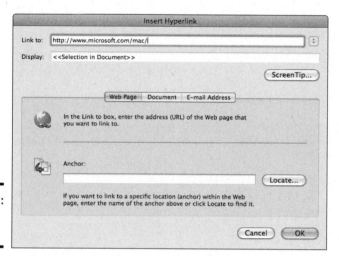

Figure 10-11:
Linking to a
Web page.

Hyperlinking to a local file

You can link to any file on your computer. There are two kinds of links:

+ **Absolute:** This kind of link contains the entire file path to your content. The URL starts with *file://localhost/Users/* and links to a file anywhere on your computer. This kind of URL works only for a single user account. If you move the document, workbook, or presentation to another computer, the hyperlink won't work. Use this kind of link only if you know your link will never have to work on another computer.

+ **Relative:** A relative link contains only the filename of content that is linked within the same folder (at the same directory level) as the document, workbook, or presentation before you make the link. If you copy the folder itself that contains the document, workbook, or presentation file that also contains the content file, you can put the copy of the entire folder onto any media such as a flash drive, CD, or DVD, and the link will work on any computer. To set up your document to make a copy that can be distributed with relative hyperlinks, take these steps:

 1. **Press ⌘-S, or click the Save button on the Standard toolbar to save your document in its current location.**

 2. **Choose File⇨Save As and click the New Folder button to make the folder that will contain your document and content prior to linking.**

 3. **Save a copy of your document, workbook, or presentation in the new folder.**

4. **Make copies of your content: In Finder, Option-drag copies of any content you want to link to into the folder.**

   Now you can make links (following the directions in the next section) to the content that you put into the shared folder.

To hyperlink to a local file on your computer, here's what you do:

1. **Display the Insert Hyperlink dialog by right-clicking selected text or an object and then choosing Hyperlink from the pop-up menu, or press ⌘-K.**

2. **Click the Document tab. (See Figure 10-12.)**

Figure 10-12: Linking to a file.

3. **Click the Select button.**

   The Choose a File to Link To dialog displays. Navigate to the file you want to open when the hyperlink is clicked. The file can be an Office file, a picture, a PDF, or even a file belonging to another application.

4. **Choose a file and then click Open to create the link and close the dialog.**

5. **(Optional) Click the ScreenTip button to display a dialog where you can type a ScreenTip that appears when someone hovers a mouse pointer over the hyperlink.**

6. **(Optional) Click the Locate button.**

   If the Web page has anchors (bookmarks), the Select Place in Document dialog displays and lists the anchors. If you're linking to a Word document, a list of bookmarks displays. If you're linking to an Excel workbook, you can link to a sheet name, named range, or named object. PowerPoint offers a list of slides to link to. (See Figure 10-13.)

Choose a bookmark from the list in the Select Place in Document dialog and then click OK to close it.

7. **Click OK to close the Insert Hyperlink dialog.**

   The hyperlink displays.

Figure 10-13:
Locating an
anchor in
Excel.

Hyperlinking to an e-mail address

When you create an e-mail address hyperlink in Word, Excel, or PowerPoint, the computer's default e-mail program opens a blank, pre-addressed e-mail message. This works great as long as you've chosen a default e-mail program, such as Microsoft Outlook, and configured it to work with your e-mail server. If you only use e-mail in a Web browser and haven't configured a default e-mail application, you won't be able to send the message from your e-mail program.

To hyperlink to a new, pre-addressed e-mail message in Word, Excel, or PowerPoint, follow these directions:

1. **Display the Insert Hyperlink dialog by right-clicking selected text or an object and then choosing Hyperlink, or press ⌘-K.**

2. **Click the E-Mail Address tab. (See Figure 10-14.)**

3. **In the To field, type or paste an e-mail address.**

   Be sure to include the @ sign. The e-mail message will be sent to the e-mail address that you enter here. The Link To field at the top is filled in automatically as you fill in the To and Subject fields in the dialog.

4. **In the Subject field, type a subject for the e-mail that will be sent.**

5. **(Optional) Click the Launch E-Mail Application.**

   Click this button if you need to find out which e-mail application is the default e-mail application on your computer. After you click this button, the default e-mail program opens. You have no control over what e-mail program will be used on any other computer, so if you share your file with someone else or open it on a different computer, a different e-mail application may open.

6. **Click OK to finish making the hyperlink.**

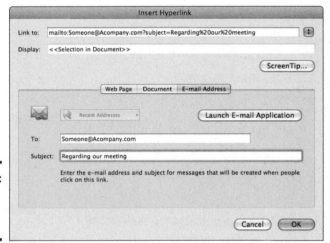

Figure 10-14:
Linking to
an e-mail
message.

Chapter 11: Making Great Tables

In This Chapter

✔ **Starting a table**

✔ **Choosing table options**

✔ **Formatting with a table style**

✔ **Making a table style**

*O*ffice now brings a consistent way to make and work with tables in Word, Excel, and PowerPoint, thanks to the Tables tab of the Ribbon. Tables are simply gridlines that form boxes, or *cells,* that you can fill in, usually with text and numbers. You can format the cells so that the appearance is pleasing and the display is informative to the audience. When made in Excel, tables can take advantage of Excel's powerful formulas and calculation capabilities.

Making a Table

Just to remind anyone who's used to Insert⇨Table, this feature still works in Office 2011, along with the Table menu and pop-up menu commands you're used to. There's no need to fret! In this chapter, we discuss how the new Table tab on the Ribbon makes and formats tables. Both methods work just fine — use the one you like.

Making a new table with the Ribbon

You can make a new table from scratch in several different ways. Even using the Ribbon, it's a bit different depending upon the Office 2011 application you're using.

Making a table using the Ribbon in Word and PowerPoint

The steps to make a brand-new table in Word and PowerPoint are the same:

1. **Position your cursor in your Word document or PowerPoint slide at the position where you want the upper-left corner of the table to be.**

In Word, you can't make tables in Notebook Layout view using the Ribbon. You can still use the Table menu, though.

2. **On the Ribbon, click the Tables tab. In the Table Options group, click the New button.**

   When you click the New button (shown in the margin), the pop-up menu shown in Figure 11-1 appears.

3. **Drag over the grid for the number of rows and columns to make.**

   Don't worry about getting this just right. It's easy to add and remove rows and columns after you make your table.

4. **When you're finished dragging, click over the grid to insert your table.**

   The table appears in your document or presentation.

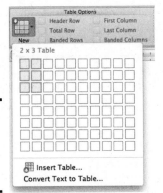

Figure 11-1: Making a Word or PowerPoint table.

Making a table using the Ribbon in Excel

Making a table in Excel is almost the same as in Word and PowerPoint, but not quite. Here's what to do (see Figure 11-2):

1. **Select a range of cells to turn into a table.**

   The cells can be empty or already filled in.

2. **On the Ribbon, click the Tables tab, find the Table Options group, and click the small triangle to the right of the New button.**

   A pop-up menu appears. Choose from these two options:

   • *Insert Table with Headers:* Tells Excel to use the top row of the selected cell range as headers.

   • *Insert Table without Headers:* Tells Excel there is no header row.

   The cells become a table object within the worksheet. Notice that when making a table without headers, Excel puts a generic set of column headers above the table by default, as shown in Figure 11-2.

Figure 11-2:
Making
a table in
Excel.

a		b		c		a		b		c		a		b		c	
1		2		4		1		2		4		1		2		4
3		5		6		3		5		6		3		5		6

Making a new table with a dialog

We promised that the familiar menus still work, and here's the proof. The
table dialogs are all still right here:

✦ **In Word,** choose Table➪Insert➪Table; alternatively, on the Ribbon's
  Tables tab, in the Table Options group, click New. At the bottom of the
  pop-up menu, choose Insert Table.

✦ **In Excel and PowerPoint,** choose Insert➪Table.

The Insert Table dialog lets you choose how many rows and columns your
table will have. In Excel, you choose how many rows and columns you want
by first selecting a cell range, as shown in in Figure 11-2. When using Word,
you enter the number of columns and rows you want in the Number of
Columns and Number of Rows fields, respectively. The Insert Table dialog in
Word offers these additional options, as shown in Figure 11-3:

✦ **Autofit Behavior:** Choose from these options:

  • *Initial Column Width:* Choose Auto or type in a value.

  • *Autofit to Contents:* Autofits table cell width to the content within
    the cell.

  • *Autofit to Window:* Autofits table to the width of the document
    window.

✦ **Set as Default for New Tables:** You can make any changes you apply in
  this dialog the default for new tables inserted.

Figure 11-3:
Making a
table using
a dialog.

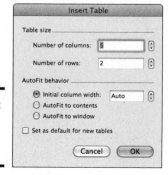

Making a new table from text in Word

Not to be outdone, Word can make a table instantly from delimited text. Occasionally, you may find yourself faced with text that's been laid out using tabs, commas, or other delimiters. Paragraph marks denote the ends of the rows. Converting this information to a table is very easy. Simply select the range of text containing the tab separated text. Then display the Insert Table dialog shown in Figure 11-3 by using either of these two methods:

✦ **(Word only) On the Ribbon, click the Tables tab. In the Table Options group, click New. Choose Convert Text to Table near the bottom of the resulting palette.** This option is shown earlier in Figure 11-1.

✦ **Choose Table⇨Insert⇨Table.**

Choosing Table Options

New for Word and Excel is the ability to use table styles to format text and table cells, an ability that PowerPoint gained in Office 2008. You get many attractive, built-in styles from which to choose. In Word and Excel, you can create your own styles and add them to your collection.

Next to the New button in the Table Options group of the Ribbon of Word and Excel are check boxes (refer to Figure 11-1) that affect how your table displays. If your window isn't widened enough, you might not see the buttons. In this case, click the Options button (shown in the margin) to display the same options:

✦ **Header Row:** When selected, this option displays the header row.

When this option is selected in Word and PowerPoint, special formatting is applied to the header row. When selected in Excel, you see special formatting with filter buttons that when clicked, activate the Filter dialog as shown in Figure 11-4. Look in Book III, Chapter 5 for more about these filters.

Figure 11-4:
Turning off
the Header
Row option.

✦ **Total Row:** When selected, this option displays a row at the bottom of the table that can be used for the results of calculations on data in the table.

In Word, Excel, and PowerPoint, the Total row can be formatted. In Word, you can use Word fields (explained in the Book II, Chapter 8) to perform calculations on data in table cells.

In Excel, you can use the power of Excel formulas to put calculation results into the Total row. To display the pop-up menu shown in Figure 11-4, click into any cell in the Total row and click the formula button that appears. Choose a formula from the pop-up menu, as shown in Figure 11-5.

✦ **Banded rows:** Displays or hides color bands for rows. (See Figure 11-6.)

✦ **First Column:** Highlights the first column in the table. (See Figure 11-7.)

✦ **Last Column:** Gives the last column in the table a highlight color.

✦ **Banded Columns:** Displays or hides color bands for columns.

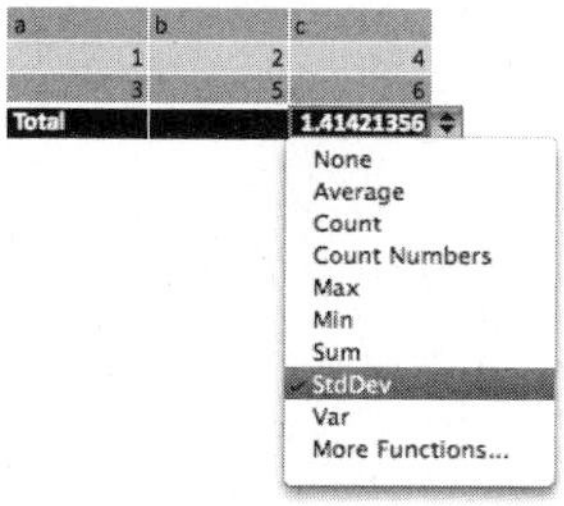

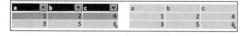

Figure 11-5:
Adding a
Total row.

Figure 11-6:
Turning row
banding on
and off.

Figure 11-7:
Accenting
the first
column.

Formatting with Table Styles

Table styles are new for Word and Excel in Office 2011. The Ribbon's Table Styles gallery and submenu, shown in Figure 11-8, make it very easy to apply great formats to your tables, so we're sure you'll like them.

Applying a style

All you do to apply a table style is click into a table and then click on a table style in the gallery or its submenu. The Clear Table Style option restores your table's original format. The colors of the options in the gallery are influenced by the current theme.

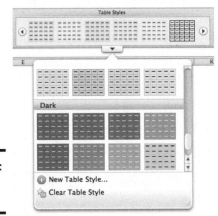

Figure 11-8:
Applying a
table style.

Making a new table style

In Word, you can use the elaborate Styles dialog, which is discussed in Book II. PowerPoint doesn't let you make new table styles. The option to make a new table style is available at the bottom of the Table Styles submenu in Excel, shown in Figure 11-8. Choosing this option displays the New Table Style dialog shown in Figure 11-9. When using the Excel New Table Style dialog, here's what you need to know:

✦ **Name:** Enter a name for your new table style.

✦ **Table element:** Select which table element you want to format or clear.

✦ **Format:** Opens a secondary dialog with font, border, and fill formatting options for the selected table element.

✦ **Clear:** Clears the formatting for the selected table element.

✦ **Set as Default Table Style for This Workbook:** If you choose this option, the current table style will be applied to any new tables you make in the active workbook.

Applying direct formatting

In addition to the table elements you can control using styles and themes, you can apply formatting directly to a table and use Table Layout controls. These controls work differently in Word, Excel, and PowerPoint. You can find explanations of these controls in the corresponding minibook for each application.

REMEMBER

If you apply a theme after applying a table style, the theme colors and fonts override your table style. You can apply direct formatting to a table even after you have applied a style or theme.

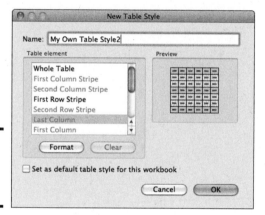

Figure 11-9:
Creating a
new table
style.

Chapter 12: Using VBA

In This Chapter

✓ Discovering VBA

✓ Finding and using add-ins

✓ Using the Visual Basic Editor

✓ Recording macros

You can use Office without ever confronting any VBA (Visual Basic for Applications) code. At some point, though, we bet that you'll get tired of doing a repetitive task. This chapter shows you how to record *macros* (the steps you took saved in a fairly easy-to-learn Basic computer language) to automate those repetitious tasks. Perhaps after recording a few macros, you'll discover that you can do coding of some sort after all!

VBA is a programming language for Microsoft Office applications such as Word, Excel, and PowerPoint. Outlook's programming language on the Mac is AppleScript, a scripting language built with the Mac OS X. This chapter explores VBA, and as such, this entire chapter is Technical Stuff!

In this chapter, we show the new Visual Basic Editor (VBE) in Office for Mac. If you've made macros, you'll find the new VBE familiar, yet improved. In case you've made VBA projects in Windows, we explain how the Mac VBE differs and help you get over the shock of seeing your applications while looking at your code. If you made VBA code work in Windows, you'll almost always be able to do the same thing or an equivalent in Mac VBA. We explain the major things to watch for so that your code can be either completely cross-platform or have a Mac version as well as a PC version.

Discovering VBA

Unlike other programming languages, most people who use VBA learn it on their own to help with a specific task. Few people making extensive use of VBA fall into the geek or nerd category. People use VBA most commonly to automate repetitive chores. Don't be afraid to give VBA a try. Getting started with VBA is more about writing than it is about math. VBA code, also known as macro or macrocode, consists of instructions for your computer to follow. These instructions are stored as text, which is written in syntax similar to simplified English.

VBA version 6.5

When Apple switched from PowerPC processors to Intel processors, VBA got the kibosh on the Mac. VBA is a compiled language, meaning a compiler turns the VBA text into zeros and ones the processor can deal with. Unfortunately for Mac users, the VBA compiler is processor-specific and had to be rewritten from scratch.

The new compiler and VBE in Office 2011 are built around VBA version 6.5. The new compiler is souped-up a bit to seamlessly handle 64-bit code written in VBA version 7 on Windows, execute AppleScript, exchange variables with AppleScript, and work with Mac-only features of Office.

Because Office has VBA, you can make your own macros (instruction sets) that automate repetitive tasks, such as applying formatting and adding paragraphs in Word, copying and pasting cells in Excel, or removing all the animations from a PowerPoint presentation. In addition, with a little scripting and coding help, you can make VBA *add-ins*. These add-ins plug into parent programs such as Word, Excel, and PowerPoint and add extra capabilities to their repertoire. If you get very well versed with VBA, you can even make full-blown applications.

In Word and Excel, you can record VBA macros as you perform actions within the applications. These recordings are saved as code that you can further edit on your own. PowerPoint doesn't allow you to create macros by recording.

Displaying the Developer Ribbon

To get started, turn on the Developer tab of the Ribbon by visiting the Ribbon preferences of Word, Excel, and PowerPoint and doing the following:

1. **Choose *[Application]*⇨Preferences⇨Ribbon.**
2. **In the Preferences dialog, scroll down and select the Developer check box.**
3. **Click OK.**

   The Developer tab of the Ribbon and its VBA controls display in all their finery. We show you a part of that finery in Figure 12-1.

The Visual Basic group on the Developer Ribbon has three main controls:

✦ **Editor:** Displays the Visual Basic Editor (VBE).

✦ **Macros:** Displays a dialog that shows you available macros. See the section "Displaying Your Macros" near the end of this chapter.

✦ **Record:** Starts and stops the process of recording your actions as Visual Basic code (Word or Excel only). If you're a PowerPoint user who is now cursing Microsoft, go ahead and do it. We understand!

Figure 12-1:
Using VBA from the Ribbon.

Of course, you don't have to use the Ribbon if you don't want to. From the menu bar, choose one of the following:

✦ **Tools⇨Macro⇨Visual Basic Editor:** Displays the VBE.

✦ **Tools⇨Macro⇨Macros:** Displays the Macro dialog.

✦ **Tools⇨Macro⇨Record New Macro:** Starts recording your actions and displays a small toolbar with a button to stop recording. Recording is available only in Word and Excel.

Using Office Add-Ins

An add-in enhances or works with Office software in some way. Add-ins are sometimes called *plug-ins* or *add-ons*. Here are three examples of excellent commercial-quality add-ins that work with Mac Office:

✦ **EndNote (www.endnote.com):** A high-end bibliography product for Microsoft Word.

✦ **MathType (www.dessci.com/en/products/MathType_Mac):** The full version of Equation Editor that's included in Office. It lets you put mathematical symbols in Word, Excel, and PowerPoint.

✦ **TurningPoint (www.turningtechnologies.com):** Use clickers to capture audience responses in real time and present the results on PowerPoint slides. This software is used in classrooms, quiz shows, marketing studies, and more.

Many add-ins made for Office for Windows can work on your Mac, so be sure to check their system requirements. Almost all add-ins can be made Mac-compatible with a little effort, but you may have to request the developer of a nonfunctioning add-in to make that extra effort.

Installing Add-Ins

You can put add-ins anywhere in Finder. If you want to make an add-in available to all Mac OS X user accounts on a computer, put them into Applications:Microsoft Office 14:Office:Add-Ins. The Documents folder is a good place to put add-ins to be used by a particular OS X user account.

A few commercially produced add-ins are installed using the Mac OS X installer program. Because making an installer is an art of its own and takes extra time and effort on the add-in developer's part, you install most add-ins manually using the Add-Ins dialog in Office.

A Word add-in is a template file that contains VBA code. You can add such a template to the Templates and Add-Ins dialog. In PowerPoint and Excel, an add-in has a special file extension and is not necessarily a template. Table 12-1 gives the file extensions for add-ins in Word, PowerPoint, and Excel.

Table 12-1	Add-In Extensions	
Application	*New Add-In File Extension*	*Old Add-In File Extension*
Word	`.dotm`	`.dot`
Excel	`.xlam`	`.xla`
Excel macro enabled template	`.xltm`	`.xlt`
PowerPoint	`.ppam`	`.ppa`
PowerPoint macro enabled template	`.potm`	`.pot`

The Add-Ins dialog is shown in Figure 12-2. To open this dialog, here's what you do:

✦ **Word:** Choose Tools⇨Templates and Add-Ins.

In this chapter, only the Add-Ins portion of the dialog is of interest in Word. We cover Word templates features in Book II, Chapter 2.

✦ **Excel and PowerPoint:** Choose Tools⇨Add-Ins.

✦ **Word, Excel, and PowerPoint:** Click the Developer tab on the Ribbon and then click Add-Ins⇨Add-Ins.

Figure 12-2:
Using the
Add-Ins
dialog in
PowerPoint
(and Excel).

When you have the Add-Ins dialog open, you can do the following simple
tasks to add, remove, load, and unload add-ins, as shown in Figure 12-2:

✦ **Load:** Same as selecting the check box next to the add-in's name.
Loading also runs the add-in. (Available only in Excel and PowerPoint.)

✦ **Unload:** Same as deselecting an add-in's check box. Unloading disables
the add-in. (Available only in Excel and PowerPoint.)

✦ **Add:** Click to open the Choose a File browser, where you can browse to
an add-in template in Finder and add your add-in to the list.

✦ **Remove:** Click to remove the selected add-in from the list.

In Word, when you select an add-in's check box or click the Add button, you
load the template, thereby making the VBA routines that it has available glob-
ally within all open documents in Word. A loaded template is called a *global
template*. Revisit the Templates and Add-Ins dialog to re-load your template(s).
To disable an add-in, deselect its check box or click the Remove button.

Excel and PowerPoint add-ins are also loaded and unloaded using check
boxes. When you close Excel or PowerPoint, add-ins that were loaded at
closing reload themselves when you reopen the application.

Exploring the Visual Basic Editor

The Visual Basic Editor (VBE) is very much like a specialized word processor combined with an organization tool and some special tools to help you
make visual basic code. To display the VBE using the Ribbon, click the
Developer tab, and in the Visual Basic group, and click Editor. From the
menu bar, choose Tools➪Macro➪Visual Basic Editor.

If you're used to using the VBE in Office for Windows, you will immediately
discover you can see your application and other windows beneath the VBE
windows. On the Mac, the VBE is not constrained within a window, so you
can click to and from application windows while the VBE is running, which is
handy when stepping through code while debugging.

The VBE has menus, toolbars, and keyboard shortcuts, but there is no Ribbon. As with Office applications, VBE toolbars and menus are context sensitive. You can customize VBE menus and toolbars using code, but that's beyond the scope of this chapter.

Displaying the VBE interface

As with Office applications, you can turn VBE interface components on and off using the View menu, shown in Figure 12-3. Be sure to toggle on the Debug, Edit, and Standard toolbars as shown. Notice that keyboard short-cuts are displayed on the View menu.

Figure 12-3: Viewing VBE components.

The Standard toolbar

Some of the controls on the Standard toolbar in VBE (see Figure 12-4) are familiar text-editing controls. The rest are specific to working within the VBE. Refer to Figure 12-4 when going through this run-down of controls:

✦ **Host Application:** Takes you out of the VBE and displays the document, spreadsheet, or presentation view. Alternatively, you can click into a document, spreadsheet, or presentation window to return to the host application, or go to another application window for that matter. This control does not stop code execution when stepping through code, so you can make changes in the host document, workbook, or presentation while stepping through code.

✦ **Insert:** Inserts into the current Project a new UserForm, Module, Class Module, or Procedure. This button remembers which you inserted last and offers the most recently used as its default.

✦ **Save:** Saves the document, workbook, or presentation of the Project that is currently selected in the Project Explorer. Hover the mouse cursor over the Save button for a ScreenTip that tells you which file will be saved.

✦ **Cut, Copy, Paste, and Find:** Work similar to other applications.

✦ **Run:** Click into a module (procedure) and then click Run to run your code.

✦ **Break:** Interrupts code execution. Click Run or press F5 to resume, or click Step Over on the Debug toolbar to execute one command at a time.

✦ **Reset:** When in Break mode, Reset ends the break and resets so that if you click Run again, code execution starts at the beginning.

✦ **Design Mode:** In Design mode, the Break and Reset commands are disabled.

✦ **Project Explorer:** Switches focus to the Project Explorer.

✦ **Properties Window:** Displays the Properties window.

✦ **Object Browser:** Displays the Object Browser.

✦ **Help:** Displays VBA help. VBA and the VBE have a special help system with code examples and details about each object and command.

✦ **Line and Column:** You can think of a code module as a grid, with each character that you type at a specific location (line and column) within the grid. The cursor's position is always displayed here. This is blank if your selection cursor is not in a code module.

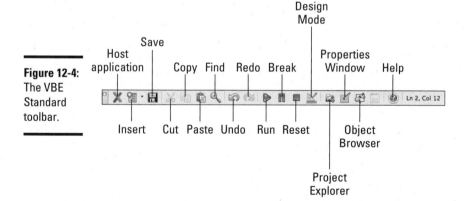

Figure 12-4:
The VBE
Standard
toolbar.

The Edit toolbar

This toolbar focuses on editing code and making it easier to read with indenting. Figure 12-5 shows these controls:

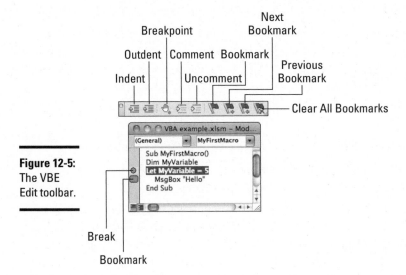

Figure 12-5:
The VBE
Edit toolbar.

+ **Indent/Outdent:** Applies to selection. Indenting is not automatic.

+ **Breakpoint toggle:** Adds or removes a breakpoint at the selection and is represented by a circle in the margin. If you run code, execution halts at a breakpoint. Press F5 or click Run to resume. Clicking in the margin adds a breakpoint. Clicking a breakpoint in the margin removes it.

+ **Comment/Uncomment:** Comment turns selection into a comment, which is text that does not execute when run. Uncomment undoes the comment.

+ **Bookmark Toggle:** Sets or removes a bookmark, represented by an oval in the margin.

+ **Next Bookmark/Previous Bookmark:** Navigation for bookmarks.

+ **Clear All Bookmarks:** Removes all bookmarks from the module.

The Debug toolbar

The VBE Debug toolbar shares several tools in common with the Standard and Editing toolbars. Here we discuss only the controls that are unique to the Debug toolbar, shown in Figure 12-6:

Figure 12-6:
The VBE
Debug
toolbar.

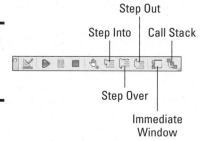

Step Out

Step Into   Call Stack

Step Over

Immediate
Window

✦ **Step Into:** Sets code execution at the first line of code.

✦ **Step Over:** Executes one line of code each time it is pressed. This is the same as ⌘-Shift-O.

✦ **Step Out:** Stops code executing. Same as ⌘-Shift-T.

✦ **Immediate Window:** Displays the Immediate Window, where you can enter a code snippet followed by a question mark to see its result.

✦ **Call Stack:** Displays the Call Stack dialog, an advanced debugging tool that you won't need to worry about until you're an expert.

Coding

The first option on the View menu shown earlier in Figure 12-3 is the Code option, which is grayed out until you make at least one Code window visible in the VBE. A common way to open a new code window is to use Insert⇨ Module. A module is like a new word processing document window — it's blank. Nothing interesting happens until you start writing. To make our example code window shown in Figure 12-7 more interesting, we declared a variable and typed two simple macros. Although this example was made in Excel, the same VBE features apply to Word and PowerPoint.

Exploring the Code Window

Referring to Figure 12-7, notice that horizontal lines separate the declarations section and each of the two macros. The lines are drawn automatically by the VBE. Each macro section is called a procedure. More about Code windows:

✦ **Object pop-up menu:** This is the pop-up menu on the left side of the window; it provides a list of shortcuts to objects.

✦ **Procedure pop-up menu:** This is the pop-up menu on the right side of the window; it provides a list of shortcuts to procedures and declarations. When an object is chosen in the Object pop-up menu, the procedures that are applicable to the selected object are displayed.

✦ **Declarations section:** (Optional) Public declarations appear at the top of a Code module.

✦ **Macro modules:** Each macro, or procedure, is separated by a line.

✦ **Procedure view button:** Click to limit the display to the declaration or procedure section that has the insertion cursor.

✦ **Full Module view button:** Click to display all Code window contents.

Declarations

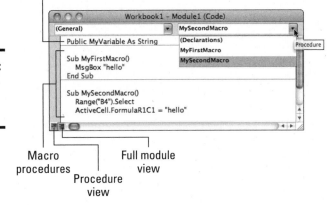

Figure 12-7:
Using
a Code
window.

Macro
procedures

Procedure
view

Full module
view

Writing VBA code

As with a word processor, in a Code window the editor knows which commands are legal and which are not, and the editor gives you feedback as you type. New for VBA in Office 2011 is *Intellisense,* a feature that helps you automatically complete your code as you type. To see how Intellisense works, declare a public variable in an empty Code window (refer to Figure 12-7):

1. **Choose Insert⇨Module to display a blank Code window.**

2. **Type the following code exactly as you see it here and press Return at the end of the line:**

```
Public MyVariable as String
```

Notice that after you type **as**, a pop-up menu appears, as shown in Figure 12-8. This is Intellisense at work. If you know what you want to type, you can keep right on typing. But if you want to see all the possible options, use the pop-up menu. As you type, the offerings in the list narrow down. Use arrow keys or the scroll bar in the list. Click an option or press the spacebar to choose it. If you're stepping through code, you can display the current value of a variable by positioning the mouse cursor over the variable.

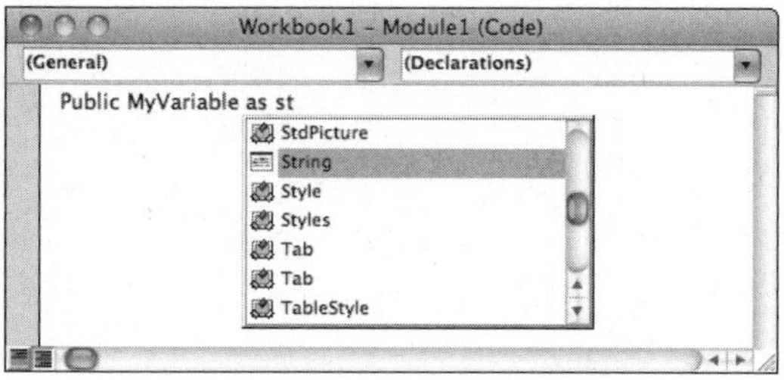

Figure 12-8:
Working
with
Intellisense.

In order to get through the rest of this chapter, you'll need a Macro Procedure to refer to. All macro procedures begin with *Sub* and end with *End Sub*. To write a simple macro, do the following:

1. **Choose Insert⇨Module to display a blank Code window.**

2. **Type the following code exactly as you see it here and press Return at the end of each line:**

```
Sub MyFirstMacro()
Msgbox "Hello"
End Sub
```

Figure 12-7 includes this macro, but all you have to type here is three lines.

Running a macro in the VBE

In this example, the name of the macro is *MyFirstMacro*. If you want to run your macro within the VBE, click anywhere within the macro and then press F5 on the keyboard, or choose Run⇨Run Sub/UserForm. If you typed our example correctly, you should see a "Hello" message in a window.

Right-clicking for options

When you right-click within the VBE, you're rewarded with a pop-up menu that offers all manner of context-sensitive coding assistance. When you right-click on *MsgBox*, the menu shown in Figure 12-9 displays.

Getting help with code

You can rely on the following five principal sources of code examples, syntax help, and general programming assistance:

✦ **Macro recorder:** In Excel and Word, you can record your actions and then look at the code that was recorded inside the modules. Often, the same or similar actions give you enough hints to make or copy code for PowerPoint, as well.

✦ **Object browser:** A handy treasure trove of information about the objects, methods, and properties of Office.

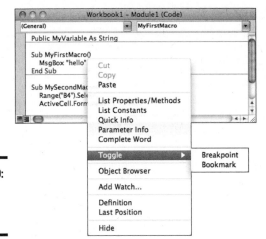

Figure 12-9:
Right-
clicking on
code.

+ **Help:** The Help system within the VBE is minimal. Microsoft plans to provide VBA help for Excel only.

+ **Internet:** Search the Internet for VBA code examples. Chances are good that someone has already asked the question you're trying to answer.

+ **Books on VBA:** You can find plenty of books about VBA. Although almost all of them are Windows-centric, consider what you learn in this chapter, and you should be able to use these books to your advantage.

Using VBA with AppleScript

VBA can run AppleScript code. AppleScript can run VBA code. The two languages can exchange variable values with each other. Here's a Web page with examples:

```
http://word.mvps.org/mac/applescript-vba.html
```

Making code cross-platform

You may want to make Mac or Windows specific code, yet have the same module work on both platforms. You can use the `Like` operator with `"*Mac*"` or `"*Win*"` using an `If` statement to make specific code segments for Windows or Macintosh, as in this example:

```
If Application.OperatingSystem Like "*Mac*" Then
```

Exporting and importing code

New in the VBE on the Mac is File➪Export File. You can now export and import code modules using the File menu. The File➪Import File path is still there. Now you can export frequently used code modules and save them so that you can reuse them or share them.

Being cross-platform aware

If you're certain your VBA code will be run only on Macs running Office 2011, you can skip this sidebar. Everyone else, please pay close attention!

When programming in VBA, you must have an awareness of which features are available in which versions of Office if you want your code to run successfully across versions. Code that calls an AppleScript will fail on Windows. Code that calls the 32- or 64-bit kernel in Windows will fail on a Mac. You can almost always make your code run on both Macs and PCs for current and older versions of Office if you use conditional branching. For example, to check which operating system is being used, use this line:

```
If Application.OperatingSystem
    Like "*Mac*" Then
```

To customize your code for specific versions of application use a variant of, add this line:

```
If Application.Version = 14
    Then
```

When your code doesn't run as expected on one platform or another, as a programmer you've created disappointment. You can almost always make any add-in or VBA code work on Macs or PCs, but it may take some extra work to learn the other platform as well as the one you are accustomed to. If you are building a commercial application, it can really hurt your reputation if you don't go that extra mile.

Watching

Power programmers will be glad to know that the Debug menu has Add Watch, Edit Watch, and Quick Watch, along with their corresponding dialogs in the Mac VBE.

Organizing with Project Explorer

The Project window is the Project Explorer. It lets you explore all objects and Code windows that are open within the Office application you're using. In our example shown in Figure 12-10, two Excel files are open. By default, the filenames are used as the name for a project. Select things within the Project Explorer and then click the controls, use the View menu, toolbars, right-click, or double-click. One little oddity about the Project Explorer is that by design, you can't close it. Project Explorer has the following:

✦ **Code view:** Shows the code window for the selection. Worksheets and other objects can have their own code. You can attach code to almost any object.

✦ **View object:** Displays the selected object.

✦ **Toggle folders:** Opens or closes all of the folders in the Project window.

✦ **Disclosure triangle:** Opens or closes one of the folders in the Project.

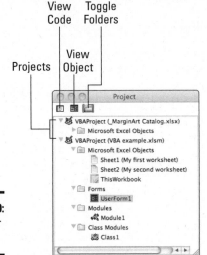

Figure 12-10:
Seeing your
projects.

Viewing and changing properties

Choose View↵Properties Window or press F6 to display the Properties
window. When you select something in the Project Explorer or select the
window of an object in the VBE, the Properties window (shown in Figure
12-11) updates to display the properties of the selected item. You can view
or change properties in various ways:

✦ **Select Object pop-up menu:** When one object, such as a UserForm, contains other objects, such as Toolbox controls, you can choose which
object's properties to display.

✦ **Alphabetic:** Displays the list of property names alphabetically.

✦ **Categorized:** Displays the list of property names in groups.

✦ **Ellipsis:** When you click an ellipsis, a dialog displays. A new feature for
Office 2011 is that you display the Mac OS X color picker when setting
colors.

✦ **Type in fields:** Some properties are set by single-clicking the property
and waiting for the field to change to editable, as when changing file
names in Finder. The (Name) and Caption fields, among others, work
this way.

✦ **Pop-up menus:** Some properties have pop-up menus for available
options.

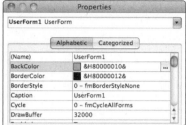

Figure 12-11:
Viewing
and setting
properties.

Getting immediate results

Choose View➪Immediate Window or press ⌘-Control-G to display the
Immediate Window. The Immediate window allows you to try code snippets
and see the results without having to bother creating a procedure. You can
also view or set the value for variables while in Break mode. Figure 12-12
illustrates these:

✦ **Executing a command:** As shown, type the following and then press Return:

```
MsgBox "Hello"
```

The command displays the "Hello" message box.

✦ **Displaying a variable's value:** Type a question mark followed by a
space and then the name of the Variable. Press Return to display the
value, which starts off as 5 in the example shown.

✦ **Changing a variable's value:** The Let statement changes the variable's
value from 5 to 10 in the example shown.

Figure 12-12:
Using the
Immediate
window.

Browsing in the Object Browser

Click the Object Browser button on the Standard toolbar or choose
View➪Object Browser to display the browser. The Object Browser, shown in
Figure 12-13, is where you can find details about the objects, their properties
and methods, as well as user-defined procedures. Use the Object Browser
in conjunction with Help within the VBE to determine where in the object
model hierarchy a command or object is. When using the Object Browser,
you can use the following features:

✦ **Libraries:** Pop-up menu that displays the libraries currently being referenced.

✦ **Search field:** Searches library/libraries chosen in Libraries.

✦ **Forward & Backward:** Navigation buttons for search history.

✦ **Copy:** Copies selection to the Mac OS X Clipboard.

✦ **Definition:** Displays definition of selection.

✦ **Search Results:** Toggles a pane that displays Library, Class, and Member for the active search.

✦ **Help:** Opens VBA help. If the selected topic is not automatically found in Help, try searching for it manually.

✦ **Classes pane:** Displays classes of the selected library.

✦ **Members pane:** Displays the members of the selected Class.

✦ **Detailed description and links.** Displays syntax rules and context and has links you can click for more information.

Right-click the Members pane and choose Show Hidden Members from the pop-up menu to display hidden classes and members. These hidden items are for backwards compatibility. There's no guarantee that hidden items will work correctly or even at all, now or in the future. Just the same, there are some gems in there that do work.

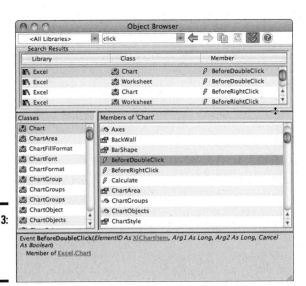

Figure 12-13:
Browsing
VBA
objects.

Making UserForms

UserForms are windows that you can configure as dialogs, input forms, or whatever strikes your fancy. Choose Insert⇨UserForm or click the Insert UserForm button on the Standard toolbar to display a new, blank UserForm, as well as the Toolbox, shown in Figure 12-14. The UserForm is just a gray window with grid dots. You select tools from the Toolbox and drag them onto a UserForm. Then you associate code with the control from the Toolbox and adjust the properties of the control and the UserForm using the Properties window. When a UserForm is the active window, formatting and aligning options are available on the Format menu. Using the Toolbox controls is beyond the scope of this book.

Figure 12-14: Displaying the UserForm Toolbox.

Viewing the Locals window

The Locals window is a debugging tool, which you display by choosing View⇨Locals Window. As you step through code, at each step the Locals window updates to let you know the values of the variables and expressions in your project, as shown in Figure 12-15.

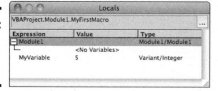

Figure 12-15: Viewing the Locals window.

Setting Project properties

You can set properties for a Project within the VBE by choosing Tools⇨ VBAProject Properties or by right-clicking the project name in the Project Explorer and choosing VBAProject Properties from the pop-up menu. This displays the Project Properties dialog, which has two tabs: General and Protection. The General tab (shown in Figure 12-16) offers three input fields:

✦ **Project Name:** You can change your project's name.

✦ **Project Description:** A short description suffices.

✦ **Conditional Compilation Arguments:** You can declare arguments so that you can enable or disable sections of your code at will.

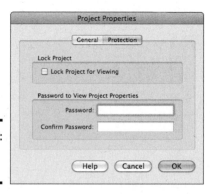

Figure 12-16:
Setting
General
properties.

On the Protection tab, if you select the Lock Project for Viewing check box and then enter a password, you will need that password to view the project in the VBE. Consider doing this as a final step in a completed project. Make a copy of the entire project first. Set the password only on the copy of the project. Keep an unprotected version of your project. See Figure 12-17.

Be sure to keep track of the password. You *will* need it.

Figure 12-17:
Locking a
project.

Displaying Your Macros

The Macros dialog is accessible in the Excel, Word, or PowerPoint interface by choosing Tools⇨Macro⇨Visual Basic Editor and from the Ribbon: click the Developer tab, find the Visual Basic group, and click the Macros button. You can also access macros from within the VBE by choosing Tools⇨Macros. The Macros dialog is a shortcut to projects and macros. In the Macros dialog, shown in Figure 12-18, you can do the following:

✦ **Macro Name:** Type a macro procedure's name or choose from the list.

✦ **Macro list:** Choose from this list.

✦ **Run:** Run the selected macro.

✦ **Step Into:** Displays the code window and selects the first command.

✦ **Edit:** Displays the macro's code window in edit mode.

✦ **Create:** If you choose a different project from the Macros In pop-up menu while in the VBE, you can click Create to make a new module in the selected project.

✦ **Delete:** Deletes the selected macro.

✦ **Options:** Lets you type a description for your macro and assign a keyboard shortcut to run the selected macro.

✦ **Description:** Displays the description you gave to your macro.

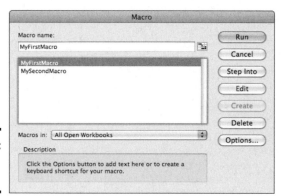

Figure 12-18:
The Macro
dialog.

Recording Macros

An easy way to get code examples is to turn on the macro recorder in Word or Excel, perform some actions, end recording, and then head to the VBE and take a peek at the module that the recorder made. The recorder does not record the keystrokes you make. Instead, it records the actions you took, changes you make to object properties, and text that you typed. Even if you only change one property of an object, the recorder will capture all the object's properties.

Start recording

To start recording a macro, click the Developer tab on the Ribbon, find the Visual Basic group, and click Record. When you start recording, the red circle in the Record button becomes a black square, and the Record Macro dialog shown in Figure 12-19 displays. When you click OK to close the Record Macro dialog, the recorder continues to run until you click the black square. In the Record Macro dialog, you can do the following:

✦ **Macro name:** Type a name for your macro or accept the default. Macro names can't have spaces or special characters.

✦ **Shortcut key:** (Optional) Set a keyboard shortcut for your macro.

✦ **Store Macro In:** Choose a file or project for your macro.

✦ **Description:** (Optional) Type a description. What you type displays in the description section of the Macros dialog when it is displayed.

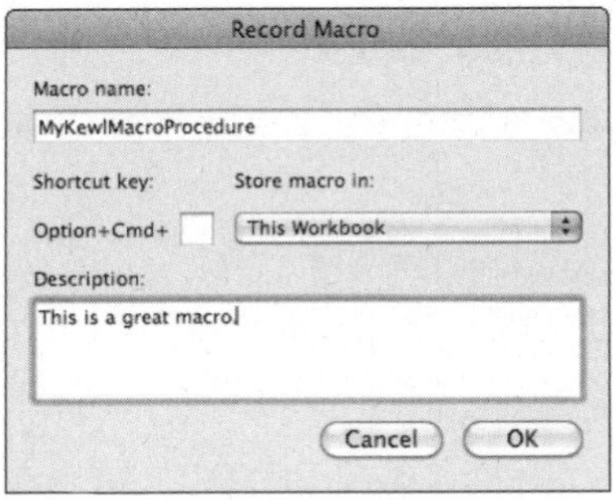

Figure 12-19:
Getting
ready to
record a
macro.

> Record Macro
>
> Macro name:
> MyKewlMacroProcedure
>
> Shortcut key: Store macro in:
> Option+Cmd+ [ ] [This Workbook ▼]
>
> Description:
> This is a great macro
>
> (Cancel) (OK)

Stop recording

 Click the Start button while it has a black square to end the recording session. After you stop recording, click the Developer tab of the Ribbon. In the Visual Basic group, click Macros. Your new macro is in the list. Select it and then click the Edit button to visit the VBE and examine your fresh code.

Adjusting VBE Preferences

When you're in the Visual Basic Editor, if you choose *[Application]*⇨Preferences instead of seeing the application's preferences, you will display the Visual Basic Editor Preferences, as shown in Figure 12-20. The Editor and General tabs are for advanced users, so we skip those. On the Editor Format tab, you can set the code window appearance and code font. There's no Reset button, so before you get carried away with making changes, make a note of the way things are by default.

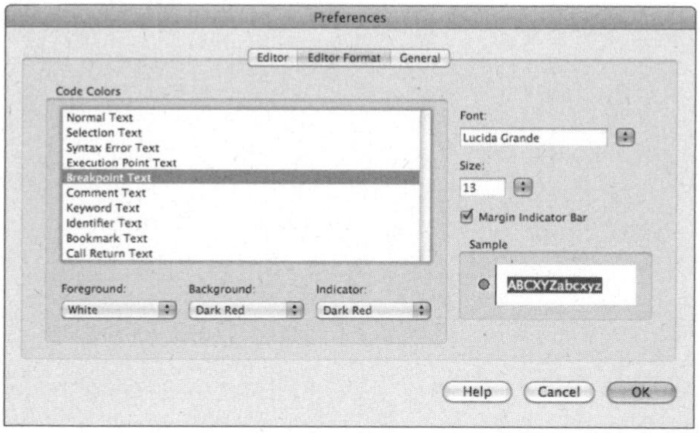

Figure 12-20:
The
Preferences
dialog.

Book II

Word 2011

The 5th Wave

By Rich Tennant

"Needlepoint my foot! These are Word fonts. What I can't figure out is how you got the pillow cases into your printer."

Contents at a Glance

Chapter 1: Exploring Word's Interface

In This Chapter

✓ Opening Word

✓ Using the new Word Document Gallery

✓ Choosing the right view

✓ Getting things done in Print Layout view

✓ Making layouts in Publishing Layout view

✓ Customizing toolbars and menus

✓ Becoming a Word master

✓ Taking advantage of keyboard shortcuts

*W*elcome to the Word 2011 minibook. In this minibook, we explore features that are unique to Word 2011.We begin by making you aware of the various layouts you can find in Microsoft Word. From there we encourage you to explore and customize as you go.

Word on the Mac does triple duty. It's a word processor, a page-layout program, and a note-taking tool all bundled into the same application. Whether you need to send a short note, write some prose or poetry, or even write an entire book, Word is the tool for you. The book you're reading right now was written completely in Word 2011. The authors took advantage of Word's powerful capabilities, and so can you!

And if you're used to working with an older version of Word or using a Windows version, you'll find that Word 2011 is compatible!

Opening Word for the First Time

The very first time you open Word, you're greeted with a beautiful welcome screen, as shown in Figure 1-1. You can start learning about the six major new features highlighted on the welcome screen immediately by clicking the Explore Word button. When you click the Close button, the welcome screen becomes the Word Document Gallery, which we discuss in the next section. You can redisplay the welcome screen by choosing Help➪Welcome to Word from the menu bar when working in Word.

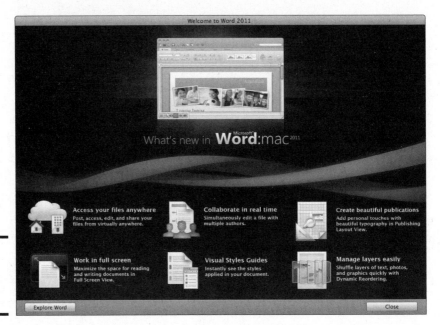

Figure 1-1:
Greetings
from Word
2011!

Opening the Word Document Gallery

The default behavior for opening Word is that it displays the All Templates option of the Word Document Gallery, as shown in Figure 1-2. You can also display the Templates Gallery by choosing File⇨New from Template from the menu bar or by pressing ⌘-Shift-P.

The first three templates in the All Templates category are the three main kinds of editing layouts in Word: Word Document, Word Notebook Layout, and Word Publishing Layout. We start with these and then describe the rest of the gallery:

✦ **Templates list:** The Templates list contains the following:

- *All:* Displays all templates stored on your computer.

- *My Templates:* Displays templates you saved in the My Templates folder, specified in Word's Preferences pane.

    You also see other categories of built-in templates such as those for Print Layout, Publishing Layout, and Notebook Layout that are included within Word 2011.

- *Online Templates:* Click the disclosure triangle next to Templates to hide the local templates; then click the disclosure triangle next to Online Templates to display the many categories of online accessible templates. This feature is new for Office 2011 and requires a live Internet connection.

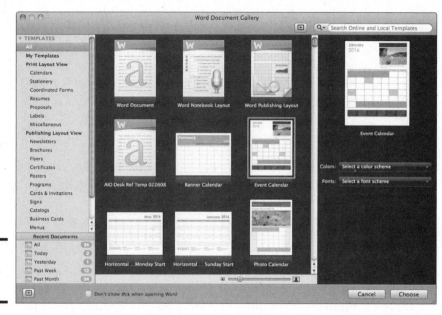

Book II
Chapter 1

Exploring Word's
Interface

Figure 1-2:
Choosing a
template.

✦ **Recent Documents:** Up to one month's worth of recently opened documents are available. You can show all the recent documents or filter by Today, Yesterday, Past Week, or Past Month. When any Recent Document option is selected, the Search field works on Recent Documents instead of local templates.

You can set the number of recently used files in the Word File menu by choosing Word⇨Preferences⇨General⇨Settings⇨Track Recently Opened Documents from the menu bar. Type in a number you want in the dialog.

✦ **Show/Hide Recent Documents:** A toggle button. Can also be changed in Word Preferences.

✦ **Word Document:** Choosing this option opens Word to a new, blank document that's the most common way many people use Word. This layout is based upon a global template within Word called `Normal.dotm`. `Normal.dotm` is Word's default document template type.

✦ **Word Notebook Layout:** Choosing this option starts a new, blank document in Notebook Layout view, which is distinctly different from the blank page layout you see in the Word Document layout. Notebook layout looks like lined paper and is used for taking notes with audio coordinated with your text as you type in meetings, classes, legal proceedings, and more. Notebook Layout view is a Mac-only feature and is not found in Word for Windows.

Word Notebook Layout on the Mac is similar to the Microsoft OneNote application for Windows.

✦ **Word Publishing Layout:** Choosing this option starts a new, blank document in Publishing Layout view. You can use Publishing Layout to create reusable page layouts for newsletters, newspapers, magazines, and books. Publishing Layout view is a Mac-only feature and is not found in Word for Windows.

Word Publishing Layout on the Mac has the core functionality of the Microsoft Publisher application for Windows.

✦ **Don't Show This When Opening Word:** When this check box is selected, the Word Document Gallery won't display when Word is opened.

✦ **Size:** Drag the slider left and right to change the size of previews in the larger pane, or click the icons at the left and right to choose the smallest and largest size, respectively.

✦ **Show/Hide Right Pane:** Choose to show or hide the template preview.

✦ **Search field:** By default, this field searches template names and keywords of local templates. The search includes online templates if the online disclosure triangle has been activated. When one of the Recent Document timeframes is selected, this field searches Recent Documents instead of templates.

✦ **Preview and Navigation:** Displays a preview of the template selected in the larger pane. If the template is not a blank document template, click the navigation arrows to scroll through the template. Nonblank templates display theme color and font selections from which to choose for the document.

✦ **Cancel:** If Word is starting, clicking Cancel takes you to a new, blank Word document. If Word was already running when you opened the Word Template Gallery, Cancel closes the gallery without opening a document.

✦ **Choose:** Chooses the selected template.

Choosing a View

You can choose from seven different views when working within Word 2011. Each view is designed to provide a different environment, optimized for the task and your working preference. The moment you open a new, blank document, your eyes are drawn immediately to the ScreenTip above the view buttons at the lower-left corner of the window. (Look ahead to Figure 1-3 to see the Print Layout view ScreenTip.)

Click the X close button to close the ScreenTip for the first time. After that, move the mouse cursor over the view buttons to display ScreenTips, and move away to hide the ScreenTips. The view buttons are part of the horizontal scroll bar, which you can turn on and off by choosing Word⇨Preferences⇨ View⇨Window from the menu bar. The same window view options are found on the View menu of the menu bar at the top of the screen.

You can choose from the following views:

Book II
Chapter 1

+ **Draft:** Shows a simplified view of your document along with the names of text styles that have been applied. Content isn't displayed the way it will look when you print.

+ **Web Layout:** Word approximates what your document will look like if you save it as a Web page and then open it in a Web browser.

+ **Outline:** With heading levels, you can organize your document into an outline. (See the "Typing an outline" section later in this chapter.) Text can be promoted and demoted in a level that you specify with the Outline tools group on the Ribbon, which displays automatically when you choose Outline view.

+ **Print Layout:** Print Layout view shows you how your document will look when you print. See the section "Working in Print Layout View," later in this chapter for more.

+ **Notebook Layout:** Notebook Layout view enables you to take notes and record audio that's synchronized with your text while you type. We discuss this in the section "Taking Notes in Notebook Layout View," later in this chapter.

+ **Publishing Layout:** Newsletters, brochures, flyers, and even small magazines can be created in Publishing Layout View. We discuss the Publishing Layout view in the section "Designing in Publishing Layout View," later in this chapter.

+ **Full Screen:** This new view lets you read or edit without the distraction of toolbars, the Ribbon, or other interface clutter. See "Reading and Working in Full Screen View," later in this chapter.

Working in Print Layout View

Print Layout view is a good starting point for beginners because what you see onscreen is closest to what you get when you print. We use this view as an example to explain the general layout of Word's interface. Figure 1-3 shows a document in Print Layout view.

Draft and Outline views in Word have many of the same basic interface characteristics as Print Layout view, although each has minor variations.

Menu bar   Standard toolbar   Ribbon

Figure 1-3:
A blank
Word
document in
Print Layout
view.

View buttons

We draw your attention to these specific interface elements:

✦ **Menu bar:** Contains commands and shortcuts to dialogs (Mac only).

✦ **Script menu:** Here you find the Word Automator Actions that come with all Office package bundles except the Home and Student Edition.

✦ **Show/Hide Toolbars:** This button is near the upper-right corner of the window and toggles toolbars on and off.

✦ **Document title:** This is the filename of your document. A new document has a generic name, such as Document1, until you save it. Right-click the title for a pop-up menu of shortcuts to places in Finder.

✦ **Standard toolbar:** Figure 1-3 shows the default toolbar buttons for Page Layout view. Different tools appear when you switch views.

✦ **Ribbon:** Click the tabs to access groups and galleries. Click at the right end of the Ribbon for Ribbon Preferences and customization options.

✦ **Sidebar:** Choose View➪Sidebar➪*[sidebar name]* from the menu bar to display the sidebar. Drag the divider between the sidebar and the document area to resize the sidebar. Click the circle with the X to close the sidebar. The sidebar has its own toolbar buttons, shown in the margin. The sidebar houses the following items:

• *Thumbnails Pane:* A small thumbnail of each page is visible with the page number. Click a thumbnail to view that page.

• *Document Map Pane:* This option shows a map of your document based upon the heading levels you've used within your document. Right-click the Document Map to limit the map to specific headings. This view doesn't show a map until you apply heading styles to text in your document. You can apply text heading styles with the Styles group of the Ribbon, Styles tab of the Toolbox, or by choosing Format➪Styles from the menu bar. We discuss styles in Chapter 4 of this minibook.

**Book II
Chapter 1**

Exploring Word's
Interface

• *Reviewing Pane:* Can be toggled on and off in the View menu or you can click the Ribbon's Review tab, and in the Changes group, click the Review Pane button. This pane helps you move around in multiple page documents. The Reviewing feature is covered in Chapter 5 of this minibook.

• *Search Pane:* Click the triangle to reveal the Find and Replace search tools, as shown in Figure 1-3. Enter a search term and then click the Find button to locate instances of matching text in your document, which are listed in the Matches pane. Click a match to locate the instance in your document. Click the wheel for search filters. Type replacement text and choose Replace All or Replace to automate replacing text.

✦ **Ruler:** You have horizontal and vertical rulers. Adjust margins and indents by dragging ruler elements. Click in the horizontal ruler to add tab stops. Double-click rulers for additional options. You can toggle the ruler on and off in the View menu.

✦ **Blinking insertion cursor:** When you type, insert something, or paste, this is the place in your document where it happens. You can click anywhere in text or text boxes to set the cursor's location.

✦ **ScreenTip:** Hover the mouse cursor over toolbars and buttons to find out what they do. Some ScreenTips are big, but most are small and yellow.

✦ **Toolbox:** Apply styles, manage citations, use the Scrapbook, look up references, and check compatibility here. Toggle the Toolbox on and off with the Toolbox button on the Standard toolbar or using the View menu.

✦ **Media browser:** Allows you to insert shapes, sounds, movies, symbols, and photos. Supports Mac programs such as iPhoto and iMovie. Toggle the Media browser on and off with the Media button on the Standard toolbar or in the View menu.

✦ **Scroll bar:** The vertical scroll bar appears automatically when needed. Drag scroll bars with your mouse. The horizontal scroll bar is always on. You can customize your scroll bars by modifying the Appearance settings in Mac OS X preferences. You can enable and disable the scroll bars by choosing Word➪Preferences➪View from the menu bar.

✦ **Scroll buttons:** Click, or click and hold these buttons to scroll through your document.

✦ **Next/Previous Page buttons:** Click these buttons to view the next or previous page.

✦ **Select Browse Object button:** This small button is between the Next/Previous Page buttons. When you click this button, a pop-up menu offers various ways to browse your document. (See Figure 1-4.)

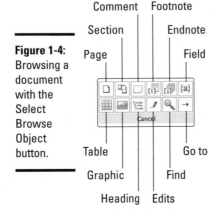

Comment Footnote
Section   Endnote

Figure 1-4:
Browsing a
document
with the
Select
Browse
Object
button.

Page   Field

Table   Go to

Graphic   Find

Heading   Edits

✦ **View buttons:** Click these to switch from one view to another, which is the same as choosing a different view in the View menu. Hover the cursor over each button to see what it does.

✦ **View name:** The name of the currently active view appears to the right of the view buttons.

✦ **Page Information and the Find/Replace/Go To button:** Displays page number and total number of pages (Mac only). When clicked, displays the Finding/Replace/Go To dialog. Many of this dialog's features are now in the sidebar, discussed earlier in this chapter.

✦ **Spell Check button:** Click this button to initiate a spell check beginning at the current cursor location or check the spelling of text you selected. When clicked, checking grammar is also an option.

✦ **Word Count button:** The number of words in your document is updated on this button as you type. Click this spot to display the Word Count dialog, as shown in an example in Figure 1-5.

Figure 1-5:
Viewing
statistics
about the
text in your
document.

Taking Notes in Notebook Layout View

The Notebook Layout view in Word (see Figure 1-6) has so many uses; where should we begin? Notebook Layout View is great for students who jot notes, office workers who attend meetings, assistants who track tasks, and professionals who need to record meetings with clients.

The Notebook Layout view allows you to record sound while you type. What you type is linked to the audio so that Word annotates the audio. You can play back the audio that was recorded when you typed the text by clicking anywhere in the text of the document and then clicking the speaker icon that appears.

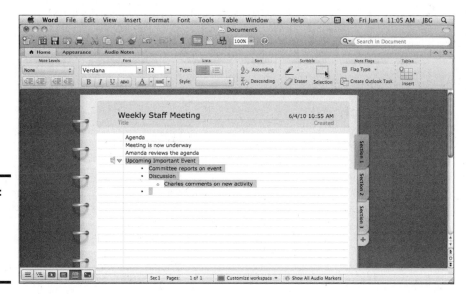

Figure 1-6:
The
Notebook
Layout
view for
meetings.

Word Notebook Layout versus Microsoft OneNote

If you work on both Macs and PCs, you should be aware of some platform limitations. Notebook Layout view in Word for Mac offers the core functionality of the Microsoft OneNote Windows program, but without the requirement of a different file format. On Word for Mac, audio and typed annotations are stored in standard Word documents. Word for Mac can't open Windows OneNote files. Word for Windows can open files made in Word for Mac Notebook Layout view, but can't use any of the Notebook Layout view features. Word for Windows displays only the typed text — it won't play audio unless you save the Notebook Layout audio as a file and then manually insert the sound file into Word by choosing Insert⇨Audio.

Notebook Layout has its own special tabs on the Ribbon: Home, Appearance, and Audio Notes, which we discuss next. Notebook Layout view has the following features:

✦ **Section tabs:** Click a tab to choose a section of your document.

✦ **Add section:** Click the plus sign to add a section to your document.

✦ **Show Audio Markers:** Click this button to display or hide all the audio markers within a document. Click in the left margin next to any text to display the audio marker associated with that text.

✦ **Customize Workspace:** Choose a workspace beautification option.

To see how Word Notebook Layout view looks and works, open a new, blank Word document in Notebook Layout view by following these quick steps:

1. **Choose File⇨New from Template from the menu bar.**

   The Word Document Gallery opens displaying all templates.

2. **Double-click Word Notebook Layout.**

Right away you can see that Notebook Layout view is very interesting; it looks just like a notebook, complete with (optional) spiral bindings and (optional) lined notebook paper. (Refer to Figure 1-6.) The Ribbon looks different, too, with all sorts of new controls on it. If you take a quick peek at the Word menus, you'll see that many of the menu items are different. You can use most, but not all, of Word's Print Layout features in Notebook Layout view.

Typing an outline

When you're typing in Notebook Layout, think in terms of writing an outline. Here are some guidelines that will help:

✦ **Use Return to end a paragraph.** If you're using the microphone to record, pressing Return adds an audio marker. We cover recording audio in the next section.

✦ **Use the Tab key to indent; use Shift-Tab to outdent.** Think of each level of indenting as a Note Level. No indenting is Note Level 1; the first indent is Note Level 2, and so on. Note Levels are styles, so you can see and set them in the Style tab of the Toolbox as well as on the Ribbon. In addition to using the Tab key to indent and Shift-Tab to outdent, you can select text and then click the Promote and Demote buttons on the Ribbon to change indentation and Note Levels. If you want to move selected text up or down in your document, select the text and then click the Move Up or Move Down buttons.

Audio notes will *not* move with the text, so audio might play out of sequence if you move text around.

Figure 1-7 shows the Note Level group on the Ribbon's Home tab and the corresponding Note Level on the Styles tab of the Toolbox.

Book II
Chapter 1

Exploring Word's
Interface

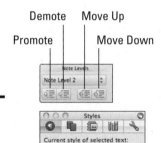

Figure 1-7:
Working in
an outline.

Recording audio

All Mac laptops and iMacs are equipped with built-in microphones that offer surprisingly good sensitivity in meetings. Other Macs require a microphone to record audio notes. The Recording Status indicator of the Audio Notes tab on the Ribbon always displays the current audio status. Follow these steps to get started with a recording session:

1. **Click the Audio Notes tab on the Ribbon.**

This action displays the tab contents, the left-end portion of which is shown in Figure 1-8.

Figure 1-8:
Recording
audio.

Figure 1-8:
Recording
audio.

2. **Adjust the Input Volume slider.**

   Try starting with the Input Volume slider adjusted so that the sound input level indicator shows the volume is about ¾ of full volume. Take a sound sample before you do your real recording to get the best level for the meeting room.

3. **Click the red Record button and then type notes while you record the session.**

   Audio is synchronized automatically with your notes as you type. Press Return or Enter as you type while recording to make it visually apparent in your document when a new topic or something noteworthy you want to differentiate appears. Keep an eye on the sound input level indicator and try to keep it at about ¾ volume with the Input Volume slider. You can adjust indenting levels later. Pressing Enter or Return adds an audio marker and denotes a new paragraph. Press Tab to indent and Shift-Tab to outdent.

4. **Click the black Stop button to stop recording the audio.**

   To continue recording, click the Start button again.

Playing audio

After you record audio, you can have some fun playing it back. If you move your mouse over the margin to the left of anything you typed, an audio icon appears. Click that icon to hear the audio that was recorded while the text on that line was being typed. If you see a disclosure triangle, click it to show or hide indented Notes Levels. To find the following playback options, go to the Ribbon, click the Audio Notes tab, and look for the Audio Playback group (shown in Figure 1-9):

✦ **Play:** Starts audio playback at the beginning of the document, resumes playing when paused, or plays from the time chosen in Seek.

✦ **Pause:** Halts playback until you click Play again.

✦ **Seek:** Lets you go to a specific time in the audio timeline as follows:

   • Click the button at the left to move closer to the beginning of the audio.

   • Click the button at the right to move more to the end of the audio.

   • Drag from the left side of the Seek timeline to move the timeline indicator to a specific time.

   • Click into the Seek control. Click or drag the mouse to adjust the time.

✦ **Rate:** Drag the slider left for slower playback, or right for faster playback.

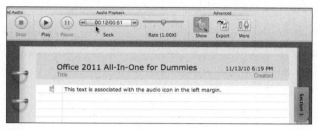

Figure 1-9:
Playing audio in Notebook Layout view.

Using advanced audio features

The Advanced group of the Audio Notes tab (shown in Figure 1-9) has three controls:

✦ **Show:** Toggles the audio notes indicators on and off. This is the same as the Show All audio notes markers button at the bottom of the window.

✦ **Export:** Choose to save the recorded audio as an .mp4 file.

✦ **More:** A shortcut for Word⇨Preferences⇨Audio Notes, which brings up a dialog where you can make adjustments to the following:

- *Quality:* Choose from preset levels of low, medium, medium-high, high, or custom.

- *Audio Type:* Choose MP4 (default), AIFF, or WAV.

- *Channels:* You can choose Mono or Stereo. (Stereo requires a stereo microphone.)

- *Sample size:* Your choices are 8-bit or 16-bit. The 16-bit option is higher quality, but it makes bigger files.

- *Sample rate:* Choose from 8 KHz to 48 KHz presets. Bigger is better quality audio, but makes bigger files. Slow processors may have problems with skipping at higher settings.

- *Note Playback:* When selected, you can specify the number of seconds you want to elapse before linked audio starts to play.

Just having fun

Sometimes Microsoft does extra special things just for Mac users so that we enjoy using our Macs. That's what most of the features on the Appearance tab of the Ribbon are for. See Figure 1-10. Use the Appearance controls to customize your workspace. Go ahead and spoil yourself! You deserve it. Of course, some of these have practical use. Customize with these controls on the Appearance tab:

✦ **Type:** Choose different styles for the notebook appearance.

✦ **Background:** Choose backgrounds for your visual pleasure.

- ✦ **Color:** Choose from five splendiferous colors, or even none at all!

- ✦ **Rename:** Lets you edit the name of the current section's tab. You can double-click a tab to change its name, too.

- ✦ **Delete:** Deletes a section and its contents.

- ✦ **Style:** Change the rule lines style to Standard or None.

- ✦ **Distance:** If you choose Standard, choose how far apart the rules are.

- ✦ **Include:** If you want to have a footer, choose either Page Number or None.

- ✦ **Restart Numbering per Section:** When this check box is selected, Word restarts page numbers on each section.

Figure 1-10:
Appearances need not always be deceptive.

For a document that's long and in sections, when you press ⌘-F to move the cursor to the Search in Document field and enter a search term and press Return to find text, section tabs that contain your search criteria light up if a match to the search criteria is in that section.

Designing in Publishing Layout View

Welcome to the Word Publishing Layout view! We could shout, "Extra! Extra! Read all about it! Ordinary computer user discovers complete publishing program in Office for Mac!" But we'd rather be understated about Word's publishing capabilities.

Headlines aside, Office for Mac contains a publishing program that you can use to create and publish a newspaper, newsletter, or any story-based communication periodical. With Word Publishing Layout view, you can design and create professional-looking publications that can be distributed via e-mail or print. The best part is you don't need special skills, a different program, or a special file format. Word does it all in standard Word documents with the traditional Word tools you're used to.

True, Publishing Layout view doesn't give you the capabilities of publishing programs such as Adobe InDesign or QuarkXPress, but that would only be a problem if you need to print something on a press such as brochures that have been created with four-color separations. If you don't understand the language of *color separations,* you'll love Word's Publishing Layout and the ability to use a language most can understand.

Word includes professionally designed templates that help you with layout. The templates available on the Word Document Gallery, and include options such as Newsletters, Brochures, Flyers, and Invitations to name a few. The templates give you a hint at the wide variety of tasks for which Word Publishing Layout view is designed. Because Word Document Gallery is highly interactive and so easy to use, if you want to create a document that falls into any of these categories, take these simple steps:

1. **Choose File⇨New from Template from the menu bar.**

2. **When the Word Document Gallery opens, choose a template.**

The Publishing Layout view screenshots in this book use the Advantage Newsletter template, in case you were wondering. See Figure 1-11.

If you're an experienced user who wants to start from scratch, open a new, blank document in Publishing Layout view as follows:

1. **Choose File⇨New from Template from the menu bar.**

2. **When the Word Document Gallery opens, under Templates, choose All⇨Word Publishing Layout.**

**Book II
Chapter 1**

**Exploring Word's
Interface**

Publishing toolbar

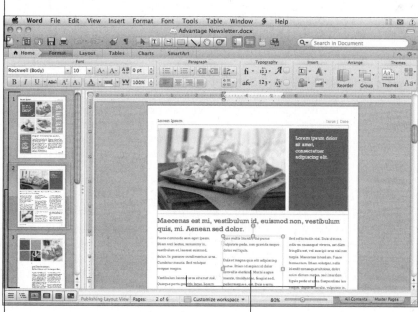

Figure 1-11:
Working in
Publishing
Layout view.

Navigation pane   Story boxes

Publishing Layout versus Microsoft Publisher

Publishing Layout view in Word for Mac offers the core functionality of the Microsoft Publisher Windows program, but without the requirement of a different file format. On Word for Mac, Publishing Layout view documents are stored as standard Word documents. Word for Mac can't open Windows Publisher files. Word for Windows can open and work with files made in Word for Mac Publishing Layout view, but Word for Windows doesn't have the Publishing Layout view's Standard toolbar or Publishing Layout view.

When you distribute documents made in Publishing Layout view in Word for Mac, consider using the PDF format to preserve the formats and layouts that you create. To create a PDF from your document, choose File➪Save As from the menu bar. In the Format pop-up menu, choose PDF. This way people using Word for Windows (or other versions of Word for Mac) or those folks who may not have the same fonts that you do can still enjoy the full fidelity of your published documents.

Notice that the Standard toolbar is different in Word Publishing Layout view. You can't customize the Standard toolbar in Word Publishing Layout view. You can, however, customize the workspace with the Customize Workspace button in the horizontal scroll bar at the bottom of the document window.

Text boxes in Word Publishing Layout view are very interactive. Just hover the mouse over the story text boxes, as shown in Figure 1-11, and you'll notice box numbers appear and disappear as the mouse passes over the text boxes. These numbers tell you that the text boxes are part of a story in which text flows from one text box to another. If you click inside box 1 and start typing, when box 1 fills up, the text continues into box 2, and then into box 3, and so on. If you drag a story text box, you see guides and measurements that appear to help you precisely lay out your publication. Also, notice that different toolbar buttons become active depending upon which story box you click. The first text box and the last text box within a story have different options from text boxes that are between them.

Making the Most of Toolbars and Menus

The Ribbon, menus, and toolbars are *context-sensitive:* Office knows what layout you're using and what's currently selected in your document. The options available are updated automatically to offer what's appropriate at any given moment. Right-clicking or Control-clicking in the interface produces a context-sensitive menu that relates to wherever you click. Double-clicking objects usually displays the Format tab on the Ribbon.

Sometimes, context-sensitive menus and toolbars don't quite give you the options you want at your fingertips. If that's the case, you'll want to customize your toolbars and menus. If you read Book I, Chapter 3 about customizing toolbars, you know that we encourage you to add and remove commands as well as to make your own toolbars. Remember to visit this feature regularly.

Choose View➪Toolbars➪Customize Toolbars and Menus from the menu bar to display the Customize Toolbars and Menus dialog, as shown in Figure 1-12. When this dialog is open, you can drag commands to any menu or toolbar, remove commands, and move commands. You can turn toolbars on and off, add, remove, name, and rename toolbars and menus. The Commands list is alphabetized, and you can press a letter of the alphabet to jump to the first letter of a command in the list. You can assign macros to command buttons and menus. On the Toolbars and Menus tab is a shortcut that displays the keyboard shortcuts dialog.

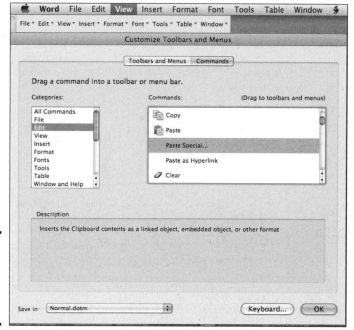

Figure 1-12: Customizing Word's toolbars and menus.

Making Word Behave the Way You Want It To

Wouldn't it be great if you could force your unruly teenager to behave just the way you want by saying a few special words? Well, Word can't make your teenager act any better, but you can do some simple things to make Word behave the way you want it to.

Finding Help in Word

In each minibook, we encourage you to explore a topic using Help so that you get to try the new Office 2011 Help system. Reading about how to create a newsletter, for example, is as easy as searching Help:

1. **Click the purple Help button on Word's Standard toolbar.**

   The Word Help window displays.

2. **In the Search field, type** Newsletter **and then press Return or Enter.**

   The Help Topics display.

3. **Choose Lay Out a Newsletter in Publishing Layout View.**

   A complete tutorial about making a newsletter appears. Click disclosure triangles to expand topics.

Finding what you want in Word's Preferences pane

Do you get irritated when Word corrects spellings and formats bulleted lists without being asked? That's the AutoCorrect feature working more than you want it to. Word's Preferences pane is where you head when you wonder why Word is doing what it's doing, and it's where you can change the settings. You access Word's settings by choosing Word⇨Preferences from the menu bar.

If you have an inkling of a preference's name that you want to find, type it into the Search Word Preferences field, and the Preferences pane shows you where to find it, as shown in Figure 1-13.

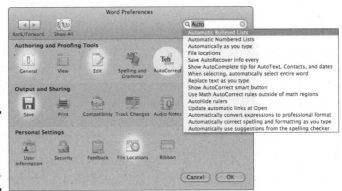

Figure 1-13: Setting Word preferences.

As you work in Word, you can make changes to various preferences without visiting the Preferences pane. Options that you choose from pop-up menus, widgets, toolbars, and Toolbox controls sometimes affect preferences without making a big deal about it.

Turning AutoCorrect on and off

A lot of people wish Word weren't so presumptuous about how things ought to be. In particular, when Word is autocorrecting things, maybe it'd be better if Word started by asking you what you want done. Unfortunately, Word isn't a mind-reading, context-sensitive robot. You have to turn correction features on or off on your own.

Now there just happens to be a simple setting in AutoCorrect that allows you to turn off the entire AutoCorrect feature. Choose this magical sequence: Word⇨Preferences, and then click the AutoCorrect button and deselect the Automatically Correct Spelling and Formatting as You Type check box. When you have time, you should go through *all* of Word's settings and decide which ones you want to turn on and which ones you want to turn off so that Word behaves exactly the way you want it to.

Setting compatibility preferences

AutoCorrect isn't the only feature that affects how Word behaves. In addition to the AutoCorrect preferences, take a peek at the compatibility preferences by way of choosing Word⇨Preferences⇨Compatibility. The Compatibility preferences dialog (shown in Figure 1-14) lists a wide variety of specific behaviors of Word that have changed over the years. Turn specific behaviors on and off here, such as the following:

✦ **Font Substitution:** If you open a document that used a font that isn't available on your computer, Word substitutes a font that you do have for the font that you don't have. If you'd rather choose the font, click the Font Substitution button and then choose the font you want.

✦ **Recommended Options For:** This pop-up menu has preconfigured combinations of settings from the behavior options. You can change Word 2011 to behave like older versions of Word or even WordPerfect.

✦ **Options:** You can turn individual Word behaviors on and off in this list by selecting or deselecting check boxes. The choices are eclectic. As you make choices, the Recommended Options For pop-up button changes to let you know which set an individual choice you check belongs to.

✦ **Default:** Click this button to use the settings you've made as the default behavior for Word from now on. If you click this button, you must allow the `Normal.dotm` template to be modified in order to permanently change Word's behavior.

✦ **Compatibility Report:** In this section, select the Check Documents for Compatibility check box to activate the Compatibility Report feature. Click the Reset Ignored Issues button to tell the compatibility checker to recheck the entire document and also flag problems you had previously told it to ignore. Click Reset All Issues button to tell compatibility checker to recheck all documents for incompatibilities even if you told the checker to never check for errors again.

If you want to check whether a document is compatible with other versions of Word, choose Toolbox⇨Compatibility Report.

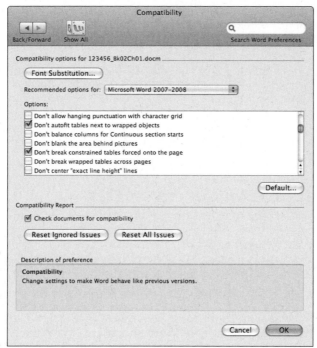

Customizing Word's keyboard shortcuts

Being able to speed up your work is always a good thing. Keyboard short-cuts are one of the best ways to increase your productivity, and customizing these shortcuts makes your computer more personalized.

Mac OS X has its own keyboard shortcuts in addition to Word's keyboard shortcuts. When you press a key or a key combination, Mac OS X searches first to see whether a task is assigned to that shortcut in Mac OS X system preferences. If Mac OS X has a shortcut defined for what you pressed, the keyboard shortcut is carried out by the operating system. However, if Mac OS X keyboard shortcuts aren't defined for what you pressed, Mac OS X tells Word what you pressed on the keyboard. If you want to use a particular key-board shortcut in Word, you have to check to make sure that your desired shortcut isn't already assigned to do something else by Mac OS X.

Showing keyboard shortcuts

Apple has a lot of nice keyboard shortcuts already defined for Mac OS X, and you can easily get a complete list of them:

1. **In Finder (the Desktop), choose Help⇨Mac Help.**

2. **In the Ask a Question search box, type** shortcuts **and then press Return or Enter.**

Help responds with a list of relevant topics.

Likewise, Word also has a generous assortment of keyboard shortcuts right from the start. If you switched to the Finder application in the preceding steps, switch back to Word. The shortcuts in Word are available by searching Word's Help for Keyboard Shortcuts. You can set up Word so that it automatically displays keyboard shortcuts in menus and toolbar ScreenTips:

1. **In Word, choose View⇨Toolbars⇨Customize Toolbars and Menus from the menu bar.**

2. **On the Toolbars and Menus tab of the resultant dialog, select the Show Shortcut Keys in Screen Tips check box.**

3. **Click OK.**

Making your own shortcuts

You can assign keyboard shortcuts to Word commands and change the ones that Microsoft assigned. Word doesn't force you to stick with the default shortcuts. You can assign and reassign shortcuts as you wish. Figure 1-15 shows the Customize Keyboard dialog. To access the Customize Keyboard dialog and set a keyboard shortcut, take these steps:

1. **Choose Tools⇨Customize Keyboard.**

This opens the Customize Keyboard dialog, shown in Figure 1-15.

2. **In the Categories list, select a category, and in the Command list, choose a command.**

For example, we selected Edit in the Categories list and EditPasteSpecial in the Commands list.

3. **To assign (or reassign) a keyboard shortcut for the selected command, type in a customized keyboard shortcut combination for the selected command and then click the Assign button.**

4. **Click OK twice.**

Save a document with one or more custom shortcuts as a template so that when you open that template, the keyboard shortcuts you customized apply only to the documents created from that template.

**Book II
Chapter 1**

Exploring Word's Interface

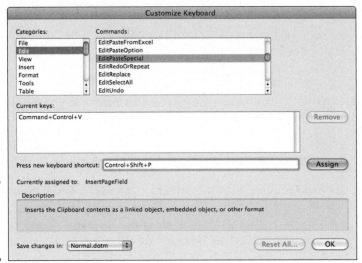

Figure 1-15:
Customizing
keyboard
shortcuts.

As shown in Figure 1-15, these features and commands are available while using the Customize Keyboard dialog:

✦ **Categories:** Lists general categories of Word commands that can accept keyboard shortcut assignments.

✦ **Commands:** Lists commands within categories that can accept keyboard shortcut assignments.

✦ **Current Keys:** If the selected command already has a keyboard assignment, it's displayed here.

✦ **Press New Keyboard Shortcut:** Press a key combination for the command, then click the Assign button to assign the combination as a shortcut. If you try to use a shortcut already assigned by Mac OS X, the shortcut will execute, or you may hear a beep instead of seeing the keyboard combination appear.

✦ **Currently Assigned To:** If you type a shortcut that has already been assigned, the current assignment is displayed. You can override the current assignment by clicking the Assign button.

✦ **Description:** Describes the selected command in the Commands list.

✦ **Save Changes In:** Select from this pop-up menu to determine whether the keyboard shortcut is saved in the current Word document or in Word's `Normal.dotm` template:

• *If you save to a document,* the assignment works only for that particular document.

- *If you save to* `Normal.dotm`, the assignment works from now on whenever you open a new Word document. Choose this option to save in your copy of Word so that it works on your computer from now on.

You can transfer shortcuts from one document template to another and to the `Normal.dotm` template with the Organizer tool. We explain the Organizer tool in Chapter 3 of this minibook.

Reading and Working in Full Screen View

**Book II
Chapter 1**

Exploring Word's
Interface

There's a new Full Screen view in Word 2011 that lets you edit or simply read a document without the clutter of the Ribbon, rulers, and other distractions. Full Screen view is actually two views in one: You can choose Reading mode or Writing mode. In Reading mode, there's little to disturb you as you turn pages and read a document. Writing mode provides a sleek, minimalist, unobtrusive toolbar.

Switching to Full Screen view

You can display your document in Full Screen view. As described earlier in this chapter, you can click the Full Screen view button in the lower-left portion of the window.

The toolbar hides itself. Move the mouse to the top of the window to display the toolbar while working in Full Screen view. You can navigate by clicking the mouse, clicking in the Navigation pane, using arrow keys, and by using the navigation controls at the top of the window.

You can use the Media browser, the Toolbox, and custom toolbars in Full Screen view if you turn them on before switching to Full Screen view.

Full screen view uses a lot of video resources on your computer. If switching between Read and Write modes is sluggish or doesn't work, try to make more video RAM available by closing other windows.

Working in Writing mode

Writing mode, shown in Figure 1-16, reaches out to people who want a single, simplified toolbar to make basic Word documents. This simplified workspace is great for beginners. If you're one of the people who find Word's regular interface daunting, give Writing mode in Full Screen view a try. Another group likely be attracted to this new view is people who know keyboard shortcuts well enough that they don't rely on menus or toolbars and want to work in a clutter-free environment. Remember, you can use keyboard shortcuts and right-click in your document while in Writing mode.

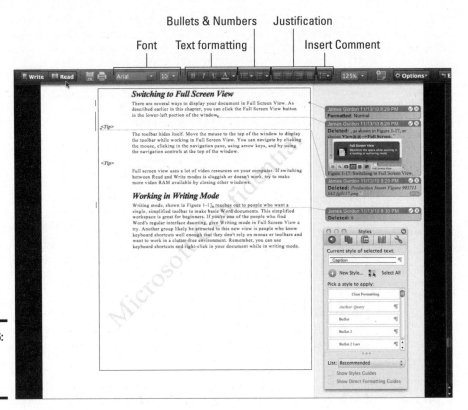

Font   Text formatting   Bullets & Numbers   Justification   Insert Comment

Figure 1-16:
Exploring
Writing
mode.

These controls appear only in Full Screen view:

✦ **Write:** Switch to Writing mode (also called Writing view). Nothing happens when you click this button if you are already in Writing mode.

✦ **Read:** Switch to Reading mode (also called Reading view), discussed later in this chapter.

✦ **Options:** Figure 1-17 shows a close-up of these Options:

   • *Find:* Changes the toolbar into the Search input field.

   • *Track Changes:* Toggles track changes on or off.

   • *Show Comments and Changes:* Submenus take you through tracked comments and reviewing.

   • *Show Original / Final Document:* Submenus let you accept and reject tracked changes.

   • *Toolbox and Media Browser:* Toggle these tools on or off.

   • *Background:* Choose a background from the pop-up menu, which is larger than shown in Figure 1-17.

Figure 1-17:
Choosing an option.

Reading in Reading mode

Reading mode is the simplest of Word's views, shown in Figure 1-18. Word's Navigation pane displays to the left. If your screen is wide enough, your document displays as two pages side-by-side as shown in Figure 1-18, but you can toggle the display to Show One Page on the Options menu.

In Reading mode, you have most of the options of Writing mode. Instead of Toolbox and Media Browser, there is a Margin control menu. When a single page is displayed you can choose from these turning animations: fade through, page curl, or none.

When in Reading mode, you can't edit your document, but you still have access to lookup and research functions by right-clicking in the document.

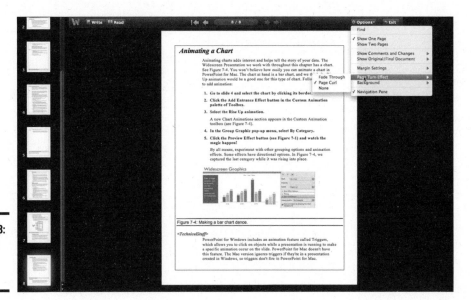

Figure 1-18:
Reading in Reading mode.

Chapter 2: An Open and Shut Case

In This Chapter

- ✔ Opening up with Word
- ✔ Saving ordinary and secure files
- ✔ Modifying Word's default Normal template
- ✔ Saving in compatible formats

*W*ord has some pretty slick ways of dealing with a wide variety of file formats, from the known to the mysterious. As you'd normally expect, Word can open and save its own files, but Word can work with other kinds of files as well. Every once in a while you might receive a document that you just can't get to open. Word can often help with this problem. Some file formats are widely shared, such as RTF (Rich Text Format) files. Word can open and save files as RTFs and in other formats. You also have ways to protect the information inside your Word files. And of course, Word has a master `Normal.dotm` template that can make styling your text a breeze.

Opening the World in Word

You'd think that opening files would be an old hat by now to most everyone who has ever touched a computer, but a lot of people still don't know about some of the ways to open files in Word. You might use some of these methods all the time, whereas you might use others once in a blue moon, but it's good to know they're available just in case!

Opening Web pages

Surfing the Web is great, but at times, you may want to edit those Web pages in Word. Several approaches bring all or part of a Web page into Word.

Word is all about words. Web browsers can have all sorts of content that Word can't deal with, so don't expect Word to faithfully reproduce a Web page. Be happy if you get the text you want.

Copying and pasting

Copying and pasting is a fast, easy way to get Web page content into Word. To do so, take these steps:

1. **Select what you want in your Web browser and then choose Edit⇨Copy from the menu bar, or press ⌘-C.**

2. **Switch to Word and choose Edit⇨Paste from the menu bar, or press ⌘-P.**

   If the result isn't good enough, try the steps in the next section.

Saving and opening a Web page

Word can open Web pages that have been saved as .htm, .html, or .mht (Web archives). For example, say you're using a Web browser and you find a Web page that you want to edit in Word. Use the Web browser to save the Web page as a file on your computer and then open the saved file in Word. Here's how:

1. **In the Web browser, choose File⇨Save As.**

   The Web browser's Save dialog opens.

2. **Choose a location.**

   Remember the filename or give the file a name of your choosing.

3. **Click Save to save the file.**

After you save the Web page, you need to know how to open it. To open the saved Web page in Word, follow these steps:

1. **In Word, choose File⇨Open from the menu bar.**

   The File Open dialog appears.

2. **Choose All Files from the Enable pop-up menu.**

3. **Navigate to and select the file you saved in the preceding steps.**

4. **Click the Open button or double-click the filename.**

   Word does its best to open the Web page you saved. Bear in mind, many Web page elements (such as Flash, Silverlight, style sheets, and various scripts) are ignored by Word. Just the same, you may be able to get the content you want into Word so that you can take it from there and do your own editing magic.

If your first attempt didn't turn out well, you can try using a different Save As format in your Web browser. Web browsers and Web pages vary widely. In Word, a Web page saved by one browser, such as Safari, may look completely different from the same page saved by a different Web browser, such as Opera or Firefox. Each Web browser has different Save As formats from which to choose, so don't give up after just one attempt. Try saving the page again with a different browser and/or format.

Sometimes the results just aren't good no matter what format or browser you choose. This is a limitation of opening Web pages in Word.

Saving a document as a Web page

Twenty years ago, the Internet was something exciting and new to most people. Everyone wondered how the Internet would shake out, and Microsoft wanted to be a leader in the field. At that time, the best way to distribute Word documents on the Web was to save them as *HyperText Markup Language* (HTML) files, the native file format understood by Web browsers. The idea was to save a Word document in HTML and upload it to a Web server; then anyone with access to the server could download the file, and that Word copy would reconstruct the document exactly as it was before.

Recently, new Internet technologies have made this scenario passé. Today you have better ways to share documents online, such as SkyDrive and SharePoint, discussed in Book I, Chapter 4.

You can see approximately how a document will look when saved as a Web page by choosing View⇨Web Layout from the menu bar while working on your document. Word is better at creating Web pages from scratch than it is at rendering Web pages made with other tools. To turn a Word document into a Web page, choose File⇨Save as Web Page from the menu bar. In the Save As dialog is a Web Options button for advanced users. Click the Save button to make the .htm file and folder with linked content files, such as photos, movies, and sounds.

Extracting text from any file

Every so often, you might come across a mystery file and you can't figure out what it contains or maybe even which file format it uses. Maybe the file was corrupted, or maybe it's in a Microsoft Windows format that has no equivalent on the Mac side. Don't worry. Even if you don't know what application created the file, Word might be able to help. If text is in a file, Word can extract the text no matter what application created the file. To do so, follow these steps:

1. **Choose File⇨Open from the menu bar.**

The Open dialog appears.

2. **Choose Recover Text from Any File in the Enable pop-up menu.**

3. **Select the file that you want to extract the text from and then click Open.**

Alternatively, you can double-click the file you want to extract the text from.

A new Word document opens. The Word document contains the text, if any, that was in the file you selected. You might now know what the mystery document was, have a hint about what kind of file it was, or you may have rescued the text from a corrupt file and can now use the rescued text.

Finding files in Finder

Your file's gone! You knew right where that file was a minute ago, but now it's gone. Now is the time to use Spotlight. Whether you use the Word Open command or you're browsing your files with Finder, find the Spotlight Search box with its little magnifying glass icon in the upper-right corner of the window. Type a search term into the Search box, and Spotlight instantly displays the files containing that term.

If you're browsing in Finder, turn on Cover Flow view by pressing ⌘-4. Select a document and press the spacebar to enlarge the Cover Flow preview and then scroll through your entire document with the Mac OS X QuickView without even opening the file, as shown in Figure 2-1.

Of course, you can use any of more than 20 different ways to open the file at this point, including double-clicking the QuickView window.

Cover Flow view

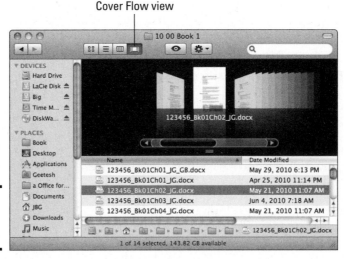

Figure 2-1:
Finding a
missing file.

Recovering AutoRecover files

Uh oh — the power went out, or Word crashed, and you were right in the middle of writing an important document! If that ever happens to you, and we hope it never does, all you have to do is open Microsoft Word again. Word looks for and opens any AutoRecover files for the document(s) that you were working on when the crash occurred. Your document(s) open(s) with Recovered appended to the filename. Choose File⇨Save As from the menu bar to restore the original filename and location. Word can recover files that were open because, by default, Word autosaves your document every ten minutes while you're working on it. If you want, you can change the save time interval within the AutoRecover setting as follows:

1. **Choose Word⇨Preferences⇨Save from the menu bar.**

   Word's Save preferences are displayed, as shown in Figure 2-2.

2. **Change the number of minutes in the Save AutoRecover Info Every: [X] Minutes setting.**

   The default is 10 minutes. Entering a lower number saves more often, but you may notice Word is more sluggish when it saves so often. Entering a higher number may make Word perform better, but you may lose more changes if a power outage or computer crash occurs.

   You can deselect this check box if you don't want Word to save an AutoRecover file. You might do this for extremely large documents that take a long time to save. Of course, if you experience a power outage or computer crash, you will lose all your changes since the last time you manually saved the file.

   You don't need to select the Always Create Backup Copy check box. With AutoRecover and Time Machine, the bases are covered. The option is there only for backward compatibility.

3. **Click OK when you're finished.**

Rarely, Word might not automatically display the AutoRecover file for the document(s) you were working on the next time you open Word. In that case, do the following in Word to open the AutoRecover file:

1. **Choose File⇨Open from the menu bar.**

   The Open dialog appears.

2. **Type** AutoRecover **or type a keyword or phrase in the Spotlight Search box in the top-right corner of the Open dialog.**

   Spotlight lists all AutoRecover files on the selected volume. Click Computer if you don't see one or more AutoRecover files. Of course, if you deselected AutoRecover in Word Preferences, you probably won't have anything to recover.

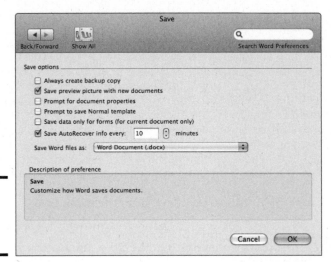

Figure 2-2:
Finding
your Save
options!

3. **Double-click the most recently saved AutoRecover file, or select the file and click Open. If you did a keyword or phrase search, use the Last Opened information to help you choose a likely file to open.**

    If the file you want is grayed-out, choose All Files in the Enable pop-up menu, which allows you to open any file type.

You can also use Mac OS X Time Machine to recover any file that you've saved at least once. When you use Word for Mac, it's nearly impossible to lose more than a few minutes' worth of work thanks to AutoRecover and Time Machine.

Saving Word Documents

Most of the time, saving a file in Word is a very simple task. But at times, you may want to limit access to a particular file. Or maybe you want to save a document so that it's compatible with older versions of Word; or perhaps you want to save your document in a format that's compatible with other programs. Or maybe you want to send a document via e-mail or Microsoft Messenger, or put it online as a Web page. The Word Save As options can accommodate all these needs and more.

Just close me

This may seem somewhat obvious, but Word keeps track of whether a document's been changed since it was opened last. If you close a document after making any changes at all, Word displays a dialog asking whether you want to save changes.

✦ **If you click Save,** Word replaces the old version of your document with the current version.

✦ **If you click Don't Save,** well, Word doesn't save your changes (and yes, at times, you don't want your changes made and would rather start over with the original document). Word closes your document, and any changes you made since the last save are discarded.

✦ **If you click Cancel,** you're telling Word that you really didn't mean to close the window, and it keeps the document open just as it was before you tried to close the window.

Giving a document a new name, a new location

When you open a new, blank document, it starts off with a generic name, such as Document1. That's not much help when you want to find your file again later, but it's easy to fix:

1. **Choose File⇨Save As from the menu bar.**

   The Save As dialog appears. By default, Word uses whatever you typed in the first line of the document as the filename.

2. **(Optional) In the Save As field, type in a new name.**

3. **Navigate to the desired location and click Save.**

   A good place to store documents is in the Documents folder. Save As dialogs have a New Folder button in the lower-left corner in case you want to create a new folder in which to save your document.

Making documents secure and private

Sometimes you absolutely don't want anyone, including Aunt Millie and her 16th nephew, opening or editing a document. Different levels of security are available. A low-security method lets you control who can do what with a particular document by bringing up the Save preferences dialog, shown in Figure 2-3, using any of these methods:

✦ Choose Word⇨Preferences⇨Security from the menu bar

✦ Choose File⇨Save As⇨Options⇨Show All⇨Security from the menu bar

✦ Press ⌘-, (comma) and click the Security button

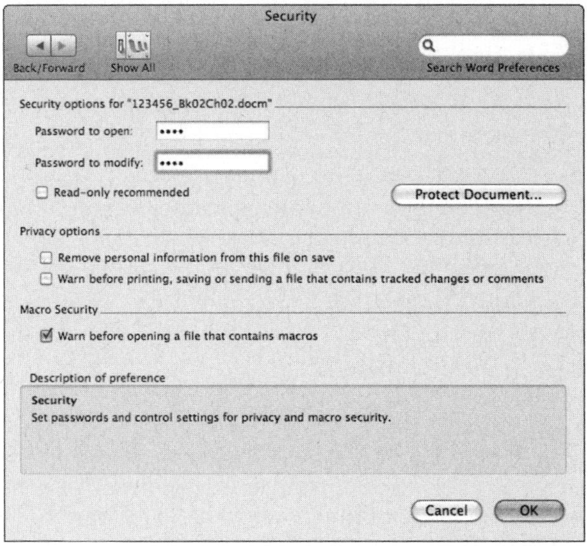

Security

Back/Forward   Show All   Search Word Preferences

Security options for "123456_Bk02Ch02.docm"

Password to open: ••••

Password to modify: ••••

☐ Read-only recommended   (Protect Document...)

Privacy options

☐ Remove personal information from this file on save
☐ Warn before printing, saving or sending a file that contains tracked changes or comments

Macro Security

☑ Warn before opening a file that contains macros

Description of preference

Security
Set passwords and control settings for privacy and macro security.

(Cancel)   (OK)

Figure 2-3:
Setting document security options.

File protection

Choose from the following file security options in the Security dialog to protect your document. Because macros to crack any password are freely available on the Internet; we consider these options to be very low security. These options apply only to the document listed next to Security Options for *[Document name]*:

✦ **Password to Open:** Type a password to be required to open this document.

✦ **Password to Modify:** The password you type will be required to modify this document.

✦ **Read-Only Recommended:** If you select this check box, when you open the document, a dialog is displayed recommending that the document be opened in read-only mode. This helps prevent accidental overwriting of the file.

✦ **Protect Document:** Same as choosing Tools⇨Protect Document from the menu bar and clicking the Ribbon's Review tab, and in the Protection group, clicking Document. Requires a password to modify specified content within the document.

A document can be protected against changes for any one of the following:

- Tracked changes (See Chapter 5 in this minibook.)
- Comments (See Chapter 5 in this minibook.)
- Forms (See Chapter 8 in this minibook.)

File privacy

Choose these privacy options, which apply only to the document listed next to Security Options for *[Document name]*:

✦ **Remove Personal Information from This File on Save.** Select this check box to remove most personal information from a file. By default, Word retains the username and certain user activity within a file. You can see and control what's in a document by choosing File⇨Properties and Word⇨Preferences⇨User Information from the menu bar. Of course, private information contained in the body or filename of a document is not affected by this setting.

✦ **Warn before Printing, Saving, or Sending a File That Contains Tracked Changes or Comments.** Select this check box when you're working with documents that may have hidden comments or tracked changes that should not get into the wrong hands. Word can't stop you from saying things that might prove embarrassing later, but it can warn you that your document has comments or tracked changes. You might want to make a template with this setting turned on. If you want to turn on this setting for every document you open, consider making a macro (see Book I, Chapter 12) that turns on this setting for all documents.

Credentials permissions

If you work for an organization that uses an Information Rights Management (IRM) server, you can require that your Word document be authenticated against the IRM server. Click the Review tab on the Ribbon. In the Protection group, click the Permissions button and then choose Manage Credentials to add your credentials so that they are remembered. The first time you access a licensing server, you're prompted to enter your username and password. If you select the check box to save your username and password in the Mac OS X Keychain application, you have to enter the info only once. From then on, to restrict your Word document by requiring authentication to the IRM server before opening, go to the Review tab on the Ribbon, find the Protection group, and click Permissions; or choose File⇨Restrict Permissions⇨Manage Credentials from the menu bar.

Macro security

The Warn before Opening a File That Contains Macros check box causes the macro warning dialog to display whenever a file that contains macros is opened. Deselect this option setting at your peril. Deselecting allows macros from all documents to run. A macro can be designed to damage your system, so don't run macros from sources you don't trust. If you turn off macro warnings, you can turn warnings back on by choosing Word➪Preferences Security to access the settings. Choose the check box Warn before opening a file that contains macros.

Changing Word's Default Document

Perhaps you've suspected that Word must have a special template some-where that you can use as a default when you create that seemingly plain, blank document. Well, you're right; this special template is Normal.dotm, and it has all the settings that control what you see when you create a new, blank document.

The special file Normal.dotm is the template that Word uses to create new documents when you choose File➪New Blank Document from the menu bar or open a new, blank document from the Word Document Gallery. As you work, things such as toolbars, AutoText, and certain preferences can be saved into Normal.dotm.

To make a pristine Normal template, locate the file by choosing Word➪Preferences➪File Locations➪User Templates➪Location from the menu bar. Then quit Word. Then rename or delete the existing Normal.dotm file. The next time Word opens, it creates a new Normal.dotm file based on default settings. Do we detect new car smell?

You can overwrite the Normal.dotm template to use as Word's default for new documents. Before starting the procedure, we suggest making a copy of the existing Normal.dotm file. You also need to know where the Normal template is located. You can find (and modify) the Normal template by choosing Word➪Preferences➪File Locations➪User Templates➪Location from the menu bar. When you know where Normal is, take these steps:

1. **In Word, choose File➪Open from the menu bar.**

   A file Open dialog displays.

2. **Switch the Enable pop-up menu to Word Templates.**

3. **Navigate to Normal.dotm and open the file.**

4. **Make the modifications you desire.**

5. **Choose File⇨Save from the menu bar, click the Save button, or close the window and choose Save when prompted.**

   Any new documents you make from then on will be based on the modified `Normal.dotm` template you saved.

After customizing, make a copy of your new Normal template in case you decide subsequent changes to Normal are not desired. If you want to create an official default template for your organization, create a custom Normal template and distribute it.

Being Compatible with Others

Being aware and respectful of other people's tastes is key to getting along with everyone in this world. Microsoft promotes this concept well in Word by giving you a lot of file format choices.

You have Word 2011, but remember, not everyone else does. At times, you may need to save your files in a format that people with other software can open. Knowing the software capabilities of the people you're communicating with helps you choose the most appropriate format. Fortunately, almost every word processor can use certain file formats.

The Word 2011 default format files have an *x* at the end of the filename to signify that they're eXtensible Markup Language (XML) documents. The following list gives a rundown on the various extensions you find in the Save As dialog:

✦ **Word Document (`.docx`):** This is Word 2011's default, regular format. It's the international standard format for word processing documents, also known as standard open XML format. This format is fully compatible with Word 2008 (Mac), Word 2007 (Windows), and Word 2010 (Windows). This format has fair compatibility with Word 2004 (Mac) and Word 2003 (Windows) when Microsoft's free Office updates are installed. You can open, view, save, and print the DOCX format with Word 2003 and 2004 versions — but you can't edit them with the same capabilities. OpenOffice, NeoOffice, Lotus Notes, and Apple Pages (part of iWork) can open these documents, but their conversion process changes how documents look and work. SkyDrive, Google Docs, and Docs.com display these documents well, but they have minimal editing capabilities.

✦ **Word Template (`.dotx`):** Same compatibility benefits and issues as explained for Word Document (DOCX).

✦ **PDF (Portable Document Format; `.pdf`):** The PDF format is a great way to distribute a Word document when you want the recipient to be able to view and print your document just the way you saved it, regardless of what fonts or printer driver the recipient has installed on her Mac. Your document retains its fonts and formatting on just about every computer. This is also a good file format when you don't want anyone editing or changing your document in any way.

+ **Word Macro–Enabled Document (.docm):** This file format is supported for Word 2003 through 2011, both Mac and PC, except Word 2008 (Mac). The macros contained in these documents must be written properly in order to work on all platforms.

+ **Word Macro–Enabled Template (.dotm):** Same compatibility characteristics as Word Macro–Enabled Document (DOCM).

+ **Word 97–2004 Document (.doc):** All versions of Microsoft Office from 97 to 2011 for both Mac and Windows can open this format, but new 2007 and later features aren't supported fully.

+ **Word Document Stationery (.doc):** When you choose Word Document Stationery in Word's Save As dialog, your document is saved as a Stationery file in Word 97–2004 file format. This is the same as using Finder's Get Info command to turn a document into a Mac OS X Stationery template.

+ **Word 97–2004 Template (.dot):** Same compatibility as Word 97–2004 (DOC).

+ **Rich Text Format (.rtf):** This is the best choice to use when you want to cover the widest possible audience. Although RTF isn't a formal standard, most word processors do a decent job of working with this format. Do remember, though, that after you save to the RTF format, you lose the editing ability for Word-specific features, such as WordArt, Picture Styles, and so on.

+ **Word 4.0–6.0/95 Compatible (.rtf):** This RTF variant has support for specific features of Microsoft Word versions 4, 6, and 95. Use this format if you know your recipient is using one of these older versions of Microsoft Word, either Mac or Windows.

+ **Plain Text (.txt):** Saves only the text portion of the Word document. Everything else is discarded.

+ **Web Page (.htm):** Turns your Word document into a Web page (HTML) document and also creates a supporting folder of linked objects, such as pictures or movies. Web browsers, such as Safari and Firefox, can open the result.

+ **Single File Web Page (.mht):** Similar to Web Page (HTM), Single File Web Page creates a single file also known as a Web archive. Web browsers, such as Safari and Firefox, can open the result.

+ **Word 2003 XML Document (.xml):** Creates an XML document without compressing it, specifically for Word 2003.

Standard format XML Word documents are zipped folders that contain XML files, which are simply text files containing HTML and XML. If you're really into this sort of thing, you can unzip and open the actual XML files by changing the file extension in Finder from (.docx) to (.zip). Then, in Finder, double-click the (.zip) file. The resulting folder is your Word document, but you can now see all the stuff that is normally hidden by looking inside the folder. You could (optionally) edit the contents; zip the folder and change the file extension back to (.docx) to go full circle and make the folder a regular Word document again.

Chapter 3: Formatting and Typography

In This Chapter

✔ Formatting whole paragraphs

✔ Controlling pagination

✔ Stopping at tabs

✔ Dropping your caps

✔ Trying out typography features

A fter you have your document underway, you discover how important it is to format and fine-tune your document. Although what formatting and fine-tuning you do depend on the type and purpose of your document, some things are surprisingly universal. Foremost among these similarities is an observation: It's one thing to get down words, but you want them to look their best. Readers appreciate the time that writers spend to make their work readable. Some writers enjoy creating documents that pay attention to finer details, such as the spacing among lines and characters, as well as kerning and paragraph formatting. This chapter covers Word's ability to help you create documents with style.

Formatting Paragraphs

Sometimes you want the placement of your text on a page to be aesthetically pleasing. Consider how important it is to have a poem or a quotation look just right to create the desired ambience on the page. In these situations, you might need to adjust values for line spacing and paragraph spacing. When working with the options in the Paragraph group of the Home tab on the Ribbon, the settings apply to entire paragraphs. (See Figure 3-1.)

Figure 3-1:
Changing
paragraph
properties.

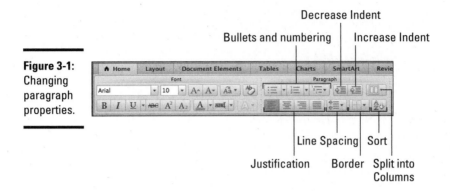

Click anywhere in a paragraph or select multiple paragraphs when you apply these formatting options.

✦ **Decrease Indent or Increase Indent:** Click Decrease Indent to make the indent smaller or remove it; click Increase Indent to make the indent bigger.

✦ **Split Text into Columns:** Select the text you want arranged as columns, then click this button and choose how many columns.

✦ **Justification:** To apply justification to a paragraph, click the desired justification. Your choices are Align Text Left, Center, Align Text Right, or Justify.

✦ **Line Spacing:** Choose from the pop-up menu. Choosing Line Spacing Options displays the Indents and Spacing tab of the Paragraph formatting dialog, shown in Figure 3-2.

✦ **Border Formats:** Select a format from the pop-up menu.

✦ **Sort:** Click to alphabetically order a column of text.

Although using the Ribbon is quick and easy, Word offers a more complete version of the same controls over the spacing and indentation of your text. To get at the full line and paragraph spacing and the page break controls, take these steps:

1. **Select the text you want to fine-tune and then choose Format⇨ Paragraph from the menu bar, or choose the Line Spacing Options at the bottom of the Line Spacing pop-up menu in the Paragraph group. (Refer to Figure 3-1.)**

The Paragraph dialog appears, as shown in Figure 3-2.

2. **Make adjustments as desired and click OK when you're finished.**

You can use negative numbers for negative indentation.

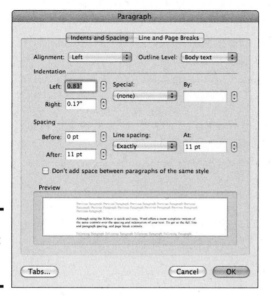

Figure 3-2:
Spacing out
in a good
way.

Controlling Paragraphs

Whether prose or poetry, a business report, or a science project, you can have a paragraph call attention to itself by changing the paragraph's formatting. Conversely, you have a potential problem on your hands when a paragraph inadvertently calls attention to itself by crossing a page boundary.

In the previous section, we discuss indents and spacing paragraph controls. Here we delve into different aspects of paragraph control. A paragraph that starts with a single line at the bottom of a page and continues onto the next is a *widow;* its counterpart, the *orphan,* occurs when the last line of a paragraph ends at the top of a page.

It's good to know that Word allows you to control paragraph formatting so that you can call attention to paragraphs when you want to avoid unhappy problems like widows and orphans. To get at these paragraph formatting controls, take these steps:

1. **Choose Format⇨Paragraph from the menu bar.**

The Paragraph dialog opens.

2. **Click the Line and Page Breaks tab.**

Line and page break settings become available, as shown in Figure 3-3.

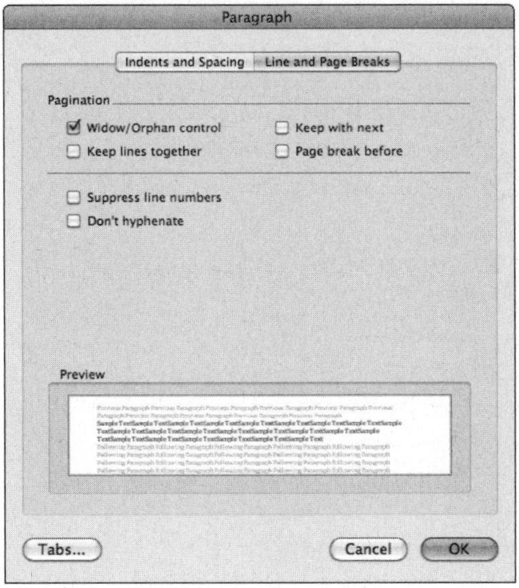

Figure 3-3:
Keeping
paragraphs
under
control.

These check boxes affect paragraphs:

✦ **Widow/Orphan Control:** Prevents widows and orphans.

✦ **Keep Lines Together:** Sometimes Word's paragraph spacing can cause text that ought to stay together to get separated. For example, you might have a heading near the end of a page and you want the heading to stay associated with the paragraph that follows. Word wants to put the heading at the bottom of a page and then the associated text winds up all by itself at the top of the next page. To prevent this problem, select both the heading and the following paragraph and then select this check box. Word keeps the text and the heading together.

✦ **Keep with Next:** You may want to make sure two paragraphs are always kept together. Select both paragraphs and then select this check box. Word won't allow a page break to come between them.

✦ **Page Break Before:** If you have a paragraph that you want to always start at the top of its page, select a paragraph and then select this check box. Word makes sure a page break always occurs before the selected paragraph.

Here are some other options you can choose from the Paragraph dialog:

✦ **Suppress Line Numbers:** This works if you've turned on line numbering, which we discuss in the section "Starting a bulleted or numbered list automatically," later in this chapter. The lines that are selected when you choose this option aren't included in the page count.

✦ **Don't Hyphenate:** This check box does what it says. Select paragraphs that you don't want Word to use hyphenation with and then select this check box.

✦ **Tabs:** Click this button to display the Tabs dialog (described in the section "Precision tab placement," later in this chapter).

Tinkering with Tabs

The old-fashioned idea of a basic *tab stop* is that when you press the Tab key, the cursor jumps to the next tab stop that's set on the ruler and then you start typing. In Word, this kind of tab stop is the left tab stop. These days, tabs do a lot more than just act as a position to stop the cursor. Read on!

Working with the Tabs menu

Word has five types of tab stops. To see the list of tabs, you must use a view that supports rulers. Follow these steps:

1. **Choose either View➪Draft or View➪Print Layout from the menu bar.**

Both views support rulers.

2. **Choose View➪Ruler from the menu bar if the ruler isn't turned on already.**

You can see Word's rulers.

3. **Click the Tabs button to the far left of the horizontal ruler.**

The Tabs menu, as shown in Figure 3-4, appears.

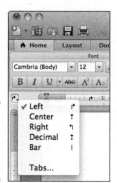

Figure 3-4:
Displaying
the Tabs
menu.

Notice the five kinds of tabs in Figure 3-4, each with its own icon. Left is the default tab. If you choose a different kind of tab, the Tabs menu displays the selected kind of tab.

Setting a tab stop

Tabs work at the paragraph level; when you set tab stops, they work with the currently selected paragraphs. You can select an entire document before you set tabs if you want your tab stops to work for the whole thing. The actual steps to set a tab stop are simple:

1. **Select one or more paragraphs.**

   If you want to select the entire document, choose Edit⇨Select All from the menu bar or press ⌘-A.

2. **Click the Tabs menu (see Figure 3-4) and choose one of the five tab stops.**

   See the following section for more detail about each tab stop option.

3. **Click in the horizontal ruler wherever you want a tab stop.**

   Each time you click, the symbol for the tab stop you chose is placed into the ruler.

When you work with tabs, be sure to toggle paragraph marks on and off with the Show All Non-Printing Characters button on the Standard toolbar. This button is simply labeled Show on the toolbar. When paragraph marks are turned on, you see an arrow pointing to the right appear in the text whenever you press the Tab key. (See Figure 3-5 for several examples.)

The five kinds of tab stops

Your paragraph behaves differently for each of the five kinds of tab stops. Here are descriptions of each kind of tab stop (see Figure 3-5):

✦ **Left:** By default, each document has a left tab stop every ½ inch, unless you click in the ruler to add your own stops. If you press the Tab key, the cursor advances to the next tab stop. If you start typing at a left tab stop, your text begins at that tab stop.

✦ **Center:** After you set a center tab stop, press the Tab key to move to the stop. When you start typing, your text is centered below the tab stop.

✦ **Right:** After you set a right tab stop, press the Tab key to move to the right tab stop and start typing. Use a right tab to right-align text, perhaps when making a column.

✦ **Decimal:** As the name implies, use this tab stop when you're typing decimal numbers. Word lines up the numbers at the decimal point. Even if you don't type an actual decimal point, Word assumes the decimal point.

✦ **Bar:** Danger: Using a bar tab stop may cause inebriation. Okay, not really. A bar tab stop is much the same as a left tab stop, except Word puts a vertical bar at the tab stop. After you set a bar stop and start typing, your text is to the right of the bar.

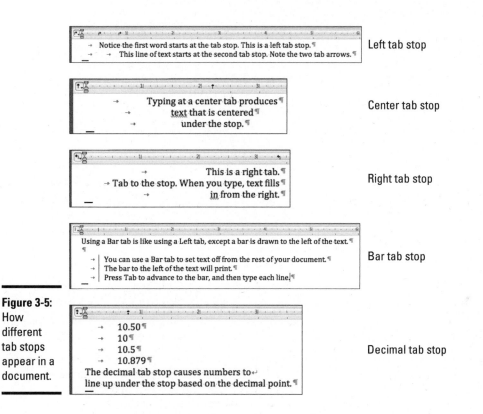

Left tab stop

Center tab stop

Right tab stop

Bar tab stop

**Book II
Chapter 3**

Formatting and Typography

Figure 3-5:
How different tab stops appear in a document.

Decimal tab stop

Precision tab placement

Although clicking in the ruler to place tabs is fast and easy, you may have a need for precise tab positioning. You can approach this in several ways, but we suggest you try to click into the ruler to place your tab stop(s) first. You can drag tabs in the ruler to reposition them. If that placement isn't precise enough for you, choose Tabs from the Tabs menu (refer to Figure 3-4) to open the Tabs dialog, as shown in Figure 3-6, where you can fine-tune to thousandths of an inch.

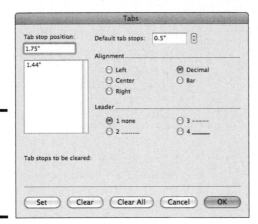

Figure 3-6: Precision placement of tabs in the Tabs dialog.

The Tabs dialog has lots of tab settings that you can control. When working with this dialog, your changes aren't committed until you click OK. Here's the rundown:

✦ **Tab Stop Position:** Enter a position in inches, and then

   • *To clear the entered tab stop position,* click the Clear button.

   • *To create a new stop at the entered tab stop position,* select the Alignment and Leader settings and then click the Set button.

   • *To modify a stop at the entered tab stop position,* click the Alignment and Leader settings and then click the Set button.

✦ **Default Tab Stops:** When you open a new, blank document, a tab stop exists every ½-inch — even though there's no tab stop marker to show this in the ruler. You can press the Tab key in a blank document if you don't believe us. You can adjust the default setting, but we can't think of any particular reason to do so.

✦ **List of tabs:** Clicking tab stops here enters the stop into the Tab Stop Position field so you don't have to type.

✦ **Clear:** Adds the entered tab stop position to the Tabs Stops to Be Cleared area. The tabs clear when you click OK.

✦ **Clear All:** Marks all tab stops for the current paragraph and notes this in the Tab Stops to be Cleared area. The stops clear when you click OK.

✦ **Leader:** When you select left, right, center, or decimal tab stops, you add the selected style as a fill between the tab stops.

To remove a tab stop, you can simply drag a tab stop from the ruler and release the mouse button anywhere. This works only about half the time, though. Use the Tabs dialog (see Figure 3-6) if you come across a stubborn tab that won't go away.

Shooting Bullets and Numbing Numbers

Bullets and numbers are special paragraph styles that visually separate lists from the body of your text. You can configure bullets and numbers in a nearly limitless number of ways.

Starting a bulleted or numbered list automatically

Word's default AutoCorrect setting automatically detects when you're starting a bulleted or numbered list. Word looks for consecutive paragraphs that start with either an asterisk (*) or a number. To make Word think you're starting a list, do the following:

1. **Type some text and then press Return or Enter.**

2. **Type either of the following:**

   - **1** followed by a period, a space, and some text.

   - An asterisk (*****) followed by a space and some text.

3. **Press Return or Enter.**

   Word indents the number and the text, turns on numbering or bullets, and displays a widget. Click the widget for the following options:

   - *Undo Automatic Numbering (or Bullets):* Undoes the automatic number or bullet format that was just applied.

   - *Stop Automatically Creating Numbered (or Bulleted) Lists:* Tells Word to stop using the Automatic Numbering and Bullets feature.

   - *Control AutoFormat Options:* Displays the AutoFormat as You Type tab in the AutoCorrect preferences dialog. See the next heading.

If your document already has a numbered list somewhere, Word may display a small widget. If you click the widget, you can start the numbering over.

Telling Word to stop adding bullets or numbers

The easiest way to turn off bullets and numbering is by choosing Tools⇨AutoCorrect⇨AutoFormat as You Type from the menu bar. Under Apply as You Type, deselect the options for Automatic Bulleted Lists and Automatic Numbered Lists.

If you're typing a bulleted list and you want to tell Word that you've typed the last entry for the list, simply press Return or Enter twice after the last entry in the list. Word returns to normal text.

Formatting existing text as a list

Turning a series of paragraphs into a list is easy as pie with the Ribbon. Try this simple example:

1. **Type a simple list.**

   For example, enter this text:

   > **First item**
   >
   > **Next item**
   >
   > **Last item**

2. **Select the list.**

   You can use any sequence of small paragraphs in a document.

3. **On the Ribbon's Home tab, go to the Paragraph group. Click either the Bulleted List or Numbered List button.**

   Your list has the bullet style or number style you chose. You can increase the indenting of a selected item in your list to a new level by pressing the Tab key or clicking the Indent button in the Paragraph group on the Ribbon. (Refer to Figure 3-1.) To outdent a listed item, select it and press Shift-Tab or click the Decrease Indent button in the Paragraph group on the Ribbon. This is similar to working in an Outline. Bulleted lists can have up to eight levels of indentation.

Making special bullets and numbers

Each time you press Return or Enter, you create a paragraph mark. When working in a list, you use a paragraph mark to tell Word you want a new bullet or number. For each level of indentation, your indented bullet or number can display a different style. A list can have one of four different bullet and numbering schemes:

✦ **Bulleted:** An asterisk or special character marks each bullet point. Each indentation level can display a different bullet.

✦ **Numbered:** A number denotes each new item in the list.

✦ **Outline Numbered or Multilevel:** A number denotes each new item in the list. Indents invoke formatting rules for sub-numbering.

✦ **List Styles:** Create and save list customizations as styles. See Chapter 4 of this minibook for more about styles.

The existing style for each of the eight bullet indentation levels and various number formats can be viewed and customized. You can create new styles so that you can apply them to other lists later.

Customizing bullets

You can fine-tune the formatting of your bullets right on the Ribbon. First, put the insertion cursor within a bullet level in your document. To display bullet styles, click the small triangle to the right of the Bulleted List button shown in the margin. This displays the Bullet gallery. Choose a bullet style to apply to the list's current indentation level from Recently Used Bullets, the Bullet Library, or Document Bullets.

Choosing the Define New Bullet option at the bottom of the Bullet gallery displays the Customize Bulleted List dialog shown in Figure 3-7. This dialog lets you customize bullets.

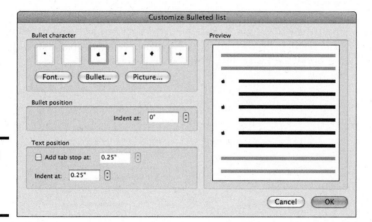

Figure 3-7:
Making
a custom
bullet.

Across the top of the Customize Bulleted List dialog is the Bullet Character section, where you see the existing bullets for each level currently in the document. To change a bullet, select one of them, click one of the following buttons, and observe the preview:

✦ **Font:** Displays the Format Font dialog. You can choose from any font on your system and format the character precisely.

✦ **Bullet:** Displays the Symbol dialog discussed in Book I, Chapter 8. Choose from many special characters contained within your fonts.

✦ **Picture:** Displays a file Open browser, where you can choose a (hopefully very tiny) picture to be a bullet.

Use the spinner control under Bullet Position to set how much the bullet will be indented.

The Text Position portion of the dialog gives you these options:

✦ **Add Tab Stop At:** When selected, this option adds a tab stop at the position you specify using the spinner control.

✦ **Indent At:** Use the spinner control to set the bullet's indentation.

Customizing numbered lists

You can choose custom number formats on the Ribbon. First, put the insertion cursor within a number level. To display number styles, click the small triangle to the right of the Numbered List button shown in the margin. It's the one in the middle of the three buttons in the Paragraph group. This button displays the Numbered List gallery. Choose a number style from Recently Used Number Formats, the Numbering Library, or Document Number Formats.

Choosing the Define New Number Format option at the bottom of the Number style palette displays the Customize Numbered List dialog shown in Figure 3-8. This dialog lets you customize number styles.

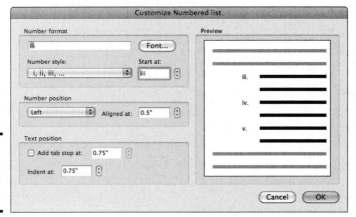

Figure 3-8:
Customizing a numbered list.

In the Number Format area of the dialog is a field that displays the current number format. You can replace what you see with a potential number candidate, such as a letter or number from your keyboard, and then choose Font to display the Format Font dialog to customize that letter or number.

In the Number Format area, you get these options:

✦ Choose a style from the Number Style pop-up menu.

✦ If you want the numbered list to start with a number other than 1 or the letter a, use the Start At spinner control or type in the input box to set the starting number for the list.

The Number Position area gives you a couple more options:

✦ Choose Left, Centered, or Right from the pop-up menu to determine how the numbers are aligned.

✦ Use the Aligned At spinner control or type in the input box to set the number position alignment.

You're not out of options yet. Here are the Text Position options:

✦ Select the Add Tab Stop At check box to add a tab stop at the position you specify using the spinner control.

✦ Use the Indent At spinner control to set the indentation.

Making a multilevel (outline numbered) list

An easy way to make a multilevel list is to start with a list that's been indented using tabs. Take a look at Figure 3-9 as you follow these steps:

1. **Type a simple list, as shown on the left side of Figure 3-9.**

   Use the Tab key to indent the text in your list.

2. **Select the list.**

   You can use any sequence of small paragraphs in a document.

3. **On the Ribbon's Home tab, go to the Paragraph group and click the Numbered List button (the middle of the three bullet and number buttons).**

   Word automatically senses you have a multilevel list and formats it as shown on the right side of Figure 3-9.

Indented list   Multilevel numbered list

Figure 3-9:
Making a
multilevel
list.

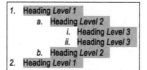

Customizing multilevel (outline numbered) lists

To apply a new multilevel style, click anywhere in your list and choose the Multilevel List button shown in the margin. It's the button at the right of the group of three bullet and numbering buttons on the Ribbon. Clicking the button displays the Multilevel List gallery. Choose a multilevel style from Current List, List Library, or Lists in Current Documents.

You can create your own multilevel list formats. Choosing the Define New Multilevel List option on the Multilevel style palette displays the Customize Outline Numbered List dialog shown in Figure 3-10. This dialog lets you customize multilevel lists and outline styles by level.

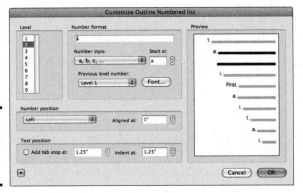

Figure 3-10:
Customizing a multilevel list.

From the Level list, choose which indentation level you want to format.

In the Number Format area, choose from the following options:

✦ Enter a potential number candidate, such as a letter or number from your keyboard, in the text box.

✦ Choose a style from the Number Style pop-up menu

✦ Use the Start At Spinner if you want the numbered list to start at a number other than 1 or letter a.

✦ Select a level from the Previous Level Number pop-up menu to bring the number format from the chosen level to the level you're formatting.

✦ Click the Font button to display the Format Font dialog. Choosing this applies formatting to the level being formatted, not the Previous Level.

Under Number Position, you find these options:

✦ Choose Left, Centered, or Right from the pop-up menu to change the alignment.

✦ Use the Aligned At spinner control or type into the input box to set the number position alignment.

The Text Position area offers these goodies:

✦ Select the Add Tab Stop At check box to add a tab stop at the position you specify using the spinner control.

✦ Use the Indent At spinner control to set the bullet's indentation.

Clicking the Show/Hide More Options button exposes more options. See the next section.

Loving legal beagles and authors of long documents

The Customize Outline Numbered List dialog has a special button that will be of particular interest if you need to make legal documents that follow legal numbering style. This feature also applies to you if you included ListNum field codes in a long document. (See Chapter 8 for info on how to use Word field codes.) Click the Show/Hide more options button to display additional formatting options, shown in Figure 3-11.

**Book II
Chapter 3**

**Formatting and
Typography**

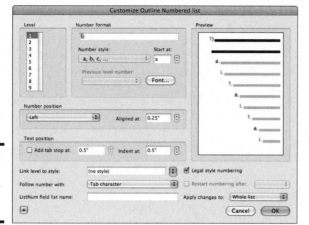

Figure 3-11:
Choosing
additional
options.

These additional formatting options apply to the level you're formatting:

✦ **Link Level to Style:** Select an option from this pop-up menu to link the formatting of the selected level with the formatting of an existing style.

✦ **Follow Number With:** Numbers have a tab after them by default. Select an option from the pop-up menu to change the default Tab character to something else.

✦ **ListNum Field List Name:** Enter a name to tag this field code.

✦ **Legal Style Numbering:** When selected, this check box restricts the level to Arabic numbers, preventing Roman Numerals from being used.

✦ **Restart Numbering after Level:** Select this check box and choose a level after which numbers will automatically start over at 1.

✦ **Apply Changes To:** Your options are Whole List (Default), This Point Forward, and Selected Text.

Starting over in the middle of a list

You may need to start over your numbering in the middle of a list. To restart numbering, follow these steps:

1. **Select the text where you want numbering to restart.**

2. **Right-click or Control-click and then choose Restart Numbering from the contextual menu.**

   Word starts the numbers from the first number that you have in the Start field of the Bullets and Numbering section of the Formatting palette.

Dropping a Cap

The Drop Cap feature isn't about losing your hat; it's just about adding beauty to your text with an option that's familiar from print design. In the days of yore, a typesetter would painstakingly use wooden blocks and then drop in a large, fancy capital letter at the beginning of the first sentence of a new chapter. In typesetting jargon, this embellishment is known as a *drop cap.* To make a drop cap, select the first character of the first paragraph in a document and choose Format⇨Drop Cap from the menu bar. Figure 3-12 shows a drop cap for T.

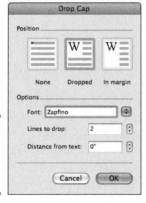

Figure 3-12:
Making a
drop cap the
easy way.

As shown in Figure 3-12, the character that becomes the actual drop cap doesn't have to be the same font as the rest of the paragraph. You can find special, embellished fonts that work very well as drop caps.

When you create your drop cap, you can set the number of lines of text that the drop cap uses, and whether the cap will appear dropped, as shown in Figure 3-12. The None option restores a drop cap to the character that it was before you turned it into a drop cap.

Turning on Typography

Typography is the art and business of making the shapes of characters that are printed or displayed on screen. A professional typographer prepares text for publication for a living, with a focus on the text's appearance.

A quick Web search on any of the Typography terms used in the following sections will produce a large body of resources.

The Typography features in Word work only on fonts that are specifically designed to support them. Very few of the fonts that are on your system now are likely to support more than one or two of these features. If you want to use these features, install fonts that support each feature by name. For example, a font's description must state that it supports Contextual Alternatives if you expect this feature to work with this font. Perhaps some entrepreneurial font seller will market a collection of fonts specifically designed to work with all of the Office 2011 Typography features.

To use these features, simply select some text and apply the formatting. If nothing happens when you try, the font you chose does not support the feature you tried to apply. For example, Apple Chancery and Zapfino support Ligatures. Office 2011 comes with Gabriola, a font specifically designed to take advantage of the new typography features.

Applying advanced typography on the Ribbon

The Ribbon's new Typography group shown in Figure 3-13 displays automatically on the Home tab when you're using Publishing Layout view, but you can turn it on in other views by choosing it in the Ribbon preferences. If you aren't aware of what Publishing Layout view is, you might want to read Chapter 1 of this minibook to understand Word's different views.

To turn on the Typography group in the Ribbon, choose Word⇨Preferences and then click the Ribbon button. In the Customize area, select the Typography option. You can now find this group on the Home tab of the Ribbon.

Office 2011 has improved support for typography. If you've switched from Windows, you may find some additional controls that are not in Word for Windows.

✦ **Ligatures:** The combining of two letters in a fancy way, such as the letters *fi* on the Ribbon.

✦ **Stylistic Set:** Select some text, then click this pop-up menu. If your font supports this feature, you can choose a style. The font illustrated in Figure 3-13 is Zapfino, which comes with Mac OS X.

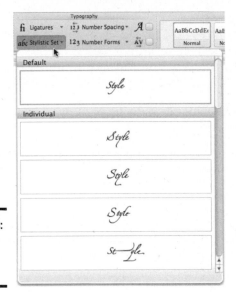

Figure 3-13:
Displaying
stylistic
sets.

✦ **Number Spacing:** Select some numbers and choose default, proportional, or tabular.

✦ **Number Forms:** Select numbers and choose default, lining, or old style. Old style is supported by many fonts.

✦ **Contextual Alternatives:** When selected, displays alternative font styles based on the sentence context. Your best bet is to select text and select this check box to see what happens.

✦ **Kerning:** When selected, applies kerning. By default, a font must be at least 72 points or larger for this feature to work.

Adjusting typography controls

In addition to the Typography group on the Ribbon, you can select text and apply precise formatting by choosing Format➪Font from the menu bar. When the Font dialog displays, click the Advanced tab, as shown in Figure 3-14.

On the Advanced tab of the Font dialog, you can choose from the following:

✦ **Scale:** Adjust using the spinner control. This option makes characters fatter or thinner.

✦ **Spacing:** Choose normal, expanded, or condensed, and number of points. This option adds or removes space between characters.

✦ **Position:** Choose normal, raised, or lowered, and by how many points. This can be a way to control how much subscript or superscript to apply to text.

✦ **Kerning:** Choose on or off and set the minimum number of points. Your font must support kerning to see any effect when this feature is applied.

✦ **Advanced Typography:** These controls duplicate the controls found when you use the Typography group in the Ribbon.

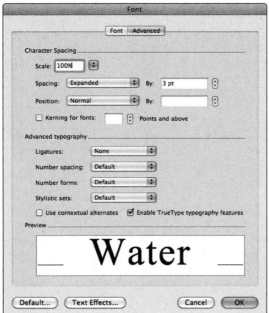

Figure 3-14:
Fine-tuning advanced typography.

Chapter 4: Working with Document Layout

In This Chapter

✓ Adding pages in Publishing Layout view

✓ Setting up pages and adjusting margins

✓ Getting layout just right

✓ Displaying layout gridlines

✓ Formatting headers and footers

✓ Making bookmark shortcuts

✓ Applying and making styles

✓ Copying items with Organizer

✓ Numbering your lines automatically

*W*hen you think of a document as a whole, elements such as columns, margins, and page breaks come to mind. Knowing how to manage these elements helps you create a better, more consistent layout. In this chapter, we also discuss controls that when applied, affect the entire document.

Adding Pages

The concept of a page in Word is a bit flexible. Word formats your document based on the fonts used, margin settings, and also on the capabilities of your computer's default printer. You can set up everything just perfectly on your computer, but when the document is opened on another computer, the formatting can change.

If you think your document will be opened on a computer other than your own, choose File➪Page Setup. In the resulting Page Setup dialog, change Settings to Page Attributes, and change Format For to the Any Printer option.

The same exact version of each font you used in your document must be on any other computer that opens the document in order for it to look exactly the same. Word for Mac does not let you embed fonts, so coordination between you and your collaborators regarding fonts is essential. Word will substitute missing fonts, and substitute fonts are always slightly different.

In all views except Publishing Layout view, document text is fluid. You can click anywhere in a document and start editing. As you add or remove text, the changes increase or decrease the document size unless you've put in specific page breaks.

When you're working in Publishing Layout view, your text will be mostly in story text boxes, where text flows from one box to another in a chain of boxes for a given story. The boxes remain in fixed positions, and a page is easier to define. To manage pages in Publishling Layout view, click the Layout tab on the Ribbon. In the Pages group, click the Add button's triangle to bring up the menu shown in Figure 4-1:

✦ **New Page:** Adds a new page.

✦ **New Master:** Adds a new master page.

✦ **Duplicate Page:** Creates a duplicate of the selected page.

Figure 4-1:
Adding and removing pages.

Configuring Page Setup

For convenience, page setup options are now on the Ribbon. Click the Layout tab. Look for these options in the Page Setup group, shown in Figure 4-2. Choose from the following:

✦ **Orientation:** Portrait (tall) or landscape (wide).

✦ **Size:** Choose a size. More sizes and custom sizes are available when you choose File➪Page Setup and then click the Paper Size button.

✦ **Break:** Choose a break option from the gallery shown in Figure 4-2.

Click the Show All Nonprinting Characters button (the one that looks like a mirrored P) on the Standard toolbar to toggle on and off your ability to see breaks in your document.

To remove a page break, make sure that you've enabled the Show All Nonprinting Characters option. Then double-click the page break so that it's highlighted and press the Delete key.

If you choose to display nonprinting characters by clicking the Show All Nonprinting Characters button on the Standard toolbar, you can see the break indicator at the beginning or end of a section. Break formatting information is contained within the indicator, so you can copy and paste breaks as a way to copy and paste formatting within a document, or even from one document to another.

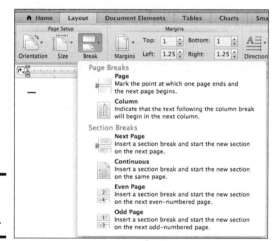

Figure 4-2:
Adjusting
page setup.

Ruling Margins

Most people are accustomed to seeing a perimeter style margin surrounding the text in documents. You'd have a hard time reading a book if the type went from edge to edge on each page. In a book or magazine in which the sheets are bound, you need extra white space, or *gutter,* in addition to a margin. Even normal documents that need to be printed need that gutter.

Paper can become tattered, which is one more reason to keep the text away from the edges. Even when reading on a computer screen or a handheld device, your eyes prefer the definition a clean margin provides.

Ruling by the Ruler and Ribbon

You can adjust the margins by clicking the Layout tab on the Ribbon and using the options in the Margins group, as shown earlier in Figure 4-2, or by dragging the margin sliders in the rulers. Of course, first you need to turn on the rulers at the top and left edge of the document area in Word: To do so, choose View⇨Ruler when in Draft View or Print Layout View.

In the ruler, you can do the following:

✦ **Margin:** Drag the line that divides the shaded part from the white part to adjust the margin setting.

✦ **First line indent:** Adjust by dragging the ruler's top triangle horizontally.

✦ **Hanging indent:** Drag the lower triangle on the horizontal ruler to set where the first line of the paragraph starts.

✦ **Left indent:** Drag the lowest button situated immediately under the hanging indent triangle to adjust the left indent.

Ruling by a dialog

Even with the rulers and Ribbon at their disposal, many users find it easier to adjust margins with a dialog. Follow these instructions to display the margin settings in the Document dialog:

1. **Choose Format⇨Document from the menu bar.**

The Document dialog (shown in Figure 4-3) opens.

2. **Click the Margins tab.**

You can type in exact values for the margins so that you can keep consistent margin values in all your documents.

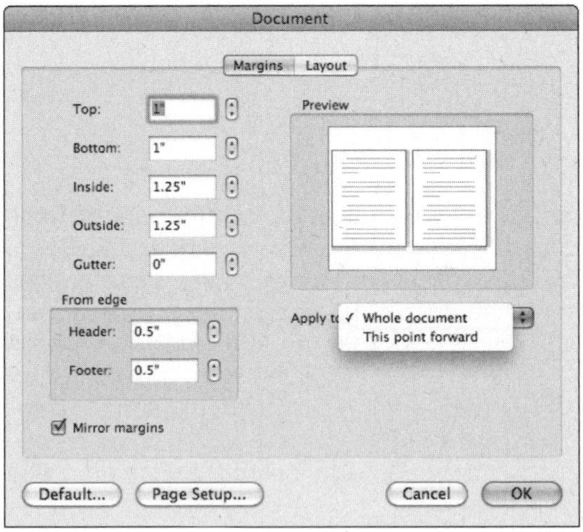

Figure 4-3:
Managing
margins
with ease.

The Margins tab of the Document dialog is straightforward. Enter decimal values for distances or use the spinner control next to the input fields. You need to know about the following other aspects of the Margins tab:

✦ **Mirror Margins:** Select this check box to use mirror margins and a gutter when you set up a document to be printed with facing pages, such as a book or a magazine. If a regular physical book is open, the extra gutter on the page to your left is mirrored on the page to your right so that the text is kept away from the binding by an equal amount on both pages.

✦ **Apply To:** Choose from the following:

   • *Whole Document:* The settings apply to the entire document.

   • *Selected Text:* The settings apply to whatever text you selected before opening the Document dialog.

   • *This Point Forward:* If you have no text selected, you get this option instead of Selected Text. This lets you apply settings from where your insertion point is placed in the document.

✦ **Default:** Default turns the current settings into Word's default settings to be used from now on when creating new, blank documents. This setting is stored in Word's `Normal.dotm` template.

✦ **Page Setup:** Displays the Page Setup dialog.

Arranging Text Layout

The Text Layout group on the Layout tab of the Ribbon, shown in Figure 4-4, offers popular layout tools:

✦ **Direction:** Rotate all text 90 or 270 degrees.

✦ **Columns:** Select text and then choose the number of columns.

✦ **Line Numbers:** Choose options for line numbers, which appear in the left margin when turned on. Choose None to turn them off.

✦ **Hyphenation:** Choose to display the Hyphenation dialog, which lets you adjust hyphenation rules for your document.

Figure 4-4:
Adjusting
page setup.

Formatting Page Background and Borders

A presence lurks behind the Word text. No, this presence isn't a ghost or a snake; it's just the background. Normally the background is white, but you can change that and even apply document theme colors to it. You have to use Print Layout view for this to work, so if you're not already in Print Layout view, click the Print Layout view button at the lower-left corner of the document window to switch to it. When you modify the background in Print Layout view, Word can convert it into Notebook Layout view and Publishing Layout view. Three formatting tools are in the Page Background group of the Ribbon's Layout tab, shown in Figure 4-5:

Figure 4-5:
The Page
Background
group.

◆ **Color:** Click to display the color palette. Color formats the background layer that's furthest to the back. Refer to Book I, Chapter 7 for details about layers.

◆ **Watermark:** Above the background layer but still behind the text layer is a layer that you can use if you want to add a watermark. You can choose from two watermark types, Picture and Text. (See Figure 4-6.) The controls speak for themselves, so we don't need to elaborate.

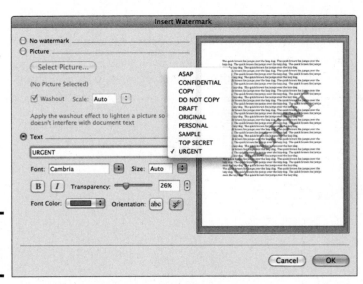

Figure 4-6:
Creating a
watermark.

✦ **Borders:** Displays the Page Border tab of the Borders and Shadings dialog, shown in Figure 4-7. This dialog is a creative person's playground for customizing borders.

- *Setting:* Choose from None, Box, Shadow, 3-D, or Custom.

- *Custom:* Use the Interactive Preview to choose which edge(s) to apply or remove a border.

- *Style:* Choose a line style for your border.

- *Color:* Choose a color for your border.

- *Width:* Specify a width for your border.

- *Art:* Choose from an enormous variety of artwork.

- *Apply To:* Choose Whole Document or a section option.

- *Options:* Displays the Border and Shading options dialog that lets you adjust margin and placement of your border.

- *Horizontal Line:* Displays an Open dialog that lets you choose a picture of a line to use as your border's line style.

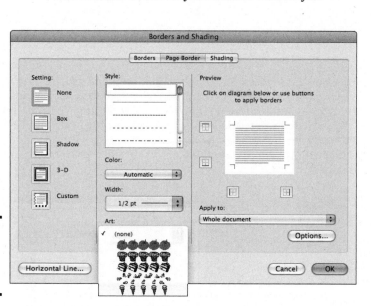

Figure 4-7:
Adding
a page
border.

Activating Gridlines

You can activate gridlines in several of Word's views to help you align objects on your page. On the Ribbon's Layout tab, go to the Grid group and click the Options button, as shown in Figure 4-8. The Options button displays a Grid Formatting dialog that lets you customize your grid display and set it as Word's default if you like.

Grid
Gridlines
Snap Objects to Others
Options
Snap Objects to Grid

Figure 4-8: Turning on the grid.

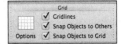

Tickling Footers and Watching Your Header

People seem to really enjoy customizing headers and footers because they're versatile and can be used to contain page numbers, dates, and logos for formal stationery. You can work with headers and footers in several of Word's views. The quick way to work with headers and footers is by way of the Header and Footer group on the Ribbon's Document Elements tab, shown in Figure 4-9.

Header and Footer
Header
Footer
Page #

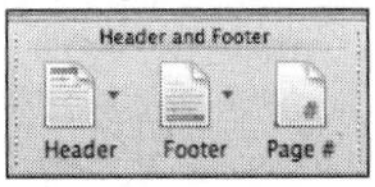

Figure 4-9: The Header and Footer group.

Clicking either the Header or Footer button displays a gallery, as shown in Figure 4-10, from which you can choose a style for your header or footer. The basic layout of three positions (left, center, and right) is the first style on the palette. Notice that some styles affect only odd-numbered or even-numbered pages. Some of the styles apply tables to the header or footer, so if you click into one of these styles, the Format Tables tab on the Ribbon will activate.

Built-In
[Text] [Text] [Text]
[Document Title]
[Date]
| Text
Basic (All Pages)
Conservative (All Pages)
Contrast (Even Page)
Company name | #
Document title
DOCUMENT TITLE
DOCUMENT TITLE
Contrast (Odd Page)
Edge (Even Page)
Edge (Odd Page)

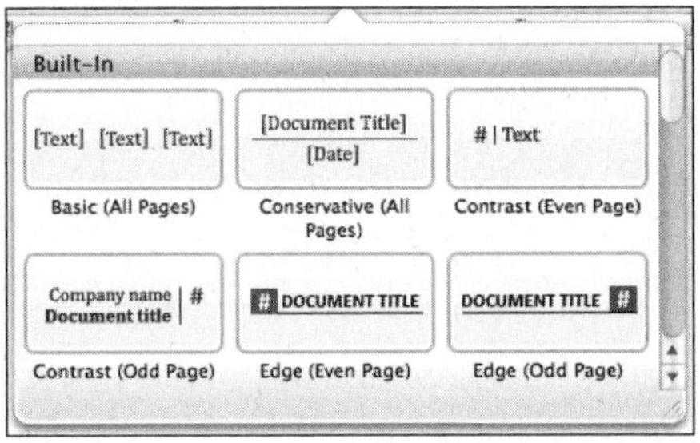

Figure 4-10: Choosing a header or footer.

When you choose a header or footer style, Word changes the interface so that you can type in your header or footer. You can display this view by choosing View⇨Header and Footer without having to choose a style from the Ribbon. To work with the interface, simply click into it and type. Click the Page # button on the Ribbon to display the Page Numbers dialog, which you can use to choose alignment and formatting options for your page numbers.

To exit Header and Footer view, choose a view from the views listed in the topmost group of the View menu, or double-click the document body. You can also click the small Close button below the Header or above the Footer area. (See Figure 4-11.)

You may want to format your Header or Footer to display Page # of #, as shown in Figure 4-11. To make this custom format starting without a Header or Footer style, do the following:

Book II
Chapter 4

Working with
Document Layout

Figure 4-11:
Making
custom
page
numbers.

1. **Choose View⇨Header and Footer from the menu bar.**

This displays the Header and Footer view.

2. **Click within either the Header or Footer area.**

Your cursor will be at the left. Press Tab once or twice to move to the center or right, if desired.

3. **Type the word** Page, **followed by a space.**

4. **Choose Insert⇨Field from the menu bar.**

The Insert Field dialog displays.

5. **Make sure that Categories is set to (All). Under Field names, choose Page and then click OK.**

You will now see the current page number in your document.

6. **Add a space and then type** of **followed by another space.**

7. **Choose Insert⇨Field from the menu bar.**

The Insert Field dialog displays a second time.

8. **Under Field Names, choose NumPages and then click OK.**

   Your document now displays the "Page # of #" phrase, as desired.

Getting around with Bookmarks

You have a lot of ways to get from one place to another in a long document. One of the best ways is to create *bookmarks,* electronic markers that you can use to identify specific places in your document. Follow these steps to create a bookmark:

1. **Click at the point in the document where you want to create a book-mark and then choose Insert⇨Bookmark.**

   The Bookmark dialog opens.

2. **In the Bookmark Name field, type a name that will make sense to you later (no spaces are allowed) and click the Add button.**

   Your bookmark is added to the list of bookmarks for that document. You can view these at any time by summoning the Bookmark dialog.

Follow these steps to go to your bookmarks:

1. **Press F5.**

   The Find and Replace dialog appears. (See Figure 4-12.)

2. **Click the Go To tab if it isn't selected already.**

3. **In the Go to What list, choose Bookmark.**

4. **Click the Enter Bookmark Name pop-up menu to choose a bookmark or type a name of a bookmark in the field if you already know it.**

5. **Click the Go To button or press Return.**

   Word takes you to the place in your document where the bookmark resides. Click the red Close button to close the Find and Replace dialog.

Figure 4-12:
Going to a
bookmark.

Writing with Style

A *style* is the way in which content is formatted, and the format is made up of a collection of attributes, for a font, paragraph, tabs, border, language, frame, numbering, shortcut key, or text effects. Styles are like fine wines: You have an almost unlimited variety, different kinds are best for different occasions, they're fun to use, and you don't have to be a connoisseur to appreciate a good one. We think that homemade styles can be the best of all.

The Ribbon helps you apply all kinds of styles including text formatting, table styles, header and footer styles, as well as others. In the following sections, we stick with styles that can be formatted using Word's Styles dialog (choose Format⇨Styles to open it), which are the same styles as displayed on the Styles palette of Word's Toolbox.

Applying slick styles

It's great that styles, one of the most powerful features in Word and Office, are so easy to work with. Styling your document is as intuitive as 1–2–3. Follow these steps to apply a style:

1. **Select some text to apply a style to.**

2. **Click the Toolbox button on the Standard toolbar to display the Toolbox if it isn't already being displayed. (See Figure 4-13.)**

3. **In the Toolbox, click the List button to reveal All Styles if they aren't visible already, or choose a style filter.**

4. **In the Pick a Style to Apply list, choose a style that you want to apply to the selected text.**

   The style is applied to your selection.

After you've applied some styles, click into the text of various portions of your document. Notice that the Styles palette tells you which particular style has been applied to that selection. The current style of selected text is kept constantly refreshed. You can see this displayed as the first thing in the Current Style of Selected Text section.

Showing style guides

Choosing Show Styles Guides in the Styles Palette (see Figure 4-13) turns on colored numbers in the left margin that are color-coordinated with the Styles palette, as shown in Figure 4-14. This makes it easy to see which styles have been applied and where they are in your document. These Style Guides then show even if you close the Toolbox. This new feature is Mac-only.

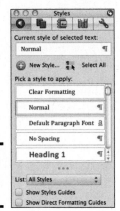

Figure 4-13:
Applying a
style.

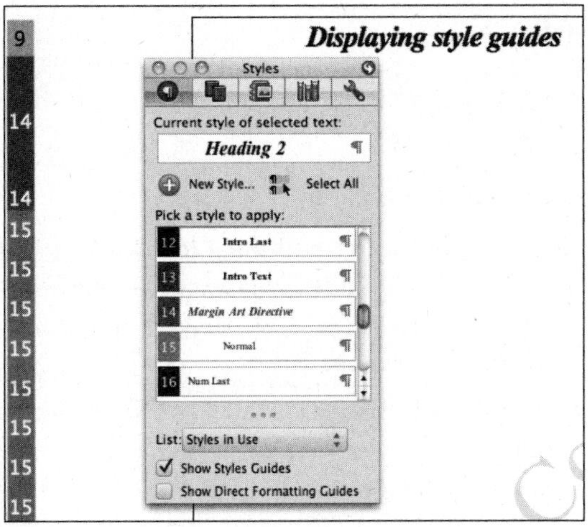

Figure 4-14:
Displaying
style guides.

Word enables you to display the style names in the left margin instead of
using numbers and colors. To do this, switch the view in the View menu to
either Draft or Outline. Take these steps to display the descriptions:

1. **Choose Word⇨Preferences.**

2. **In the Word Preferences dialog, in the Authoring and Proofing tools
group, choose View.**

3. **Below the Window section, find the option for style area width.
Enter a number or use the spinner control to enter a value greater
than zero.**

Showing Direct Formatting Guides

Sometimes you will override a style by applying formatting directly to text. For example, you may increase a font size or change a word's color. This is called *direct formatting*. Show direct formatting guides is a new, Mac-only feature that lets you highlight all instances in your document where you have applied direct formatting (such as changing text to italic) in place of a style. Choose Show Direct Formatting Guides in the Styles palette (refer to Figure 4-13) to highlight passages where the style was altered by direct formatting, shown in Figure 4-15.

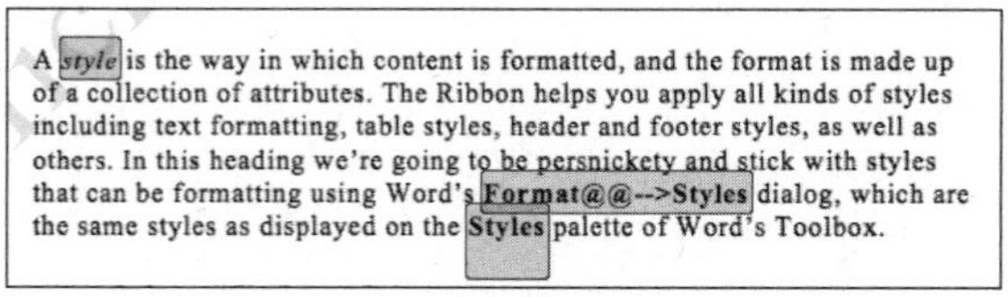

Figure 4-15: Displaying style guides.

> A *style* is the way in which content is formatted, and the format is made up of a collection of attributes. The Ribbon helps you apply all kinds of styles including text formatting, table styles, header and footer styles, as well as others. In this heading we're going to be persnickety and stick with styles that can be formatting using Word's **Format@@-->Styles** dialog, which are the same styles as displayed on the **Styles** palette of Word's Toolbox.

Book II
Chapter 4

Working with Document Layout

After you've applied some styles to your text, you can change the theme of your entire document by choosing a document theme by clicking the Ribbon's Home Tab. In the Themes group, click the Themes button to display the gallery of themes. While you apply different document themes, watch the styles you applied in your document instantly adopt the new theme colors and fonts. Notice that the Toolbox's Style palette also updates to match the document theme you apply.

Creating a new style from formatted text

The real power of styles comes from creating your own. Word has a fast and easy way to save a new style. Say you spent some time formatting text just the way you want it and you want to save that format as a style so you can use it again in this document or another document. Here's what you do:

1. **Select the formatted text.**

2. **In the Styles Palette of the Toolbox, click the New Style button.**

   This button is oversized, green, and has a plus sign so you can't miss it!

   The New Style dialog opens, as shown in Figure 4-16. The formatted attributes of your selection are displayed in this dialog.

3. **Below Properties, in the Name field, type a name for your style and then select the Add to Template check box.**

   If you leave this option deselected, your style is saved only with the current document. If you select the check box, the changes are saved to Word's `Normal.dotm` template so that it's available from now on in all documents.

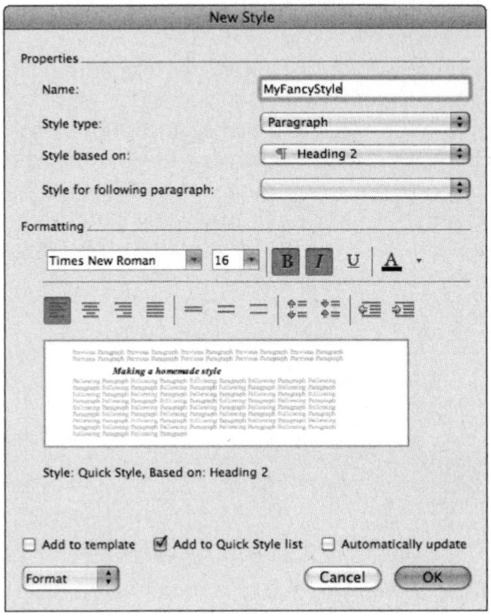

Figure 4-16:
Making a
new style.

4. Click OK.

Your new style appears in the Styles Palette of the Toolbox in the Pick Style to Apply section. If it doesn't, you probably need to choose In Current Document or All Styles in the List filter at the bottom of the Styles toolbox, or scroll up or down in the list of styles.

Creating new styles from scratch

The Style dialog allows you to create new styles, modify existing styles, delete styles, and organize styles. To create new styles from scratch or from existing styles, follow these steps:

1. Choose Format⇨Style from the menu bar.

The Style dialog opens. Here you see a list of the styles you already have.

2. Click the New button.

The New Style dialog opens. (See Figure 4-16.)

When you open the New Style dialog, you can create styles from one of four style types in the Style Type pop-up menu:

+ **Paragraph:** Affects entire paragraphs. These are the most commonly used styles.

+ **Character:** Affects any character attribute, such as font, size, and italics.

+ **Table:** Creates new styles for tables.

+ **List:** Creates styles for bulleted or numbered lists.

Notice as you change style types in the New Style dialog's Style Type pop-up menu, the other options in the New Style dialog change as well. Click the Format pop-up menu in the lower-left corner of the New Style dialog, as shown in Figure 4-16, to find specialized formatting tools. Here's a list of formatting customizations that you can save with a style:

**Book II
Chapter 4**

**Working with
Document Layout**

+ **Font Formatting:** Displays the Font dialog.

+ **Paragraph Formatting:** Displays the Paragraph dialog.

+ **Tabs:** Displays the Tabs dialog.

+ **Border:** Displays the Borders and Shadings dialog.

+ **Language:** Displays the Language dialog.

+ **Frame:** Displays the Frame dialog.

+ **Numbering:** Displays the Bullets and Numbering dialog.

+ **Shortcut Key:** Displays the Customize Keyboard dialog.

+ **Text Effects:** Displays the Text Effects dialog.

Selecting Add to Template saves your style in Word's `Normal.dotm` template (the default template used when Word opens). If you save a style in `Normal.dotm`, your new style will be available to all documents from then on. Selecting Add to Quick Style List adds your style to the Styles gallery on the Home tab of the Ribbon. If you select Automatically Update, Word automatically refreshes the style to include any formatting changes you make to objects that were formatting with this style.

Using Organizer

Organizer is an amazing Mac-only tool that can copy the following things from one template to another or from a document to another template:

+ **Styles,** covered in the previous sections

+ **AutoText,** which we cover in Chapter 6 in this minibook

✦ **Toolbars,** which we cover in Book I, Chapter 2

✦ **Macro Project items,** such as modules and UserForms from one Visual Basic for Applications Project to another, covered in Book I, Chapter 12

You can also use Organizer to rename or delete the preceding items, but copying styles seems to be the most common use for Organizer.

Opening Organizer

Use the Styles dialog to fire up Organizer. Follow these steps:

1. **Choose Format⇨Style from the menu bar.**

The Style dialog opens.

2. **Click the Organizer button.**

The Organizer dialog, as shown in Figure 4-17, opens. You can now copy styles from one template to another as detailed in the next section.

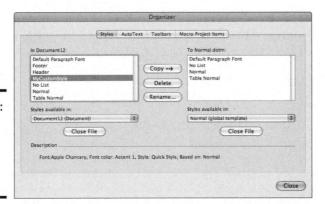

Figure 4-17: Copying styles with the Organizer dialog.

Copying styles, AutoText, toolbars, and VBA items

Organizer is quite simple. In Figure 4-17, Document 12 has a custom style that we want to copy to our `Normal.dotm` (also called the *global template*) file so we can use it whenever we open a new, blank Word document.

Here's how to copy from one document or template to another template:

1. **On either the left or right side of Organizer, select an open document or template from the Styles Available In pop-up menu.**

The Styles Available In pop-up menu changes to AutoText, Toolbars, or Macro Project Available In as appropriate for the tab you chose at the top of the dialog.

2. **On the opposite side, select a different document or template from the Styles Available In pop-up menu.**

3. **On either side, select something (style, AutoText, toolbar, or VBA item) to copy to the other document or template.**

   The Copy button arrow will always point to the document that will be copied to.

4. **Click the Copy button to copy your selection to the destination.**

   The item list of the destination document or template will automatically update to show that the item was added.

Word's `Normal.dotm` template determines all formatting aspects when opening new, blank Word documents. Styles, AutoText, and toolbars saved in `Normal.dotm` are always available to you in Word. In Organizer, the `Normal.dotm` template is referred to as Normal (global template).

Even though Word for Windows doesn't have the Organizer feature, the documents templates you make on your Mac using Organizer should work just fine in Word for Windows.

AutoText copy works only between two Word templates (`.dotm` or `.dotx`). AutoText can't be copied to or from regular Word documents. Of course, you can use Save As to turn an ordinary Word document into a template and then copy the AutoText.

If you're into using VBA to automate processes, you can get a code sample of the Organizer tool by turning on the macro recorder and then copying something from one document or template to another.

Renaming or deleting Organizer items

In addition to copying, you can select an item from either side of Organizer and then click either of the following (refer to Figure 4-17):

+ **Delete:** Deletes the selected item from either side of Organizer.

+ **Rename:** Causes a small window to open that lets you type a new name for the selected item, which can be on either side of Organizer.

AutoFormat as You Type

By default, most of Word's AutoFormat options are turned on. These options control many of Word's automatic features such as headings and bulleted or numbered lists. You can get at the list of AutoFormat options by taking these two steps:

1. **From Word's Tools menu, choose AutoCorrect.**

The AutoCorrect preferences dialog opens.

2. **Click the AutoFormat as you Type button at the top of the dialog.**

The AutoCorrect options appropriate for automatic formatting display, as shown in Figure 4-18.

The preferences shown in Figure 4-18 are options with check boxes that you can turn on and off at will. Most people probably don't need to adjust these, but if Word is automatically formatting something as you type and you don't want it to, this is the place to look first to look to see whether you need to turn off a setting. Moving the mouse cursor over the items updates the description. Click OK to tell Word to use your new preference settings or click Cancel to leave without making changes.

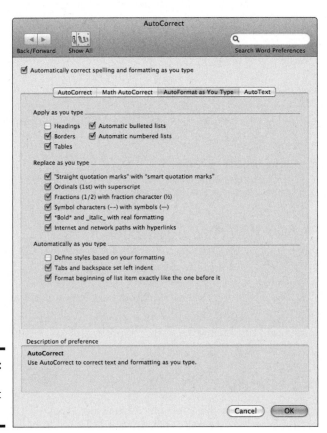

Figure 4-18:
Displaying
AutoFormat
options.

Automatically Numbering Lines

Word can automatically number the lines in your documents. This can be handy when referring to specific places within a document without having to use bookmarks, which we discuss earlier in this chapter. To add or remove line numbers, your document must be in Print Layout view. You can turn on line numbers for an entire document or selected portions of a document. Here's how:

1. **Select a portion, section, or several sections of a document.**

If you want to number an entire document, skip this step.

2. **Choose Format⇨Document from the menu bar.**

The Document dialog opens.

3. **Click the Layout tab.**

4. **Click the Line Numbers button.**

The Line Numbers options appear. See Figure 4-19.

5. **Click the Add Line Numbering check box to activate the line-numbering options.**

Choose options as desired.

6. **Click OK twice to return to your Word document.**

To remove line numbers, repeat these steps, but in Step 5, deselect the Add Line Numbering check box.

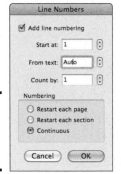

Figure 4-19:
Turning
on line
numbering.

You can control the following settings as you like:

- ✦ **Start At:** Sets the number of the first line.
- ✦ **From Text:** Sets the distance of the line numbers from the text.
- ✦ **Count By:** Skips the display of line numbers by however many you choose. If you count by two, only the numbers next to every other line appear.
- ✦ **Numbering:** You get three options. The Continuous option means the numbering won't restart at page or section breaks and will be continuous throughout the entire document or selection.

Chapter 5: Collaborating on and Proofing Documents

In This Chapter

✔ Sharing and tracking changes

✔ Coauthoring in real time

✔ Cleaning your edited document

✔ Casting spells and checks

✔ Working with dictionaries

✔ Choosing your language

✔ Taming the grammar checker

Sharing documents and reviewing them is an everyday activity in all kinds of companies and organizations, from businesses to universities to governments to churches. Sometimes you receive a document you're expected to contribute to, and other times you create a document that others need to add to and comment on. At times, multiple users are working on the same document, or maybe just one additional person is helping to edit a document. Whatever the situation may be, Word has you covered on all fronts.

Word's new, live coauthoring capability lets you edit your Word document with coauthors in real time, so you no longer have to do a round robin. People can work on a document simultaneously in a meeting or across the globe!

After you've pulled a document together (perhaps by collaborating with a coauthor), you need to make sure the words are spelled properly and your sentences are grammatically correct. Word has some nifty automatic spelling, grammar, and AutoCorrect features to help you proofread your document before you call it finished.

Keeping Track of Changes

So you find yourself on a committee at work and you have to prepare a report about something substantial. Everyone on the committee is supposed to contribute to the report, but nobody has time to meet. The solution could be a shared document. You decide to start with a Report template from the Word Document Gallery (choose File⇨New from Template), customize it for your committee, and then type your portion of the report. When sharing, the Review tab on the Ribbon and the new, live file sharing option are two features you will come to rely upon, along with your SkyDrive or SharePoint cloud services. (See Book I, Chapter 4)

Setting up Track Changes

Collaboration is where the Word Track Changes feature comes into play. Word can keep track of the changes made, who made them, and when the changes were made. But — and you knew there was a *but* — these changes aren't tracked until you turn on the Track Changes feature; then you can send the document to your committee members, and their changes are tracked. After the members have made changes and added comments, they return the modified document to you. With this nifty feature, you can see who made which change!

Before you turn on track changes and start sharing your document with everybody, all sharing participants must check their Word preferences to make sure that their names are known to Word. Check your own Word preferences to make sure your own information is accurate. Here's how:

1. **Choose Word⇨Preferences from the menu bar.**

The Preferences dialog opens.

2. **In the Personal Settings section, choose User Information.**

The User Information preferences pane is displayed. (See Figure 5-1.)

3. **At the top of the pane, verify that the First, Last, and Initials show your actual name.**

Fill in this information and make corrections as needed. No other fields in User Information need to be adjusted in order to use track changes.

4. **Click OK to save your changes and close the pane.**

Sometimes IT departments clone Office installations, and everyone winds up with the same name or no name at all. Word can't detect different users if two or more people have the same name in the User Information preferences.

So how do you turn on the Track Changes feature for a document? Click the Ribbon's Review tab, find the Tracking group. Click the Track Changes button, shown in the left margin to toggle tracking on or off.

Here's a second way to activate track changes:

1. **Choose Tools⇨Track Changes⇨Highlight Changes.**

This brings up the Highlight Changes dialog. See Figure 5-2.

Figure 5-1:
Make
sure the
username is
correct.

2. **Make sure the last three check boxes are selected, as shown in Figure 5-2.**

   You may prefer to check all four check boxes.

3. **Click OK.**

   Word returns you to your document and starts tracking changes.

Figure 5-2:
Activating
Highlight
Changes.

That's all there is to it. When you're ready to distribute your document, you can go to the Review tab and find the Share group to send your document as an e-mail attachment or via Microsoft Messenger, or choose File⇨Share and save to SkyDrive or SharePoint. This is a good time to choose Flag for Follow Up on Word's Tools menu to set a reminder to make sure the document actually does get worked on. For more about calendar, task, and reminder features of Office 2011, see Book V, Chapters 6 and 7.

After you receive a document with other people's changes in it, you can either accept or reject those changes — more on this in the section "Accepting and rejecting changes," later in this chapter.

Track Changes

You can fine-tune the Track Changes preferences, although the default settings are fine for most purposes. To access Track Changes preferences, choose Word⇨Preferences⇨Track Changes. In the Track Changes preference pane (shown in Figure 5-3), you can change the color of each author's changes, and you can set how changes are highlighted. In fact, you can make a lot of adjustments to the way track changes displays changes and comments in Word's interface. We show you the preference pane here, but we think you should bother with these settings only if you're using track changes every day (maybe you're a copy editor at a large publishing house) and you have time to experiment with various setting combinations.

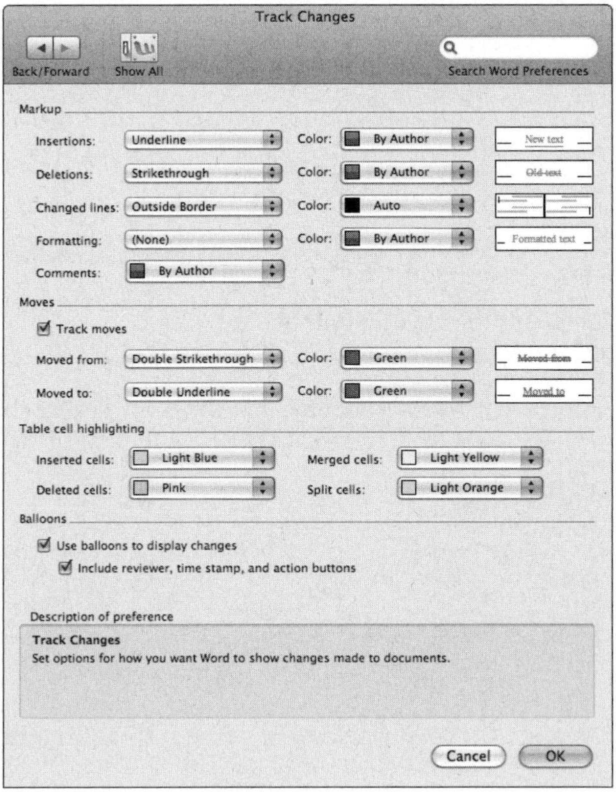

Figure 5-3:
Adjusting
Track
Changes
preferences.

If you do want to experiment (refer to Figure 5-3), click the pop-up menus for nearly endless combinations of settings. When you move the mouse cursor over preference controls, you see a description for each option.

In addition to tracking changes, the Track Changes feature also keeps track of comments for all reviewers. Any reviewer can click the New button in the Review tab's Comments group to add comments to the document.

Merging changed versions into the original

Picture this: You've sent out your document to two committee members, and they've made changes and returned the document to you. Now you have three copies of the same document — the original one plus two returned documents that contain changes. You want to consolidate all the changes into the original document. In a folder that you can find easily, save the returned documents with new filenames, perhaps named after the person who worked on the revisions, so you can tell the returned files apart from each other and the original.

After you save your changed documents under new filenames, you're ready to merge the changed documents into the original so that you can have a single document in which to work. See Chapter 2 of this minibook for instructions.

Accepting and rejecting changes

When you're ready, you can go through the changes that people made to the document and work toward creating a final document.

Keep in mind that although text changes and comments are tracked, not every change made to a document is tracked. For instance, changes made to SmartArt objects aren't tracked.

As years have passed, Microsoft has attempted to make the ideal interface to accomplish accepting and rejecting changes. Each attempt, though, has plusses and minuses. One interface works better on a large screen; another works better when there are few comments; yet another when there are a lot of comments.

Our advice is to start with balloons because they're so visible. If you find these balloons hard to read, too crowded, or clumsy to work with, try using one of the other methods, such as using the Reviewing sidebar or the Accept and Review Changes dialog that we discuss shortly. You can turn the balloons on or off in the Track Changes preferences pane. (Refer to Figure 5-3.)

The Reviewing pane is an alternative to balloons for viewing changes. The Reviewing pane shows up as a pane to the left of your Word interface. Toggle the Reviewing pane on and off by one of these methods:

✦ Choose View⇨Sidebar⇨Reviewing Pane.

✦ Choose the Sidebar button on the Standard Toolbar, and then choose Reviewing Pane.

✦ Click the Review Pane button in the Changes group of the Review tab.

**Book II
Chapter 5**

**Collaborating
on and Proofing
Documents**

We show the Reviewing pane, the Review tab, and Balloons in a single screen shot in Figure 5-4. You would normally display either Balloons or the Reviewing pane, unless you have a really big screen.

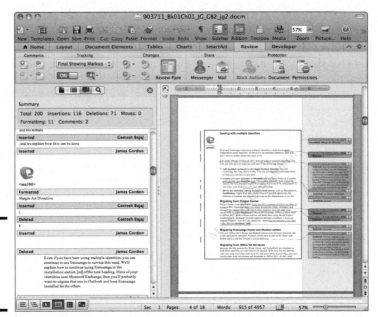

Figure 5-4:
The
Reviewing
pane and
Balloons.

The Changes group of the Review tab (see Figure 5-4) has every control needed to manage tracking changes. The buttons in the Comments group allow you to move from change to change within the document as well as buttons to accept or reject changes.

 On each change balloon, you can click either the checkmark to accept a change or the X to reject the change, as shown in the margin.

When working in the Reviewing pane, right-click a change and choose to accept or reject the change from the pop-up menu.

An alternative to both balloons and the Ribbon's Review tab is the now-discontinued Accept or Reject Changes dialog. If you really liked it, you can still use it by way of a VBA macro (see Book I, Chapter 12):

```
Sub OldTrackChangesDialog()
Dialogs(wdDialogToolsAcceptRejectChanges).Show
End Sub
```

Finishing up

While you work on a document with track changes, Word internally keeps a history of these changes and allows you to see them via the Review tab of the Ribbon. In the Tracking group (see Figure 5-4), choose from the following views:

✦ **Original:** This view shows what the document looked like before any changes. Switching to this view shows the original document, but the tracked changes remain in the document, hidden from view. This view is what your document will look like if you choose to reject all changes.

✦ **Original Showing Markup:** This view shows the original text and formatting changes, and it displays deleted text inline.

✦ **Final:** This view shows how the document would look if you were to accept all changes. Deleted text isn't displayed. Switching to this view hides original text that was changed or deleted by reviewers, but it's still retained within the document.

✦ **Final Showing Markup:** Shows inserted text and formatting changes. Deleted text appears in balloons.

After you have your document with everybody's changes, clean up the text by accepting or rejecting those changes. Start at the beginning of your document and work your way to the end with balloons, the Reviewing pane, or the Changes group on the Review tab. Decide whether to accept or reject each and every change in the document. When you accept or reject revision marks, the revision marks are removed. In the end, your final document has no revision marks at all.

After you finish going through the document accepting and rejecting changes, follow these steps to properly prepare a document for final delivery:

1. **Start with your document closed. In Finder, right-click or Control-click the file's icon; then choose Duplicate from the pop-up menu.**

A copy of your document containing revisions is made. You now have a copy of the document in case you want to refer to the revisions later.

2. **Open the document containing tracked changes in Word.**

3. **On the Review tab, in the Tracking group, change the Final Showing Markup pop-up menu to Final.**

This is how your document will look if you complete the next step. Look through the document and make sure everything looks right. If everything is okay, proceed to Step 4.

4. **On the Review tab of the Ribbon, in the Changes group, click the small triangle on the Accept button. From the pop-up menu, choose Accept All Changes in Document.**

When you accept all changes, your changed text replaces the original text, and deleted text is removed from the document. This is important because unless you take this step, tracked changes will remain in the document and be read by anyone who has the document.

(Optional) You can reject all changes, which would restore the document to its original state before any changes were made. To reject all changes, use the Reject button triangle's pop-up menu.

5. **Delete all comments in your document by finding the Comments group on the Review Ribbon and clicking the small triangle on the Delete button and choosing Delete All Comments in Document. (See Figure 5-5.)**

Figure 5-5:
Deleting all comments from your document.

6. **Choose Word⇨Preferences from the menu bar.**

The Preferences pane appears.

7. **Choose Security.**

The Security preferences pane appears.

8. **Select the Remove Personal Information from This File on Save check box.**

9. **Select the Warn before Printing, Saving, or Sending a File That Contains Tracked Changes check box.**

10. **Click the Save button on Word's Standard toolbar.**

Your document is now safe for distribution. If you receive a warning that track changes are in the file, you didn't accept or reject all the revisions. Cancel the save; then repeat the steps beginning with Step 4.

Occasionally people forget to remove comments and edits, which can cause much embarrassment and even legal liability. Always make sure you have all the edits resolved by searching for track changes one last time to finalize your document.

Coauthoring Simultaneously

Word 2011 brings a new wrinkle to collaborating with others. SkyDrive or SharePoint enables you to use the expansive capabilities of Microsoft Word while collaborating on a document online and in real time.

Coauthoring requirements

You can coauthor a document that was saved in Microsoft Word (.docx) format with a collaborator who has Word 2011 for Mac or Word 2010 for Windows. No other versions of Word support coauthoring.

The document to be coauthored must be saved on a SkyDrive account (free and open to the public) or Microsoft SharePoint 2010, which is installed on a private network (typically used in large corporations). The SharePoint option is limited to Microsoft Office for Mac Home and Business 2011, Microsoft Office for Mac Academic 2011, and Microsoft Office for Mac Standard 2011. Book I, Chapter 2 explains how to put your document into SkyDrive or SharePoint 2010. All collaborators must have permission to read and write files to the SkyDrive or SharePoint 2010 folder in which the Word document is located.

Start sharing

Each collaborator opens the Word document that has been stored on the SkyDrive or SharePoint as described in the following sections.

Opening a Word document stored on SkyDrive

Each collaborator opens the Word document file using a Web browser. Safari, Firefox, and Internet Explorer are supported. The collaborator opens the URL of the stored document. The URL of the stored Word document can be sent to collaborators directly from SkyDrive by choosing Share⇨Send a Link, as shown in Figure 5-6.

Figure 5-6:
Sending the shared document's link.

Book II Chapter 5

Collaborating on and Proofing Documents

If a collaborator uses different methods to open the file to be shared on SkyDrive, other collaborators may not be allowed to open the file and will receive a message saying that the file is locked for editing.

After a collaborator opens the Word document in the Web browser, the collaborator chooses the Open in Word option. After clicking OK to a message explaining that your computer needs to have a compatible Office program, the Word document will open in Microsoft Word 2011 (on a Mac) or Microsoft Word 2010 (on a PC). The download process can take a while, even with a fast Internet connection. After your Word document has finished downloading, you're ready to start editing.

Opening a document stored on a SharePoint server

Collaborators will need to know the URL of the file to be shared. This can be obtained by navigating to the stored Word document using a Web browser.

Each collaborator does the following to start the sharing session:

1. **Copy the URL of the file on the SharePoint Server.**

2. **In Word, choose File⇨Open URL.**

    An Open URL field displays.

3. **Paste the URL of the Word file and then click OK.**

    The document opens and you are ready to edit in Normal View.

After you've opened a document from the server, you can quickly open it again by choosing it in the recently used file list on the File menu or in the recent documents list in the Word Document Gallery.

Editing together

Working together, collaborators can be fairly independent, or they can be in constant communication with each other via Messenger, Communicator, iChat, or even an old-fashioned telephone. Microsoft Word behaves normally, and its interface is as responsive as it is when not coauthoring. You can switch views and change the content. Work with media, charts, tables, and Word fields. You can even work with masters in Publishing Layout View.

Detecting coauthors

While collaborating, the status bar at the bottom of the window indicates how many people are collaborating and whether any collaborators have saved updates (changes) to the server, as shown in Figure 5-7. Clicking the coauthor's button displays a list of coauthors. Clicking the name of a coauthor displays the Presence Indicator for that author.

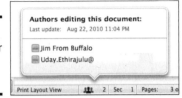

Figure 5-7:
Checking for
authors and
updates.

When a new coauthor joins the collaboration, his or her name flashes briefly at the author's button, and the number of authors changes in the author's button.

Editing

When a coauthor starts editing, an indicator displays to the left of the paragraph that is currently being edited. Figure 5-8 is a screen shot showing how Word puts dotted lines to the left of a paragraph you are editing.

Figure 5-8:
Word marks
your own
edits.

> This paragraph is being authored in Word 2011 for Mac.
>
> The dotted lines let you know
> that you are in control of this paragraph
>
> The quick brown fox jumps over the lazy dog. The quick brown fox jur
> brown fox jumps over the lazy dog. The quick brown fox jumps over th
> jumps over the lazy dog.
>
> *This paragraph is being edited in Word 2010 for Windows.*

When one of your coauthors makes a change, Word displays the name of the coauthor in the left margin and puts a bracket along the left side of the paragraph that was changed, as shown in Figure 5-9. Click the coauthor's name to display the Presence Indicator for that author. When you see a coauthor's name and a bracket, you know that updates are available.

Figure 5-9:
Discovering
a change
was made.

Another way Word indicates that updates are available is by displaying a double-arrow indicator to the left of a paragraph, as shown in Figure 5-10. Holding the mouse over the indicator displays a ScreenTip.

Figure 5-10:
Updates are available.

Any collaborator can block other authors from making changes to parts of the document being coauthored. To block or unblock paragraphs, do the following:

1. **Select the paragraph or paragraphs for which you want to disallow editing by other authors.**

2. **Choose on the Ribbon's Review tab, go to the Protection group, and click Block Authors. (See Figure 5-11.)**

   a. *To block authors, choose Block Authors from the pop-up menu.*

   b. *To unblock areas that you previously protected, choose Unblock All My Blocked Areas from the pop-up menu.*

3. **Save the document.**

Figure 5-11:
Blocking and unblocking authors.

Paragraphs that have been blocked for editing display a bracket with a small "no" symbol. A symbol by itself indicates a paragraph that you have blocked for other authors, as shown in the margin, but you can edit within the paragraph. The symbol displayed with a coauthor's name and a slightly darker bracket indicates a paragraph that you can't edit because the coauthor has blocked editing. The Block Authors feature is independent from the Protect Form feature discussed in Chapter 8 of this minibook.

Synchronizing

When any coauthor is ready to share their changes, Word's Save feature activates the synchronization process. Any coauthor can send changes to the server and at the same time incorporate other coauthor changes by using Save (not Save As) by doing one of the following:

✦ **Click the Save button on the Standard toolbar.**

The Save button has little arrows on it while in coauthoring mode, as shown in the margin.

✦ **Press ⌘-S.**

✦ **Click the Updates Available button** located in the status bar at the bottom of the document window.

Every time you synchronize a document that was changed by a coauthor, Word displays a dialog explaining that changes made by another author were incorporated into the server copy of the Word document. By all means, click the check box in the dialog so you don't have to see it every time!

It's entirely possible that two or more coauthors may modify the same paragraph if Block Authors was not used. This is not a problem because when you save and synchronize, Word notices any conflicts and offers to help you resolve them. Word has an orderly process to help you resolve conflicts in Print Layout view:

1. When Word detects a conflict, it displays a yellow band at the top of the document to alert you, as shown in Figure 5-12. Click the Resolve Conflicts button. If for some reason you don't want to resolve the conflicts, click the X button at the left end to postpone resolving.

Figure 5-12:
Resolving
conflicts
Step 1.

2. When you click Resolve Conflicts in Step 1, Word enters Conflict Mode with a special Conflict tab and interface, as shown in Figure 5-13. The conflicts will be listed in a pane at the left. The changes made by coauthors are highlighted in light green. Your changes are underlined, and the font turns purple.

3. Click a conflict in the Your Conflicting Changes list. The corresponding text or object is selected in the document area to the right. Text is highlighted in a shade of red, as shown in Figure 5-13 with the label Choosing a Conflicting Change. Choose one of the following options:

- *Accept My Change:* Your change is kept and the coauthor's change is discarded. The next change in the list is automatically selected.

- *Reject My Change:* The coauthor's change is kept, and your change is discarded. The next change in the list is automatically selected.

- *Previous:* Select the previous (higher in the list of conflicting changes pane) change without accepting or rejecting the change.

- *Next:* Select the next (lower in the list of conflicting changes pane) change without accepting or rejecting the change.

While working in Conflict Mode, you can insert and review comments in a similar fashion, which is described earlier in this chapter.

Figure 5-13:
Resolving
conflicts
Steps 2
and 3.

4. When all conflicts have been either accepted or rejected, Word automatically displays a message bar (see Figure 5-14) alerting you that no conflicts remain and offering to Save and Close View, which refreshes the server copy of the Word document and alerts your coauthors that an update is available to them.

Figure 5-14:
Step 4: Save
and close.

While resolving conflicts, you can abort the process at any time by clicking the End Conflict Mode button, shown in Figure 5-13. The conflicts message bar may display again to allow you to resume resolving conflicts.

As with the Track Changes feature, not every kind of change is flagged as a conflict. Conflicting changes to a picture's format by multiple authors, for example, will not trigger Conflict Resolution mode. In these cases, the most recently saved version is applied to the copy on the server.

Resolving connection problems

If a coauthoring session terminates abnormally, perhaps due to a network problem or you quit Word before the Save synchronization has completed, Word has you covered. A small application called Upload Center runs in the background, but it shows itself if there's a problem. (See Figure 5-15.) Upload Center gives you an opportunity to try saving to the server again or to cancel the attempt to synchronize your changes.

Figure 5-15:
Taking
care of
interruptions.

Casting a Spell Check

> *Eye strike a key and type a word*
> *And weight four it two say*
> *Weather eye am wrong oar write*
> *It shows me strait a weigh.*
> — Sauce unknown

One of the miracles of Microsoft Office is spell check. By now, most everyone who has ever used a word processor or typed an e-mail knows that a red, squiggly underline means you might have a spelling error. The concept is simple, yet extremely effective. When you finish typing a word, Office compares your spelling to a list of known words in the Word spelling dictionary. If what you typed isn't in the list, Office puts a red squiggle under your word. In Word, when you finish typing a sentence, that sentence is compared to grammar rules. If you violate a rule, Word puts a green squiggle under your sentence.

Knowing how to spell is still important!

Yes, we text message. We know that language is evolving, and our technologies are shaping it. But remember: Phonetic spellings and abbreviations are fine for text messages, but that's it. Sorry. It still pays off big time to know words and their proper spellings and meanings, including nuances and context.

Consider this small example:

They are so deer.

Word shows no red or green squiggles, but you probably wanted to say

They are so dear.

As you can see, no computer substitute exists for knowing proper spelling and word usage.

Running a spelling and grammar check

Instead of looking through your document to find all the squiggles, Word can check all spelling and grammar for you in a single pass.

If you haven't already, get in the habit of running a spell check before you finish a document. You may have missed something.

To activate spell checking, do either of the following:

✦ Choose Tools⇨Spelling and Grammar.

✦ Use the keyboard shortcut ⌘-Option-L.

Spell checker runs, and if it doesn't find errors, it gives you a clean bill of health. Yay! But more often than not, spell check reminds you that you're fallible. When that happens, the Spelling and Grammar dialog opens, highlights a word or portion of a sentence in the document, and offers several choices for correcting the perceived problem. (See Figure 5-16.) Most of the time the correct spelling is highlighted under Suggestions, and all you have to do is click the Change button to fix the spelling and continue to the next misspelled word.

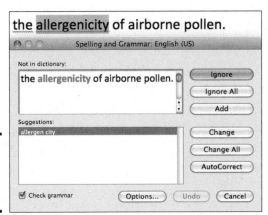

Figure 5-16: Fixing spelling and grammar.

But wait a minute! You're pretty darn sure that *allergenicity* is spelled correctly in Figure 5-16, but the spell checker says it's not. You look through the list of suggested spellings. You definitely don't want to replace *allergenicity* with *allergen city.* If this were the only time you used *allergenicity,* you'd click the Ignore button and be on your way. If you used *allergenicity* a lot in this document but don't think you'll ever use the word again, you could click the Ignore All button so that *allergenicity* doesn't get flagged again within this open document.

For this example, what you really want to do is add *allergenicity* to the custom dictionary so that Word knows from now on how to correctly spell it. After all, you might use this word often in your documents. To teach Word a new word, all you have to do is click the Add button.

If Word displays a spelling suggestion that you like, select it. Click the Change button, and Word fixes the mistake and goes on to the next one.

If you want Word to automatically correct your misspelling to a suggested spelling from now on, select the correct spelling from the suggestion list and then click the AutoCorrect button.

Adding a custom dictionary

Word lets you create, edit, and add new dictionaries to its collection of dictionaries. Perhaps your discipline, science, or profession uses a lot of specialized terms not found in the Word default dictionary, or maybe you need to add a dictionary for a language not supplied with Office.

A *dictionary* is simply a list of words with a paragraph mark after each word (created by pressing Return or Enter) in which the words are saved as a file with a .dic extension. Dictionary files aren't different for Mac or Windows, but beginning with Word 2011, Word on the Mac may demand dictionaries that were saved a special way (we tell you how to do this just ahead) in order to support UniCode fonts.

You can find custom dictionaries and foreign language dictionaries on the Internet by searching for them, and many are free. To add a custom dictionary file, take these steps:

1. **Choose Word⇨Preferences from the menu bar.**

   The Preferences pane displays.

2. **In the Authoring and Proofing Tools section, choose Spelling and Grammar.**

   The Spelling and Grammar preferences pane opens.

3. **In the Spelling section, click the Dictionaries button.**

   The Custom Dictionaries dialog opens.

4. **Click the Add Button.**

   A special Add Dictionary dialog opens.

5. **Navigate to the `.dic` dictionary file and select it.**

   If the `.dic` file you want to use is grayed out, switch the Enable pop-up menu to All Files.

6. **Click Open.**

   Your custom dictionary appears with a check box that's selected in the Custom Dictionaries dialog.

7. **Click OK to close the Custom Dictionaries dialog and then click OK to close the Spelling and Grammar preferences pane.**

   Your new dictionary is now available to Word, Excel, and PowerPoint. Outlook uses the Mac OS X dictionary.

Editing a custom dictionary

Because dictionaries are simply text files, you can open them in Word, add and remove words, and save them again. If you ever accidentally add a misspelling to a custom dictionary or if you want to add or remove words, follow these steps:

1. **In Word, choose File⇨Open.**

2. **Select All Files from the Enable pop-up menu.**

3. **Choose the `.dic` file you want to use and click Open.**

   A list of words appears in the Word document.

 4. **Click the Show button on Word's Standard toolbar to toggle on the ability to see paragraph marks if they aren't showing already.**

5. **Add or remove words from the list:**

   • Type a new word to add to the list. Press Return or Enter after each new entry to add a single paragraph mark after the new word.

   • Delete misspelled or unwanted words (and their associated paragraph marks) from the list.

   Each word in the list must be followed by a single paragraph mark.

6. **Click the Save button on Word's Standard toolbar to save your changes; then click the Close button to close the document.**

Making a new custom dictionary

If you found a list of words, or you don't mind typing your own list, you can start from scratch with an empty dictionary, and then add your list to it using the steps to edit a dictionary from the previous section. Here's how to make a new, blank custom dictionary:

1. **Choose Word⇨Preferences from the menu bar.**

    The Preferences pane displays.

2. **In the Authoring and Proofing Tools section, choose Spelling and Grammar.**

    The Spelling and Grammar preferences pane opens.

3. **In the Spelling section, click the Dictionaries button.**

    The Custom Dictionaries dialog opens.

4. **Click the New Button.**

    A file Save dialog opens. Give your dictionary a name and then save it. Your custom dictionary appears with a check box that's selected in the Custom Dictionaries dialog.

5. **Click OK to close the Custom Dictionaries dialog and then click OK to close the Spelling and Grammar preferences pane.**

    Your new, empty dictionary is now available to all Office applications. Follow the steps in the previous section, "Editing a custom dictionary," to populate your new dictionary.

Setting a new default language for proofing

Word comes with many different language dictionaries. The default dictionary determines which language's proofing tools Word uses for spelling and grammar. You can change Word's default language dictionary:

1. **Choose Tools⇨Language.**

    The Language dialog opens. You see a list of languages, as shown in Figure 5-17.

2. **Select the new language to use and click the Default button.**

    A dialog appears asking whether you're sure you want the change, and notifying you that your change will be saved in the Normal.dotm template.

3. **Click Yes to change Word's default spelling and grammar checking language to the language you selected.**

4. **Click OK to close the Language dialog.**

   The language dictionary you selected is now Word's default language for spelling and grammar.

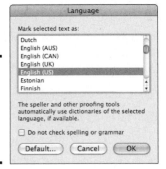

Figure 5-17:
Changing
the Spelling
and
Grammar
language.

Using a different language for proofing a selection

There may come a time where you want to use a different language for only a portion of your document. You can also use the Language feature (refer to Figure 5-17) to change the language of just the selected text:

1. **Select a word or passage in the text.**

2. **Choose Tools⇨Language from the menu bar.**

   The Language dialog opens.

3. **Select a language to use.**

4. **Click OK to close the Language dialog.**

5. **Choose Tools⇨Spelling and Grammar.**

   The selection will have a different spelling and grammar language applied to them and will be checked against the proofing tools for the language selected using the Language dialog. The rest of the document will be checked against Word's default spelling and grammar language.

Just for fun, we selected a few words in an English sentence and set spelling and grammar to French for these words with the Language dialog. As expected, the spell checker encountered many misspelled words. *Note:* The language being used for a passage is always shown in the title bar of the Spelling and Grammar dialog, as shown earlier in Figure 5-16.

Enabling Japanese for proofing

Japanese is a special case. Before you can use Japanese to check spelling and grammar, you must enable Japanese. To enable Japanese language features in the English version of Office, do the following:

1. **In Finder, in the Applications folder open the Microsoft Office 2011 folder. In the Additional Tools folder locate Microsoft Language Register.**

2. **Double-click the Microsoft Language Register application.**

   The Microsoft Register application opens.

3. **Switch the pop-up menu from English to Japanese and click OK to enable Japanese and close the Microsoft Register application.**

Making these modifications to the Language setting doesn't change the language that's used for the Office interface. If you want the entire Office interface to be in a particular language, you have to purchase and install an Office version that's customized for the particular language you want to use.

Choosing a writing style

Word has writing styles in the Spelling and Grammar preferences. A writing style tells word what rules to follow when checking spelling and grammar. Choose a writing style to be Word's default by following these instructions:

1. **Choose Word⇨Preferences from the menu bar.**

   The Preferences pane displays.

2. **In the Authoring and Proofing Tools section, choose Spelling and Grammar.**

   The Spelling and Grammar preferences pane opens.

3. **In the Grammar section, click the Writing Style pop-up menu and select a writing style.**

   You can tune the settings coarsely by choosing any of these built-in writing style preferences:

   - *Casual:* Word lets a lot of possible mistakes slide.
   - *Standard:* The grammar checker gets a bit pickier.
   - *Formal:* Word will be extremely picky.
   - *Technical:* Grammar checking isn't as picky as Formal, but different things are looked for than with Standard.
   - *Custom:* A set of choices that you make.

4. **Click OK to close the Spelling and Grammar preferences pane.**

Creating a custom writing style

Choosing a writing style from the pop-up menu is okay, but you don't get to see exactly what grammar rules are being checked in your document. If you want, you can fine-tune each of these writing styles to create your own totally customized writing style. All this is done in Word's Spelling and Grammar preferences pane. To see and adjust grammar settings, take the following steps:

1. **Choose Word⇨Preferences from the menu bar.**

   The Preferences pane displays.

2. **In the Authoring and Proofing Tools section, choose Spelling and Grammar.**

   The Spelling and Grammar preferences pane opens.

3. **To the right of the Writing Style pop-up menu, click the Settings button.**

   The Grammar Settings dialog opens, as shown in Figure 5-18.

4. **Choose an option from the Writing Style pop-up menu and click Settings to view the default settings for that style.**

   Feel free to modify the settings. Changing presets for a default writing style creates a custom writing style. Another way to create a custom style is to choose Custom from the Writing Style pop-up menu and choose settings as desired.

5. **Click OK to close the Grammar Settings dialog.**

   You return to the Spelling and Grammar preferences pane.

6. **Select a writing style.**

   If you customized a writing style and want to use it, choose Custom.

7. **Click OK to close the Spelling and Grammar preferences pane.**

Incidentally, if you follow these steps while you have text selected that has a proofing language other than Word's default, the grammar rules and choices will be in the language of the selected text. Each language has its own set of writing styles.

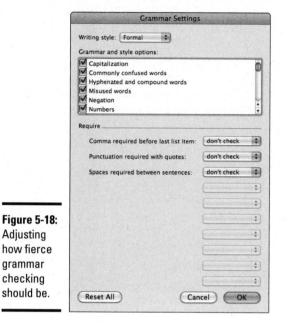

Figure 5-18:
Adjusting
how fierce
grammar
checking
should be.

Chapter 6: Making Great Tables and Charts

In This Chapter

↙ **Picking your table tools**

↙ **Making tables quickly**

↙ **Styling your tables**

↙ **Working with tables on the Web**

↙ **Graphing and charting your way**

↙ **Framing and anchoring**

*T*ables and charts have two virtues: They look great and help portray your information in a more visual and aesthetic way. Of course, they also have the added virtue of making a good impression while conveying important information. Whatever your message, Word makes it easier than ever before to make great-looking info-graphics with tables and charts.

Tables in Word 2011 are now fully compatible with table styles used in Word 2010 for Windows. You can now use VBA, Office's built-in programming language, to automate operations with tables.

Deciding Which Table Tools to Use

Microsoft realizes that tables are one of Word's most-used features. Consequently, Word lets you work with tables using a variety of different interface tools. In the next few sections, we show three ways to create a table:

✦ Using the Ribbon

✦ Using your mouse with the Draw Table feature

✦ Using Word's Insert Table dialog

Each of these methods comes with an entire set of tools that you can use when working on your tables. This presents us, your authors, with a particular problem. If we were to cover all the possibilities, we'd need more than 1,500 bullet points just to cover the basics. Instead, we explain how most of the controls, buttons, formatting, and basic table functions appear within each interface tool grouping. You can mix, match, and work with the tools from any of the groupings. If we point out something on the Tables menu, chances are good that you can find the same tool on the Ribbon, in a dialog, or in the pop-up menu you see when you right-click things. No one single place has every table control.

Here's the rundown on the major interface tool groupings:

✦ **Tables tab on the Ribbon:** An array of table controls in groups.

✦ **Dialogs:** The Table menu gives you access to table creation and formatting dialogs.

✦ **Menus:** The Table menu has many options and is great for people who prefer using menus. Additional menus are available if you right-click within a table.

In addition, if you need to create and edit tables frequently, you may want to consider adding your most-often-used table commands as keyboard shortcuts (described in Chapter 1 of this minibook) or adding the commands to a custom toolbar (covered in Book I, Chapter 3).

Here's an example of various options you can choose from to accomplish the same task. To adjust the sizes of rows, columns, or cells in a table, you can do any of the following:

✦ Drag the column and row dividers.

✦ Right-click and choose Table Properties to open the Table Properties dialog.

✦ Access the Table Layout tab of the Ribbon, and use the controls in the Cell Size group.

✦ Drag the border indicators in the rulers.

We leave it up to you to decide which way is best. Just remember that if we show you one way to do something, chances are good that you can accomplish the same thing in other ways. Find the way that works best for you.

Making a Table

Word allows you to make a new table quickly and easily. You can make a table in any view except Notebook Layout view. When you make a table, not only does the table display in your document, but you can also see the row and column indicators in the Rulers if you have them turned on. The following sections describe how to make a table with different methods.

Using the Ribbon

Here's how to insert a plain table by using the Tables tab of the Ribbon:

1. **Click in your document to set the insertion cursor at the position where you want the new table to be placed.**

2. **Select the Tables tab on the Ribbon. In the Table Options group, click the New button.**

   A grid will display in the form of a small drop-down gallery.

3. **Move the mouse cursor down and to the right across the grid.**

   Cells highlight in the grid as you drag, showing the number of rows and columns you'll get when you release the mouse. (See Figure 6-1.)

4. **Release the mouse to choose the number of rows and columns for your new table.**

   A new table appears in your document.

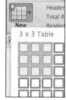

Figure 6-1:
Creating a
new table.

Using the mouse

If you prefer to use the mouse whenever possible, you'll love this method of creating and editing tables because it's mostly click-and-drag. Here's how to make a new table with your mouse:

1. **Choose Table⇨Draw Table from the menu bar. Alternatively, click the Draw button in the Draw Borders group of the Ribbon's Tables tab.**

   The mouse cursor changes into a pencil when it's over your document so that you can start drawing.

2. **Drag the mouse diagonally to create a dotted box shape and then let go of the mouse button.**

   The box shape is the outside border of your new table.

3. **Continue drawing row and column dividers by dragging the mouse horizontally and vertically. (See Figure 6-2.)**

4. **Click the Draw button in the Draw Borders group of the Tables tab of the Ribbon to restore normal mouse operation.**

Whenever you want to use the mouse to draw more rows, columns, or even another table, just click the Draw button. It's a toggle switch between Word's regular cursor and the table-drawing cursor.

Figure 6-2:
Drawing a
new table.

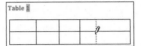

When you want to add, remove, or format the borders and lines of the cells in your table, the Draw Borders group on the Tables tab, shown in Figure 6-3, is at your service. The settings you choose here determine how the lines you draw will look:

+ **Borders:** Choose a border for visual emphasis from a pop-up menu.

+ **Line style:** Choose a line style for your border.

+ **Line weight:** Choose a thickness for your border.

+ **Draw:** Toggles the drawing cursor on and off.

+ **Erase:** Toggles the Erase cursor, shown in Figure 6-4, on and off.

You can save time by setting line weight, style, and color before adding borders and drawing table cells.

Figure 6-3:
The table-
drawing
tools.

To use the Erase tool, click the Erase button. The cursor turns into an eraser. Drag over table lines you want to remove and then let go of the mouse, as shown in Figure 6-4. To erase a cell's border, click the eraser on it.

Figure 6-4:
Erasing cell
dividers.

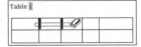

Using the Insert Table dialog

This method uses a dialog to set the number of rows and columns to insert into your document:

1. **Click in your document to set the insertion cursor at the place where you want the new table to appear.**

2. **Choose Table⇨Insert⇨Table. Alternatively, go to the Ribbon's Table tab and choose New⇨Insert Table.**

The Insert Table dialog displays, as shown in Figure 6-5.

3. **Enter the number of rows and columns you want in the appropriate text boxes.**

4. **(Optional) Decide on Autofit options:**

- *Initial Column Width:* This defaults to Auto. When Auto is chosen, the table takes up as much room as is available in the document. Alternatively, use the spinner control to adjust the column width to a fixed amount. All columns will be equal width. You can resize the widths after you make the table if you decide they're not just right.

- *Autofit to Contents:* When you click inside the table and start typing, the cells will automatically size themselves to fit the contents.

- *Autofit to Window:* The same as Initial Column Width set to Auto.

(Optional) If you know you'll create more tables with these options, select the Set as Default for New Tables check box.

5. **Click OK to close the Insert Table dialog.**

A new table appears in your document at the insertion cursor.

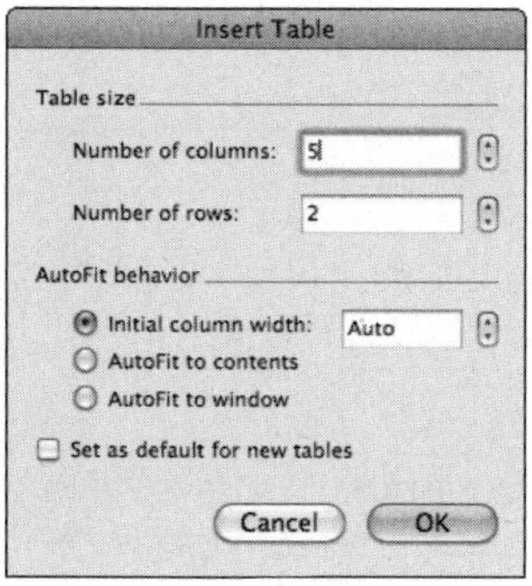

Book II
Chapter 6

Making Great
Tables and Charts

Figure 6-5:
Using the
Insert Table
dialog.

Basic Table Tips

After you format your tables to your liking, it's time to do some actual work. Filling in a table is a snap:

✦ Click inside any cell and start typing.

✦ To move to the next cell, press the Tab key.

✦ If you press the Tab key while in the bottom-rightmost cell, a new row is added to the bottom of the table.

Here are some general tips and hints for adjusting and fine-tuning your tables:

✦ **Adjusting row heights and column widths:** Double-click row and column borders to automatically size rows and columns to fit their contents. You can easily adjust column width and row height by dragging borders, or dragging the table indicator marks in rulers.

✦ **Selecting a range of cells:** You can apply formatting to cell ranges — highlight more than one cell at a time by dragging inside the table with your mouse. (See Figure 6-6.)

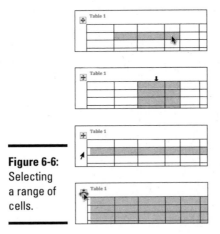

Figure 6-6:
Selecting
a range of
cells.

✦ **Selecting one or more columns at a time:** Position the mouse cursor at the top border of the table; it turns into a downward-pointing arrow. Click to select a single column, or click and drag to select multiple columns, as shown in Figure 6-6.

✦ **Selecting one or more rows at a time:** Position the mouse cursor at the left border of the table. It will turn into a rightward-pointing arrow. Click to select a single row or click and drag to select multiple rows. See Figure 6-6.

✦ **Selecting an entire table:** Click the table handle, as shown in Figure 6-6, to select the entire table.

✦ **Table handle menu:** If you right-click the table handle (see Figure 6-6), a pop-up menu lists things that you can do with or to the entire table, as shown in Figure 6-7.

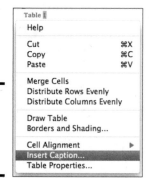

Figure 6-7:
Displaying
the table
handle
menu.

✦ **Repositioning a table:** Drag the table handle (see Figure 6-6) to reposition the table within the document.

✦ **Captioning a table:** Word has a built-in captioning system. If you choose Insert Caption from the table handle pop-up menu, you can get a sneak peek at the table Caption dialog, as shown in Figure 6-8. For more about captions, turn to Chapter 7 in this minibook.

Figure 6-8:
Setting
the table's
caption.

✦ **Converting selected text to a table:** You can select a range of *delimited* text (in which the table elements are separated from each other by spaces, commas, or some other character) and convert it into a table. Choose Table➪Convert➪Convert Text to Table.

✦ **Converting selected table to text:** You can select a table in Word and turn it into plain old text. Choose Table➪Convert➪Convert Table to Text.

Formatting Tables

Every aspect of a table's appearance can be formatted. You can merge cells together to form bigger cells, unmerge them, change border colors, create cell shading, and more. Join us as we explore the various ways to improve the way your tables look.

Applying a table style from the Ribbon

The Tables tab of the Ribbon is the most obvious place to begin our table-formatting discussion. To apply a built-in table style, click anywhere in your table, then choose a table style from either the Table Styles gallery or palette, as shown in Figure 6-9. Word offers you plenty of beautiful built-in styles from which to choose. You can easily modify the shading or line colors by clicking the Shading or Lines buttons next to the gallery.

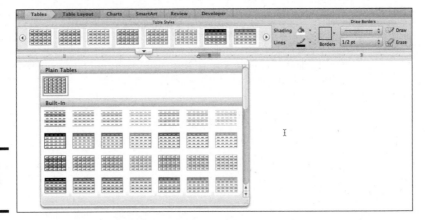

Figure 6-9:
Formatting
a table.

Applying a table style from the Styles dialog

Hang on to your hat because we're going to up the ante! This time you get to choose from more than 140 different table styles using the Style dialog, which has the 44 AutoFormats from the old Table AutoFormat feature from previous versions of Word. We show you how to apply a table style, and then how to modify these built-in styles and add your own styles to the collection.

Applying a style

To get at all the table styles Word has to offer, click anywhere within the table you want to format and then follow these steps:

1. **Choose Format⇨Style from the menu bar.**

   The Style dialog opens, as shown in Figure 6-10.

2. **Click the List pop-up menu and choose All Styles to remove the filter from the style list.**

3. **Click in the Styles list and then press T to get to the table styles.**

   When you select any style with a description that starts with *Table,* you see a preview of the selected table style in the Table Preview area.

4. **Select the style you want to apply to your table and click the Apply button.**

   The style you selected is applied to your table.

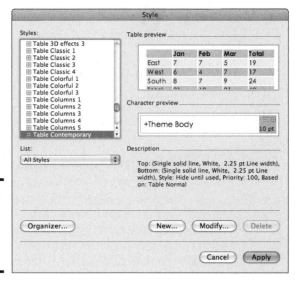

Figure 6-10:
Formatting
a table with
the Style
dialog.

Modifying a table style

If you like a style but want to tweak it just a bit or even a lot, you'll be pleased to know that table styles can be modified easily. To modify an existing table style, follow these steps:

1. **Click anywhere in a table.**

2. **Follow Steps 1–3 in the preceding section (refer to Figure 6-10).**

3. **Select the style you want to modify and then click the Modify button.**

The Modify Style dialog opens, allowing you to customize the style. (See Figure 6-11.)

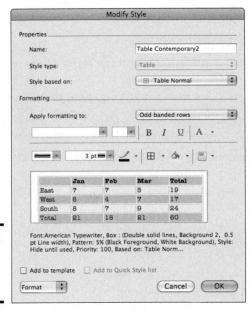

Figure 6-11: Modifying an existing style.

The Modify Style dialog allows you to customize the existing table styles. Go ahead and investigate the Modify Style dialog shown in Figure 6-11:

✦ **Name:** This name appears in lists of styles in the Style dialog and in the Style Gallery on the Ribbon.

We suggest that you always give your modified style a new name unless you specifically want to overwrite an existing style. Word doesn't allow you to overwrite or delete built-in styles, so if you started with a built-in style, you most definitely need to type in a new name for your modified style. We recommend you start any table style name with the word *Table* so that it's easy to find in the Styles list.

✦ **Style Type:** Table. Well, of course!

✦ **Style Based On:** Lets you select an existing style to use as the basis for your modifications. Don't change this unless you want to pick a different style to modify.

✦ **Apply Formatting To:** Click this pop-up menu to choose which table elements you want this table style formatting to affect. For example, you could make a style for striped row formatting that when applied doesn't affect the other table elements listed in the pop-up menu, such as headers.

✦ **Formatting:** A set of formatting tools for text, line, border, fill, and alignment is provided for your convenience.

✦ **Preview:** A live preview updates as you make formatting choices.

✦ **Description:** A description of the style updates as you make formatting choices.

✦ **Add to Template:** When selected, your modifications are saved as a new style in the `Normal.dotm` template unless you have opened a particular template for editing, in which case your modifications are saved in that template. Your customized style is always available to you as a style in the Style dialog and in the Table Style Gallery on the Ribbon. If you don't select this check box, your customization remains with the current document only.

✦ **Add to Quick Style list:** This adds your style to the Table Styles gallery on the Tables tab of the Ribbon.

Creating a new table style

You can create new table styles from within the Style dialog. Take these steps:

1. **In Word, choose Format⇨Style.**

The Style dialog opens. (Refer to Figure 6-10.)

2. **Click the New button.**

The New Style dialog opens, which is practically identical to the Modify Style dialog, shown earlier in Figure 6-11.

3. **Type a name for your new style in the Name field.**

4. **From the Style Type pop-up menu, choose Table.**

5. **(Optional) Click the Style Based On pop-up menu to base your new style on an existing table style.**

6. **In the Formatting section, choose formatting options as desired.**

7. **Select the Add to Template box if you want to use this style again.**

When Add to Template is selected, your modifications are saved as a new style in the `Normal.dotm` template unless you have opened a particular template for editing, in which case your modifications are saved in that template. Your customized style is always available to you as a style in the Style dialog and in the Table Style Gallery of the Ribbon. If you don't select the Add to Template check box, your customization remains only with the current document.

8. **Click OK to create the new style or click Cancel to close the New Style dialog.**

If you have applied style formatting to a table, when you subsequently apply a document theme, the document theme's colors are applied to your table.

Applying special formatting to labels and totals

A common practice is to use the first row of a table as labels for the columns. Often, the first row of a table is called the header row because each label represents a column header. Another practice is to use either the first column or the last column as labels for information contained in the row's cells. Word gives you the opportunity to apply special formatting to these rows and columns. An array of check boxes is in the Table Options group (found on the Ribbon's Tables tab), shown in Figure 6-12. Select the check box next to each item to activate or deactivate the switch:

✦ **Header Row:** Applies special formatting to the top row of the table.

✦ **Total Row:** Applies special formatting to the bottom row, which is often used for calculation results such as the total or average for a column.

✦ **First Column:** Applies special formatting to the leftmost column.

✦ **Last Column:** Applies special formatting to the rightmost column.

✦ **Banded Rows:** Turns the shading in alternate rows on or off.

✦ **Banded Columns:** Turns the shading in alternate columns on or off.

Figure 6-12:
Setting
table format
options.

Performing Table Manipulations

As you populate your table, you may discover you need more rows or columns, or perhaps you will want to merge some cells to enhance the layout. You might want to adjust the row height, column width, or maybe even split a table in two. You can adjust table, row, column, and cell settings by using the Ribbon and dialogs.

When you click anywhere within a table, the Table Layout tab displays on the Ribbon. Click the Table Layout tab to display the groups we discuss in the following sections.

Displaying gridlines and setting properties

The *Settings* group of Table Layout tab has only two buttons:

✦ **Gridlines:** Toggles grid lines on and off. You can see the effect of this control only on borders not having a border style. To remove border styles, select a cell, range of cells, or the entire table, and then click the Tables tab on the Ribbon. In the Draw Borders group, click the Borders pop-up menu and choose None.

✦ **Properties:** Displays the Table Properties dialog, described later in this chapter.

Adding a row or column

Click in your table and then click an appropriate button from the Rows and Columns group on the Table Layout tab, as shown in Figure 6-13. Each time you click a button, a new row or column is added relative to the selected table cell. Pressing Tab in the last cell of a table adds a new row.

Figure 6-13:
Adding
a row or
column.

Deleting a row, column, or cell

Click in your table and then select a cell, row, column, or drag over the desired cells. Then click the Ribbon's Table Layout tab, find the Rows and Columns group, and click the Delete button. A menu displays. Choose from the following:

✦ **Delete Cells:** Deletes the selected cell or cells.

When you delete cells, you may need to tell Word what to do with the remaining cells in the Delete Cells dialog shown in Figure 6-14.

✦ **Delete Columns:** Deletes the selected column or columns.

✦ **Delete Rows:** Deletes the selected row or rows.

✦ **Delete Table:** Deletes the entire table and all of its contents.

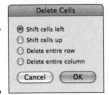

Merging and splitting

The Merge group on the Table Layout tab, shown in Figure 6-15, offers the following options:

✦ **Merge:** Select a range of cells and then click this button to remove the cell borders to create a single, larger cell.

✦ **Split cells:** Select a cell or range of cells and then click this button to display a small dialog where you specify how many cells to split the selection into.

✦ **Split table:** Select a cell and then click this button to split the table into two tables. The table breaks above the selected cell.

Figure 6-15:
Merging or
splitting.

Automatically adjusting cell size

You can adjust cell sizes automatically using the buttons in the Cell Size group of the Table Layout tab, shown in Figure 6-16. The three formatting options are:

✦ **AutoFit:** These are the same formatting options offered by Insert Table discussed earlier in this chapter (refer to Figure 6-5).

✦ **Distribute Rows:** Select two or more rows and then click this button to make the row height uniform for the selected range using the average height of the rows selected.

✦ **Distribute Columns:** Select two or more columns and then click this button to make the column width uniform for the selected range using the average width of the selected columns.

Figure 6-16:
Autosizing
cells.

Aligning cell contents

Unless the content of your cells fits exactly, there's room within cells to position the contents. In the Alignment group of the Table Layout tab, shown in Figure 6-17, you can use the following options:

✦ **Align:** Select a cell or cells and then choose a content alignment option from the pop-up menu.

✦ **Direction:** Select a cell or cells and then choose a text direction from the pop-up menu. Vertical text is harder to read, but gets attention.

✦ **Margins:** Displays the Table Options dialog that lets you specify how much space to have around the content within the selected cell or cells. You can make cells larger than the contents so that you can take advantage of visual appearance of content positioning.

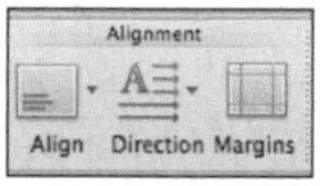

Figure 6-17:
Setting cell
internals.

Sorting, calculating, and converting

When data is arranged so that the top row, and only the top row, is the column labels, and there are no merged cells, Word can do some common spreadsheet functions with your data. Word is certainly not Excel, but here are the things you can do with a data table using the Data group of the Table Layout tab, shown in Figure 6-18:

✦ **Sort:** Displays a Sort dialog that lets you make a single sort or successive sorts.

✦ **AutoSum:** If you have a column containing numbers that you want to add up and put the total in a cell at the bottom, here's what you do:

1. *Click into the empty cell at the bottom of your column containing numbers.*

2. *Click the AutoSum button.*

Word calculates the total for you automatically and inserts a Word field to perform the calculation. (We discuss Word fields and how to perform additional calculations in Chapter 7 of this minibook.)

✦ **Repeat Header Row:** Click into the first row of your table and then click this button so that when your table spans more than one page, the header is replicated on the top row of each page.

✦ **Convert Table to Text:** Click to remove all the table elements and leave just the text separated by tabs.

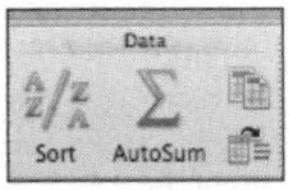

Figure 6-18:
Working
with data.

Using the Tables Properties dialog

If you prefer working with dialogs or if you're interested in precisely formatting tables, columns, rows, and cells, nothing beats the options found in the Table Properties dialog, shown in Figure 6-19. First select your table and then you can get to this dialog by using one of these methods:

✦ On the Ribbon's Table Layout tab, find the Settings group and click Properties.

✦ Right-click or Control-click a table cell and then choose Table Properties from the pop-up menu.

✦ Choose Table⇨Table Properties.

On the Table tab of the Table Properties dialog, you can control the following:

✦ **Size:** Select the check box and click the spinner control arrows to adjust the overall width of the table as measured on the ruler. Choose from inches or percentage measure with the Measure In pop-up menu.

✦ **Alignment:** Choose Left, Center, or Right alignment for a table that doesn't fill the entire width between margins. For precision, use the Indent from Left spinner control to adjust exactly how far in from the left margin you wish the table to be placed.

✦ **Text Wrapping:** Choose None or Around. If you choose Around, the Positioning button becomes active so that you can control exactly how text flows around the table.

✦ **Positioning button:** Activates the Table Positioning dialog, as shown in Figure 6-20.

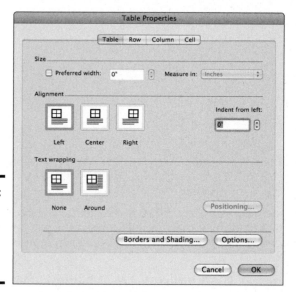

Figure 6-19:
Fine-tuning
with the
Table
Properties
dialog.

The Table Positioning dialog allows precision positioning of the table within your document, either in inches or relative to other document properties in these ways:

- *Horizontal:* Click the buttons to activate pop-up menus or type a numeric value to specify a position.

- *Vertical:* Click the buttons to activate pop-up menus or type a numeric value to specify a position.

- *Distance from Surrounding Text:* Type numeric values or use the spinner controls.

- *Move with Text:* When you select this check box, the table stays in the same relative position to text as you add and remove text while working in the document.

- *Allow Overlap:* Select this check box if you want the table to overlap other objects in your document.

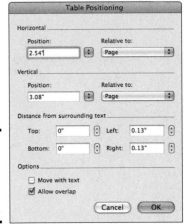

Figure 6-20:
Setting
precision
table
positioning.

✦ **Borders and Shading button:** Activates the Borders and Shading dialog, as shown in Figure 6-21. You can also open this dialog by choosing Format⇨Borders and Shading.

• *Borders tab:* This tab offers the same border-formatting options you find on the Table Layout tab on the Ribbon. You can apply borders to tables, cells, and paragraphs, as explained in Chapter 4 of this minibook.

• *Page Border tab:* This tab offers the same border-formatting options you find on the Page Background group of the Layout tab on the Ribbon. With the Page Border tab, click the Apply To pop-menu to choose from Whole document, This section, This section – First Page Only, or This Section – All Except First Page.

• *Shading tab:* This tab, shown in Figure 6-21, lets you choose fill and pattern options that you can apply to the selected table, selected cell, and current paragraph.

✦ **Row tab:** Back in the Table Properties dialog (refer to Figure 6-19), the Row tab allows you to adjust row settings, one row at a time.

• *Size:* Has the same size controls found on the Cell Size group of the Table Layout tab on the Ribbon.

• *Allow Row to Break Across Pages:* If you select this check box, Word allows a row to break at a page break. The default is that rows don't break at a page break.

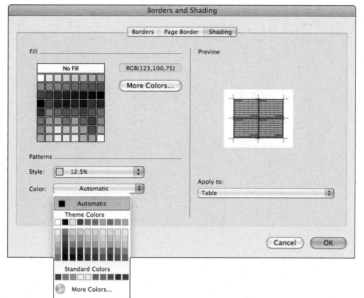

Figure 6-21:
Formatting
with the
Borders and
Shading
dialog.

- *Repeat as Header Row at the Top of Each Page:* If you select this check box, Word repeats the currently selected row as the column header when a table is large enough so that a page break passes through the table. Usually you use the first row of a table for this purpose.

- *Previous Row and Next Row buttons:* These buttons allow you to navigate through the current table so you can set row options row by row.

✦ **Column tab:** Column allows you to set column widths, one column at a time. Use the Previous Column and Next Column buttons to navigate through the current table.

✦ **Cell tab:** This tab lets you set these properties for the selected cell or range of cells:

- *Width:* Set width precisely by typing a number or using an increase/decrease control. Width is measured in inches or percentage.

- *Vertical Alignment:* Choose Top, Center, or Bottom.

- *Options button:* Displays the Cell Options dialog. (See Figure 6-22.)

Word defaults to using the same cell options for all the cells in a table, but you can deselect the Same as the Whole Table check box and format a select cell or a range of cells. By default, Word wraps text in cells, but you can deselect the Wrap Text check box to turn off wrapping.

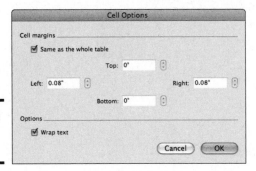

Figure 6-22:
Setting cell
options.

Handling Tables from the Web

Word can open Web pages that you saved from your Web browser, which we discussed in Chapter 2 of this minibook. If a Web page contains an *HTML* (HyperText Markup Language) table, you can use Word's Table features. You might find it easier to copy just the table portion of the Web page from the Web document and paste it into a working Word document.

At some point, you might come across a *PDF* (Portable Document Format) file that has valuable table information in it that you want to extract. If the table information within the PDF is text-based and not a scanned image, you can use the Mac OS X Preview application to take a stab at getting the table information. Follow these steps:

1. **Open the PDF file in Mac OS X Preview application.**

2. **In Preview, choose Edit⇨Select All.**

3. **In Preview, choose Edit⇨Copy.**

4. **Switch to Microsoft Word by clicking Word's Dock icon or use which-ever way you usually use to switch or launch applications.**

5. **Make sure you have a new or existing document open.**

6. **In Word, choose Edit⇨Paste.**

   You may need to manually delete extraneous information. If text wasn't pasted, the PDF probably doesn't contain any text, or is locked, and you can't use this method to grab the data. If that's the case, you have to stop here. If text was pasted, continue on.

7. **In Word, select the pasted text that needs to be converted to a table.**

8. **Convert text selection to a table by choosing Table⇨Convert⇨Convert Text to Table.**

   Word makes a table out of the data.

PDFs can contain tables that have been saved as images, as can Web pages and other documents you might find online. If that's the case, you need Optical Character Recognition (OCR) software to convert the pictures of text into actual text. OCR software isn't included with Office. Cheap scanners have been known to ship with high-quality OCR software that's worth even more than the scanner. ReadIris (www.readiris.com) is excellent for OCR.

Working with Charts

Hold your horses! Whether you're working in Word, Excel, or PowerPoint, Excel handles all the charts. Because charts work the same way in all applications, we include a comprehensive section about charts in Book III, Chapter 5. In this chapter, we cover the intricacies that apply to charts specifically within Word. If necessary, read the information about charts in Book III, Chapter 5 before proceeding because we assume you already know how to create a chart using the Charts tab of the Ribbon.

In Office, charts and graphs are the same thing. Even the dictionary agrees you can use *chart* and *graph* interchangeably. We point this out because in Office, these two words are both used to describe the same objects at times. We try to stick with *chart* unless something that we're discussing in the Office interface uses *graph*.

Whoa! It's way too big!

The first thing you're likely to notice when you start making a new chart in Word is that the chart might span the entire width of the page. Although that might be okay occasionally, most of the time, you'll want to resize the chart. To resize the chart, grab any corner handle and drag it diagonally with your mouse cursor. Be careful not to make it so small that the chart distorts or loses information.

Getting unstuck

After you resize the chart, you might wonder how you can move the chart around on the page. When you first make a chart, it's locked to the left margin. If you try dragging the chart's border, it doesn't budge. Follow these steps to cure this problem:

1. **Select the border or any part of the chart.**

2. **On the Ribbon's Chart Format tab, look for the Arrange group, and click the Wrap Text button and change the style from In Line with Text to one of the other options, as shown in Figure 6-23.**

Now you can drag the chart and position it wherever you want on the page. Of course, this wrapping trick can work for other things, such as pictures and movies!

Figure 6-23: Free your chart by changing the way text wraps around it.

When you make a chart using the Ribbon, your chart is not linked to an external Excel file. Your chart is in an Excel workbook that is contained by your Word document. We call this arrangement *embedding*.

This Is a Frame-Up!

A *frame* is a container that surrounds objects, such as pictures and charts. You use a frame when your text or graphic contains comments, comment marks, or note reference marks so that you can position them within a document precisely and control text flow around the frame. Frames are handy containers because you can put all sorts of stuff inside them. Here is some handy information about frames:

✦ **You can position frames anywhere on a page by dragging.**

✦ **You can wrap text around a frame, although you only get two of the numerous wrapping options for frames: None and Around.**

✦ **You can anchor a frame to a specific position on a page so that it doesn't move with the text.** This feature is useful for page layout, especially if you want something to stay put in Publishing Layout View.

The Ribbon doesn't contain an Insert Frame button. If you use frames often, we suggest adding the Insert Frame command to a toolbar as follows:

1. **In Word, choose View⇨Toolbars⇨Customize Menus and Toolbars.**

The Customize Menus and Toolbars dialog opens.

2. **Select the Commands tab and in the Category list on the left, select Insert.**

3. **In the Commands list on the right, scroll down until you find the Horizontal command. Drag this command to the Standard toolbar and release the mouse button when you see the insertion cursor.**

The Insert Frame button appears on the Standard toolbar. Don't worry that it's Horizontal in the Commands list and Insert Frame on the toolbar — it works just fine.

4. **Click OK to close the Customize Menus and Toolbars dialog.**

The Insert Frame command is now ready for you to use.

In this example, we insert an empty frame and position it in the middle of some text. Working with a frame while it's empty is easier. After you put something into a frame, it can be nearly impossible to select just the frame. Follow these steps:

1. **Click the Insert Frame button (which you create in the preceding steps).**

Your cursor turns into a crosshair, as shown in the margin.

2. **Hold down the mouse button and then drag diagonally to make the frame.**

3. **Release the mouse button when you're done.**

An empty box with a shaded border appears; this is the frame, as shown in the margin.

Before you put something inside the frame, take a moment to size and position the frame and to set its properties. Right-click or Control-click the frame and choose Format Frame. The Frame becomes selected, as shown in the margin, and the Format Frame dialog appears, as shown in Figure 6-24. You can control the exact size and position of the frame with each section of the Frame dialog:

✦ **Text Wrapping:** Choose None or Around.

✦ **Horizontal:**

  • Specify an exact position from the left edge of the margin, page, or column.

  • Specify that the distance from the frame text will be in the horizontal direction.

✦ **Vertical:**

  • Specify an exact position from the top edge of the margin, page, or column.

  • Specify that the distance from the frame text will be in the vertical direction.

  • *Move with Text:* Selecting this check box makes the frame's position relative to the paragraph.

  • *Lock Anchor:* Selecting this check box causes text to flow around the frame instead of the frame moving as the text preceding it is added or removed.

✦ **Size:**

  • *Width:* Specify an exact width or let Word automatically size the frame.

  • *Height:* Set a minimum height, an exact height, or let Word decide the frame's height with the Auto option.

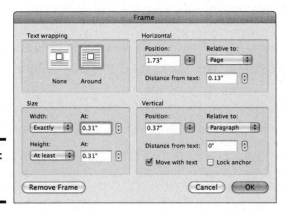

Figure 6-24:
Formatting
a frame.

You can use frames as placeholders. For example, you can insert a frame into a document where you plan to put a picture later. When you're ready, you can drag a picture from the Media Browser into the frame, and the picture size adjusts to fit the frame.

Select a range of text or a picture and then click the Insert Frame button. The selection will then be contained within a frame that is easily positioned anywhere in your document.

Book II
Chapter 6

Making Great Tables and Charts

Chapter 7: Saving Time in Word

In This Chapter

✔ Teaching Word to remember with AutoText

✔ Inserting things with AutoText keystrokes

✔ Making a Table of Contents

✔ Generating an Index

✔ Making a Table of Figures

✔ Automating making a Table of Authorities

✔ Documenting citations

Pilots use AutoPilot to help them fly aircraft. Word has that power! Just like an aircraft captain, you can turn Word's automatic features on and off individually and fly by your own visual flight rules.

An intelligence of a sort exists in Word, and yes, we're dead serious. Word can figure out how to finish typing words and phrases for you. You can give Word standard document tasks, such as captioning pictures and other objects in a long document, creating a Table of Contents, and generating an index. Just don't expect Word to pay your bills. Not yet, anyway.

Automating with AutoText

Word's AutoText feature is so simple, yet so powerful, you might wonder how you got along without it. You teach Word to remember text that you use often and don't feel like typing over and over. Word can then type that text for you. If we had to choose one feature in all of Word that we think everyone should know, AutoText is the one! (If you switched from Word 2007 or 2010 for Windows, AutoText was called a Building Block, but that term isn't used on the Mac.) We start with a simple example.

Teaching Word a lesson

Before we get started, we want to remind you that you can click the Show button on the Standard toolbar to show or hide paragraph marks and other nonprinting characters while you work. Many people find it useful to see these marks while they work. Don't worry; these don't print!

As we drive through this section, we use five Autos:

✦ **AutoText:** When you type certain text, this feature instantly inserts an AutoText entry.

✦ **AutoText name:** Each AutoText entry has a name so that you can refer to an AutoText entry by typing its name in a document and so you can manage them all in AutoText preferences, which we explain shortly.

✦ **AutoComplete:** This is the process whereby a saved AutoText entry is added to a document when its name is typed.

✦ **AutoCorrect:** This is the technology that the AutoText feature uses. You can consider AutoCorrect to be the parent of the AutoText feature.

Maybe you have to type your organization's name often. Maybe you have to type a word or an expression that's cumbersome, such as *Nuclear Factor-Kappa B and Placental Apoptosis.* To teach Word a word or expression, all you have to do is this:

1. **Type the word or expression that you use often and select it.**

You can also select a word or expression you already have in an existing document.

You can select as much text as you like. An entire paragraph isn't out of the question. If you select the ending paragraph mark with the text, Word knows both the text and the current text's formatting.

2. **With the text selected, choose Insert⇨AutoText⇨New.**

This step summons the Create AutoText dialog with a suggested name for your AutoText entry, as shown in Figure 7-1.

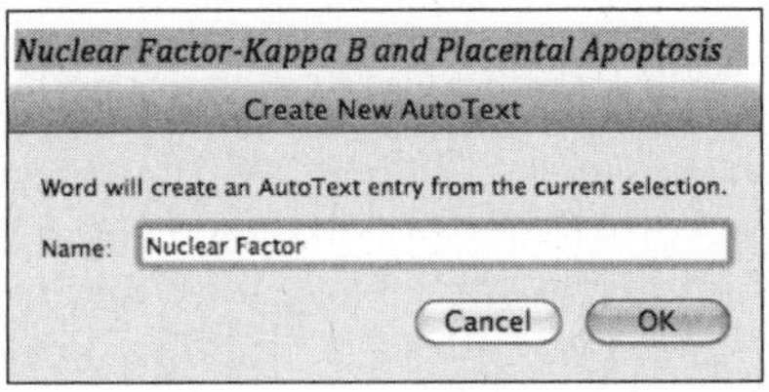

Figure 7-1: Teaching Word a new expression.

Nuclear Factor-Kappa B and Placental Apoptosis

Create New AutoText

Word will create an AutoText entry from the current selection.

Name: Nuclear Factor

Cancel   OK

3. **(Optional) If you don't want to use Word's suggestion, type a new name in the Name field.**

4. **Click OK to close the Create AutoText dialog and add the entry to Word.**

Word looks for the names of AutoText entries as you type, and when you begin to type the first few letters, AutoText displays a tooltip showing the first few words of the AutoText entry. Pressing Return or Enter fills in the rest of the text for you.

In this example, whenever you type **Nuclear Factor**, Word knows you want to use the long, awful *Nuclear Factor-Kappa B and Placental Apoptosis* expression in your document. You don't have to use any of the words of the saved AutoText in the name you give to AutoText. You can invent your own AutoText naming scheme.

Using AutoText on a daily basis

Word always enables you to choose between accepting the AutoText displayed as a tooltip and continuing to type. Because you taught Word the text you want and set up a name, whenever Word sees you typing that name, it displays a tooltip (as shown in Figure 7-2) with the full or abbreviated AutoText. If you want to use the AutoText, all you have to do is press Return or Enter. Word instantly does the tough typing and inserts the full text. (This automated way of typing is *AutoComplete.*) If you don't want to use the AutoText suggestion, you can keep right on typing, and Word doesn't bother you about it.

Figure 7-2:
Activating
an AutoText
prompt.

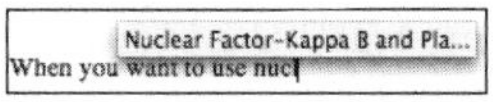

> Nuclear Factor-Kappa B and Pla...
> When you want to use nucl

Some people find AutoText tooltips distracting. You can reduce the distraction by using a prefix when you give your AutoText a name. For example, you could use a prefix, such as *Atext,* for all your AutoText entries so that the AutoText appears only when you type **Atext** along with the rest of the name.

Teaching Word even more

Turns out Word is pretty smart. You can teach Word more than just text. Word for Mac can save just about anything you come across as AutoText. The neat thing about AutoText is that you don't even have to open a template, apply a style, or even use the Ribbon — you just keep typing, and AutoText autocompletes it for you on demand. Here's a short list of things you might want to turn into AutoText entries (these are all things you commonly use or need to type):

✦ Plain text (excluding paragraph marks)

✦ Formatted text, paragraphs, or more (including paragraph marks)

✦ Your favorite formatted tables

✦ Equations you use frequently

✦ Graphs that you've customized

✦ Pictures or logos that you use often

✦ Word fields

✦ WordArt and SmartArt

✦ A form or form letter

✦ Frequently used logos, figures, and expressions

✦ Just about anything you want to have at your fingertips

Taming AutoText

You manage AutoText by choosing Tools⇨AutoCorrect. Click the AutoText tab in the AutoCorrect preferences dialog. If you're wondering why AutoText is under AutoCorrect preferences even though AutoText has nothing to do with making corrections, it's because Word uses its AutoCorrect technology to accomplish AutoText automatic insertion. In the AutoCorrect preferences dialog, you can adjust settings for these additional features, as shown in Figure 7-3:

✦ **Automatically Correct Spelling and Formatting as You Type:** This check box is an on/off switch for all the automatic Word behaviors shown on all the tabs of AutoCorrect preferences. Deselect the check box to turn off all aspects of AutoCorrect.

✦ **Show AutoComplete Tip for AutoText and Dates:** This check box is probably the most important one for AutoText because it's an on/off switch for AutoText's AutoComplete feature. Deselecting this check box pretty much defeats the purpose of AutoText unless you want to turn off AutoText for a particular demonstration. If you deselect this, you can still use the AutoText toolbar All Entries pop-up menu or choose Insert⇨AutoText to manually put AutoText entries into your document. Also, you can turn AutoComplete back on by selecting the check box.

Review the other check boxes and make changes to suit your preferences. If you write many business letters with long text entries that are often repeated, you might want to leave most of these options selected.

✦ **Look In:** This is a pop-up menu that lets you filter what AutoText entries are displayed in the AutoText entries list. You can choose from any currently open document template. AutoText entries are stored in templates.

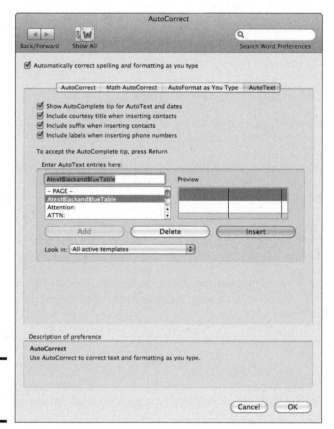

Figure 7-3:
Managing
AutoText.

♦ **Enter AutoText Entries Here:** Take a look at the list of entries, as shown in Figure 7-3. If you see things in the list that you want to have AutoComplete finish, leave them. Otherwise, delete the entries you don't need. Click OK when you're done cleaning AutoText entries. Click a name to see a preview of the entry.

♦ **Delete:** Select an AutoText entry; then click Delete to permanently remove it. AutoText entries are saved to `Normal.dotm` template. Changes to Normal template are saved when you quit Word.

♦ **Insert:** Inserts the selected AutoText into your document at the position of the insertion cursor.

♦ **Add:** If you select something before opening these preferences, you can type a name and click Add to create a new AutoText entry.

If you ever need to find your own AutoText entries, they're stored in Word's Normal template (`Normal.dotm`). You can use Organizer (which we discuss in Chapter 4 of this minibook) to copy AutoText entries from one template to another.

Choose Insert⇨AutoText and choose any existing AutoText entry to insert at the current cursor location. Your own custom AutoText entries will be found in the *Normal* submenu.

Automating Long Document Chores

If you're creating a particularly long document, such as a book manuscript, you can take advantage of some clever automation features in Word.

Your document may have plenty of illustrations, charts, equations, or other things that need to be labeled and kept track of. That's when Word's Index and Tables feature comes in handy.

Whenever you work with the Index and Tables dialog, work on copies of your files instead of the originals. You might go through several trials before you find the result you want.

The Index and Tables dialog has four tabs (look ahead to Figure 7-5), each representing a wonderful timesaving operation that Word can perform for you. The four tabs are

✦ **Index:** Automatically creates an index using marked entries.

✦ **Table of Contents:** Automatically creates a table of contents using Heading styles.

✦ **Table of Figures:** Automatically creates a table of figures using figure captions.

✦ **Table of Authorities:** Automatically creates a Table of Authorities based on styles.

Making an instant Table of Contents

Word 2011 features a fast, new way to make a Table of Contents (TOC). If you've been using Heading styles throughout your document, the process is entirely automatic. Choose to make a Table of Contents automatically; otherwise, select the Manual Formatting option. Follow these steps to make a TOC:

1. **Click in the document where you want the TOC to appear.**

2. **In the Document Elements tab of the Ribbon, look in the Table of Contents group and click the tab at the bottom-center of the gallery. (See Figure 7-4.)**

A gallery with TOC heading samples displays.

3. **Choose a TOC style from the Automatic Table of Contents group in the gallery.**

   • Choose *Heading Styles* if your document contains Heading styles.

   • Choose *Manual* if your document does not contain Heading styles.

   If you choose an Automatic option, based on the heading styles you used in the document, Word creates a quick TOC for you! If you choose the Manual option, Word guesses at your document's structure and presents you with a generic TOC based on your format choice from the gallery that you can customize manually.

Book II
Chapter 7

Saving Time
in Word

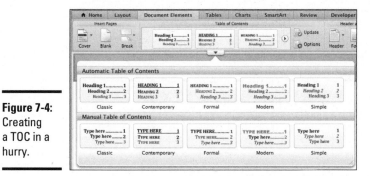

Figure 7-4:
Creating a TOC in a hurry.

How fast and easy is that? As long as your document is well-structured based on Heading styles, Word's TOC feature saves you a ton of work. But what if you want more TOC style choices? No problem! Select the entire TOC that you put into your document. In Word, choose Insert⇨Index and Tables and then select the Table of Contents tab in the Index and Tables dialog that appears, as shown in Figure 7-5.

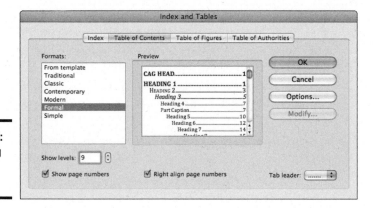

Figure 7-5:
Expanding your TOC options.

Here you can choose from additional formatting options:

✦ **Formats:** Shows built-in and your own custom TOC format styles.

✦ **Show Levels:** Sets how many heading levels will be used in the TOC.

✦ **Show Page Numbers:** This check box shows or hides page numbers.

✦ **Right Align Page Numbers:** This check box aligns page numbers left or right.

✦ **Tab Leader:** This pop-up menu offers more choices for the type of leader line that will be inserted between headings and page numbers.

✦ **Options button:** This button opens the Table of Contents Options dialog. (See Figure 7-6.)

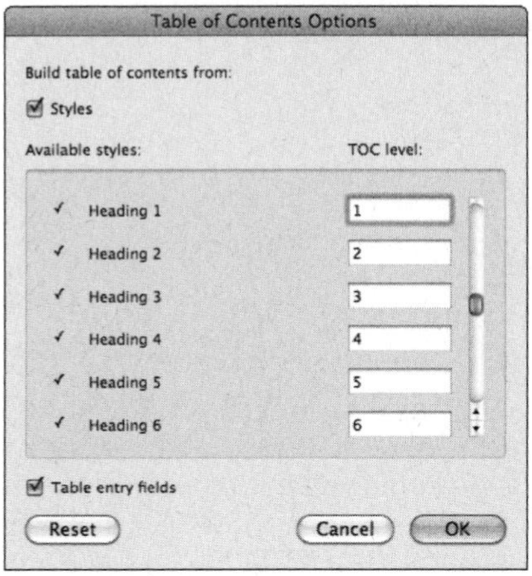

Figure 7-6: Setting Table of Contents heading level options.

With the Table of Contents dialog, you can manually map styles to TOC levels by typing in TOC level values in the fields to the right of the Available Styles list. You can determine which styles to make available:

• *Styles:* Selecting this box allows you to choose from TOC styles from `Normal.dotm` and other open templates.

• *Table Entry Fields:* Select this box to allow mapping of TOC Word field codes in your document to TOC levels in a TOC. (We explain Word field codes in Chapter 8 of this minibook.)

✦ **Modify:** Available if you choose From Template in the Styles list.

Using Index and Tables styles

Each tab of the Index and Tables dialog represents a specific kind of index or table. Because all the Index and Tables formats use styles, you can use the same techniques to create, customize, and delete your own styles as you do for table styles in Chapter 6 of this minibook.

To enable the ability to customize any index or table, select From Template in the Index and Tables Formats list of any tab to activate the Modify button. Click Modify to open the Style dialog. In the Style dialog, click Modify Style to open the Modify Style dialog.

Creating an index

Perhaps you're working on a long document in which you want an index with page numbers. Word can automate this task for you. This procedure entails three steps:

1. **Generate a table of words or phrases to be indexed, saved as a special file called a *concordance file.***

2. **Mark the words or phrases to be used in the index.**

3. **Generate the index.**

Making a table of words and phrases to index

Word is pretty smart, but you need to tell Word the words or phrases to use in the index, and which index headings to make. You tell Word the words or phrases to be used in the index by creating a concordance file. Don't let that word scare you; a *concordance* file is a fancy name for a Word document that consists of a one- or two-column table. (For information on how to create other kinds of tables, see Chapter 6 in this minibook.) Follow these steps to create a concordance table:

1. **In Word, choose File⇨New Blank Document.**

    A new, blank Word document appears.

2. **From the menu, choose Table⇨Insert⇨Table.**

    The Insert Table dialog appears.

3. **In the Insert Table dialog, set Number of Columns to 2.**

    For now, the number of rows you have is irrelevant. The other default settings are fine and don't need to be changed.

4. **Click OK to close the Insert Table dialog.**

   A two-column table appears in your document.

5. **Fill in the cells as described here (see Table 7-1):**

   - *Left column:* Put all the words from your document that should be marked for indexing into the left column, one word or phrase per cell.

   - *Right column:* Enter the appropriate document index heading corresponding to each word in the left column.

   - *Don't use column headings:* Nothing else can be in the concordance file except your two-column table.

     In this example, any occurrence of *Formatting, Web, PDF,* or *Table* will appear under the Tables index heading. Any occurrence of *AutoFormat* or *Formatting* will appear in our index under the Styles index heading. You don't have to group the words or the index headings. Word figures it all out for you.

6. **Choose File➪Save to save the table as a Word document and then choose File➪Close to close the concordance table document.**

The following table shows a concordance table we made to use on a draft version of a chapter of this minibook. The left column is a list of the words we want to mark for indexing. The right column is the index heading that's used for our marked words.

Formatting	Tables
Web	Tables
PDF	Tables
AutoFormat	Styles
Table	Tables
Formatting	Styles

Marking the words or phrases to use in the index

After you save your concordance file, you can use it to create an index from a long document; in this case, the draft of a chapter in this minibook. Follow these steps to use a concordance file:

1. **In Word, choose File➪Open.**

   The File Open dialog displays.

2. **Select the Word document you want to index but don't open it yet.**

For this example, we select a chapter in this minibook.

3. **In the File Open dialog, choose Copy from the Open pop-up menu and then click the Open button to open a copy of the document that you want to index.**

A copy of the document you chose opens.

4. **In the copy of your document, choose Insert⇨Index and Tables.**

The Index and Tables dialog opens. (See Figure 7-7.)

Book II
Chapter 7

Saving Time
in Word

Figure 7-7:
Indexing
with the
Index and
Tables
dialog.

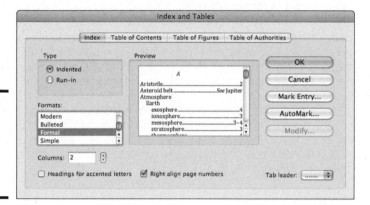

5. **Click the Index tab and then click the AutoMark button.**

The Choose a File dialog opens.

6. **Navigate to the concordance file you saved earlier and then click the Open button.**

Word marks the indexed words with { XE "Index" }. You have to turn on paragraph marks to see these index codes by clicking the Show button on Word's standard toolbar. The Index and Tables dialog closes. All the words in your document that will be used in the index have now been marked.

Generating the index

The following steps create the index:

1. **Click in your document to set the insertion cursor to the place where you want to create the index.**

2. **In Word, choose Insert⇨Index and Tables.**

   The Index and Tables dialog opens again. (See Figure 7-7.)

3. **Click the Index tab if it isn't selected already.**

4. **Choose the type, format, tab leader style, and so on; or go with the default settings to format your index.**

   The choices you make are updated instantly in the preview.

5. **After you make all your choices, click OK.**

   The Index and Tables dialog closes. Your index appears in your document.

Your basic index is all fine and well, but what if you want subheadings in your index? Word has that covered, too! With a colon (:), you can tell Word to create a subheading. Try this out with a new concordance table separating main headings from subheadings with a colon, as shown in the right column of the following table. Notice the overall main heading (*Tables* in this example) stands alone without colons so that the subheadings appear beneath the main heading. Also notice that Styles gets its own heading and is also listed as a subheading under Tables with our scheme. Look at the following table to see the headings and subheadings we used to produce the results, as shown in Figure 7-8. Figure 7-8 is in Draft View (in Word, choose View⇨Draft) with Show Hidden Marks turned on. (Click the Show button on the Standard toolbar.)

Formatting	Styles:Tables
Web	Tables:Web
PDF	Tables:Web
AutoFormat	Styles:Tables
Table	Tables
Formatting	Tables:Styles

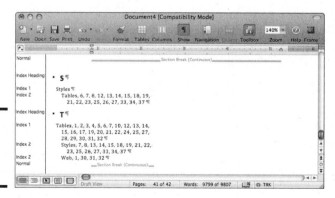

Figure 7-8: Your index inserted in Word.

When you make your index, think about how you want subheadings to work in your document. Experiment freely until you get just the right result.

Producing a Table of Figures

Many long documents have plenty of figures in them, and whether the figures are tables, pictures, graphs, drawings, SmartArt, WordArt, or embedded objects, you can list them all in one place in your document by creating a Table of Figures with the Index and Tables dialog. Before you can create a Table of Figures, you have to put a caption style onto each of the figures you want included in the table. To put a caption on a figure, follow these steps:

1. **Select a figure and then choose Insert⇨Caption.**

   The Caption dialog appears, as shown in Figure 7-9.

2. **Type a caption in the Caption text box and make any other changes.**

3. **Click OK when you're done and repeat the process for other figures in the document.**

Figure 7-9:
Captioning
a figure.

After you caption all the figures, take the following steps to create the Table of Figures:

1. **In Word, choose Insert⇨Index and Tables and select the Table of Figures tab.**

   In Figure 7-10, you see the Table of Figures tab of the Index and Tables dialog with the following options:

   - *Caption Label:* Select which objects in the document to include in the table.

   - *Formats:* This is a list of the styles available.

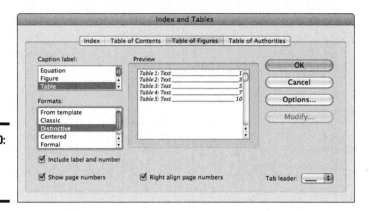

Figure 7-10:
Making a
Table of
Figures.

- *Tab Leader:* Select a tab leader style.

- *Include Label and Number:* Select this check box to include the caption's label and number.

- *Show Page Numbers:* When selected, shows page numbers in the Table of Figures.

- *Right Align Page Numbers:* When selected, page numbers are right aligned; otherwise, they're left aligned.

- *Options button:* Displays the Table of Figures Options dialog shown in Figure 7-11, where you can modify the Style, Table Entry Fields, and Table Identifier.

Figure 7-11:
Fine-Tuning
Table of
Figures
Options.

2. **Select a Label in the Caption Label list.**

   For this example, we chose Figure to create a table of figures. This selection limits the output to captions labeled as Figure.

3. **In the Formats area, select a format that you like.**

   Click the various styles and check boxes, and Preview updates.

4. **Select or deselect the check boxes as desired, and when you're done, click OK.**

   Preview updates as you select and deselect options. The Table of Figures appears in your document.

Accelerating a Table of Authorities

If you're an attorney, lawyer, paralegal, law student, or some other sort of legal beagle, this is just for you! Creating a Table of Authorities is a two-stage process. First, you mark selected text to be indexed; then Word uses the marked text to create the table.

Marking text to include in the table

Follow these steps to mark text to include in the Table of Authorities:

1. **In Word, choose Insert➪Index and Tables.**

   The Index and Tables dialog opens. (See Figure 7-12.)

2. **Select the Table of Authorities tab.**

Book II
Chapter 7

Saving Time
in Word

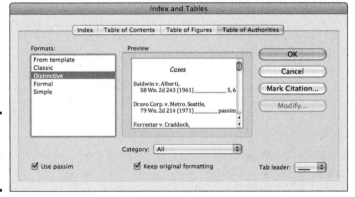

Figure 7-12: Inserting a Table of Authorities.

In this tab, you can choose from the following to play around with Preview:

- *Formats:* Lists format styles from which to choose.

- *Use Passim:* If one of the citations is referenced on five or more pages, you can display the word passim instead of displaying the actual page numbers by checking this check box.

- *Keep Original Formatting:* Select or deselect, and observe Preview.

- *Tab Leader:* Choose from the pop-up menu and observe Preview.

3. **Click the Mark Citation button to open the Mark Citation dialog.**

The Index and Tables dialog disappears and is replaced by the Mark Citation dialog, as shown in Figure 7-13. When this dialog is open, you can go back and forth between the dialog and the document.

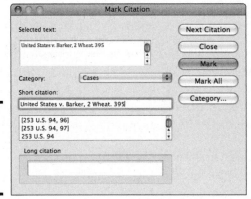

Figure 7-13:
Marking
text for a
Table of
Authorities.

4. **Click the Next Citation button.**

Word searches the document for anything that looks like a citation and then selects the likeliest character. If you want to mark the surrounding text as a citation, drag over it in the document to select it; otherwise, click the Next Citation button again to move on.

5. **Click anywhere on the Mark Citation dialog.**

The text you highlighted in your document displays in Selected Text.

6. **Choose a category from the Category pop-up menu.**

7. **Click the Mark button to mark the selected text.**

You can also click the Mark All button to tell Word to mark all the matching text everywhere in the document.

8. **Click the Next Citation button to move to the next unmarked possible citation, or click Close to exit the Mark Citation dialog.**

While in the Mark Citation dialog, you can click the Category button to display the Edit Category dialog, as shown Figure 7-14. Here you can change the default category names that appear in the Category pop-up menu.

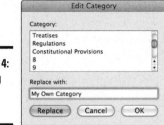

Figure 7-14:
Managing
category
names.

Building the Table of Authorities

After you finish marking the citations, follow these steps to create a Table of Authorities:

1. **Click in the document to set the insertion cursor at the place where you want the Table of Authorities to appear.**

2. **In Word, choose Insert➪Index and Tables and click the Table of Authorities tab.**

The Index and Tables dialog opens. (Refer to Figure 7-12.)

3. **Select Formats, Category, and other options as desired.**

Preview updates instantly as you make choices.

4. **Click OK to create the Table of Authorities.**

Citations are grouped by category.

You may notice in Figure 7-13 (shown earlier) that Word allows you to index long citations. When you use the Table of Authorities feature, you might not like the way Word uses page numbers for citations in paragraphs that extend over a page break. Word uses the page number from the end of the para-graph rather than the beginning. To fix this, manually drag the { XE... } marker to the start of the paragraph.

Inserting a Citation

We sure wish this feature had been around when we were in college! If you need to insert citations for a paper, Word has another feature to help. Citations describe the source of a quotation, passage, figure, or data, and they follow a particular formatting style. To activate the citation feature, follow these steps:

1. **Switch to a view that supports the Toolbox, such as Print Layout view, by clicking the Print Layout button at the lower-left corner of the doc-ument window.**

Toolbox

2. **If Toolbox isn't showing already, click the Toolbox button on the Standard toolbar to display it.**

3. **Click the Citations button (second from the left in the top toolbar) to activate the Citations tab, as shown in Figure 7-15.**

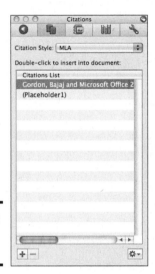

Figure 7-15:
Inserting
citations.

In the Citations tab of the Toolbox, you have the following options:

✦ **Citation Style:** Click this pop-up menu to choose from four different styles: APA, Chicago, MLA, and Turabian.

✦ **Citations List:** Word maintains a list of your citations. This option shows Word's master citations list filtered by the selected style. Select a citation; then double-click it to insert it in your document at the insertion cursor.

✦ **Add Citation:** Displays the Add New Citation dialog for your master citations list. You can enter appropriate data for the currently selected citation style.

✦ **Delete Citation:** Removes the selected citation from Word's master citation list.

✦ **Edit Source or Use Citation Source Manager:** You have two options when you click this button:

- *Edit Source:* Displays the Edit Citation dialog.

- *Citation Source Manager:* Displays the Citation Source Manager. Here you can copy citations to and from open documents and share citations with others.

Word maintains a master list of citations, but you have to add or copy at least one citation to your master citations list before you can insert a citation into a document.

In the Edit Citation dialog, you have these options:

✦ **Type of Source:** Click this pop-up menu to choose from a list of many source types.

✦ **Bibliography Fields:** Enter data as applicable for the citation style selected in the Toolbox pop-up menu.

✦ **Example:** Shows an example for the currently select input field.

Use the Citation Source Manager dialog to set the following features:

✦ **Master List:** Your Word master list of citations.

✦ **Current List:** Citations in the currently active document.

✦ **Copy:** Copy a selected citation to or from either list. The Copy direction arrow changes depending upon which list has the currently selected citation.

✦ **New:** Opens the Create New Source dialog.

✦ **Edit:** Opens the selected citation in the Edit Source dialog.

✦ **Delete:** Deletes the selected source from your master list.

Chapter 8: Advanced Word Stuff

In This Chapter

✔ **Wrapping text**

✔ **Getting text to flow with text boxes**

✔ **Publishing a newsletter or periodical**

✔ **Ferreting out fields**

✔ **Managing several open documents at once**

✔ **Making smart electronic forms that look great**

✔ **Embedding objects**

A lot of people call these topics *advanced,* but for the most part, these topics are better categorized as *extra stuff you could know* rather than *difficult* or *complicated.* Understanding the tasks and concepts in this chapter can make your experience with Word more productive and enjoyable. Who knows? Maybe you'll wind up using one of these features every day after you discover how much it can help.

Wrapping Text around Objects

From pictures and graphs to SmartArt, you can easily add all sorts of objects to a Word document. But after the object is inserted in your Word document, you'll probably need to control how text wraps around it. You can adjust text wrapping in Print Layout, Notebook Layout, Publishing Layout, and Full Screen views.

Using contextual menus to wrap text

The fastest way to get at the Wrap Text options is to right-click an object. This produces a pop-up menu from which you can choose Wrap Text. The menu and submenus are similar to those shown in Figure 8-1.

Wrap text using the Ribbon

When you select an object, the Wrap Text button in the Arrange group on the Ribbon's Format tab becomes available, as shown in Figure 8-1. The Wrap Text button offers the same wrapping options as the Advanced Layout dialog, but you choose them using a pop-up menu, like this:

1. **Select an object.**

The border surrounding the object becomes prominent, usually with dots called *handles* that you can drag to resize the object.

2. **On the Ribbon's Format Picture tab, find the Arrange group; click Wrap Text and choose a wrapping option from the pop-up menu.**

Text wraps around your object based on your style choice.

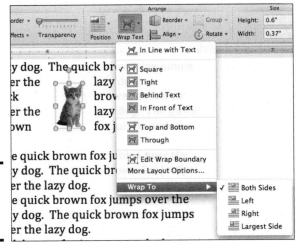

Figure 8-1:
Wrapping
is easy with
the Ribbon.

Using the Advanced Layout dialog

To see all of Word's text wrapping styles, first select an object in a document. Then, on the Ribbon's Format tab, find the Arrange group and choose Wrap Text⇨More Layout Options to display the Text Wrapping tab of the Advanced Layout dialog, shown in Figure 8-2.

The Advanced Layout dialog is divided into three groups:

✦ **Wrapping Style:** Text wrapping denotes how text in a Word document flows around the periphery of other objects, such as pictures and graphs. The following available styles are well referenced by descriptive icons:

  • *Square:* Text flows around all sides of the object.

  • *Tight:* Same as square, but the text is closer to the object.

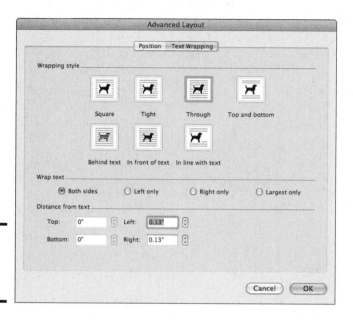

Figure 8-2:
Getting all
the wrap
options.

- *Through:* Text wraps to the wrap boundary instead of the selection indicator boundary (the default for all other wrapping options). Through works with objects such as certain SmartArt or ClipArt objects with clear space (or transparent backgrounds).

- *Top and Bottom:* White space appears to the left and right of an object. Text appears only above and below the object.

- *Behind Text:* Places the object in a layer behind the text. The text does not change position and behaves as if the object weren't there. This works best if you have a faded object that contrasts with the text color.

- *In Front of Text:* Places the object in a layer in front of the text. The text does not change position and behaves as if the object weren't there, but the text beneath the object is obscured. You can adjust the object's transparency to allow some see-through.

- *In line with Text:* This is the default for inserting pictures and other objects. The object is placed at the beginning of the paragraph containing the selection cursor. The first line of text displays to the right of the inserted object.

To change Word's default picture insertion setting, choose Word➪Preferences➪Authoring and Proofing Tools➪Edit. In the Preferences dialog's Editing Options group, click the pop-up menu button for Insert/Paste Pictures As. You can find the same seven options that we discuss in the preceding bullet.

✦ **Wrap Text:** This setting determines the side or sides that text is allowed to wrap around your object. Choose from Both Sides, Left Only, Right Only, or Largest Only. Largest means text will appear on the side that is the greater distance from the object to the margin.

✦ **Distance from Text:** Use spinner controls to manually set the distance of text from the Top, Bottom, Left, and Right boundaries of your object.

Setting an object's wrap boundary

Every object around which you wrap text ends up with a text-wrapping boundary, which you can see in Figure 8-3. These boundaries look different depending upon the type of text wrap you opt for.

Figure 8-3:
Adjusting
the text-
wrapping
boundary.

You can control the size and shape of the boundary so that your text flows around any object exactly as you wish. To adjust the text-wrapping boundary, first select the object. (We selected a picture.) The selected indicator with resize handles will display. Then, on the Ribbon's Format Picture tab, find the Arrange group and click the Wrap Text button. Then choose Edit Wrap Boundary from the drop-down gallery.

This turns on the wrap boundary line and its points, as shown in Figure 8-3. You can drag the boundary line points to control precisely how text flows around the object. Click the boundary line to add a drag point. Click away from the object to return to your document.

Positioning and Anchoring an Object

Word gives you shortcuts to position an object in your document. Here's how to get at them:

1. **Select an object.**

2. **On the Ribbon's Format tab, go to the Arrange group and click the Position button.**

   The drop-down gallery shown in Figure 8-4 displays.

3. **Choose a position from the gallery.**

   The object moves in your document to the chosen position.

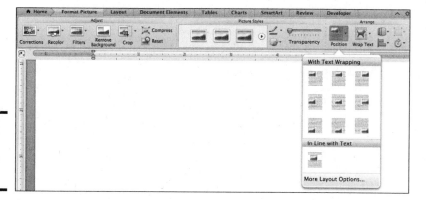

Figure 8-4:
Taking a
shortcut to
a position.

When you put an object into a Word document and then add text or other content earlier in the document, your object moves down along with the text in the document. A word-processing document flows that way so that your objects stay in the same relative position to the text as you add or delete text and objects. You can change this behavior, though.

You can make an object stay in an exact position in the document so that text flows around the object, and it doesn't move with the text — this is known as *anchoring*. Think of this as dropping a boat anchor — water flows by, but the boat stays in the same position relative to the shore. In Word, if you anchor an object to a margin, the object stays in the same relative position. Nonanchored objects and text flow around the object. This anchoring capability is a basis of publishing programs, so it's natural to use it in Word's Publishing Layout and Print Layout views. Follow these steps to anchor an object in Word:

1. **Select an object.**

2. **On the Ribbon's Format tab, go to the Arrange group and choose Position⇨More Layout Options.**

   The Advanced Layout dialog opens.

3. **Click the Position tab. See Figure 8-5.**

4. **(Optional) Set the position of an object precisely using controls in this dialog.**

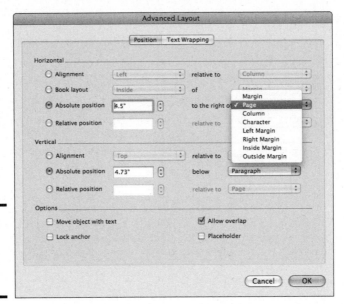

Figure 8-5:
The
Advanced
Layout
dialog.

5. **Under Options, select the Lock Anchor check box.**

6. **Click OK to close the Advanced Layout dialog and then click OK to close the Advanced Layout dialog.**

   Text now flows according to the settings you made, and the object is anchored to the position you selected. Although you can still drag the object to new positions on the page, it won't move when you add or delete text.

Flowing Text from One Text Box into Another

So far in this chapter we discuss how text flows around objects, such as pictures and charts, placed in a Word document. In this section, we show you how to make text flow from one text box into another so that text does not disturb your layout. You would use this when making a newsletter or magazine.

This process works with plain, empty text boxes or text boxes that are for-matted already with niceties and ornamentation. Try thinking of a chain of linked text boxes as a story in a newspaper, newsletter, or magazine. You can link several text boxes together so that text flows automatically from one box to another in a story. This maintains layout and prevents nontext objects from moving from one page to another. The text boxes in a story are numbered, so you can tell the order in which they will be filled. Each chain of linked boxes has its own color and independent numbering scheme.

When you combine linked text boxes with the ability to anchor objects, you have the foundation of page layout programs right within Microsoft Word. For you, this means that you don't need an additional page layout program, such as Microsoft Publisher, because you have Word 2011.

Creating text boxes

Start with a single, plain text box. You can make a text box by clicking in the body text of your document and then clicking the Ribbon's Home tab, finding the Insert group, and clicking Text Box. Alternatively, choose Insert⇨Text Box from the menu bar.

 The mouse cursor turns into a special cursor, shown in the margin. Position the mouse where you want to start drawing and then click and hold down the mouse button while dragging diagonally in your document. Release the mouse button when the box is the shape you want. (See Figure 8-6.) If you hold down the Shift key while dragging, you get a perfect square.

Figure 8-6:
Making a
plain text
box.

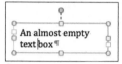

 As you start typing in the box, notice that the text inside the box wraps automatically. You may have to make the box larger or use a small font size to make the text fit the box just right. In addition to line spacing options, you can use hard returns and soft returns to control paragraph formatting in Word. Click the Show button on the Standard toolbar to show paragraph marks to see the difference between these two:

✦ **Hard return:** When you press Return or Enter, Word inserts a paragraph mark and moves the insertion cursor to the next paragraph.

✦ **Soft return:** When you hold down Shift as you press Return or Enter, Word moves the cursor to the next line without adding a paragraph mark. This is indicated by a little arrow symbol.

Linking text boxes in Publishing Layout view

Text boxes work a little differently in Publishing Layout view than in other views, where text boxes have tools to help you position them on a page. Switch to Publishing Layout view and then have a look at these tools.

Follow these steps to create two (or more) linked text boxes:

1. **Make sure you're in Publishing Layout view.**

   If you aren't in Publishing Layout view, choose View➪Publishing Layout.

2. **Make a text box.**

   See the section "Creating text boxes," earlier in this chapter.

   A Text Box button is available on the Standard toolbar in Publishing Layout view, and you can use this button to quickly insert a new text box.

3. **Click the Forward Link button (as shown earlier in Figure 8-6) on your text box.**

   The cursor changes to a crosshair when you click the Forward Link button.

4. **Drag a new text box with this crosshair cursor.**

   This action creates a new text box linked to the first text box.

5. **Type (or paste) enough text in the first text box so that it overflows into the second box, as shown in Figure 8-7.**

Figure 8-7:
Text flowing from the first text box to the second.

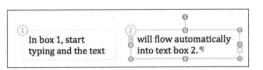

With this example, you can create text boxes that span from the second to the third, and the third to the fourth text box, and so on to create a story. Word helpfully shows you the sequence number of all text boxes in a story, as shown in Figure 8-8.

After you create a new text box, clicking the Previous Link and Forward Link handles takes you instantly to the neighboring link within the story's chain. If you drag entire text boxes, guides appear to help you line up the boxes with each other.

To add more text boxes to a story, click a box's Forward Link (to link to a lower number box) or Backward link button (to link to a higher number box), and then click on another text box.

If you decide to break a link in a story, the remaining links are retained and you will then have two stories. To break a link, select the text box that is to be the end of the first story. Click the Format tab in the Ribbon, and then in the Text Box group, click the Break Link button.

Publishing Newspapers, Newsletters, and Periodicals

Get ready because if you read the sections before this one, you have all the elements you need to create superb publications. (If you haven't read them yet, we'll happily wait right here for you.) You know how to make text flow around objects, how to anchor objects, and how to make text flow in a story. Here we explore Publishing Layout view in more detail to see how this feature can help you in your quest. We start with the Publishing Layout view's Standard toolbar, shown in Figure 8-8.

**Book II
Chapter 8**

**Advanced
Word Stuff**

Figure 8-8:
Getting to
know the
Publishing
Layout
view's
Standard
toolbar.

Discovering more Publishing Layout tools

Almost everyone knows the Hand tool. A hand grabs the page and moves it up or down as you drag the mouse in Publishing Layout view. These steps open a template so you can see how the Hand tool works:

1. **Choose New from Template on the Standard toolbar.**

The Word Document Gallery opens.

2. **In the Templates list, in the Publishing Layout View group, choose any multipage template.**

The School Newsletter template works nicely for this example.

3. **Click the Hand tool on the Standard toolbar.**

The cursor changes to a hand.

4. **Click and hold down the mouse button while dragging the mouse up or down within the document.**

You can easily move the page without accidentally selecting individual objects and moving them!

5. Press the Esc key.

The Hand tool turns off.

Another handy tool helps you zoom in and out. It's called the Zoom Loupe (pronounced *loop*) tool. Here's how it works:

1. In Publishing Layout view, click the Zoom Loupe tool on the Standard toolbar.

The cursor becomes loopy, as shown in the margin.

2. Click and hold down the mouse button while dragging the mouse in various directions within the document.

You can easily zoom in and out.

3. Press the Esc key.

The cursor returns to normal.

Mastering master pages

Word takes the concept of a master page to a new level in Publishing Layout view. A *master* page is a kind of template page within a Word document. Whatever you put on the master page is duplicated on any pages that are based on it. Master pages are a way to maintain a consistent feel throughout your document as you add new pages. If you use master pages, you can save time by not having to re-create page elements, such as page numbers, headers, and footers, with each new page as you build your publication.

The School Newsletter template in the Word Document Gallery uses Master Pages, so we use it as an example. To see the master pages, click the Master Pages tab near the bottom-right corner of the window, shown in Figure 8-9. Remember that these tabs show only in Publishing Layout view. The Insert button in the Layout tab of the Ribbon assists you with adding pages while maintaining the layout. To insert a new page based on the master, take these steps:

1. With a document open in Publishing Layout view, click the All Contents tab in the lower-right corner of the document window.

The All Contents tab shows you the contents of the document you're building.

2. On the Ribbon, click the Layout tab. In the Pages group, click the little triangle to the right of the Add button, as shown in the margin.

Choose from one of the following options:

- *New Page:* Inserts a new page based on a master template.

- *New Master:* Allows you to create a new master page out of the current page. You can have multiple masters.

- *Duplicate Page:* Creates a duplicate of the current page.

Figure 8-9:
Mastering
master
pages.

Switch back and forth between all contents and master pages by clicking the tabs at the lower-right corner of the document window. When you select the Master Pages tab, the Master Pages Options group on the Layout tab of the Ribbon becomes available (see Figure 8-10) and offers three options:

✦ **Different First Page:** Allows the first page to be formatted independently of the rest of the master.

✦ **Different Odd and Even Pages:** Use this when setting up documents that will have pages that face each other when printed and you want to use a gutter or opposing page numbers.

✦ **Link Previous:** Keeps formatting the same as the previous master page when you add a new master page. If you only have one master page, this option is grayed out.

Figure 8-10:
Choosing
Master
Page
Options.

Using static guides

You can add *static guides,* which are guide lines to help you align objects in Publishing Layout view. You can see the guides by clicking the Ribbon's Layout tab, finding the Guides group and clicking the Show button, and then choosing whichever guides setting suits you best. See Figure 8-11.

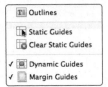

Figure 8-11:
Choosing
guides.

Follow these steps to add static guides to your document:

1. **Make sure your rulers are visible.**

   If your rulers aren't visible, choose View⇨Ruler to toggle them on.

2. **Position the mouse cursor over a ruler and then drag a guide line from the ruler into the document.**

   It's as if there are static guides secretly waiting for you to drag them out of the rulers! While you drag, Word tells you the location of the line on the ruler. Position the static guide as desired and then release the mouse button. You can drag static guides to reposition them.

To remove static guides, click the triangle next to the Show button on the Guides group of the Layout tab of the Ribbon and then choose Clear Static Guides from the resulting drop-down gallery.

Static guides placed on the Master Pages tab appear when you're viewing both the Master Pages tab and the All Contents tab. Static guides placed on the All Contents tab don't appear on the Master Pages tab. When removing static guides, you need to remove guides placed on the All Contents tab independently from the Master Pages tab.

Having a Field Day

Whether you're new to Word or an old hand, Word fields can help you accomplish a wide variety of tasks, including all sorts of automation. We briefly discuss fields in relation to mail merge in Chapter 10 of this minibook. Here we take a closer look at fields and see what's going on under the Word hood.

In their broadest definition, Word *fields* are special codes that perform various tasks. We have a hard time describing them better than that because they do so many different things. Word fields are an essential part of mail merge, page numbering, and other tasks. Some fields are very simple; others are quite complex. We show you how fields work with the Word field for Time as an example.

Getting to know Word fields is probably easiest if you start with a new, blank Word document in Print Layout view.

In the following steps, we collect three tools and then put them onto a toolbar so that we can use them later. You can drag them to the Standard toolbar or any other toolbar. (Follow the instructions in Book I, Chapter 2 to create your own toolbars.) Follow these steps to drag these commands onto any toolbar of your choice:

1. **In Word, choose View⇨Toolbars⇨Customize Toolbars and Menus.**

   The Customize Toolbars and Menus dialog appears.

2. **Select the Commands tab and make sure that the left pane shows All Commands.**

   Click in the right panel and then press the first letter of the command to bring you to that letter of the alphabet and save time.

3. **Drag the ViewFieldCodes, InsertFieldChars, and UpdateFields commands to any toolbar.**

4. **Click OK to close the Customize Toolbars and Menus dialog.**

Adding a field

Now it's time to find out where Word fields hide on your computer. They quietly reside in a small, but powerful, dialog; choose Insert⇨Field. The Field dialog, as shown in Figure 8-12, appears. Here you can insert a special code, dubbed a *field code,* into your Word document. The field code categories are listed on the left side of the dialog in the Categories list. The Field Names list on the right side of the dialog allows you to select a field code to insert into a document.

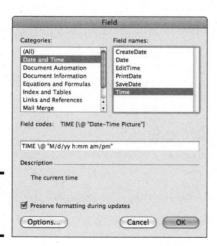

Figure 8-12:
The Field
dialog.

We're going to grab the Time Word field and put it into a blank document so we can pick it apart and see how it works. For this example, see Figure 8-12 and follow these steps:

1. **Click the New button on Word's Standard toolbar to open a new, blank Word document.**

2. **Choose Insert⇨Field.**

   The Field dialog, shown in Figure 8-12, appears.

3. **In the Categories list, choose Date and Time.**

4. **In the Field Names list, choose Time.**

   The description in the dialog changes to The Current Time.

5. **Click OK to close the Field dialog.**

   The current time appears in the document.

Updating a field

After you have the time in your document, the time doesn't change. You can refresh the time by updating the field code in this two-step process:

1. **Wait until the computer time is different than when you inserted the time field. (You might have to wait for at least a minute.) Then select the time in your document.**

   This tells Word that you want to do something with the time field. By selecting the time (the result of the field code's action), you also select the field code. If you're really observant, you might notice that the field part of the selection looks darker, which lets you know it's not just text.

2. **Click the Update Field button that you placed on a toolbar earlier in this section.**

   Alternatively, right-click the time and choose Update Field.

   The time refreshes.

The first step in the preceding list is very important. If you don't select the field code first, nothing happens when you click the Update Field button.

Peeking inside a field code

In this section, you look at the actual code inside a field. This, too, requires that you first select the field code:

1. **Select the Time field code by selecting the time in your document.**

2. **Click the View Field Codes toggle button that you placed on a toolbar earlier in this section.**

Alternatively right-click and choose Toggle Field Codes.

The actual code (instead of the field's result) toggles on.

You can now see the actual field code, which is always contained within two curly brackets. From left to right, this list describes a field code:

✦ **Opening bracket:** This begins the field code.

✦ **Field name:** In the following example, TIME is the field name. The Time field is followed by the * MERGEFORMAT switch. This switch instructs Word to keep the previous formatting when updating the field.

    {TIME *MERGEFORMAT}

✦ **Switches:** Additional items that control how the field works.

The switches for Time allow you to control how time will be formatted in the document. Switches for other Word fields can specify file paths, hyperlinks, symbols, and all kinds of different things!

✦ **Closing bracket:** This completes the field code.

You can type inside the field code's special brackets. The brackets are special because they can't be typed in from your keyboard, even though they look like the regular curly brackets. You can insert an empty pair of field code brackets into any document by clicking the Insert Field Characters button you put on a toolbar earlier in this section, or press ⌘-F9.

Adding more options to a field

Create another Word field that displays the time, but this time add some optional formatting. Start with a new, blank document:

1. Click the New button on Word's standard toolbar to open a new, blank Word document.

2. Choose Insert⇨Field.

The Field dialog, as shown earlier in Figure 8-11, appears.

3. In the Categories list, choose Date and Time.

4. In the Field Names list, choose Time.

The description in the dialog changes to The Current Time.

5. Click the Options button.

The Field Options dialog opens, as shown in Figure 8-13.

6. Choose MMMM d, yyyy in the Date-Time Formats list.

If you live somewhere other than the United States, you may have to choose d MMMM, yyyy. You'll have to drag the scroll bar down slightly to see this format. This just swaps the placement of the month and date! In the following list, *m* stands for *month, d* stands for *day,* and *y* stands for *year* (just like in Excel):

- *M* displays the number of the month.
- *MM* displays a two-digit number for the month.
- *MMM* displays a three-letter abbreviation for the month.
- *MMMM* displays the month spelled out.
- *d* displays the number of the date.
- *dd* displays the date as a two-digit number.
- *ddd* displays the day of the week as a three-letter abbreviation.
- *dddd* displays the day of the week spelled out.
- *yy* displays a two-digit year.
- *yyyy* displays a four-digit year.

7. **Click the Add to Field button to add the formatting to your field.**

8. **Click OK to close the Field Options dialog and then click OK to close the Field dialog.**

   The current time appears in your document with the switch formatting. If you view the field code after completing step 8 you see \@ plus the chosen format is added to the field code as TIME \@ " MMMM d, yyyy ". When you add options to a Field code they are shown after a backslash and are called *switches.*

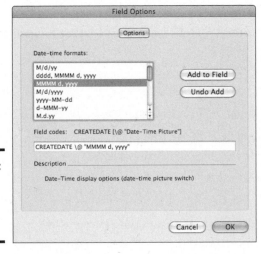

Figure 8-13:
Adding an optional switch to a field code.

Take a look at your new field code and compare the differences before and after adding the formatting switch, as shown in the following example. You could've typed in all that formatting stuff, but Word typed it for you. Go ahead and experiment with the format code. Try the different variations that are listed in the Field Options dialog, such as M.d.yy, and notice the placement of quotation marks, if any. Quotation marks within Word fields tell Word to do certain things. In this case, they specify the formatting to apply.

```
11:57 AM
{TIME \*MERGEFORMAT}

June 18, 2010
{TIME \@ "MMMM d, yyyy" \*MERGEFORMAT}
```

Time is a fairly typical Word field. If you've followed along so far, you know quite a bit about Word fields and can fully customize page numbers, dates, and times in headers and footers.

Managing Multiple Open Documents

Sometimes you might work with several documents open at once; Word has some features that can help. The most common way of switching from one open document to another is simply to click from one document window to another. The document window you click comes to the front. This takes some getting used to for people switching to a Mac from a PC, in which you commonly use the Windows taskbar for this purpose. To keep Windows users from getting homesick on your Macs, you can hold down the mouse button on the Word Dock icon. This displays previews from which you can choose to switch from one document to another, as shown in Figure 8-14.

Word's Window menu (see Figure 8-15) has a similar switching capability as well as other features:

✦ **Arrange All:** Arranges open document windows horizontally on your screen.

✦ **Split:** Divides the currently open document window into a top and bottom half so you can see and work in two portions of the document at the same time. Split is a toggle. To remove the Split, choose the Split option a second time from the Window menu.

✦ **List of open documents:** At the bottom of the Window menu, you can choose from a list of open documents to switch from one document to another.

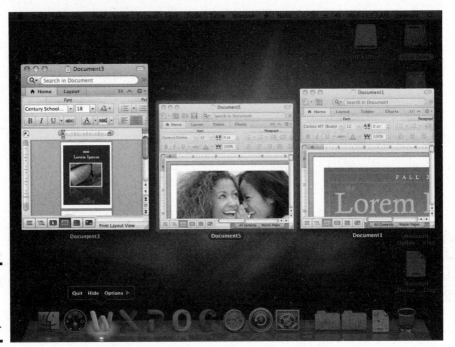

Figure 8-14: Switching documents on the Dock.

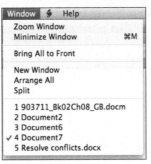

Figure 8-15: Switching documents from the Window menu.

Creating an Electronic Form

Word can create not only paper forms, but electronic ones, too! After you figure out how to create an electronic form in Word, you can distribute the form, and the recipients can fill it in on their computers and then return it to you. You create forms in Word's Print Layout view.

Accessing the form controls

Form controls live on the Developer tab of the Ribbon. (See Figure 8-16.) However, the Developer tab doesn't appear by default — you have to tell Word you want to see it. To access the Developer tab, follow these steps:

Figure 8-16:
Exploring
the
Developer
tab.

**Book II
Chapter 8**

**Advanced
Word Stuff**

1. **Click the small wheel at the right end of the Ribbon's tab bar (as shown in Figure 8-16).**

2. **Choose Ribbon Preferences from the pop-up menu.**

   The Ribbon Preferences dialog displays, as shown in Figure 8-17.

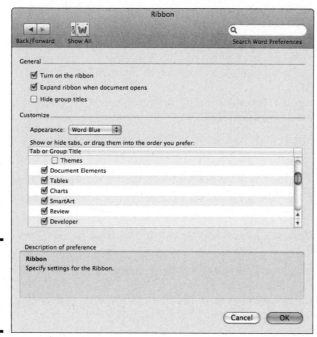

Figure 8-17:
Turning
on the
Developer
tab.

3. **In the Customize area, look under the Print Layout section and select the Developer check box.**

4. **Click OK to close the Ribbon Preferences dialog.**

    The Developer tab of the Ribbon displays (refer to Figure 8-16).

Making and enabling a form

Making a form in Word is as simple as choosing appropriate form controls from the Developer tab of the Ribbon, placing them in your Word document, and then enabling your form by turning protection on. We cover the details of each form control in the following sections.

A ground rule for forms is that you edit them in *unprotected* (or *unlocked*) mode. When the form is done and ready to be used, *protect* (or *lock*) the form to enable the form controls. You can toggle between Lock and Unlock modes for your form by clicking the Protect Form button on the Form Controls group of the Ribbon's Developer tab (refer to Figure 8-16). Expect to toggle back and forth often as you design your form.

Use a table to keep your form fields organized neatly in your document.

Inserting a text input form field

The text input field is the most common form field. You might have filled in thousands of them in your lifetime. Name, address, and phone number are appropriate for text fields. To add a text input field to a document:

1. **In an open Word document, place the insertion point where you want to insert a text form field.**

    This insertion point can be within a table, in a frame, or basically anywhere in the document.

2. **Click the Text Box Field button on the Developer tab of the Ribbon.**

    A gray box (the form field) appears in your document at the insertion cursor position, and the fun begins.

3. **Click the gray box to select it and then click the Options button on the Ribbon.**

    The Text Form Field Options dialog opens, as shown in Figure 8-18.

Double-clicking a form control (while the form is not protected) displays the Options dialog for that form control.

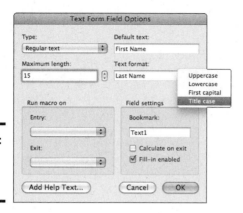

Figure 8-18:
Setting up
a text box
form field.

The Text Form Field Options dialog is devilishly simple, yet brilliant. When
you click the Type pop-up menu and choose a text field type, the rest of the
Text Form Field Options dialog changes to offer appropriate choices based
on your selection. Here are the six types of text form fields from which to
choose:

✦ **Regular Text:** Word displays whatever is typed.

✦ **Number:** Numbers can be formatted and used in calculations.

✦ **Date:** Dates can be formatted.

✦ **Current Date:** Displays the current date in your form.

✦ **Current Time:** Displays the current time in your form.

✦ **Calculation:** Calculates values based on entries made in numeric fields.

In Figure 8-18, we show you the default arrangement of the Text Form Field
Options dialog, which allows these options for Regular Text:

✦ **Type:** Choose a field type as described in the previous paragraph.

✦ **Maximum Length:** Specify the number of characters allowed in the field.

✦ **Default Text:** This text appears as a prompt in the field.

✦ **Text Format:** Choose a text formatting option from the pop-up menu.

✦ **Run Macro On:** If macros are available to this document, you can
choose one to be triggered as the form field is clicked into or exited.

✦ **Field Settings:** These settings are available:

• *Bookmark:* Add a bookmark name to your form field.

• *Calculate on Exit:* If you have calculated fields, select this check box
to have them calculate when exiting the form field.

- *Fill-In Enabled:* Select this check box so your field can be typed in.

- *Add Help Text button:* This opens the Form Field Help Text dialog that enables you to add a prompt or explanatory text about the form field. This help text appears in the status bar at the bottom of the document window, or you can have it appear when the user presses the Help button on the keyboard (but not from the Help option you see when you right-click or Control-click the field).

Work with form fields and set their options while the form is unprotected (or unlocked). You have to protect (or lock) a form before you can fill in the form fields.

Inserting a check box on a form

Adding a check box to a form is a piece of cake! Follow these steps:

1. **Click at the point in your document where you want this form control to be located.**

2. **Click the Check Box Form Field button (shown in the margin) on the Developer tab of the Ribbon.**

A little square appears.

3. **Click the Form Fields Options button (shown in the margin) on the Developer tab of the Ribbon.**

The Check Box Form Field Options dialog opens. (See Figure 8-19.)

Figure 8-19: Checking out a check box.

The following options in this dialog are

+ **Check Box Size:** You have two choices here:

  - *Auto:* Let Word decide.

  - *Exactly:* Type a value or use the increase/decrease control.

✦ **Default Value:** Select Checked or Not Checked.

✦ **Run Macro On**: If you have macros available to this document, you can choose one to be triggered as the form field is clicked into or exited.

✦ **Field Settings:** Three options exist in this area:

- *Bookmark Field:* Give the check box a name ending with a number. We suggest that numbers you assign be sequential.

- *Calculate on Exit:* If you use calculations, you can select this box to cause Word to perform the calculations after the control is used. We explain calculated form fields in just a bit!

- *Check Box Enabled:* Deselect to disable this check box.

Upgrading to a combo

Want to upgrade to a combo meal? Yum! (Okay, so we shouldn't write while we're hungry.) In a form, a combo field is a pretty neat thing. Use a combo when you want the user to choose an entry from a list of choices. The *Combo Box* field is also referred to as a *Drop-Down Form* field. Follow these steps to create a combo box:

1. **Click in your document at the position to insert the form field.**

2. **On the Developer tab of the Ribbon, click the Combo Box button (shown in the margin).**

A small gray box appears.

3. **Click the Form Fields Options button (shown in the margin) on the Developer tab of the Ribbon.**

The Drop-Down Form Field Options dialog opens. (See Figure 8-20.)

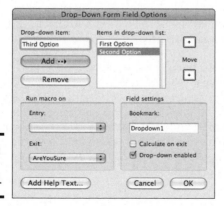

Figure 8-20:
Adding a
combo field.

The top half of this dialog lets you build the list of choices that will appear when the Drop-Down button is clicked in your finished, protected form.

✦ **Drop-Down Item:** Type an item to appear in the drop-down list.

✦ **Add:** Adds your typed Drop-Down item to the Items in Drop-Down List.

✦ **Remove:** Removes a selected item from the Items in the Drop-Down List.

✦ **Items in Drop-Down List:** These items appear in the drop-down list of choices that appears when the Drop-Down button is clicked in your finished, protected form.

✦ **Move:** Select an item in Items in Drop-Down List. Click an arrow to move it up or down in the list.

✦ **Field Settings:** Here are the field settings:

  • *Bookmark:* Give the drop-down list a name ending with a number. The numbers you assign should be sequential.

  • *Calculate on Exit:* If you use calculations, you can select this check box to cause Word to perform the calculations after the control is used. We explain calculated form fields in the following section.

  • *Drop-down Enabled:* When selected when the user clicks a button in the form field, a pop-up menu displays showing the items in the drop-down list.

When you're done setting up the combo box and you select it within the form, it works like a regular pop-up menu.

Doing the math in Word forms

One more thing! Form fields are also Word fields. Figure 8-21 shows an example of a simple calculation. The figure shows the Word document on the left side, and the Text Form Fields Options dialog on the right. Notice that the answer, 25, is selected and highlighted. The Text Form Field Options dialog changes in response to what is currently selected.

We made three text box fields named Number1, Number2, and Answer1. In Figure 8-21, you see these three fields with labels to their left. Underneath the three fields, we show the Answer1 field as it looks when Display Field Codes button is clicked so that you can see the Word field code that does the calculation. This Word field code represents the entry shown in the Field Text Form Fields Options dialog in the Expression field. You can see from the dialog that the Type is set to Calculation, and on the left side, you can see that the result of the calculation is 25.

You can modify the formula in a field code by typing in the Word field, which we recommend if the formula is long. Table 8-1 shows the operators supported by Word fields in calculated form fields.

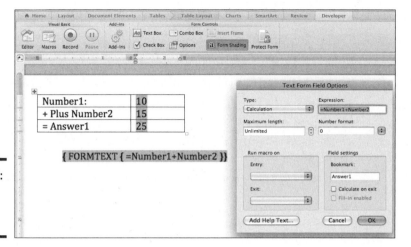

Figure 8-21:
Fielding
a math
problem.

Table 8-1	Doing Math in Word Form Fields
Operator	*Description*
+	Add
−	Subtract
*	Multiply
/	Divide
%	Percent
^	Power or root
=	Equals
<	Is less than
>	Is greater than
<=	Is less than or equal to
>=	Is greater than or equal to
<>	Not equal to

Grabbing just the form field data

Word has a special feature that allows you to save just the data from forms
in a document, instead of saving the entire document. This is handy when all
you need to have is the data, instead of the entire form. To make this special
text file, start off in Word with a filled-in form document open:

1. **Choose File⇨Save As.**

   The Save As dialog opens.

2. **Click the Options button.**

   Word's Save dialog opens.

3. **Select the Save Data Only for Forms (for Current Document Only) check box and click OK.**

   Word's Save dialog reappears. Note that the file format has changed to Plain Text (.txt).

4. **Give your data file a name and a location and click Save.**

When you open the resulting file in Word, you see all the form answers separated by commas. You can import this file into a database as a record or even open it within Microsoft Excel.

If you're handy with VBA and HTML, you can use the resulting text file with the HTML Post method to add a record on a server.

Embedding All Kinds of Things

A Word document is a very versatile thing; so versatile that you can actually embed other kinds of object types, such as tables and charts, right inside a Word document. You can even embed another Word document.

The Object dialog shown in Figure 8-22 displays a list of things you can embed in a Word document. To access this dialog and insert one of the objects, take these steps:

1. **In an open Word document, choose Insert⇨Object.**

   The Object dialog displays, as shown in Figure 8-22.

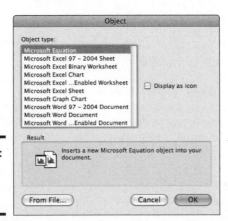

Figure 8-22: Embedding objects in Word.

2. **Select or deselect the Display as Icon check box as desired.**

   If you select this option, the embedded object appears in your document as an icon that can be double-clicked to open the embedded object.

   If you *don't* select this option, the embedded object itself or a preview of the object displays in the Word document.

3. **Select an object type from the Object Type list or click the From File button:**

   • *Object Type list:* Choose one of the types listed to embed it into your Word document, which is described in the Result section. Click OK to embed the object and close the Object dialog.

   • *From File button:* Closes the Object dialog and opens the Insert as Object dialog (shown in Figure 8-23), where you can navigate or use Spotlight to locate a file object to embed into your Word document. Click Insert to embed the selected file. You can embed only the files of the object types that you see listed in the Object dialog shown in Figure 8-22. More about From File follows.

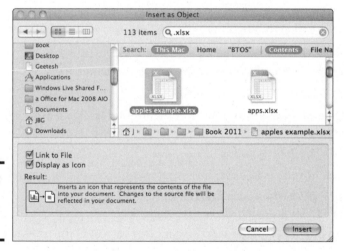

Figure 8-23:
Insert as
Object
dialog.

If you choose to open the Insert as Object dialog (shown in Figure 8-23), it has two option buttons:

✦ **Link to File:** Word internally remembers the file path information, and a reference (link) to the source document is created. If the source document is renamed, moved, or for some other reason, the path changes, the link breaks. If the original changes, the changes are reflected whenever the linked object's icon or preview is double-clicked.

If you don't select this option, a copy of the file is embedded, and the original is left untouched. If the original changes later, the embedded object isn't updated.

✦ **Display as Icon:** If you select this option, the embedded object appears in your document as an icon that can be double-clicked to open the embedded object.

You might think that having an embedded object in a Word document, especially if it's another Word document, is confusing. If so, select the Display as Icon check box before you click OK in either the Object dialog or the Insert as Object dialog. If you've inserted an object and displayed it as an icon, you can choose a picture instead of the default icon by following these steps:

1. **Right-click or Control-click the icon (or the blank spot where the icon is supposed to be) and from the pop-up menu, choose Format⇨Object.**

   The Format Object dialog appears.

2. **If it's not selected already, in the Format Object dialog, select the Colors and Lines tab.**

   Colors and lines formatting options display.

3. **In the Fill area, click the Color pop-up menu and choose Fill Effects.**

   The Fill Effects dialog appears.

4. **Select the Picture tab and then click the Select Picture button.**

   The Choose a Picture dialog displays.

5. **Navigate or use Spotlight to find and then select a nice, small picture (JPEG or another format) to use as the icon.**

6. **Click the Insert button.**

   The chosen picture displays in the Fill Effects dialog.

7. **Click OK to close the Insert Picture dialog and click OK to close the Format Object dialog.**

   The picture is on the icon placeholder for your embedded object. Double-click the picture to activate the embedded object.

Chapter 9: Printing for Posterity

In This Chapter

- ✓ Setting up Page Setup
- ✓ Preparing to print
- ✓ Printing your document just right

*T*oday's printers are just amazing. Not only do they print all your beautifully crafted documents, but some of them scan, copy, and fax, too. Yet others can show you previews of photos before printing them, and some even work wirelessly with your computer! The good news is that whether your printer is a desktop model or a big, fancy networked behemoth, your Word documents can come out just the way you like.

When it comes to printing, Word and Mac OS X interact with each other to a high degree. When Word opens, it checks to see what the default printer is and what its capabilities are. When you open or create a document in Word, some of the Page Setup options are determined by the default printer's capabilities. The same document may have slightly different page breaks and font spacing when opened on a computer with a different default printer. Some printers can print from edge to edge, but others can't. Word is smart; it reformats your document to the current default printer, which is a reason why a document can look a wee bit different from one computer to another.

The choices you're offered when you print a document depend upon the printer's brand and model and the printer driver version that's installed. Certain options are available only if your printer supports them. These include *duplex* (printing on both sides of a sheet of paper), booklet layout, *full bleed* (edge to edge), collating, paper quality, print quality, and printer ink levels. And if all that printer terminology left you bewildered, don't worry because we explain these features in this chapter.

Keep in mind that the figures in this chapter probably won't match exactly what you see when you use your printer (unless you happen to have the exact same printer we do!). That's because every printer works with driver software to communicate with Mac OS X, and each printer brand thus has drivers that show dialogs a little differently. The good news is that all these dialogs are populated with options that generally work the same across all printers.

Sizing Up Things with Page Setup

To start, take a look at the dialog that comes up when you choose File⇨Page Setup. A very simple-looking Page Setup dialog (see Figure 9-1) appears, and most of the time you'll use it to choose Portrait or Landscape orientation only and then go on your way. But take a closer look at all the options, starting from the top. Although some of these settings are the same as the Page Setup settings on the Ribbon, which we discussed in Chapter 4 of this minibook, you can do more with the dialogs we show here:

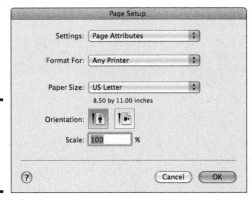

Figure 9-1:
Setting up
with the
Page Setup
dialog.

The Page Setup dialog provides access to the following controls:

✦ **Settings:** A pop-up menu where you can choose from the following:

- *Microsoft Word:* This option takes you to Word's Margins dialog.

- *Save as Default:* If you choose this option, when you're done making adjustments to all Page Setup's settings, your saved settings become the default for Page Setup.

✦ **Format For:** Enables you to format your document for a specific printer, any printer, or you can open the Mac OS X Print and Fax settings dialog. See the next section for all the details.

✦ **Paper Size:** Allows you to change the paper size. See the section "Choosing a paper size," later in this chapter.

✦ **Orientation:** Choose portrait or landscape.

✦ **Scale:** You can scale the document larger or smaller by typing a new percentage value.

Formatting for a particular printer

Word looks at the Format For setting in the Page Setup dialog (see Figure 9-1) and adjusts document formatting according to the chosen printer's capabilities.

When you click Format For, a pop-up menu appears where you see a list of printers that are currently attached to your computer. If you want your documents to be formatted with a specific printer in mind, choose the printer from the list of printers in the pop-up menu.

You can set Format For to Any Printer if you want Word to use a standard set of formatting options. This is the best option to choose if you plan to share your document with other people who may use other printer brands and models. This is also the only choice available if you don't have a printer installed and connected to your computer.

In the same Format For pop-up menu, you can choose the Print & Fax preferences option. The Print & Fax dialog shown in Figure 9-2 is provided by Mac OS X and your particular printer driver, not Microsoft Word. Therefore, your Print & Fax preferences may look substantially different from ours unless you happen to be using the same printer. As shown in Figure 9-2, you can open the print queue and check the printer's ink or toner supply levels.

Figure 9-2:
Printing
and fax
preferences.

Choosing a paper size

The Paper Size pop-up menu has a lot to offer to a curious printing aficionado. A click of this pop-up menu offers some common size formats. Our printer can do borderless printing, but the current selection in Figure 9-3 is for US Letter size paper with a border. The Paper Size pop-up menu is nice enough to show you the border that will be used by the printer — in this case, 0.12 inch.

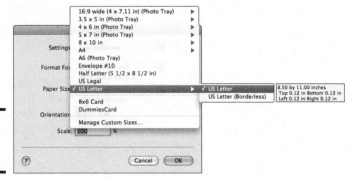

Figure 9-3:
Choosing a
paper size.

At the bottom of the Paper Size pop-up menu is the Manage Custom Sizes option. This option takes you to the Custom Page Sizes dialog, as shown in Figure 9-4, where you can create a custom paper size. Keep in mind that the custom paper sizes you create here are available to all applications, not just Microsoft Word.

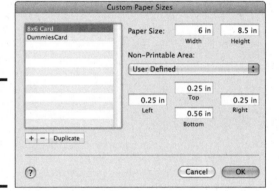

Figure 9-4:
Creating
a custom
paper size
for your
printer.

Printing Like a Pro!

Word has a couple of not-so-hush secrets that can make your printing fast and easy. We show you where to look to find the printing option that's right for your situation.

Make it fast!

When you just want a printout of the current document on the default printer and you don't want to be bothered with any settings, click the Print button on the Standard toolbar. (See Figure 9-5.) You aren't pestered by any printer dialogs, and your document goes straight to the printer. Life is simple and easy!

Figure 9-5:
The fastest
way to print.

Getting a few more options

When you want more than a printout with the default of every setting, you can find more options by choosing File⇨Print or pressing ⌘-P to bring up the Print dialog, as shown in Figure 9-6. You can even find an option here to expose every possible printer control. We talk more about that later in this chapter. For now, we focus on the default options.

Figure 9-6:
Printing with
the default
Print dialog.

Picking a printer

The Printer pop-up menu enables you to choose from three options:

✦ **List of printers:** All available printers are shown, and you can choose which one to use.

✦ **Add Printer:** Opens the Mac OS X printer options dialog and allows you to add a printer.

✦ **Print and Fax Preferences:** Opens the Mac OS X Print & Fax system preferences dialog. (Refer to Figure 9-2.)

Picking a set of preset printing options

The Presets pop-up menu enables you to choose from several different printing presets:

✦ **Standard:** Most of the time, this is the best one to use.

✦ **Last Used Settings:** Might be the one for you if you have some special customized presets.

✦ **List of Customized Presets:** If you've created customized presets in the advanced printing options (see the section "Seeing all the possible print options," later in this chapter), you can choose one of them.

Printing to PDF

One of the really neat things about having a Mac is that every application that can print prints to PDF (Portable Document Format). Word is no exception, except that in Word, you can choose File⇨Save As and in the Format pop-up menu, choose PDF.

Unless you need one of the other PDF options in the following list, you don't have to go through the Print dialog to make a PDF. Here's a rundown on the PDF printing options (refer to Figure 9-6):

✦ **Save as PDF:** Opens the Save dialog to save your document as PDF.

✦ **Save as PostScript:** Opens the Save dialog to save your document as a `.ps` postscript file. A PostScript printer is needed to print the file.

✦ **Fax PDF:** Opens the Print dialog to a Mac OS X Fax cover sheet. If your Mac has a dialup modem, you can use this option to fax your file.

✦ **Mail PDF:** Opens an e-mail message in Apple Mail, not Microsoft Outlook, and adds the PDF as an attachment.

✦ **Save as PDF-X:** This option flattens transparency and changes colors to CYMK.

✦ **Save PDF to iPhoto:** Creates a PDF and sends the PDF to iPhoto.

✦ **Save PDF to Web Receipts Folder:** Creates a PDF and puts it into your Web Receipts folder.

✦ **Edit Menu:** Allows you to add custom PDF workflows. Click the Help button in the Print dialog for more details.

Previewing in Mac OS X Preview

The Print dialog is standard for all applications that can print. Mac OS X offers a preview of your document when you click the Preview button. (Refer to Figure 9-6.) The File⇨Print Preview command path is no longer available.

Seeing all the possible print options

In the Print dialog, click More Printing Options (the downward-pointing triangle to the right of the Printer pop-up menu shown earlier in Figure 9-6) to display the complete Print dialog, as shown in Figure 9-7.

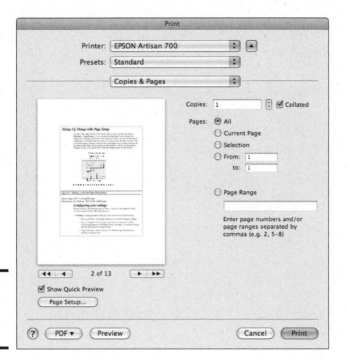

Figure 9-7:
Advanced
printing
options.

The settings for Printer, Presets, Preview, and PDF output, which we
describe in the previous sections, are the same in the advanced options
dialog shown in Figure 9-7. However, there are plenty of other options that
we discuss next.

Using Copies & Pages

In its larger, advanced options incarnation, the Print dialog has the Copies &
Pages sheet shown as the default. Notice in Figure 9-7, you can choose how
many pages to print and which pages (or range of pages) to print.

An optional Quick Preview with forward and backward arrows is on the left
to help you find specific pages in your document. You don't have to wait
for Quick Preview to finish working before you click the Print button. Quick
Preview can slow the Print dialog a bit, so you can turn off Quick Preview.
(Just deselect the Show Quick Preview check box.)

Using special Microsoft Word printing options

When you click the Copies & Pages pop-up menu in the advanced options
dialog, you find a special Microsoft Word option. When you choose this
option, which results in the dialog shown in Figure 9-8, you're offered a variety of specific printing options that you might need. For example, if your

printer can't print on both sides of the paper at once (*duplex* printing), you can print all the odd pages, turn the paper over, and run it through a second time to print all the even pages.

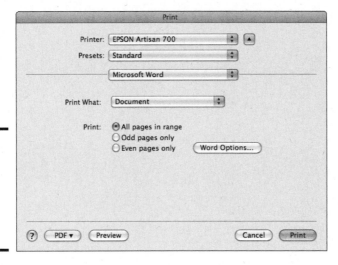

Figure 9-8: Using special Microsoft Word printing options.

The Print What pop-up menu deserves a bit of attention here. The choices in this pop-up menu enable you to print the entire document or specific parts of your document that are listed in the pop-up menu.

When you click the Word Options button, Word's Print preferences dialog (shown in Figure 9-9) appears, where you can choose from a variety of specific printing options.

The Reverse Print Order check box is a popular choice. Many older printers print the first page so that it's on the bottom of the pile when you're done. This feature tells Word to print the document from last page to first page so that when you're done printing, page one is on top of the pile.

Select the Print Background Colors and Images check box to enable these options that are set on the Ribbon's Layout tab.

Using special printer features

When you click the Copies & Pages pop-up menu, all the options below Microsoft Word in the menu are tailored to the brand and model printer that you choose. The options available depend upon what capabilities your printer has and upon the skill of the folks who wrote the printer driver. We don't cover each feature (and some options differ from printer to printer), but we do point out some things most Word users want to know about:

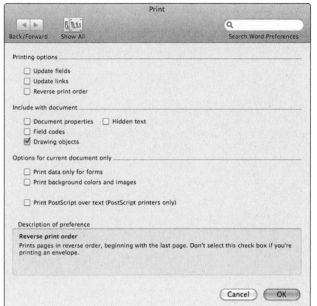

Figure 9-9:
Adjusting
Word's print
preferences.

✦ **Layout:** Here you might find the duplex printing option if your printer
supports this. This option can be grayed out if your printer does not
support two-sided printing, or if your printer uses a separate dialog specifically to support duplex printing.

Our printer happens to have its own dialog to manage two-sided printing
options. Again, each brand and model comes with its own drivers and
options. Your printer may not have these options.

✦ **Paper Handling:** You probably don't need to adjust this one. You can
use this feature to choose reverse print order instead of using Word's
preferences.

✦ **Cover Page:** This adds a cover page to your document (almost like
adding a cover page for faxes you might send, especially since some
printers have fax capabilities). You might also choose this option if more
than one person is sharing a printer.

✦ **Scheduler:** If you want to schedule your document to print at a certain
time or put your print job on hold, choose this option.

✦ **Print Settings:** This dialog offers many choices. Choose a paper type,
speed, and quality of the print job. For a quick draft, adjust the settings.
Lately, some printers default to speed over quality. If you find that some
things in your documents aren't printing right, you probably need to
raise the quality setting. Your printer may have other options here.

Chapter 10: Managing a Mail Merge

In This Chapter

✔ Meeting the Mail Merge Manager

✔ Making the data right

✔ Running the merge

✔ Merging to labels and envelopes

People use Mail Merge to accomplish many tasks. The most popular is to make personalized form letters along with labels and envelopes to put them in. If you're looking to go green, you can use Merge to Outlook E-mail and save paper and postage. If you're in business and you want to get really fancy, you can make personalized product catalogs that contain just the products you think your customers might want. You can even use Mail Merge to generate periodic reports.

If you need to send mailings on a schedule, choose Tools⇨Flag for Followup from the menu bar to set a schedule. Word will remind you to run the Mail Merge.

Word 2011 for Mac's Mail Merge Manager lets you see all six merging steps at once, so you can easily follow through the process.

Making Magic with Mail Merge

If one major area exists in which Office for Mac beats all the others by a country mile, mail merge is it! Sending form letters and customized messages to a group of people in one fell swoop has never been so easy.

Your guide to mail merging in Word is Mail Merge Manager. You can invoke Mail Merge Manager by choosing Tools⇨Mail Merge Manager from the menu bar. It's designed to be used starting at the top in Step 1, and you work your way down to Step 6. The six steps to making a mail merge are shown in Figure 10-1.

Figure 10-1:
Looking
over the
Mail Merge
Manager.

The steps in the Mail Merge Manager are as follows:

1. **Select a Document Type.**

   Choose from four types of mail merge:

   - *Form Letters:* Customize a letter with personal information or data.

   - *Labels:* Make mailing labels, tent cards, book labels, and DVD labels.

   - *Envelopes:* Print envelopes of any size.

   - *Catalog:* Choose this option to build custom, personalized catalogs, brochures, and price sheets. For example, you could pull pictures from a database to create individualized custom catalogs based on customer purchases, category, or some other criteria.

2. **Select Recipients List.**

   Choose a data source for the mail merge.

3. **Insert Placeholders.**

   Choose the field names (for example, column names, headers, and column headers) and position them in your document.

4. **Filter Recipients.**

   Set rules as to which records will be retrieved from the data source.

5. **Preview Results.**

   See exactly how your document looks with data before running the mail merge.

6. **Complete Merge.**

   Run the merge. You can merge to a printer, a single Word document, personalized Word documents, or e-mail messages.

We go through an example of each of the four types of mail merges that can be performed in Step 1 of the Mail Merge Manager, but because all four use data sources, we start our discussion with mail merge data sources.

Getting Good Data for Your Mail Merge

It may seem odd to start with Step 2 of the Mail Merge Manager, but no matter which option you choose in Step 1, you need to choose a data source. When you get to Step 2 in the examples in this chapter, refer to this section.

Mail merge works by bringing data stored in a data table into Word. A good data table's first row (and only the first row) has the headers, also called *fields* or *column names.* All subsequent rows contain data. There are no merged cells in a data table, and there are no completely empty rows or columns, although empty cells are allowed.

The headers will be used as placeholders in your Mail Merge document. Placeholders display the data gleaned from the data source for each record as the merge is run in Step 6.

Word can use many different data sources to perform a mail merge:

✦ A table in Word.

✦ An Excel worksheet or data range.

✦ A FileMaker Pro database file.

✦ Advanced users can use ODBC and VBA to connect to practically any data source, including Microsoft Access, SQL Server, Oracle, and MySQL.

After you've chosen the document type in Step 1 of the Mail Merge Manager, you need to choose a data source in Mail Merge Manager Step 2: Select Recipients List, and then choose the Get List option to display options, as shown in Figure 10-2. We discuss each Get List option in the following sections.

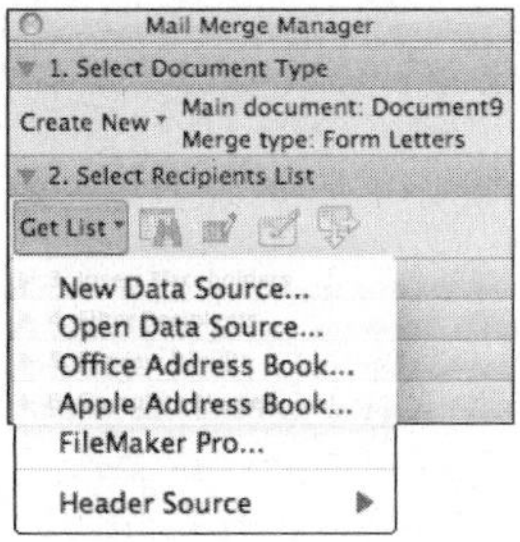

**Book II
Chapter 10**

**Managing a
Mail Merge**

Figure 10-2:
Choosing a
data source.

New Data Source

If you don't have a data table, the New Data Source option lets you make a data table from scratch in a new Word document using a series of dialogs. This option is fine for small databases up to a few thousand records.

Be aware that using a Word document as a data source doesn't cut it for large data sources. If you find that Word becomes slow when you're working with the data source, move your table to Excel, which can handle over a million records per worksheet. You can copy the data from Word and paste it into Excel.

Choosing fields

When you choose New Data Source, you're presented with the Create Data Source dialog, shown in Figure 10-3. First, you define fields for your new data. By default, you're presented with some commonly used fields. In the Placeholder List field, you can type new header names and add them to the list by clicking the Add Placeholder button.

To re-order the field names, choose a field name in the list and then click the up or down arrows. To remove a field name from the list, select it and then click the Remove Field Name button.

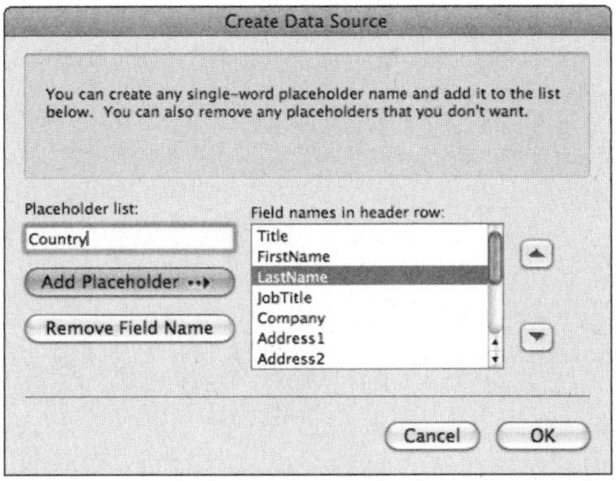

Figure 10-3:
Choosing
field names.

When you're done choosing field names, click the OK button and you will be prompted to save the new Word document. Give your new data source a name and then save the file.

Filling in the data

As soon as your file is saved, you'll be presented with an easy-to-use database input form called Data Form, shown in Figure 10-4.

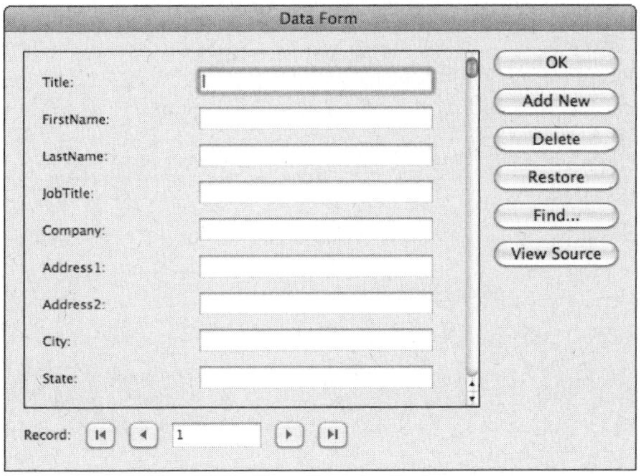

Book II
Chapter 10

Managing a
Mail Merge

Figure 10-4:
Entering
data
records.

The left side of Data Form shows your field names. Drag the scroll bar if all the fields don't fit in the dialog. In the center column, you type the data entries for the current record. The current record's number is shown in the Record navigation at the bottom of the Data Form. Use these controls in the data form:

+ **Add New:** Add a new record to the end of the table.

+ **Delete:** Deletes record currently displayed.

+ **Restore:** If you've started to make changes to an existing record, this cancels the changes if you haven't saved the record (by clicking OK).

+ **Find:** Displays a dialog that lets you find a specific record by searching keywords within a field in the data table.

+ **View Source:** Displays the Word document that is the data source. Your table will be quite plain, so you might want to visit the Tables tab of the Ribbon to spruce it up.

+ **Record:** Click the navigation buttons to display individual records in your data table. You can type a record number there and then press the Tab key to view a specific record.

In the Data Form dialog, press Tab or the down-arrow key to advance to the next field within a record. Press Shift-Tab or the up-arrow key to select the previous field.

When working with your data table in Word, you can edit directly in the table. Turn on the database toolbar, shown in Figure 10-5, by choosing View➪Toolbars➪Database from the menu bar. The controls on the Database toolbar are as follows:

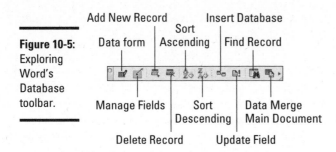

Figure 10-5:
Exploring
Word's
Database
toolbar.

◆ **Data Form:** When the selection cursor is in a table, displays the Data Form shown in Figure 10-4. This same button is also located in Step 2 of the Mail Merge Manager.

◆ **Manage Fields:** When the selection cursor is in a table, displays the Manage Fields dialog, which lets you choose nondefault separators, which is probably not a good idea to do.

◆ **Add New Record:** When the selection cursor is in a table, adds a new, blank row to the bottom of the table.

◆ **Delete Record:** When the selection cursor is in a table, deletes the row (the record) containing the cursor.

◆ **Sort Ascending:** When the selection cursor is in a table, sorts the column containing the cursor alphabetically or from lowest to highest numeric value.

◆ **Sort Descending:** When the selection cursor is in a table, sorts the column containing the cursor in reverse alphabetical order or from highest to lowest numeric value.

◆ **Insert Database:** When starting with a new, blank document, you can use this option to create a database connection link to an existing database file in Finder. In the process, you can choose multiple filters for records. The queries are saved as part of the database connection. You can use this table as an intermediate table for a mail merge, or you can use Insert Database to make a standalone table that's connected to a data source.

◆ **Update Field:** Refreshes the data in a table that was made by Insert Database.

◆ **Find Record:** Search records by keyword within a specified field.

◆ **Data Merge Main Document:** When the selection cursor is in a table, and that table is used as the data source for a Word mail merge document, clicking this button opens that mail merge main document.

Don't let bullies try to say you shouldn't do these things in Word. If you like Word and are comfortable with these tools, it's perfectly fine to use Word for a basic database. You can use the Tables tab of the Ribbon with the Database toolbar to manage your table's style, options, and borders.

Open Data Source

The Open Data Source option (refer to Figure 10-2, which shows Step 2 of the Mail Merge Manager) enables you to choose a file in Finder to use as the data source for your mail merge. It displays the Choose a Data File dialog, which behaves as an Open dialog. Navigate in Finder to any file was saved as a database. You can choose a Word document, such as one made using New Data Source in the Mail Merge Manager, a text file (usually in .csv format), an RTF document, or an Excel workbook.

Book II
Chapter 10

Office Address Book

The Office Address Book option (refer to Figure 10-2) allows you to use your Outlook contacts as the mail merge data source. Choosing this option displays Step 3 in the Mail Merge Manager and gives you instant access to the field names you have in your Outlook Contacts.

Managing a
Mail Merge

Apple Address Book

New for Word 2011 is the ability to choose contacts from your Apple Address book. Choosing the Apple Address Book option in Step 2 immediately displays Step 3 in the Mail Merge Manager, which gives you instant access to the field names in your Apple Address Book.

FileMaker Pro

The FileMaker Pro option (refer to Figure 10-2) within the Get List area of the Mail Merge Manager displays the Choose a File dialog. Navigate in Finder to a FileMaker Pro file that's already set up as a mailing list or a data source list.

Making a Form Letter

While personalizing form letters fools no one, they are popular just the same and can also be useful to generate automated reports within an organization. You can start from an existing Word document or a blank document. Either way, the steps are the same. Make sure the Mail Merge Manager is available by choosing Tools⇨Mail Merge Manager from the menu bar. Then follow these steps in the Mail Merge Manager:

1. **In the Mail Merge Manager, click Select Document type and then choose Create New➪Merge Type: Form Letters.**

   The Mail Merge Manager displays the name of the main mail merge document and the chosen merge type.

2. **In the Mail Merge Manager, click Select Recipients List and then click Get List.**

   See the earlier section, "Getting Good Data for Your Mail Merge," which can help you decide whether to make a new data source or choose an existing data source for the merge. After you've selected a data source, additional options may become available to you in Step 2 of the Mail Merge Manager.

   • *Find Record:* Displays an input field that lets you search for a record within a field.

   • *Data Form:* Displays the Data Form dialog.

   • *Edit Data Source:* If the data source is a Word table, choose this to display the table.

   • *Add or Remove Placeholders on Labels:* If you choose labels in Step 1, this option becomes available.

   • *Fill in the Items to Complete Your Merge:* If you chose Labels in Step 1, this option copies a picture that you put in the first label to all the labels.

3. **In the Mail Merge Manager, click Insert Placeholders.**

   Drag placeholders from the Mail Merge Manager to the position within your document where you want the data to be merged. The tabs available and the fields you can choose from depend upon the data source you've chosen, but the method is the same — drag and drop. (See Figure 10-6.) Chevrons denote inserted mail merge fields.

Inserted placeholders   Drag a placeholder into the document.

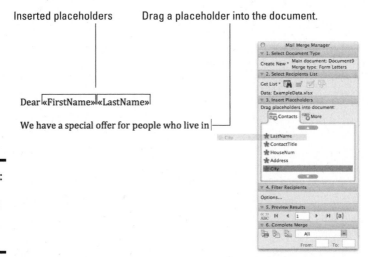

Dear «FirstName» «LastName»

We have a special offer for people who live in

Figure 10-6:
Dragging a merge field into a form letter.

4. **(Optional) In the Mail Merge Manager, click Filter Recipients.**

By default, Word's mail merge does its merging in the order in which the records are in the source data table and merges all records. Click the Filter Recipients step in the Mail Merge Manager and then click the Options button to display the Query Options dialog, which lets you filter records and change the order in which the merge will run.

On the Filter Records tab of the Query Options dialog, you can impose up to six criteria on your data by choosing options from the pop-up menus. See Figure 10-7.

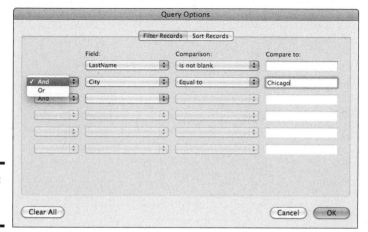

Figure 10-7: Filtering records.

Click the Sort Records tab of the Query Options dialog to change the order in which records will be run in the mail merge. Sorting for up to three levels is available. See Figure 10-8.

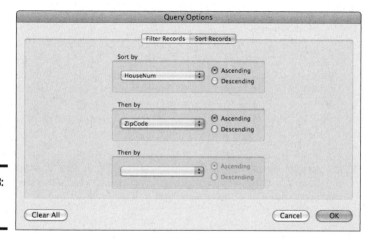

Figure 10-8: Sorting records.

5. **In the Mail Merge Manager, click Preview Results.**

You can see the merged data so you can decide whether your merge works as planned. The placeholders you inserted in Step 3 are the field names displayed with chevrons. When you see chevrons, you know you're seeing the field names. A common set of field names is `<< First Name >> << Last Name >>`.

This is when the magic of previewing your results comes in. (See Figure 10-9.) You can display your merge fields in one of three ways:

• If you don't click any buttons, you see the field names with chevrons.

• If you click the View Merged Data button (<<ABC>>), Word displays the actual data that will be merged from the database instead of the field codes.

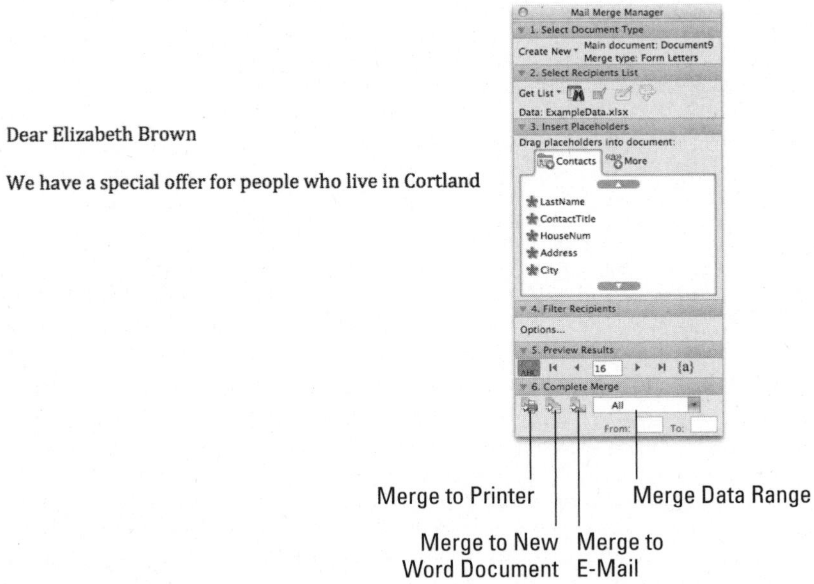

Dear Elizabeth Brown

We have a special offer for people who live in Cortland

Figure 10-9:
Previewing
the merge.

Merge to Printer   Merge Data Range

Merge to New   Merge to
Word Document   E-Mail

If you click the View Merged Data button (<<ABC>>), you can see your document in live preview mode. You can type a specific record number into the Go to Record box and then press Return or Enter to see that particular record. The same box shows you which record is displayed currently.

• If you click the View Field Codes button ({a}), field codes look like this:
`{ MERGEFIELD First Name } { MERGEFIELD Last Name }.`

6. **In the Mail Merge Manager, click Complete Merge.**

By the time you get to the last step in the Mail Merge Manager, you have a very smart document on your hands; it knows what database you want to use, what fields to bring in, where to place the data within the document, and any special instructions you've given. The completed mail merge document is like having an electronic printing press that's ready to roll.

7. **Before you print a large mail merge, do a sample run.**

   The Merge Data Range pop-up menu can help you. (See Figure 10-10.) Doing a test run is probably a good idea, especially if you have lots of data to merge. Here are the options to control your sample run:

   • *All:* Use this setting to complete the entire merge.

   • *Current Record:* With the record indicated in Mail Merge Manager Step 5, this option merges only one record.

   • *Custom:* Enter a range of records.

8. **Give Word the green light to process the mail merge.**

   As mentioned earlier, you can choose to merge to a printer, to a new Word document, or to Outlook, as shown in Figure 10-10.

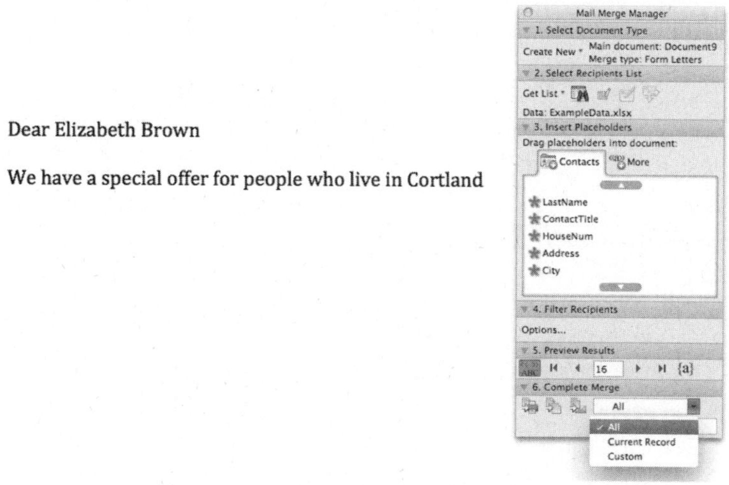

Dear Elizabeth Brown

We have a special offer for people who live in Cortland

Figure 10-10:
Completing
the mail
merge.

• *Merge to Printer:* When you click the Merge to Printer button, Word sends the final product to the printer. Be sure you have plenty of paper and toner handy if you're printing a lot of pages!

• *Merge to a New Document:* When you click Merge to a New Document, Word creates a fresh, new document that has all the merged information in it. If you print this document, it's the same as if you click the Merge to Printer button.

Living happily with your ISP

Merge to E-Mail is a very powerful capability. If you merge 10 or 20 e-mail messages, no one will bother you. If your merge involves hundreds of records or more (Word can merge more than one million messages at a time from an Excel table!), make sure your Outlook rules are set up sensibly. A flood of e-mails into a Sent Items box can make your account exceed your quota. Even 100 messages might cause those IT people or your Internet service provider (ISP), to shut down your account. Make sure your ISP or IT folks know ahead of time that you plan to send a large merge so that you don't get into trouble with them. They may have to make special arrangements to allow more than a certain number of your messages be sent and delivered.

This new document is a regular Word document. This merged document doesn't have any merge fields in it — it displays the result of the merge as ordinary text. Consequently, this merged document isn't connected to the data source, and it won't change when the data source is updated. It's a good way to make a record of the output of your mail merge and provides a merged document that you can distribute to other people.

- *Merge to E-Mail:* Click the Merge to E-Mail button to send the output to your Outlook Outbox and then to open the Mail Recipient dialog. (See Figure 10-11.)

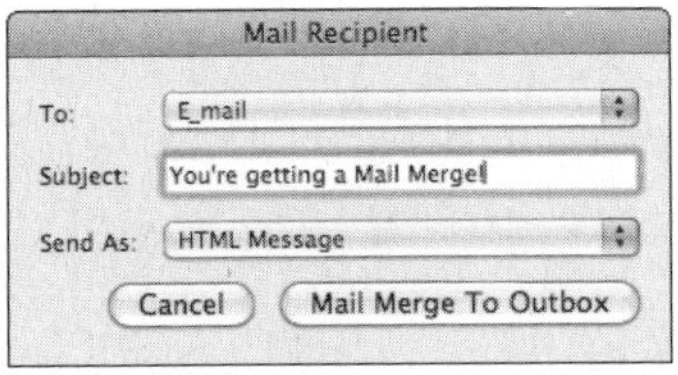

Figure 10-11: Making final preparations for merging to e-mail.

Mail Recipient	
To:	E_mail
Subject:	You're getting a Mail Merge!
Send As:	HTML Message
	Cancel Mail Merge To Outbox

9. **(Optional) If you're sending your mail merge to Outlook, choose the following options and then click the Mail Merge To Outbox button:**

- *To:* Choose the mail merge field that contains the recipients' e-mail addresses from the To pop-up menu.

- *Subject:* Type a subject for each message in your mail merge.

- *Send As:* Choose Plain Text, Attachment, or HTML from this pop-up menu. If you choose Plain Text, only text and numeric characters from your document will be sent. All formatting is discarded. Text in text boxes, WordArt, figures, charts, objects (organization charts, equations, and so on) may be discarded. If you choose Attachment, a copy of the Word document is sent as an e-mail attachment. Use this to ensure the recipient gets a full fidelity document. If you choose HTML, Word sends the document as HTML (the language of Web browsers). Modern e-mail clients can render HTML, some better than others. To see what your document might look like when it's received, switch to Web Layout view in Word before you send it in HTML format. This is the option you'll probably use the most.

There's a trick to getting mail merge to work for e-mail. In your main mail merge document, you must put a field that has the e-mail address to use for sending. How else would Office know who to send the merged document to? You can hide that address by selecting the e-mail address field, choosing Format⇨Font from the menu bar, and then in the Effects section of the Font dialog, choosing Hidden. The field will still be there, but your recipients won't see it.

**Book II
Chapter 10**

**Managing a
Mail Merge**

Before you send the whole batch as HTML, take a moment to merge just one record to make sure it looks okay in Outlook. Some of the gorgeous templates in Project Gallery are too complex for Outlook and other e-mail programs. If you're not happy with the HTML rendering, choose Send as Attachment.

When you click the Mail Merge to Outbox button to create the mail merge documents, they go to the Outlook Outbox. The documents will go out on your next scheduled send time in Outlook, or you can click the Send/Receive button on the Outlook toolbar to send them immediately. Off they go!

Merging to Envelopes

After you print your letters, make envelopes for them. You might want to make a mail merge for envelopes for other purposes, too, such as sending out holiday cards or invitations. The general procedure is the same for merging to envelopes as for merging to a form letter, which we describe in the preceding section.

We start a fresh example with a new, blank Word document. Make sure the Mail Merge Manager is visible; if not, in Word, choose Tools⇨Mail Merge Manager from the menu bar to turn it on. To merge to envelopes, only the first step of the Mail Merge Manager needs special instructions. The rest of the steps are the same as for merging to a letter (which we describe in the preceding section). Follow these steps to choose your envelope's size for the mail merge:

1. **In the Mail Merge Manager, click Select Document Type and then choose Create New⇨Envelopes.**

   The Envelope dialog appears. (See Figure 10-12.)

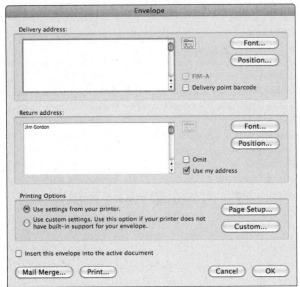

Figure 10-12:
Choosing
an envelope
size.

   Word creates a #10 standard business size envelope by default. If that's the envelope size you need, click OK to close the Envelope dialog and then go on to Step 2 of the Mail Merge Manager, which we describe in the preceding section.

   If you want to use an envelope size other than #10 standard business size, keep reading.

2. **Click the Page Setup button.**

   The Page Setup dialog opens. (See Figure 10-13.)

3. **Choose a paper size from the Paper Size pop-up menu.**

4. **Click OK.**

   The Envelope dialog (refer to Figure 10-12) returns.

   • If the envelope size you need is in the Paper Size pop-up menu, click OK to close the Envelope dialog. Complete the merge starting with Step 2 of Mail Merge Manager, as described in the preceding section.

   • If the envelope size you need isn't in the Page Setup dialog, click OK to close the Page Setup dialog to return to the Envelope dialog where you can try these additional steps.

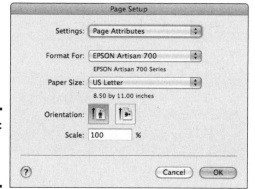

Figure 10-13:
Using Page
Setup's
paper size.

5. **In the Envelope dialog, click the Custom button.**

The Custom Page Options dialog opens, as shown in Figure 10-14.

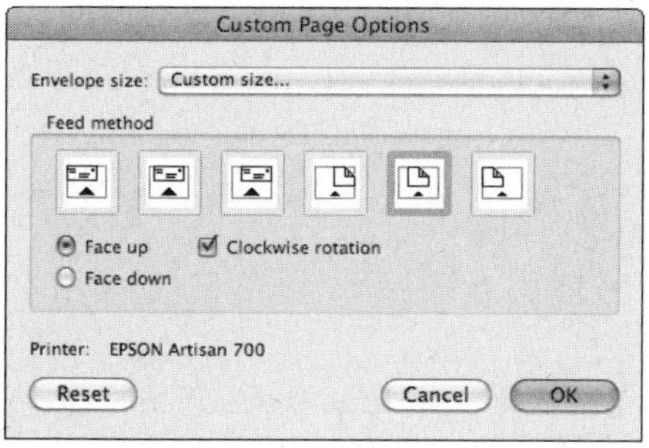

Figure 10-14:
Choosing
Custom
page
options.

6. **In the Envelope Size pop-up menu, choose a size from the pop-up menu.
(Move the mouse cursor to the top of the list to find the envelopes.)**

- *If the envelope size you need is in the Envelope Size pop-up menu in
the Custom Page Options dialog,* click OK. Then click OK to close the
Envelope dialog. Complete the merge starting with Step 2 of Mail
Merge Manager, as described in the preceding section.

- *If the envelope size you need* isn't *in the Envelope Size pop-up menu
in the Custom Page Options dialog,* at the bottom of the pop-up menu,
choose Custom. Word allows you to provide width and height attributes for your envelope in the Envelope Size dialog, as shown in
Figure 10-15. No matter what size envelope you have, Word can use
it! You may have to experiment with your printer's feed method to
get the custom envelope orientation right.

Figure 10-15:
Create a
custom
envelope
size.

7. **Click OK to close the Envelope Size dialog; click OK to close the Custom Page Options dialog; and click OK to close the Envelope dialog.**

   Complete the merge starting with Step 2 of the Mail Merge Manager, as described in the preceding section.

Making Labels

Generally, when it comes to mailing labels, you want one of two things:

+ A sheet in which all the labels are exactly the same (to send to one person or address)

+ To make labels from a data source in which each label has a different address obtained from the database

Word can do both kinds of labels.

Don't try to cram too much text onto a small label. Please don't try to put five or more lines of information or long lines on little mailing labels. Please don't shrink the font to 8 points or smaller! If you find you can't get the information you need on the label without resorting to these no-no's, you need bigger labels.

Making a sheet of identical labels

In this example, we start with a new, blank Word document that will contain a set of identical labels on a sheet of mailing labels in less than three minutes! Follow these steps and substitute your own paper size and the number of labels you want to fit on a page:

1. **In Word, choose Tools⇨Labels from the menu bar.**

   The Labels dialog appears, as shown in Figure 10-16.

2. **Enter an address and selection options in the Labels dialog as follows:**

   • *In the Address field in the upper left, type the name and address you want placed on each label.* If you like, you can use an address from your Outlook contacts by clicking the small contacts icon to the right of the Address block to open a Contacts dialog that lets you pick a contact from your Outlook Address Book.

     You could also select the Use My Address check box to use your Me contact address in your Outlook Address Book. (See Book V, Chapter 5 for information about the Me contact.)

   • *Click the Font button to open Word's Font dialog to customize text formatting.*

   • *Choose a label size from the Label Products pop-up menu.* Hundreds of different sizes and preset labels from more than 14 different manufacturers are available.

   • *Click the New Label button to open the New Custom [laser or dot matrix] dialog,* which allows you to create a completely customized label from scratch.

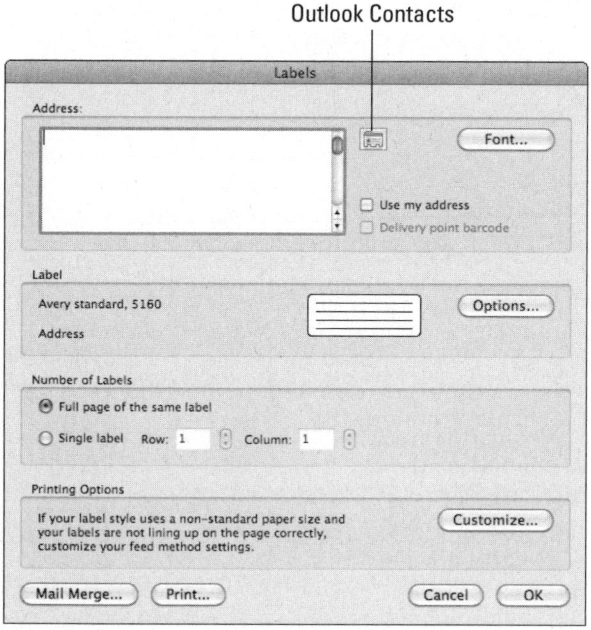

Book II
Chapter 10

Managing a
Mail Merge

Outlook Contacts

Figure 10-16:
The Labels
dialog.

3. **Click the Options button to bring up the Label Options dialog, as shown in Figure 10-17.**

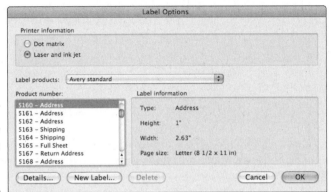

Figure 10-17: Choosing a label size.

4. **Select the product from the Label Products pop-up menu, select the label number from the Product Number list, and then click OK.**

Really, 99 percent of the time, all you have to do is just look on the box of labels you have and select the brand and product number from the Label Products pop-up menu.

5. **Click OK to close the Labels dialog.**

You now have a full sheet of perfect labels!

It's that easy. Pretty cool, huh? The rest of this section explains how you can customize your label in just about every way imaginable.

When printing labels, try printing on a sheet of plain paper first. Hold your test sheet up to the light with a sheet of blank labels behind it to see how everything lines up. You can adjust the margins by dragging them in the ruler, or click the Customize button in the Labels dialog to fine-tune everything so your labels line up perfectly.

Merging to labels

You can use an Excel workbook as your mail merge data source. Get ready by preparing the following:

✦ An Excel workbook with a data range or table that's set up as a mailing list

✦ A new, blank document in Word

To make labels from Excel or another database, take the following steps:

1. In the Mail Merge Manager, click Select Document Type and then choose Create New⇨Labels.

The Label Options dialog (see Figure 10-10) appears.

2. From the Label Products pop-up menu, choose the product.

For example, we chose Avery Standard.

3. From the Product Number list, select the correct number for your labels.

We selected 5160 — Address.

4. Click OK to close the Label Options dialog.

A table appears. Don't make any adjustments to the table or click in the table. The insertion cursor should be blinking in the upper-leftmost cell, which will be the only empty cell in the table. You may have to drag the bottom scroll bar to see the blinking cursor. Section 1 of Mail Merge Manager now displays the name of the Main Document and which type of merge you're performing.

5. In the Mail Merge Manager, click Select Recipients List and then choose Get List⇨Open Data Source.

A File Open window appears.

6. Navigate to the Excel (.xlsx) workbook you're using as the data source and click Open.

A dialog appears with a pop-up menu that lists all the sheets and named ranges in the workbook.

7. Select the worksheet or range that has the names and addresses for the data source, and then click OK.

Your Word mail merge document is now linked to the worksheet or data range data source in the Excel workbook. The Edit Labels dialog appears, as shown in Figure 10-18.

8. In the Mail Merge Manager, click Edit Labels.

When the Edit Labels dialog opens, you see an empty Sample Label with a blinking insertion cursor.

9. Click the Insert Merge Field pop-up menu and choose the field that will be on the left of the top row of the label.

In Figure 10-18, the first field is <<FirstName>>. Word puts chevrons surrounding the field name to indicate that it's a merge field.

In this example, we pressed the spacebar once to put a space between First Name and Last Name.

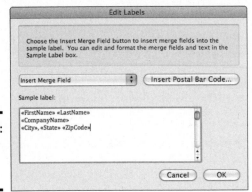

10. **To add more lines to your label, press Return or Enter and then select another field from the Insert Merge Field pop-up menu.**

    Continue the same way to add remaining fields. You can type characters as needed, such as a comma to separate City from State.

    Do not click the Insert Postal Bar Code button. The U.S. Post Office changed how it generates postal bar codes, and Word doesn't conform to the new specification.

11. **Click OK to close the Edit Labels dialog.**

    You return to your Word document, and your table grid is now filled with a whole bunch of field names in chevrons. Step 3 of Mail Merge Manager opens, but don't use anything from Mail Merge Manager Step 3 because the Edit Labels dialog takes care of inserting placeholders when making mail merge labels. Step 2 of Mail Merge Manager now shows the filename of the data source document.

12. **(Optional) In the Mail Merge Manager, click Filter Recipients.**

    Filter data and order records.

13. **In the Mail Merge Manager, click Preview Results.**

14. **In the Mail Merge Manager, click Complete Merge.**

    You're done!

Merging to a catalog

Merging to a catalog is a bit beyond the scope of this book. Using this option to its best effect requires you to be familiar with using advanced Word fields so that you can include pictures along with text. The basic idea is to make a document that can be automatically filled in with pictures and text that comes from a database. Here are three tips in case you want to try when merging to a catalog:

✦ Set up your Word document using page layout features. Use frames and text boxes as placeholders and put your merge fields into them.

✦ Find out how to use the INCLUDEPICTURE Word field.

✦ Have a column in your data source that has the complete file path for each picture to be used with INCLUDEPICTURE in the merge.

Book III

Excel 2011

The 5th Wave   By Rich Tennant

"I've used several spreadsheet programs, but this is the best one for designing quilt patterns."

Contents at a Glance

Chapter 1: Working Every Day in Excel

In This Chapter

✔ Opening Excel

✔ Opening the Excel Workbook Gallery

✔ Getting a good view of Excel

✔ Making your own keyboard shortcuts

✔ Making worksheets

✔ Setting preferences

*E*xcel is Microsoft's calculation and data powerhouse application. With endless business, accounting, scientific, reporting, and other uses, Excel is the cornerstone of data storage, calculations, and analysis for millions of users. Excel 2011 is the most robust version of Excel ever on the Mac, with full support for Visual Basic for Applications (VBA) and AppleScript, two computer languages that give Excel exceptional *extensibility,* meaning you can extend Excel's capabilities even further with your own code.

Excel is also the Microsoft database solution on the Mac. With the included Microsoft Query application and a third-party ODBC driver, you can use Excel worksheets as data tables for SQL (Structured Query Language) queries in a fully relational database.

Opening Excel for the First Time

The very first time you open Excel, you're greeted with Excel's beautiful welcome screen, shown in Figure 1-1. You can start learning about Excel's six major new features highlighted in the welcome screen immediately by clicking the Explore Excel button. When you click the Close button, the welcome screen becomes the Excel Workbook Gallery, which we discuss next. You get to see the welcome screen only once, but don't worry that you missed the tutorials; you can find them by choosing Help➪Welcome to Excel any time you want them.

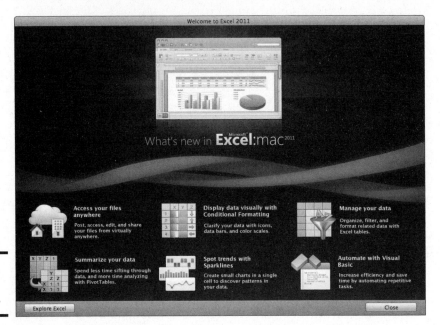

What's new in **Excel**:mac²⁰¹¹

Figure 1-1:
Greetings
from Excel.

Opening the Excel Workbook Gallery

The default behavior for opening Excel is the display All Templates option of the Excel Workbook Gallery, as shown in Figure 1-2. You can also display the Templates Gallery by choosing File➪New from Template from the menu bar or by pressing ⌘-Shift-P.

The first template in the All category is Excel Workbook, the template that you use to start a new, blank workbook. The rest of the templates are categorized and searchable, so you can browse or search to find a template to use or customize. Other Excel Workbook Gallery tools are as follows:

✦ **Show/Hide Right Pane:** Choose to show or hide the Template preview.

✦ **Templates list**

- *All:* Displays all templates stored on your computer.

- *My Templates:* Displays templates you saved in the My Templates folder, specified in Excel's preferences.

- *Built-In Templates:* Many categories of built-in templates are included with Office such as those for Time Management, Business Essentials, Personal Finance, and so on.

- *Online Templates:* Click the disclosure triangle next to Templates to hide the local templates. Then click the disclosure triangle next to Online Templates to display the many categories of online templates. This feature requires a live Internet connection, and is new for Office 2011.

Preview and navigation

Show/Hide right pane

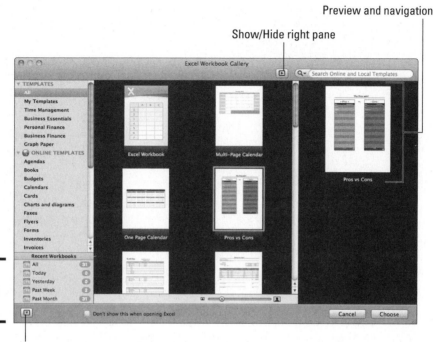

Figure 1-2:
Choosing a
template.

Show/Hide recent workbooks

✦ **Search:** By default, this text box searches template names and keywords of local templates. You can also search online templates if the online disclosure triangle has been activated. When one of the Recent Workbook time frames is selected, this text box searches Recent Workbooks instead of templates.

✦ **Preview and Navigation:** Displays a preview of the template selected in the larger pane. If the template has multiple pages, click the navigation arrows to scroll through the template.

✦ **Recent Workbooks:** Up to one month's worth of recently opened workbooks are available. You can show all, or filter by Today, Yesterday, Past Week, or Past Month. When any Recent Workbook option is selected, Search works on Recent Workbooks instead of local templates.

✦ **Show/Hide Recent Workbooks:** This toggle button displays or hides this section of the gallery.

✦ **Don't Show This When Opening Excel:** When checked, the Excel Workbook Gallery will not display when Excel is opened. You can still access it by choosing the File➪New from Template.

✦ **Size:** Drag the slider left and right to change the size of previews in the larger pane. Click the icon on the left end to choose the smallest size. Choose the icon on the right end of the slider to choose the largest.

✦ **Cancel:** If you just opened Excel, clicking Cancel takes you to a new, blank Excel Workbook. If Excel was already running when you opened the Excel Workbook Gallery, clicking Cancel closes the gallery without opening a workbook.

✦ **Choose:** Opens the selected template in Excel.

Choosing a View

A *workbook* is a container for a collection of worksheets. A standard *worksheet* is a grid composed of cells arranged in columns and rows, but you can use other kinds of sheets, which we discuss in the section "Working with Sheet Types," later in this chapter.

When you're working in Excel, you have your choice of two views: Page Layout view and Normal view. We discuss these views in the following sections.

You can find general interface discussion about menus, toolbars, the Dock, Elements Gallery, and the Formatting Palette in Book I, as well as how to open and save files.

Using Normal view

Normal view (shown in Figure 1-3) is similar to Page Layout view, except the entire sheet is continuous. Instead of seeing distinct visual differentiation between pages, you see dotted lines that indicate page boundaries after you select any Page Setup or Print function. Normal view maximizes the amount of worksheet that you see on the screen. You can display Normal view by clicking the Normal View button in the lower-left corner of the window or by choosing View⇨Normal.

If you're moving from Excel for Windows (or if you use Excel both on Windows and Mac), Normal view on the Mac looks just like it does in Windows.

Using Page Layout view

Page Layout view, shown in Figure 1-4, displays your workbook so that you can see how it will look when you print it. Page breaks are clearly visible in this view. You can display Page Layout view by clicking the Page Layout View button in the lower-left corner of the window, or by choosing View⇨Page Layout from the menu bar.

Ribbon

Standard toolbar

Menu bar

Formula bar

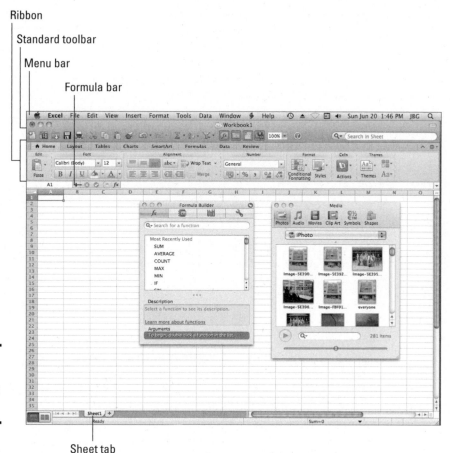

Figure 1-3:
Viewing
with Normal
view.

Sheet tab

In the interface in Figure 1-4, pages with data are brighter than the rest, and the page break indicators look like physical breaks. Any sheet that has content appears bright, and sheets that contain no content are slightly grayed and display Click to Add Data. In this view, you can easily see whether text or other objects will be cut off or spill over breaks when you print the sheet.

Figure 1-4 also shows these features of Page Layout view:

✦ **Ruler:** Choose View➪Ruler to toggle the rulers off and on. You can drag rulers to resize margins. Double-click the ruler to the left of the work-sheet to display the Page Setup dialog, which we discuss in Chapter 11 in this minibook.

✦ **Header and Footer:** Double-click the white space above and below the sheets to add header and footer controls, which we also talk about in Chapter 11 of this minibook.

✦ **View buttons:** Click a view button at the lower-left corner of the window to switch between Normal view and Page Layout view. The Page Layout view button is selected in Figure 1-4.

✦ **Page break indicator:** As soon as you enter any data into a cell or add an object to a sheet, the page break indicator updates.

Using the common interface

Whether you prefer to work in Page Layout view or Normal view, most interface components are the same in both views. We highlight these common features in Figure 1-3 and Figure 1-4:

✦ **Workbook:** Each filename in Excel is the title of its corresponding workbook. Each workbook contains at least one worksheet.

Rulers   Page Break

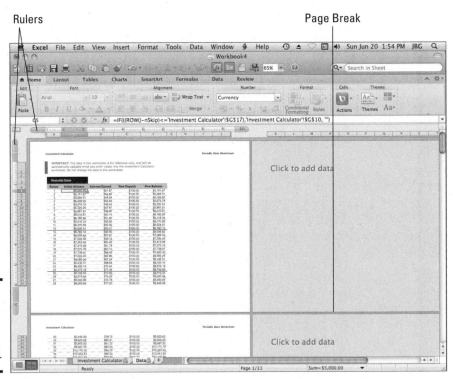

Figure 1-4:
Looking at a
worksheet
in Page
Layout view.

✦ **Menu bar:** This is the topmost set of controls. The menu bar is Mac only. Menus are customizable (see Book I, Chapter 2) and programmable via both VBA and AppleScript.

✦ **Standard toolbar:** The Standard toolbar is at the top part of each document window, along with standard Open, Minimize, and Close buttons. The Standard toolbar is customizable within Excel and roughly equivalent in that respect to the Quick Access Toolbar of Office for Windows.

If you want to do more with the Standard toolbar, it's also programmable via VBA and AppleScript.

✦ **Show/Hide Toolbar:** This tablet-shaped button toggles the Standard toolbar's visibility off and on.

✦ **Ribbon:** The Ribbon is new to Excel 2011. The Ribbon is tabbed and displays between the Standard toolbar and the Formula bar.

✦ **Formula bar:** Major changes were made to Formula bar for Excel 2011. Instead of one Formula bar for the entire Excel application, there is now a Formula bar in each workbook's window. When working with more than one open workbook at a time, pay attention to which window's Formula bar you're using. This takes getting used to.

✦ **Worksheet:** Figures 1-3 and 1-4 show a standard Excel worksheet, where you can enter text and formulas, perform calculations, and store data. Each open worksheet has its own window.

✦ **View buttons:** Click these buttons to switch between Page Layout view and Normal view.

✦ **Sheet tab:** Each sheet in a workbook has a name that appears on its tab near the bottom of the window. Double-click a sheet tab to edit that sheet's name. Right-click a sheet tab to display a pop-up menu of sheet operations and formatting options. You can drag the horizontal scroll bar all the way to the left to hide sheet tabs, as shown in the left margin. Drag the scroll bar to the right to unhide.

At long last, the most requested feature from Windows Excel has come to the Mac — color sheet tabs. To change a sheet tab's color, right-click the tab and then choose Tab Color from the contextual menu. This displays the Color palette that contains Theme Colors. If you click the More Colors option, you see the Mac OS color picker, where you can choose from millions of colors.

✦ **+ (Add Sheet):** Click the plus sign to add a new, blank standard worksheet to your workbook. You can add as many worksheets as you want until your computer runs out of memory. You could potentially add thousands of them!

✦ **Range tool:** Also known as the name box, this tool allows you to name a range of cells in a worksheet. (See Book III, Chapter 3 for details.)

Book III
Chapter 1

Working Every
Day in Excel

✦ **Toolbox:** Click the Toolbox button on the Standard toolbar to display the Toolbox. (See Book I, Chapter 3 for more.)

✦ **Media browser:** Click the Media button on the Standard toolbar to display the Media browser. (See Book I, Chapter 8 for more.)

✦ **Rows:** Excel has 1,048,576 rows on each worksheet. Row numbers display at the left side of a worksheet. When used as a database, each row with data is a record.

✦ **Columns:** Excel offers 16,384 columns in a worksheet. Column letters display at the top edge of the worksheet.

✦ **Cells:** A worksheet in Excel has 17,179,869,184 cells. Yes, that's more than 17 billion cells per sheet!

If you find you're pushing Excel's limits and want to know exactly what they are, search Excel's Help for the "Specifications and Limits for Excel" topic. You can find such information as how many characters fit into one cell and how many nested levels you can have in a function.

Like other Office applications, you can find context-sensitive menus just about everywhere you right-click in Excel.

Customizing Keyboard Shortcuts

Choose Tools⇨Customize Keyboard from the menu bar to display the Customize Keyboard dialog shown in Figure 1-5. To make a new shortcut, choose a command and then press a keyboard combination. Click the Add button to add your shortcut to Excel's keyboard shortcuts. To delete a shortcut, select the command and then press the Delete button.

Getting the perfect interface

Book I, Chapter 2 discusses how to customize menus and toolbars. Excel has its own keyboard shortcuts and shortcut organizer. The complete list of built-in keyboard shortcuts is in Excel Help; search for the "Excel Keyboard Shortcuts" topic to find the list.

To get to the Keyboard Shortcut dialog, choose Tools⇨Customize Keyboard from the menu bar. The shortcut organizer is another way to discover Excel's built-in shortcuts, as well as a way to change, add, or remove your own keyboard shortcuts. You aren't allowed to delete Excel's built-in shortcuts. Also remember that if Mac OS X is already using a particular keyboard shortcut, Excel can't use it.

The ability to customize Excel keyboard shortcuts is Mac-only — Excel for Windows doesn't have this feature.

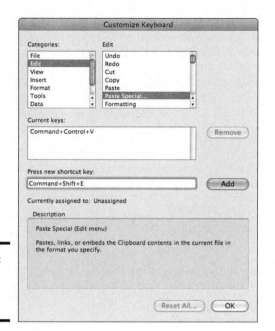

Figure 1-5:
Making a
keyboard
shortcut.

Working with Sheet Types

Excel sheets can be general or dedicated to a specific purpose. You don't have to be an expert to use the various sheet types, but you should know their names and each sheet type's purpose.

You can mix different sheet types within a single workbook.

Sheet types

Here's the rundown of the kinds of specialized sheets in Excel:

✦ **Blank sheet:** This general-purpose standard worksheet has cells, rows, and columns; the cells can hold text, formulas, and data. You can place objects such as charts, WordArt, SmartArt graphics, objects from the Media browser, pictures, sounds, and even movies in layers on worksheets.

✦ **Chart sheet:** A chart sheet contains a single graph or chart. We discuss charts in Chapter 6 of this minibook.

✦ **Excel 4.0 Macro sheet:** Before VBA, there was the Excel 4.0 XLM macro language. Excel 2011 supports the Excel 4.0 macro language. If this applies to you, search Excel Help for *Excel 4* and then download the entire Excel 4.0 Macro Language Reference; click the Download link in the Excel 4.0 (XLM) Macro Commands topic.

✦ **Excel Dialog sheet:** Excel dialog sheets let you customize your own dialogs. You could make your own wizard or devise an input form for your database. Dialog sheets make use of VBA.

Ledger Sheet and List Sheet types are discontinued. When you open a workbook that contains either of these, Excel will automatically convert these to standard Excel worksheets. Each data range will be formatted into an Excel Table using the new Excel Table feature. Don't be flustered by the dialogs you get when you open one of these older style workbooks. So far, all our workbooks converted nicely despite dire warnings about possible loss of tables.

Making blank worksheets

Because you often need to create new, blank standard worksheets, Excel provides you with several ways to do so. Here are two easy methods:

✦ Choose Insert⇨Sheet⇨Blank Sheet from the menu bar.

✦ Click the plus sign (+) sheet tab to add a new, blank standard worksheet to your workbook (as shown earlier in Figure 1-3).

And here are two ways to make a chart sheet:

✦ Make an Excel chart; then move the chart to a chart sheet, as we explain in Chapter 6 of this minibook.

✦ Select the data range for your chart. Then choose Insert⇨Sheet⇨ Chart Sheet from the menu bar. A new chart sheet displays your data.

To make an Excel 4.0 macro sheet, choose Insert⇨Sheet⇨Macro Sheet from the menu bar.

To make a dialog sheet, choose Insert⇨Sheet⇨Dialog Sheet from the menu bar.

Discovering and Setting Excel Preferences

Although it's true that you can gain a better knowledge of any application if you visit its preferences and try to figure them out, it's almost essential for Excel. Choose Excel⇨Preferences from the menu bar to display the Preferences dialog shown in Figure 1-6. When you have an inkling or thought about a setting you want to change, just type into the Search field.

Here are some selected settings not covered elsewhere in this minibook:

✦ **General:**

• *Sheets in New Workbook:* The spinner sets the number of blank worksheets a new workbook will have by default.

- *Standard Font:* Choose a default font. Unless you have a compelling reason to change this, leave this as "body font," which is roughly the same as the default font.

- *Preferred File Location:* Set the default location for Excel files.

- *Show This Number of Recent Documents:* Set the number of recently used workbooks shown in Excel's File menu by typing in a figure here. Recently used items in the File menu don't disappear after a month. This list is based on the quantity you set.

✦ **View:**

- *Comments:* Adjust how comments are displayed.

- *Show Formulas:* Display formulas instead of calculation values.

- *Show Zero Values:* Displays a 0 instead of an empty cell when selected.

- *Show Sheet Tabs:* Deselect to hide all the sheet tabs with the horizontal scroll bar. Selecting redisplays the scroll bar.

✦ **Edit:**

- *Automatically convert date systems*: When selected, Excel automatically corrects for differences between the 1900 (Windows) and 1904 date systems (Mac) during copy and paste. The destination workbook's format is adopted.

✦ **AutoCorrect:** See Book II, Chapter 1 for details about AutoCorrect. You can have Excel fix your common typing blunders automatically.

✦ **Calculation:** When not set to *Automatically,* working with large spreadsheets with lots of complicated formulas can be faster and easier.

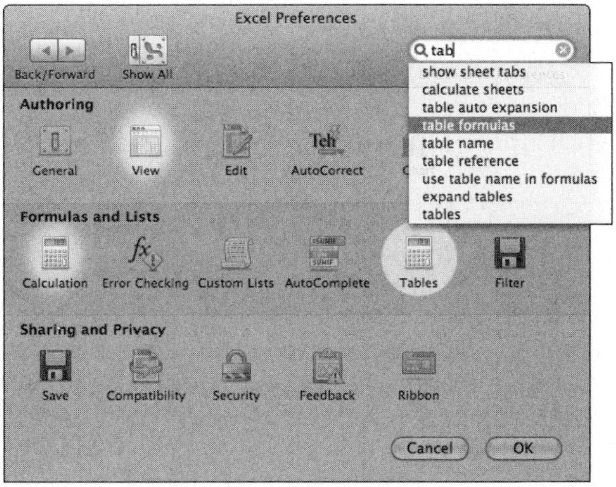

Figure 1-6:
Setting
Excel's
preferences.

If you turn off Excel's automatic calculation capability, you need to turn it back on again, or Excel's formulas won't calculate. This is especially important if you turn off automatic calculation using a macro. Be certain your code turns the Automatically option back on under all circumstances.

Chapter 2: Opening and Saving Files in Excel

In This Chapter

✔ Using current Excel formats

✔ Looking into a variety of file formats

✔ Using the AutoRecover feature

*O*ne of Excel's strengths is the large number of file formats that it under-stands. Another is its ability to share files simultaneously with up to 256 other users in real time. Excel can open content from Web pages and Web tables and can make Web pages of any workbook. In this chapter, we explore the unique file capabilities of Excel that go beyond the ordinary.

Working with Excel Workbook .xlsx Format

The Excel workbook .xlsx format is the default format for Excel workbooks. Although Excel can work with a plethora of file formats, this format preserves all aspects of your workbook. Use this file format if you need to comply with standard open XML (eXtensible Markup Language) requirements.

Excel has used Excel workbook .xlsx format as the default file format since Excel 2007 (Windows) and Excel 2008 (Mac). The file format is identical for Macs and PCs. You don't need to use any translators or third-party software to share this file format across platforms.

Versions of Excel as far back as Excel 2003 (Windows) and 2004 (Mac) will open the .xlsx format as long as Microsoft's free software updates have been installed.

Many important features in Excel 2011 are not supported in old versions of Excel or in products billed as "compatible" with Excel. For best compatibil-ity, we recommend that IT departments standardize on Excel 2011 for Mac and Excel 2010 for Windows. (Excel 2007 has reasonably good compatibility with Excel 2011, but older versions are obsolete.)

Working with Various File Formats

You expect Excel to open Excel files, of course, but the program can do more than that. You can actually open, work on, and save a file in several formats. Choose File⇨Save As and then click Format to open the pop-up menu. Excel can open and save in the formats listed in this Format pop-up menu.

Excel keeps your file in the format it has when you open it. For example, if you open an old Excel .xls workbook, it opens normally, and you can work on it. The title bar will indicate Compatibility Mode, and many Excel features will be grayed out and unavailable. When you save the workbook, the format remains in old .xls format unless you intentionally change the format by choosing File⇨Save As and then choosing a different format from the Format pop-up menu.

Current Excel formats

You have several options for file formats besides Excel's default (.xlsx) format:

✦ **Excel Template (.xltx):** Saves the workbook as a template, which you can open in the My Templates section of the Excel Workbook Gallery. You can also open templates by choosing File⇨Open and selecting Excel Templates from the Enable pop-up menu. This format does not have macros and is another open XML format.

✦ **Excel Macro-Enabled Workbook (.xlsm):** Workbooks in this XML format contain Visual Basic for Applications (VBA) programming language code, or Excel 4.0 macro code. When opening this format file, Excel displays a prompt, as shown in Figure 2-1, asking whether you want to remove the macros contained in the file. The default is Disable Macros. You must instead click Enable Macros if you want macros to run.

✦ **Excel Macro-Enabled Template (.xltm):** The same as .xlsm, except this is a template. The macro warning dialog shown in Figure 2-1 displays when you open a workbook in this format, and you must click Enable Macros if you want macros to run.

Figure 2-1: Enabling macros.

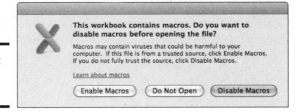

This workbook contains macros. Do you want to disable macros before opening the file?

Macros may contain viruses that could be harmful to your computer. If this file is from a trusted source, click Enable Macros. If you do not fully trust the source, click Disable Macros.

Learn about macros

(Enable Macros)   (Do Not Open)   (Disable Macros)

Save time with Excel binary workbook (.xlsb)

From an efficiency point of view, Excel's new default XML file format isn't the optimal way to save computer files. XML is text, and text files become huge and bloated very quickly. Zipping and unzipping XML text files adds overhead and takes time. Even though XLSX files are zipped and unzipped automatically for you, they're usually much larger than when you save them in Excel binary workbook .xlsb file format.

Saving in the .xlsb format will result in much smaller files that open and save faster. You can save workbooks with or without macros in (.xlsb) format. You can even make saving in the .xlsb format the default for Excel so that you always save in the most efficient file format. Follow these steps:

1. **In Excel, choose Excel⇨Preferences from the menu bar.**

   The Excel Preferences dialog appears.

2. **Click the Compatibility icon.**

3. **Click Save Files in This Format in the Transition area and choose Excel Binary Workbook (.xlsb) from the pop-up menu that appears.**

4. **Click OK.**

If you need to fiddle with the XML code of a workbook that was saved in the .xlsb file format, you can always choose File⇨Save As and then choose a different Excel XML workbook format from the Format pop-up menu.

✦ **Excel Add-In (.xlam):** Saves a macro-enabled workbook as an Excel add-in. See Book I, Chapter 12 for details about add-ins.

✦ **Excel Binary Workbook (.xlsb):** This is the most compact file format, and is recommended for large files. See the "Save time with Excel binary workbook (.xlsb)" sidebar. This format doesn't conform to open source standards.

✦ **Comma Separated Values (.csv):** Saves a worksheet data table as text separated by commas. This format is text only. All other content is discarded.

✦ **Web Page (.htm):** Save the workbook in a format that Web browsers understand and can display. Excel creates a file in HTML format, along with a supporting folder. Upload both the file and folder to a Web server if you want to share your workbook via the Internet.

Excel can open and save Web pages in HTML (HyperText Markup Language) format and do great things with Web tables and data from the Web, but don't uninstall your HTML (Web page) code editor. Excel can't replace that.

Book III Chapter 2

Opening and Saving Files in Excel

Automating a Web page

Suppose you post daily updates to spreadsheets and charts that you save as Web pages for your intranet. You can set up your Mac so that the Web site is refreshed automatically on any schedule you want. Of course, the Mac must have read/write access to the Web server's folders. Here's how to set Excel to automatically update a Web page:

1. **Prepare a workbook with updated information to present on the Web site.**

2. **Choose File⇨Save As Web Page.**

   The Save As dialog displays.

3. **Click the Automate button.**

   The Automate dialog shown in Figure 2-2 displays.

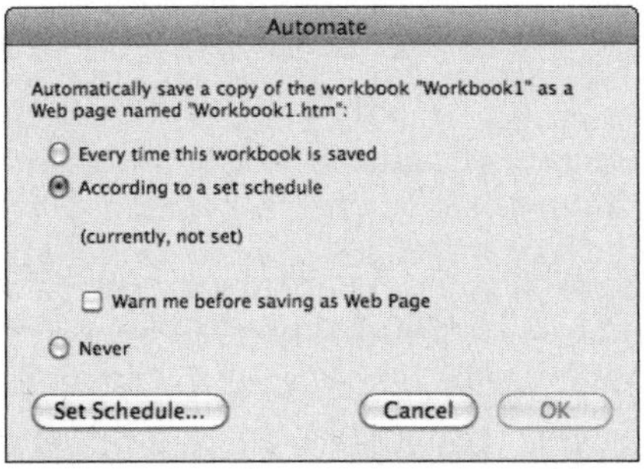

Figure 2-2:
Automation help from Excel.

> **Automate**
>
> Automatically save a copy of the workbook "Workbook1" as a Web page named "Workbook1.htm":
>
> ○ Every time this workbook is saved
> ◉ According to a set schedule
>
>   (currently, not set)
>
>   ☐ Warn me before saving as Web Page
>
> ○ Never
>
> (Set Schedule...)   (Cancel) (OK)

4. **To have the Web page updated at a particular time, select the According to a Set Schedule check box.**

5. **Click the Set Schedule button.**

   The Recurring Schedule dialog shown in Figure 2-3 displays.

6. **Choose the options that suit the schedule you want Excel to follow, and then click OK to close the Recurring Schedule dialog.**

7. **Click OK to close the Automate dialog.**

8. **Choose a save location and then click the Save button.**

   Excel now saves the current version of this workbook according to the rules you established.

You can combine this technique with a Web query or a database query, and create a Web page that's completely automatic! Of course, you can also add additional automation procedures with VBA.

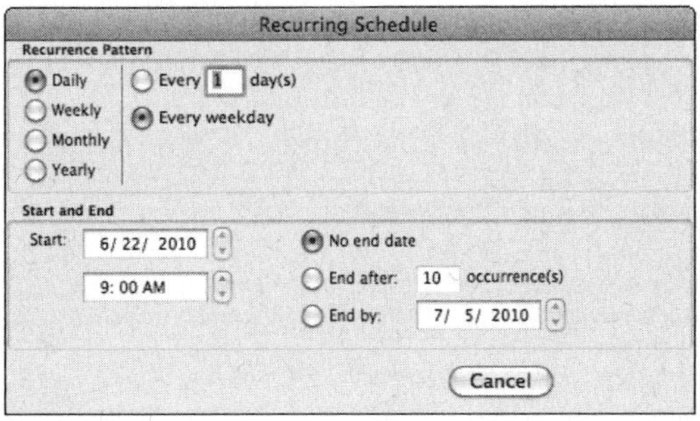

Figure 2-3:
Automating
a Web site.

Old Excel formats

Excel lets you save a workbook in the following old Excel formats for someone who has a version of Excel prior to Excel 2007:

✦ **Excel 2004 XML Spreadsheet (.xml):** Excel 2004 and Excel 2008 can use
  this XML format. This was a precursor to the open source standard XML
  format that is now Excel's default.

✦ **Excel 97–2004 Workbook (.xls):** Save in a format that was used by
  these old versions of Excel.

✦ **Excel 97–2004 Template (.xlt):** Save a template in a format that was
  used by these old versions of Excel.

✦ **Excel 97–2004 Add-In (.xla):** Save a macro-enabled workbook as an
  Excel add-in for these old versions of Excel. Excel 2008 can't run macros
  or add-ins.

✦ **Excel 5.0/95 Workbook (.xls):** Save in a format that was used by these
  old versions of Excel.

These old formats are worth trying when sharing files with people using programs that are ostensibly "compatible" with Excel.

Saving in these old formats will cause data loss with worksheets larger than
65,536 rows or 256 columns. Many objects will turn into pictures and not be
editable. Expect compatibility problems with pivot tables, tables, graphs,
charts, conditional formatting, protection, collaboration, and other Excel
features that have been significantly upgraded. Old formats are not recommended for every day use.

Delimited

In the delimited format type, data arranged in tables with rows and columns is
saved in text files that use a specified character, called a *delimiter,* to indicate
the beginning of a new column. People have mostly settled on using a comma

as the delimiting character, and Comma Separated Value (CSV) is a popular file format. However, other delimited file formats can specify any character:

✦ **Tab Delimited Text (.txt):** Save row and column headers, and data, in a text file that uses the tab character as its delimiter. This format saves only the text within cells.

✦ **Windows Comma Separated (.csv):** Save row headers, column headers, and data in a text file that uses the comma character as its delimiter in a format that's slightly different from standard CSV.

✦ **MS-DOS Comma Separated (.csv):** Save row headers, column headers, and data in a text file that uses the comma character as its delimiter in a format that's slightly different from standard CSV.

✦ **Space Delimited Text (.prn):** Save only the text within cells using a text file format for old dot-matrix and line printers.

When opening files, Excel can deal with any delimiter, as long as you tell Excel which delimiter was used in the preparation of your delimited file.

More old formats

Excel still offers these formats, but it may not for long. If you have any of these files, save them in one of the current formats in case Excel stops supporting these formats:

✦ **Data Interchange Format (.dif):** Save row and column headers, along with data, in a format designed specifically for data.

This format often works better than delimited formats because it's not fussy about which characters are in the data.

✦ **Symbolic Link (.slk):** Use this old Microsoft-specific format to exchange data. It requires special handling of semicolons.

All the other formats

Here are the additional file formats you have to choose from:

✦ **Single File Web Page (.mht):** Save the workbook as a single-file Web page that you can upload to a Web server for distribution via the Internet and view in a Web browser. This format can be automated the same way as (.htm) discussed earlier in this chapter.

✦ **UTF-16 Unicode Text (.txt):** Save only the text within cells using the UTF-16 standard.

+ **Windows Formatted Text (.txt):** Save only the text within cells using Windows text file format.

+ **MS-DOS Formatted Text (.txt):** Save only the text within cells using MS-DOS text file format.

Using AutoRecover

Although crashes in Excel are extremely rare, it doesn't hurt to make sure Excel is backing up your changes as you work. The following sections tell you what to do to ensure Excel is making backups and how to retrieve the backup if you need to.

Setting up AutoRecover

Take a moment to make sure your preferences automatically save an emergency backup file of your work. Before you do that, remember that AutoRecover is not a substitute for saving your files often! To set up AutoRecover, follow these steps:

1. **Choose Excel⇨Preferences from the menu bar.**

   The Excel Preferences dialog appears.

2. **In the Sharing and Privacy section, select Save.**

   The Save preferences appear.

3. **Select the Save AutoRecover Information After This Number of Minutes check box.**

4. **Enter the number of minutes that you want between AutoRecover file saves, or use the increase/decrease control.**

5. **Click OK.**

   After you turn on AutoRecover, Excel saves your work at the specified interval so that you can recover in the event that the system or Excel crashes.

Retrieving an AutoRecover file

If your computer or Excel crashes, you can recover your work up to the most recent AutoRecover save, but only if you turned on AutoRecover saves. (See the preceding section.) Take these steps to restore any workbooks that were open at the time of the crash:

1. **Click the Excel Dock icon.**

   Excel presents any documents that you're working on that have been saved at least once. Recovered documents have (Recovered) in the title bar.

2. **To keep the recovered version, choose File⇨Save As.**

   The Save As dialog appears. Take one of the following actions:

   - *To replace the existing file with the recovered version:* Navigate to the file or use Spotlight to locate the existing file. Then, click the filename to change the recovered file's name to the existing filename. Click Save to overwrite the existing file.

   - *To save the recovered file without overwriting the original:* Select a location to save the recovered file and enter a name for the file in the text box. Then click Save.

To discard a recovered workbook, click the red Close button to close the workbook. When prompted, don't save changes.

To permanently remove AutoRecover files from your computer, follow these steps:

1. **Quit all open Office applications.**

2. **In Finder, press ⌘-F.**

   The Spotlight search dialog appears.

3. **Enter AutoRecover in the text box.**

   Spotlight displays a list of matching files, if any.

4. **Select all AutoRecover files.**

5. **Drag the files to the Trash.**

6. **Empty the Trash.**

Chapter 3: Getting into Cells and Worksheets

In This Chapter

✔ Selecting, editing, naming, and clearing cells

✔ Dragging text, numbers, and dates

✔ Customizing automated lists

✔ Entering things in general

✔ Using cell formulas

✔ Putting Formula Builder to work

✔ Referring to cells relatively and absolutely

A s the name implies, a *cell* is a small part of a larger whole. You work with Excel *cells,* which are small rectangles arranged in rows and columns on a worksheet. Cells, rows, and columns in Excel work just like a table in Word or PowerPoint, but have many more capabilities.

This chapter focuses on the things you can do in Excel's cells, rows, and columns. Excel conforms to standard behaviors that you're probably already used to in other applications. Even if you've never needed to do calculations on a worksheet before, it's a fairly easy task to get Excel to carry out your wishes.

Interacting with Excel

Excel constantly gives you feedback as you work. You can follow the discussion in the following sections by simply opening Excel. Click Excel's Dock icon to open Excel and display a blank, standard worksheet.

Selecting a cell or range of cells

Click a cell to select it. Excel indicates the selected cell in several different ways, as shown in Figure 3-1:

✦ **Highlighted row number and column letter:** We selected the cell that intersects Column B and Row 2, referred to as the *address* of the cell. In Figure 3-1, the selected cell's address is B2.

+ **Heavy border:** The selected cell has a thicker border.

+ **Fill handle:** The lower right-corner of the selected cell is a dark square, which you can drag to copy the cell's contents.

+ **Name box:** Also known as the *Range tool*, this displays the *address* of the cell. The address is the column letter followed by the row number.

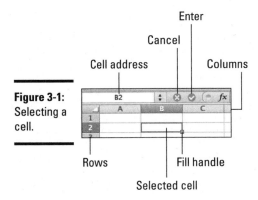

Figure 3-1:
Selecting a
cell.

You can change the color of the selected cell's border in Mac OS X System preferences. To change the color of the selection indicator, choose Apple Menu⇨System Preferences⇨Personal⇨Appearance to display the Appearance dialog. Click the Highlight Color to display a pop-up menu from which to choose a different color. This setting applies not only for Excel, but for all installed applications on your Mac. If you have Excel open when you make these changes, you have to close and restart Excel to see the change in the cell border color.

You can select or refer to more than one cell at a time. When more than one cell is selected or referred to at a time, it's called a *cell range.*

To select a group of cells, drag the mouse cursor across the cells you want to select. When you release the mouse button, the range of cells becomes highlighted, and the row numbers and column headers are darkened to indicate the selected range.

Excel uses a colon (:) to indicate a contiguous cell range. Type **A1:C5** in the cell address box (see Figure 3-1), in cell formulas, or in dialogs to indicate a range of cells whose top-left position is A1, and whose bottom-right position is C5. Cell ranges can be named. See the next section.

To select noncontiguous ranges of cells, hold down the ⌘ button as you drag the mouse cursor over cell ranges or select individual cells by clicking them.

Near cell A1 (left of A column header and above the 1 row header) is a special button that looks like a small triangle. Clicking this button selects all the cells of a worksheet at once. When you hover the mouse cursor over this button, it takes on a different arrow. (Look ahead to Figure 3-3.) Click this button to select all cells on the worksheet. This is the same as pressing ⌘-A. With the whole sheet selected, you can apply formatting options to the entire sheet.

Using the Range tool

The Range tool is also called the *Name box,* as shown in Figure 3-1. This tool has multiple uses:

✦ Select a cell or range of cells and then type a name into the Name box. Press Return or Enter to assign the name to the cell or cell range. You can refer to a *named range* in cell formulas and VBA macros. Valid names have no spaces or special characters.

✦ After you assign a name to a cell or cell range, you can type its name into the Range tool and then press Return or Enter to select and show the range.

✦ Click the Names pop-up menu of the Range tool (refer to Figure 3-1) to display a list of named ranges in the worksheet. Choose a name from the list to select the cell or cell range.

✦ Select a cell or many cells. For example:

  • Type **C12** in the Name box and then press Return or Enter to select cell C12.

  • Type **A1:C5** in the Name box and then press Return or Enter to select the range of cells from cell A1 through C5. The colon (:) tells Excel to select the first cell, the last cell, and all the cells in between.

✦ Drag the small gray dot to the left of the Formula Builder button (see Figure 3-1) to increase or decrease the size of the Range tool/Name box.

✦ Select an object, such as a cell, shape, picture, movie, text box, or SmartArt, and then observe the Name box. The name of the object is displayed.

Naming cells or a range of cells

Select a cell or cell range and choose Insert➪Name➪Define from the menu bar to display the Define Name dialog shown in Figure 3-2.

The Define Name dialog lets you manage the named ranges on your worksheet as follows:

✦ **Add:** Type a name for the selection and then click the Add button to add the current selection to the list.

✦ **Delete:** Select a name in the list and click Delete to remove it.

✦ **Refers to:** Click the button beside the Refers To text box to collapse the dialog. You can then select a cell or range of cells by using the mouse. Click the button again when you're done selecting cells.

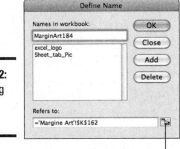

Figure 3-2: Managing named ranges.

Click to select cells.

Editing a cell

When you start typing in a cell, the border gets a nice, soft shadow and seems to be closer to you than the rest of the sheet, as shown in Figure 3-3, where we typed **something**. The blinking insertion cursor displays inside the cell so you can see and control where text will appear as you type or paste. When you type in a cell, you're performing what's called *in-cell editing*. What you type in a cell appears simultaneously in the Formula bar, and vice versa. When you're done editing in a cell, the cell displays the calculation result, and the Formula bar displays the cell's formula.

Figure 3-3: Typing something in a cell.

Excel doesn't know when you're done typing in a cell unless you take specific action to let Excel know you're no longer working with a cell.

When you're done editing in a cell or the Formula bar, take any of the following actions to let Excel know you've finished:

✦ Press Return or Enter.

✦ Press an arrow key.

✦ Press the Tab key.

✦ Click the Enter button beside the cell address box. (Refer to Figure 3-1.)

✦ Click the Cancel button beside the cell address box. (Refer to Figure 3-1.)

✦ Click a different cell.

After you select something other than the cell you're editing, the cell you were editing returns to its normal appearance. Double-click any nonempty cell to return to in-cell editing. Excel displays the insertion cursor in the cell, and you can resume editing the cell's contents.

An alternative to in-cell editing is to edit in the Formula bar. To use the Formula bar to edit, first select a cell. You can then start typing in the Formula bar. The Formula bar was redesigned in Excel 2011 so that each workbook window gets its own Formula bar. When you get going with Excel, you'll likely need more room than one line to type in the Formula bar. New features to deal with this possibility are shown in Figure 3-4:

✦ Drag the top edge of the column letters down or up to expose or hide more room for the Formula bar.

✦ Click the triangle at the far right of the Formula bar to expand or contract the size of the Formula bar.

Figure 3-4:
Making
more room
in the
Formula bar.

Clearing one or more cells

Want to get rid of something inside a cell? All you have to do is click that cell and press the Delete key.

That's handy for a single cell, but if you select a range of cells and press the Delete key, only the contents of the first cell in the range will be deleted. To clear a range of cells, select the range of cells and then hold down the ⌘ key down while you press the Delete key. (On some Macs, you may need to press the Function key as well for this to work.)

Using the Delete key method deletes cell content, but not formatting or comments. You can clear formats, contents, or comments by using this method:

1. **Select the cell range you want to clear.**

   Select by dragging the mouse or entering the name of the cell range into the Name box.

2. **Choose Edit⇨Clear from the menu bar. Alternatively, click the Ribbon's Home tab, and in the Edit group, click Clear.**

   Either way, you get to a submenu with several options. Choose one of the following:

   • *All:* Clears contents, formats, and comments.

   • *Formats:* Clears formats without disturbing contents or comments.

   • *Contents:* Clears contents without disturbing formats or comments.

   • *Comments:* Clears comments without disturbing contents or formats.

   • *Hyperlinks:* Clears hyperlinks without disturbing contents or formats. If there are no hyperlinks in the cell(s) you selected, this option is grayed out.

Inserting cells, rows, and columns

Adding rows and columns is almost as easy as pressing a button:

✦ **Inserting a cell:** Select a cell (or multiple cells) and then choose Insert⇨Cells from the menu bar. Alternatively, click the Ribbon's Home tab; in the Cells group, choose Insert⇨Insert Cells. A small dialog asks you which way to push the existing cells.

✦ **Inserting a row:** Select a cell (or multiple cells row-wise) and then choose Insert⇨Rows from the menu bar. Alternatively, click the Ribbon's Home tab; in the Cells group, choose Insert⇨Insert Rows. Your new, blank row(s) push(es) the current row and the rows beneath down one (or more) row(s).

✦ **Inserting a column:** Select a cell or multiple cells column-wise and then choose Insert⇨Columns from the menu bar. Alternatively, click the Ribbon's Home tab; in the Cells group, choose Insert⇨Insert Columns. Your new, blank column(s) push(es) the current column and columns one (or more) column(s) to the right.

Deleting cells, rows, and columns

You can delete cells, rows, or columns in the following ways:

Delete

 ✦ **Deleting a cell:** Select a cell and then choose Edit⇨Delete from the menu bar. Alternatively, click the Ribbon's Home tab; in the Cells group, choose Delete⇨Delete Cells. A small dialog asks you which way to move the existing cells.

 ✦ **Deleting a row:** Select a row number and then choose Edit⇨Delete from the menu bar. Alternatively, click the Ribbon's Home tab; in the Cells group, choose Delete⇨Delete Rows. Your selected row vanishes, and the rows beneath move up one row.

 ✦ **Deleting a column:** Select a column letter and then choose Edit⇨Delete from the menu bar. Alternatively, click the Ribbon's Home tab; in the Cells group, choose Delete⇨Delete Columns. Your column disappears, and columns to the right move one to the left.

Making Sense of Cursors

Excel is always trying to tell you what it can do. When you're in a worksheet, the cursor changes as you move the mouse around. The cursor's appearance reveals what you can do:

 ✦ **Open cross:** This is the mouse cursor you see most of the time in Excel. When you see the open cross, Excel expects you to do something.

 ✦ **Hand:** When you see the hand, you can hold down the mouse button and drag a cell or cell range from its current location to any other location on the worksheet.

 ✦ **Dark arrow:** This arrow cursor appears only if the mouse pointer moves over a column or a row indicator. Although pointing is certainly bad manners under normal circumstances, Excel is just being helpful in this case. The arrow points down when the mouse pointer is in a column indicator, or it points to the right when the mouse pointer is over a row indicator. (See Figure 3-5.)

   • Click when this arrow is visible to select the entire row(s) or column(s).

   • Drag when this arrow is visible to select multiple rows or columns. A tooltip displays to show how many rows or columns you're about to select when you release the mouse button.

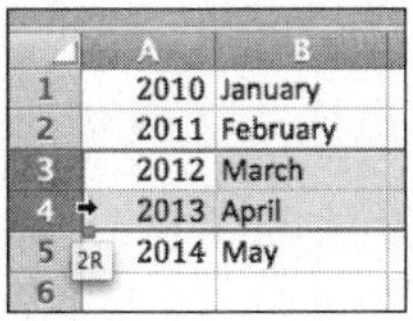

Figure 3-5:
Selecting
two rows.

✦ **Double arrow:** The double arrow appears when the mouse pointer is over the divider between cells, between rows and columns, and in various windows to let you know you can move pane dividers and other dividers. When you see this cursor, hold down the mouse button and drag the divider to resize, or double-click the mouse to automatically size the row or column.

✦ **Solid cross:** To see this cursor, the mouse pointer has to be positioned over the fill handle. To drag the fill handle, hold down the mouse button when you see the solid cross and then drag to copy the selection across or down. See the "Dragging a Series of Text, Numbers, or Dates" section, later in this chapter, for details about special fill handle capabilities.

✦ **Format Painter:** Make a selection and then click the Format Painter button on the Standard toolbar. The cursor changes to a paintbrush to let you know that whatever you click next will receive the formatting from whatever was selected when you clicked the Format Painter button.

✦ **Insertion cursor:** This blinking cursor tells you where text will appear when you type.

✦ **Shape cursor:** Blue dots, which you can drag, surround a selected shape accompanied by a green dot that you can drag to rotate the object.

Moving a Row or Column

Although you can't drag rows or columns, they're still pretty easy to move. To move a row or column, follow these steps:

1. **Select a row number or column letter.**

The entire row or column is highlighted.

2. **Choose Edit⇨Cut from the menu bar or press ⌘-X.**

3. **Select the cell in column A of the destination row or in row 1 of the destination column.**

4. **Right-click and choose Insert Cut Cells.**

Your row or column appears, and the existing row or column and all others below or to the right move over.

Dragging a Series of Text, Numbers, or Dates

Excel is pretty smart because it can automatically fill in a series of either numbers or dates, and it can even make intelligent guesses about a series of numbers.

Filling in a series

We use an example to show how Excel can fill in a range of cells for you. Follow along on your computer to watch what happens:

1. **With Excel open, start with a blank, standard worksheet.**

2. **Type** January **in a cell and then select a different cell.**

3. **Click the cell that has the word January in it.**

   The selection cursor appears, as shown in the margin.

4. **Position the mouse cursor over the lower-right corner of the selected cell (the fill handle) so that it becomes the solid cross cursor.**

5. **Drag the fill handle down or to the right and watch Excel do some magic.**

   As you drag across the cells, you see the tooltip note each month in the series.

Release the mouse a few cells over, and Excel enters all the month names for you. Your screen looks like Figure 3-6. Additionally, when you let go, a little widget appears. Resist the urge to click the widget! If you're curious about what's in the widget, look at Figure 3-6 and read the sidebar "Wondering about widgets," but don't choose any options from the widget right now.

Figure 3-6: Auto- matically filling in a series.

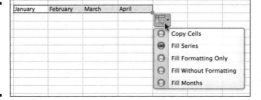

Filling in a complex pattern

Excel can do more than fill in a series of consecutive numbers or dates. While it can manage to divine months of a year or days in a week from just one cell, Excel can also figure out most series of numbers from just two or three starting numbers. Series can be in rows, such as the example we use, or in columns. Follow these steps to see how Excel deduces what number values to fill in (see Figure 3-7):

1. **Enter** 1 **in cell B2 and enter** 3 **in cell C2.**

   Typing in a cell dismisses the widget. Notice that 1 and 3 are odd num- bers in sequence in adjoining cells.

2. **Select B2:C2.**

   The trick here is to select both cells (drag over both cells) so that Excel notes the first two values of the series.

3. **Without clicking anything else, grab the fill handle's cross cursor and drag it to the right.**

   Excel deduces from the selected cells that you want a series of odd numbers and then fills in the series (1, 3, 5, 7, 9, and more).

Figure 3-7:
Making
a series
of odd
numbers.

Filling a column

Sometimes you want an entire column of the same thing. To do this, take these steps:

1. **Type text or a formula in row 1 of your column.**

2. **Select the cell in row 1.**

3. **Press Control-Shift-↓.**

   The entire column becomes highlighted.

4. **Press Control-D.**

   The entire column fills with the contents of the cell in row 1. The sheet has over a million rows, so give Excel a second or two to fill in.

Using the Custom Lists Feature to Fill Cells

The Custom Lists feature is about making lists that Excel can refer to when filling in a series by dragging a selected cell's fill handle (the solid crosshair cursor), which results in an automatic series fill.

Not only can Excel figure out number and date series on its own, but you also can teach Excel to figure out just about any series.

You have two easy ways to make a new series with Custom Lists:

✦ Type a custom list from scratch, making entries in Excel Preferences.

✦ Start with an existing series of cells in a workbook.

For example, say you frequently make reports that have a series of reoccurring days. The following sections provide examples of how to create a custom list in Excel Preferences and from a series of cells.

Making a custom list in Excel Preferences

To make a custom list to use in fills, follow these steps:

1. **Choose Excel⇨Preferences from the menu bar.**

Excel Preferences displays.

Custom Lists

2. **In the Formulas and Lists section, click Custom Lists.**

The Custom Lists preferences pane, shown in Figure 3-8, displays. You see a handful of built-in series. You can't change these.

3. **Select New List in the Custom Lists list.**

4. **In the List Entries list, type the series entries in order.**

If you have both Return and Enter keys, press Return (*not* Enter) after each entry. If you have just one Return key that says Enter as well, press this key.

5. **Click the Add button when the list is complete.**

Your series is added to the Custom Lists list.

6. **When you're done adding lists, click OK.**

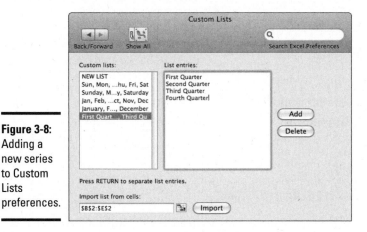

Figure 3-8:
Adding a
new series
to Custom
Lists
preferences.

Wondering about widgets

Occasionally Excel displays little widgets to offer you alternatives to the default behavior. They appear whenever Excel thinks it got it right but knows that there's an alternative behavior that you might prefer over the default behavior. You see a widget in Figure 3-6. Although Excel got it right (we wanted the default, which is Fill Series), we could have chosen an option from the pop-up menu, such as Copy Cells, Fill Formatting Only, Fill without Formatting, or Fill Months.

To dismiss a widget, click a cell away from the series and type a character.

Making a custom list from a series of cells

If you have a worksheet with a series in a range of cells that you want to add, follow these steps to add the series to Custom Lists:

1. **In the Custom Lists window (see the preceding section), click the small grid button next to the Import List from Cells pop-up menu.**

   The small grid button is to the immediate left of the big Import button.

   Custom Lists preferences pane shrinks so you can see your worksheet. The cursor changes to a plus (+) sign.

2. **Select the cell range that contains the list.**

   To do so, drag over the cells that contain the series you want to add to the Custom Lists preferences. A dotted line indicates the selected cell range, and Excel automatically types the selected range into Custom Lists preferences pane. Each cell's contents becomes a list entry.

3. **Press Escape or Return when you're done selecting.**

   Preferences displays. The Import List from Cells pop-up menu displays the range you selected.

4. **Click the Import button.**

   The selected series appears under List Entries.

5. **Click the Add button.**

   The selected series is added to Custom Lists list.

Understanding General Format

In some respects, Excel is a bit like a word processor. You can format text in many of the same ways as you can in Word or PowerPoint. You can check spelling by choosing Tools⇨Spelling from the menu bar. However, Excel has no concept of a sentence or paragraph, so it can't check grammar like Word can.

Sometimes, Excel may do something unexpected when you type into a cell. For example, if you type a fraction (say, **1/3**), you might be surprised when Excel converts your fraction into a date (3–Jan in this case). When a cell is using the General format (the default cell format), Excel interprets entered text and numbers in a certain way. It's important to understand how Excel automatically formats what you enter into a cell. (In Chapter 4 of this minibook, we describe how to change the General format to other formats.) Table 3-1 lists some of the common ways Excel interprets what you enter into a cell.

Table 3-1	Knowing What Excel Thinks of What You Type	
Enter This	*Excel Displays*	*Reason*
A	A	Anything that starts with a letter is treated as text.
1	1	Any cell that has a number is treated as the value of that number.
–1	–1	Negative numbers display the minus sign.
'15	15	A single quotation mark makes Excel treat the cell content as text.
½	2–Jan or February 1st	Numbers separated by / are interpreted as a date.
January 1	1–Jan	Excel displays the date in its standard date format.
.5	0.5	Excel displays the mathematical value for a decimal.
0 1/2	1/2	A zero and a space before a fraction lets Excel know you want the mathematical fraction and not a date.
12 o'clock	12 o'clock	Most combinations of letters and text are treated as text.
=A1	The value of cell A1	A cell beginning with an equals sign signals a cell reference or formula.
=SUM(A2:A5)	The sum of the values of cells A2 through A5	A cell beginning with an equals sign signals a cell reference or formula.

Book III Chapter 3

Getting into Cells and Worksheets

Entering Cell Formulas

Cell formulas are equations that perform calculations or logical operations. You can enter a formula on your own, or you can use the Formula Builder, which helps you build formulae by using a step-by-step structured wizard-like method. We cover both ways to enter a formula in the following sections.

These words have special meaning in Excel:

✦ **Function:** A specific calculation, such as SUM, MULTIPLY, or COSINE. A function can be a logical operator, such as IF. Functions are represented in uppercase in Excel documentation.

✦ **Argument:** A variable in a calculation or logical operation. This is the kind of argument you may remember from math class; not the kind of argument you have when someone disagrees with you!

✦ **Formula:** These are the instructions that tell Excel what you want to calculate. Formulas start with the equals sign (=) and include functions and/or arguments. A formula entered in a cell is a *cell formula*.

✦ **Syntax:** These are specific rules that explain what should be entered and the order in which to enter arguments in a cell formula.

If you're new to Excel, don't feel bad if what you type doesn't produce the expected result at first. Chances are good that a stray or missing character got mixed in. Table 3-1 (shown earlier) may help you understand what went wrong when you tried to enter a formula.

Typing a formula

We start with a very easy example to show you the structure of a formula and that Excel treats numbers as values within a formula:

1. **Start with a blank worksheet.**

2. **Type =1+1 in cell A1 and then press Return, Enter, Tab, or an arrow key to exit the cell.**

   If you select the cell again, you see that Excel displays the *value* (2) of the formula in cell A1 and displays the *formula* (=1+1) in the Formula bar.

The cell's appearance changes while you type. Observe and see how the cell appears while you type and after you exit the cell. You can use the value represented in a cell and refer to it in a formula in a different cell.

Here's another example. This time we use values from cells in the worksheet instead of using numbers in the formula. This gives you experience figuring out various ways to refer to cells and cell ranges in formulas:

1. **Start with a blank worksheet.**

2. **Type 1 into cells A1 and B1.**

    The value of 1 displays in cells A1 and B1, as shown in Figure 3-9.

3. **In cell C1, type** =A1+B1.

    Your screen looks exactly like Figure 3-9. Excel color-codes the cell references within your formula to match the referenced cells A1 and B1, which are now highlighted to match the color code in the formula. Your formula now displays in the Formula bar.

4. **Click the green Enter button when done.**

    Excel displays the value of the formula in cell C1 and displays the formula in the Formula bar.

The moment you start typing in a cell or the Formula bar, the red Cancel and green Enter buttons become activated. You can click Cancel to erase your cell entry or click the green Enter button to accept your entry. These buttons are new for Excel 2011.

Figure 3-9:
Making a
simple cell
formula.

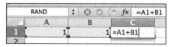

Letting Excel type a formula for you

Here's an example that shows you how to let Excel type for you so you're less likely to make a typing mistake in a formula:

1. **Start with a blank worksheet.**

2. **Type 1 into cells A1 and B1.**

    The value of 1 displays in cells A1 and B1, as shown in Figure 3-9.

3. **In cell C1, type the equals sign (=), click cell A1, type the plus sign (+), and then click cell B1.**

After you type the equals sign and move the mouse, the cursor changes. A cell selection indicator moves with the mouse. When you put the selection indicator over cell A1, clicking the mouse tells Excel you want to use the value of cell A1 in the formula and types it for you. You can do the same with cell B1. Again your screen looks identical to Figure 3-9.

4. **Click the green Enter button when done.**

   Excel displays the value of the formula in cell A1 and displays the formula in the Formula bar.

You're allowed to select ranges of cells, which is a great help when working with complicated formulas.

Entering a function manually

This example shows how to use a built-in cell function within your formula. You use the SUM worksheet function to add the values of two cells:

1. **Start with a blank worksheet.**

2. **Type 1 into cells A1 and B1.**

   The value of 1 displays in cells A1 and B1, as shown in Figure 3-9.

3. **In cell C1, type = SUM(A1:B1).**

   Excel displays the value of the calculation in cell C1 and the formula in the Formula bar.

4. **Click the green Enter button when you're done.**

   Excel displays the value of the formula in cell A1 and displays the formula containing the SUM function in the Formula bar.

In this example, SUM is the function, and the cell range A1:B1 is the argument. The argument of a function is placed in parentheses. Entering a function and its arguments manually may be useful when you refer to cells that are widely dispersed on a worksheet. You can refer to named ranges, as in =SUM(rangename).

Letting Excel type functions and arguments

Excel has hundreds of built-in functions that you can use in cell formulas. While you type a function in a cell formula, a pop-up menu appears. In the following example, we use Excel's built-in SUM function. See Figure 3-10 while you explore this sequence.

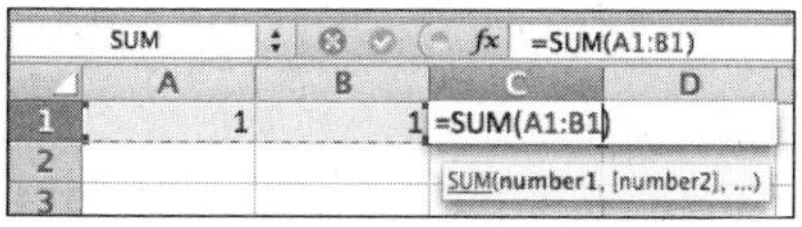

Figure 3-10:
Letting
Excel do the
typing.

	A	B	C	D
1	1	1	=SUM(A1:B1)	
2			SUM(number1, [number2], ...)	
3				

SUM ≎ ⊗ ⊘ ⌢ *fx* =SUM(A1:B1)

1. **Start with a blank worksheet.**

2. **Type 1 into both cells A1 and B1.**

   The value of 1 displays in cells A1 and B1, as shown in Figure 3-10.

3. **In cell C1, type =S.**

   Wow! While you type, a pop-up menu showing all worksheet functions beginning with the letter S displays. Look at all the functions that start with the letter S! Right now, you're interested in the SUM function.

4. **Choose SUM from within all those S options in the pop-up menu with the arrow keys on your keyboard; then press the Enter or Tab key. Don't type anything else for now.**

   Excel displays =SUM(|) with the vertical bar indicating the insertion cursor is ready to fill in the argument.

5. **Drag over the range A1:B1.**

   Excel enters the cell range for you and you don't have to worry about making a typing mistake. (See Figure 3-10.) Is that neat or what?

   (Optional) You can manually type the argument.

6. **Click the green Enter button to finish.**

   Excel displays the value of the formula in cell A1 and displays the formula containing the SUM function in the Formula bar.

The SUM function is so popular that it has its own button! You can find it by clicking the Ribbon's Formulas tab, and in the Function group, clicking AutoSum. Click a range of contiguous numbers and then click the button and choose a SUM function. Excel deduces the range for you and enters the formula.

When you enter a cell formula that includes a function, Excel shows you the function's name and its syntax, as shown in Figure 3-10. The function's name is blue and is underlined like a hyperlink. That's because it's a link to the Help topic for that particular function.

**Book III
Chapter 3**

**Getting into Cells
and Worksheets**

Each function is thoroughly documented with complete sample data and examples so that you can easily see how to use it. To display the complete list of all functions by category, click the Ribbon's Formulas tab, and in the Function group, click Reference. (See Figure 3-11.) Click a disclose triangle to display a list of that category's functions. In the disclosed list, clicking a function name displays detailed information about the function, including how to properly use the function's arguments. Some topics explain the calculations used by the function to arrive at its result.

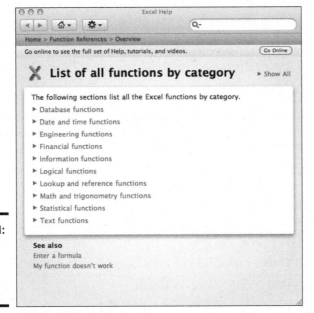

Figure 3-11: Getting the details about a function.

Building a formula with the Formula Builder

Formula Builder is a tool in Toolbox designed to help you build cell formulas. You start at the top of the Formula Builder and work your way down to put a finished cell formula into an empty cell. Refer to Figure 3-12, where we build a formula to count the number of times the word *apple* is in a list. To follow along, type data into cells as shown in A1:D5 in Figure 3-12 (or enter your own list where a word appears more than once). Then follow these steps:

1. **Click in an empty cell.**

Choose the cell that will display your formula's result. In our example, we selected cell A6.

2. **To activate the Formula Builder, choose one of the following:**

   - Click the Formula Builder button on the Formula bar.
   - Click the Toolbox button on the Standard toolbar.
   - Click the Ribbon's Formulas tab, and in the Function group, click Formula Builder.

   The Formula Builder opens, as shown in Figure 3-12. At this point, you can use the scroll bar to browse all of Excel's functions. Drag the divider down to expose more formulas at once.

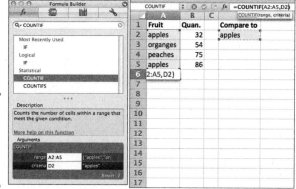

Figure 3-12: Building a formula with the Formula Builder.

3. **In the Formula Builder, enter a search term in the search field to filter the list of functions.**

   You can enter the name of a function if you already know it. Otherwise, enter a term you think might be a function. As you type, the list filters. We looked for COUNTIF and clicked the COUNTIF function to see its description.

4. **Double-click COUNTIF in the search results list to choose it for your formula.**

   The function is added to your worksheet with the insertion cursor ready for your input from the Formula Builder. The Formula Builder displays empty fields for arguments specific to the function you selected.

5. **Click into the topmost argument field in the Formula Builder.**

   The insertion cursor blinks in the empty argument field. When you click into an argument field, the Description updates to display information about the argument. Some functions let you add and remove arguments by clicking plus or minus sign buttons to the right of argument fields.

Some functions, such as the popular IF worksheet function, offer pop-up menus of options to choose from.

6. **Do one of the following to satisfy an argument:**

   - Type text or values to satisfy the argument.

   - Click a cell to satisfy the argument.

   - Drag a range of cells to satisfy the argument.

   Doing any of these actions results in the display of your argument's value or formula in the Formula Builder and in the Formula bar. More than one argument may be needed for your calculation. Click the More Help on This Function link if you need specific information about the function you've chosen, including details about required arguments or how your function calculates its result. Formula Builder displays the current value of your function based upon the arguments you've provided. Don't press Return or Enter until you've finished satisfying all arguments unless you want to quit the Formula Builder.

   In this example for COUNTIF, we first selected cells A2:A5, then clicked the Criteria box in the Formula Builder, and finally clicked cell D2. (Refer to Figure 3-12.)

7. **After satisfying the arguments, press Return or Enter or click the green Enter button in the Formula bar.**

   The finished formula appears in the Formula bar. The cell that you selected in Step 1 displays the formula's resulting value. You can double-click the cell to perform manual in-cell editing if needed, or you can refine your formula in the Formula bar.

In the example shown in Figure 3-12, when you're done, the value of A6 depends upon the value of D2. Type a different fruit from the list into D2 and then click elsewhere. Watch as the count in A6 updates instantly.

You can use the Formula Builder to learn new functions. Suppose someone gives you a workbook that uses a function you're unfamiliar with, and you want to understand how it works. Turn on the Formula Builder and then click on the mysterious formula. The Formula Builder shows you how the formula and its arguments were constructed. Click into each argument to display a description of the argument.

Knowing When to Be Absolute, Relatively Speaking

Usually, you simply press ⌘-C or choose Edit➪Copy to copy things. Likewise, you press ⌘-V or choose Edit➪Paste to paste. Copying and pasting cells and cell formulas works differently from text and other objects, so they can be a little bit puzzling if you don't know the secret about *relative* versus *absolute* references.

Making a relative reference

Say you want to use the value of cell A1 in a formula, so you type =**A1** in your formula to use the value of cell A1 and away you go. Your formula works, and all seems well.

What Excel is actually thinking when you type =**A1** is that you want to use the value of the cell that's the number of rows and columns away from the cell in which you're typing your formula. Your formula works as expected in its original location, but if you copy the cell containing your formula and then paste that cell somewhere else, the formula in the pasted cell no longer refers to the value in cell A1. Instead, it refers to the cell in the relative location (the same number of rows and columns away from the copied cell). This concept of relativity is why this reference style is a *relative* reference.

Here's a fun little example with a relative reference. Start with a blank worksheet and refer to Figure 3-13 while you follow these steps:

1. **Click in a cell, any cell.**

   For this example, we clicked in cell A1.

2. **Type something in the cell.**

   For this example, we typed *Hello.*

3. **Click in any other cell.**

   For this example, we clicked in cell B2.

4. **In the cell you chose in Step 3, type a formula to equal what's in the cell from Step 1 and then click the green Enter button.**

   For example, we typed =**A1**. The example in Figure 3-13 shows that our cell B2 displays *Hello,* which equals the value of cell A1. Cell B2's formula has a relative reference to cell A1, which is one column to the left and one row up.

5. **Select the cell that you just typed in and then press ⌘-C.**

   This copies the cell you just put the formula into.

6. **Click in any unused cell and choose Edit⇨Paste or press ⌘-V.**

   We pasted into cell B4. Notice that the pasted cell shows zero instead of the value of cell A1. The pasted cell refers to empty cell A3 as you can see in the Formula bar in Figure 3-13, and by choosing Trace Empty Cell in the error widget (the widget with the exclamation in Figure 3-13). Cell A3 is one row up and one row over from the pasted cell B4. That's because the copy/paste operation pastes a relative reference by default.

Excel notices two things and displays two widgets:

+ **Exclamation Point widget:** Indicates an error of some sort. Click to display an alert that the formula references an empty cell.

+ **Clipboard widget:** When clicked, the Clipboard widget displays Paste Special options. By choosing Link Cells from the pop-up menu, we can use an absolute reference (see next heading) instead of the default relative reference type.

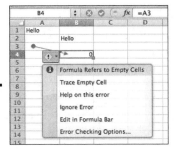
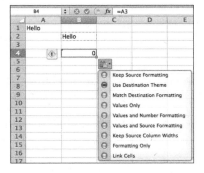

Figure 3-13: Copying a relative reference.

Using an absolute reference

An *absolute* reference always uses the exact cell referred to in the formula. You do this by adding a dollar sign ($) to the row, the column, or both in a formula. If you want to always refer to the value in cell A1, type =$A$1. A good way to remember how to make an absolute reference is to think of the dollar sign ($) as *always.* When you read =$A$1, think "equals always column A, always row 1."

In rare circumstances, you might need an absolute value reference to either a row or a column. If you want to refer to the value in column using an absolute reference A but use a relative reference for rows, type =$A1.

To toggle a cell's reference style between relative and absolute reference, click the Ribbon's Formulas tab, and in the Function group, click Switch Reference.

Displaying row and column reference style

The default for Excel is to display using column letters and row numbers, but you can change the display so that you see row and column numbers instead. Choose Excel➪Preferences. Click the General button in the Authoring area and then select or deselect the first item. Use R1C1 Reference Style to switch the display.

If you're referring to cells with VBA, you will find this option to be handy because, in VBA, you often use this R1C1 method of addressing cells. You would read a relative reference that looks like this =R[-1]C[-1] as "Refer to the cell that's one row less than the current row and one column less than the current column." The same cell with an absolute reference would be =R2C2.

Chapter 4: Formatting and Conditional Formatting

In This Chapter

✔ Taking out your formatting tools

✔ Coloring and shading cells for emphasis

✔ Figuring out and formatting dates and times

✔ Formatting with conditions

✔ Formatting the worksheet background

*I*f you hold this book for five minutes in your hands each day, Excel auto-matically starts behaving. Jokes aside, we start this chapter by pointing out some interesting formatting options, including how to control borders, shading, and patterns. We explain the mysteries behind Excel's date and time calculations and how Excel can apply formatting for you based on a cell's contents.

This chapter's focus relates to features that are unique to Excel. You can find info about formatting text, text boxes, shapes, pictures, WordArt, and other objects that can be placed on worksheets in Book I, Chapter 6.

Before you can format anything, you must first select it. In general, to select something, click it. The interface responds by changing the display to indi-cate your selection, usually by changing the selection's border or outline.

Formatting Cells

One of the things you might find you do frequently is change the way cells look, and you do so with options on the Home tab of the Ribbon, shown in Figure 4-1. Refer to Figure 4-1 as we discuss the organization of the Home tab in the following sections.

You can apply many operations such as formatting to more than one work-sheet at a time. Hold ⌘ down as you click on worksheet tabs to select multi-ple worksheets. As you apply formatting, the corresponding cells in the selected sheets are also formatted. Click a worksheet tab without pressing ⌘ to return to having a single sheet selected.

Figure 4-1:
Formatting
cells from
the Ribbon.

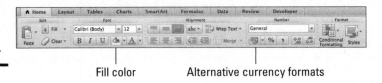

Fill color   Alternative currency formats

Applying number and text formats

Other than the visual effect, format also means how a cell treats the content
that's typed inside it. General format is the default cell format. (Look in the
Number group on the Home tab shown in Figure 4-1.) In Chapter 3 of this
minibook, we provide a table that explains how General format treats characters when you enter them. Briefly, the General format applies formatting
by using these simple rules:

✦ A cell that contains any text characters is formatted as text.

✦ A cell containing numbers only is formatted as a number or date.

✦ A cell that begins with an equals sign (=) is a formula.

You can override General format and apply any other format that you want
to a cell. If you change a cell's format from one of the number or date formats into Text format, you can no longer use the number value or date in
formula calculations.

The Number group on the Home tab offers quick formatting options:

✦ **Number Format:** This is a pop-up menu that lets you apply the default
format for each of the major format categories.

✦ **Alternate Currency:** This pop-up menu lets you apply accounting formats for specific currencies.

✦ **Percent:** Displays decimal values as a percent.

✦ **Thousands:** Click to toggle commas on or off as thousands separators.

✦ **Reposition decimal point:** Click a button to move the decimal point one
position to the left or to the right.

To display the complete list of available number formats, press ⌘-1 (or
choose Format⇨Cells from the menu bar) and in the Formal Cells dialog,
click the Number tab, as shown in Figure 4-2. We have a step-by-step example using Date custom formatting codes in the section "Formatting a date,"
later in this chapter.

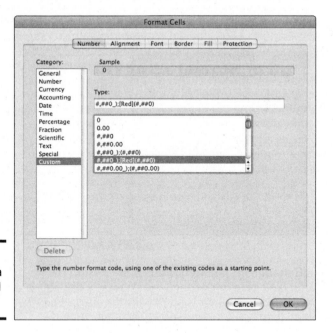

Figure 4-2:
Designing a custom cell format.

Fitting and positioning content

Similar to the controls for formatting a table, you can align and position cell contents using the Alignment group on the Ribbon's Home tab (refer to Figure 4-1):

✦ **Horizontal:** Select from left, center, or right justification for a cell.

✦ **Vertical:** Select top, center, or bottom.

✦ **Orientation:** Tip and turn cell contents.

✦ **Wrap Text:** Choose Wrap Text from this pop-up menu to allow text to wrap within a cell. Select some contiguous rows and then select Shrink to Fit from the pop-up menu. The text in rows with more text will be made smaller to match the length of the shortest text entry among the selected rows.

✦ **Merge:** Select two or more cells and then click this button to merge the selection into a single cell. You retain only the content of the upper-left cell. Select an already merged cell and then click this button to unmerge the merged cell.

When you type text that extends past the right edge of the cell, your text displays. If you then enter text or a formula into the cell immediately to the right, the contents of the second cell will cover the text in the first cell. This is normal. Adjust the column width and row heights by using the double-arrow cursor, as described in Chapter 3 of this minibook. The Wrap Text button has a pop-up menu from which you can choose to either Wrap Text or Shrink Text to Fit, which you can use to solve overlap problems.

You can access additional cell alignment options by pressing ⌘-1 and clicking the Alignment tab, as shown in Figure 4-3. The Orientation area gives you a couple fun options:

✦ **Stacked letters:** Click this button to stack letters as shown in Figure 4-3.

✦ **Angled orientation:** Drag the angle line or use the spinner control to tilt text to any angle.

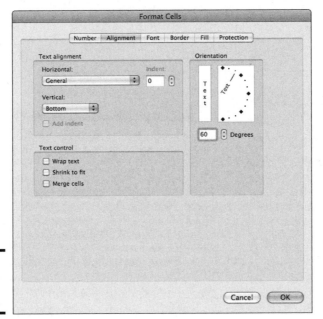

Figure 4-3:
Setting cell
alignment.

Formatting cell borders

Formatting cells and cell ranges is like formatting tables, as we describe in Book I, Chapter 11. In the Font group of the Ribbon's Home tab, clicking Borders button displays a drop-down gallery of border styles.

Experienced Excel users may yearn for the old floating Borders toolbar. Happily, you can find the Borders option on the Formatting toolbar, which you turn on by choosing View⇨Toolbars⇨Formatting from Excel's menu.

You can find more presets for borders in the Format Cells dialog, which you can display by pressing ⌘-1 and choosing the Border tab, shown in Figure 4-4. If you select a cell range before opening the Format Cells dialog, you format the outer border as well as the inner borders.

Use the following order when you're formatting a range of cells using the Border tab of the Format Cells dialog:

1. **Color:** Choose a color for your border from Excel's color picker. The color you choose is displayed in the Style pane.

2. **Style:** Select a solid, dashed, thick, thin, or double-style border.

3. **Border:** For the border, you work in either the Presets area or the Border area.

In the Presets area, choose from these options:

- *None:* Clears borders from the selected cell or cell range.

- *Outline:* Applies a border to the selected cell or around the outside border of a range of cells.

- *Inside:* Applies borders to cells within a selected range, but doesn't put a border around the entire range.

In the Border area, click in the preview, or click toggle buttons to turn individual outside, inside, or diagonal borders on and off.

You can apply multiple colors and line styles. You have to choose a new color and style for each border you turn on.

Formatting cell fill color and shading

Choosing a theme and sticking with its color set is usually a safe way to add colors to cells. Whether it's to match a color key, corporate theme, or to add emphasis, Excel helps you by making cell fill easy to apply quickly — on the Home tab, find the Font group and click the Fill Color button and choose a color from the color palette. More fill options are available as follows:

1. **Select the cell or range of cells you want to format.**

2. **Press ⌘-1.**

The Format Cells dialog appears.

3. **Click the Fill tab, as shown in Figure 4-5.**

4. **Choose a background color from the color picker.**

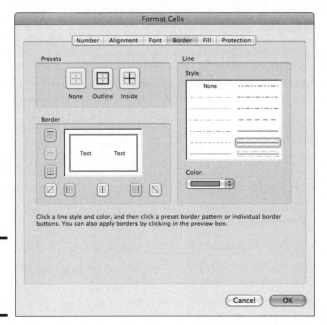

Figure 4-4:
Building
better
borders.

5. **(Optional) Choose a Foreground Color and a Foreground Pattern from the color and pattern pickers to apply on top of the background color.**

   The Sample area shows you a preview of your cell. Remember, you may have text in a cell. Choose colors and patterns to complement, not conflict with, your cell contents.

Applying and saving cell format styles

Although applying all these formatting options is fun, you might find that the built-in styles will suit you fine, or at least give you a starting point from which you can refine to your taste. In the Home tab's Format group, click the previews in the Styles gallery, or click the downward-pointing button to display a drop-down gallery that has many preconfigured styles from which to choose.

You can give your own cell format a name, which you can save as a cell style in the workbook. At the bottom of the Ribbon's Style gallery, choose New Cell Style to display the New Cell Style dialog shown in Figure 4-6. Choose which properties to include and give your style a name.

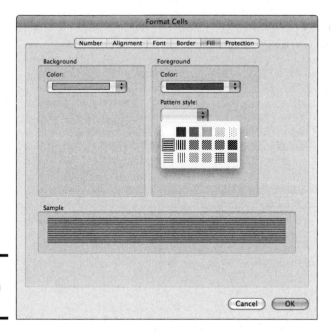

Figure 4-5:
Choosing a
cell fill.

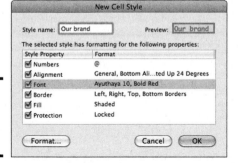

Figure 4-6:
Saving a
custom cell
style.

At the bottom of the Ribbon's Style gallery, choose Import Cell Styles to
display the names of custom cell styles that are in other open workbooks.
Choose one of the styles to copy from the other workbook.

Formatting Dates and Times

Excel has fantastic date and time calculation capabilities. You need to know
just two secrets:

✦ Each day is represented by a whole number, called a *serial number*.

✦ Portions of days are represented by decimal fractions.

Finding today

Some days, you wake up and don't even know what day it is. Excel doesn't have this problem. To have Excel return the current date, select the cell you want Excel to show the current date in and type the cell formula =**TODAY()** and then click the green Enter button. The selected cell displays today's date, and Excel automatically changes the format of the cell to Date.

Getting today's serial number

Each day has its own serial number in Excel. If you follow the steps in the preceding section, you don't see the serial number in the selected cell because Excel knows the formula represents a date. If you want to see the serial number instead of a date format, you can manually change the format of the selected cell to Number by selecting Number in the Ribbon's Number Format pop-up menu (as shown earlier in Figure 4-1).

Knowing that each day is represented by a whole number makes adding and subtracting dates easy.

When you have a date serial number displayed in a cell, you can change that serial number as follows:

✦ Subtract whole numbers from the serial number to change it to an earlier date. If you subtract 1 from the serial number for today's date, you get yesterday's date. For example, the cell formula =**TODAY()-5** displays the date five days ago.

✦ Add whole numbers to the serial number to advance to a later date. If you add 1 to the serial number for today's date, you get tomorrow's date.

In Excel, to add and subtract any number of days, just add and subtract whole numbers. You're probably wondering how Excel arrived at the serial number of today. To find out, enter **1** in a cell and apply the Date format. The date changes to January 1, 1900 — the first day that Excel knows about. Every day in Excel is the number of days after 1/1/1900.

Finding the time of day

Because Excel works with days as whole numbers, you might guess that portions of days are fractions. Well, you'd be right! Starting with a whole number representing a date, append **.5** (one-half day) to a date serial number to represent noon. Apply the Time number format, and the time changes to 12:00 PM. Go ahead and try some different decimals.

The first-day mystery

The beginning of time in Excel is the date with the serial number one. Starting with Excel 2011 on the Mac, Excel uses the same starting date as Excel for Windows; that date is January 1, 1900. In previous versions of Excel for Mac, that date was January 1, 1904. There used to be a difference because Excel for Mac was on the market many years before Excel for Windows. Actually, Excel for Mac was sold years before Windows even existed! During the time before Windows, Excel for Mac had to compete against the spreadsheet runaway market leader on the IBM platform, which was Lotus 1-2-3.

Microsoft knew about a leap-year bug in Lotus 1-2-3 and had to make choices. To avoid the Lotus 1-2-3 leap year bug, Excel for Mac's first serial number date was January 1, 1904.

When making Excel for IBMs and compatibles, Microsoft could be accurate but incompatible with Lotus and risk losing market share, or include the Lotus 1-2-3 error and be compatible. Microsoft chose compatibility over correctness. Excel eventually eclipsed Lotus 1-2-3 to become the market leader.

Ordinarily, Excel handles the date system for you automatically, regardless of whether a workbook was created in Excel for Mac or Excel for Windows. You can manually switch the date system in a workbook; choose Excel⇨Preferences. In the resultant dialog, click the Calculation button. In this sheet, in the Workbook options area, you can select the option that says Use the 1904 Date System, but only select this option if you need to fix a workbook in which all the dates displayed are off by four years.

Formatting a date

You have at least three different ways to apply a date format. Perhaps the fastest is to select a cell or cell range, and then click the Home tab of the Ribbon. In the Number group, click the pop-up button under the Number group title and choose Date to display the date as m/d/yy, where *m* represents the month's number, *d* represents the day number, and *yy* represents a two-digit year.

Excel has many more built-in date formats, which you can apply by displaying the Format Cells dialog (shown in Figure 4-7) by pressing ⌘-1 and then clicking the Number tab. You can also display the Number tab of the Format Cells dialog by clicking the Home tab on the Ribbon. Then click the pop-up button under the Number group title and choose Custom from the pop-up menu.

When the Format Cells dialog displays, select the Date category. Choose a Type from the list. Choosing a different Location (language) or Calendar type changes the date types offered.

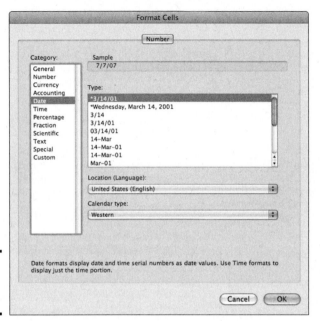

The Custom category at the bottom of the Categories in the Format Cells dialog (see Figure 4-2) displays Type as an input field. See Table 4-1 for custom formatting codes.

If a custom date format in a cell is too wide to display in the column, Excel shows hash marks (##) in the cell. To fix, click the Home tab, and in the Cell group, choose Format➪AutoFit Column Width.

If you experiment with custom formatting codes in the Format Cells dialog's Custom tab (refer to Figure 4-2), you may notice some patterns. Table 4-1 has some example format code that you can try.

Table 4-1	Date and Time Format Examples
Format Code	*Result*
h:mm	18:00
h:mm AM/PM	6:00 PM

Format Code	Result
h:mm:ss AM/PM	6:00:00 PM
Yyyy	2009
Yy	09
Mmmm	February
Mmm	Feb
Mm	02
M	2

Conditional Formatting

You can set Excel to change the format of a cell, cell range, table, or pivot table based on conditions you specify. You can use these settings when you want a cell's appearance to change as the result of a formula or when someone types in a worksheet. Conditional formatting was improved in many ways for Excel 2011. There are more conditions from which to choose. Conditions can be external to the cell you're formatting, and conditions can be based on criteria on other worksheets. Excel 2011 has new formatting options, such as borders, solid fills, icon sets, plotting negative values, and data bars.

There are literally billions of possible combinations, so to save space we show you only a few million possibilities. There are five major styles of conditional formatting, which you can find when you go to the Home tab's Format group and click the Conditional Formatting button, as shown in Figure 4-8. We have an example for each option in this chapter. Each option has a submenu, palette, or dialog associated with it.

If you apply a rule to a data set and then apply another rule, both rules will be in play. Use the Clear Rules option near the bottom of the Conditional Formatting pop-up menu to remove conditional formatting. We show you how to use the Manage Rules option after we discuss each style of conditional formatting.

If you select a cell, cell range, or table before choosing an option, the formatting you apply will affect the selection. If you do not make a selection first, the conditional formatting applies to the entire worksheet.

Figure 4-8:
Choosing a
conditional
format
option.

We use the data set shown in Figure 4-9 for our conditional formatting examples. Of course, you should try these with your own data, too!

Figure 4-9:
Our sample
data.

Highlight Cells Rules

The Highlight Cells Rules option lets you format cell font, borders, and fill. It's the same kind of conditional formatting from previous versions of Excel and is called the *Classic* style. When you choose Highlight Cells Rules, you then choose from a submenu with these options:

✦ **Greater Than:** Highlights any value greater than a number you specify.

✦ **Less Than:** Highlights any value lesser than a number you specify.

✦ **Between:** Highlights any values between two numbers you specify.

✦ **Equal To:** Highlights any value equal to a number or text you specify.

✦ **Text That Contains:** Highlights any values that include text you specify.

✦ **A Date Occurring:** Highlights any values that include a date you specify.

✦ **Duplicate Values:** Highlights repeated values in your selection.

✦ **More Rules:** Displays the New Formatting Rule dialog directly.

As soon as you choose from the submenu, the New Formatting Rule dialog displays using the Classic style, and the logical operator field is prepopulated based on your choice, as shown in Figure 4-10. The New Formatting Rule dialog changes configuration depending upon the choices you make.

When entering the argument, you can type an entry such as a number, date, or formula such as *="text"* or click the little button next to the entry field, which changes the cursor as shown in Figure 4-11 so that you can select a cell or range in the workbook. Your selection can be on any worksheet.

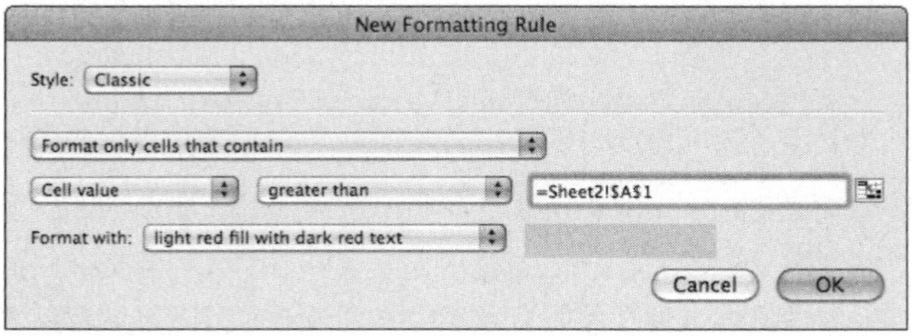

Figure 4-10: Making a new conditional format rule.

New Formatting Rule		
Style: Classic		
Format only cells that contain		
Cell value	greater than	=Sheet2!$A$1
Format with: light red fill with dark red text		
	Cancel	OK

Using the sample data from Figure 4-9, we chose to format cells with a value greater than zero to produce the result shown in Figure 4-11. To do that, follow these steps:

1. **Select the cells that you want to use for the conditional formatting.**

   In this example, we used the data shown in Figure 4-9 and selected cells A1:A5.

2. **Click the Ribbon's Home tab, and within the Format group, click the Conditional Formatting button to bring up the menu shown in Figure 4-8.**

3. **Choose Highlight Cells Rules➪Greater Than to bring up the New Formatting Rule dialog shown in Figure 4-10.**

4. **In the empty text box next to the pop-up menu with the "greater than" option chosen, type 0 (the number 0). Click OK.**

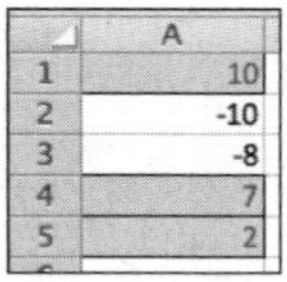

Figure 4-11: Applying Classic formatting.

	A
1	10
2	-10
3	-8
4	7
5	2

Top/Bottom Rules

The Top/Bottom Rules option (found in the Conditional Formatting pop-up menu on the Home tab) defaults to Classic style and results in formatting that looks similar to Figure 4-12. Although the submenus all specify 10 — as in 10 percent or "Top 10" — you can change this value in the New Formatting Rule dialog. The submenu options are as follows:

✦ **Top 10 Items:** Formats the 10 highest numeric values in a list. Use with lists of more than 10 items.

✦ **Top 10%:** Formats only list members in the top 10 percent of the list's values.

✦ **Bottom 10 Items:** Formats the 10 lowest numeric values in a list. Use with lists of more than 10 items.

✦ **Bottom 10%:** Formats only list members in the bottom 10 percent of the list's values.

✦ **Above Average:** Formats list members above the average value.

✦ **Below Average:** Formats list members below the average value.

✦ **More Rules:** Displays the New Formatting Rule dialog preselected to Classic style, as shown in Figure 4-12.

  • *Top/Bottom pop-up menu:* Choose comparison type from this pop-up menu.

  • *Value text box:* Enter a number to use as a quantity or percent.

  • *Percent check box:* Select this check box to use a percent value instead of quantity.

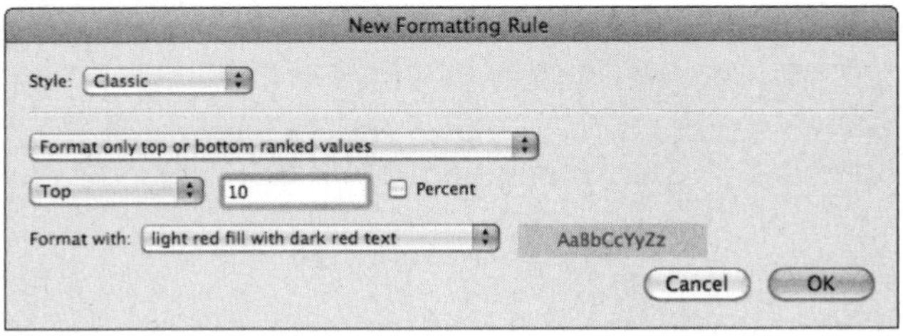

Figure 4-12: Formatting top and bottom.

Data bars

For data bars to display nicely, your cells need to be wide enough to accommodate not just your data, but some fancy formatting as well. When you choose the Data Bars option from the Conditional Formatting pop-up menu, you're offered the palette of preformatted gradient-fill and solid-fill options shown in Figure 4-13.

Figure 4-13:
Choosing
a data bar
format.

If your data contains both positive and negative values, the bars originate from the middle of each cell as shown in the gradient-filled Figure 4-14.

Figure 4-14:
Gradient
filled data
bars.

Choosing More Rules from the Data Bars pop-up menu displays the New Formatting Rule dialog for data bars, shown in Figure 4-15, where you can choose solid and gradient bars, borders, and axis colors.

Color Scales

You can format your data using either 2-color or 3-color scales by choosing Color Scales from the Conditional Formatting pop-up menu. Use color scales when you have large data sets. The 3-color option is good if you have enough records to add a third color for visual clarity and emphasis. The Color Scales option produces the pop-up menu shown in Figure 4-16. You should apply this formatting only to data that is arranged in ascending or descending order.

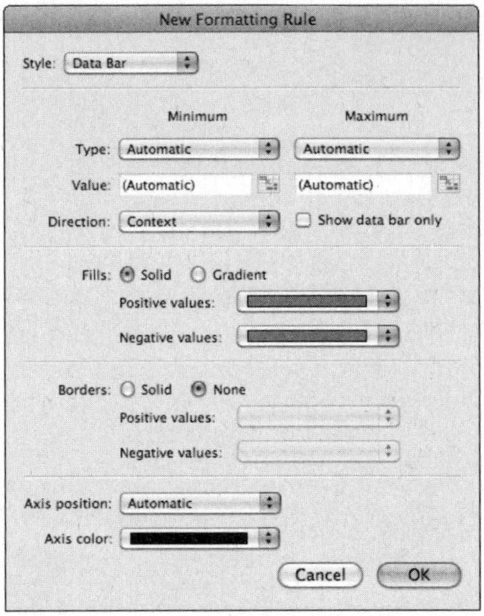

Figure 4-15:
Formatting
data bars.

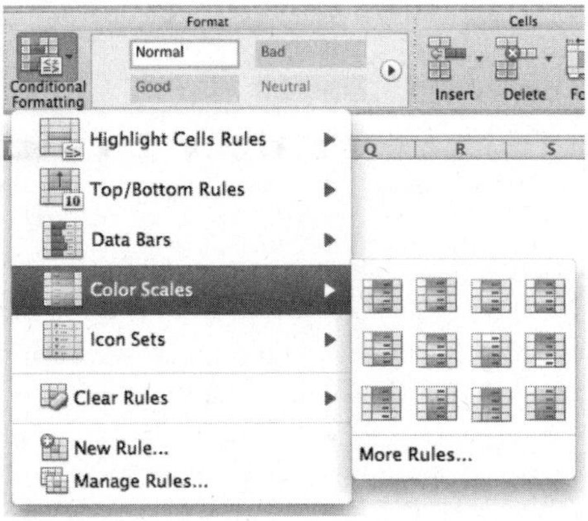

Figure 4-16:
Choosing a
color scale.

Choosing More Rules from the Color Scales submenu displays the New Formatting Rule dialog for Color Scales. The dialog is the same for 2-color and 3-color scales, except that 2-color scales don't have a color for the mid-point range. See Figure 4-17.

Icon sets

Use icon sets when you have large data sets. Icon sets may be better for color-blind people because in addition to color, you add the distinction of shape. The Icon Sets option produces the pop-up menu shown in Figure 4-18. Use the Icons pop-up menu to choose an icon set.

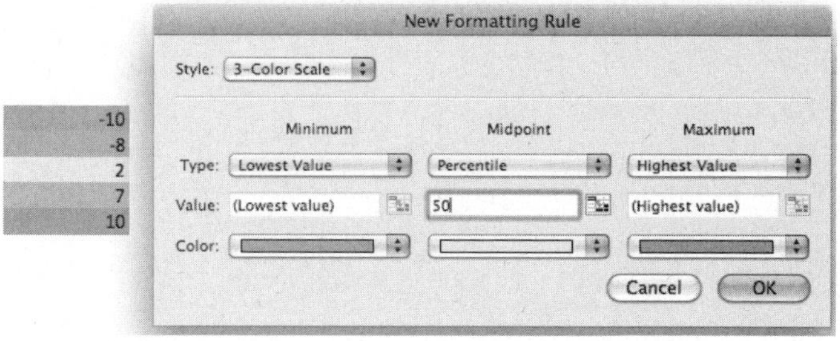

Figure 4-17: Formatting a color scale.

Figure 4-18: Choosing an Icon Set.

Choosing More Rules from the Icon Sets submenu displays the New Formatting Rule dialog for Icon Sets. You have options to reverse the icon order or show only the icon. Click a Display pop-up menu to choose a specific icon to use when the selected cell matches the value and type of criteria you choose. See Figure 4-19.

Managing conditional formatting rules

Choosing Manage Rules from the Conditional Formatting pop-up menu (refer to Figure 4-8) displays the Manage Rules dialog. Here you can set the order in which rules will be executed and even stop rules from firing if previous rules are satisfied. You can edit the rules and change the cell ranges that the rules apply to, as shown in Figure 4-20. Formatting rules are executed in the order presented in Manage Rules starting from the top.

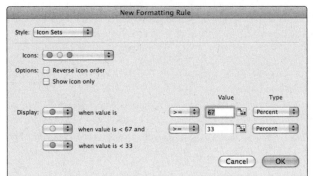

Figure 4-19:
Formatting
an Icon Set.

The Show Formatting Rules For pop-up menu lets you choose from Current Selection; This Sheet; or choose a sheet, table, or pivot table in the workbook.

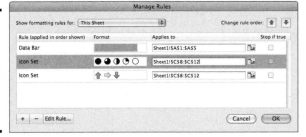

Figure 4-20:
Manage
rules to
control the
display of
conditional
formatting.

Adding a Picture to a Worksheet Background

Behind the cells on each worksheet is a background layer that you can format. There's not a lot of customization to this feature, but you can place an image on the background layer by following these steps:

1. **Choose Format⇨Sheet⇨Background from the menu bar, or go to the Ribbon's Layout tab, find the Page Setup group, and click Background. (This button may not appear on the Ribbon if your workbook window is small in size.)**

   The Choose a Picture dialog appears.

2. **Click the Browse button and navigate to a picture you want to use as a tiled background.**

   While you can use any image, keep in mind that Excel will tile the image, which may not be the desired effect. Also, images that are busy or too dark will make it hard to read any data in your worksheet. You may want to stick to light-colored, simple images.

3. **Click OK to place the image.**

If you decide you don't like the image in the background, you can remove it by going to the Ribbon's Layout tab, and in the Page Setup group, click the Background button. Remember that this Background button is a toggle.

Chapter 5: Making, Formatting, and Filtering a Table

In This Chapter

- ✓ Setting table ground rules
- ✓ Making a table quickly
- ✓ Choosing options for table display
- ✓ Formatting tables
- ✓ Sorting and filtering in Excel
- ✓ Calculating totals in columns
- ✓ Getting rid of duplicates
- ✓ Making a PivotTable

Although it's true that a worksheet has all the characteristics of a table, there's a special kind of table object in Excel. You can designate a cell range as a table, which is easily formatted and used for calculations.

Tables in Excel 2011 are fully compatible with table styles used in Excel 2010 for Windows. You can use VBA, Office's built-in programming language, to automate operations with tables. In this chapter, we cover how to work with the tables themselves. In Chapter 8 of this minibook, we explain how to link tables to data sources. While we're on the topic of tables, we introduce the newly revised PivotTable feature. We show you how to make versatile reports quickly from your data.

Listing the Table Rules

A *table* is a cell range on a worksheet that contains tabular data. You can name your table using any of the naming methods for cells and ranges discussed in Chapter 1 of this minibook.

Excel can figure out whether you have a table if your data follows these simple rules:

✦ The first row — and only the first row — includes column names (field names in database parlance). Those names are unique.

✦ The end of the table is the first adjoining empty row and/or the first completely empty column.

✦ No cells in the table are merged cells.

Even if you don't turn data that obeys the preceding rules into a table, Excel considers it a *data range*. You can use data features such as sorts and filters with data ranges as well as with tables.

The table shown in Figure 5-1 obeys the preceding table rules. You can use this data to follow along in our examples in the following sections by typing the data anywhere on a worksheet. Better yet, use your own data if it follows Excel's table rules.

Figure 5-1:
Typing some sample data.

Experiment	Date	Result 1	Result 2	Result 3
Trial 1	3/12/12	9	0	12
Trial 2	3/15/12	6	9	10
Trial 3	4/1/12	4	8	3

Making a Table

Making an Excel table is so easy. You can make a table in Normal or Page Layout view. Note that when you make a table, not only does the table display in your document, but you can also see table row and column indicators on the rulers in Page Layout view. Here's how to make a table:

1. **Select any cell in a data range.**

Of course the range must obey the table rules in the previous section.

2. **Choose Insert⇨Table from the menu bar. Alternatively, on the Ribbon's Tables tab, find the Table Options group and click New.**

A grid displays, as shown in Figure 5-2. That's your table!

Figure 5-2:
An Excel table.

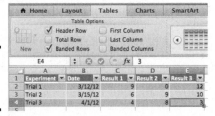

Choosing Table Options

A common practice is to use the first row of a table as labels for the columns. The first row of a table is called the *header row* because each label is at the head of the column. Another practice is to call the column labels *field names, data fields,* or *fields.*

An array of check boxes is available in the Table Options group on the Ribbon's Tables tab, as shown in Figure 5-2. Although Excel's table option controls look just like the ones you find in Word and PowerPoint, the Header row and Total row work differently. Select the check box next to each item to activate or deactivate the switch:

- ✦ **Header Row:** Displays or hides the header row. The header row displays Excel's Filter buttons.

- ✦ **Total Row:** Displays or hides this special row, which has enormous calculation capabilities.

- ✦ **Banded Rows:** Turns the shading in alternate rows on or off.

- ✦ **First Column:** Applies special formatting to the leftmost column.

- ✦ **Last Column:** Applies special formatting to the rightmost column.

- ✦ **Banded Columns:** Turns the shading in alternate columns on or off.

Formatting Tables

You can format every aspect of a table's appearance. You can change line colors, create cell shading, and more, but don't merge cells, or you'll break key functionality of your table. In the following sections, you can explore the various ways to improve the way your table looks.

Book III
Chapter 5

Making, Formatting, and Filtering a Table

Remembering List Manager

Excel's Table feature got its start in Excel 98 on the Mac as the List and List Manager feature. Twelve years later, the feature was finally fully ported to Excel for Windows 2010, as the "new" Table feature, updated with new text styles capabilities. If you already know how to use Lists from previous versions of Excel for Mac, then you already know the new Table feature, except you use the Ribbon instead of the List Manager toolbar. If you open a workbook containing a list, Excel converts the list into a prettier table.

If you need to know about cell formatting, head to Chapter 4 of this mini-book. You can use those tools to customize your table's font, borders, and shading.

Applying a table style from the Ribbon

The Tables tab on the Ribbon has built-in table styles. Click anywhere in your table, then choose a table style from either the Table Styles gallery directly on the Ribbon or the drop-down galleries, as shown in Figure 5-3. There are plenty of beautiful built-in styles from which to choose, categorized by custom, light, medium, and heavy. We'd like to point out the following:

+ There's a sweet spot you can click along the bottom edge in the middle of the style gallery to display the style palette.

+ You won't see custom styles unless you make a new table style of your own. Custom styles belong to the workbook.

+ Many of the styles you see are based on the theme that is applied to the workbook. If you change the theme, the styles (especially the colors) change too. Look at the section called "Applying a document theme," later in this chapter, to find out how you can change the theme.

+ Choose any cell in a table and then choose the Clear Table Style option to remove all style formatting from the table.

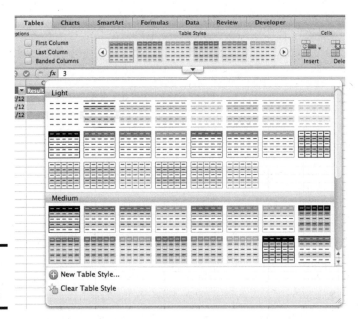

Figure 5-3:
Applying a
table style.

Making a new table style

After you have customized a table to your liking, do the following to save your customizations as a new table style:

1. **Select a cell in your table.**

2. **On the Ribbon's Tables Styles tab, click to open the Table style gallery (refer to Figure 5-3) and then choose New Table Style.**

   The New Table Style dialog opens, as shown in Figure 5-4.

3. **Type a name for your new style in the Name field.**

4. **(Optional) Adjust other settings in the dialog if needed.**

   You have a couple options to consider:

   • *Set as Default Table Style for This Workbook:* Select this check box to use your new custom style as the default for this workbook.

   • *Format:* Click to display the Format Cell dialog. You probably shouldn't do this if you're already happy with your format.

5. **Click OK to save your new table style.**

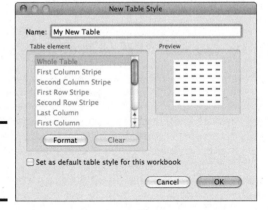

Figure 5-4: Saving a new table style.

Applying a document theme

Because table formatting, such as line color and shading, is actually a style and since you can format styles with document themes, you can apply document themes to format tables:

1. **Select a cell for the table you want to format.**

2. **On the Ribbon's Home tab, click the Themes button.**

   This brings up the drop-down Themes gallery.

3. **Choose a theme.**

   Your table instantly adopts the selected theme. You don't see changes unless your table already has some formatting, such as shading or a table style applied.

Changing a theme has repercussions beyond just the look of your table. A theme stipulates the look of your entire workbook. Changing the theme may change the look of your charts, the fonts used in the cells, and the colors of other objects. See Book I, Chapter 10 for more about themes.

Adding or Deleting Rows and Columns

As you populate your table, you may discover you need more rows or columns. You can adjust table, row, column, and cell settings by using the options available on the Ribbon and in dialogs.

Click in your table at the point you wish your new row or column to appear, and then choose an appropriate button from the Tables tab's Cells group. Each time you click the Insert button, a new row or column is added relative to the selected table cell. Likewise, clicking the Delete button removes the row and its contents. Each button has self-explanatory submenus.

Sorting and Filtering in Tables and Worksheets

When sorting your tables and worksheets, you're likely to use ascending and descending sort orders most often. The quick way to sort a table or data range is to select a cell in the column you want to sort. Then go to the Ribbon's Data tab, find the Sort and Filter group, and click Sort. The first time you click this button, the sort is lowest to highest or alphabetical. Click the button again to sort highest to lowest or reverse alphabetically.

Don't click the column letter before sorting. If you do, the sort will be applied only to the contents of the column, not the entire table or data range.

Can you believe that after 27 years, Microsoft changed the name of this feature from *AutoFilter* to just *Filter*? R.I.P., AutoFilter. The Filter feature places a button to the right of each cell in the header row of a table or data range. Filter is turned on by default when you make a table, and you can see these buttons in the header row of a table. You can toggle Filter on or off by pressing ⌘-Shift-F. When you click the Filter button in a column header, the Filter dialog shown in Figure 5-5 displays. The column header label is the title of the dialog. Filter lets you sort and filter.

Custom sorting

You can use a custom sort to specify multi-level sorts that progress in successive order. Choosing this option displays the Custom Sort dialog. Someone at MacBU (the Mac Business Unit at Microsoft) must have been thinking they wanted to make the coolest multiple sort dialog ever, and here it is. Cross-platform users may notice custom sorting on the Mac offers more sorting options than Excel for Windows. To display this dialog, click the Data tab on the Ribbon. In the Sort & Filter group, click the small triangle to the right of the Sort button and choose Custom Sort from the pop-up menu.

1. **Click the + plus sign to add a sort condition.**

   Each new sort is marked "Then by" to indicate the sorting sequence.

2. **Click the little button under the Column heading to choose a column to sort.**

3. **Click the little button under Sort-on to set sorting criteria.**

4. **Click the little button under Order to set the sort order conditions.**

5. **Click the little button under the Color/Icon heading to apply sort conditions based on these characteristics if they exist in the column.**

6. **To remove a sort, select it and then click the (–) minus sign.**

Options: You can change the default sorting scheme from top to bottom so that sorting rules are executed from left to right, and you can check a box to make your sort case sensitive.

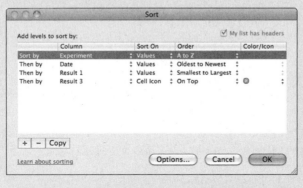

Book III
Chapter 5

Making, Formatting, and Filtering a Table

Sorting

The upper portion of the Filter dialog is for sorting:

✦ **Ascending:** Click this button to sort the column from lowest to highest or alphabetically.

✦ **Descending:** Click this button to sort the column from highest to lowest, or reverse alphabetically.

✦ **By Color:** If you have applied color formats to a table, you can use this pop-up menu to sort by cell color or font color. If you have applied conditional formatting (see Chapter 4 of this minibook), then you can sort by the symbol you applied. If you haven't applied colors or conditional formatting, this button is inactive.

Figure 5-5:
Displaying
the Filter
dialog.

Filtering

Beneath the Sort functionality is the Filter section of the Filter dialog. (Refer to Figure 5-5.) Usually, you know what you're looking for in a column, so the first thing to do is either type what you want in the search filter or choose it from the Choose One pop-up menu and form field. Starting at the top of the Filter options shown in Figure 5-6 you can choose:

✦ **By Color:** Show records in your column that match the cell color, font color, or cell icon. If you haven't applied colors or conditional formatting, this pop-up menu is inactive.

✦ **Choose One:** Select a criterion from this pop-up menu. Then, in the pop-up menu to the right, you can select a record from the column that matches the set of conditions. When you make your first condition set, the dialog changes to enable you to select And or Or to add a second set of filter criteria, as shown in Figure 5-6. As you change your criteria settings, observe that the filter check boxes are turned on and off for you to match your criteria.

✦ **Check boxes:** You can select and deselect these boxes to display only rows that match the selected items.

✦ **Clear Filter button:** Removes all criteria from the entire Filter dialog so that no filter or sorting is performed.

Figure 5-6:
Filtering
with logic.

Calculating Columns

Table Options is one of the most useful Excel tools because of its ability to quickly do mathematical and statistical operations on table columns by displaying the Total row. A *Total row* lets you perform any calculation (even advanced statistical calculations) for the cells in the column.

To display the Total row, go to the Ribbon's Tables tab, find the Table Options group, and then select the Total Row check box. The Total row displays at the bottom of your table, as shown in Figure 5-7. Click in any cell of the Total row to display a button that produces a pop-up menu from which to choose popular functions. Excel uses the SUBTOTAL worksheet function for many of these calculations.

By choosing the More Functions option, you display the Formula Builder (see Chapter 3 of this minibook), which gives you easy access to all the functions in Excel for the Total row.

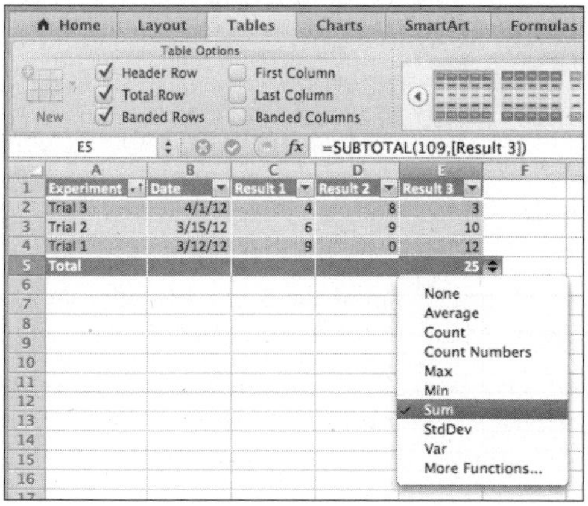

**Book III
Chapter 5**

**Making, Formatting,
and Filtering a Table**

Figure 5-7:
Formulating
in the Total
Row.

Managing Tables

Sometimes, tables need some maintenance. Perhaps a row was accidentally duplicated. Maybe you need to rename the table, or the table isn't useful anymore and you want to change it back to normal Excel cells. The following sections show you how to do all these table management tasks.

Removing duplicate rows

A common task is to identify and then remove duplicate records (a row is a record) in a table. You can use the Remove Duplicates tool to make that task easier. First select a cell in a table. Then go to the Ribbon's Tables tab, find the Tools group, and click Remove Duplicates to display the Remove Duplicates dialog shown in Figure 5-8. Choose a column to analyze by selecting its field name check box. Excel will instantly report how many duplicates it found and put a marker to the right of each row containing a duplicate record. Click the Remove Duplicates button to delete rows containing duplicate records.

By default, the Remove Duplicate option analyzes all the columns in your table, and it finds duplicates only if entire rows (records) have the same data.

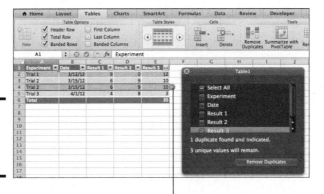

Figure 5-8:
Removing duplicate records.

Duplicate row

Renaming a table

Like everything you put on a worksheet, a table has a name. The default name is something nondescript, such as Table1. (See Figure 5-8.) To give your table a descriptive name so that you can select it using the Name box or a macro, go to the Ribbon's Tables tab, find the Tools group, and click Rename. No dialog comes up to rename the table. Instead, the current name of the table will be highlighted in the Name box, where you simply type a new name for your table, and then press Return or Enter.

If you rename a table after you've referred to its name by formula, the formula will update, but if you rename a table after using its name in a macro, you have to manually edit the name of the table in your macro. If you don't update the macro, it won't work.

Untabling a table

We know *untabling* isn't a word, but we couldn't come up with a better one to describe the process of converting a table into an ordinary spreadsheet range. The official terminology for this process is to convert a table to a range object. It's easy enough to do. Select a cell in the table and then go to the Ribbon's Tables tab. Find the Tools group and click Convert to Range. Say goodbye to those nice number formats, but your Total row formulas will persist.

Making a PivotTable

A *PivotTable* is a special kind of table that summarizes data from a table, data range, or database external to the workbook. If you're PivotTable aficionado, you will be in seventh heaven with the new PivotTable capabilities in Excel 2011. Using the example data from Figure 5-1 (shown earlier), we generated the nice PivotTable report shown in Figure 5-9 in just a few seconds. Here's how to make a PivotTable:

**Book III
Chapter 5**

Making, Formatting, and Filtering a Table

1. **(Optional) Select a cell in your data range or table.**

    Your data range must obey the table rules we set out in the earlier section, "Listing the Table Rules."

2. **Choose Data➪PivotTable. Alternatively, on the Ribbon's Tables tab, go to the Tools group and click Summarize with PivotTable.**

    The Create PivotTable dialog displays, as shown in Figure 5-9.

3. **Choose the data to analyze:**

    Make choices from the following options:

    - *Location:* If you performed Step 1, your table or range is already filled in for you. If you didn't start with a table or range, you can select a data range or table using the mouse.

    - *Use an External Data Source:* Displays the Mac OS X ODBC dialog, which we describe in Chapter 8 of this minibook.

4. **Choose where to put the PivotTable:**

    - *New Worksheet:* If selected, adds a new sheet to the workbook and places your PivotTable in Cell A1 of the new worksheet.

    - *Existing Worksheet:* Choose a cell on your worksheet. The cell will be the upper-leftmost corner of your PivotTable. Make sure there's enough room so your PivotTable doesn't overlap existing cell ranges.

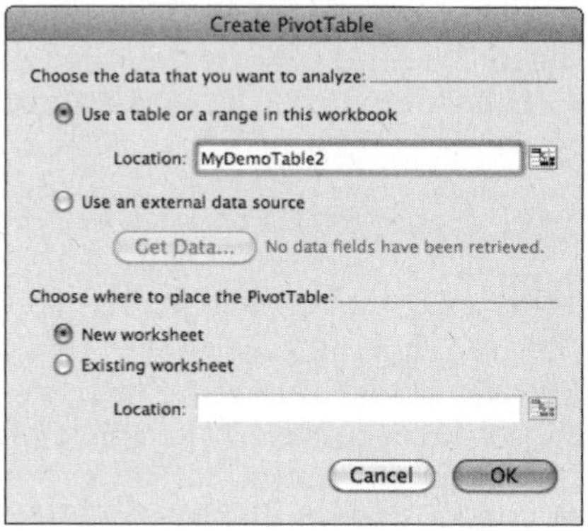

Create PivotTable

Choose the data that you want to analyze:

⦿ Use a table or a range in this workbook

Location: | MyDemoTable2 |

◯ Use an external data source

(Get Data...) No data fields have been retrieved.

Choose where to place the PivotTable:

⦿ New worksheet

◯ Existing worksheet

Location: | |

(Cancel) (OK)

Figure 5-9:
Choosing
the data
and report
location.

5. **Click OK.**

   The PivotTable Builder displays, as shown in Figure 5-10.

6. **Drag field names from the Field Name section at the top to the panes below.**

   - Selecting and deselecting the field names includes or excludes the columns from the pivot table.

   - Clicking the pop-up buttons within the pivot table displays Filter dialogs appropriate for the data type in your pivot table.

   - You can filter the Field Name list by typing field names in the search box in the Pivot Table Builder dialog.

   - Drag fields from one pane to another to generate new pivot table variations.

Click to filter

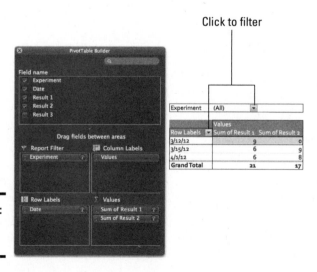

Figure 5-10:
Building a
PivotTable.

You can change the column names, calculations, and number formats provided by the PivotTable Builder. There's a little information button at the right end of each field name in the panels at the bottom of the PivotTable Builder. Click the information button to display the PivotTable Field dialog, shown in Figure 5-11. The properties displayed are for the field name of the button you clicked:

✦ **Field Name (Optional):** Type a new field name.

✦ **Summarize By:** Choose which type of calculation to use.

✦ **Show Data As:** Select how you want to show the data from the pop-up menu. You can choose from Normal, Difference From, % Of, % Difference From, Running Total In, % of Row, % of Column, % of Total, or Index.

✦ **Base Field and Base Item:** If you choose Difference From in the Show Data As pop-up menu, choose which fields you're comparing.

✦ **Delete:** Removes this field from the PivotTable report.

✦ **Number:** Displays the Number tab of the Format Cells dialog so you can choose a number format or make a custom number format.

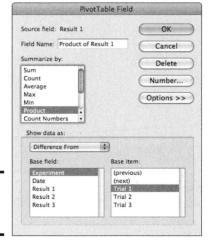

Figure 5-11:
Building a
PivotTable.

 When you select a cell in a PivotTable, look at the Ribbon to find the PivotTable tab, which you click to display all sorts of PivotTable tools. The PivotTable tab is for experts. PivotTable Ribbon offers additional formatting options and still more controls for your PivotTable, but it goes beyond the scope of this book. If you find PivotTables to be useful, then by all means explore the PivotTable Ribbon.

Chapter 6: Making Charts

In This Chapter

✓ Making and customizing charts

✓ Saving a chart template

✓ Making sparklines

✓ Sprucing up your chart

✓ Making error bars and trendlines

✓ Moving to a chart sheet

✓ Adding charts to other applications

Charts are an Excel strongpoint. Students, businesses, scientists, news organizations, economists, and many other groups use charts. When you make charts in Office 2011, you find a brand-new set of Chart tabs on the Ribbon that guide you with the latest Microsoft charting technology.

The terms *chart* and *graph* are interchangeable. We stick with *chart* while acknowledging that *graph* is the preferred term.

In Office, Excel handles all chart making. If you're starting a chart in Word or PowerPoint, you'll immediately be brought to Excel. We cover all aspects of making charts in this chapter.

Making a Chart in Excel

If you have some data to chart, by all means use it as you go through these examples. Figure 6-1 shows the data we used so you can type it in and follow along if you prefer. Our data shows percent change in Gross Domestic Product as reported by the USDA in case you're interested.

Typing in the data was the hard part. Now for the easy part: making the chart! Take a look at Figure 6-1 as you take these steps:

1. **Select a cell in the data range.**

2. **On the Ribbon's Charts tab, go to the Insert Chart group and then choose a chart type.**

Marked Line

A palette displays, showing various subtypes of charts. Choose one you think will display your data well. Excel figures out the boundaries of the data range and instantly displays your chart. To follow with our example, choose Line➪2-D Line➪Marked Line.

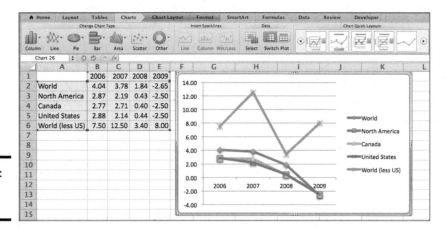

Figure 6-1:
Making a chart.

If the chart looks right you could stop right here and not bother with the rest of this chapter, but then you'd miss out on our great charting tips. If the chart looks wrong, chances are Excel's guess about which rows and columns to use for the axis was wrong. It's a 50-50 proposition. To fix this problem, on the Ribbon's Charts tab, locate the Data group and choose whichever Switch Plot button is not selected to switch row and column data source. If you used our sample data, you probably need to click the Switch Plot button and choose Plot Series by Row, and your chart will look just like Figure 6-1.

When you select a chart, the Chart menu activates, the data range is highlighted, and you have three extra tabs on the Ribbon to enjoy: Charts, Chart Layout, and Chart Format. You can right-click individual chart elements like series, plot area, legend, and so on to display pop-up menus that lead to more formatting options. If you're into designing great-looking stuff, welcome home!

Customizing a Chart with Ease

Welcome to chart design's magical playground. There are many ways you can customize a chart, but we can help you do it in an organized fashion. To use these tools, be sure to click the chart's border to select the chart before applying the tool.

You can customize a chart in the following ways:

✦ **Change the chart type.** You'll want the chart type that displays your data in the most effective visual format. On the Ribbon's Charts tab, find the Change Chart Type group and try various chart types by clicking the buttons. Some chart types, such as financial charts, require data to be in a specific arrangement. Check Excel help for details.

✦ **Change the chart layout.** The next stop is the Chart Quick Layouts gallery on the Ribbon, shown in Figure 6-1. Click different layouts to see how they look. Click the scroll buttons at each end of the gallery, or click the "sweet spot" at the middle of the bottom border to display a drop-down gallery. Some layouts include chart titles and other data labels, which are text boxes you can type in to customize your chart.

✦ **Apply a chart style.** The Chart Styles gallery on the Ribbon (see Figure 6-2) has intriguing and beautiful styles based on the theme applied to your workbook. The icons that are available vary by chart type.

By the time you make it this far with chart formatting, most of the time we think you'll have found the perfect chart for your data. Of course, that doesn't mean you have to stop here. You can continue customizing your chart to perfection. See the section "Perfecting Your Chart," later in this chapter.

**Book III
Chapter 6**

Making Charts

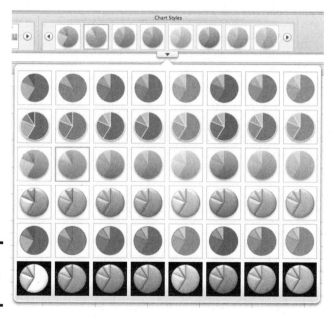

Figure 6-2:
Customizing
your chart.

Saving Your Chart as a Template

After you've tweaked to your heart's desire and settled on your chart design, you can save it as a chart template so you can use it again or share it with others. To save your chart, take these steps:

1. **Right-click the border of your chart and choose Save As Template from the contextual menu.**

A Save dialog displays. By default, the dialog is set up so that you'll save the template in the Chart Templates folder, which is where you should save your chart templates.

2. **Give your template a name and then click the Save button.**

To apply your custom chart template to any selected chart, click the Charts tab of the Ribbon, and within the Change Chart Type group, click the Other button to show a drop-down gallery. Scroll right to the bottom of this gallery to find the Templates category populated with any templates you create. Click any of the available templates to apply it to a selected chart.

Making Sparklines

If you're really in a hurry, or if space on your worksheet is at a premium and you want a quick visual representation of your data, sparklines are worth investigating. It only takes a few seconds to make sparklines. Here's what to do:

1. **Select the data range.**

Don't select any column or row headers in your data range — just the actual data.

2. **On the Ribbon's Charts tab, find the Insert Sparklines group and choose a sparkline style. (See Figure 6-3.)**

You get three choices for sparkline styles:

- *Line:* Displays a mini-line chart of your data in a cell.

- *Column:* Displays a mini-column chart of your series.

- *Win-Loss:* Displays a bar above the cell's midline for positive numbers, or a bar below the midpoint for negative numbers.

After you choose a sparkline style, the Insert Sparklines dialog, also shown in Figure 6-3 displays.

3. Drag over the empty cells that you want to display your sparklines.

Usually you want an adjoining range of empty cells.

4. Click OK to close the Insert Sparklines dialog.

Your sparklines display.

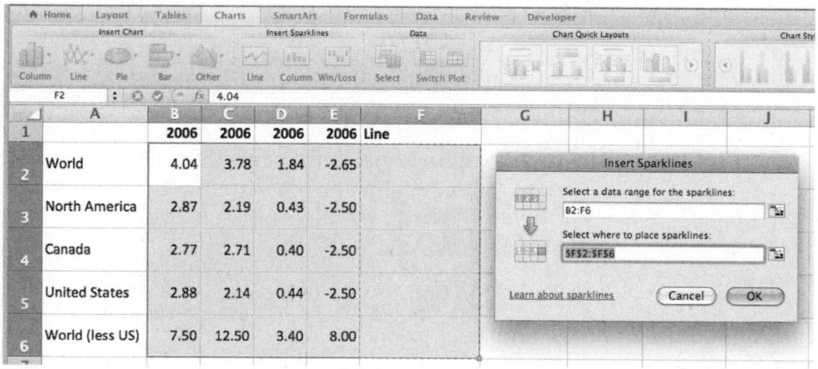

Figure 6-3:
Inserting
sparklines.

	A	2006	2006	2006	2006 Line	F
1						
2	World	4.04	3.78	1.84	-2.65	
3	North America	2.87	2.19	0.43	-2.50	
4	Canada	2.77	2.71	0.40	-2.50	
5	United States	2.88	2.14	0.44	-2.50	
6	World (less US)	7.50	12.50	3.40	8.00	

Insert Sparklines
Select a data range for the sparklines:
B2:F6
Select where to place sparklines:
$F$2:$F$6
Learn about sparklines   Cancel   OK

Now you have sparklines, but the rows are too skinny to display them properly. You need to increase the row height and center the text in the cells. Here's what to do:

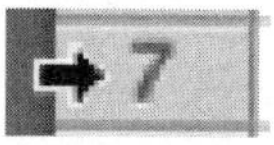

1. Drag over the row numbers to select the rows you want to format.

As you drag up or down to select a set of entire rows, the mouse cursor should be a right-pointing arrow, as shown in the margin.

2. Drag any divider between two row numbers down within the selected rows to increase the row height.

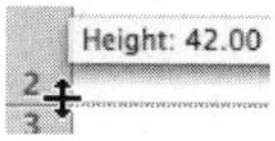

As you drag, the mouse cursor is a double-pointed arrow, and the row height displays as you drag, as shown in the margin. All selected rows heights are increased at once.

3. Reselect the data range.

4. On the Ribbon's Home tab, go to the Alignment group and click Align Text Middle.

Now your sparklines should look almost like ours in Figure 6-4, which shows sparklines for our sample data from Figure 6-1. Notice that when you select a sparkline cell or cell range, the corresponding data lights up in your data range, and if you look up at the Ribbon, there's a Sparklines tab you can click.

To add data points and make our sparklines a bit more sparkly, we selected a sparkline cell and then clicked the Sparklines tab. For our Line sparklines, we turned on markers by going to the Sparklines tab and clicking Markers and then selecting the All check box. Then we visited the Sparklines tab's Format group and, in the Sparklines gallery, we chose nice grayscale styles. You can find plenty of self-explanatory options to play with on the Sparklines tab. Just don't spend all day there because we have more about charts coming right up!

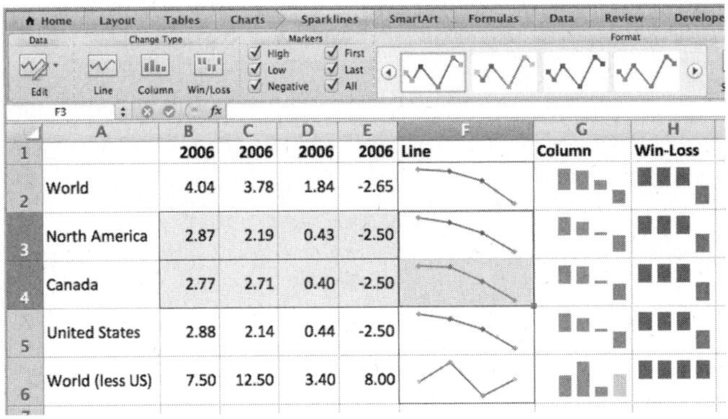

Figure 6-4:
Sparklines get highlighted.

Perfecting Your Chart

Don't read the rest of this chapter unless you want to become 100 percent addicted to making charts in Excel. Like we did. It's fun and habit-forming for sure. You could wind up playing with these tools for days. If you turn into a chart-aholic, don't say we didn't warn you!

One of the more subtle things to master with charts is training yourself to be aware of what is selected at any given moment. The Ribbon can help you with this. When you click anywhere on a chart, the Ribbon displays three tabs from which to choose (refer to Figure 6-1):

✦ **Charts:** This is where you start with your chart. This Ribbon tab has chart types, quick layouts, chart styles, sparklines, and data source controls.

✦ **Chart Layout:** This Ribbon tab is where you fine-tune chart customization. Here you find a selection indicator and chooser, selection formatting options, analysis options, label options, and 3-D rotation options.

✦ **Format:** More fine-tuning using the selection indicator and chooser, chart element styles, text styles, arrangement, and size tools.

Selecting chart elements

To select a chart element, you can either click the element or click the Current Selection pop-up menu found within the Chart Layout tab of the Ribbon. (See Figure 6-5.) All the formatting options adjust automatically to activate only those options that are applicable to whatever is selected.

Figure 6-5: Choosing a chart Ribbon.

When you select a chart series within a chart, the corresponding data series and data labels are selected in your data range. Selection indicators display on the chart series elements in the chart.

Deleting a chart series

A *chart series* represents the data found within a row or column To delete a chart series, select it and then press the Delete key. The corresponding row or column in the data source is not deleted.

Formatting chart elements

You have your choice of using the formatting tools on the three Ribbon tabs, or you can display a dialog by clicking the Format Selection button. The formatting options work the same in charts as for other objects. An example of the dialog that displays if you choose to format the chart area is shown in Figure 6-6. You have countless formatting options from which to choose.

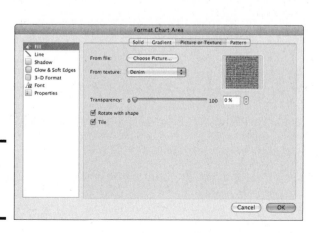

Figure 6-6: Formatting a chart selection.

Labeling your chart

The Labels group on the Chart Layout tab of the Ribbon is where you can find the controls for the labels and title in your chart, as shown in Figure 6-7. Each button lets you choose from a pop-up menu of position and formatting options. You can choose whether or not to have a label on your chart at all; you can choose No Chart Title, for example. The final option in each menu displays a dialog with precision control over the chart element being formatted.

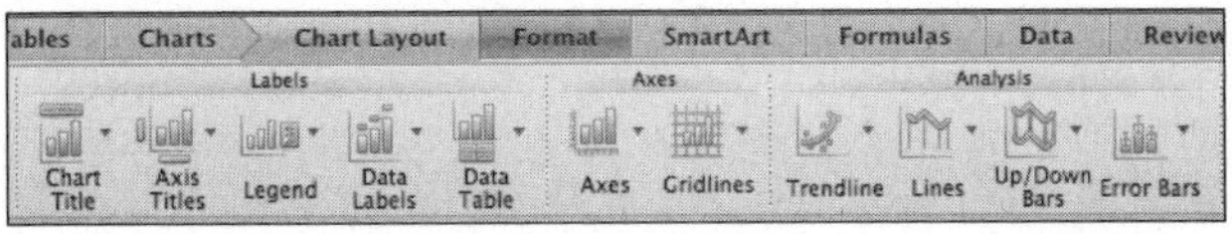

Figure 6-7:
Labels,
Axes, and
Analysis
groups.

| ...ables | Charts | Chart Layout | Format | SmartArt | Formulas | Data | Review |

Labels — Axes — Analysis

Chart Title | Axis Titles | Legend | Data Labels | Data Table | Axes | Gridlines | Trendline | Lines | Up/Down Bars | Error Bars

Formatting chart axes

The axes on your chart can be formatted, adjusted for scale, and turned on and off. To do so, click the Axes button in the Axes group of the Chart Layout tab of the Ribbon. (See Figure 6-7.) You can set the unit of measurement and switch from scalar (the default) to log scale using the Axes button.

The Gridlines button lets you turn horizontal and vertical gridlines on and off independently. The final option in each button's drop-down menu displays a dialog with precision control over the axis being formatted.

Performing Chart Analysis

Real power is lurking in the chart analysis tools, but using them requires some knowledge of the math behind the features.

Adding a trendline

Excel can add a line called a *trendline* that calculates and projects the trends into the past or future indicated by your data.

Used improperly, a trendline can present a false picture of what's going on with your data, so make sure you and your audience are clear about the calculation choices you made to produce your trendline.

It's best to start with a line or bar chart. Not all chart types support trendlines. Using a single data series makes your chart much easier to understand. To add a trendline, choose the Trendline option from the Chart

Layout tab of the Ribbon. This brings up the Trendline gallery with options to choose from. If you want more control, choose Trendline Options to display the Format Trendline dialog displayed in Figure 6-8.

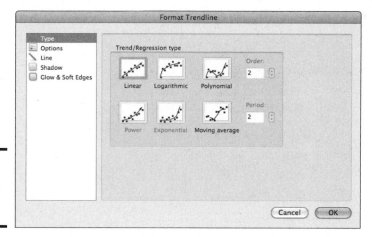

Figure 6-8:
Choosing a trendline type.

After you've added a trendline, double-click the trendline to display the Format Trendline dialog. If you display the Format Trendline dialog again using the Ribbon button, you add an additional trendline to the chart, which you probably don't want to do.

Book III
Chapter 6

Making Charts

Choosing a trendline type

The Type tab of the Format Trendline dialog lets you choose which mathematical calculation will be used for generating your trendline. The Polynomial calculation lets you choose which order calculation will be used. The Moving Average calculation is generally used with financial data from a stock market. You can specify the number of periods.

Choosing trendline options

Click the Options tab on the left pane of the Format Trendline dialog as shown in Figure 6-9, where you can adjust the following:

✦ **Trendline Name:** You can assign a custom name to your trendline so you can refer to it via the Name Box or in VBA.

✦ **Forecast:** Use the spinner controls to predict the future or the past. This is more accurate for the future than a fortuneteller, but not by much!

✦ **Set Intercept:** Sets the Y-axis intercept.

✦ **Display Equation on Chart:** Excel displays the formula it used to calculate the trendline in a text box on the chart.

✦ **Display R-Squared Value on Chart:** Excel displays this value in a text box on the chart.

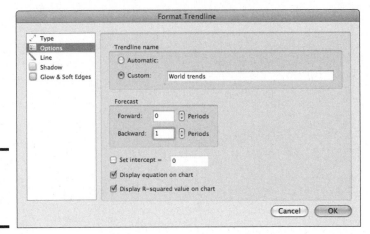

Figure 6-9:
Choosing
trendline
options.

Text boxes placed on charts can be formatted and moved by dragging. Label positions are controlled by the formatting options on the Ribbon and dialogs.

Double-click a trendline to display the Format Trendline dialog where you can format Line, Shadow, Glow, and Soft Edges for your trendline.

Adding drop lines and high-low lines

Two special kinds of lines can be added to your line chart: drop-lines and high-low lines.

On the Ribbon's Chart Layout tab, go to the Analysis group and choose Lines⇨Drop Lines to add lines from your data points to the X-axis, as shown in Figure 6-10.

Hi-low lines connect the highest value and lowest value of each data point with a line, as shown in Figure 6-11. In the Chart Layout tab's Analysis group, choose Lines⇨High-Low Lines to add these.

Adding up-down bars

Up-down bars automatically highlight the differences between the topmost and second topmost values of your chart, as shown in Figure 6-12. On the

Ribbon's Chart Layout tab, go to the Analysis group and click Up/Down Bars to turn these on or off. Double-click one of the bars to display the Format Up Bars dialog, where you can customize these bars.

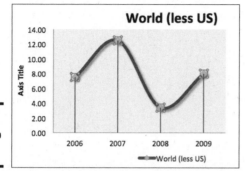

Figure 6-10:
Adding drop lines.

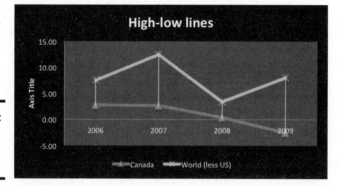

Figure 6-11:
Adding high-low lines.

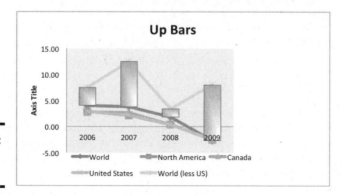

Figure 6-12:
Adding up/ down bars.

Adding Error Bars

In the Chart Layout tab's Analysis group, click Error Bars to display a pop-up menu where you can choose from standard error, percentage, or standard deviation to add error bars, as shown in Figure 6-13.

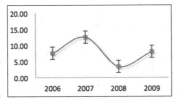

Figure 6-13: Adding error bars.

Double-click an error bar to display the Format Error Bars dialog, shown in Figure 6-14. You can format your error bars in this dialog. You can specify custom error values by clicking the Specify Value button and choosing cells.

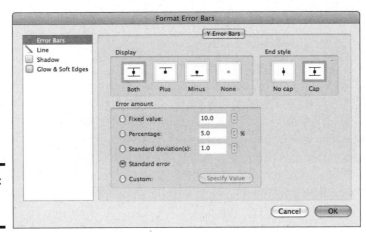

Figure 6-14: Formatting error bars.

Moving to a Chart Sheet

Excel has a special kind of worksheet called a *chart sheet* that you can use to showcase a chart. A chart sheet can have only one thing: a single chart. On a chart sheet, you can format the chart by using the same tools as when you have the chart on a conventional worksheet. If you want to move the chart back onto a worksheet, you can use the Move Chart tool again.

To move a chart to a chart sheet, follow these steps:

1. **Select the chart.**

   Selecting the chart activates the Chart menu.

2. **On the menu bar, choose Chart⇨Move Chart.**

   The Move Chart dialog opens, as shown in Figure 6-15.

3. **Click the New Sheet radio button.**

4. **In the New Sheet text box, type a name for the Chart Sheet tab.**

5. **Click OK.**

Figure 6-15:
Moving
a chart
to a new
residence.

Instantly, your chart appears as a full sheet on a new tab that has the name you typed in the Move Chart dialog. The source data remains on the worksheet you started from, and the chart is still linked to the data. If the data changes, the chart is updated instantly, even if the data is the result of a formula or a query.

**Book III
Chapter 6**

Making Charts

Adding Charts in Other Applications

You'll be glad to know that it's easy to move your charts to Microsoft Word, PowerPoint, and Outlook. You can even create a chart directly in Word and PowerPoint. Easy is good!

You can also add them to the Scrapbook, which we discuss in Book I, Chapter 3.

Copying from Excel to Word or PowerPoint

The process of copying Excel charts into Word or PowerPoint is straightforward. Follow these steps:

1. **Make sure that Excel and the destination application (Word or PowerPoint) are open.**

   In Excel, the currently open workbook needs to contain the chart you want to copy to Word or PowerPoint.

2. **Select the chart in Excel by clicking its border.**

   The selection indicator is a thick, blue outline replacing the border.

3. **Copy the chart.**

   Use any of the usual methods: Click the Copy button on the Standard toolbar, press ⌘-C, or choose Edit⇨Copy.

4. **Switch to the Microsoft Word document or PowerPoint presentation.**

   Use the Dock or press ⌘-Tab.

5. **Paste the chart.**

   Use any of the usual methods: Click the Paste button on the standard toolbar, press ⌘-V, or choose Edit⇨Paste.

6. **Click the small widget in the lower-right corner of the chart.**

   A drop-down menu appears, as shown in Figure 6-16. The widget for Word is on the left, and the widget for PowerPoint is on the right.

The Word widget   The PowerPoint widget

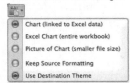

Figure 6-16:
Choosing
chart paste
options.

7. **Choose how you want the chart to behave while it's living in your Word document or PowerPoint presentation:**

   • *Paste as Picture* or *Picture of Chart:* Office converts your chart to a picture, and then pastes a picture of the chart into your document or presentation.

   • *Excel Chart (Entire Workbook):* Pastes a copy of the entire workbook as an embedded OLE (Object Linking and Embedding) object into the Word document or PowerPoint presentation, displaying the chart. Chart colors and fonts adopt document theme colors of the paste destination.

   • *Chart (Linked to Data):* This is the default option and pastes a chart object in your document or presentation. The data is linked to the Excel source workbook, which remains an independent Excel file.

After updating the chart in Excel, in Word you refresh the chart by choosing Edit➪Links➪Update Links. PowerPoint links update automatically. Selecting the pasted chart in Word or PowerPoint activates the Charts and Format tabs on the Ribbon.

- *Keep Source Formatting:* Word or PowerPoint doesn't apply its existing document theme but instead retains Excel's source colors and fonts.

- *Use Destination Theme:* This is the default paste. The chart adopts the Word document or PowerPoint presentation's theme.

8. **Click outside the drop-down list to close the widget.**

Copying from Excel to Outlook

If you're composing an e-mail message in Outlook, and if the message is in HTML format, you can simply copy and paste a chart from Excel into your message. An alternative is to save the chart as a picture, which you can do by right-clicking your chart and choosing Save As Picture from the pop-up menu. Then, either insert the picture into your message, or attach it.

Pasting special for charts

If you prefer, when you copy and paste a chart from Excel to Word or PowerPoint, you can choose Edit➪Paste Special to open the Paste Special dialog, which offers you more paste formats and link options. Each time you select a different combination of format and paste options, the description in the Result section interactively updates so that you know what will happen when you click OK. Click OK to confirm your selection. Word's Paste Special dialog is shown in the following figure. PowerPoint's dialog has similar options and operations.

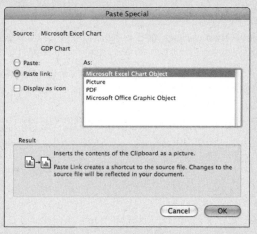

Making a chart in Word or PowerPoint

Starting a chart from Word or PowerPoint is almost the same as starting one in Excel, but not quite. Here are some tips to keep in mind when making a chart in Word or PowerPoint:

1. **Select your data table.**

    If you have data in a Word or PowerPoint table you want to turn into a chart, you must first select the data table.

    -   In Word, click anywhere in your table and then choose Table⇨ Select Table.

    -   In PowerPoint, click the table's border.

    -   If your data is in some other application or on the Web, select the data in the other application or Web browser.

2. **Copy the data.**

    Use any copy method: Click the Copy button on the Standard toolbar, press ⌘-C, or choose Edit⇨Copy.

3. **Select where the chart is to be placed.**

    Click in the Word document or on the PowerPoint slide where you want the chart to be inserted. Optional: In Word, you can click into a frame to contain the chart, and in PowerPoint, you can click into a slide place-holder to contain the chart.

4. **Choose Insert⇨Chart or go to the Ribbon's Charts tab, find the Insert Chart group, and choose a chart type.**

    Excel opens and displays a sample data set, with cell A1 selected.

5. **Paste your data into cell A1.**

    Use any of these paste methods: Click the paste button on the standard toolbar, press ⌘-V, or choose Edit⇨Paste.

6. **Close Excel's window by clicking the red close button or by pressing ⌘-W.**

    Your chart is now visible in your Word document or PowerPoint presentation.

You can perform all the chart customization and formatting operations we discuss earlier in this chapter by using the Ribbon. You need to know only one more trick, and that's how to edit the data:

1. **Select the chart by clicking its border.**

2. **Choose Edit⇨Select Data in Excel or right-click and choose Select Data in Excel from the contextual menu.**

If you missed the border in Step 1, chose Edit Data, which also works!

Chapter 7: Controlling Excel

*E*xcel has unique behaviors that enable you to do special tasks. This chapter shows you how to take advantage of Excel's ability to take ordinary features and extend them to extraordinary levels so that you have more flexibility. You also end up getting so used to these features that you might wonder how you managed without them all this time! In fact, you can twist Excel into many positions, like a rubber band. This chapter is loaded with tips on how to get Excel to work (and stretch) in many special ways.

Copying and Pasting

The first thing to consider when copying and pasting content into Excel from Excel (or some other application) is to think about the nature of what you're attempting to copy. Cells, cell ranges, and formulas are treated differently from other kinds of things, such as SmartArt, equations, and charts. We start by showing you how to copy cells, formulas, and ranges. After that, we show you what happens when you copy other kinds of things.

If you're not familiar with SmartArt and Equation Editor, flip to Book I, Chapter 5 and Book I, Chapter 10, respectively, to read more about these shared Office features.

Simply copying and pasting

If you're used to copying and pasting, you know that if you select some text and then copy and paste, the default settings paste the text, along with the text format — such as blue (or another font color), bold, or italic.

In addition to the copy and paste methods we describe here, you can use the Scrapbook feature, which is described in Book I, Chapter 3.

Follow this simple example to copy and paste in Excel:

1. **Select a nonempty cell or any worksheet object to copy.**

2. **Use one of the usual copy methods.**

   Click the Copy button on the Standard toolbar, press ⌘-C, or choose Edit⇔Copy.

3. **Click in the cell where you want to paste and choose any of the typical paste methods.**

   Click the Paste button on the Standard toolbar (or the Home tab of the Ribbon), press ⌘-V, or choose Edit⇔Paste.

   Your content appears along with a small widget, as shown in Figure 7-1. Choosing Edit⇔Paste Special produces a Paste Special dialog, described in the following section.

4. **Click the widget.**

   When you click the widget, you can see all your pasting options. The paste from Clipboard widget is context-sensitive, offering various options related to the kind of content or object you are pasting.

   When copying and pasting, you have to click the widget before you start working in another cell; otherwise, the widget goes away.

Figure 7-1: Pasting from clipboard widget.

Pasting Special

Here we describe using Paste Special with cells and cell ranges. Figure 7-2 displays the data we used for our examples, in case you want to type it into Excel and follow along with us.

Figure 7-2:
Getting
ready for
examples.

	A	B	C	D	E
1	Experiment	Date	Result 1	Result 2	Result 3
2	Trial 1	3/12/12	9	0	12
3	Trial 2	3/15/12	6	9	10
4	Trial 3	4/1/12	4	8	3

The simple Paste option from the Clipboard widget described in the previous section handles most of your ordinary pasting requirements, but it's a one-shot deal — you can choose only a single option. On the other hand, Excel's Paste Special feature lets you pick and choose exactly what individual or combination of attributes you want to paste.

1. **Select the cell or cell range to copy and choose Edit⇨Copy.**

   Alternatively, you can press ⌘-C or click the Copy button on the Standard toolbar.

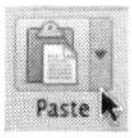

2. **Click in the cell where you want to paste and then choose Edit⇨Paste Special.**

   Alternatively, right-click and choose Paste Special, or select the Ribbon's Home tab, click the triangle on the right side of the Paste button, and then choose Paste Special from the resulting pop-up menu.

   The Paste Special dialog, as shown in Figure 7-3, appears.

3. **In the Paste section of the dialog, select the option that you need.**

   Figure 7-3 shows these options.

4. **Click OK.**

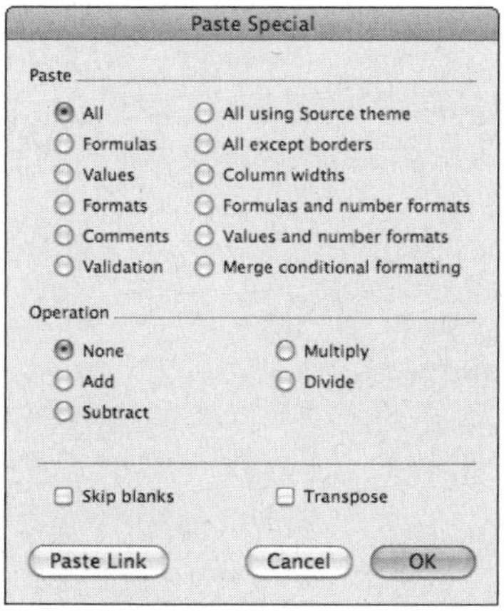

Paste Special

Paste

- ◉ All
- ◯ Formulas
- ◯ Values
- ◯ Formats
- ◯ Comments
- ◯ Validation

- ◯ All using Source theme
- ◯ All except borders
- ◯ Column widths
- ◯ Formulas and number formats
- ◯ Values and number formats
- ◯ Merge conditional formatting

Operation

- ◉ None
- ◯ Add
- ◯ Subtract

- ◯ Multiply
- ◯ Divide

☐ Skip blanks   ☐ Transpose

(Paste Link)   (Cancel)   (OK)

Figure 7-3:
Pasting the
special way.

The Paste Link button becomes active depending on what you copied and which paste option you chose in the Paste Special dialog. The Paste Link button pastes a cell formula that refers to the cell you're copying.

Turning rows into columns

Many times, you may wish you could easily change the layout of data from horizontal to vertical, or vice versa. Fortunately, Excel's Paste Special Transpose option does exactly that.

To change columns into rows quickly, follow these steps (and look at Figure 7-4 as you go along):

1. **Select a cell range and choose Edit⇨Copy.**

   Alternatively, you can press ⌘-C or click the Copy button on the Standard toolbar.

2. **Select a destination cell.**

   This cell becomes the upper-left cell of the pasted range.

3. **Choose Edit⇨Paste Special.**

   The Paste Special dialog opens.

4. **Select the Transpose check box and then click OK.**

   See Figure 7-4, where we pasted into cell A6.

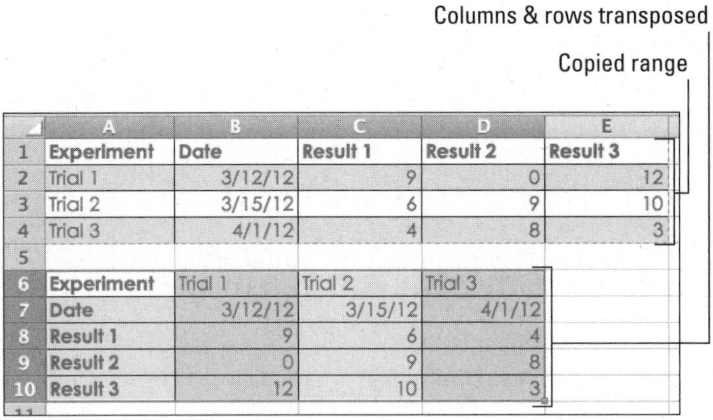

Columns & rows transposed

Copied range

	A	B	C	D	E
1	**Experiment**	Date	**Result 1**	**Result 2**	**Result 3**
2	Trial 1	3/12/12	9	0	12
3	Trial 2	3/15/12	6	9	10
4	Trial 3	4/1/12	4	8	3
5					
6	**Experiment**	Trial 1	Trial 2	Trial 3	
7	**Date**	3/12/12	3/15/12	4/1/12	
8	**Result 1**	9	6	4	
9	**Result 2**	0	9	8	
10	**Result 3**	12	10	3	

Figure 7-4: Turning columns into rows.

Using Paste Special with objects

In Chapter 6 of this minibook, we have an example of using Paste Special with charts, with screen shots of the Paste Special dialog you see when pasting objects. If you copy an object, rather than a cell or cell range, the Paste Special dialog offers paste options appropriate to the kind of object you are pasting. Charts, tables, and pictures all have unique Paste Special options, each described within the description portion of the Paste Special dialog.

You can use the Paste Special feature in Excel by using content that you copied from another open application, such as Word, PowerPoint, or even a Web browser. Options in the Paste Special dialog change depending on what you've copied to the Clipboard.

Copying as a picture in the first place

You can easily copy a picture of an object, a cell, or a cell range, but you have to know about the secret Edit menu. Follow these steps to use the modified Edit menu:

1. **Select a cell, a range of cells, or an object on a worksheet.**

A range of cells can include a mixture of cells and objects or just cells.

2. **Hold down the Shift key and click the Edit menu.**

Here's the secret! When you hold down the Shift key, the Edit menu offers Copy Picture and Paste Picture options.

3. **Choose Edit⇨Copy Picture.**

A small Copy Picture dialog displays.

4. **Click one of the choices:**

- *As Shown on Screen:* What you see is what you get.

- *As Shown When Printed:* The picture is formatted based on your current selections in Page Setup.

Now, you have a picture on the Clipboard that you can use in Excel or any other application that can paste pictures.

You can also hold Shift and choose Edit⇨Paste Picture to paste the Clipboard contents as a picture, regardless of its origin.

Moving and Copying Entire Sheets

You can move or copy one sheet at a time, or select multiple worksheets and move or copy them all at once. You can move or copy sheets within a workbook or from one workbook to another.

1. **Click a sheet tab to select the sheet you want to copy.**

   Hold ⌘ while clicking sheet tabs to select multiple worksheets.

2. **Choose Edit⇨Move or Copy Sheet.**

   Alternatively, carefully right-click over the selected tabs (so that they don't get deselected) and choose Move or Copy.

   The Move or Copy dialog, as shown in Figure 7-5, opens.

Figure 7-5:
Moving and copying entire worksheets.

3. **In the To Book pop-up menu, choose the destination for the worksheet(s) you plan to move or copy.**

   You can choose these destinations:

   * Within the Currently Active Workbook
   * To Any Other Open Workbook

     The open workbooks are listed in the destination pop-up menu.

   * To a Brand New Workbook

   The Before Sheet section lists all the sheets currently in the workbook. The sheets you move or copy are inserted in front of the sheet that you select.

4. **(Optional) To make a copy (instead of moving the entire sheet), select the Create a Copy check box.**

   If you don't select this check box, Excel uses the default move behavior instead. The Move option deletes the worksheets from the source workbook.

   Consider the cell references and hyperlinks on the sheets you're moving or copying. If you have references to other sheets, you may be creating links. When you're done with the Move or Copy tool, choose Edit⇨Links in the destination workbook. The Edit Links dialog appears. You can break unwanted links in the Edit Links dialog.

Did you want to move worksheets within the same workbook, as in reordering the worksheet tabs? You can just click a worksheet tab to select it and then drag and reorder them within a workbook.

Creating Camera Magic

The Camera command creates a "picture" of a range of cells. "Picture" is in quotation marks because these pictures aren't static; they're *dynamic* — they change. Pictures are linked to the range you select, and they update when the range changes.

You can use the Camera command in a variety of ways:

✦ **Display the calculation results of numbers or charts when the calculations and charts are on hidden worksheets (but not hidden rows or columns), other worksheets, or cell ranges that are off-screen.** You can keep your formulas out of sight so unwanted visitors are less likely to tamper with them. Because the result is a linked picture, updated results are displayed automatically.

✦ **Precisely size and position the picture of the cell range.** The Camera command creates an object that you can size and format like a picture. You can position the Camera picture anywhere on a worksheet.

✦ **Position live snapshots of various ranges from distant places in a workbook.** You can make them fit close together on a worksheet.

Customizing to get the Camera tool

Before you can use this magical tool, you have to turn it on. In Book I, Chapter 2, we explain how to customize menus and toolbars. Here's a quick refresher:

1. **Choose View⇨Toolbars⇨Customize Menus and Toolbars.**

The Customize Menus and Toolbars dialog appears.

2. **Click the Commands tab.**

3. **Drag the Camera command to any toolbar (or menu) and click OK.**

Using the Camera tool

To use the Camera tool, take these steps:

1. **Drag over a range of cells and then release the mouse button.**

   Everything within the selection range becomes part of a Camera picture. Objects (such as graphs or PivotTables) completely within the selection area are included in the resulting Camera picture.

2. **Click the Camera button on the toolbar (or select Camera from the menu if you put the command on a menu, as mentioned in the preceding section).**

   The cursor changes to a plus sign (+).

3. **Move the mouse cursor to a new location and then drag the mouse to create a Camera picture.**

   The new location can be on the same worksheet, on another worksheet in the same workbook, or a worksheet in another open workbook (which creates a link).

When using the Camera option, the camera's linked picture location shouldn't overlap the original selection range.

Hiding and Unhiding Worksheets, Rows, and Columns

Being secretive can be fun in Excel. You can hide entire worksheets or just some columns or rows. And you can unhide them, too. This control over what can be seen or not can be helpful in hiding content such as:

✦ Content that needs to be used in a formula, but need not be visible

✦ Content that you link from, but you don't need to show it to everyone

Just remember that you can also wind up having secrets that others know how to discover with these methods! Use these options to hide or unhide a complete worksheet:

✦ **To hide a worksheet:** Choose Format➪Sheet➪Hide.

✦ **To unhide a worksheet:** Choose Format➪Sheet➪Unhide.

You can also right-click any worksheet tab to bring up a menu that has a Hide option. Similarly, right-click any visible worksheet tab to bring up the same menu with an Unhide option.

If your workbook has just one unhidden worksheet, or even just one work-sheet in the entire workbook, you won't be able to hide it.

✦ **To hide a row or rows:** Select a complete row or multiple rows. Then choose Format⇨Row⇨Hide. Or right-click the row header and choose the Hide option.

✦ **To hide a column or columns:** Select a complete column or multiple columns. Then choose Format⇨Column⇨Hide. Or right-click the column header and choose the Hide option.

✦ **To unhide rows or columns:** You must first select the surrounding rows or columns by using the dark arrow cursor in the row number or column heading before you can unhide by choosing Format⇨Row (or Column)⇨Unhide. You can also select surrounding rows or columns, right-click the row or column header, and choose the Unhide option in the resultant menu.

There's a super-secret `xlSheetVeryHidden` property in VBA if you want to hide a worksheet so that hardly anyone can find it!

Calculation Ordering with Nesting and Nest Building

The beautiful Andorinha-dáurica bird builds nests with multiple chambers. Not unlike this bird, you can make a nest with multiple chambers right in Excel. To make your nests, use parentheses within your cell formulas.

If you want Excel to control calculation order, put what you want calculated first within parentheses (called *nesting*) inside your cell formula.

First things first

You might want to nest a formula so that you can control the order in which calculations are completed, which is *precedence*.

Here's the order in which each part of the formula is calculated:

1. Innermost parentheses to outermost parentheses
2. Multiplication and division
3. Addition and subtraction
4. Left to right

Precedence can be illustrated by the simple examples in Figure 7-6:

✦ In the formula =5+(2*3), parentheses cause multiplication to happen first.

✦ In the formula =(5+2)*3, parentheses force the addition to happen first.

As shown in Figure 7-6, the same numbers and operations in each formula result in entirely different values when those operations have different precedence.

Figure 7-6:
Parentheses
take
precedence.

Formula	Value
=5+(2*3)	11
=(5+2*3	21

Applying logic

The Excel IF formula enables you to perform logical operations:

IF (a condition is met) THEN (do this) ELSE (do something else).

Figure 7-7 shows a simple example of an IF formula — =IF(A1=1,TRUE,FALSE) — which means, "If the value of cell A1 is equal to 1, the logical value of the cell is TRUE; if cell A1 isn't equal to 1, the logical value of cell A1 is FALSE." In this formula, the parentheses simply provide clarity.

Figure 7-7:
Making
simple logic.

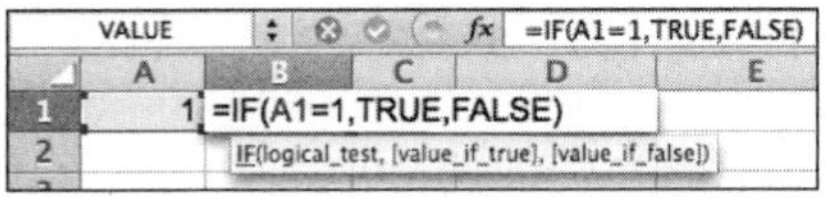

VALUE			*fx*	=IF(A1=1,TRUE,FALSE)	
	A	B	C	D	E
1	1	=IF(A1=1,TRUE,FALSE)			
2		IF(logical_test, [value_if_true], [value_if_false])			

The nested IF statement in Figure 7-8 — =IF(A2>=90,"A",IF(A2>=80,"B","C")) — wants to display a letter grade based on a student's numeric score. The formula means, "First, if the student attains a score of 80 or higher, the student gets a B; next, any score that's lower than 80 gets a C; and finally, if the score is 90 or higher, the student gets an A."

The innermost parenthesis is processed first. You can display *text* as the result of an IF formula, as long as you put quotation marks around the text.

Figure 7-8:
Nesting
for logic,
clarity, and
brevity.

When nesting in a formula, you need the same number of open parentheses as closed parentheses — use parentheses in pairs. Excel helps you by color-coding pairs of parentheses in the formula bar while you type.

You don't have a specific limit as to how many sets of parentheses you can nest within a formula, but it's usually less than 13 pairs. However, because the final ELSE can refer to another cell's value, which can have even more nesting, you really don't have a limit to the number of nests you can have in a chain.

If we take our earlier example to another nested option, it might look like this: =IF(A2>=90,"A",IF(A2>=80,"B",IF(A2>=50,"C","D"))).

Now, the formula means, "First, if the student attains a score of 50 or higher, the student gets a C; next, any score that's lower than 50 gets a D; then, if the score is between 80 or higher, the student gets a B; finally, if the student score is 90 or higher, the student gets an A."

Troubleshooting Formulas

The idea of *errors* is a misnomer. In actuality, some of these so-called errors are just messages from Excel, saying it had trouble doing what you asked. We tackle the most common error messages.

Getting rid of hash marks

The error message you're most likely to see is a set of hash marks in a cell. (See Figure 7-9.) These marks simply mean the cell isn't wide enough to display a value that's the result of a formula. You can cure hash marks in three ways:

✦ **Widen the column by dragging or double-clicking the column divider.** You use the double-arrow cursor, as shown in Figure 7-9.

✦ **Widen the column by choosing Format➪Column➪AutoFit Selection.**

✦ **Change the number format to show fewer decimal places by using the Ribbon.** On the Ribbon's Home tab, go to the Number group and then click the Decrease the Number of Decimal Places button.

Figure 7-9:
Expanding
a cell gets
rid of hash
marks.

Drag divider to widen cell.

Tracing precedents and dependents

After working for a while within Excel, you have many *dependents* (formulas on sheets) that take values from *precedents* (other formulas), which is a good thing. Keeping track of which dependent cells get influenced from values within other precedent cells is handled automatically. The new Audit Formulas group on the Formulas tab of the Ribbon, shown in Figure 7-10, has tools that will help you. The general procedure is as follows:

1. **Select a cell with a formula.**

2. **Click the Ribbon's Formulas tab and then click a Trace button.**

Dependency or precedent trace lines with arrows display. Click Trace repeatedly until you hear a beep to show all precedents or dependencies in a chain of formulas.

3. **Double-click a trace line to select the cell containing the next cell formula in the precedent or dependency chain.**

Use the Remove Arrows button to remove precedent and dependency arrows. Saving the workbook also remove the arrows.

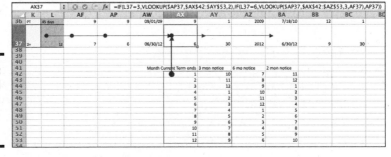

Figure 7-10:
Tracing cell
precedents
and depen-
dencies.

Circular references

As you make worksheets more and more complex, you're likely to accidentally link cells so that you have an endless loop. Excel dubs this predicament a *circular reference*.

Fixing circular references

If you accidentally make a circular reference, a warning appears, threatening you with dire consequences. Okay, we made that up, but Excel does come darn close to that!

If you get such a warning, you may not remember where in the chain you went wrong. If you want to wait 'til later to investigate, you can continue. If you do continue, Excel makes a big deal about it by showing plenty of warning signs and dialogs. Excel simultaneously highlights all the cells in the chain, opens the Excel Help topic on how to get rid of circular references, hoping that you can analyze your formulas and get rid of the circular reference.

In Figure 7-11, we set three cells equal to each other, creating a circular reference, for your viewing pleasure! And, of course, it's so much fun to see Excel panic. To replicate the example in Figure 7-11, start by typing **6** into cell A2. Next, in cell A1, enter **=A2**. (Now both cells have a value of 6.) In cell B1, enter **=A1**. (Now all three cells equal 6.) Now go back into cell A2 and enter **=B1**. Now each cell formula refers to the others in an endless loop.

Figure 7-11:
Tracing a
circular
reference.

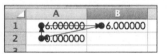

Keeping your circular reference

If you insist, we show you how you can force Excel to allow you to keep your circular reference. But you have to pay a ransom: You have to tell Excel how many times you want Excel to perform the calculation (the number of *iterations*) before it exits the endless loop.

To specify your iterations, follow these steps:

1. **On the Ribbon's Formulas tab, go to the Calculation group and choose Settings⇨Calculation Options.**

    Calculation preferences appear, as shown in Figure 7-12.

2. **In the Iteration area, select the Limit Iteration check box.**

3. **Set the number of iterations you want Excel to perform before exiting the loop.**

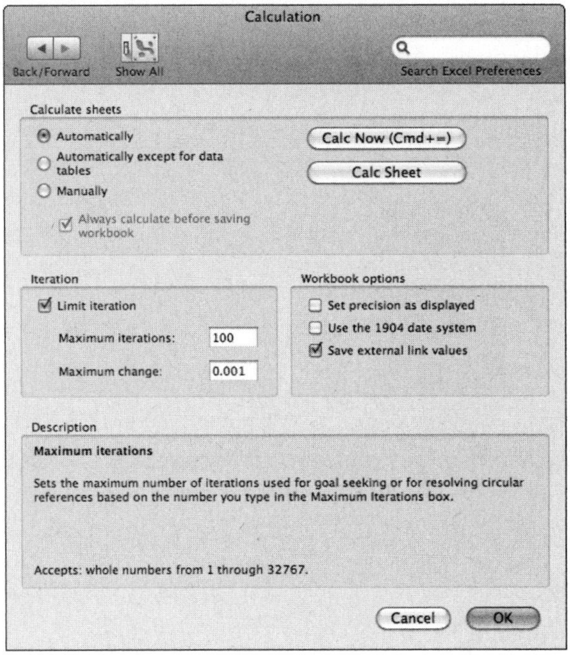

Figure 7-12:
Forcing
Excel to
calculate
a circular
reference.

Clearing #DIV/0

You get the #DIV/0 message if a formula is asked to divide a number by 0. Remember math class? You can't divide by 0.

Other Error Messages

You encounter other cell messages less frequently. You can get details about them by searching Excel Help for *error messages*. To check a worksheet for errors, go to the Ribbon's Formulas tab, find the Audit Formulas group, and choose Check for Errors➪Check for Errors to display a dialog that helps you locate cell formulas that result in errors and correct those errors in an organized fashion.

Even if you don't manually check for errors using the Check for Errors option, Excel puts little green triangles in cells that have error messages, and sometimes those triangles can be annoying, rather than helpful. You can turn them off entirely or select the kinds of things you want to be notified about:

1. Choose Excel⇨Preferences to bring up a dialog of the same name.

2. Click the Error Checking button to bring up a sheet that comprises a Rules section.

3. Deselect any rules that you don't want to be flagged with the little green triangles.

4. Click OK when done to get back to Excel.

Chapter 8: Delving Deeper into Data

In This Chapter

✔ Cutting out the jargon

✔ Playing what-if

✔ Getting data from outside sources

✔ Getting rid of duplicate rows

✔ Grouping and ungrouping tables

✔ Building a Web query

Dealing with data is fraught with mystery and jargon, not to mention thought and anticipation. Our goal is to take the mystery away and help you use the amazingly powerful tools available in Excel to analyze your data. You find data analysis and presentation features on the new Ribbon tabs, and we're pleased to be able to focus on them in this chapter.

In Chapter 5 of this minibook, we cover the Table tab of the Ribbon, sorting, filtering, and PivotTables. We continue our exploration of data in this chapter by focusing on features in the Data tab of the Ribbon. Unfortunately, we don't have enough room to go into minute detail about each of these features — even in a book of this size! The Excel Help documentation and an Internet search engine are good stops for more information about features we don't have room to cover.

Simplifying Database Jargon

Sometimes, a word's meaning changes depending on context. In this chapter, we use the following words with these meanings:

✦ **Table:** A collection of data arranged in rows and columns that you can use to display and analyze sets of data.

✦ **Database:** A collection of tables.

✦ **Query table:** A table that is the result of a query.

Advanced filtering

When you click the Ribbon's Data tab, go to the Sort & Filter group and click the Filter button's triangle. A pop-up menu displays that includes Advanced Filter. Although we could devote half a chapter to this filter, it goes a bit beyond the scope of the book. You can use Advanced Filter to base your filter conditions on a cell's value (which can be the result of a formula), and you have the option to put the filter's results elsewhere on the active worksheet or another worksheet.

The tables we talk about in this chapter conform to the rules for tables we set out in Chapter 5 of this minibook, but now we add further restrictions:

✦ The first row — and only the first row — includes column names. Those names are short, unique, and contain no special characters, such as dashes, slashes, or exclamation points. Spaces are discouraged.

✦ The end of the table is the first adjoining empty row and/or the first completely empty column.

✦ Merged cells don't exist.

Performing a What-If Analysis

 Accountants, economists, scientists, and students can take advantage of Excel's data analysis tools. Excel has tools that not only display data; these tools let you experiment with the data to see how experimental data affects your analysis. Excel can even help you determine a value you need to obtain a specific result. On the Ribbon's Data tab, in the Analysis group, you find the What-If button. Clicking this button displays a pop-up menu from which you can choose three different "what-if" tools, as described in the following three sections.

Making and merging scenarios

Choosing What If⇨Scenario Manager launches the Scenario Manager dialog. You add a scenario that specifies cells that you change using experimental values. Each scenario has a different set of individual cells used for experimentation. Workgroup teams can create their own scenarios, which can be merged. Scenarios can be summarized in scenario PivotTables.

Goal seeking

Choosing What If⇨Goal Seek launches the Goal seek tool. The Goal Seek tool changes a designated cell's value so that the result of a calculation matches a specified desired result. We show an example in Figure 8-1. If you have a complex chain of formulas or a hard calculation to work backwards from such as a standard deviation or cotangent, Goal Seek can save you a lot of time by computing the value needed to achieve a specified result. You need specify only three parameters:

1. **Set Cell:** Choose a cell that calculates a value that is the result of a formula. This cell can be the final result or any cell in a chain of formulas.

2. **To Value:** Specify the value that you desire to have in the set cell.

3. **By Changing Cell:** Choose a cell in the Set Cell's precedence chain. This cell's value will be changed by Goal Seek to produce the value specified in Step 2.

Figure 8-1 shows the setup needed so that Goal Seek will determine the value cell C2 needs to contain to produce the value 10 in cell C5. When we click OK, Goal Seek figures out the value needed in cell C2 based on the calculation that's in cell C5. When you click OK using our example, Goal Seek changes the value of C2 to –5.

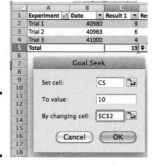

Figure 8-1:
Achieving a
goal.

Making a data table

Choosing What If⇨Data Table launches the Data Table tool, which you can use to produce a table of results from varying one of the cells within the calculation's precedence. This may be easier to understand with an example, such as the one shown in Figure 8-2. We set up the table in Figure 8-2 as follows:

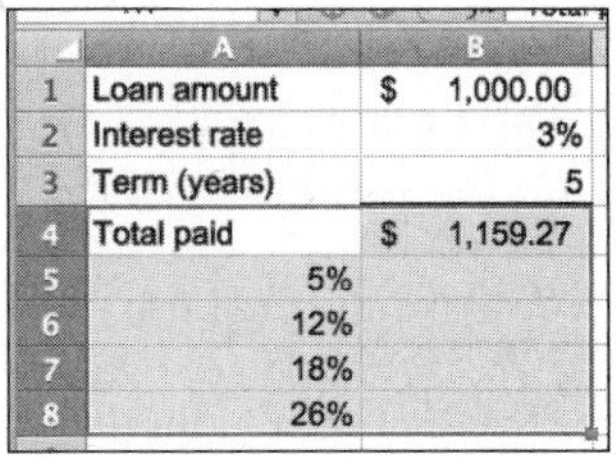

	A	B
1	Loan amount	$ 1,000.00
2	Interest rate	3%
3	Term (years)	5
4	Total paid	$ 1,159.27
5		5%
6		12%
7		18%
8		26%

Figure 8-2:
Setting up a
data table.

1. On a blank worksheet, we formatted cells B1 and B4:B8 as currency.

2. We filled in the text and values shown in Figure 8-2.

3. In cell B4, we entered this formula: **=B1*(1+B2)^B3.**

4. Finally, we selected the cell range A4:B8.

To create a table of results from your data using the Data Table tool, follow these steps:

1. **Choose Data⇨Data Table. Alternatively, select the Ribbon's Data tab, go to the Analysis group, and choose What If⇨Data Table.**

   The Data Table dialog displays, as shown in Figure 8-3.

2. **Click Column Input cell and then choose the desired cell.**

   This is the value we want to vary to produce a data table. In our example, we choose cell B2 (Interest rate).

3. **Click OK.**

   In our example, Excel fills in the total amount owed for 5 years for the various interest rates we typed in cells A5:A8.

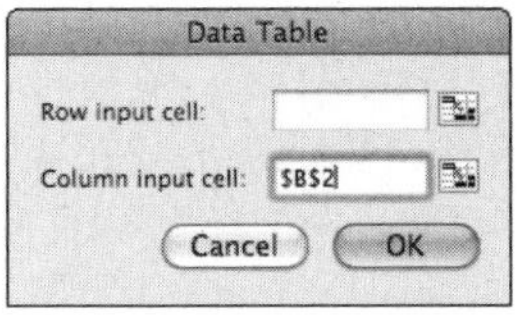

Figure 8-3:
Choosing
the variable
for a data
table.

Data Table	
Row input cell:	
Column input cell:	$B$2
Cancel	OK

Getting Data from External Sources

You can find data in many different places and bring it into Excel workbooks in whole, or as the result of a query in a query table. The tools on the External Data Sources group of the Data tab in the Ribbon, shown in Figure 8-4, facilitate importing and refreshing data from sources that are external to Excel.

Figure 8-4:
Working
with
external
data.

Refreshing a data table

If your query table is linked to a data source, you can update the data in your workbook on demand so that it reflects the current state of the data source. On the Ribbon's Data tab, go to the External Data Sources group and click Refresh button's triangle to display a pop-up menu, where you can choose from the following options:

✦ **Refresh All:** Refreshes all linked query tables in your workbook.

✦ **Refresh Data:** Select a cell in a query table and then choose this option to refresh only the table containing the selected cell.

✦ **Refresh Status:** A large data set can take time to complete. Choose this option to display the status of your refresh.

✦ **Cancel Refresh:** A large data set can seem to take forever. Tired of waiting? Choose this option to get on with your life.

✦ **Parameters:** Excel supports parameter queries. This option displays the parameters so you can edit them for a parameter query.

Opening a CSV or other text file containing data

The most common type of text file containing data is Comma Separated Values (.csv). Excel can open these straight away if you choose File⇨Open. If you have a text file that was saved using a character other than a comma as the column delimiter, you can open it by using the Text button on the Database tab of the Ribbon. Note that you need to be able to tell Excel which character was used as the delimiter when the file was saved. Clicking the Text button opens a wizard that helps you establish the content boundaries of each column.

Connecting to a database

If you have a database you want to connect to so that you can build a query, you start by clicking the Database button. You need to take some preparatory steps before you can successfully use options in the External Data Sources group in the Data tab of the Ribbon. First, you need to install an ODBC driver on your computer. (ODBC stands for Open Database Connectivity and is a standard that allows communication of data records between different database systems.)

You must also add at least one data source to the ODBC manager before you can get data into Office. When you have a data source, you launch Microsoft Query, an Office application that visually builds the query for you and brings the results of your query into Excel.

Building SQL (Structure Query Language) queries is beyond the scope of this book. If you need to build queries in Excel, visit this Web site, where you can find out how to use Excel as a fully relational database, and as a report generating tool connecting to Microsoft Access, SQL Server, and other databases:

`www.agentjim.com/MVP/Excel/RelationalOffice.htm`

Importing HTML data

On the Ribbon's Data tab, go to the External Data Sources group and click HTML to display an Open dialog. From this dialog, you can open a Web page that you saved from a Web browser. Excel imports the data in the Web page.

Importing from FileMaker Pro

On the Ribbon's Data tab, go to the External Data Sources group and click the FileMaker button to display a Choose a Database dialog where you can choose a FileMaker Pro file to use as your data source.

Putting Tools to Work

The Tools group on the Data tab of the Ribbon is a collection of assorted useful tools:

✦ **Text to Columns:** Choose a cell that has a whole bunch of data in it that you could swear was delimited — or maybe not. A wizard guides you from a jumble of text and puts your data into nice, neat columns.

✦ **Consolidate:** So easy to say! This is a complex tool that can perform consolidations by position, category, or formula. Refer to this Web site for details: `http://technet.microsoft.com/en-us/library/cc750889.aspx`.

✦ **Validate:** We discuss this option in Chapter 10 of this minibook.

Grouping and ungrouping

Use the Group tool to identify ranges of rows that can be turned on and off using switches in a new margin that is displayed when Group is active, as shown in Figure 8-5. Group is particularly useful when you have large tables with Total Rows turned on because it lets you hide data rows to reduce visual clutter on a busy worksheet. To group a worksheet that has multiple data tables that all begin flush left (or at least in the first few columns), do the following:

1. **Select the rows that contain the tables with Total Rows turned on.**

   Tables need at least one empty row between them as separators. Contracted rows may not be included in Total Row calculations.

2. **On the Ribbon's Data tab, go to the Group & Outline group and choose Group⇨Auto Outline.**

   Excel turns on the group controls in a new margin.

To use the new controls, here's what you do:

✦ Click the 1 button at the top of the new margin to contract all groups. A plus sign displays next to the Total Row of each contracted group.

✦ Click the + and – signs in the margin to expand or contract individual tables.

✦ Click the 2 button at the top of the new margin to expand all groups.

Contract groups

	A	B	C	D	E
1	Experiment	Date	Result 1	Result 2	Result 3
5	Total	#DIV/0!	#DIV/0!	0	0
6					
7	Experiment	Date	Result 1	Result 2	Result 3
8	Trial 1	3/12/12	9	0	12
9	Trial 2	3/15/12	6	9	10
10	Trial 3	4/1/12	4	8	3
11	Total	3/19/12	2.5166115	9	25
12					
13	Experiment	Date	Result 1	Result 2	Result 3
17	Total	#DIV/0!	#DIV/0!	0	0

Figure 8-5: Grouping rows to hide them.

Expand groups

You can select a range of adjacent rows within a single table and on the Ribbon's Data tab; go to the Group & Outline group and choose Group⇨Group to group just the selected rows.

To ungroup, go to the same Group & Outline group on the Data tab and choose Ungroup⇨Ungroup or Clear Outline.

Using a Web Query

Excel can try to load tables from a Web page directly from the Internet via a Web query process. A *Web query* is simple: It's just a Web-page address saved as a text file, using the .iqy, rather than .txt, file extension. You use Word to save a text file that contains just a hyperlink and has a .iqy file extension. Excel reads that file and performs a Web query on the URL that is within the .iqy text file and then displays the query results.

You can easily make Web queries for Microsoft Excel in Microsoft Word. Follow these steps:

1. **Go to a Web page that has the Web tables that you want to put in Excel.**

2. **Highlight the Web address in the address field and choose Edit⇨Copy.**

3. **Switch to Microsoft Word and open a new document.**

   Launch Word if it's not open already.

4. **Choose Edit⇨Paste.**

   The URL is pasted into the Word document.

5. **In Word, choose File⇨Save As.**

   The Save As dialog appears.

6. **Click Format and choose Plain Text (.txt) from the pop-up menu that appears.**

7. **Type a filename, replacing .txt with .iqy as the file extension.**

   Don't use the .txt extension. The .iqy file extension signifies that the file is a Web query for Microsoft Excel.

   If you encounter the File Conversion dialog, as shown in Figure 8-6, select the MS_DOS radio button, and then click OK.

8. **Select the Documents folder.**

9. **Click the Save button.**

After you save your Web query, follow these steps to run the Web query:

1. **Open Excel.**

2. **Choose Data⇨Get External Data⇨Run Saved Query.**

3. **Open the .iqy file you saved in Word.**

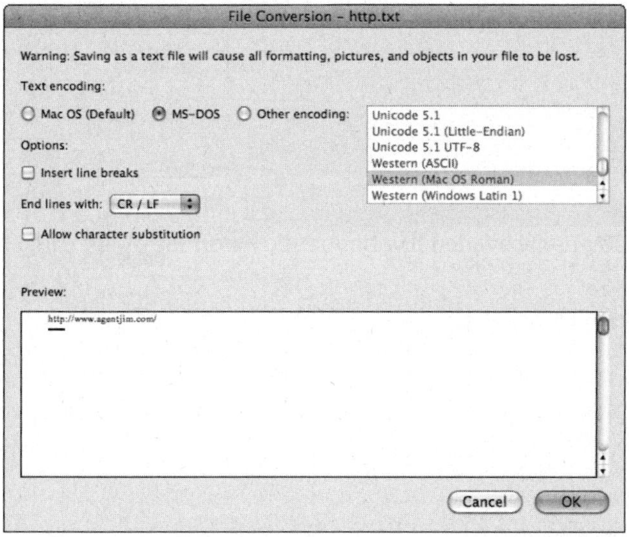

File Conversion – http.txt

Warning: Saving as a text file will cause all formatting, pictures, and objects in your file to be lost.

Text encoding:

◯ Mac OS (Default)   ⦿ MS–DOS   ◯ Other encoding:

Options:

☐ Insert line breaks

End lines with: [CR / LF ▾]

☐ Allow character substitution

Unicode 5.1
Unicode 5.1 (Little-Endian)
Unicode 5.1 UTF-8
Western (ASCII)
Western (Mac OS Roman)
Western (Windows Latin 1)

Preview:

http://www.agentjim.com/

(Cancel) (OK)

Figure 8-6:
Saving a
Web query.

Excel attempts to open the Web page for you, which creates a query range formatted as a table. Web queries work with HTML tables, not pictures of tables, Adobe Flash, PDF, or other formats. The fancy Web query browser found in Excel for Windows is not available in Excel for Mac.

You can refresh a Web query quickly by first positioning the selection cursor anywhere in the data table and then choosing Data➪Refresh Data.

**Book III
Chapter 8**

Delving Deeper
into Data

Chapter 9: Sharing and Collaborating

In This Chapter

✔ Sharing your workbooks

✔ Reviewing the Review tab

✔ Making comments

✔ Keeping track of your changes

*E*xcel for Mac has many great features, including the ability to share a workbook with hundreds of users simultaneously. Excel even has a Mac-friendly, free, online SkyDrive version, too, so you can share workbooks with people who don't even have Excel.

When you share an Excel workbook with others, you likely want to let others know what a formula does, or you want to know who made what changes — that's where comments and track changes come in. We show you how to add, edit, format, and delete comments, and how to track changes, accept or reject changes, merge changes, and even create a history report of all the changes made to a workbook.

Simultaneous Workbook Sharing

Excel was the first Office application to allow more than one person at a time to make changes in a shared file live, in real time. The Share Workbook feature is useful if more than one person needs to update data in a real-time environment. Excel has built-in rules you can select that decide which changes to accept in case of conflicts.

Up to 256 people can share a single workbook at one time, and they can use any mix of Macs or PCs. Not only can Excel deal automatically with conflicting information, but you can tell Excel to keep a history of the changes for as many as 32,767 days (the default is 30 days). Truly amazing stuff!

Although you're not prohibited from sharing various versions of Excel, we do recommend that all users sharing have only Excel 2011 on their Macs and Excel 2010 on PCs. There are so many new features in Excel 2011 that we advise against sharing with anything older than Excel 2010 to avoid compatibility problems.

Before using Share Workbook, consider turning on the Protect Shared Workbook feature so that the change history can't be deleted. See the section "Protecting a shared workbook," later in this chapter.

Activating Share Workbook

To start sharing a workbook, follow these steps:

1. **Choose Tools⇨Share Workbook⇨Editing. Or, if you feel Ribbony, click the Review tab. In the Share group, click the Share Workbook button and then choose Share Workbook from the menu.**

The Share Workbook dialog opens on the Editing tab. See Figure 9-1.

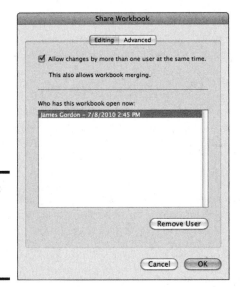

Figure 9-1: Enabling multiple-user workbook sharing.

2. **Select the Allow Changes by More Than One User at the Same Time check box.**

Selecting this box activates Share Workbook.

3. **Click the Advanced tab.**

The Share Workbook Advanced tab appears, as shown in Figure 9-2.

4. **Select a Track Changes option:**

   • *Keep History for [Number] Days*

   Enter a number in the text box or use the spinner control to adjust the number. We recommend increasing this setting to 90 days.

   • *Don't Keep Change History*

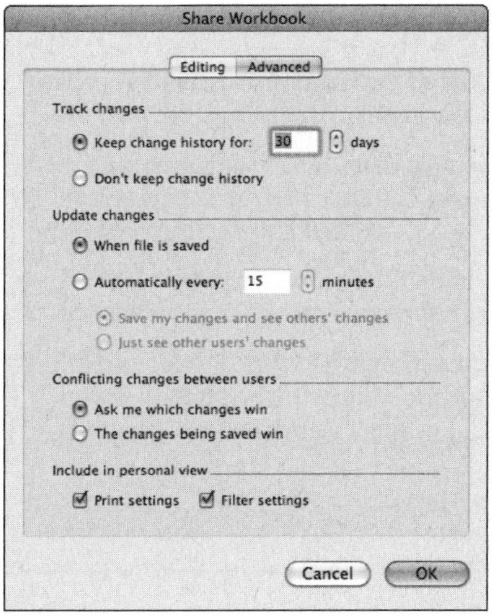

Figure 9-2:
Setting up
sharing
rules.

5. **Select an Update Changes option:**

   • *When File Is Saved*

   • *Automatically Every [Number] Minutes*

     Fill in the number of minutes or use the spinner control to adjust the number. If you save automatically at regular intervals, you can select either Save My Changes and See Others' Changes or just See Other Users' Changes.

6. **For the Conflicting Changes Between Users section, select one of the two options:**

   • *Ask Me Which Changes Win*

   • *The Changes Being Saved Win*

7. **In the Include in Personal View section, select the Print Settings and Filter Setting check boxes to include print and filter settings.**

8. **Click OK.**

   The Save As dialog opens.

9. **Navigate to a shared network directory that's read/write accessible to all who need to share and then click Save.**

   Up to 256 users who have permission to read and write to the directory can now open the workbook at the same time.

Workbook Sharing mode

The Track Changes and Share Workbook features put your workbook into Workbook Sharing mode. While a workbook is in Workbook Sharing mode, you can't change certain aspects of the workbook. You can use these features *before* you turn on sharing, and they work again after you turn off workbook sharing. But shared workbooks don't allow you to add or change any of the following: merged cells, conditional formatting, data validation, tables, charts, pictures, SmartArt Graphics, WordArt, subtotals, hyperlinks, scenarios,

data tables, PivotTables, embedded objects, text boxes, or error checking.

Before sharing your workbook, tell everyone to choose Excel⇨Preferences⇨Authoring⇨General. In General preferences, each person should make sure that his name appears in the User Name field. Sometimes, IT departments clone images, and everyone winds up with the same name (or no name at all). If that happens, Excel may not be able to record useful tracking and history information, or worse, you may end up with useless info.

Everyone who needs to share a workbook simultaneously must have read/ write permissions to a shared directory in Mac OS X Finder and/or Windows Explorer on a high-speed network.

Administering a shared workbook

You return to the Editing tab of the Share Workbook dialog often when you're administrating a shared workbook. To access this tab, simply choose Tools⇨Share Workbook. The Share Workbook dialog automatically opens with the Editing tab displayed (as shown earlier in Figure 9-1). You can see who's sharing the workbook at any given time in the Who Has This Workbook Open Now list.

The Who Has This Workbook Open Now list may indicate someone's still sharing even if you know that she isn't. (Maybe her connection failed while sharing.) When this happens, remove the name of the user from the list manually. Just select the user in the list and then click Remove User.

Protecting a shared workbook

Turning on protection before putting a workbook into Workbook Sharing mode prevents others from deleting the change history. Follow these steps:

1. **Open the workbook that you plan to share and choose Tools⇨ Protection⇨Protect and Share Workbook; or, from the Ribbon, select the Review tab, go to the Share Workbook group, and click Protect and Share Workbook.**

The Protect Shared Workbook dialog appears.

2. **Choose the Sharing with Tracked Changes check box, as shown in Figure 9-3.**

3. **Type a password into the Password text box and click OK to close the Protect Shared Workbook dialog.**

   If a user attempts to turn off track changes, which would delete the history change log, Excel opens a dialog demanding the password. If you lose the password, you can't turn off workbook sharing.

Figure 9-3: Protecting the workbook's track change history.

Reviewing with the Ribbon

The new Review tab of the Ribbon makes sharing your workbook easier than ever. When coupled with SkyDrive and SharePoint file services, Excel 2011 offers the latest in collaboration and file sharing. Check out these great tools:

✦ **Comments:** This simple feature lets you put comments into comment boxes that float above your worksheet.

✦ **Track Changes:** A much more robust commenting and tracking system. When you have track changes turned on, Excel automatically records changes, who made them, and when they were made.

✦ **Share Workbook:** Up to 256 users can use the same workbook together in real time. Excel for Mac and Excel for Windows users can share a single workbook simultaneously.

✦ **Co-authoring:** Using SkyDrive or SharePoint, two users can work simultaneously in real time, sharing all Excel features.

Commenting

Working with comments is a breeze with the Comments group of the Ribbon's Review tab. In the following sections, we show you how to add, edit, and delete a comment, as well as how to change a comment's appearance.

Inserting a comment

You can easily add comments to a worksheet, without disturbing contents or formatting, by using Excel's New Comment feature.

To insert a comment, follow these steps:

1. Select a cell and choose Insert⇨New Comment or go to the Ribbon's Review tab and click the New button in the Comments group.

A text box opens, displaying your name.

2. Type your comment in the text box.

You don't even have to click in the box. Just start typing. Your typed text appears in a little box with selection handles.

3. Click outside the text box when you finish typing.

A red triangle appears in the upper-right corner of the cell, as shown in Figure 9-4, to indicate the cell has a comment.

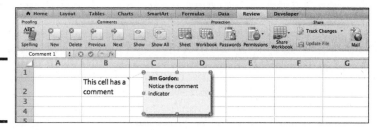

Figure 9-4: Reading a comment.

Viewing a comment

Here are the ways to view a comment:

✦ Hover your mouse over a cell that contains a comment to display it.

✦ Select a cell, go to the Comments group on the Review tab, and click Show to make a comment persistent. Clicking Show a second time hides the comment.

✦ Click the Show All button in the Comments group to display all comments on the worksheet. Clicking Show All a second time hides all comments.

Editing a comment

To edit a comment, follow these steps:

1. **Select a cell that contains the red-triangle comment indicator.**

2. **Choose Insert⇨Edit Comment. Alternatively, select the Ribbon's Review tab, go to the Comments group, and click New.**

   The comment box selection handles appear. Note that the New button acts as an Edit Comment option if the selected cell already has a comment.

3. **Click into the comment box and then make your edits.**

4. **Click anywhere outside the comment box.**

Formatting a comment box

You might consider this feature a bit over the top, but you can format comment boxes to an incredible degree. Here's how to format a comment box:

1. **Select a cell that contains the red-triangle comment indicator.**

2. **Choose Insert⇨Edit Comment. Alternatively, select the Ribbon's Review tab, go to the Comments group, and click New.**

   Resize selection handles appear to let you know the comment box is selected and that you can drag the handles to resize it. If you move to an edge of the comment box that doesn't have resize handles, the cursor changes to a hand that lets you reposition the comment without resizing it.

3. **If you're up for a challenge, double-click the comment box's border. Or take the easy way and choose Format⇨Comment.**

   The Format Comment dialog displays, as shown in Figure 9-5. Okay, it's insanely difficult to get to the Format Comment dialog by clicking the border! One of the authors of this book could never double-click the Comments box without making it disappear.

   The Format Comment dialog offers a surprisingly large number of options that you can apply to your comment box — you can format the font and alignment of the text; change the color and lines of the comment box; change the size of the box; and more. See Chapter 4 of this minibook for more about formatting.

4. **Make the changes you want in the Format Comment dialog, and click OK to see your changes.**

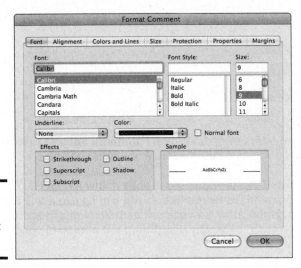

Figure 9-5:
Formatting
a comment
box.

To change when comments appear, choose Excel⇨Preferences. In the Authoring group of the Excel Preferences dialog, click the View button. Select one of three options:

+ **No Comments or Indicators:** The interface displays no indication that comments exist. You can still add, edit, and delete comments.

+ **Indicators Only, and Comments on Hover:** This is the default behavior for inserted comments.

+ **Comments and Indicators:** Red-triangle comment indicators and comment boxes are always visible. You don't have to hover the cursor over comment indicators to see comment boxes.

Finding comments

Jumping from one comment to the next is quick using the Review tab of the Ribbon. On the Ribbon's Review tab, go to the Comments group and click either Next Comment or Previous Comment to make your move.

Deleting a comment

You can remove a comment from a cell as easily as you can insert a comment. Select the cell that contains a comment and then go to the Review tab's Comments group and click Delete. You can also choose Edit⇨Clear⇨Comments.

Tracking Changes

Say that you want multiple people to work on a workbook that you plan to distribute via e-mail, SkyDrive, SharePoint, or other means. To make this situation even more fun, you're in charge of this project. You distribute a workbook to several people. Each person makes changes and then returns the changed workbook to you. After that, you decide which changes to accept or reject for the final version. Although we use a multiperson example, the process works just as well if you're working with only one or two other people.

Before you use the Share Workbook, consider turning on the Protect Shared Workbook feature so that only you have the authority to delete the change history. See the section "Protecting a shared workbook," earlier in this chapter.

Turning on track changes

To turn on track changes, follow these steps:

1. **Open a workbook.**

2. **Choose Tools⇨Track Changes⇨Highlight Changes. Or, on the Ribbon, select the Review tab, go to the Share group, and choose Track Changes⇨Highlight Changes.**

   The Highlight Changes dialog opens. (See Figure 9-6.)

3. **Select the Track Changes While Editing check box.**

   Your workbook is now in Workbook Sharing mode. Some features are disabled in Sharing mode. See the earlier sidebar "Workbook Sharing mode" for the scoop.

4. **In the Highlight Which Changes section, select the When check box to display a pop-up menu (as shown in Figure 9-6) and choose an option.**

   Tell Excel when to begin tracking changes. Generally, you choose All, meaning Excel tracks changes all the time.

5. **Select the Who check box and then click the pop-up menu and choose whose changes you want Excel to track.**

6. **To limit tracking to a particular range, select the Where check box and type the name of an existing cell range or table into the Where field.**

   You can also select the range by clicking the select cells button beside the Where field and dragging over the desired area in the worksheet.

7. **(Optional) Select the Highlight Changes on Screen option if you want Excel to highlight changed cells.**

   If you select this option, Excel gives changed cells special borders and blue-triangle comment indicators that you can hover over to reveal the changes.

8. **Select List Changes on a New Sheet to create a new sheet that displays a report of the changes made.**

   We talk about history reports in the section "Generating a history report," later in this chapter.

9. **Click OK to close the Highlight Changes dialog.**

   Excel prompts you to save your workbook. Your workbook can now be opened simultaneously by everyone who has access to the folder.

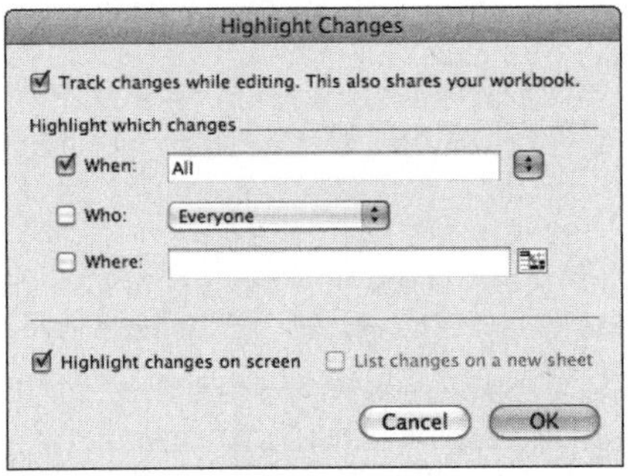

Figure 9-6:
Turning on track changes in Excel.

Now, you're ready to distribute your workbook. After you turn on track changes, send copies of the workbook via e-mail (or Messenger, CD, USB drives, or what have you).

When the Track Changes feature is turned on and a user changes a cell, a balloon appears, telling you the following:

✦ What was changed

✦ Who made the change

✦ When the change was made

Merging tracked changes

After people finish doing what they need to do with your workbook, they return their edited copies to you. Now you need to merge copies of the edited workbooks into a copy of the original. Follow these steps to merge the changes from everyone else's edited workbooks into a copy of the original workbook:

1. **Create a new folder in Finder.**

2. **Put a copy of the original workbook into the new folder.**

3. **Put copies of the edited workbooks into the same folder.**

4. **In the new folder, open the copy of the original workbook.**

5. **With the original workbook open, choose Tools⟹Merge Workbooks.**

   The Select File to Merge into Current Workbook dialog appears.

6. **Navigate or use Spotlight to locate a copy of an edited workbook located in the new folder that you made in Step 1 and then select that edited workbook.**

7. **Click OK.**

   Repeat Steps 5–7 until you merge all the workbooks into your copy of the original workbook.

Deciding whose changes to review

You need to decide whose changes to review, what date to use as a starting point for the review, and how much of the workbook you want to review. Because Excel allows you to merge an unlimited number of workbooks, you may have changes from many individuals to deal with. Excel gives you an opportunity to filter changes before you accept or reject changes.

You can set criteria that Excel uses when it displays changed cells before you accept or reject those changes. Follow these steps:

1. **Choose Tools⟹Track Changes⟹Accept or Reject Changes. Or, from the Ribbon, select Review tab, find the Share group, and choose Track Changes⟹Accept or Reject Changes.**

   The Select Changes to Accept or Reject dialog opens. (See Figure 9-7.) Excel knows you have merged workbooks, so even though you took the same steps as in the previous heading, the dialog is different.

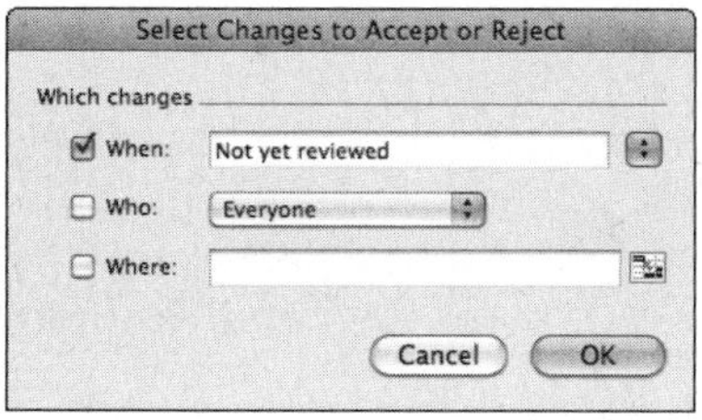

Figure 9-7:
Filtering
whose
changes to
consider.

2. **Make any appropriate changes to the When option.**

   You can accept the default, enter a date, enter All, or select various options from the pop-up menu to the right of the entry field. Excel doesn't display changes made prior to the date entered when you review the workbook.

3. **Select the Who check box and select whose changes you want to review from the pop-up menu that appears.**

   Choose Everyone to review everyone's merged changes at the same time.

4. **To limit your review to a range, click the selection button to the right of the Where field and enter a cell range or named range.**

5. **Click OK to close the Select Changes to Accept or Reject dialog.**

   Excel goes through your workbook and finds all the cells that your collaborators changed.

The settings you select in the Select Changes to Accept or Reject dialog apply to all the merged workbooks at the same time.

Accepting and rejecting changes

If you followed our example from the preceding section, each changed cell is highlighted, and the Accept or Reject Changes dialog appears. (See Figure 9-8.) If Excel detects more than one change in a cell, you see a list of the cell's original content, plus all the suggested changes. When you click the Accept or Reject buttons, the dialog moves on to the next cell that has changes. The Accept or Reject Changes dialog remains onscreen until you deal with all changes. The changes you accept are retained in your final version, and the changes you reject are removed.

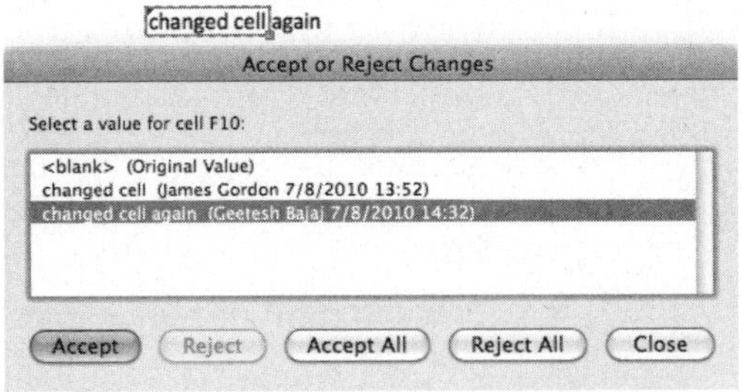

changed cell again

Accept or Reject Changes

Select a value for cell F10:

<blank> (Original Value)
changed cell (James Gordon 7/8/2010 13:52)
changed cell again (Geetesh Bajaj 7/8/2010 14:32)

(Accept) (Reject) (Accept All) (Reject All) (Close)

Figure 9-8:
Accepting one change from several.

Accepting and rejecting track changes works like this:

1. **Choose Tools⇨Track Changes⇨Accept or Reject Changes. Alternatively, select the Ribbon's Review tab, go to the Share group, and choose Track Changes⇨Accept or Reject Changes.**

The Accept or Reject Changes dialog opens. Excel knows that merged workbooks are being used, so it displays the appropriate dialog here.

2. **Click the button that suits your needs.**

You can select from the following:

• *Accept:* Accept that change only.

• *Reject:* Disregard that change only.

• *Accept All:* Accept all changes.

• *Reject All:* Disregard all changes.

3. **Click Close when you're done.**

Excel displays the final version of your workbook.

Finishing up

You need to turn off sharing to change your final version into a regular workbook. The following steps turn off track changes and delete the history file, as well as turn on the features that were disabled when you began sharing the workbook. To turn the shared workbook back into a regular workbook, follow these steps:

1. **Choose Tools⇨Track Changes⇨Highlight Changes. Or, on the Ribbon, select the Review tab, go to the Share group, and choose Track Changes⇨Highlight Changes.**

The Highlight Changes dialog appears.

2. **Deselect the Track Changes While Editing check box.**

Excel automatically saves the workbook as a fully enabled regular workbook. Excel no longer tracks changes and discards the change history.

Generating a history report

After people have made entries in the shared workbook, the question arises, "How do you see the entire change history all at the same time?" We have the answer, of course. Our favorite way is to view the changes in a separate worksheet called a *change history report,* as shown in Figure 9-9.

Figure 9-9:
Viewing
the change
history
report.

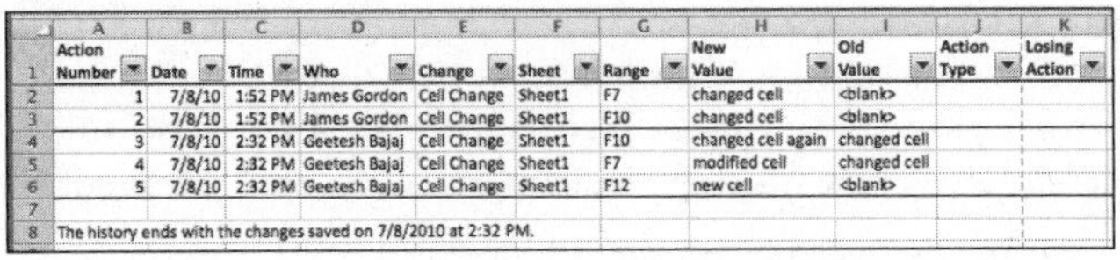

	A	B	C	D	E	F	G	H	I	J	K
1	Action Number	Date	Time	Who	Change	Sheet	Range	New Value	Old Value	Action Type	Losing Action
2	1	7/8/10	1:52 PM	James Gordon	Cell Change	Sheet1	F7	changed cell	<blank>		
3	2	7/8/10	1:52 PM	James Gordon	Cell Change	Sheet1	F10	changed cell	<blank>		
4	3	7/8/10	2:32 PM	Geetesh Bajaj	Cell Change	Sheet1	F10	changed cell again	changed cell		
5	4	7/8/10	2:32 PM	Geetesh Bajaj	Cell Change	Sheet1	F7	modified cell	changed cell		
6	5	7/8/10	2:32 PM	Geetesh Bajaj	Cell Change	Sheet1	F12	new cell	<blank>		
7											
8	The history ends with the changes saved on 7/8/2010 at 2:32 PM.										

If you want to see a combined history, you must select the List Changes on a New Sheet option in the Highlight Changes dialog (which we talk about in the section "Turning on track changes," earlier in this chapter).

You can't retrieve the change history from a workbook after you accept and reject changes.

You can make a history report for any individual workbook by opening it and then following these steps:

1. **Choose Tools⇨Track Changes⇨Highlight Changes. Or, on the Ribbon, select the Review tab, go to the Share group, and choose Track Changes⇨Highlight Changes.**

   The Highlight Changes dialog appears. (Refer to Figure 9-6.)

2. **Select the List Changes on a New Sheet check box.**

   This option isn't grayed out if changes have been made in the workbook.

3. **Click OK.**

   You get an amazing report detailing exactly what changes were made, by whom, when, and a lot more, as shown in Figure 9-9.

Chapter 10: Making Forms in Excel

In This Chapter

✔ Activating Excel's Developer tab

✔ Adding more form preparation tools

✔ Locking and protecting methods

✔ Adding form controls to a worksheet

✔ Touching on dialog sheets

When it comes to making forms, Office gives you many options. In Book II, Chapter 8, we discuss how to build a form in a Word document. In Excel, you build your form within the grid of a worksheet. Making a form in Excel allows you to take advantage of conditional formatting, data validation, and Excel's incomparable calculation capabilities. Excel also has radio button and combo-list form controls not found in Word.

Go ahead and try your hand at making a form in Excel. Forms are actually fun to make, and we show you that working with Excel form controls need not be complicated at all. This chapter covers the buttons that you find on the Developer tab of Excel's Ribbon. Near the end of this chapter, we introduce some advanced concepts regarding Excel dialog sheets.

Displaying the Developer Tab

Excel's form controls are not displayed by default. To see them, you must display the Developer tab on the Ribbon. Here's how:

1. **Choose Excel⇨Preferences⇨Sharing and Privacy⇨Ribbon.**

   Ribbon preferences display.

2. **In the Customize section, scroll to the bottom of the Tab or Group Title section and select the Developer check box.**

3. **Click OK to close Excel preferences.**

   You now see the Developer tab on the Ribbon, as shown in Figure 10-1. Refer to Figure 10-1 throughout this chapter.

Figure 10-1:
The
Developer
tab is at your
service.

We cover the Form Controls group in this chapter. The Visual Basic group and Add-Ins group are covered in general in Book I, Chapter 12. (The Relative References button isn't directly related to Visual Basic, so we wonder a little bit why it's mixed in with the Visual Basic group on the Developer tab of the Ribbon.)

Making More Tools Available

When you use Excel to make forms, you use certain toolbar commands extensively in addition to the buttons on the Developer tab of the Ribbon. We recommend you display the Formatting toolbar so you don't have to switch Ribbon tabs as often. To display the Formatting toolbar, choose View➪Toolbars➪Formatting. The Formatting toolbar displays beneath the Standard toolbar.

We also recommend that you download and install the free Excel 2011 MVP Toolbar because it has all of the form controls you see on the Ribbon's Developer tab. The toolbar *floats* (is always available) so you don't have to keep switching back and forth to the Ribbon. Get the toolbar here: www. agentjim.com/MVP/Excel/xl2011toolbar.html.

We also recommend you add a few controls to the Formatting toolbar. Not every control you need for working with forms is on the Developer tab of the Ribbon; you can add the toolbar buttons you need to the Formatting toolbar as follows:

1. **With the Formatting toolbar visible, choose View➪Toolbars➪ Customize Toolbars and Menus.**

   The Customize Menus and Toolbars dialog displays. See Book I, Chapter 2 for details on how to use this dialog.

2. **Click the Commands tab.**

3. **In the Categories list, choose All Commands.**

4. **In the Commands list, drag the Lock Cell and Protect Sheet commands to the Formatting toolbar.**

5. **When you're finished adding commands to the Formatting toolbar, click OK.**

Protecting Worksheets and Locking and Unlocking Cells

When you make forms, you'll be turning worksheet protection on and off frequently. You must turn off worksheet protection when you want to build a form. Turning off sheet protection enables you to use the form controls on the Developer tab of the Ribbon and allows you to edit worksheet content. When you're done building the form, you must turn on protection so that people can tab through the input fields. Turning on protection activates form controls, and at the same time it disables your ability to edit the controls on your form. Also, turning protection on prevents the users of your form from changing the contents of locked cells while allowing them to enter data in the unlocked cells.

By default, all cells on a worksheet are locked. You unlock cells that you want to designate as *input fields,* which are the cells that users fill in. You also unlock the cells that will have the result of a choice made by a user in a form control.

Protecting and unprotecting a worksheet

The default state of a worksheet is that it is unprotected. When you want to create or edit a form, you need to make sure the worksheet is unprotected — if it's protected, you can't edit the form. Conversely, when you're ready to test or use your form, you must turn on protection.

To turn on protection on a worksheet, follow these steps:

1. **From the menu, choose Tools⇨Protection⇨Protect Sheet.**

   If you installed the MVP 2011 Toolbar, you can just click the Protect Sheet button on the toolbar.

   The Protect the Sheet and Contents of Locked Cells dialog shown in Figure 10-2 displays.

2. **(Optional) Type a password to be required to unprotect the form.**

3. **In the Allow Users of This Sheet To section, select the first two check boxes, Select Locked Cells and Select Unlocked Cells.**

4. Click OK to close the dialog.

The worksheet is now protected, and the form is enabled for use. The Protect Sheet button has become an Unprotect Sheet button.

You can adjust other settings in the Protect the Sheet and Contents of Locked Cells dialog as desired, but only the Select Unlocked Cells option enables a form. Excel 2011 gives you more options for Protect Sheet. To be consistent with the Protect Worksheet command in previous versions of Excel, you allow users to select locked cells by selecting that option in the Protect Sheet dialog along with Select Unlocked Cells.

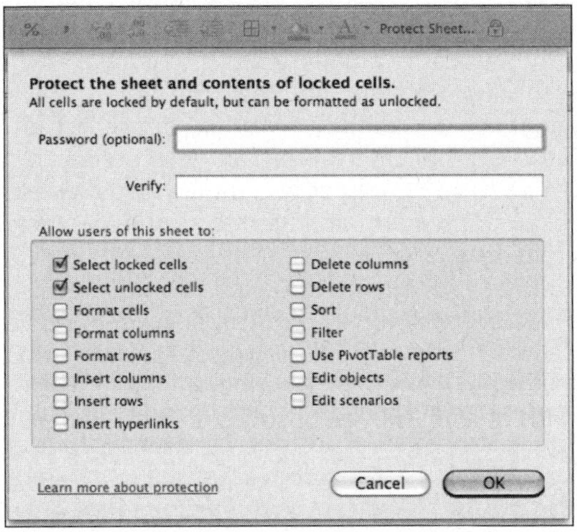

Figure 10-2: Protecting your form.

While protection is turned on, the only cells that can be changed are the cells you unlocked. While protection is turned on, pressing the Tab key takes the cursor from one input field (unlocked cell) to the next. This is a very convenient feature for filling in forms.

To turn off protection on a worksheet, from the menu choose Tools⇨Protect⇨Unprotect Sheet, or click the Unprotect Sheet button on the MVP Toolbar. Your worksheet is enabled for editing, and the Unprotect button reverts to the Protect Sheet button.

Locking and unlocking a cell

Unlock a cell by selecting it and then press ⌘-1 to display the Format Cells dialog (described in Chapter 4 of this minibook). Click the Protection tab in the Format Cells dialog and then deselect the Locked option. If you installed the MVP Toolbar, you can simply click the Lock/Unlock Cell toggle button on the toolbar. On the MVP Toolbar, the Lock Cell button acts as status indicator. When it appears as a depressed button, the selected cell(s) is (are) locked. It always indicates the lock state of the current selection.

Alternatively, you can right-click on a form control and choose Format Control from the contextual menu. In the Format Control dialog, click the Protection tab and deselect the Locked option.

Making a Form on a Worksheet

You can use Excel form controls on Excel worksheets and on Excel dialog sheets. All the controls we talk about in the following sections can be placed onto either a regular worksheet or a dialog sheet. The remaining controls work only on Excel dialog sheets, discussed later in this chapter.

The form controls on the Developer tab of the Ribbon behave similarly in some respects. To make a control, click its button on the Ribbon and then drag diagonally on a worksheet. When you let go, the control appears. You right-click the control and then choose Format Control from the pop-up menu to display the options available for that particular control. Forms that produce an output require that you choose a linked cell for that output. Right-click a control to select it. Use arrow keys to move a selected control in small increments. To delete a control, select it and then press the delete key.

There's a 3-D Shading control in most of the dialogs involving form controls. It's there for backwards compatibility. It doesn't have much effect anymore, so you can simply ignore it.

Making an input field

An *input field* is simply an unprotected cell or merged cell. It's an almost trivial task to make an input field:

1. **Select the cell that is to be the input field.**
2. **Click the Unlock button that you put on the Formatting toolbar.**

That's all there is to it. Type a label in a neighboring cell or add a Label control (described in the "Placing a label" section, later in this chapter), and you're done. Figure 10-3 shows what it may look like.

Figure 10-3:
Making an
input field.

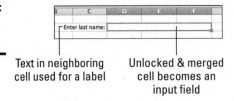

Text in neighboring
cell used for a label

Unlocked & merged
cell becomes an
input field

Restricting entry with data validation

It's always a good thing when you can help people fill out your form. One
way to lend a helping hand is to make it harder for them to make mistakes
when filling out the form. For example, by using data validation, you can
make sure that someone enters a particular kind of data (such as a date,
number, or text) into an input field. Follow these steps to use validation:

1. **Select an input field.**

2. **Choose Data⇨Validation. Or, on the Ribbon's Data tab, go to the Tools
group and click Validate.**

The Data Validation dialog opens, as shown in Figure 10-4.

3. **On the Settings tab, choose a setting from the Allow pop-up menu.**

Data Validation is an interactive dialog — its options change depending
on what you decide to allow. You can allow the following:

• *Any Value:* Allow any character, word, number, or combination.

• *Whole Number:* Apply logical operators and restrict entry to whole
numbers.

• *Decimal Number:* Apply logical operators and restrict entry to decimal numbers.

• *List:* Allow entries from a cell range that you specify on the same worksheet. Click the button to the right of the Source field and then drag
over the criteria list. Select the In-Cell Dropdown check box to display
the list that the selected cell range contains in a drop-down list.

• *Date:* Apply logical operators and restrict entry to dates. See
Figure 10-5.

• *Time:* Apply logical operators and restrict entry to time values.

• *Text Length:* Apply logical operators and restrict entry by the length
of the input string.

• *Custom:* Restrict entry based on a cell formula.

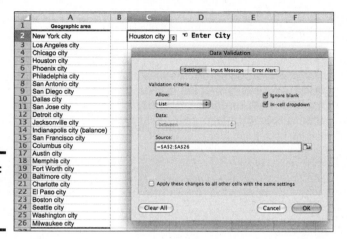

Figure 10-4:
Using a list
to restrict
entries.

To require a valid entry, deselect the Ignore Blank check box. Pressing
the Tab key won't advance to the next field until a satisfactory entry is
made. This setting applies to all data validation Allow choices. Other
methods of selecting cells are not disabled, however.

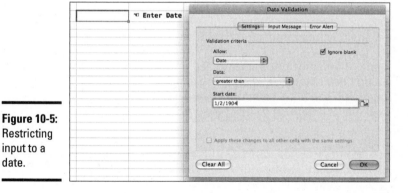

Figure 10-5:
Restricting
input to a
date.

**Book III
Chapter 10**

Making Forms
in Excel

4. **(Optional) On the Input Message tab, give your message a title and
type an input message in the Input Message field. (See Figure 10-6.)**

   The input message appears in a ScreenTip when you select the input
   field in a protected form.

5. **(Optional) On the Error Alert tab, select an error alert style and then
type an error message in the Title and Error message field. (See
Figure 10-7.)**

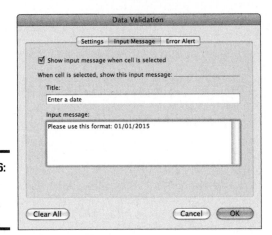

Figure 10-6:
Setting
an input
prompt.

Customize the error message that a user gets if he fails to follow the data validation rule you create. Try not to be sarcastic in these messages. After all, you don't want to hurt feelings or ruffle feathers.

6. **Click OK to apply the validation rules and close the Data Validation dialog.**

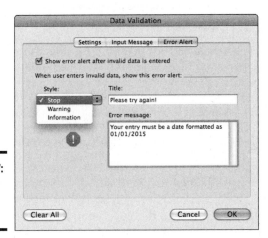

Figure 10-7:
Setting the
error alert
message.

You can also use conditional formatting (discussed in Chapter 4 of this minibook) to further enhance your form.

Running a macro from a button

The *button* control runs a macro when clicked on a protected form. To make a button, take these steps:

1. **While your form is unprotected, click the button control on the Developer tab of the Ribbon (shown in the margin).**

2. **Drag diagonally and then let go of the mouse.**

   Your button appears and a dialog opens that lists available macros.

3. **Select a macro and then click OK; or choose New to display a new module in the VB Editor; or choose Record to start the Visual Basic Macro Recorder. Click OK to close the dialog.**

4. **(Optional) Right-click the new button and choose Format Control from the pop-up menu.**

   Adjust formatting options as desired. You can make fancy buttons. To assign a different macro to the button, you can right-click the button and choose Assign Macro from the pop-up menu.

Making check boxes

Check boxes are handy things in surveys and questionnaires where multiple answers are provided and more than one choice is allowed. Each check box control is linked to a cell on your worksheet. To make a check box, take these steps:

1. **While your form is unprotected, click the Check Box control on the Developer tab of the Ribbon (shown in the margin).**

2. **Drag diagonally and then let go of the mouse.**

   A check box appears and is selected on your worksheet.

3. **Right-click the new button and choose Format Control from the pop-up menu.**

   The Format Control dialog displays, as shown in Figure 10-8.

4. **On the Control tab of the Format control dialog, set a cell link by clicking into the empty Cell Link field and then clicking a cell on any worksheet.**

   The linked cell is indicated in the Cell Link field in the dialog.

5. **Unlock the linked cell.**

   See "Locking and unlocking a cell," earlier in this chapter.

The control won't work when you protect the worksheet unless you unlock the linked cell. Adjust other formatting options as desired. Repeat Steps 1 through 4 for each Check Box control you want to add to your worksheet.

To prevent a user from tabbing into a linked cell, put the linked cell in a hidden row or column, or on another worksheet.

6. Click OK to close the Format Control dialog.

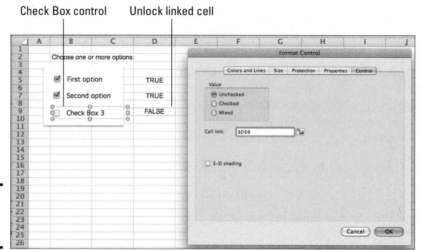

Figure 10-8: Linking a check box.

When the check box control is selected, the linked cell's value is TRUE. When the control is deselected, the linked cell's value is FALSE. (See the left side of Figure 10-8.) You can set the initial value in the Format Control dialog. If you choose an initial setting of Mixed, the linked cell's value displays #N/A until the check box is clicked in the form.

The default text when you make a check box is its official name, which will be something like Check Box 4. Change the default text by clicking into the text inside the control and then dragging over the text to select it, as shown in the margin. Then type replacement text. Typing replacement text to display does not change the control's name.

Making radio buttons

Radio buttons (also called *option buttons*) are similar to check boxes, but you use radio buttons when only one of several choices is allowed. You put a group box around each group of radio buttons that answer a given question so that Excel knows which radio buttons answer which question. Each group has a single cell link for all the radio buttons within the group, as shown in Figure 10-9. You can put as many radio buttons as you want within a group, but you do need a minimum of two radio buttons to make the choices work. First you make radio buttons and then you group them. To finish up, you make the cell links.

Grouped radio buttons

Radio Button control   Unlock linked cell

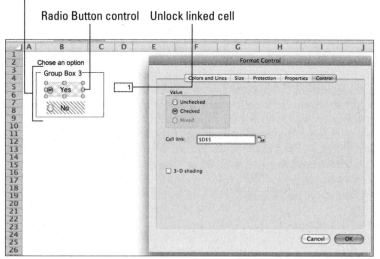

Figure 10-9:
Linking a
radio button.

Book III
Chapter 10

Making Forms
in Excel

Making a radio button

Take these steps to make a radio button:

1. **While your form is unprotected, click the Radio Button control (shown in the margin) on the Developer tab of the Ribbon.**

2. **Drag diagonally and then let go of the mouse.**

   A radio button appears and is selected on your worksheet. Repeat Steps 1 and 2 for each radio button you need. If you don't make the right number of controls, you can always make more of them or delete them any time.

To change the text inside the button, click in the text. Drag over the text to select it, and then start typing replacement text.

Grouping radio buttons

When you have your radio buttons nicely arranged on your worksheet, you need to put them into groups. (Refer to Figure 10-9.)

1. **While your form is unprotected, click the Group Box control (shown in the margin) on the Developer tab of the Ribbon.**

2. **Drag diagonally and then let go of the mouse.**

   A group box appears as selected on your worksheet. Repeat Steps 1 and 2 for each group box you need. You need one group for each set of radio buttons.

3. **Resize the group boxes and the radio buttons so that the radio buttons fit completely inside the group boxes.**

   If a radio button isn't completely contained by its group box, it isn't included in the group.

To change the text for the group box's label, click in the text. Drag over the text to select it and then start typing the replacement text or delete the text to have a continuous line for the box.

You can make a group box disappear by using Visual Basic for Applications (VBA) to change its visible property to FALSE.

Linking and unlocking

After you've grouped the radio buttons, you can link the group to a cell and then unlock that cell following these instructions. Refer to Figure 10-9 as you follow these steps:

1. **Right-click one option button within a group to select it and then select Format Control from the contextual menu.**

   Selection handles indicate the control is selected; when you select Format Control, the Format Control dialog appears.

2. **On the Control tab of the Format Control dialog, set a cell link by clicking into the empty Cell Link field and then clicking a cell on any worksheet.**

   The linked cell is indicated in the Cell Link field in the dialog. You set just one link for each group of option buttons. This is where the results of the form user's selection will display.

3. **Unlock the linked cell. (See "Locking and unlocking a cell," earlier in this chapter).**

   The control won't work when you protect the worksheet unless you unlock the linked cell. Repeat Steps 1 through 4 for each group of radio buttons on your worksheet.

4. **Click OK to close the Format Control dialog.**

Except for the cell link, each radio button can be formatted independently even though they are within a group. The linked value for radio buttons is a number based on which button in a group was selected. (Refer to Figure 10-9.)

Making list boxes

Use a list box when you have a long list of items from which a choice is to be made. The list box will report which item was selected with a number that shows how many items from the top of the list was chosen. The first item is #1, second #2, and so on. A list box comes with a built-in scroll bar. The range of cells that is being used to populate the list box can be hidden or placed on a different worksheet. To add a list box to your worksheet:

1. **While your form is unprotected, click the List Box control (see left margin) on the Developer tab of the Ribbon.**

2. **Drag diagonally and then let go of the mouse.**

   An empty list box appears and is selected on your worksheet.

3. **Right-click the new list box control and choose Format Control from the pop-up menu.**

   The Format Control dialog displays, as shown in Figure 10-10.

4. **On the Control tab of the Format Control dialog, choose a range in a column that has the values you want to use to populate the control.**

   Don't include the header; include only cells that contain data. Blanks don't look right in a control, so make sure your data is contiguous.

5. **On the Control tab of the Format Control dialog, set a cell link by clicking into the empty Cell Link field and then clicking a cell on any worksheet.**

   The linked cell is indicated in the Cell Link field in the dialog. This cell is where the form user's choice will display.

6. **On the Control tab of the Format Control dialog, choose a selection type.**

   Of the three selection types, only Single takes advantage of the linked worksheet cell. Multi and Extend selection types allow users to choose more than one item in your list box, but you need VBA to determine what was selected, which is beyond the scope of this book.

7. **Deselect the Locked check box on the Protection tab of the Format Control dialog to unlock the linked cell.**

   The control won't work when you protect the worksheet unless you unlock the linked cell.

8. **Click OK to close the Format Control dialog.**

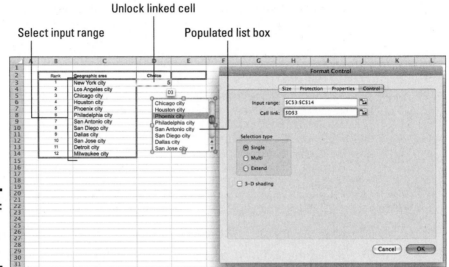

Figure 10-10:
Filling and
linking a list
box.

Making a scroll bar

A scroll bar control generates a number within a specified range, in set
increments. The form user drags the scroll bar control left and right or up
and down. As user drags the control, the number increases or decreases.
The form user can adjust the scroll bar using the arrows at the right or
bottom end, and you can click into the bar to change the control in specified increments.

You can use scroll bars in a variety of ways. Our example (see Figure
10-11) uses the result of the scroll bar's linked cell as the first argument
of a VLOOKUP worksheet function. The lookup instantly displays the corresponding value in the data range as the scroll bar is dragged. To make a
scroll bar on a worksheet, take these steps:

1. **While your form is unprotected, click the Scroll Bar control (shown in
   the margin) on the Developer Ribbon.**

2. **Drag diagonally and then let go of the mouse.**

   A scroll bar appears as selected on your worksheet.

3. **Right-click the new scroll bar and choose Format Control from the
   pop-up menu.**

   The Format Control dialog displays, as shown in Figure 10-11.

4. **On the Control tab of the Format Control dialog, set a cell link by clicking into the empty Cell Link field and then clicking a cell on any worksheet.**

   The linked cell is indicated in the Cell Link field in the dialog. This is where the results of the form user's selection will display.

5. **On the Control tab of the Format Control dialog, use spinner controls to adjust the following settings as desired:**

   - *(Optional) Current Value:* Set a default value. Displays the scroll bar's current value if it has been changed on the form.

   - *Minimum Value:* The number in the linked cell when the scroll bar is all the way to the left.

   - *Maximum Value:* The number in the linked cell when the scroll bar is all the way to the right.

   - *Incremental Change:* The incremental number for how much the number increases or decreases as the scroll bar is moved.

   - *Page Change:* How much the value will change when a user clicks into the scroll bar itself, but not on the scrollbar's drag button.

6. **Click OK to close the Format Control dialog.**

Click the Lock Cells button to unlock the linked cell. The control won't work when you protect the worksheet unless you unlock the linked cell.

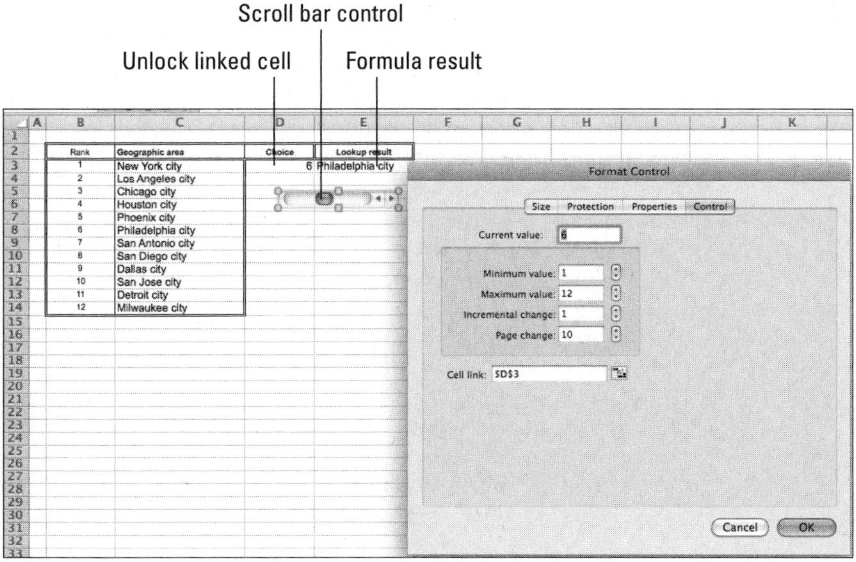

**Book III
Chapter 10**

Making Forms in Excel

Scroll bar control

Unlock linked cell   Formula result

Figure 10-11:
Sliding in a
scroll bar.

Making a pop-up menu button

The official name of a pop-up menu in Excel is *combo box*. For some reason, Web page designers seem to think this is the only kind of control there is. Don't you just hate it when you have to use a pop-up menu that's so big it doesn't even fit on the screen? Pop-up menus work best when there are at least three but no more than 20 items to choose from. Don't be like Web page designers. When you have fewer than three or more than 20 items to choose from in a list, use one of the other form control types. Thank you for listening to our public service announcement; now here's how to make a pop-up menu button:

1. **While your form is unprotected, click the Combo Box control (shown in the margin) on the Developer tab of the Ribbon.**

2. **Drag diagonally and then let go of the mouse.**

   An empty pop-up menu button appears as selected on your worksheet.

3. **Right-click the new menu button and choose Format Control from the pop-up menu.**

   The Format Control dialog displays, as shown in Figure 10-12.

4. **On the Control tab of the Format Control dialog, choose a range in a column that has the values you want to use to populate the control.**

   Don't include the header; include only cells that contain data. Blanks don't look right in a control; so make sure your data is contiguous.

5. **On the Control tab of the Format Control dialog, set a cell link by clicking into the empty Cell Link field and then clicking a cell on any worksheet.**

   The linked cell is indicated in the Cell Link field in the dialog. This is where the results of the form user's selection will display.

6. **Click OK to close the Format Control dialog.**

Click away from the control to deselect it and then click the pop-up menu button to see the list from which to choose. Make a selection, and the linked cell displays a number showing the count of how many places from the top of the list the selected item is. After a choice is made in the pop-up menu, the choice made displays within the control.

In Figure 10-12, we used the number result as the first argument in a VLOOKUP formula, so when a choice is made in the pop-up menu, the corresponding result displays in a cell.

Unlock linked cell

Input range

Formula result

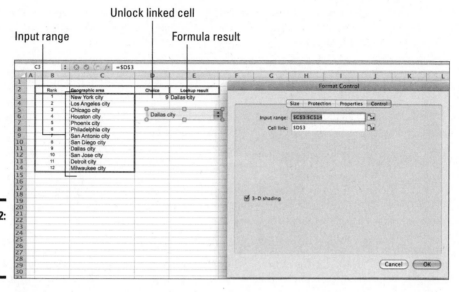

Figure 10-12:
Making
a pop-up
menu.

Going for a spin

The spin button control is similar to the scroll bar control, but is always
vertical. You can make it tall and skinny if space is tight. Spin button, also
known as a spinner control, does not have a scroll bar. This control works
well for large lists. It has two buttons that, when clicked, either increase
or decrease the numeric value in the linked cell. In Figure 10-13, we used
the value of the linked cell as the first argument in a VLOOKUP formula to
produce an instant result on the worksheet. To put a spinner control onto a
worksheet, take these steps:

1. **While your form is unprotected, click the Spin Button control (shown
    in the margin) on the Developer tab of the Ribbon.**

2. **Drag diagonally and then let go of the mouse.**

    A two-button control appears as selected on your worksheet.

3. **Right-click the new spinner control and choose Format Control from
    the pop-up menu.**

    The Format Control dialog displays. (See Figure 10-13.)

4. **On the Control tab of the Format Control dialog, set a cell link by
    clicking into the empty Cell Link field and then clicking a cell on any
    worksheet.**

    The linked cell is indicated in the Cell Link field in the dialog.

5. **On the Control tab of the Format Control dialog, use spinner controls (just like the one you're making!) to adjust the following settings to match your data source:**

   - *(Optional) Current Value:* Set a default value. If the default value has been changed by the form user, it displays the spinner's current value when you display the Format Control dialog.

   - *Minimum Value:* The lowest number in the linked cell when the spinner's lower button is clicked repeatedly.

   - *Maximum Value:* The highest number in the linked cell when the spinner's upper button is clicked repeatedly.

   - *Incremental Change:* The incremental number for how much the linked cell's value increases or decreases when a spinner button is clicked.

6. **Click OK to close the Format Control dialog.**

Unlock a form control's linked cell. (See "Locking and unlocking a cell," earlier in this chapter.) A form control won't work when you protect the worksheet unless you unlock its linked cell.

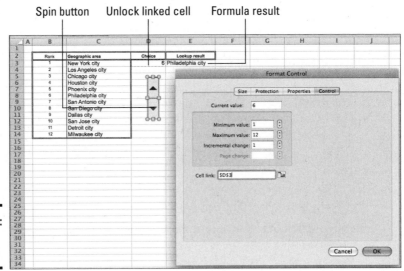

Figure 10-13: Making a Spin button.

Placing a label

There's not much to the Label form control. It's just like a text box. You click the Label button on the Ribbon and then drag diagonally across the sheet. When you let go, you get a label, as shown in the margin. Click into the label, drag over the default text, and then type replacement text. You can right-click a label control and choose Format Control to customize your label.

Making a Form on a Dialog Sheet

Excel has a special kind of sheet called a *dialog sheet,* on which you can make an input form such as the one you see when you're in an Excel table and choose Data⇨Form. You can probably make one much nicer if you put your mind to it. Another use for dialog sheets is to make your own wizards.

Dialog sheets gain new prominence by having their form controls exposed on the Ribbon in Excel 2011. Beginning with Excel 98, VBA Userforms largely replaced dialog sheets. The Text Box, Combo List Edit, and Combo Dropdown Edit form controls found on the Developer tab of the Ribbon can be placed only on a dialog sheet.

Making a dialog sheet

Making a dialog sheet is easy! Choose Insert⇨Sheet⇨Dialog Sheet to display a new, default dialog sheet cleverly called Dialog 1. Notice that all of the Form Controls on the Developer tab of the Ribbon plus the buttons we talk about in the next section are now available for you to use.

Now that we've teased you with the capabilities, we have to tell you that the rest of this chapter requires VBA. If you already know VBA, we refer you to Book I, Chapter 12, where we show you the VBA interface on the Mac. The rest of this chapter covers essential things you must do in Excel 2011 to make full use of dialog sheets.

Running a dialog sheet

After you place controls onto a dialog sheet, you run the sheet to use the controls. There's a catch! The Run button isn't on the Ribbon or even in the Customize Toolbars and Menus dialog. You can find the Run button on the free Excel 2011 MVP Toolbar we tell you about earlier in this chapter, along with the controls shown in Figure 10-14.

Book III
Chapter 10

Making Forms
in Excel

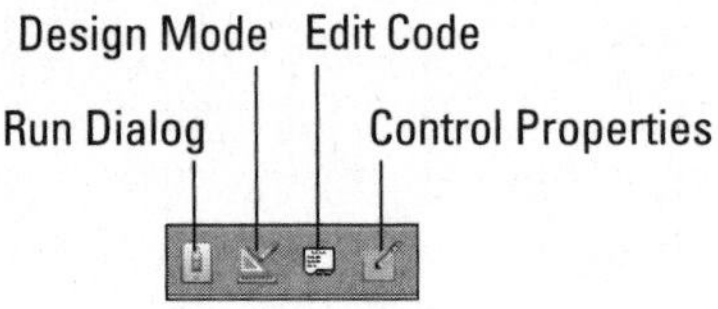

Design Mode   Edit Code

Run Dialog   Control Properties

Figure 10-14:
Using dialog
tools.

✦ **Run Dialog:** To make a dialog sheet work, you have to run it. Clicking this button runs the dialog while you're building your form. Usually you exit a dialog using a control, but you can also press the Esc key. After you've finished making your dialog, you would have a macro run it. Developers tend to hide dialog sheets (Format➪Sheet➪Hide) and display them only when they are needed.

✦ **Design Mode:** Click this toggle button to enter or exit Design mode.

✦ **Edit Code:** Select a control, and then click this button to view or edit the VBA code associated with the selected control in the VB Editor (VBE).

✦ **Control Properties:** Select a control and then click this button to display the Format Control properties dialog for the selected control.

Now you have everything you need to make and edit dialog sheets. Examples of how to program dialog sheets are on the Internet and in books dealing with programming for Excel version 5.

Chapter 11: Printing in Excel

In This Chapter

✔ **Using the Ribbon's Layout tab to prepare to print**

✔ **Turning print options on and off**

✔ **Adding headers and footers**

✔ **Adding a digital watermark**

✔ **Getting great print quality**

*P*rinting from Excel is a bit different from other Office applications in some respects. Excel's printing feature takes full advantage of Mac OS X print capabilities, and Excel supplements these with some clever tricks of its own.

Setting Up Your Pages

The Layout tab of the Ribbon offers many of the commands that are also available on Excel's Page Setup dialog so you can format your worksheet's printing output. To display the Page Setup dialog, choose File➪Page Setup. (See Figure 11-1.)

Switching to Page Layout (View➪Page Layout) view makes it easier to see page breaks.

The Layout tab of the Ribbon has a Page Setup group of options, shown in Figure 11-2, that parallel the Page Setup dialog options:

✦ **Orientation:** Choose from portrait or landscape.

✦ **Size:** Displays a drop-down gallery of popular paper sizes. The last option in this gallery is Page Setup, and selecting this option brings up the Page Setup dialog (refer to Figure 11-1).

✦ **Margins:** Choose Normal, Wide, Narrow, or Custom.

Custom Margins displays the Margins tab of the Page Setup dialog, where you may find the Center on Page check boxes of special interest:

- *Horizontally:* Provides equal amounts of blank space on the left and right sides of your printed page.

- *Vertically:* Provides equal amounts of blank space on the top and bottom of your printed page.

Select both options to center the printed area on the page.

✦ **Breaks:** Insert or delete page breaks or reset all manually set page breaks to Excel's default settings.

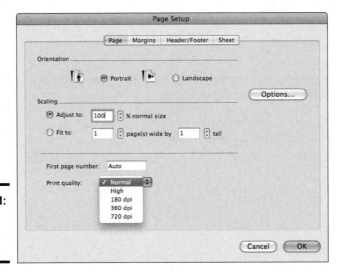

Figure 11-1:
The Page
Setup
dialog.

Figure 11-2:
The Page
Setup
group.

Choosing View Options

The Layout tab of the Ribbon has several View options, shown in Figure 11-3. These affect what is displayed onscreen, not what's printed!

Choose Page Layout view to work with a mode that shows a live preview of your sheet's layout for printing, with clearly visible page breaks. In Normal view, page breaks are displayed as dotted lines after you use a Print or Page

Setup command. The other options are all toggles. Depending upon your resolution, you'll see them as check boxes (as shown in Figure 11-3) or as a drop-down gallery. Choose an item once to turn it on with a check mark, and again to turn it off.

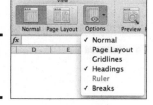

Figure 11-3:
The View
group.

Printing from Excel

The Print group on the Layout tab of the Ribbon, shown in Figure 11-4, has the printing tools you use most often:

Figure 11-4:
The Print
group.

Book III
Chapter 11

Printing in Excel

✦ **Preview:** Displays a preview of your document in the Mac OS X Preview application. Adobe Reader or Adobe Acrobat may intercept this action.

✦ **Repeat Titles:** Displays the Sheet tab of the Page Setup dialog, shown in Figure 11-5. We discuss this in the next section.

✦ **Gridlines:** Selecting this check box prints all the lines between the rows and columns.

✦ **Headings:** Prints row numbers and column letters.

✦ **Fit To:** You can shrink the width and height of the printed output separately so that the content fits in a few less pages. This works great if you find that your sheet prints an extra page just to accommodate a few rows or columns. This option is best used along with the Preview option so you know exactly how much you want to shrink the page count.

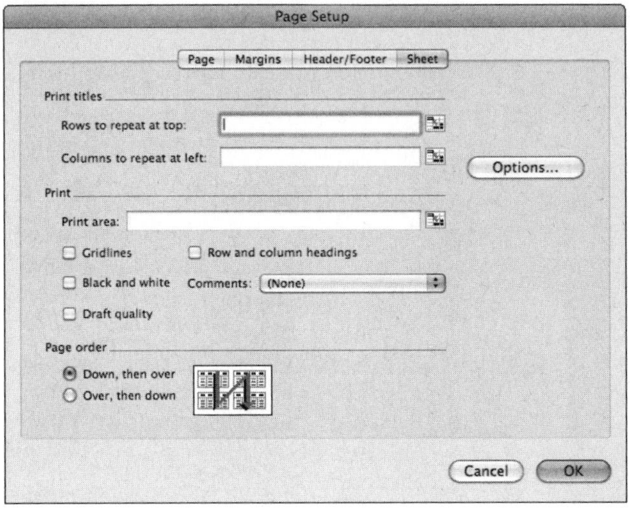

Figure 11-5:
The Page
Setup
dialog.

You have several ways to adjust the way you print Excel files on the Sheet tab of the Page Setup dialog, accessed by clicking the Repeat Titles button:

✦ **Rows to Repeat at Top:** If you want the first row (probably composed of column headings) to repeat on each printed page, use this setting, as shown in Figure 11-5. You can do either of the following:

   • Type in a row or range of rows.

   • Click the selection button to the right of the Rows to Repeat at Top field; then select row number(s) in your workbook to select entire rows. Clicking the selection button a second time returns you to the Page Setup dialog.

✦ **Columns to Repeat at Left:** This option is like setting a row to print, except you click a column instead. You can do either of the following:

   • Type in a column or range of columns.

   • Click the selection button to the right of the Columns to Repeat at Left field; then select column letter(s) in your workbook to select entire columns. Clicking the selection button again returns you to the Page Setup dialog.

✦ **Print Area:** Type in a range, name of a table, PivotTable, query table, or some other named object. Separate multiple ranges or objects with commas. Each object or range prints on a new sheet of paper.

You can also click the selection button to the right of the Print Area field, and then drag over a range. Clicking the selection button again returns you to the Page Setup dialog.

Alternatively, you can select a range directly on your worksheet; choose File⇨Print Area⇨Set Print Area. You can also choose File⇨Print Area⇨Clear Print Area to reset any print area you set, or choose File⇨Print Area⇨Add to Print Area to add an area to the print area already set.

Excel lets you limit printing to a predetermined range of cells on each worksheet. When you set a print area, Excel remembers this information when you save the workbook. And Excel prints this range when you click the Print button on the Standard toolbar or if you accept the defaults when choosing File⇨Print.

✦ **Black and White:** Prints in black and white. You will choose this option if you have some colored areas in the worksheet that you want to print as black and white.

✦ **Draft Quality:** Prints to a lower fidelity, draft output.

✦ **Comments:** The Comments pop-up menu lets you choose from these options:

  • *None:* Don't include comments.

  • *At End of Sheet:* Show all comments at the end of the printed sheet.

  • *As Displayed on Sheet:* Show comments as they appear on the worksheet.

✦ **Page Order:** You get two options within this area:

  • *Down, Then Over:* Prints pages from your worksheet, from top to bottom leftwards, and then the same way from top to bottom subsequently. Think about printing pages as in a flipped N.

  • *Over, Then Down:* Prints pages from your worksheet, from left to right topwards, and then the same way from the left to right subsequently. Think of printing pages in a sequence as in a Z.

Working with Headers and Footers

 Formatting headers and footers adds a distinctive appearance to your printed worksheets. You can also easily include important date and time information. You can work with headers and footers in Page Layout view by choosing View⇨Page Layout or clicking the Page Layout button in the Layout tab of the Ribbon.

Entering a header or footer

Follow these steps to add a header or footer:

1. **Move the cursor over the white space near the top of a page to add or format a header. Similarly, you can move the cursor over the white space near the bottom of a page to add or format a footer.**

A prompt appears, telling you to double-click if you want to add a header (or footer), as shown in Figure 11-6.

Figure 11-6: Excel coaxes you to add a header.

2. **Double-click in the white space.**

The Header/Footer text area opens, and the Header/Footer toolbar becomes available, as shown in Figure 11-7. You may have to look for the toolbar on your screen. It won't necessarily appear where you see it in the figure.

Headers and footers are divided into three distinct regions. You're in the left, right, or center region, depending on where you double-click.

3. **Type your header or footer in the text provided.**

4. **Click the Close button or press Esc on your keyboard to exit the Header/Footer dialog.**

Figure 11-7: Typing a header.

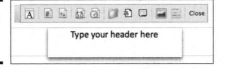

Formatting your headers and footers

When you're entering or editing a header or footer, you can use the Header and Footer toolbar buttons (left to right on the toolbar, as shown in Figures 11-8 and 11-9) to make things fancy:

✦ **Format Text:** Select text and then click Format Text to display the Format Font dialog. See Book I, Chapter 6 for font formatting options.

✦ **Insert Page Numbers:** Inserts & [Page] code. When printing, the current page number appears on your printed page where you put this code.

Figure 11-8:
Entering
page
information
into a footer.

Figure 11-9:
The Header/
Footer
toolbar.

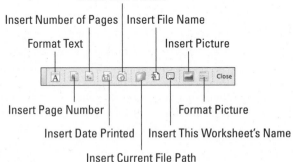

Book III
Chapter 11

Printing in Excel

✦ **Insert Number of Pages:** Inserts &[Pages] code. The number of pages in the entire document is printed on your printed page where you put this code.

You can combine codes with text. For example, use Insert Page Number and Insert Number of Pages with additional text like this: Page &[Page] of &[Pages] to print "Page # of #".

✦ **Insert Date:** Inserts &[Date] code. The current date appears on your printed page where you put this code.

✦ **Insert Time:** Inserts &[Time] code. The system time appears on your printed page where you put this code.

✦ **Insert File Path:** Inserts &[Path]&[File] codes. The file pathname and filename of the spreadsheet appear on your printed page where you put this code.

✦ **Insert File Name:** Inserts &[File] code. The filename of the spreadsheet appears on your printed page where you put this code.

✦ **Insert Sheet Name:** Inserts &[Tab] code. The name of the worksheet appears on your printed page where you put this code.

✦ **Insert Picture:** Displays the Choose a Picture dialog, where you can navigate or use Spotlight to select a background picture. Inserts &[Picture] code.

✦ **Format Picture:** Displays the Format Picture dialog, where you can control the size and other formatting aspects of your picture.

✦ **Close:** Dismisses the Header/Footer toolbar and displays the worksheet.

If you prefer the retro look of the old Header/Footer pane from previous versions of Excel, you can still access it by choosing File⇨Page Setup and then clicking the Header/Footer tab; you can also choose View⇨Header and Footer. We think using Page Layout view is more intuitive.

Making a Watermark

You can use the Picture feature of the Header/Footer toolbar to insert a picture as a watermark. A *watermark* gets its name from a paper-manufacturing process in which words or symbols are embedded in paper pages by wetting the paper. In an electronic environment, you create a watermark by formatting text and pictures to appear only faintly and then putting them into the background.

Follow this step-by-step process to insert WordArt as a watermark:

1. **Choose Insert⇨WordArt**

A text box with placeholder text appears and the Format Ribbon displays. Book I, Chapter 9 has more info on WordArt and text effects.

2. **Type the text that will be your watermark.**

It might be something like **Confidential.**

3. **Use the Ribbon to format your text to perfection.**

4. **Right-click the border of the WordArt and choose Save as Picture from the pop-up menu that appears.**

The Save dialog appears.

5. **Navigate to a handy location and click Save.**

You're now done with the WordArt you created, and you can delete it if you want.

6. **In the workbook where you want the watermark, choose View⇨Page Layout or click a Page Layout button.**

The workbook switches to Page Layout View.

7. **Double-click the center of the header area, where it says Double-Click to Add Header.**

8. **Click the Insert Picture button on the Header/Footer toolbar.**

   A Choose a Picture dialog makes its appearance.

9. **Go to where you saved your WordArt and select the image.**

10. **Click the Insert button in the Choose a Picture dialog.**

11. **Click the Format Picture button on the Header/Footer toolbar.**

    On the Size and Picture tabs of the Format Picture dialog, set rotation, brightness, and other settings to make your picture a subtle watermark.

12. **Click OK to close the Format Picture dialog and then click Close to close the Header/Footer toolbar.**

Adjusting Print Quality

Adjusting the quality of the print jobs you get from Excel can be a two-stage (but several-step) process:

✦ In the first stage, you adjust the quality level Excel sends to your printer.

✦ In the second stage, you adjust your printer's quality level.

Stage 1: Setting Excel's print output quality

The following steps determine your Excel print settings:

1. **Click the Repeat Titles button on the Layout Ribbon.**

   The Sheet tab opens in the Page Setup dialog (refer to Figure 11-5).

2. **Select the appropriate settings.**

   Select from the following options:

   • *Black and White:* Produces black-and-white printed output.

   • *Draft Quality:* Prints quickly at low quality. Fine lines and details, such as gridlines, may not print, even if selected in other settings.

3. **Click the Page tab (refer to Figure 11-1).**

4. **In the Print Quality pop-up menu, choose from options offered by your printer driver.**

   Options vary by brand and model of printer. See Figure 11-12. These settings affect the quality of the output that Excel sends to the printer.

5. **Click OK to close the Page Setup dialog.**

Do you want it fast? Or, do you want it sharp? You have the following choices:

✦ **For the fastest printing:**

- Choose the Draft Quality check box on the Sheet tab.

- Pick the lowest-quality option that your printer offers in the Print Quality field on the Page tab.

✦ **For the highest-quality printing:**

- Deselect Draft Quality on the Sheet tab.

- On the Page tab, select the highest-quality setting that your printer offers in the Print Quality field.

You can experiment with settings in between until you get the right balance of quality and speed with your printer.

Stage 2: Setting your printer's quality level

If you want to set the quality level in your printer's settings, you've come to the right section. Options vary by brand and model printer, so you may not see everything we illustrate available for your own printer. To tell your printer the quality level you want, follow these steps:

1. **Choose File⇨Print.**

The first time you choose Print, a condensed Print dialog opens, much like the one shown in Figure 11-10.

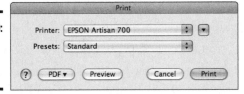

Figure 11-10: The condensed Print dialog.

2. **Click the downward-pointing triangle.**

The full Print dialog opens. (See Figure 11-11.)

3. **From the Copies & Pages pop-up menu, select Print Settings.**

The Print Settings dialog provided by your printer appears. Each brand and model of printer will offer different options in this dialog. The Print Settings dialog shown in Figure 11-12 is for an Epson Artisan printer.

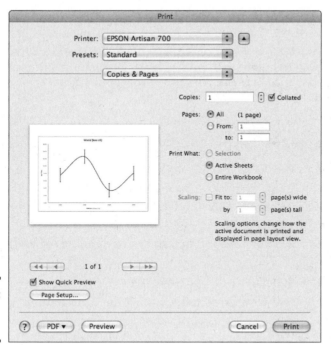

Figure 11-11:
Setting print
options.

Even if you set Excel to print highest-quality output in the preceding
section, you may need to adjust the printer's settings to get the highest-
quality print. Some printer brands default to the lowest-quality setting
to provide the highest speed. Gridlines and other content may not print
properly or at all at low-quality print settings.

4. **Make any changes you want to the print options in the Print dialog.**

You have these options:

- *Printer:* Select a printer from your available printers in this pop-up
  menu.

- *Presets:* This pop-up menu lists the names of combinations of print
  settings that you've previously saved. Select one or select Standard
  for the default set of printing options.

- *Copies & Pages:* Choose settings provided by your printer driver.

- *Copies:* Type or use the Increase/Decrease control to set the number
  of pages to print.

- *Collated:* Select this check box to print all the pages in order for each
  copy.

- *Pages:* Select All or type beginning and ending page numbers that you want to print.

- *Print What:* You can select Selection (which prints what's currently selected in the workbook), Active Sheets (prints the currently selected sheet tabs), or Entire Workbook (prints all sheets of the workbook).

- *Scaling:* Scaling options change how the active document is printed and displayed in Page Layout View. For example, you can choose settings such as Fit to *[Number]* Pages Wide by *[Number]* Pages Tall.

- *Show Quick Preview:* Select this check box to display a small preview in the Print dialog.

- *Page Setup:* Select this button to display the Page Setup dialog. (Refer to Figure 11-1 earlier in this chapter.)

- *PDF:* Select this button to display PDF printing options.

- *Preview:* Select this button to display a print preview of your document in the Mac OS X Preview application.

5. **After you set your print options, click the Print button.**

   Your workbook prints with the settings you just chose.

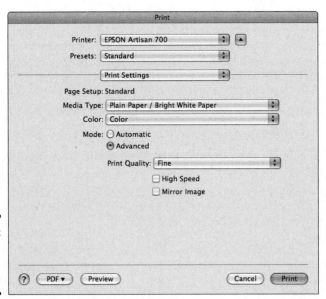

Figure 11-12: Adjusting the printer's print quality.

Book IV

PowerPoint 2011

The 5th Wave

By Rich Tennant

"Okay-looks like the 'Dissolve' transition in my presentation needs adjusting."

Contents at a Glance

Chapter 1: Profiling PowerPoint's Interface

In This Chapter

✔ Viewing the PowerPoint Presentation Gallery

✔ Finding templates

✔ Working in Normal view

✔ Sorting in Slide Sorter view

✔ Making smooth transitions

✔ Automating slide timings

✔ Setting PowerPoint preferences

✔ Putting Notes Page view to work

*P*owerPoint is a tool that presenters of all kinds rely on to help communicate with an audience. Initially, PowerPoint was used to create the framework that aided presenters. Then, PowerPoint widened its scope to encompass the creation of self-running kiosk presentations. In the present scenario, PowerPoint's role has further expanded into the cloud horizons, with educators, businesspeople, students, and others incorporating Web content into PowerPoint and sharing PowerPoint presentations online.

Our goal is to help you feel comfortable with PowerPoint and also with yourself as a presenter. Throughout this minibook, we include bits of helpful advice on giving your presentation as we show you how to use the exciting features of PowerPoint. We put you at ease and make presenting to an audience fun. At the very least, we aim to make presenting less stressful for you, even if it's your first time in front of an audience.

Opening the PowerPoint Presentation Gallery

The default behavior for opening PowerPoint is to display the All Themes option of the PowerPoint Presentation Gallery, as shown in Figure 1-1. You can also display this Presentation Gallery by choosing File⇨New from Template or by pressing Shift-⌘-P.

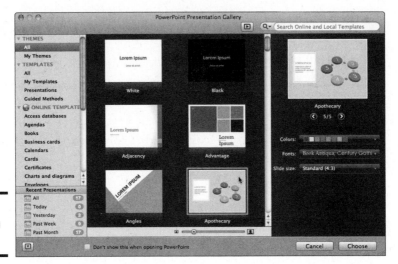

Figure 1-1:
Choosing a
template.

The first two themes in the All Templates category are White and Black, themes that you use to start a new, blank presentation. The rest of the themes and templates are categorized, searchable, and can be browsed, so you can always find a great theme or template to use or customize. The Presentation Gallery also offers these tools:

✦ **Show/Hide Right Pane:** Choose to show or hide the Template preview.

✦ **Themes section of left pane**

- *All:* Displays all themes stored on your computer.

- *My Themes:* Displays themes you saved on your computer. You can choose from theme color sets and theme fonts installed with PowerPoint or your own color sets and fonts.

✦ **Templates section of left pane**

- *All:* Displays all templates stored on your computer.

- *My Templates:* Displays templates you saved in the My Templates folder, specified in Word's (not PowerPoint's) preferences.

- *Guided Methods:* Ready-made presentations that inform; include great tips.

- *Presentations:* Many great templates are included with Office.

✦ **Online Templates:** Click the disclosure triangle next to Online Templates to display the many categories of templates accessed from Microsoft's online template collections. This requires a live Internet connection and is a new feature for 2011.

✦ **Search online and local templates:** Search templates includes online templates if the online disclosure triangle has been activated. When one of the Recent Presentation time frames is selected, this searches Recent Presentations instead of templates.

✦ **Preview:** Displays a preview of the template selected in the larger pane. In the Preview pane, you can apply Theme colors, Theme fonts, and choose the size (ratio of height-to-width) of the slide show to the selected theme or template before opening it.

✦ **Recent Presentations:** In the gallery, up to one month's worth of recently opened presentations are available. You can show them all or filter them by Today, Yesterday, Past Week, or Past Month. When any Recent Presentations option is selected, Search works on Recent Presentations instead of local templates.

Set the number of recently used presentations visible in the File menu by choosing PowerPoint➪Preferences➪General. Be sure the Track Recently Opened Documents check box is selected and then use the spinner control to set how many documents to display in Open Recent. Recently used items in the File menu do not disappear after a month.

✦ **Show/Hide Recent Presentations:** This toggle button displays or hides the Recent Files section of the gallery.

✦ **Don't Show This Gallery When Opening PowerPoint:** When this option is selected, the PowerPoint Presentation Gallery will not display when PowerPoint is opened.

✦ **Size:** Drag the slider left and right to change the size of previews in the middle pane. Click the icon on the left end to choose the smallest size. Click the icon on the right end of the slider to choose the largest.

Move the mouse cursor over the thumbnail to see mini previews of the slides contained in a template or theme.

Choosing a View

After you've made a theme or template choice in the Presentation Gallery, you'll be in PowerPoint proper, ready to edit in Normal view. You can switch views by clicking the view buttons in the lower-left corner of the window. (See Figure 1-2.) For more view options, use the View menu.

✦ **Normal:** Normal view is where you assemble, edit, and customize your presentation. You can find out more about Normal view in the next section.

✦ **Slide Sorter:** Displays a thumbnail preview of each slide in your presentation. Re-order, copy, and paste slides in this view. Here you can also add and preview transitions. Slide Sorter view is covered later in this chapter.

✦ **Notes Page:** Each slide has a notes page, which you can edit in this view. See the later section, "Taking Advantage of Notes Page View," for more about adding and using notes.

✦ **Presenter:** Present your slide show on a projector and see your notes on your own computer. See Chapter 7 in this minibook for more about Presenter view.

✦ **Slide Show:** Runs your presentation as a slide show. See Chapter 7 in this minibook for more about slide shows.

✦ **Master views:** Format themes, slide designs, Notes pages, and handouts. These views are covered in Chapter 5 in this minibook.

Building and Editing Slides in Normal View

The workhorse editing view in PowerPoint is the Normal view. In Normal view, you build presentations by adding slides, titles, text, and rich content, and then animating them judiciously. Figure 1-2 shows Normal view's default title slide on a small screen, as you might see it on a 13-inch MacBook. When working with a small screen, hide and display the Ribbon by clicking the Ribbon button on the Standard toolbar. Show and hide the Standard toolbar by clicking the little button in the upper-right corner of the window.

When working in a smaller window, some Ribbon controls become smaller or their labels disappear. Use PowerPoint's Ribbon preferences to turn Ribbon groups on and off to control overcrowding on the Ribbon.

In Normal view, you have the following options and features:

✦ **Presentation:** The filename in PowerPoint is the presentation title you see at the top of the screen.

✦ **Menu bar:** This is the topmost set of controls.

✦ **Standard toolbar:** The Standard toolbar is at the top part of each document window, along with standard close (red), minimize (yellow), and maximize (green) buttons. The Standard toolbar is programmable via VBA and AppleScript. It's roughly equivalent to the Quick Access Toolbar (QAT) of Microsoft Office for Windows.

✦ **Show/Hide Toolbar:** This tablet-shaped button toggles the Standard toolbar's visibility off and on.

✦ **Ribbon:** The Ribbon is new to PowerPoint 2011. The Ribbon displays beneath the Standard toolbar.

✦ **Slide:** Figure 1-2 shows Normal view, where you edit individual slides by adding text, sounds, moves, pictures, and graphics in layers. You can order layers and animate everything.

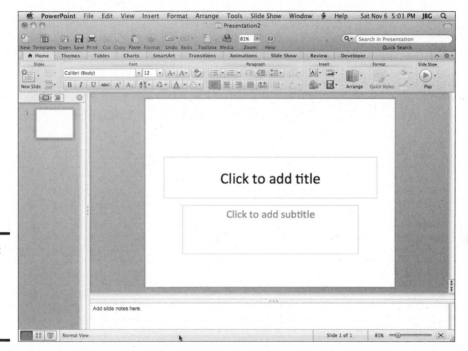

Figure 1-2:
Building
presenta-
tions in
Normal
view.

✦ **View buttons:** Click these buttons to switch the view to Normal view, Slide Sorter view, or Slide Show view. (See Figure 1-2.) Use the View menu for more options.

✦ **Zoom:** In addition to the zoom control on the Standard toolbar, use the slider and fit to pane X button in the bottom-right corner of the window.

✦ **Toolbox:** Click the Toolbox button on the Standard toolbar to display the Toolbox.

✦ **Media Browser:** Click the Media button on the Standard toolbar to display the Media Browser.

Like other Office applications, you can find context-sensitive pop-up menus just about everywhere you right-click in PowerPoint.

The following list lets you in on a couple of minor secrets about using Normal view that can make working smoother:

✦ **To run the presentation starting with the slide you're working on,** click the miniature screen button, the rightmost view button in the lower-left corner of your screen.

✦ **To end a running presentation,** press the Escape key.

✦ **To change to Outline view in the left pane,** click the Outline View button at the top of the pane.

**Book IV
Chapter 1**

**Profiling
PowerPoint's
Interface**

Organizing Your Presentation in Slide Sorter View

Shown in Figure 1-3, the Slide Sorter view (choose View➪Slide Sorter) is used for several purposes. You can use it to do the following:

✦ Organize and reorder your slides by dragging them into the proper order.

✦ Organize your presentation by grouping slides into separate sections.

✦ Organize your presentation as a storyboard.

✦ Copy, paste, duplicate, and delete slides.

✦ Select sequential or nonsequential slides.

✦ Hide and show selected slides.

✦ Control transition effects that play when your presentation advances from one slide to the next.

✦ Set and adjust slide timings.

Using slide timings is optional. You can set the amount of time a slide will be shown, and then PowerPoint advances to the next slide automatically during your presentation. Setting timings is useful when setting up a self-running kiosk presentation. If you or someone else will be giving the presentation, you most likely won't use slide timings.

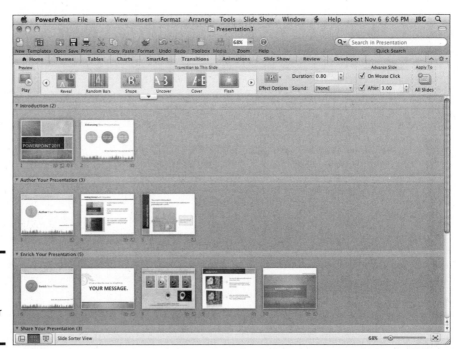

Figure 1-3:
Looking over the Slide Sorter view.

Selecting slides

Here are some guidelines that can help you select slides in Slide Sorter view:

+ To select one slide, click the slide.

+ To select a range of slides, hold the (left) mouse button down while you drag across and over slides like a marquee. Dragging in a diagonal direction can be helpful.

+ To select a contiguous range of slides, click the first slide, hold down the shift key and then click the last slide.

+ To select multiple, noncontiguous slides, hold the Command (⌘) key down and then click the slides you want to select.

+ To select all the slides in the presentation, press ⌘-A or choose Edit➪ Select All, or click the All Slides button on the Ribbon.

+ To select all but a few slides, first select them all and then ⌘-click individual slides to deselect them.

Changing slide order

Changing the slide order is drag-and-drop easy. Just select one or more slides and then drag them in front of the slide where you want them inserted. As you drag, the slides rearrange themselves.

Inserting, copying, pasting, and deleting

Here are three ways to add a new slide following the active slide in your presentation:

+ Click the Ribbon's Home tab. In the Slides group, and click New Slide.

+ Choose Insert➪New Slide.

+ Press ⌘-Shift-N.

Copying, cutting, and pasting is very intuitive. To copy, select one or more slides and use any common copy method, such as choosing Edit➪Copy or pressing ⌘-C. Click at the desired insertion point and then choose Edit➪ Paste or press ⌘-V. Of course, you can use the Scrapbook as well. (See Book I, Chapter 3 for Scrapbook details.) You can cut (deleting the selected object and placing it on the Clipboard) by choosing Edit➪Cut or pressing ⌘-X. To delete one or more slides, select them in Slide Sorter view or in the slides pane of Normal view and then press the Delete key. You can click between the thumbnails to set the insertion point between two slides if you want to paste a slide at a specific position.

You can combine copy and paste by duplication — to do that, press ⌘-D in Slide Sorter view with your slide(s) selected.

Grouping slides into sections

To group slides into a section, first select a contiguous range of slides. Then click the Home tab of the Ribbon, and in the Slides group, click Section. From the pop-up menu, choose Add Section. A dialog appears asking you to name the section.

To manage a section, click the name of the section in Slide Sorter view, then on the Home tab of the Ribbon, go to the Slides group and click Section to display the Section pop-up menu. In Normal view, right-click on the section name in the Slides pane to display the same menu, shown in Figure 1-4.

Clicking the disclosure triangle next to a section name in Slide Sorter view or in the Slide pane in Normal view expands or collapses the section.

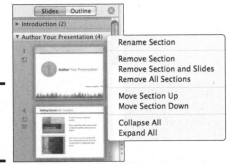

Figure 1-4: Working with sections.

Using keyboard shortcuts in PowerPoint

Although you can customize keyboard shortcuts in Word and Excel, the keyboard shortcuts available in PowerPoint are built in and can't be customized within PowerPoint. But that doesn't mean you can't create your own shortcuts by using Mac OS X.

Click PowerPoint's Help button on the Standard toolbar and search for the term *keyboard shortcuts*. Be sure to check out each of these very nicely produced topics:

✔ **Create or delete a keyboard shortcut:** Describes how to customize Mac OS X.

✔ **PowerPoint keyboard shortcuts:** Lists all the keyboard shortcuts available in PowerPoint.

✔ **Common Office keyboard shortcuts:** Lists many keyboard shortcuts used throughout Office.

You'll be glad that the PowerPoint Help section has been completely redone for 2011. You can even have Help open while you work in PowerPoint!

Transitioning from One Slide to the Next

Transitions are effects that add animation or sound to the movement of the change between one slide and another, depending on which transition style you choose. We discuss transitions in the following sections, but first it's important to remember that when you're using transitions, you must keep both your audience and the content in mind. Think about the reason that you're adding a transition in the first place. Transitions can be overdone or underused.

A presentation that moves from slide to slide every time with a *jump cut*, meaning without transitions, can be dull and look like it's not done yet. Appropriate transitions make presentations easier to watch. At times, you use transitions that are more visually active to help draw attention naturally to transitions in the content that you're delivering. However, remember that if you use too many high-motion transitions, your audience will be reeling from motion sickness.

Choosing a transition

It's fast and easy to apply transitions to display when a slide changes to the next during a slide show. To do so, follow these steps:

1. **While in Slide Sorter view, Normal view, or Slide Master view, select one, several, or all of the slides.**

2. **Click the Transitions tab of the Ribbon.**

The Transition to This Slide gallery displays, allowing you to choose a transition. Click the "sweet spot" in the middle of the gallery along the bottom border to display the full palette of transitions, as shown in Figure 1-5.

3. **Click a transition thumbnail to apply it.**

The transition plays as the slide begins to display.

Book IV Chapter 1

Profiling PowerPoint's Interface

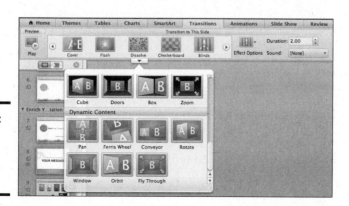

Figure 1-5: Applying a change-slide transition.

Formatting a transition

You can customize the behavior of a transition. Select a slide or slides having a transition, and you can do any of the following:

+ **Change the transition effect's options:** The Effect Options buttons of the Transitions tab becomes available when you choose a slide or slides with a transition that offers variations. Click the button to display a pop-up menu of effect options that are specific to the transition that's associated with the slide. The button's icon changes to indicate which transition is applied.

+ **Add a transition sound effect:** Sounds can act as punctuation points, exclamation points, or incidental music in your presentation. A handful of sounds are located on the Transitions tab's Sound pop-up menu, but if you go to the very bottom of the pop-up menu, you can select Other Sound. This option causes a File browser to open, so you can choose any sound available on your system, or even sounds from your iTunes music library. Choose transition sounds of short duration, lasting only a few seconds.

+ **Set a transition's duration:** The Duration spinner control of the Transitions tab in Slide Sorter view lets you control how long the transition will take. The time is given in seconds.

Advancing to the Next Slide

The Advance Slide grouping lets you choose from the following settings:

+ **On Mouse Click:** When this check box is selected, you can click the mouse in a running presentation to advance to the next slide. Selecting the On Mouse Click check box doesn't affect Presenter View, but it does affect presentations that run by using the other methods.

+ **After [Number of] Seconds:** Select this check box to turn on automatic slide timings. The presentation advances to the next slide automatically after this amount of time has elapsed — you don't have to click the mouse.

If you have items on your slide that take a certain amount of time to run, such as animations or a movie, you should choose an automatic transition time value that's longer than it takes for everything to play. Then add a few seconds as a cushion because not every computer is as fast as yours, and you want your slide to finish without being cut off.

You can also add timings by choosing Slide Show⇨Record Narration and Slide Show⇨Rehearse Timings, features which we cover in Chapter 7 in this minibook.

Making a Blank Presentation

Because this is something done often, you have several ways to make a new, blank standard presentation from within PowerPoint:

+ Choose File⇨New Presentation.

+ Press ⌘-N.

+ Click the New button on the Standard toolbar.

Setting PowerPoint Preferences

Unlike other Office applications, you probably won't need to visit the PowerPoint preferences very often. There aren't many settings, and most can be set once and then be forgotten. To display the Preferences dialog, shown in Figure 1-6, choose PowerPoint⇨Preferences, or press ⌘-, (the Command key followed by a comma). We think the default settings are fine for most users. Check these just in case:

+ **General:** Be sure the Track Recently Opened Documents check box is selected so that recently used files show in the File menu.

+ **Save:** Be sure the Save AutoRecover Info check box is selected so that if PowerPoint crashes, the files you were working on will automatically be displayed upon re-opening PowerPoint.

+ **Advanced:** Be sure your name and initials are correct and that the default file locations are the ones you want to use when you save your files.

Taking Advantage of Notes Page View

Every presentation has a secret alter-ego of sorts, and that alter-ego is none other than Notes Page view, shown in Figure 1-7, which you display by choosing View⇨Notes Page. Notes pages have many uses:

+ **Speaker notes:** Putting notes to yourself in the Notes section of either Notes Page view or Normal view is a good way to add reminders about topics that you want to talk about, but don't want to clutter your slides with. You can display notes as the presentation is running using Presenter view (see Chapter 7 in this minibook), but the notes aren't visible to your audience.

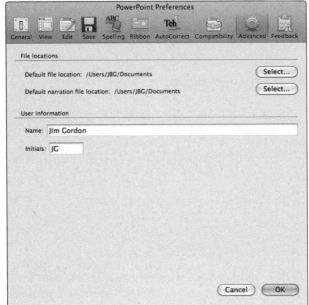

Figure 1-6:
Setting
PowerPoint's
preferences.

✦ **Notes:** The Notes Page view is a place to put all that extra text that you want to put onto your slides and read to your audience, but you wisely choose not to abuse your audience that way. Plus you can rearrange the layout of Notes Page view, as we did in Figure 1-7. When you choose to distribute your presentation, in the Print dialog you can choose Notes under Print What and then choose PDF to make a version to print or share. You can find out more about using the Print dialog in Chapter 8 in this minibook.

✦ **Documentation and annotation:** It's always advisable to cite your sources. Put hyperlinks and citations into your notes to keep your slides clutter-free, yet have the information immediately available.

✦ **Supplemental content:** You can put more than just text into Notes. As you can see in Figure 1-7, you can have charts. Other objects work just as well, and you can format just about everything. Supplemental material is visible only in Notes Page view, and is not seen in Normal view.

You can drag the placeholders in Notes Page view to rearrange and resize them, as we did in Figure 1-7. You can use the Notes Master, discussed in Chapter 5 in this minibook, to make a custom Notes layout for your entire presentation.

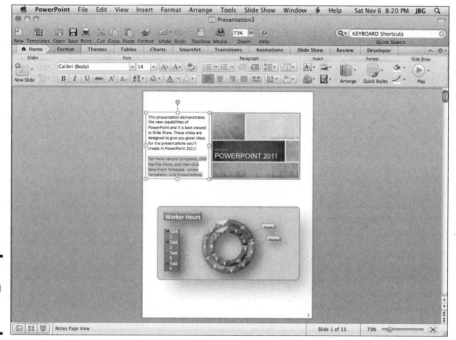

Figure 1-7:
Rearranging
Notes Page
view.

Chapter 2: Opening and Saving a Presentation

In This Chapter

✔ Opening presentations

✔ Discovering special ways to save your presentations

✔ Protecting your presentations

*P*owerPoint has some special file-handling features up its ornamented sleeve. In Book I, Chapter 4, we cover the general ways to open and save files, and that info applies to PowerPoint as well. In this chapter, we cover special ways to open and save files in PowerPoint.

Opening Password-Protected Presentations

The Windows version of PowerPoint provides the ability to password-protect PowerPoint files. This feature gives PowerPoint for Windows users a sense of security, although some critics complain that it does little to prevent hackers from opening and editing password-protected files. PowerPoint 2011 for Mac users who know the password can open these files. Mac users can save previously protected files and keep the password; however, they can't change the password or add password protection to an unprotected presentation.

Saving in Various Formats

The switch to standards-based open XML file formats has brought a much-needed revolution in the way Office stores multimedia in its documents. No longer are audio and video linked with the resulting loss when moving a presentation from one computer to another. Upgrading is an enormous advancement in convenience and compatibility. We strongly recommend using the XML file format (the default PowerPoint 2011 PPTX file format) whenever possible. By far, your best cross-platform compatibility scenario is Office 2011 for Mac and Office 2010 for Windows.

Table 2-1	PowerPoint XML File Format Compatibility
Compatibility With	*Compatibility Rating*
2011 (Mac) and 2010 (Windows)	Excellent. The only cross-platform support for QuickTime.
Microsoft SkyDrive and Docs.com	Fair but could get better. QuickTime support plans unknown.
2008 (Mac) and 2007 (Windows)	Good.
2004 (Mac) and 2003 (Windows)	Fair. Requires free Office updates from Microsoft.
Office v.X (Mac), 2002 (Windows), or earlier Microsoft Office versions	Fair. Requires saving in old format or using a file converter.
"Compatible" products such as OpenOffice and Lotus Symphony	Fair.

When sharing presentation files with Windows users, remember that only PowerPoint 2010 for Windows supports QuickTime. If you plan to share files with Windows users of any older Windows PowerPoint version, convert your movies to .wmv and sounds to .wav before inserting them.

When you choose File⇨Save As and click the Format pop-up menu, you'll find many options. Knowing your audience's capabilities will help you decide which format to use. The following sections explain when to use each of these options.

Saving as XML

All the XML formats listed in File⇨Save As are packages that contain the presentation and copies of embedded media files (pictures, sounds, and movies). File formats are identical on PowerPoint for Windows and Mac, and XML formats are the default file formats for PowerPoint 2007 (PC), 2008 (Mac), 2010 (PC), and 2011 (Mac). Users of PowerPoint 2003 (PC) and 2004 (Mac) need only install the free software updates from Microsoft to work with these files. These are the PowerPoint XML file formats to choose from in the Save As dialog:

✦ **PowerPoint Presentation (.pptx):** The default format. When you open the file, it opens in Normal view for editing.

✦ **PowerPoint show (.ppsx):** When this file type is double-clicked in Finder or Windows, the presentation starts to play. When opened by choosing File⇨Open in PowerPoint, it opens in Normal view for editing.

✦ **PowerPoint template (.potx):** You open this type of file using the PowerPoint Presentation Gallery. The template remains unchanged because a copy is opened with a new filename in Normal view for editing.

✦ **PowerPoint Macro Enabled Presentation (.pptm):** Same as PowerPoint presentation (.pptx), except the letter *m* on the extension alerts you that there is VBA macro code included in the presentation.

✦ **PowerPoint Macro Enabled Show (.ppsm):** Same as PowerPoint show, but contains macros.

✦ **PowerPoint Macro Enabled Template (.potm):** Same as PowerPoint template, but contains macros.

✦ **PowerPoint add-in (.ppam):** This is a PowerPoint add-in created with VBA.

✦ **Office Theme (.thmx):** A theme consists of a color scheme, font family, slide masters, and slide design masters.

Saving in old PowerPoint formats

In a professional setting, you may not need to mess with older file formats. But not everyone has the latest software, so you may have to save in old file formats on occasion. You'll loose a lot of capabilities, and you'll have to compensate for linked content with these formats. PowerPoint 2011 lets you save in these old formats:

✦ **PowerPoint 97-2004 Presentation (.ppt):** The former default format.

✦ **PowerPoint 97-2004 Show (.pps):** The old PowerPoint show format.

✦ **PowerPoint 97-2004 Template (.pot):** The old template format.

✦ **PowerPoint 97-2004 Add-in (.ppa):** The old VBA add-in format.

Because the XML file format contains all embedded media, linking is not a problem in 2011. Movies and many sounds in old formats were linked, and there used to be a Save As PowerPoint Package to deal with the problem of linked media, but that option is gone. If your presentation has linked media, for old time's sake you can make a home-made PowerPoint Package by following these steps:

1. **Choose File⇨Save.**

This saves your presentation in its existing state so you can edit it later.

2. **Choose File⇨Save As.**

The Save As dialog displays.

3. **Choose the old file format you want to use from the Format pop-up menu.**

4. **Navigate to the folder where you want to create your package.**

5. **Click the New Folder button.**

Type a name for your PowerPoint package folder.

6. **(Optional) Click the Compatibility Report button.**

A compatibility report displays, letting you know what features you used in your presentation are likely to be degraded by the old format.

7. **Click the Save button.**

Your presentation is now saved in the package folder.

8. **In Finder, Option-drag each linked media file into the package folder.**

This creates a copy of each linked media file in the package folder.

9. **Go through your presentation, deleting each linked media content and then re-inserting the media using the copies from the package folder.**

This creates a relative link that will work on any computer, whether it's a Mac or PC.

10. **Choose File⇨Save.**

This re-saves and overwrites your presentation with relative links to your media files.

11. **Quit PowerPoint.**

12. **In Finder, right-click the package folder and choose Compress.**

This makes a copy of the folder as a Zip file. Distribute this zip file.

This is the sort of thing that making a PowerPoint add-in is well suited for if you have to do it often.

Saving as a movie

You can save your presentation as a movie, complete with narrations, audio, movies, transitions, and animations if you use a screen capture utility. To prepare for recording, you set PowerPoint to play your presentation in a window instead of full screen by choosing Slide Show⇨Set Up Show⇨ Browsed by an Individual Window. Playing in a window keeps the file size reasonable and allows you to capture other parts of your screen simultaneously, if desired. The Set Up Show button is available from the Slide Show tab of the Ribbon as well. Here are four popular screen capture utilities for your Mac:

✦ **QuickTime 10:** Captures the full screen only. Comes with Mac OS X Snow Leopard.

✦ **Ambrosia Snapz Pro X:** The traditional Mac screen capture software, available at www.ambrosiasw.com/utilities/snapzprox.

- ✦ **Camtasia:** The new kid on the Mac block. It has lots of Windows fans. Available at `www.techsmith.com/camtasiamac`.

- ✦ **Screenr:** A free Web service with a 5 minute limit. Available at `http://screenr.com`.

Although all versions of PowerPoint for Mac can use QuickTime, only Windows users who have PowerPoint 2010 can use QuickTime. On Windows, users of old versions of PowerPoint need movies in (`.wmv`) format.

PowerPoint has a built-in File⇨Save as Movie feature that can turn your presentation into a QuickTime movie. This is of very limited use, as the resulting movie will have no audio, narration, movies, or animations. Transitions in the saved movie are often different from the transitions that were used in the presentation.

Saving as an outline

Many people like working in an outline in Word and then bringing that outline to PowerPoint. PowerPoint can open files that were saved in Outline format. Sometimes, you start with a presentation and want to bring it back into Word to work on it as an outline. In PowerPoint, choose File⇨Save As and in the Format pop-up menu, choose Outline / Rich Text Format to save your presentation's text as an outline that Word can use. Only the text in the Outline pane will be included in the outline.

Protecting your presentation

Sometimes, you'll want to distribute handouts of your presentations as non-editable PDF files. The File⇨Print option is a fast, easy way to get your presentation into a password-protected, copy-protected PDF format.

You can password protect your presentation, using the PDF options from the Print dialog. It might seem odd to be saving from the Print dialog. Think of it as printing to a file instead of to your printer. Follow these steps:

1. **Choose File⇨Print.**

The Print dialog appears.

2. **In the Print What section, choose what you want to save as a PDF.**

You may choose slides, handouts, notes, or outline.

3. **Click the PDF button in the lower-left corner of the Print pane and choose Save As PDF.**

The Save dialog opens, as shown in Figure 2-1.

**Book IV
Chapter 2**

Opening and Saving
a Presentation

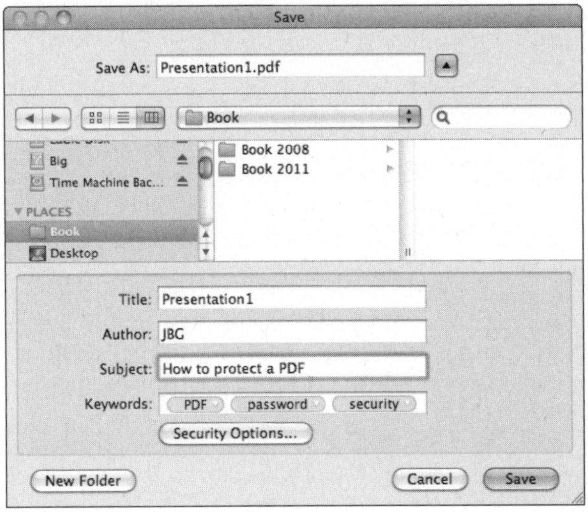

Figure 2-1:
Setting PDF
password
protection.

4. **Click in the Save As text box and enter a filename that includes the file extension .pdf.**

5. **Enter any optional information that you want to.**

   You can fill in Title, Author, Subject, and Keywords. Keywords become Spotlight search buttons as you enter them.

6. **Click the Security Options button.**

   The PDF Security Options dialog opens, as shown in Figure 2-2.

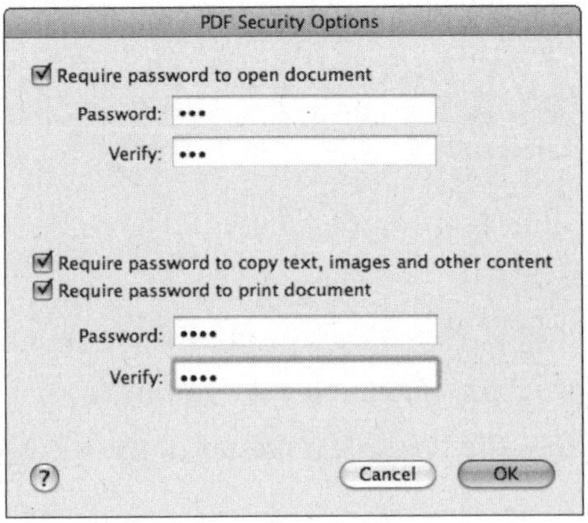

Figure 2-2:
Setting
password
security
options.

7. **Make any changes you want in the PDF Security Options dialog.**

   In this dialog, you can adjust these settings:

   - *Require Password to Open Document.* If you select this check box and enter a password, the operating system requires that you enter the password to open the file.

   - *Require Password to Copy Text, Images, and Other Content.* Select this check box to disable these commands in the interface.

   - *Require a Password to Print Document.* Select this check box and enter a password if you want to use that password when you print.

8. **Click OK to close the PDF Security Options dialog.**

   You can now access the Save dialog.

9. **Click Save to save the password-protected PDF document and close the Save dialog.**

This method can create un-editable documents that are readable on both Macs and PCs. Still, someone can capture the screenshots of PDFs or take a picture of the presentation with a camera or cellphone, so they're not entirely secure.

Saving as a Pile of Pictures

The last five File⇨Save As options save the slides of your presentation as a folder full of pictures in the format that you select — JPEG, PNG, BMP, GIF, and TIFF are the supported file formats.

In addition to being able to turn your presentation into picture files, you can make pictures of your presentation appear directly in iPhoto by choosing File⇨Share⇨Send to iPhoto.

Chapter 3: Feeling at Home on the Ribbon

In This Chapter

✔ **Slide layout options**

✔ **Formatting text**

✔ **Inserting content**

✔ **Aligning and Distributing slide objects**

✔ **Adding tables**

After you're familiar with the basics, you can let your creative juices start flowing. In this chapter, you discover the process of building content-rich slides that audiences enjoy. And of course, having great slides can make you feel more confident as a presenter. We also cover how you can create a presentation from a design template or start from scratch with a blank design, as we introduce you to using PowerPoint's rich slide building interface.

To make a great presentation, you need more than just good PowerPoint skills. Great presentations require time and thought, and we can help by showing you how to use PowerPoint more effectively. You can use all that saved time to create compelling stories and flows for your presentation slides.

A slide presentation is composed of two phases: the creation phase and the presentation phase. You might be responsible for either creating or presenting the slides, or maybe you play both roles. Either way, you have to know the topic of your presentation well. But remember, PowerPoint can only help you present your content well; it can't do the thinking for you and create content from thin air!

Starting with a Title Slide

PowerPoint offers many options to help you begin a presentation; you can choose from whichever you think suits you best. The PowerPoint Presentation Gallery holds the default blank theme, built-in themes and templates, templates from Microsoft's online repertoire, and themes and templates you've saved yourself.

Whether you start with a theme, template, or blank presentation, the first slide by default is the Title slide, and PowerPoint starts in Normal view displaying the Home tab of the Ribbon, as described in Chapter 1 of this minibook. You see two text placeholders, one for the Title and another for the subtitle. Click within each of these placeholders and type to replace the boilerplate text. As you do so, formatting options become available on the various tabs of the Ribbon. When PowerPoint is in Normal view, you can use all the Ribbon tabs to build and format your slides.

Choosing a Slide Layout

Each time you add a new slide to your presentation, it will have a slide layout consisting of placeholder boxes. The default slide layouts are shown in Figure 3-1. The Blank layout has no placeholders. You can choose a slide layout when inserting a new slide. On the Ribbon, click the Home tab. In the Slides group, click the small arrow to the right of the New Slide button to display the slide layout gallery. To switch to a different layout, click the Ribbon's Home tab, and then in the Slides group, click Layout to display the Layout gallery, as shown in Figure 3-1.

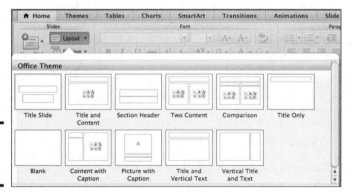

Figure 3-1:
Changing
slide layout.

You can change the layout of any slide by selecting it and then clicking a different layout from the gallery shown in Figure 3-1. We tell you how to add, remove, and customize slide layouts when we get to Masters in Chapter 5 in this minibook. For now, know that there are two basic kinds of placeholders:

✦ **Text placeholder:** Similar to a regular text box, text placeholders have text in them and can be formatted just like text boxes. Unlike regular text boxes, most text placeholders have bullets and numbering turned on by default so you type in an outline.

✦ **Content placeholder:** You can recognize a content placeholder because it has six buttons in it that you click to insert an object such as a table or picture, as shown in Figure 3-2. A content placeholder does double duty. If you click into a content placeholder and then start typing, the buttons disappear and it turns into a text placeholder.

All placeholders on a new slide start in a single layer. When you add text or content to a placeholder, each content item or text placeholder box becomes its own layer.

While you type in the outline pane to the left of the slide area, text in the slide updates automatically in the placeholders on the slide. Conversely, if you type in the text placeholders of the slide, the outline pane automatically populates. The outline and the slide panes are always synchronized.

Text that you put into other kinds of objects, such as Charts, SmartArt, and WordArt, doesn't appear in the Outline pane.

Insert table, chart, or SmartArt

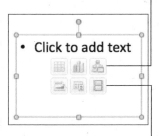

Figure 3-2: Choosing a content placeholder.

Insert picture, Clip Art, or movie

You can format placeholders using the same techniques described for text boxes and pictures in Book I, Chapters 9 and 7, respectively. Be sure to watch the Ribbon tabs because they'll offer formatting options as you select placeholders. Here's how to work each of the content placeholder's six buttons:

+ **Insert Table:** Clicking this button displays a small dialog where you enter the number of rows and columns for your table. Click OK, and your table is placed on the slide. We explain tables in Book II, Chapter 6.

+ **Insert Chart:** Click this button to activate the Chart tabs of the Ribbon. We explain charts in Book III, Chapter 6.

+ **Insert SmartArt:** Clicking activates the SmartArt tab of the Ribbon. SmartArt is covered in Book I, Chapter 5.

+ **Insert Picture:** Displays the Choose a Picture file browser, where you can choose any picture file in Finder.

✦ **ClipArt browser:** Displays the Media tab of the Media Browser. Drag a clip from the Media Browser into the content placeholder. The Media Browser is discussed in detail in Book I, Chapter 8.

✦ **Insert Movie:** Displays the Choose a Movie file browser. Choose a movie file from anywhere in Finder.

In addition to using content placeholders, you can add content items directly at any time using the Media Browser, menu commands, and toolbars.

When you insert an object that's larger than your content placeholder, you may activate a floating toolbar that lets you choose how you want to handle the excess size:

✦ **Manual:** You manually resize and crop the inserted object.

✦ **Crop:** Turns on the crop tool so you can decide what to chop off.

✦ **Resize:** Scales the object to fit the placeholder.

Working with Text Placeholders

Formatting the text as well as the borders and fill of text in PowerPoint placeholders works the same as with any other text box. You use the Font group on the Ribbon's Home tab to format text. When you select a placeholder, you can click the Format tab on the Ribbon to display even more formatting options. Text and other formatting is covered in detail in Book I, Chapter 6.

A bulleted or numbered list is text arranged as an outline. Levels are indicated by how many notches the text is indented. Each time you press Return or Enter, you insert a paragraph mark, which signifies the end of a bulleted or numbered point and probably the start of another bulleted or numbered point.

Here we discuss the unique way in which the Home tab of the Ribbon lets you control bulleting and numbering aspects of the bullet points in your text placeholders. Refer to Figure 3-3 as we explore the PowerPoint Paragraph formatting features. To follow along with us, you may want to set up your PowerPoint as follows:

1. **Open a new, blank presentation.**

You see a new, empty title slide in Normal view.

2. **Click the Ribbon's Home tab. In the Slides group, click the Layout button and then choose Title and Content from the gallery.**

Your slide's layout changes to a text title placeholder at the top, and a content placeholder covers most of the slide.

3. **Type text into your slide's placeholders and then experiment with controls in the Paragraph group on the Ribbon's Home tab, as explained in the following sections.**

Figure 3-3:
The Home
tab's
Paragraph
group.

Formatting bullets

Click the Ribbon's Home tab, and in the Paragraph group, you find the Bulleted List button. This is a dual control. Select some text and then click either the left portion or triangle button part of this control.

 By default, bullets are on. To turn off bulleting, click the left portion of the Bulleted List button. Click it a second time to toggle the bullets back on.

 Click in a bullet point, or select text that spans more than one bullet, and then click the triangle on the right side of the Bulleted List button to display the Bullet Styles gallery shown in Figure 3-4. Choose a bullet style from the gallery to format your bullet point.

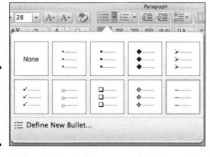

Figure 3-4:
Choosing
a different
bullet.

**Book IV
Chapter 3**

Feeling at Home on the Ribbon

If you choose the Define New Bullet option at the bottom of the gallery, you display the Bullets and Numbering portion of the Format Text dialog, shown in Figure 3-5. In this dialog, you see the same styles shown in the gallery, but you have three additional customization options:

✦ **Color:** Displays the Office color palette.

✦ **Size:** Use the spinner control to increase or decrease the size of the bullet.

✦ **Custom Bullet:** Click to display a pop-up menu where you can choose:

- *A bullet.*

- *Character:* Displays the Mac OS X Character Viewer dialog, which is discussed in Book I, Chapter 8.

- *Picture:* Displays the Choose a Picture dialog, where you can browse Finder for a picture to use as a bullet. Choose a very small picture.

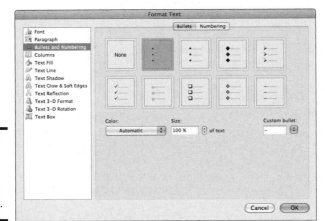

Figure 3-5:
Formatting bullets in the Format Text dialog.

Formatting numbers

Click the Ribbon's Home tab, and in the Paragraph group, you find the Numbered List button. This is a dual control. Select some text and then click either the left portion or triangle part of this button.

 By default, numbering is on. To change the formatting to a numbered list, click the left portion of the Numbered List button. Click it a second time to toggle the numbers off.

 Click in a bulleted or numbered point or select text that spans more than one point, and then click the triangle on the right side of the Numbered List button to display the Number Styles gallery shown in Figure 3-6. Choose a numbering style from the gallery.

Figure 3-6:
Choosing
a number
style.

If you choose Numbering Options at the bottom of the gallery, you display
the Bullets and Numbering portion of the Format Text dialog, shown in
Figure 3-7. In the Format Text dialog, you see the same styles shown on the
palette, but you have three additional customization options:

✦ **Color:** Displays the Office color palette.

✦ **Size:** Use the spinner control to increase or decrease the size of the
number.

✦ **Start At:** Use the spinner control to choose the first number for the numbered list.

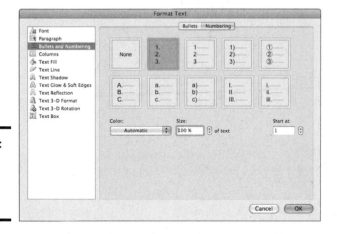

Figure 3-7:
Making
a custom
number
format.

Indenting

Paragraph

Directly beneath the word Paragraph in the Paragraph group (on the
Ribbon's Home tab), you find the Decrease Indent and Increase Indent buttons, which logically enough, decrease or increase the indenting level of
your bullets or numbers. (Refer to Figure 3-3 and the left margin.)

Click into a bullet or number level between the bullet or number and the text or select text that spans more than one level and then click the Indent button. Each time you click the button, you increase the indent level one notch. Click the Decrease Indent button to decrease indenting by one level. You might find pressing Tab to indent and pressing Shift-Tab to decrease indenting a bit handier.

Setting line spacing

To change the line spacing of a bullet or number level, click in that line or select text that spans more than one level. Then click the Ribbon's Home tab, and in the Paragraph group, click the Line Spacing button. From the pop-up menu, choose a value to apply. Choose Line Spacing options at the bottom of the menu to display the Paragraph tab of the Format Text dialog, shown in Figure 3-8.

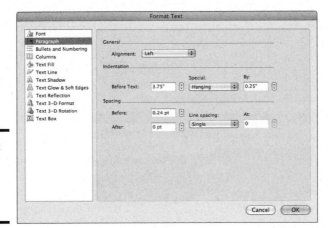

Figure 3-8:
Making
a custom
number
format.

In addition to using the Ribbon, after you select something, you can right-click and choose Format or use the Format menu from the top menu bar.

Splitting text into columns

In Figure 3-3, you find the Split Text into Columns button. Clicking it displays a pop-up menu where you can choose from one, two, or three columns. Choosing Column Options gives you a spinner control where you can adjust the spacing between the columns. Columns should be used to help with the layout, but you should never have enough text on a slide to fill more than two columns.

Obeying the 7 x 7 rule

An important way to avoid *death by PowerPoint* (that is, boring your audience to sleep, or worse, into leaving during your presentation) is to never put more than seven words into a bullet (paragraph) and never put more than seven bullets (paragraphs) on a slide. We searched in vain for the originator of this most important rule to give him or her credit, so we tip our collective hats to whomever it was.

If you have so much text on a slide that you think it's okay to break this rule, you should think again. In fact, your audience may be even happier with four bullet points in a slide rather than seven! Also remember that if you have lengthy text, you should use slide notes rather than the slide itself. And if you still want more text, you should be probably using Word, not PowerPoint!

Aligning your text

In Figure 3-3, you find the Align Text Left, Center, Align Text Right, and Justify buttons, which perform standard text justification. The default is left justified. (If you have enough text that the Justify option makes a visible difference, you probably have way too much text in your paragraph — see the "Obeying the 7 x 7 rule" sidebar for helpful tips about writing text for slides.)

Distributing text

If you want to spread the characters of your text evenly across the slide, select it and then click the Distribute Text button, shown in Figure 3-3. If your font supports ligatures, the result can be quite distracting. You certainly won't use this control very often, but there could be that one time when it hits the spot! See Book II, Chapter 3 for more about ligatures.

Changing text direction

Click the Text Direction button in the Paragraph group, as shown in Figure 3-3 (the button shows *A* next to lines pointing down), to display a pop-up menu of text directions from which to choose for your selected paragraph. Choose Text Direction Options to display the Text Box tab of the Format Text dialog, shown in Figure 3-9. You'll be surprised at how much control you have over your text.

Aligning text in a placeholder or textbox

The Align Text button (refer to Figure 3-3) in the Paragraph group really doesn't apply to the selected paragraph. Instead, it applies to all the paragraphs as a group within a text placeholder. Click this button to choose Top, Middle, or Bottom from a pop-up menu. Choose Text Alignment Options to display the Format Text dialog as shown in Figure 3-9. There you can choose centered options from the Vertical Alignment pop-up menu in the Text Layout section.

Book IV Chapter 3

Feeling at Home on the Ribbon

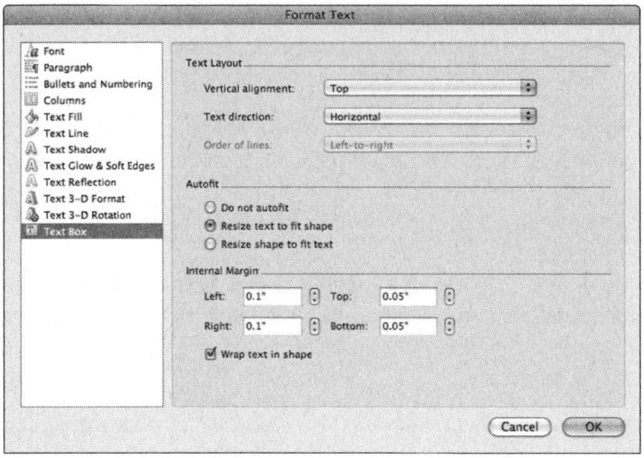

Figure 3-9:
Turning
text every
which-way.

Inserting More Content

Earlier in this chapter, we explain how to use Content Placeholders to add media and other objects to a slide. The Ribbon lets you add content, too, using the options on Home tab, in the Insert group, shown in Figure 3-10. Be sure to visit Book I, Chapter 6 for details about formatting shapes.

Each time you add something to a slide, it's placed in a layer on top of all existing objects on the slide.

Figure 3-10:
Inserting
all kinds of
things.

Inserting text stuff

Click the Ribbon's Home tab, and in the Insert group, click the Text button to display a pop-up menu with the following choices:

✦ **Text Box:** Inserts a regular text box rather than a text placeholder. The text you type into a regular text box is not added to the Outline in the Outline tab of the left-side preview pane, and is not included when the presentation is saved in Outline format.

✦ **WordArt:** Inserts a WordArt placeholder and activates the Format tab on the Ribbon.

✦ **Header and Footer:** When clicked, displays the Header and Footer dialog shown in Figure 3-11. The controls are similar for the Slide tab and the Notes and Handouts tab.

Slides don't have headers; they just have footers. However, notes and handouts can have both headers and footers. That's just a little trivia.

✦ **Date and Time:** Displays the Header and Footer dialog. See Figure 3-11. If your cursor is inside the footer, displays date and time format options.

✦ **Slide Number:** Displays the Header and Footer dialog. If your cursor is in text in a placeholder, inserts the slide number.

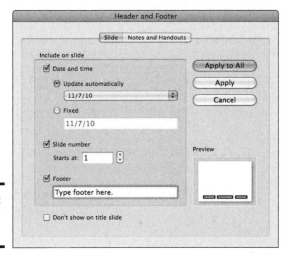

Figure 3-11:
Adding a
footer.

✦ **Hyperlink:** Select text or any object and then choose this option, or press ⌘-K to display the Insert Hyperlink dialog. Hyperlinking is explained in Book I, Chapter 10.

✦ **Symbol Browser:** Choosing this option displays the Mac OS X Character Viewer application. This application is described in Book I, Chapter 8.

Inserting shapes, AutoShapes, and Action Buttons

When clicked, the Shape button displays the gallery shown in Figure 3-12. Each submenu item displays a palette from which you can choose stock shapes. The Action Buttons are unique to PowerPoint. We cover how to use Action Buttons in Chapter 4 of this minibook. For now, remember that this is where they're located. If you choose the Shape Browser option, the Shapes tab of the Media Browser opens. We cover the Media Browser in Book I, Chapter 8.

**Book IV
Chapter 3**

Feeling at Home on
the Ribbon

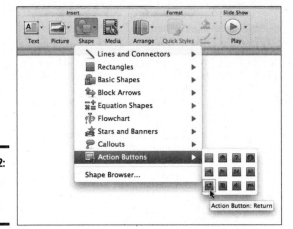

Figure 3-12:
Inserting
an action
button.

Inserting Pictures and ClipArt

Clicking the Picture button on the Ribbon displays a pop-up menu with four options:

✦ **Photo Browser:** Displays the Photos tab of the Media Browser. The Media Browser is described in Book I, Chapter 8.

✦ **Picture from File:** Displays the Choose a Picture file dialog.

✦ **ClipArt Browser:** Displays the ClipArt tab of the Media Browser, described in Book I, Chapter 8.

✦ **ClipArt Gallery:** Displays the full ClipArt Gallery application, described in Book I, Chapter 8.

Inserting Sounds and Movies

The media button displays a pop-up menu with five options:

✦ **Movie Browser:** Displays the Movies tab of the Media Browser. The Media Browser is described in Book I, Chapter 8.

✦ **Movie from File:** Displays the Choose a Movie file dialog.

✦ **Audio Browser:** Displays the Audio tab of the Media Browser. The Media Browser is described in Book I, Chapter 8.

✦ **Audio from File:** Displays the Choose Audio file dialog.

✦ **Record Audio:** Displays the Sound dialog, which is discussed in Chapter 8.

Formatting

On the Home tab of the Ribbon, the Format group (shown in Figure 3-13) offers some shortcuts that you're sure to use often. In the following sections, we discuss the many ways PowerPoint helps you place and order the many objects on a slide. You can use these tools when working in Normal view, on a master slide, or on a slide design layout in Slide Master view.

Figure 3-13: Arranging and formatting.

Aligning with visual aids

You can toggle several alignment features on and off. These features are designed to help you place objects in alignment with each other or to an invisible grid on a slide.

Rulers

Toggle Rulers on and off by choosing View⟡Ruler on the menu bar or by right-clicking in the slide area (but not on an object) and choosing Ruler from the contextual menu. When nothing is selected, a line in each ruler indicates the current cursor position. When an object is selected, its position is shown in the ruler.

Guides

You can toggle certain guide tools on and off by choosing View⟡Guides from the menu bar or by choosing Guides from the contextual menu you see when you right-click in the slide area in Normal, Slide Master, or slide design layout in Slide Master view. From the Guides sub-menu, toggle any combination of the following on or off:

✦ **Dynamic Guides:** When these guides are turned on, as you drag objects slowly on your slide, guide lines will automatically appear when the selection border of the object you are dragging is perfectly aligned with another object on the slide. In Figure 3-14, we have two objects of identical height. We dragged the glass on the left down and to the right slowly until three dynamic guide lines appeared at the top, middle, and bottom, which let us know the two objects were in perfect alignment so we could let go of the mouse button.

Original position   New position   Dynamic guides

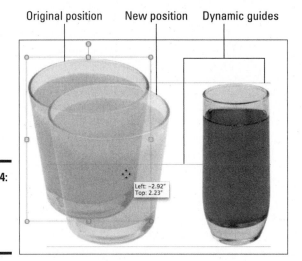

Figure 3-14:
Aligning
with
dynamic
guides.

Left: –2.92"
Top: 2.23"

✦ **Static Guides:** Turn these on to display a blue horizontal line and vertical line — the static guides. Notice that as you drag an object, its current position is displayed in a tooltip, as shown in Figure 3-15. After positioning an object, drag the static guides to match the position of the object. The guides stay put so you can align other objects along the same line. Click and hold the mouse button down on a static guide to display its exact position.

Position

Left: 1.61"
Top: 1.38"

Figure 3-15:
Positioning
static
guides.

Static guides

✦ **Snap to Grid:** When toggled on, this option causes objects to automatically align to an invisible grid as you drag them slowly. You can see this effect easier if you zoom in to 300% or more and slowly drag an object. When toggled on, as you drag an object it will move in small increments rather than smoothly. The Snap to Grid option is pretty subtle, but it's enough to save you time because your objects will line up to the grid automatically, and you don't have to give it much thought. Hold the ⌘ key down while dragging to override snap to grid.

✦ **Snap to Shape:** When Snap to Shape is turned on, take these steps:

  a. *Drag an object to a position that's close to being aligned with another object on the slide.*

  If Dynamic Guides are also on, the Dynamic Guides appear a little sooner than when Snap to Shape is turned off.

  b. *When you see a Dynamic Guide, you can let go of the mouse, and the object you're dragging aligns itself to the other object.*

  It might feel as if the Dynamic Guide is pulling the object you're dragging away from your control. The Snap to Shape option is subtle, but it could have just enough effect to make life easier when aligning shapes to each other.

Arranging in three dimensions

As you drag text and objects around on a slide, you become aware that each object is on its own layer, as if it were on a transparent sheet. The sheets are stacked on top of each other, but when viewed head-on, which is how people normally see things, the slide can look flat. If an object closer to the top has either some transparency or is without fill, the objects behind can be seen through the closer object. You can create entire 3-D landscapes using shapes, masks, pictures, movies, graphs, charts — virtually anything and everything you can do visually and with audio on a computer. Using animation effects, timings, and transitions, you can make some pretty amazing stuff!

Dynamic reordering

Say you have a slide and you put three or four pictures on it, and you also want some visible text, so you want your text on the top of the pile of pictures. But as you add pictures, the text ends up behind the pictures, and you can't even see the text box, much less select it. No problem! Click the Ribbon's Home tab, and in Format group, just click the Arrange button and choose Reorder Objects. (Refer to Figure 3-13.) PowerPoint displays each layer as a clear sheet, which you can drag. In our example, we dragged the text layer to the right to move it to the top (rightmost position) of the pile of layers, as shown in Figure 3-16. We can't imagine a simpler, more beautiful way to reorder objects. This has to be one of the best software inventions ever.

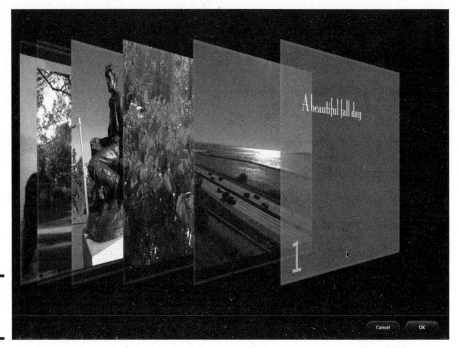

Figure 3-16:
Dynamic
reordering.

The second option on the Arrange button is Reorder Overlapping Objects, which detects which objects on your slide overlap each other and displays the Dynamic Reordering screen showing just those objects.

You can activate Dynamic Reordering even if you don't have the Ribbon's Home tab selected. Right-click a slide object and then choose Reorder Objects or Reorder Overlapping Objects from the contextual menu.

Reordering the old-fashioned way

Sure, you can still reorder the position of objects the old-fashioned way:

1. **Select an object.**

2. **Choose any of the following to display a pop-up menu:**

   • Click the Ribbon's Home tab, and in the Format group, click Arrange.

   • Right-click and choose Arrange.

   • Click the Arrange menu item on the menu bar.

3. **From the pop-up menu, choose one of the following:**

   • *Bring to Front:* Moves selected object to the top layer.

   • *Send to Back:* Moves selected object behind all other slide objects, but it's still in front of the background layer.

Applying a Quick Style

Because you're likely to spend quite a bit of time on the Home tab of the Ribbon, you'll probably find the Quick Styles button in Format group to be a very handy tool. Select anything that can be formatted (such as a picture, chart, graph, table, SmartArt, or WordArt) and then click the Quick Styles button to display a gallery of formatting options.

* *Bring Forward:* Moves the object one layer closer to the top.

* *Send Backward:* Moves the object one layer away from the top.

Aligning and distributing objects

You can access the Align or Distribute submenu in three ways:

✦ Click the Ribbon's Home tab, and in the Format group, click Arrange and choose Align or Distribute.

✦ Select an object and then click the Ribbon's Format Picture (or other object) tab. In the Arrange group, click Align and choose Align and then choose an option from the menu.

✦ Choose Arrange⇨Align or Distribute from the menu bar.

The trick to using these tools is that before you choose one of the tools, you must first choose one of these two options from the bottom of the menu:

✦ **Align to Slide:** The selected object or objects will be aligned with respect to the boundary of the slide area.

✦ **Align to Selected Objects:** Select two or more objects to align with respect to the relative positions of the objects on the slide.

The Distribute options require that you select two or more objects before you choose either Horizontally or Vertically.

Making and Formatting Tables

A table in PowerPoint is a much simpler affair than in Word or Excel. In PowerPoint, a table is formatted to look nice, but it can't have Word fields or Excel formulas. If you need a more powerful table in your slide, create the table in Word or Excel and then choose Insert⇨Object from the menu bar and select the Word document or Excel workbook to embed into your presentation.

Adding a table to a slide

You can add a table to a slide in several ways:

✦ **Choose Insert⇨Table:** Displays a small dialog where you specify how many rows and columns will be in your table.

✦ **In a content placeholder, click the Insert Table icon:** Displays a small dialog where you specify how many rows and columns will be in your table. The content placeholder is shown in the margin.

✦ **Click the Ribbon's Tables tab, and in the Table Options group, click New:** Drag the mouse cursor over a grid to choose how many rows and columns will be in your table, as shown in Figure 3-17.

Drag to select the number of rows and columns.

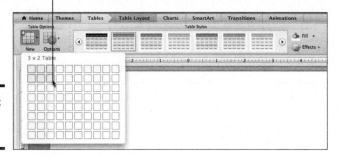

Figure 3-17:
Making a
new table.

Setting table options

After you've made a table, click anywhere in the table to select it to activate the Table Options group of the Ribbon's Tables tab. When you click the Options button, you can toggle different formatting on and off for rows and columns. The Total Row option applies only a different format to the bottom row — PowerPoint has no formulas or calculations. You may see check boxes instead of a menu if your screen is wide enough.

Applying a table style

The default blue table gets boring pretty fast. While your table is selected, visit the Tables Styles group on the Table Layout tab of the Ribbon to apply a new style. See Figure 3-18. Click the left and right scroll arrows at either end of the Table Style gallery or click the "sweet spot" at the bottom center to display all styles on a palette. If you want a completely plain table, choose Clear Table Style, which is also the first table in the Table Style gallery and on the Table Style palette.

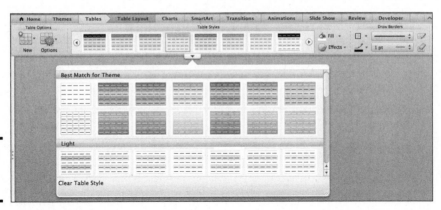

Figure 3-18:
Applying a
table style.

Applying direct table formatting

Select the table and then visit the Table Layout tab of the Ribbon to choose Fill, Effects, and border formats, as shown in Figure 3-19. (These tools are described in detail in Book I, Chapter 6.) You can add and delete rows and columns using the Draw and Erase tools. First, click anywhere in your table; then choose from the following:

+ **Draw:** When you click Draw, the cursor changes to a pencil. Draw lines within the selected table to make more rows, columns, and cells. The style of the line is determined by the Line Style and Line Weight pop-up menus to the left of the Draw button. Press the Escape key to return to a normal cursor.

+ **Erase:** Click Erase to turn the cursor into an eraser. Click row and column borders to remove the borders and merge cells. Press the Escape key to return to a normal cursor.

Figure 3-19:
You can
draw
borders in
a table.

But you've only scratched the surface! Notice that when you've selected a table or any table element, the Table Layout tab becomes available on the Ribbon, as shown in Figure 3-20. We examine each group in the following sections.

**Book IV
Chapter 3**

**Feeling at Home on
the Ribbon**

Figure 3-20:
Lay out a
table with
the Ribbon.

For even more precise formatting control, right-click your table and choose Format Table or Format Cell to display a dialog with more options.

View

Click into your table and then choose from the following options:

✦ **Select:** This button makes it easy to select specific elements in your table. Choose an option:

   • *Select Table:* Selects the entire table.

   • *Select Column:* Selects the entire column that has the cursor.

   • *Select Row:* Selects the entire row that has the cursor.

✦ **Gridlines:** Click this button to toggle gridlines on and off in your table. This doesn't affect cell border formatting, so you will most likely see these lines only if you've cleared the table of all formatting.

Rows & Columns

This Ribbon group makes it easy to control how many rows and columns your table has. Click into a table and then use these controls:

✦ **Rows and Columns:** Use the spinner controls to add or remove rows or columns from your table.

✦ **Above and Below:** Add a row above or below the cell containing the selection cursor.

✦ **Left and Right:** Add a column to the left or right of the cell containing the selection cursor.

✦ **Delete:** Delete selected columns, rows, or an entire table.

Cells

The Cells group is another way to merge and split cells. Select a cell or range of cells and then click either Merge or Split. The Distribute buttons make the rows of the selected cells or columns uniform in height or width.

Alignment

Align text within selected cells with the click of a button:

✦ **Left, Center, and Right Justify:** Justify the text within selected cells.

✦ **Top, Center, and Bottom Alignment:** Align the text within selected cells.

✦ **Direction:** Select cells, and then choose one of the options from the pop-up menu.

✦ **Margins:** Adjust the margins in your table.

Chapter 4: Adding Audio and Movies

In This Chapter

- ✔ Adding audio and movie content
- ✔ Preparing your audio
- ✔ Recording audio to a slide
- ✔ Preparing a movie
- ✔ Making movie adjustments
- ✔ Applying a movie style
- ✔ Minding cross-platform distribution issues

*R*ich media, also known broadly as *multimedia,* encompasses music, sounds, and movie clips. You can add these to your PowerPoint presentations, and you can even add your own voice narrations to individual slides. PowerPoint is a venerable program, but it's been keeping up with the times and PowerPoint 2011 knows the latest technologies. This chapter helps you incorporate multimedia content that can make your presentations interesting. We remind you that we covered media basics in Book I. In this chapter, we cover aspects of audio and movies unique to PowerPoint.

Adding an Audio Clip

You can easily add sounds and music to a slide. Choose either of two ways to activate the Insert Audio dialog:

- ✦ **From the Media Browser:** Use the Audio tab and drag from the browser into PowerPoint. The Media Browser is described extensively in Book I, Chapter 8.

- ✦ **From the menu bar:** Select one of the following three commands:

  - *Insert⇨Audio⇨From File:* When you select this option, the Choose Audio dialog appears. Navigate to a sound file or use Spotlight to search for a file. Choose Music from the OS X Places list in Finder to navigate to your iTunes library.

- *Insert⇨Audio⇨Media Browser:* Displays the Media Browser on the appropriate tab.

- *Insert⇨Audio⇨Record Audio:* We cover this option in the "Recording a sound directly onto a slide" section, later in this chapter.

In addition to adding a sound clip or music to a slide using the dialog, you can add a sound by dragging it onto a slide from Finder.

After you've inserted audio, you see a sound icon, as shown in Figure 4-1.

Previewing audio

While you're preparing your slide, you can preview the audio you added in Normal view. To preview audio, simply select the sound icon (shown in Figure 4-1) and then click the Play button underneath the sound icon. You can have fun with the sound icon in more ways:

Figure 4-1:
Previewing audio.

✦ **Change Picture:** Right-click the sound icon and choose Change Picture to display the Choose a Picture file dialog. Choose a small picture to replace the standard speaker icon. Make sure you have a valid reason to change the picture though; audiences do expect to see the familiar speaker icon to indicate a sound clip.

✦ **Play/Pause:** Click the Play button to start playing your audio. Click the button again to pause or to restart playing.

✦ **Scrub:** Drag the playhead left and right to reposition the playhead and play audio from any point. The precise time of playback is displayed.

✦ **Mute/Unmute Volume:** Click this button to toggle muting on or off. Mouse-over this button to display the volume slider, shown in the left margin.

Formatting audio

While the Audio icon is selected, take a peek at the Ribbon. There you can find the Format Audio tab, as shown in Figure 4-2. In the Preview group, click the Play/Pause button to start playing audio. Click the button again to pause or to restart playing.

Figure 4-2:
Formatting
audio.

Use the Audio Options group of the Format Audio tab of the Ribbon, shown in Figure 4-2, to set how your sound will behave when you run the presentation.

✦ **Start:** Choose among these options:

- *Automatically:* Your sound starts to play as soon as the slide plays during a presentation.

- *On Click:* This is the default. The sound plays when the sound icon is clicked while a slide show is running.

- *Play Across Slides:* The sound continues to play across successive slides until it ends or you quit the slide show.

✦ **Playback Options:** Choose among the following options:

- *Hide Icon During Show:* Use this option to prevent the sound icon from being visible when your presentation plays. This option can be used when your sound is set to start automatically, or using an animation setting, action setting, or macro to start playing the sound. Don't use this option with Start On Click because the icon won't be visible to be clicked!

- *Loop Until Stopped:* When combined with Play Across Slides, your presentation will have music or sound continuously.

- *Rewind After Playing:* When this option is selected, the audio will set itself to rewind position after playing. This means that if you get back to the slide that contains the audio, it will start playing from the beginning all over again.

You're not limited to playing sounds by using the standard icon. You can have a sound play when you click any type of object, such as a picture, clip art, SmartArt, or WordArt. (See Figure 4-3.) To make an object clickable for sound, follow these steps:

1. **Insert an object on your slide.**

2. **Right-click the object and select Action Settings from the contextual menu that appears.**

   The Action Settings dialog appears, as shown in Figure 4-3. Make sure the Mouse Click tab of this dialog is showing.

   For example, we added a picture of an old-fashioned alarm clock to a slide and right-clicked it.

**Book IV
Chapter 4**

**Adding Audio and
Movies**

3. **In the Play Sound section, click the pop-up menu and select one of the sounds from the list, or scroll down to the bottom and select Other Sound.**

   If you choose Other Sound, you're presented with the Choose a Sound dialog, which lets you navigate Finder to select a sound file.

   For this example, we just chose the Ring option from the list of PowerPoint's built-in sounds.

4. **Click OK to apply your action setting.**

Figure 4-3:
Using an action setting to play a sound when an object is clicked.

The Action Settings dialog in Figure 4-3 includes two tabs: Mouse Click and Mouse Over. The default setting is Mouse Click. If you want to change it so that the audio plays on your slide when you move the mouse over a picture or other object (so that you don't even have to click the picture), click the Mouse Over tab before selecting which sound to play. Otherwise, the steps to add an action setting are the same as the preceding steps.

Recording a sound directly onto a slide

In addition to the ability to record narrations for your slide show (see Chapter 8), you can record a sound onto a slide by following these steps:

1. **Click the Ribbon's Home tab, and in the Insert group, choose Media⇨ Record Audio to display the Record Sound dialog shown in Figure 4-4.**

Figure 4-4:
Recording a
sound.

2. **Choose a device from the Sound Input Device pop-up menu.**

   This menu displays input devices currently connected to your computer, such as an internal microphone. You add and remove devices in the Mac OS X Sound control panel.

3. **Thereafter, choose a source from the Input Source pop-up menu.**

   The reason why you need to go through second step is because some sound input devices may have more than one input source.

4. **To record a sound, click the Record button at the top of the dialog.**

5. **Click Stop or Pause when you're done and then click Play to preview your recording.**

6. **Type a name for your sound file in the Name text box.**

   The name can be used to help you when choosing animation settings and in VBA.

7. **When you're done recording your sound, click Save to produce a sound icon on your slide.**

If you need greater control over audio recordings for PowerPoint slides, check out GarageBand, a robust sound-editing application from Apple. With GarageBand, you can record your narrations straight into the program and save them as sound files, which you then insert into PowerPoint. Garage Band comes with many Macs. Look for GarageBand in your Applications folder, or purchase iLife at `http://audacity.sourceforge.net/download`.

Adding a Movie

You can easily add movies to a slide in the following ways:

✦ **From the Media Browser:** Use the Movies tab and drag from the browser into PowerPoint. The Media Browser is described extensively in Book I, Chapter 8.

✦ **From the menu bar:** Select one of the following commands:

- *Insert⇨Movie⇨Movie from File:* When you select this option, the Choose a Movie dialog appears. Navigate to a movie file or use Spotlight to search for a file.

- *Insert⇨Movie⇨Media Browser:* Displays the Media Browser on the Movies tab.

In addition to adding a movie to a slide using the Insert Movie dialog or Media Browser, you can add a movie by dragging it onto a slide from Finder.

Previewing a movie

Almost everything about movie clips has been radically improved in Office 2011. You can rejoice that linking and embedding problems have been solved because movies are now embedded, not linked, by default. Cross platform problems go away too, as Office 2010 for Windows at long last supports QuickTime and is finally compatible with Office 2011.

To preview a movie clip inserted on your slide, click the Play button on the movie placeholder, as shown in Figure 4-5. Movies can be formatted and customized in many ways. The restriction that movie always plays "on top" has also been removed! Now you treat movie as any other layer. You can now put text and other objects on top of a movie and animate these objects as your movie plays.

Figure 4-5:
Previewing
a movie.

You can control a movie in the following ways:

✦ **Play/Pause:** Click the Play button to start playing your video clip. Click the button again to pause, or to restart playing.

✦ **Scrub:** Drag the playhead left and right to reposition it and play the movie clip from any point. The precise time of playback is displayed (shown in Figure 4-5).

✦ **Mute/Unmute Volume:** Click this button to toggle muting on or off. Mouse over the button to display the volume slider.

✦ **Resize and Rotate:** Drag the handles to resize or rotate the movie. Your movie will play at the size and position you set regardless of its original size and aspect ratio.

Formatting a movie

While the Movie icon is selected, take a peek at the Ribbon. There you find a feast of new offerings. Click the Format Movie tab of the Ribbon, shown in Figure 4-6. In the Preview group, click Play to start playing your movie. Click the button again to pause, and click yet again to restart playing.

Figure 4-6:
Formatting
a movie.

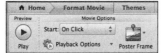

The Movie Options group of the Ribbon's Format Movie tab, shown in Figure 4-6, lets you set how your movie will behave as the presentation is running:

✦ **Start:** Choose one of these two options from this pop-up menu:

• *Automatically:* Your movie starts to play as soon as the slide plays during a presentation.

• *On Click:* This is the default. The movie plays when the movie place-holder is clicked while a slide show is running.

✦ **Playback Options:** Choose among the following options in this pop-up menu:

• *Play Full Screen:* Use this option so that when your movie plays during your presentation, the movie fills the entire screen.

• *Hide While Not Playing:* Use this option to prevent the movie place-holder from being visible when your presentation plays. This option can be used when your movie is set to start automatically or when using an animation setting, an action setting, or a macro to start play-ing the movie. Don't use this option with Start On Click because the movie placeholder won't be visible on the slide, so you can't click it!

- *Loop Until Stopped:* Your movie will loop continuously until you stop it, such as by moving to the next slide.

- *Rewind After Playing:* When selected, this option makes the movie file starts at the beginning each time it is clicked when the presentation is running. Otherwise, the poster frame of the movie ends up being the last frame of the movie.

For both movies and audio clips, you can turn off the media control bar (the semi-transparent playing controls that appear over any media while in slide show mode) by clicking the Slide Show tab of the Ribbon, and de-selecting the option called Show Media Controls.

✦ **Poster Frame:** The poster frame is the picture that you see in the movie placeholder. When you click the Poster Frame button in the Movie Options group on the Ribbon's Format Movie tab, you can choose from the following options:

- *Current Frame:* Stop the preview at any frame in the movie and choose this option to use the current frame as the poster frame.

- *Picture from File:* Displays the Choose a Picture dialog so you can choose any picture in Finder.

- *Reset:* Restores the default poster frame. It's the first frame in the movie file.

Making a movie play when moused over

The Action Settings dialog can be used to make a movie play when moused over when the slide show is running. To set this up, follow these steps:

1. **Insert a movie on a slide.**

2. **Right-click the movie placeholder and choose Action Settings from the contextual menu.**

   The Action Settings dialog appears. (Refer to Figure 4-3.)

3. **Click the Mouse Over tab.**

4. **Select Play from the Object action pop-up menu.**

5. **Click OK.**

You can record a movie on your Mac using the Photo Booth application that comes with Mac OS X.

Adjusting your movie

Have you ever wished you could make brightness, contrast, and other adjustments to a movie as easily as you could to a picture? PowerPoint has just granted your wish! Use the Format Movie tab's Adjust group, shown in Figure 4-7, to make these kinds of adjustments to your movie:

Figure 4-7:
Adjusting a
movie.

+ **Corrections:** Click to display a gallery of brightness and contrast options. Choose an option or choose Movie Corrections Options to display the Adjust Movie tab of the Format Movie dialog, shown in Figure 4-8.

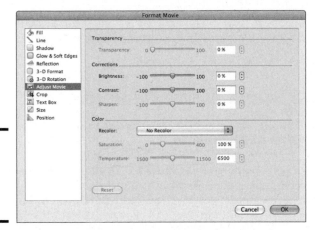

Figure 4-8:
Using the
Format
Movie
dialog.

**Book IV
Chapter 4**

Adding Audio and
Movies

+ **Color:** When clicked, displays a gallery of color tints you can apply to the movie. Select a tint or choose an option:

  • *More Colors:* Displays the Mac OS X color picker. Yes, you can choose any tint color you like from millions of colors.

  • *Movie Color Options:* Displays the Adjust Movie tab of the Format Movie dialog, shown in Figure 4-8.

+ **Crop:** Choose from the complete set of Crop and Mask options. They work the same for a movie as for a picture. These tools are discussed in Book I, Chapter 7.

+ **Reset:** Removes all adjustments you have made to the movie.

In the Format Movie dialog, you can fine-tune your settings. Figure 4-8 shows the Adjust Movie tab, where you can use sliders to adjust brightness and contrast; you can also recolor a movie from a menu containing a large number of preset colors, grayscale, and theme colors.

Applying a movie style

The Movie Format tab of the Ribbon has a Movie Styles group, shown in Figure 4-9, where you can apply wonderful borders, 3-D, reflection, glow styles, and shadow styles to your movie. Choose a style from the gallery, which you scroll by clicking the scroll button arrows at the left and right side of the gallery. Or, click the "sweet spot" at the bottom of the gallery to display a palette where you can choose from all styles at once.

A movie's line border behaves the same as any other shape's border. Line borders and effects controls are discussed in Book I, Chapter 6.

Figure 4-9:
Dressing up
your movie.

Dealing with Audio and Movie Odds and Ends

When you add audio and/or movies to a presentation, you need to keep the following odds and ends in mind:

✦ **Large file sizes:** When you use rich media, give some thought to file sizes if you're planning to distribute your presentation. Audio and movie files range from small to large. The larger the added content files, the larger your PowerPoint file becomes. For the record, it's difficult to send anything larger than 5 megabytes (5MB) via e-mail; to distribute 5MB and larger files, you need to use another option such as saving the file to SkyDrive, SharePoint, a CD/DVD, or a flash drive.

✦ **Movie compatibility:** PowerPoint on Mac doesn't actually play a movie. PowerPoint uses Apple's QuickTime as the helper application. Whatever plays in QuickTime plays in PowerPoint on the Mac. PowerPoint 2010 for Windows also supports QuickTime, but for older versions of PowerPoint for Windows, stick with Windows Media Video (.wmv).

✦ **Audio file formats (WMV):** QuickTime can understand WMV when you install a free program called Flip4Mac. Flip4Mac has other interesting capabilities that you might want if you plan to make a lot of cross-platform movie content, but at the very least, we suggest that you install the free player from this Microsoft Web site: http://www.microsoft.com/mac/downloads.

Chapter 5: Designing Masters, Slide Layouts, and Themes

In This Chapter

✓ **Customizing Slide Masters**

✓ **Making custom Slide Layouts**

✓ **Building an army of masters**

✓ **Customizing the Notes Master**

✓ **Making spiffy handouts**

✓ **Saving your own Themes**

Knowing what a theme and a Slide Master are can make you seem like a PowerPoint guru, as long as you follow the basics. With just a few hints from us, you can be in control of PowerPoint, using masters and themes in ways that make your friends look up to your PowerPoint skills.

A *master* is in charge. The idea behind a master is that you put text, adjust formatting, or add objects to the master, and the changes are instantly reflected throughout the entire presentation. PowerPoint handles these masters efficiently, so your presentation's file size doesn't grow proportionately, which is important when distributing your presentations.

In PowerPoint, you find several masters, each overlooking their respective domains (all of which we explain in this chapter). The neat part is that you're in charge of all PowerPoint's masters. They're here to do your bidding:

✦ **Slide Master:** Whatever text, formatting, or objects you apply to the Slide Master are instantly applied to the entire presentation and to the Slide Master's *slide layouts*. Using Slide Masters can save you a lot of time while you build presentations.

✦ **Slide Layout(s):** These masters let you build custom layouts for the content of your slides.

✦ **Notes Master:** Controls default formatting of Notes Page view.

✦ **Handout Master:** Formats layout for printed and PDF handouts.

Putting a Slide Master in Charge

In every presentation, one slide trumps the rest. It's called the *Slide Master*. You can see the Slide Master in any of the following ways:

✦ Choose View⇨Master⇨Slide Master from the menu bar.

✦ Press ⌘-Option-1.

✦ Click the Ribbon's Themes tab, and in the Master Views group, choose Edit Master⇨Slide Master.

You can tell which slide is the Slide Master because, as you can see in Figure 5-1, it's placed in a position of power in the upper-left corner, and it has a bigger thumbnail than the Slide Layouts, which fittingly appear below the Slide Master in the thumbnails pane.

The Slide Master has submasters called *Slide Layouts* that control various slide layouts (what else?).

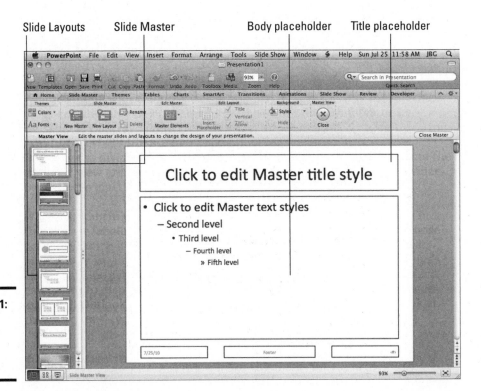

Figure 5-1: Turning on Slide Master view.

Getting Your Bearings in Slide Master View

Slide Master view is seemingly similar to Normal view in that all the regular formatting options are available. However, you can find differences if you look carefully. The Slides pane doesn't show the slides in your presentation, and there is no Outline pane co-joined to the Slides pane. (See Figure 5-1.) Instead, it shows the Slide Master at the top as a larger thumbnail, followed by smaller thumbnails that represent a master for each of the layouts that show up in the New Slide gallery on the Home tab of the Ribbon. Not surprisingly, each of these submasters is called a *Slide Layout.*

The Notes pane is absent from the Slide Master view because these aren't the actual slides you present — they're masters that influence those slides. Notes Page view has its own master, discussed in the section "Taking Note of Your Notes Master," later in this chapter.

When working with a Slide Master and its submasters, keep in mind the relationships between the slide layouts that you see in Normal view with the masters and layouts you see in Slide Master view. In particular, be aware of the following:

✦ Any change in the Slide Master affects each Slide Layout under it unless you format a specific Slide Layout differently. Changes in the Slide Master are also applied to the slides in your presentation.

✦ Any changes you make to an individual Slide Layout beneath a Slide Master doesn't affect the Slide Master. Changes made to a Slide Layout influence only slides in the presentation that are based on that particular layout.

Seeing how Slide Masters work

The following steps show how Slide Masters work by making changes to the Slide Master and watching how the layouts are affected:

1. **Access the PowerPoint Presentation Gallery by choosing File⇨New from Template from the menu bar.**

2. **Within the Presentation Gallery, choose Templates. In the Guided Methods heading, choose It Is All Too Much by Peter Walsh and then click the Choose button.**

   PowerPoint creates a new presentation with populated slides that opens in Normal view.

3. **Bring up the Slide Master view by choosing View⇨Master⇨Slide Master from the menu bar.**

   The Slide Master view displays along with the Slide Master tab of the Ribbon. (Refer to Figure 5-1.)

4. **On the Slide Master tab of the Ribbon, in the Background group, choose Styles.**

   The Background Styles gallery displays, as shown in Figure 5-2.

5. **Choose a style from the thumbnails shown in this gallery or apply a custom background format choosing the Format Background option, which brings up a dialog of the same name.**

   Your change is instantly incorporated into all the Slide Layouts, as well as the Slide Master slides.

6. **Click the big X in the Ribbon's Master View group to switch to Normal view.**

   Your slide show now has the new background.

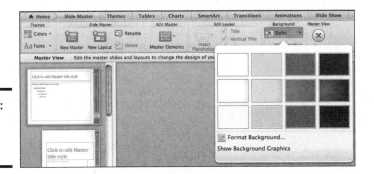

Figure 5-2:
Changing
a Slide
Master.

If you need to add a logo so that it appears on every slide in the presentation, you insert that logo in the Slide Master.

When you're working with Slide Master view, you can apply formatting, animation, add objects, and format objects just as you can in Normal view. Ribbon tabs and menus are active and are at your service in Slide Master view.

Right-click any Slide Layout or Slide Master in Slide Master view's left pane to present an amazing array of options, including options that let you add new layouts and rename existing layouts. Right-click in the main working area and see a different menu with even more options.

Looking at a new Ribbon tab

When you visit Slide Master view, a new Ribbon tab called the Slide Master (see Figure 5-3) appears, ready to get to work. When in Slide Master view, you can use options in the tab and other visible tabs of the Ribbon to add elements, apply formatting, and even add animations to your Slide Master and Slide Layouts.

Figure 5-3:
Making masters with the Slide Master tab of the Ribbon.

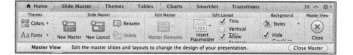

When working with a Slide Master, the Edit Master group is available and the Edit Layout group is disabled. When working with a Slide Layout, the Edit Layout group is enabled, and the Edit Master group is disabled.

Working with Slide Masters and Layouts

Use Slide Master view to add, remove, arrange, and format elements on your Slide Master and Slide Layouts. A Slide Master and each Slide Layout can be given its own name (right-click the respective thumbnails, and choose Rename Slide Master or Rename Layout).

Applying Theme Colors and Fonts

The Slide Master tab of the Ribbon (refer to Figure 5-3) begins with the Themes group. If you want your master or layout to follow a Theme Color or Font scheme, choose these options in the Themes group:

✦ **Colors:** Displays a pop-up menu listing all Theme Color sets.

✦ **Fonts:** Displays a pop-up menu of Theme Font sets.

You can apply direct formatting to objects by selecting them and then formatting them by means of options within the Ribbon tabs or conventional menus.

Adding a new set of masters

A presentation is not limited to a single Slide Master. To add a new Slide Master, click the New Master button in the Slide Master group on the Slide Master tab of the Ribbon. The new master appears with a default set of Slide Layouts beneath the default Slide Master. Scroll down the thumbnails pane to see this complete set of unformatted masters. If you format the new Slide Master, the formatting affects the new Slide Layouts, but not your other Slide Masters or their Slide Layouts.

To delete a Slide Master, select it and then press the Delete key or click the Delete button on the Slide Master group of the Ribbon. When you delete a Slide Master, you simultaneously delete all Slide Layouts associated with the master. Every presentation has at least one Slide Master, which you can't delete. So unless you have two or more Slide Masters available in a given presentation, forget all thoughts of deleting any solitary Slide Master!

Drag layouts and masters up and down in the left pane to reorder them.

Choosing Slide Master Elements

By default, a Slide Master has one each of the following elements (placeholders): Title, Date and Time, Footer, Slide Number, and Body (refer to Figure 5-1). The idea is that you select an element and then position and format it so that the formatting cascades to the master's Slide Layouts and any slides that use those layouts. In the Edit Master group of the Slide Master tab of the Ribbon, click the Master Elements button while viewing the Slide Master. You will see that the Master Elements are all on by default, and are grayed out because you would normally leave them on. These placeholders on a Master Slide are replicated when you add a new Slide Layout. You may decide you don't want a particular placeholder to appear on your Master Slide or new Slide Layouts. For example, if you don't want footers when you add a new Slide Layouts, select the footer on the Slide Master and then press the Delete key to remove the footer placeholder. Then, when you add a new Slide Layout, it doesn't have a footer.

If you delete a Master Element it will no longer be grayed out in the menu options. To restore a deleted slide element from a Slide Master, choose it from the pop-up menu you see when you click the Master Elements button in the Edit Masters group on the Slide Master tab of the Ribbon. (Refer to Figure 5-3.)

Don't click the Delete button in the Slide Master group of the Slide Master tab to delete a slide element — that button deletes the entire Slide Master or Slide Layout. Of course if you have just one Slide Master in your presentation, that button will be grayed out.

Adding and Arranging Slide Layouts

Adding a new Slide Layout is quite simple a task to perform. Follow these steps to get started:

1. **Make sure you are in Slide Master view.**

2. **Choose View⟶Master⟶Slide Master from the menu bar.**

3. **Click the Slide Master tab of the Ribbon, and within the Slide Master group, click the New Layout button.**

    PowerPoint places a new Slide Layout in the Slides pane.

Although the Slide Master is the big chief, you can arrange each of the built-in Slide Layouts independently. You should wait until you're finished formatting the Slide Master before you format any of the Slide Layouts for two reasons:

✦ The logical hierarchy is to first create a common look for all your slides and then make subtle differences in the Slide Layouts.

✦ When you format a Slide Layout so that it's different from its Slide Master, that particular layout, as well as slides in the presentation based on that particular layout, display the Slide Layout's different formatting. After you format a Slide Layout, you can get different results when you go back and reformat the Slide Master.

To add a new layout placeholder, click the Insert Placeholder button in the Edit Layout group on the Slide Master tab of the Ribbon to display a gallery. Choose one of the menu items and then drag a placeholder to establish the size and placement on the layout for your placeholder, as shown in Figure 5-4. Later, when using the layouts in Normal view, content expands to the size of a placeholder. In Slide Master view you can move, resize, and reposition these placeholders after you have them on your layout. Figure 5-4 shows how the various Slide Layout options can look on a slide. You can add any of these content placeholder types:

✦ **Content:** Makes a content placeholder for text and has six buttons, one for each kind of content.

✦ **Vertical Content:** Same as content, but sideways.

✦ **Text:** Makes a content placeholder for text, but has no buttons for other kinds of content.

Content placeholder   Vertical content placeholder

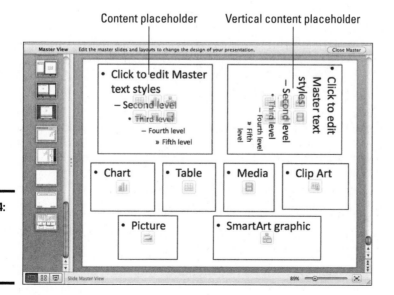

Figure 5-4:
Adding
layout
place-
holders.

✦ **Vertical Text:** Same as a text placeholder, but sideways.

✦ **Chart, Table, Media, ClipArt, Picture, or SmartArt:** Makes a single-purpose placeholder for the chosen media type.

Just like the Slide Master, you can format all the placeholders on a Slide Layout. Any slides that use that particular layout get the changes that you make to the Slide Layout. But remember that when you change formatting on a Slide Layout, you're breaking the link for the changed placeholder or element between that Slide Layout and the Slide Master. Subsequent changes to the Slide Master will not be passed on to a modified Slide Layout.

To delete a placeholder, select it and then press the Delete key.

Taking Note of Your Notes Master

If you read this chapter from the beginning, after seeing how powerful the Slide Masters and Slide Layouts are, the Notes Master may seem mundane by comparison. Here, you can select and format the layout of the Notes Page view.

Any changes you make on the Notes Master affect Notes Page view (View⇨ Notes Page) and the layout of printed Notes Pages, but do not affect the Notes portion of your slides in Normal view.

You can display the Notes master in the following ways:

✦ Choose View⇨Master⇨Notes Master from the menu bar.

✦ Press ⌘-Option-3.

✦ On the Ribbon's Themes tab, in the Master Views group, choose Edit Master⇨Notes Master.

In Notes Master view, you can select any element shown in Figure 5-5 and delete it by selecting the element and then pressing Delete on your keyboard. To restore a deleted element, select its check box in the Page Elements group on the Notes Master tab of the Ribbon. Drag elements to reposition, resize, and format them using the tools on the Ribbon or menus. You can add pictures (perhaps a logo), SmartArt, ClipArt, or other kind of object that you want to have displayed when in Notes view or when Notes are printed.

Notes can be either landscape or portrait, and this setting is independent from the rest of your slide show. On the Ribbon's Notes Master tab, in the Page Setup group, click Orientation to toggle landscape or portrait.

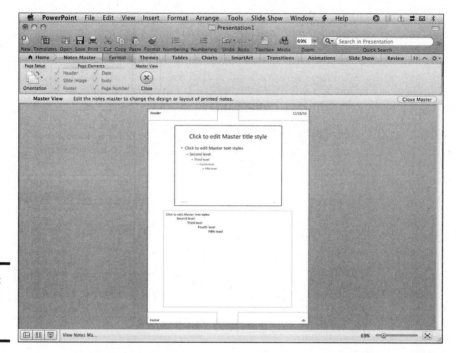

Figure 5-5:
Laying out
a Notes
Master.

Although you can make dramatic-looking Notes pages with Notes Master, remember that if you decide to print the notes, these formatting changes will apply. A dark background uses a lot of toner and ink quickly, and complicated formatting can slow your printer. On the other hand, fancy Notes pages are impressive when printed as handouts for a special audience.

Handling Handout Masters

The Handout Master affects only the background, header, and footer of slide shows when the slide shows are printed and the Handouts option is chosen in the Print dialog. Although you can click the positioning indicators on the Master toolbar, as shown in Figure 5-6, the positions can't be changed or resized. You can display the Handouts Master in the following ways:

✦ Choose View⇨Master⇨Handout Master from the menu bar.

✦ Press ⌘-Option-2.

✦ On the Ribbon's Themes tab, in the Master Views group, choose Edit Master⇨Handout Master.

You can format and reposition the handout header, footer, date and time, and slide number placeholders. You can also add objects, such as a picture.

Book IV
Chapter 5

Designing Masters, Slide Layouts, and Themes

Right-click and then choose Format⇨Background from the contextual menu to format the handout background.

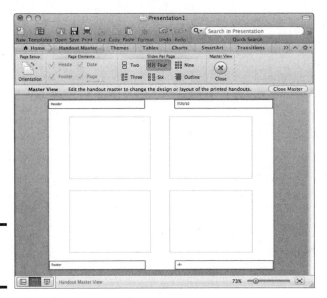

Figure 5-6:
Formatting
handouts.

Making a Theme

Whether you work alone or with a design team, PowerPoint has the tools you need to ensure consistency throughout your Office creations while making it easy to customize and save your work so you can re-use your best ideas again later. You can use built-in and downloaded themes, as well as make your own.

You should review the discussion about applying themes we have in Book I, Chapter 10 before reading this section. In this chapter, we show you how to make Theme Color and Theme Font sets, and complete Office Themes as well.

Making Theme Colors

As we mention in Book I, Chapter 10, a theme has 12 colors. Here we show you how to set those 12 Theme Colors, give your Theme Color set a name, and save it as a theme so you can apply it later. It's easy to customize a Theme Color set using the Create Theme Colors dialog. (See Figure 5-7.) Follow these steps:

1. **Open any PowerPoint presentation.**

2. **Choose Format⇨Theme Colors from the menu bar; alternatively, on the Ribbon's Themes tab, in the Theme Options group, choose Colors⇨Create Theme Colors.**

The Create Theme Colors dialog displays, as shown in Figure 5-7.

3. Double click a color square.

The Mac OS X color picker displays.

Alternatively, you can choose a color square and then click Change Color to display the color picker.

4. In the Mac OS X color picker, choose a color.

5. Repeat Steps 3 and 4 for each color you want to format.

Your Theme Colors set is ready to be saved.

6. In the Name field, type a name for your new theme.

Clicking Cancel closes the Create Theme Colors dialog without making a new theme.

7. Click Apply to All.

Your new Theme Color set is applied to your presentation and is automatically saved as a Theme Color set. You can find your new Theme Color set in the list of themes in the Colors pop-up menu (on the Ribbon's Themes tab, in the Theme Options group, click Colors) the next time you start PowerPoint. In addition, these customized color themes also show up in Word and Excel on your computer.

Before you can see a saved theme in the Themes tab of the Ribbon, you must quit and then re-open an Office application to refresh its Ribbon tabs.

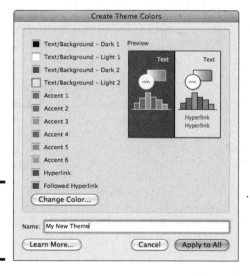

Figure 5-7:
Making
a Theme
Colors set.

Making Theme Fonts

We hate to say this, but simply put, you can't make a Theme Fonts set unless you code it yourself in a text editor and save it as XML, which is not complicated if you know some stuff about both XML and fonts. If you obtain a Theme Fonts set made in PowerPoint for Windows, you can use it if you put it into the Theme Fonts folder:

```
Hard Drive/Users/UserName/Library/Application Support/
Microsoft/Office/User Templates/My Themes/Theme Fonts
```

Theme Fonts sets put into this folder appear in the Custom group of the Fonts button of the Theme Options group of the Theme tab of the Ribbon in PowerPoint.

Use black and white for the first two colors and then use alternating light and dark colors for the third and fourth colors in the Create Theme Colors dialog. Contrasting colors should be used so that people with impaired vision can discern text from the background. Using close shades of a color for text and background may be trendy, but this is unreadable for many people. Using equal color values for red and green, or blue and yellow is also a bad idea, as colorblind people can't discern any difference within these color pairings.

Theme Colors are stored as XML files in this directory:

```
Hard Drive/Users/UserName/Library/Application Support/
Microsoft/Office/User Templates/My Themes/Theme Colors
```

Making an Office Theme

You can save Office Themes in Word, Excel, and PowerPoint. In Word and Excel, an Office Theme has Theme Colors and Theme Font information. In PowerPoint, your theme will have almost as much information as a template. An Office theme saved from PowerPoint includes Slide Masters and Layouts (including the content and formatting on both kinds of masters), and section information. By contrast, a PowerPoint template saves everything that a theme does plus the content of all your slides, custom shows, macros, and settings. Office themes have the file suffix .thmx and are stored in this folder:

```
Hard Drive/Users/UserName/Library/Application Support/
Microsoft/Office/User Templates/My Themes/
```

Using professional color tools

You can choose a color based on what's pleasing to your eyes, but everyone's eyes interpret color a little differently. Colors look different on each monitor and in various lighting conditions. If your needs require precise color control in a commercial or artistic environment, your Mac is up to the task. You can calibrate your Mac's monitor to known color values using special calibration tools that measure your monitor's output so you can adjust your Mac's video card. We suggest you start your exploration into color management at the Pantone Web site at www.pantone.com.

Office Themes in the My Themes folder are available for use by Word, Excel, and PowerPoint, appearing in the Custom section of Theme galleries and palettes on the Ribbon. Your saved themes can be applied in the PowerPoint Presentation Gallery, as well. Do understand that themes saved from within Word, Excel, or PowerPoint are available to all these Office applications on your computer.

When you've finished customizing a presentation to the point where you're ready to save it as a theme, do so on the Ribbon's Themes tab by clicking the Save Theme button and choosing Save Theme from the pop-up menu. PowerPoint automatically takes you to the My Themes folder. All you have to do is give your theme a name and then click the Save button.

To delete any theme, drag it to the trash in Finder.

In your Application/Utilities folder, you can find the Digital Color Meter application. Use the Digital Color meter application to determine the color values for pixels being displayed on your screen. Then use these values when you specify a color in the Mac OS X color picker.

Themes can be applied only to standard open XML file formats such as DOCX, XLSX, and PPTX. If you open an older DOC, XLS, or PPT file, your presentation will be in Compatibility Mode, where you can't apply a theme. You must convert your document to the current XML format if you want to use themes. To upgrade your file, choose File➪Save As and choose a current XML file format. If you're starting with a standard open XML format and then save back to an old format, applied theme formatting is likely to look substantially different when opened in an old Office version.

**Book IV
Chapter 5**

Designing Masters, Slide Layouts, and Themes

Chapter 6: Applying Animation

In This Chapter

✔ **Working with the Animations tab of the Ribbon**

✔ **Choosing animation options**

✔ **Animating text**

✔ **Animating SmartArt**

✔ **Automating sound and movie animation**

✔ **Playing audio through many slides**

✔ **Animating a chart**

*H*ave you ever experienced *death by PowerPoint?* Chances are good that you have. If you've ever sat through a presentation where every slide had 20 bullets of text, no movement, and the speaker read aloud every single word on the slide, you can claim to be a victim. Likewise, if you've seen a presentation that had every mesmerizing transition and swooshing animation possible, making you dizzy, you can also claim to be a victim. Both extremes are deadly to presenters and audiences.

There's no reason to use presentation software to simply display text, especially if each slide has oodles of text. If text is all you have, do your audience a favor and consider distributing it as a Word document or PDF file. Your audience will conclude that you're reading to them if your slides are mostly text.

Many presenters work with a 10-20-30 rule, propounded by Guy Kawasaki, which calls for 10 slides to be presented in 20 minutes with text that's at least 30 points in size. This rule and the 7 x 7 rule we mention in Chapter 3 of this minibook seem reasonable to us — and hopefully to you, as well.

PowerPoint's role is to help you present rich media content that complements the points you make while you give your presentation. Animation and transitions help your presentation flow, just like they do in movies and television programs. In this chapter, we explore how animation plays an expository role. (See Book IV, Chapter 1 for more information on transition effects.)

Applying an Animation Effect

Here's the general procedure to make something move in PowerPoint:

1. Select an object on a slide. This includes text, pictures, shapes, or anything that can be selected on the slide in Normal view.

2. Choose an animation effect on the Animations tab of the Ribbon.

3. Choose options for the applied animation effect on the Animations tab of the Ribbon or on the Custom Animations tab of the Toolbox.

Each effect offers different customization options depending upon the kind of object you're working with. You can format bulleted lists to come in as individual lines, letters, or all at once. You can animate charts by series or category.

You can apply more than one animation effect to a given object. You can apply effects to some or all objects on a slide. You can choose one object or you can select multiple objects and apply an effect to them. You control the speed of each effect and the sequence in which effects are played. Change the order of the entrance, emphasis, and exit of slide objects easily in Normal view or with the Toolbox. You can add animation while working in Slide Master view, as well.

The PowerPoint 2011 animation interface is by far the most sophisticated and powerful ever offered for PowerPoint on the Mac, yet it simplifies your work and is intuitive. It took us almost no time to adapt from the old way of animating to the new way. We hope to share our good experiences with you.

 We discovered that we were most satisfied when we combined using the Animations tab of the Ribbon with the Custom Animations tab of the Toolbox. Both are highly interactive and context sensitive, responding immediately based on what is currently selected. Sometimes we like using the Ribbon. Sometimes we like to use the Toolbox. Many of the same controls are on the Ribbon and in the Toolbox. PowerPoint's interface gives you a lot of flexibility, so experiment with it as you go and use whatever feels most comfortable.

 To access the Custom Animations tab of the Toolbox, choose View➪ Toolbox/Custom Animation from the menu bar.

Bringing the Animations Tab of the Ribbon to Life

When working in Normal view, simply select any object and then click the Animations tab of the Ribbon. The Animations tab knows what kind of object is currently selected, and it offers animation effects appropriate to that particular kind of object. The galleries on the Ribbon are in four main groups, as shown in Figure 6-1:

✦ **Entrance Effects:** Use entrance effects to bring objects into the slide while the show is running. These effect buttons are colored green.

✦ **Emphasis Effects:** During a show, emphasis effects animate objects that are already visible on your slide. These effect buttons are amber in color.

✦ **Exit Effects:** Exit effects make objects disappear from the slide while the show is playing. Exit effect option buttons are red.

✦ **Motion Path:** Your object follows a path across the screen. A line in Normal view represents the path, but the path line is invisible while the slide show plays.

Figure 6-1:
The
Animations
tab.

The Entrance, Emphasis, and Exit galleries work the same way as other Office galleries. You can click the scroll buttons at each end of the gallery, or click the sweet spot near the bottom-middle to display a gallery showing all options.

Click the Animations tab of the Ribbon, and in the Preview group, click Play to see again how your animation will look when the slide show runs. Click this button whenever you want to see how your slide will play with current animations and their settings.

Choosing Animation Options

After you apply an animation to an object on your slide, you can use the Animation Options group on the Animations tab, shown in Figure 6-2. Each effect comes with its own collection of options from which to choose. Animation Options can't be applied until you have applied at least one animation, be it either entrance, emphasis, exit, or Motion Path.

Figure 6-2:
Finding
Animation
Options.

Each effect comes with a collection of options that you can use to customize the effect's animation. After you've applied an animation effect, you can adjust its animation options.

Activating animation options

To apply animation effect options, you can use the Ribbon or the Toolbox.

To use the Ribbon to apply an animation effect, follow these steps:

1. **Click the Animations tab of the Ribbon.**

2. **Click a number associated with an animation (this is typically on the slide itself) or select the line of a motion path animation.**

   On the Animations tab of the Ribbon, you find a group called Animation Options.

3. **In the Animation Options group, you can choose individual effect options, change the start event (we explain this later in this chapter), and change the duration of the animation effects in seconds.**

To use the Toolbox to apply an animation effect, follow these steps:

1. **Click Toolbox on the Standard toolbar.**

2. **Select the Custom Animation tab in the Toolbox.**

3. **Select an animation from the list in the Toolbox.**

4. **Click disclosure triangles at the bottom of the Toolbox to display more options.**

   Using the Toolbox lets you set effect options without having to switch to the Animations tab of the Ribbon. Even when you're using the Animations tab of the Ribbon to set effect options, you may find the Toolbox to be a more convenient place to select animations in the first place.

Choosing Start options

All effects have these same three Start options, sometimes referred to as *animation events* because they determine when an effect will start playing:

✦ **On Click:** When chosen, PowerPoint waits for you to click the mouse button before starting the animation when the slide show is running. On Click is the default setting when you add a new animation to a slide.

✦ **With Previous:** When With Previous is chosen, the animation plays simultaneously with the previous animation in the list in the Animation Order section of the Custom Animation tab of the Toolbox, or as indicated with numbers in Normal view (look ahead to Figure 6-3) when the Animations tab of the Ribbon has been chosen.

✦ **After Previous:** This option tells PowerPoint to wait until the previous animation has completed before automatically starting the selected animation.

You can chain many animations together so that they play all at the same time. If you want all the animations to play without having to click the mouse, the first animation in the list should be With Previous or After Previous.

As you can see, the process of applying animation effect options is simple and intuitive. In the remainder of this chapter, we go through examples to illustrate how to apply animations and to set animation options.

Animating a Text Placeholder

One of the easiest ways to add interest to your slides is by animating your text placeholders. This method can work well because you can sequentially build one bullet after the other and the speaker can focus on the content that animated the last.

Of course, you can overdo this and wind up with a dizzying roller coaster ride instead of a presentation, so be judicious when applying animation effects.

Setting things up

You need a slide with a text placeholder that has some bulleted text in it. Use one of your own presentations or follow along with these steps to open a built-in presentation:

Templates

1. **In PowerPoint, click the New From Template button on the Standard Toolbar.**

   The PowerPoint Presentation Gallery displays.

2. **In the pane on the left, choose Templates➪Presentations.**

   The collection of built-in presentations displays.

3. **Click Project Status Report.**

   An 11-slide presentation opens in Normal view. This presentation was saved with the Slides pane larger than the work pane, which is a bit unusual — but you can drag and resize the panes! If the presentation you opened has only one slide, you opened the Project Status Report presentation *theme* instead of the similarly named *presentation*.

4. **In the Project Status Report presentation, select Slide 3 (Current Status).**

Slide 3 has a text placeholder with two bullet levels of text that doesn't have animation. In the following section, you add an animation to the text.

Applying an Entrance effect

When you have a placeholder with bulleted text to work with, you can apply an Entrance effect to the placeholder:

1. **Select a text placeholder containing bulleted text.**

In the Project Status Report presentation example, choose the placeholder (don't select individual text; just click the edge of the placeholder) that starts with "What progress has been made. . . ."

2. **Click the Animations tab of the Ribbon.**

3. **In the Entrance Effects group, click an effect.**

PowerPoint instantly displays a preview of the effect. Experiment by choosing some other effects. We chose the Rise Up Entrance effect within the Moderate category for our example shown in Figure 6-3.

Congratulations! You've successfully added an animation effect. Notice that PowerPoint puts a number to the left of each bullet in the placeholder, as shown in Figure 6-3. The numbers indicate the order in which the text will be animated. As you can see, when the Rise Up effect plays the text appears in two groups, numbered 1 and 2 in the figure. The numbers you see here show how many times you have to click to play all the animations on a slide; for this example, you have to click twice.

Click the Play button on the Animations tab of the Ribbon to see a preview of any animation you just added.

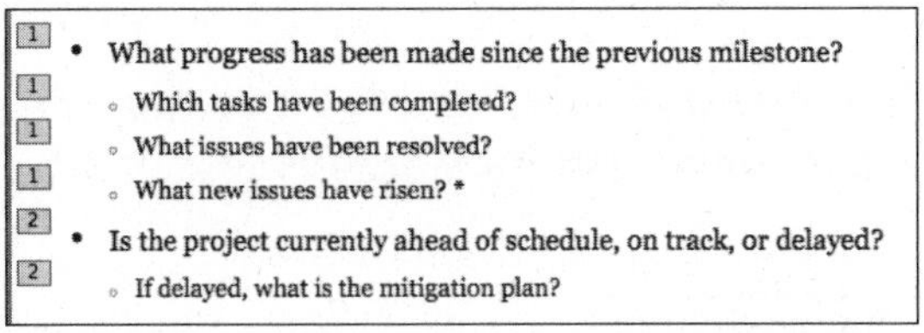

Figure 6-3:
Applying
a text
Entrance
effect.

> 1 • What progress has been made since the previous milestone?
> 1 ○ Which tasks have been completed?
> 1 ○ What issues have been resolved?
> 1 ○ What new issues have risen? *
> 2 • Is the project currently ahead of schedule, on track, or delayed?
> 2 ○ If delayed, what is the mitigation plan?

Choosing Text Effect animation options

As we mention earlier, effect options for animation can be applied using the Ribbon, the Toolbox, or a combination of these two features. We show you how to use both sets of tools as we continue with this example. First, we show how to set effect options using the Ribbon, followed by setting effect options using the Toolbox. When you're working on your own, you can freely use the Ribbon and the Toolbox in any combination.

Here we're continuing with the Project Status Report presentation from the preceding section. We've animated a text placeholder containing bulleted text using the Rise Up entrance effect.

Using the Ribbon's Animation Options group

Refer to Figure 6-2, which shows the Animation Options group on the Animations tab of the Ribbon as you go through the many options that can be applied to a text animation:

1. **Select any animation order number to the left of an animation to activate the Animation Options group on the Ribbon.**

2. **Click Effect Options.**

   A pop-up menu displays with the following options. Choose each of these options and watch how the animation changes:

   - *As One Object:* Treats the entire text placeholder as a single object. When the animation completes, there's just one animation step number displayed.

   - *All at Once:* The effect plays just like As One Object, but when the animation completes, each bullet gets its own animation step number, which you can reorder in the Toolbox.

   - *By Paragraph:* This is the default animation for Rise Up. This is a bit confusing, because it really means the animation is grouped by first level bullets, not by individual paragraph. However, each bullet (remember every paragraph is a bullet) gets its own animation step number, which you can reorder in the Toolbox.

3. **From the Start pop-up menu, choose On Click, With Previous, or After Previous, as described earlier in this chapter in the section "Choosing Start options."**

4. **Use the Duration spinner control to set the duration of the effect by setting the number of seconds it will play.**

Using the Toolbox to set Animation Options

All the effect option settings on the Ribbon described in the preceding section are available in the Toolbox, but the Toolbox has additional settings. The following steps explore what's in the toolbox for the Rise Up text animation:

1. **Select the bulleted text placeholder.**

   Our example has the Rise Up effect with the By Paragraph effect option.

2. **Display the Toolbox by clicking Reorder on the Animation Options group of the Animations tab of the Ribbon, or by clicking Toolbox on the Standard toolbar.**

3. **Select the animation you want to tweak, and then click all the disclosure triangles in the Toolbox.**

   This exposes Animation Order, Effect Options, Timing, and Text Animation groups in the Toolbox.

   Your Toolbox should look like Figure 6-4.

Figure 6-4:
Applying
animation
effect
options.

The Animation Order group of the Toolbox lists every animation on the current slide. Animations play starting with the animation at the top of the list. Each animation has its own Start setting, which is relative to the animation ahead of it in the list.

5. **To change the order in which animations play, select an animation and click an up or down arrow.**

   Each click moves the selected animations one step higher or lower in the animation sequence.

   Hold Shift to select a contiguous group of animations. Hold ⌘ and click animations in the list to select them individually.

   Clicking the X button deletes the selected animation (but not the associated object) from the animation sequence on the slide.

6. **In the Effect Options section of the Toolbox, choose from the following options (refer to Figure 6-4) in the After Animation pop-up menu:**

   • *A Theme Color:* After the animation plays, the text turns the color you choose.

   • *More Colors:* Displays the Mac OS X color picker. After the animation plays, the text turns the color you choose.

   • *Don't Dim:* This is the default. The text doesn't change after the animation plays.

   • *Hide after Animation:* After the animation plays, the text disappears from the slide.

   • *Hide on Next Animation:* After the animation plays, the text waits for the next animation in the sequence to be activated. Upon activation of the next animation, the text disappears.

7. **(Optional) Select a sound to play with the animation from the Sound pop-up menu.**

   You can have a sound play as part of the animation. If you scroll to the bottom of the pop-up menu and choose Other Sound, the Choose a Sound dialog displays, and you can choose any sound in Finder to play with your text animation.

   Adding sound can make your presentation distracting unless you have a specific reason to add sound in the first place.

8. **Adjust the timing of the Rise Up text effect by selecting from the options in the Timing section (refer to Figure 6-4):**

   • *Start:* Choose from On Click, With Previous, and After Previous.

   • *Speed:* Choose from predetermined intervals. For greater control, use the Duration setting on the Ribbon.

   • *Delay:* Use the spinner control to set the number of seconds to wait before the animation begins to play.

   • *Repeat:* Choose how many times you want the animation to repeat.

   • *Rewind When Done Playing:* Choose this option if you want the animation to start over when the slide containing the animation is shown again.

**Book IV
Chapter 6**

Applying Animation

9. **To apply fancier text animations, choose from the options in the Text Animations section:**

   - *Animate Text:* In this pop-up menu, choose from All at Once (all text that has the same animation number comes in at the same time), By Word (each word enters in succession), and By Letter (letters appear to flow into place).

   - *Group Text:* Choose how groups will play in sequence from this pop-up menu. Your options are As One Object (the entire place-holder is treated as a single entity), All Paragraphs at Once (the entire placeholder comes in at once, but each paragraph gets its own number so that you can choose individual paragraphs and then set different animation options for each paragraph), and By Bullet Level (choose a bullet level for the settings you've chosen).

More step-by-step examples can be found in the PowerPoint Presentation Gallery, accessed by choosing File⇨New From Template. Search for the word *Text* and then open the Animated Text Effects for PowerPoint Slides template. Some of the examples were made with only a Windows audience in mind. When an example says to use Ctrl-A, use ⌘-A instead. Also some templates are sourced from Microsoft's online collection, so you need to be connected to access the template in PowerPoint!

Animating a SmartArt Graphic

Sometimes it is desirable and appropriate to use a much more active visual animation. For example, you can create a simple game on a slide by animating a wheel that spins.

Setting things up

For this example, we make a circular SmartArt graphic so we can spin it:

1. **Open a new, blank presentation in PowerPoint.**

2. **Click the Ribbon's Home tab, and in the Layout group, click Blank.**

   A completely blank work area is now available.

3. **Click the Ribbon's SmartArt tab, and in the Cycle group, click Basic Cycle.**

   Basic Cycle is the first SmartArt in the Cycle gallery.

4. **Enter a word or number in each circle, as shown in Figure 6-5.**

   Your SmartArt is now ready to be animated.

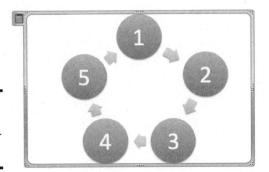

Figure 6-5:
Preparing
SmartArt for
animation.

Applying an Emphasis effect

Now you can take your SmartArt graphic out for a spin!

1. **Make sure the SmartArt placeholder is selected, as shown in Figure 6-5. Don't select an individual SmartArt shape.**

2. **Click the Ribbon's Animations tab, and in the Emphasis Effect group, click Spin.**

   The entire SmartArt spins. Observe that the Text pane goes away and the order animation number, as shown in the left margin, replaces the Text Pane button. That was easy, wasn't it?

Choosing SmartArt animation options

You can set animation options using the Ribbon, the Toolbox, or any combination of these tools.

Using the Ribbon's Animation Options group

Use the Ribbon to control the animation as follows:

1. **First click the Animations tab of the Ribbon. Then select the animation number by clicking the number visible next to an animated object on the slide.**

   The Animation Options group on the Animations tab of the Ribbon activates.

2. **From the Effect Options pop-up menu, choose one or more options. (See Figure 6-6.)**

   The pop-up menu is divided into Direction, Amount, and Sequence sections. You can select options from each group.

   This is fun. Some people get paid to do this, would you believe it?

Figure 6-6:
Spinning
SmartArt.

Using the Toolbox to set animation options

Use the Toolbox to control the animation as follows:

1. **Select the SmartArt object.**

   Our example has the Spin emphasis effect option.

2. **Display the Toolbox by clicking Reorder on the Animations Options group of the Animations tab or by clicking Toolbox on the Standard toolbar.**

3. **In the Animation Order section of the Toolbox, choose an animation step to enable the additional Toolbox sections. Click all the disclosure triangles.**

   This exposes Animation Order, Effect Options, Timing, and Text Animation groups in the Toolbox.

   Your Toolbox should look like ours, as shown in Figure 6-7. While the Toolbox looks similar to the Text Animation options shown in Figure 6-4, notice how many different options are available for SmartArt animation.

   To avoid duplication, we refer you to the Text Animation effect options described earlier in this chapter in the "Using the Toolbox to set animation options" section for explanations of options that are identical to those found in Figure 6-7.

4. **In the Effect Options section, adjust the following options:**

   • *Property:* Displays a pop-up menu that offers the number of spins: Quarter Spin, Half Spin, Full Spin, or Two Spins. (The same options are available in the Effect Options pop-up menu on the Ribbon's Animations tab.)

   • *Smooth Start:* Select this check box to have the effect accelerate up to full speed when it starts. Otherwise, the effect plays at a constant speed.

   • *Smooth End:* Select this check box to have the effect decelerate to a stop. Otherwise, the effect plays and then stops abruptly.

Figure 6-7:
Choosing
SmartArt
animation
options.

5. **From the Group Graphic pop-up menu (located at the bottom of the Toolbox) choose one of the following:**

- *As One Object:* This is the default setting.

- *All At Once:* Gives each component of the SmartArt object the same animation order number. It looks like As One Object when you play the animation, but you can select any component and give it its own animation settings.

- *One by One:* Gives each component of the SmartArt object an animation number that is grouped by the visual aspects of the diagram.

Access the PowerPoint Presentation Gallery by choosing File⇨New from Template. Then search for the term *SmartArt*. In addition to SmartArt themes, you can find two presentations with additional examples: Animated Hierarchy and Process Graphics with SmartArt and Training Presentation with SmartArt graphics. Although these presentations are for Office for Windows, most of the examples and explanations also apply to Office 2011.

**Book IV
Chapter 6**

Applying Animation

You can enable macros for Training Presentation, but as the notification tells you, Active-X controls won't work.

Animating an Audio Clip or a Movie

Including media in your animation sequence is a great idea. In PowerPoint 2011, you're no longer restricted to having movies play on top. Movies now behave nicely in their own layer and can be animated just like any other object. Movies can even overlap and follow motion paths as they play.

Just remember that as you add animations while a movie plays, a more powerful graphics card and more processing power might be required to keep things playing smoothly. Playing high-definition movies simultaneously requires a lot of computing power!

As with other animation effects, you can use the Ribbon and the Toolbox independently or together.

Inserting media, and controlling it

Media objects such as movies have some different animation effects. Although these are event-triggered actions such as play, pause, stop, and so on, PowerPoint still includes these options within the Animations tab of the Ribbon.

For this example, we insert a movie and then give it an animation effect in the next section:

1. **Open a new, blank presentation in PowerPoint.**

2. **Click the Ribbon's Home tab, and in the Layout group, click Title and Content.**

   Your slide now has a title and a content placeholder.

3. **On the Standard toolbar, click the Media button.**

   The Media Browser displays.

4. **Click the Movies tab on the Media Browser.**

   Your iMovie library displays.

5. **Drag a movie from the Media Browser into the Content placeholder.**

   Your movie is in place, and you can now animate it with event-triggered actions.

Automating media play with an Emphasis effect

When you select a media object on your slide, the Animations tab's Emphasis Effects group changes (see Figure 6-8) to allow you to control your audio or movie using an animation effect sequence, just as if you were controlling the playback using Play, Pause, and Stop controls.

Figure 6-8:
Controlling media with animation effects.

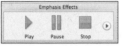

These media effects work with both movies and audio clips. To apply one of the media effect options, take these steps:

1. **Select the audio or movie object on your slide.**

2. **In the Emphasis Effects group, click Play, Pause, or Stop.**

   The chosen control is now part of the animation sequence.

When setting the duration of an audio or movie object, the Auto setting plays an audio or movie effect to completion. In the case of an audio or movie effect, setting the duration longer than the actual playback time needed is the same as choosing Auto.

Playing audio over more than one slide

The default is that your audio or movie will finish playing before you can advance to the next slide in your presentation. If you advance to the next slide before an audio object has finished, the media stops playing, and the next slide displays. You can tell PowerPoint to play audio (but not a movie) continuously over more than one slide. Here's how (refer to Figure 6-9):

1. **Select the audio object on your slide.**

2. **In the Emphasis Effects group on the Animations tab of the Ribbon, click Play.**

   The selected audio is now part of the animation sequence.

3. **Select the audio in the Animation Order list of the Custom Animation tab of the Toolbox.**

   If you have more than one animation on the slide, click arrow keys to make the audio the first animation on the slide.

4. **(Optional) In the Timing section of the Toolbox, set timing options.**

   Select options from the Start and Repeat pop-up menus as desired.

5. **In the Media Options section of the Toolbox, select the Stop Playing After # Slides radio button.**

6. **In the After # Slide text box, enter the number of slides through which you want the selected audio to play.**

   If you want to set it so the audio continues to play through to the end of the slide show, enter **999**.

Alternatively, to play an audio object continuously through the presentation, select the sound clip and then click the Format Audio tab of the Ribbon. In the Audio Options group, select Play Across Slides from the Start pop-up menu.

Figure 6-9:
Playing
audio over
many slides.

Animating a Chart

Animating your chart adds interest and helps tell the story of your data. The Widescreen Presentation you can find in the PowerPoint Presentation Gallery has a chart. You won't believe how easily you can animate a chart in PowerPoint for Mac. The chart at hand is a bar chart, and we think the Float In animation would be a good one for this type of chart. Follow these steps to add animation to a chart:

1. **In PowerPoint, click the Templates button on the Standard toolbar.**

   The PowerPoint Presentation Gallery displays.

Pulling triggers

PowerPoint for Windows includes an animation feature called Triggers, which allows you to click objects while a presentation is running to make a specific animation occur on the slide. PowerPoint for Mac doesn't have this feature.

The Mac version ignores triggers if they're in a presentation created in Windows. (Or, to put it another way, triggers don't fire in PowerPoint for Mac.)

2. **In the pane on the left, choose Templates⇨Presentations.**

   The collection of built-in presentations displays.

3. **Click Widescreen Presentation.**

   The Widescreen Presentation opens in Normal view.

4. **Go to Slide 4 and select the chart by clicking its border.**

5. **On the Ribbon's Animations tab, in the Entrance Effects group, click Float In (within the Moderate section).**

   Of course, you can try other animation effects to see how they work.

6. **Select the number of the animation next to the chart to activate the Effect Options. Then click the Ribbon's Animations tab, and in the Animation Options group, click Effect Options.**

   Try each of the various effect options and then watch the magic happen!

Moving an Object along a Path

When done artfully, the effect of moving an object along a path can add drama, change the mood, and draw attention to selected objects on your slide. As explained earlier in this chapter, you can select an object and then have it follow a path that is represented by a line in Normal view, but the line is invisible while the presentation is playing. You can draw your own lines or choose from a wide selection of built-in lines and effect options.

When you click the Motion Paths button on the Animations tab of the Ribbon, shown in Figure 6-10, you see a gallery of motion paths. Motion paths come in three categories:

✦ **Custom:** These are line drawing tools so that you can draw a path for the object to follow.

✦ **Basic:** Paths that follow simple shapes.

✦ **Complex:** Paths that follow intricate shapes.

**Book IV
Chapter 6**

Applying Animation

To make it easier to understand, we show two examples. The first example shows how to use the built-in Basic and Complex paths. The second example shows how to draw a Custom path for your object to follow.

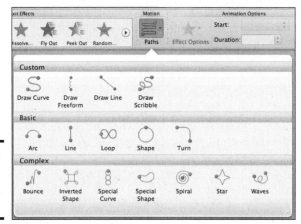

Figure 6-10:
Choosing
a path to
follow.

Inserting a shape

For our two examples, we start with a shape, although any kind of object can follow a path:

1. **Open a new, blank presentation in PowerPoint.**

2. **Click the Ribbon's Home tab, and in the Slides group, choose Layout⇨ Blank.**

A completely blank work area is now available.

3. **Click the Ribbon's Insert tab, and in the Shape group, click Rectangles.**

Choose any Rectangle on the submenu.

4. **Drag the mouse on the slide area to make a small rectangle.**

Your rectangle shape is now ready to be animated. For the following figures, we formatted the shape to have no fill to make it easier to see the motion path lines.

Applying a basic or complex motion path

As with other animations, the general procedure for applying a motion path is quite simple:

1. **Select an object.**

Any kind of object can follow a path.

2. **Click the Ribbon's Animations tab, and in the Motion group, click Paths.**

   The Motion Paths gallery displays. (Refer to Figure 6-10.)

3. **Choose a Basic or Complex motion path.**

   The following things happen as you apply a path (see Figure 6-11):

   a. A line representing the path that will be followed displays.

   b. Your shape follows the path to give you an instant preview.

   c. The Motion Paths icon and the Effect Options icon on the Ribbon change to match the icon of the path type chosen.

   d. A number is displayed that shows the path animation's number within the animation sequence.

   e. A green arrow indicates the starting point of the path and a red arrow with a bar indicates the endpoint.

Animation sequence number

Path begins   Path ends

Figure 6-11:
Editing a
motion path.

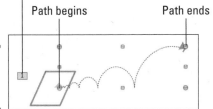

In Book I, Chapter 8, we explain in detail how to edit points on a line. Everything we talked about in that chapter about shaping and working with lines applies to motion path lines.

Right-click the line to edit points. Right-click a point to display point options in a pop-up menu. Drag the blue selection handles to resize the path line. Drag the path line or the shape to reposition the path line.

Applying a custom path

The steps to apply a custom path are the same as the previous heading except for Step 3:

1. **Select an object.**

   Any kind of object can follow a path.

2. **Click the Ribbon's Animations tab, and in the Motion group, click Paths.**

The Motion Paths gallery displays. (Refer to Figure 6-10.)

3. **Choose a line tool from Custom section of the palette.**

These are the same line drawing tools described in Book I, Chapter 8. We suggest you click the shape to set a starting point:

- *Draw Curve and Draw Freeform:* Click at the beginning of the line, move the mouse, and click again to add points as you make the line. Double-click to set an end point.

- *Draw Line and Draw Scribble:* Click and hold the mouse button down as you drag. When you let go, your line appears.

Choosing path effect options

Effect Options

Each kind of path comes with its own set of effect options. To see the options, select the path and then click the Effect Options button in the Animation Options group on the Animations tab of the Ribbon. The Effect Options button's icon changes, depending upon what type of motion path is selected. You can choose from three categories of effects:

✦ **Direction:** You might find Up, Down, Left, and Right options.

✦ **Origin:** You can anchor the path to the object, or you can position the path and the object independently. The object follows the path as placed on the slide when the show runs.

✦ **Path:** Choose either Edit Points or Reverse Direction.

Chapter 7: Delivering Your Presentation

In This Chapter

✔ Presenting your best

✔ Clicking with clickers

✔ Playing a slide show

✔ Controlling the show

✔ Using Presenter view

✔ Making an automatic presentation

✔ Making mini shows of your big show

✔ Setting playback options

✔ Broadcasting to the world

Most people speak in front of an audience every day and never think twice about it. When you talk with coworkers or fellow students, you're speaking in front of an audience. When you play cards with friends, you're speaking in front of an audience. Sometimes people become nervous about speaking before larger groups. A trick to remember is that you can engage an audience as you would your friends and acquaintances. Often, your friends are in the large audience, which makes it easier to interact with the audience as a group of your friends. And the most important fact of all is that your audience members want you to succeed: They wouldn't be there if they thought otherwise!

In this chapter, we show you how to use PowerPoint 2011 tools to deliver your presentation in person and in other formats such as a movie or on the Web. Along the way, we include tips to help make you a presenter whom audiences love. Our focus is the Slide Show tab of the Ribbon, but remember that you can use these tools from the menu bar and right-click menus if you prefer.

Presenting to a Live Audience

In the following sections, we cover how to present your slide show with confidence before a live audience. (We certainly hope the audience is alive . . . although you may find audiences aren't so lively early in the morning.)

Know your audience and your material

Near the beginning of each presentation, after describing what you're going to talk about, afford the audience members a brief opportunity to tell you what they expect from your presentation. You might need to adjust what you were planning to say to accommodate the audience's wishes.

Whether you're an instructor, a preacher, a student, or a professional presenter, be sure you understand your presentation from the audience's point of view. If you know what the audience expects, it's much easier to prepare your slides to meet those expectations. Your audience is your friend and partner.

Tailor your content to make the best use of the audience's time. Try to imagine you're in the audience looking at your show. Decide what material you want to include and exclude and how you would like to see it presented. Tell your story and please the audience. Thoughtful preparation can make you look brilliant.

Know your tools

You can use PowerPoint 2011 in many scenarios. The most common is for a presenter to be in front of an audience using a projector and sound system. If you present this way often and you present in various locations, treat yourself to a late-model MacBook Pro with lots of RAM. Carry an assortment of audio and video cables.

If you're fortunate and have a room with several multi-core Mac Pros equipped with high-end graphics cards, you can produce multimedia extravaganzas by synchronizing multiple versions of your presentation on many screens.

Sometimes presenters are faced with having to use equipment supplied by others — often older and inadequate equipment, or even another type of computer such as something that runs on Windows rather than Mac OS X. PowerPoint 2010 for Windows is compatible with PowerPoint 2011 for Mac, and you can play your PowerPoint 2011 slide show without changing anything. Any version of PowerPoint that's older than 2007 presents problems, especially with audio and movies. In this chapter, we explain how to use these two alternatives for dealing with old equipment:

✦ Capture your presentation as a movie and play the movie instead of using an old version of PowerPoint.

✦ Use the new Broadcast feature from your Mac and play the broadcast in the old equipment's Web browser. (Remember, though, that audio or movies won't work in a broadcast.)

Knowing that you've put together a good presentation and that you're acquainted with the tools available to you goes a long way to taking the stress out of presenting. Visit your presentation room ahead of time, if possible, and try out the equipment. Instead of focusing on gizmos and hardware during the show, you'll be able to focus on your audience, which is fun and why you're here.

Choosing a clicker

Remotes are available for you as a presenter. As a presenter, you use a remote to advance the slide show. You can even use specialized software and audience response keypads known as *clickers* so that your audience can actively participate with you in your presentation — more on that in just a bit.

For presenting a show, you can use a variety of methods to play slides and animations. The most obvious, of course, is to simply click the mouse button. Depending upon your equipment, you can use an Apple Remote or other brand of remote. Do you want to use your iPhone or iPod touch as a remote? Try the i-Clickr PowerPoint Remote, which you download from the App Store. i-Clickr displays your slide notes, and it even vibrates to let you know when your presentation time is running out. You can meet the creator of this bit of magic at `http://blog.indezine.com/2010/08/i-clickr-powerpoint-remote-conversation.html`.

For live audience interaction, several brands of clickers are available. One of this book's authors works at SUNY University at Buffalo where Turning Technology's Turning Point application, clickers and PowerPoint add-in are used. (See Figure 7-1.) Instructors can poll students and instantly view a graph in PowerPoint displaying the results. Your audience can use specialized clickers or even iPhones and Blackberry devices. Clickers can be used to take attendance at events and classes, and they have other uses. You can find details at the Turning Technologies site at `www.turningtechnologies.com`.

Figure 7-1: A remote for audience participation.

Playing a Slide Show to Your Audience

There are two distinctly different ways to play a slide show on a projector in front of an audience. You can use Play, and your audience sees exactly what's on the presenter's computer. The other way is Presenter View, where you as presenter see a special screen with previews and controls while the audience sees the slides.

Regardless of the method you use, when your show runs, the animations and transitions you made will activate as you specified. We discuss the Play method in the following sections; we discuss Presenter View in the later section, "Using Presenter View."

Playing a slide show

When you use the methods of playing a slide show that we describe in this section, you and your audience see exactly the same thing. Your computer's screen and the projector will match. Here are several ways to start playing your slide show:

✦ **Click the Ribbon's Slide Show tab, and in the Play Slide Show group, click one of the following (see Figure 7-2):**

  • *From Start:* The show starts at Slide 1.

  • *From Current Slide:* The show starts with the current slide in Normal View or from the selected slide in Slide Sorter view.

Figure 7-2:
Playing from the Ribbon.

✦ **Click the Slide Show button in the lower-left corner of the window.**
See Figure 7-3. This plays your show from the current (selected) slide in Normal view and Slide Sorter view.

Figure 7-3:
Playing from the View button.

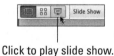

Click to play slide show.

✦ **Choose Slide Show⇨Play from Start from the menu bar or press ⌘-Shift-Return**

✦ **Choose Slide Show⇨Play from Current Slide on the menu bar or press ⌘-Return**

The following sections provide more tips about giving an in-person live presentation. We hope by now that you have the confidence to build a slide show that people will enjoy watching and that you know will do your content justice. If you still have some butterflies in your stomach, remember that your audience is almost always friendly. Only a few presenters are unlucky enough to have shoes or rotten tomatoes thrown at them. Ouch!

Using onscreen options

While a slide show is running, you will find the buttons shown in Figure 7-4 display when you move the mouse cursor. After a few seconds, the buttons dissolve away but return when you move the mouse. These buttons provide the same options that you see when you right-click anywhere on the slide while the show is running. The buttons are:

Previous   Show controls

Figure 7-4:
Controlling
your show.

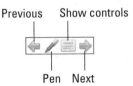

Pen   Next

✦ **Left Arrow:** When clicked, runs the previous animation. If there are no previous animations, the previous slide is displayed. When there are no previous slides, clicking causes nothing to happen unless you set your slides to loop. (See the section, "Using the Set Up Show dialog," later in this chapter.)

✦ **Right Arrow:** When clicked, runs the next animation. If there are no animations remaining on the slide, the next slide is displayed. When there are no subsequent slides, clicking causes nothing to happen unless you set your slides to loop. (See the section, "Using the Set Up Show dialog," later in this chapter.)

✦ **Pen tool:** Activates the Pen tool menu. (See the following section.)

✦ **Show controls:** Displays a pop-up menu of controls for your show. The same controls also show when you right-click on a slide. (See the later section, "Choosing show options.")

Using the Pen tool

You can draw on a slide while a slide show is running. This is useful to highlight particular things on a slide and to hide the cursor if desired. To use the Pen tool, follow these steps:

1. **In a running presentation, click the Pen shown in Figure 7-4.**

   A pop-up menu appears. (See Figure 7-5.) Pressing ⌘-P instead bypasses the menu, and you can immediately start to draw on the slide using the default pen color.

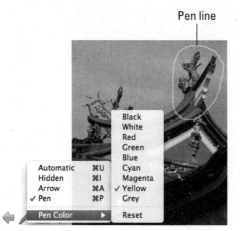

Pen line

Figure 7-5:
Writing
on a slide.

2. **From the pop-up menu, choose Pen Color⇨*Color*.**

   Be sure to choose a pen color that contrasts with your slide's content. The mouse pointer turns into a pen.

3. **Hold the left mouse button down and drag to draw on the slide.**

4. **When you're done, click the Pen Tool button on the slide again. From the pop-up menu, choose Automatic.**

   Alternatively, press ⌘-A to return the cursor to normal.

The following Pen controls are also available:

✦ **Hidden:** To hide the cursor, choose this option from the Pen menu or press ⌘-I. When you hide the cursor, you can't display the slide show buttons shown earlier in Figure 7-4, but you can activate mouse over action settings events.

✦ **Restore the Normal Cursor:** Press ⌘-A or right-click on the slide and choose Pointer Options⇨Arrow from the contextual menu.

✦ **Remove Ink:** Click the Show Controls button (refer to Figure 7-4) and then from the pop-up menu choose Screen⇨Erase Pen.

✦ **Automatic:** Choose Automatic or press ⌘-U to resume playing a slide show you are running in automatic mode using timings.

The Pen tool has the following limitations:

✦ If you're broadcasting a slide show, you can see the pen's ink on your slide, but the audience can't see the ink.

✦ You can't use the Pen tool while you're using Presenter view.

✦ You can't save your Pen drawings with the presentation.

✦ There is only one line style.

Choosing show options

When you click the Show Options button shown in Figure 7-4, you're presented with a pop-up menu that offers these groups of options:

✦ **Next, Previous, Last Viewed**

✦ **Go to Slide:** Choose any slide from the pop-up menu.

✦ **Custom Show:** Choose a custom show from the pop-up menu. This option is grayed out if you have not made any custom shows. We cover custom shows later in this chapter.

✦ **End Show:** (or press the Esc key) Ends the show and displays Normal view.

✦ **Screen:** Choose from these options:

  • *Black Screen or White Screen:* See the later section, "Blanking the Screen."

  • *Erase Pen:* Removes all lines made by the Pen tool (described in the preceding section).

Advancing to the next slide or animation

PowerPoint's default action is to advance to the next slide or animation when you click the mouse or use a remote. In addition to clicking and to using the onscreen buttons shown in Figure 7-4, pressing any of these keys also advances to the next slide or animation: Enter, Return, Page Down, right arrow, down arrow, spacebar, or N (for Next). You can also right-click the slide and choose Next from the contextual menu.

Replaying the previous animation or slide

In addition to clicking and to using the onscreen buttons shown in Figure 7-4, pressing any of these keys also replays the previous animation or, if there isn't one, the previous slide displays: P, Page Up, up arrow, left arrow, Delete, or right-click the slide and choose Previous from the contextual menu.

To display a particular slide while a slide show is running, type the slide's number on your keyboard and then press the Return key immediately. The secret here is pressing all the keys quickly in succession!

Blanking the screen

While a slide show is running, the audience is usually paying some attention to the screen. Some may be texting on a cellphone or e-mailing, but that's the way it goes these days unless you have a story that enthralls. However, there may be occasions when you're asked a question that doesn't exactly relate to what's projected on the slide, and it's better to have nothing projected rather than confuse the audience between what's onscreen and what you're saying!

Luckily, PowerPoint offers an amazing solution. When you press B or the period key, the screen goes black. Alternatively, pressing W or comma makes the screen go white. That means the audience will usually focus its attention on you, which you may want every once in a while. You can press just about any other key to resume the presentation.

Playing audio

If the audio you have put onto a slide is set to play On Click, PowerPoint waits until you click the object you've assigned the audio to. If you used the default audio icon with On Click, in PowerPoint 2011, you can do more than just click the audio icon to make the sound play. Figure 7-6 shows the new options available to you while the slide show plays.

Figure 7-6:
Playing On
Click audio.

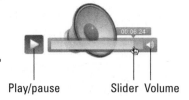

Play/pause   Slider Volume

You can click either the sound icon or the Play button to start the audio. But when you click the Play button while the audio plays it becomes a pause and resume button. When you click the Sound icon while the audio plays, the audio plays from the beginning.

You can hold the mouse button down and drag the progress bar as a slider to choose any moment on the time line. The time indicator lets you see exactly where you are in the audio. You can move the mouse cursor over the progress bar without holding the mouse down and the time indicator will still show you where you are on the progress bar.

Playing video

If the video you've put onto a slide is set to On Click, PowerPoint waits until you click the video to start it. Figure 7-7 shows the new options available while the slide show plays.

Figure 7-7:
Playing On
Click video.

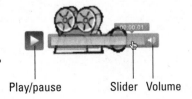

Play/pause   Slider   Volume

The video control works almost the same as the audio control. You can click either the video's poster frame or the Play button to start the video. Clicking the Play button works, or you can click the video itself because it acts as a Play, Pause, and resume button. You can drag the progress bar if you want to. Hold the mouse button down and drag the progress bar as a slider to choose any moment on the progress bar. Move the mouse cursor over the progress bar without holding the mouse button down, and the time indicator shows you where you are on the time line.

Ending the show

When you've used the default settings, to terminate a slide show while it's running press the Escape (Esc) key. Alternatively, you can right-click and choose End Show from the contextual menu, or click the Show Options button (refer to Figure 7-4) and choose End Show from the pop-up menu.

Using Presenter View

The alternative, enriched way to launch your slide show is to use Presenter view. Do remember though that you need two displays for this view to work — either two monitors or a laptop-projector combo will work.

When you use Presenter view, you see the special view shown in Figure 7-8 (typically on your laptop), while your audience sees only the slides (typically projected). To activate Presenter view, do any of the following:

✦ Choose View➪Presenter View from the menu bar.

✦ Click the Ribbon's Slide Show tab, and in the Presenter Tools group, click Presenter View.

✦ Press Option-Return.

Your slide show is now running in Presenter view.

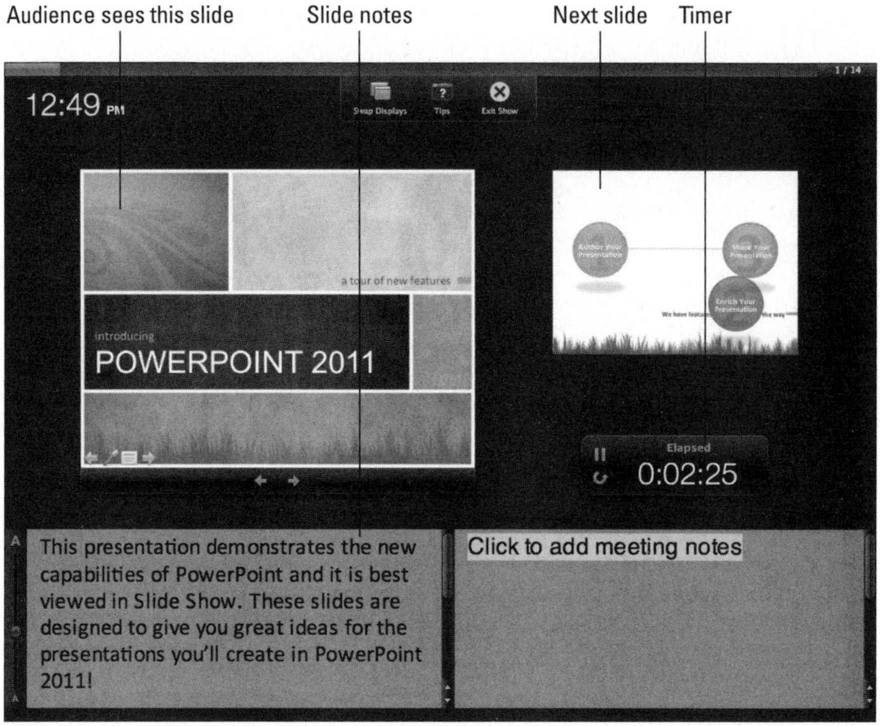

Audience sees this slide   Slide notes   Next slide   Timer

Figure 7-8:
Showing
with
Presenter
view.

Presenter view may look a bit busy at first. In actual use, Presenter view is
a simple, clean interface. The window is split into quadrants. The top-left
quadrant displays the slide as the projector is displaying it. The top-right
quadrant displays the next slide in the presentation. The bottom-left portion
displays the text of the slide notes for the slide being displayed. The bottom-
right area is where you can type slide notes as the presentation is playing.

If you add notes during a presentation, remember to save the presentation
before closing it so you don't lose those notes!

While most of the interface is self-explanatory, there are some items we
think need a bit of discussion:

✦ **Swap Displays:** If you end up seeing Presenter view on your projected
output, click this button to switch which monitor displays Presenter
view, and which monitor displays the slides.

✦ **Tips:** Click to display keyboard shortcuts you can use in Presenter view.

✦ **Exit Show:** Click to end the slide show and display Normal view.

Well that's really impressive, but what if you want to display a particular slide within your show? The secret is to move the mouse cursor to the bottom of the Presenter view window. A gallery of your slides appears, as shown in Figure 7-9. Drag the scroll bar to see more slides. Click a slide to display it to your audience. Yes, it's like being a PowerPoint DJ!

Figure 7-9:
Choosing a slide in Presenter view.

Rehearsing and Recording Your Presentation

You may want to create a narrated version of your presentation that you can distribute or broadcast. You can't be everywhere, and even though your audience members won't get the benefit of your physical presence, they'll at least be able to hear you while they enjoy your slide show. Narrated shows can be presented in PowerPoint's kiosk mode for automatic playback in screens that seem to be everywhere these days.

PowerPoint has two features that are similar: *Rehearse* and *Record Slide Show*. Both of them play the slide show while you rehearse it or speak along. While you rehearse, both features record how much time you spend on each slide. When you're done, PowerPoint offers to let you use those timings for the slide show. The difference between the two features is as follows:

+ **Rehearse** captures only the timings.

+ **Record Slide Show** captures the timings plus your audio narration.

Rehearsing

Use Rehearse whenever you want to practice your presentation. You can advance slides one after the other, and PowerPoint prompts you to save the timings. You turn on this feature by choosing Slide Show➪Rehearse from the menu bar or by clicking the Ribbon's Slide Show tab, and in the Presenter Tools group, clicking Rehearse. The slide show runs in Presenter view from the first slide. PowerPoint keeps track of how much time you take while you rehearse. (Refer to Figure 7-8.)

Clicking the Reset button resets the current slide's elapsed time to zero and adjusts the total time elapsed to the moment the current slide begins.

At the end of the show, you decide whether to keep the timings. If you opt to save these timings, they're saved as transition timings. When PowerPoint refers to an Automatic presentation, it refers to a presentation with timings, which can run unattended.

Many users work with the Rehearse Timings option to practice their PowerPoint slides aloud. They can get an idea about how long it'll take to do an actual presentation using these slides. Thereafter, they opt not to save the timings. Or they work with a copy of their presentation and then save the timings!

Even if you opt to save the timings, you can always fine-tune them later in Slide Sorter view, where you can also remove those timings altogether. (See Book IV, Chapter 1.)

If you need to adhere to strict time limits, timings keep you on track. Timings are also used for self-running presentations in kiosk mode.

Recording a slide show

Use the Record Slide Show feature when you want to make a version of your presentation that has narration included for distribution. Record Slide Show works the same way as Rehearse Timings, but PowerPoint records what you say while you rehearse. At the end of each slide, PowerPoint creates a sound file and adds it to the slide. If you're not happy with the audio, you can always go back, delete the sound icon from the slide, and re-record the slide's narration.

To start the slide show and begin recording, choose Slide Show⇨Record Slide Show from the menu bar, or click the Ribbon's Slide Show tab, and in the Presenter Tools group, click Record Slide Show. The procedure is the same as for the Rehearse feature described in the previous section.

Of course, to use this feature, you must have a microphone and speakers, or a good-quality audio headset. If you want professional-sounding narrations, you need to use a high-quality headset and record in a silent room.

Work from a script rather than try to wing it. Even with a script, expect to spend 40 minutes or more working on the audio for each 15 minutes' worth of audio that makes it into your presentation. If you're not happy with the sound of your own voice, consider hiring a professional to record the narrations.

Creating Versions with Custom Shows

We have a prediction to make. If you follow our tips, you'll make great slide shows. You'll wind up with one that takes an hour to present fully.

People will attend and love it. You're then asked to give your presentation again, but you're offered only 20 minutes in which to present. That's where PowerPoint's Custom Shows feature fits in. This feature lets you create shorter versions and different-order versions of your slide shows.

To set up a smaller version of a slide show, sometimes called a *child version*, follow these steps:

1. **In Normal view, choose Slide Show⇨Custom Shows⇨Edit Custom Show from the menu bar.**

   Alternatively, click the Ribbon's Slide Show tab, and in the Play Slide Show group, choose Custom Shows⇨Edit Custom Shows.

   The Custom Shows dialog appears, as shown in Figure 7-10.

Figure 7-10: Managing custom shows.

2. **Click the New button to create your first custom show.**

   The Define Custom Show dialog, shown in Figure 7-11, appears.

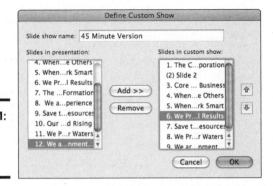

Figure 7-11: Defining a custom show.

3. **In the Slide Show Name text box, enter a name for your custom slide show.**

4. **Click the Add button to assign selected slides from the Slides in Presentation list to the Slides in Custom Show list.**

Hold Shift and click to select a range of slides. Use ⌘-click to select non-contiguous multiple slides. You can also add the same slide twice to the same custom show!

5. **(Optional) Click Remove to remove selected slides from the Slides in Custom Show list.**

6. **(Optional) Change the order of the slides in your custom show by selecting a slide and clicking the up or down arrows beside the Slides in Custom Show list.**

7. **When you're happy with the slides in the custom show and their order, click OK to close the Define Custom Show dialog, and then click Close to close the Custom Shows dialog or click Show to run the Custom Show in slide show view.**

To run a custom show, choose Slide Show⇨Custom Shows⇨*Name of Your Custom Show* from the menu bar, or click the Ribbon's Slide Show tab, and in the Custom Shows group, click the name of your custom show. Notice that the Edit Custom Shows button on the Ribbon lists your custom shows if you have any. Your show runs in Play mode. If you want to use Presenter view, see the next section.

Customizing Your Show's Setup

PowerPoint gives you even more options to choose from when presenting your show. There are options on the Ribbon, and in the Set Up Show dialog. We start with the Ribbon.

Setting up your show with the Ribbon

To set up your show using the Ribbon, you use the Set Up group. Click the Ribbon's Slide Show to access the Set Up group, as shown in Figure 7-12. Choose from these options:

Figure 7-12: The Set Up group.

✦ **Action Settings:** Select an object and then click this button to display the Action Settings dialog, which is described in Chapter 4 of this minibook.

✦ **Hide Slide:** Select one or more slides and then click this button to hide them. When the show plays, the hidden slides will be skipped. When hidden, slides have a slashed circle on them and are dimmed in the Slides list and in Slide Sorter view, as shown in Figure 7-13. To unhide a slide, select it and then click the Hide Slide button again.

✦ **Set Up Show:** A shortcut to the Set Up Show dialog, discussed in the next section.

✦ **Play Narrations:** When selected, your narrations (see Recording a Slide Show earlier in this chapter) will play when you play the slide show. Deselect this check box, and your show plays without recorded narrations.

✦ **Use Timings:** When selected, the slide transition timings you have applied will be used while the show runs. Deselect this check box to manually advance your slide show.

✦ **Show Media Controls:** By default, your audio and video set to On Click displays a volume control and you can drag the progress bar. Deselect this check box to disable the controls so you actually have to click a sound icon or the poster frame of a movie clip to play your content.

✦ **Mirror Show:** Choose this option to not show Presenter View, and play your show on multiple displays at once.

Figure 7-13:
Hidden
slides in
Slide Sorter
view.

Using the Set Up Show dialog

To display the Set Up Show dialog, click the Set Up Show button in the Slide Show tab of the Ribbon, or choose Slide Show➪Set Up Show from the menu bar. Either way, the versatile Set Up Show dialog appears, as shown in Figure 7-14. A wide variety of behaviors can be controlled, as described in the following sections.

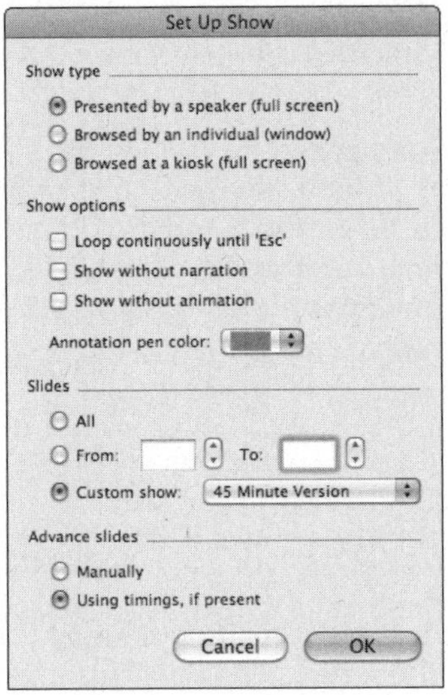

Figure 7-14:
Setting up a
show.

Choosing a show type

There are three different types of presentations you can choose from in the
Set Up Show dialog:

✦ **Presented by a Speaker (Full Screen):** This is the type audiences are
most familiar with. The presentation plays full screen, usually on a projector. This is the default type of presentation.

✦ **Browsed by an Individual (Window):** Choose this option to play your
presentation on your computer in a window. This is the option to
choose if you want to use screen-recording software to record your
presentation.

✦ **Browsed at a Kiosk (Full Screen):** Choose this option and your presentation will play full screen on your computer. If you also choose the Loop
Continuously option, PowerPoint can play your presentation endlessly.
Also your keyboard and mouse clicks are disabled in this mode, so you
will have to create navigational controls to move to the next slide or use
automatic slide timings.

To make a kiosk presentation that doesn't stall as it waits for a click, make
sure all your animations are set to With Previous or After Previous.

Choosing show options

In the Set Up Show dialog, you can choose from four quite different show
options:

✦ **Loop Continuously until Esc:** When selected, your presentation will play over and over again until the Escape key is pressed.

✦ **Show without Narration:** When selected, narrations won't play. See the earlier section, "Recording a slide show."

✦ **Show without Animation:** When selected, animations won't play.

✦ **Annotation Pen Color:** Click the pop-up menu to choose a default pen color. Choose More Colors in the pop-up menu to display the Mac OS X color picker. Choose a color that contrasts with your show's contents.

Choosing which slides to play

You can choose which slides to play in the Set Up Show dialog as follows:

✦ **All:** When you play the show or use Presenter view, all slides will play.

✦ **From – To:** Use spinner controls to set a range of slides to play.

✦ **Custom Show:** If your presentation has one or more custom shows (see the earlier section, "Creating Versions with Custom Shows"), you can choose which custom show will be presented when you play the presentation.

Advancing slides

In the Set Up Show dialog, you can choose either to require slides to play manually by selecting the Manually radio button or to use timings by selecting the Use Timings, If Present radio button. The latter option will advance slides automatically if they have transition timings applied. PowerPoint's default is to use timings.

Broadcasting a Presentation

You can run a slide show on your computer and your audience can watch as your show plays live, on-line in a Web browser. Perhaps you have an audience that's spread around the world. Perhaps you're in a classroom and you want each student to have a high-quality view of your presentation.

The audience doesn't even have to have PowerPoint, although a high-speed Internet connection is required for both the presenter and the audience. If you try this even once, you'll be hooked!

The way it works is that you run your presentation on your computer, and your audience goes to a URL to watch the show in their Web browser. You, as presenter, will need a Windows Live ID (the same ID you use for SkyDrive and Hotmail). If you don't have a Windows Live ID, you're offered an opportunity to sign up for one (they're free) in the steps that follow. Your audience doesn't need a Windows Live ID to watch the show.

Broadcasting a Presentation

Here's how to broadcast a slide show:

1. **Open your presentation in PowerPoint.**

2. **Click the Ribbon's Slide Show tab, and in the Play Slide Show group, click Broadcast Slide Show.**

   Alternatively, choose Slide Show⇨Broadcast Slide Show from the menu bar.

   A sheet appears (shown in Figure 7-15) offering additional information about slide show broadcasting, and informing you that if you use the service you're agreeing to the linked terms of service. The possibility exists that multiple providers will become available, but as we write this book, there's only the Microsoft PowerPoint Broadcast service.

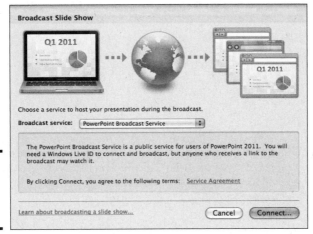

Figure 7-15: Getting ready to broadcast.

3. **Click the Connect button.**

   The Windows Live Sign In dialog displays, as shown in Figure 7-16.

Figure 7-16: Sign into the broadcast service.

4. **Enter your Windows Live ID and password in the text boxes provided.**

   If you don't have a Windows Live ID, click the Get a Live ID button and fill in the required information to sign up.

5. **(Optional) Select the check box to save your password in the Mac OS Keychain so that you don't have to enter it again in the future.**

   It may take a minute to log in.

   After you log in, the Broadcast Slide Show dialog displays and shows the Broadcast Link, as shown in Figure 7-17. You distribute this link to your audience.

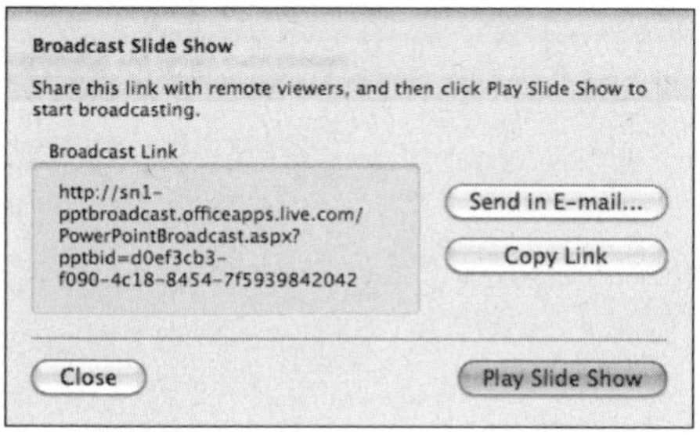

Figure 7-17: Sharing the show's URL.

6. **In the Broadcast Slide Show dialog, choose how to send your audience the link to view your slide show. You can choose:**

   • *Send in E-Mail:* Opens a new email message in Outlook, which you can address and send to your audience.

   • *Copy Link:* Puts the link onto the Clipboard so that you can paste it, perhaps into a chat window or a file that you can share with your audience.

   Allow your audience members sufficient time to go to the URL in their Web browser.

7. **When you're ready and your audience is watching, click the Play Slide Show button.**

   Your slide show starts to play. Your audience can see the slides in their Web browser.

When the show is over, the presenter's Mac shows the presentation in Broadcast view, and the show keeps running for the presenter and the audience until the presenter clicks one of the End Broadcast buttons, as shown in Figure 7-18. The presenter can keep the show alive and re-broadcast the

Book IV Chapter 7

Delivering Your Presentation

slide show using the Broadcast tab of the Ribbon (retaining the same URL) by not ending the show. Among the options on the Broadcast tab of the Ribbon:

+ **From Start:** Plays from the beginning of your presentation.

+ **From Current Slide:** Starts playing your presentation from the currently selected slide.

+ **Presenter View:** If you click this button, your audience sees only the slides.

+ **Custom Shows:** Choose a custom show, if one exists in this presentation.

+ **Email Link:** Send the link via an Outlook message.

+ **Copy URL:** Copy the URL so you can paste it elsewhere (say a chat window).

+ **Invite More:** Displays the Broadcast Slide Show dialog. (Refer to Figure 7-17.)

+ **Presenter View and Mirror Show:** Change settings for two displays. See the earlier section, "Using Presenter View," for more.

+ **Exit or End Broadcast:** End the broadcast and switch to Normal view.

Figure 7-18: Running your broadcast.

There are some limitations to broadcasting a slide show. The most important one is that sounds and movies won't play to your audience. Animations and transitions may not play. The Pen tool will display lines on the presenter's screen, but not on the audience screens.

Perhaps, as time passes, these limitations will be resolved. For a new feature, these limitations are minor. Broadcasting is outstanding!

Set your slide show up to play Browsed by an Individual (Window) in the Set Up Show Setup dialog before starting your broadcast, and then you can use all your other applications, including Messenger, Communicator, iChat, or other chat service for a truly interactive Web experience.

Developing in PowerPoint

It's fun to speculate on new ways to use PowerPoint. You can use PowerPoint to automate all kinds of shows. For example, if you owned a movie theatre, you could have PowerPoint show ads for popcorn, play the no smoking movie — everything that old slide tray does now. With a VBA macro or AppleScript, you can have presentations play at specified times. Teachers can program interactive games for their students to learn from and develop learning aids. You can have multiple Macs with multiple projectors run a complex show that's coordinated with VBA. The sky is the limit. Be sure to visit Book I, Chapter 12 if you're interested in programming PowerPoint with VBA.

**Book IV
Chapter 7**

**Delivering Your
Presentation**

Chapter 8: Printing, Sharing, and Coauthoring Presentations

In This Chapter

✔ **Printing handouts, posters, and postcards**

✔ **Sharing your presentation**

✔ **Commenting a presentation**

✔ **Comparing and reviewing presentation files**

✔ **Coauthoring with colleagues, classmates, and friends**

Sharing presentations with others is an integral part of working with PowerPoint. Audiences often expect printed handouts and online versions of your presentations as reference materials. This chapter can help you meet those expectations by showing you a wide variety of printing options and introducing you to new ways to share presentations with others.

Printing Your Presentations

Although it's most common to print handouts on regular-size paper, you can use PowerPoint to print large-scale versions of slides to use for poster sessions at booths in conferences or for wall mounting. You can also use PowerPoint to print small-scale objects, such as postcards. Your printing output can take a variety of forms, such as PDF, slides, handouts, and Notes Pages.

Printing handouts for everyone

 If you need to print handouts to give to your attendees, PowerPoint offers many options that you can access by choosing File⇨Print from the menu bar or by pressing ⌘-P rather than clicking the Print button on the Standard toolbar. If you click the Print button on the Standard toolbar (shown in the margin), PowerPoint prints full-page printouts of the slides, which may or may not be what you want.

Printing handouts with note-taking lines

This very popular arrangement prints pictures of three slides on the left, along with lines for notes on the right, on each page. This handout option is the only one that prints note-taking lines. You can find this option in the Print What pop-up menu in the Print dialog. Choose Handouts (3 Slides per Page) from the pop-up menu, as shown in Figure 8-1. The other handout options print pictures of the slides in various arrangements that you can see in the preview when you select them.

Show/Hide Print Options

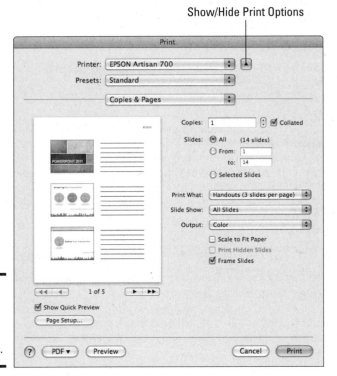

Figure 8-1:
Printing
handouts
with note-
taking lines.

Choose Page Setup⇨Orientation⇨Notes, Handouts & Outlines from the menu bar to change the orientation to landscape, where the pictures of your slides go across the page and the lines appear beneath.

You can format the handout background by choosing View⇨Master⇨ Handout Master from the menu bar as described in Chapter 5 of this minibook.

Printing handouts with slide notes

Another popular style of printing is to print the Notes view. These printouts include one slide per page. Each page has a picture of the slide, plus the slide notes for that slide, as shown in Figure 8-2. You follow the same procedure that we describe in the preceding section, except that in the Print What pop-up menu, you need to choose Notes.

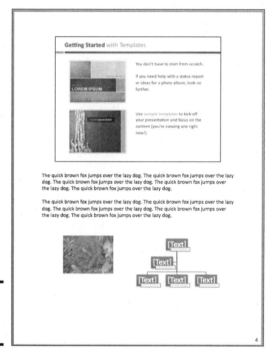

Figure 8-2:
Printing
Notes view.

Printing the slide outline

The option at the bottom of the Print What pop-up menu in the Print dialog is Outline. This option prints the text that appears in the Outline pane of the Normal view.

When it's time to print those handouts, you might want to have page numbers and other information for your audience. See Chapter 3 to find out how to include footers.

Printing on nonstandard paper sizes

If you know you're going to print to a paper size other than PowerPoint's default, choose File⇨Page Setup from the menu bar *before* you create any slides, Slide Masters, or slide layouts in your presentation. If you wait until after you build your presentation, when you change the paper size, it can cause graphic objects and even text to look squished, stretched, or otherwise distorted. PowerPoint can print large posters if you have access to a large format printer. Likewise, you can use Page Setup to choose a very small size.

Printing as PDF

We want to encourage you to be earth-friendly. Maybe you don't have to print to paper; instead, you can print to PDF files. In PowerPoint, use the Print What pop-up menu in the Print dialog to choose what aspects of your presentation to print as a PDF file, and then click the PDF button to save what you have chosen. Choosing File⇨Save As PDF saves full slides in PDF format.

Exploring Sharing Options

You can share PowerPoint presentations in many different ways. Each one is best for specific circumstances and scenarios. Know your audience members and combine that knowledge with your requirements to choose an appropriate distribution method. In Chapter 7 of this minibook, we show how to share a presentation by broadcasting live. Here, we show you how to share copies of your presentation file.

Distributing in PowerPoint format

Microsoft Office is one of the most widely installed software suites for both Mac and Windows users. That means your audience probably already has PowerPoint. Distributing in PowerPoint format is the highest-quality option to play your slide show on another computer. Use PowerPoint format to disseminate your presentation whenever possible.

Other software that can open and play PowerPoint presentations includes Apple's Keynote, Oracle Corporation's aging OpenOffice, Planamesa Inc.'s NeoOffice, IBM's Lotus Symphony, and Google Docs. Applications other than PowerPoint may substitute fonts and change or fail to play transitions or animations. Graphic objects may be altered. Effects such as soft shadows and 3D effects may look different. Charts may not look the same. In other words, stick with PowerPoint 2011 on Mac and PowerPoint 2007 or 2010 for Windows if you want your presentation to look great and play right.

Distributing as a movie

If you want to distribute your presentation as a movie, choosing File⇨Save As Movie just doesn't cut it. It won't save audio, animations, or embedded movies the same as it would if you played the slide show, but our tech editor was very happy that it did work with transitions, although many transitions will be substituted. To avoid loss of fidelity, the solution is to record a screen capture of your presentation using software such as Ambrosia's SnapZPro or TechSmith's Camtasia. The secret is to play the presentation in a window rather than at full screen so that the movie file of your presentation is no larger than it needs to be.

Here's how to set up PowerPoint to play in a window instead of full-screen:

1. **Click the Ribbon's Slide Show tab, and in the Set Up group, click Set Up Show; alternatively, choose Slide Show⇨Set Up Show from the menu bar.**

   The Set Up Show dialog displays.

2. **In the Set Up Show dialog, in the Show Type section, choose Browsed by an Individual (Window).**

3. **Click OK to close the Set Up Show dialog.**

When you're ready to record your presentation, set your screen capture program to record the screen area of just the PowerPoint window. See the instructions for your screen capture software to adjust capture quality.

Sending directly to iPhoto

An especially fun option is to send your PowerPoint slides to iPhoto. PowerPoint talks directly with iPhoto, so the process works very nicely.

Follow these steps to turn your presentation into a new iPhoto album:

1. **(Optional) With your presentation open in Slide Sorter view, select the slides you want to send to iPhoto.**

   You don't have to do this if you want to send the entire slide show to iPhoto.

2. **Choose File⇨Share⇨Send To⇨iPhoto from the menu bar.**

   The Send to iPhoto dialog appears, as shown in Figure 8-3.

3. **In the New Album Name text box, enter a name for your new album.**

4. **From the Format pop-up menu, choose JPEG or PNG.**

5. **Select either All (the entire presentation) or Selected to tell PowerPoint which slides to export to iPhoto.**

6. **Click the Send to iPhoto button.**

   PowerPoint prepares your slides and gives them to iPhoto, which creates a new album and presents the slides to you.

Figure 8-3:
Naming
your new
album.

Probably the best way to create a movie from your PowerPoint presentation is to use the Save as Video option in PowerPoint 2010 for Windows. Although the output quality is awesome, it does create the movies in the distinctly Mac-unfriendly .wmv format.

Sending by e-mail

You can send a presentation by e-mail in two ways. For small presentation files, you can send a presentation using the traditional (if not always reliable) method of attaching the file to an e-mail message. The new, better way is to send a link to your presentation on SkyDrive.

It's pretty common to receive a PowerPoint presentation by e-mail that won't open or play. Sending by e-mail is also a bit perilous because files can be altered by e-mail servers in their endless quest to protect against viruses, Trojans, and all other malware. Also, you should avoid sending by e-mail a file that's larger than 5MB.

If your presentation is larger than 5MB, or you prefer to avoid potential problems of sending your presentation as an e-mail attachment, the alternative is to save the presentation to SkyDrive or SharePoint and then e-mail a link to the presentation rather than the presentation itself. This requires a bit of preparation in that you must first set permissions on your SkyDrive or SharePoint server so that your audience has access to the presentation file.

Instructions for sending by these methods are in Book I, Chapter 4.

Exploring slide-sharing sites

Sometimes, you want others to see your presentation slides, and you may or may not want them to download the actual PowerPoint file. Whatever you prefer, a new breed of slide-sharing sites puts all these options and more at your disposal. We call this a way to get your slides in the cloud!

Here's a listing of such slide-sharing sites with their URLs:

✦ **SlideShare:** www.slideshare.net

✦ **authorSTREAM:** www.authorstream.com

✦ **SlideBoom:** www.slideboom.com

Commenting in a Presentation

If you're working with someone else to build a presentation in a collaborative environment, PowerPoint's commenting tools help you communicate with your collaborators.

The Comments group on the Review tab of the Ribbon, shown in Figure 8-4, lets you communicate to your collaborator (or yourself for that matter) without disturbing the content of your slides. Comment boxes are text boxes that float above the presentation in Normal view. Each box has its own number. When you show comment numbers, you can choose a comment by clicking its number to reveal its contents. These are the controls:

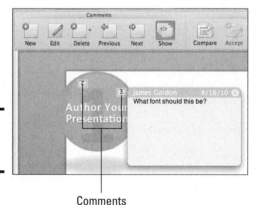

Figure 8-4:
Making
comments.

Comments

✦ **New:** Inserts an empty comment text box and its corresponding comment number indicator.

✦ **Edit Comment:** You can choose an indicator and then click this button to edit the comment.

+ **Delete Comment:** Deletes the selected comment.

+ **Previous Comment:** When more than one comment is in a presentation, displays to the next lowest comment number.

+ **Next Comment:** When more than one comment is in a presentation, advances to the next highest comment number.

+ **Show:** Toggles the visibility of comments on and off.

PowerPoint's commenting feature isn't as elaborate as Word and Excel's. There are no fancy balloons, nor can you print or format comment boxes. Despite the limitations, having the ability to insert comments is still handy.

Comparing Presentations

One of Word's best features has come to PowerPoint. Now you can easily compare the presentation you're viewing with another presentation. Additionally, you can use the Compare feature in a fashion similar to Word and Excel's Track Changes. Here's how:

1. **Open one of the two presentations you want to compare in Normal view.**

2. **Click the Ribbon's Review tab, and in the Compare group, click Compare.**

The Compare Presentations file browser displays.

3. **Choose the other presentation file you want to compare against.**

The Compare Changes floating palette displays, as shown in Figure 8-5. The Compare button on the Ribbon dims, and the review changes buttons activate.

The Compare Changes palette works in conjunction with the Normal View pane. After displaying the Compare Changes palette, you can compare individual changes this way:

1. **Select a change in the Compare Changes palette.**

The selected object, if available in the Normal view, becomes selected.

2. **Click the green check button to accept the change, or click the red crossed button to reject the change.**

You can see before and after versions in the Compare Changes palette.

Notice bottom of the Compare Changes palette displays the other presentation's version of the compared slide.

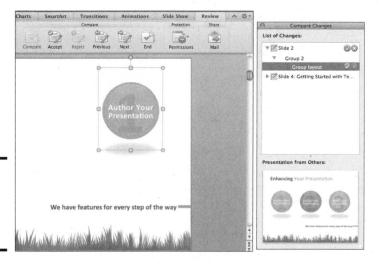

Figure 8-5:
Comparing
two
presenta-
tions.

You can also use Compare Changes buttons on the Ribbon to accept and
reject changes and consolidate two different versions of your presentation
into a single presentation. Again, after displaying the Compare Changes palette, you can consolidate changes by doing the following:

1. **Select the first change in the Compare Changes palette.**

   The selected object, if available in the Normal view, becomes selected.

2. **In the Compare group of the Review tab, click either Accept or Reject.**

   Changes you accept are incorporated into the presentation you are
   viewing in Normal view.

3. **Click Next.**

   Decide on each change until all changes have been accounted for.

You can skip a decision by clicking Next or by choosing a later revision in
the Compare Changes palette without clicking Accept or Reject. To go back
and make your decision, click Previous or choose a skipped change in the
palette.

Clicking the End button terminates the Review Changes session. Any
changes you haven't decided upon won't be included in the consolidated
version.

**Book IV
Chapter 8**

Printing, Sharing,
and Coauthoring
Presentations

Coauthoring Presentations Using SkyDrive or SharePoint

Early coauthoring schemes required using Google Docs, but you were severely hampered by the limited editing capabilities that are possible from within a Web browser. Now, the pinnacle of sharing is the new PowerPoint capability of coauthoring a presentation with multiple authors sharing PowerPoint's full set of powerful presentation editing features live, in real-time, using SkyDrive.

Coauthoring requirements

You can coauthor a presentation that was saved in PowerPoint (.pptx) format with a collaborator who has PowerPoint 2011 for Mac or PowerPoint 2010 for Windows. No other versions of PowerPoint support coauthoring.

The presentation to be coauthored must be on SkyDrive, which is open to the public, or Microsoft SharePoint 2010, which is installed on a private network. Earlier versions of SharePoint don't support coauthoring. The SharePoint option is limited to Microsoft Office for Mac Home and Business 2011, Microsoft Office for Mac Academic 2011, or Microsoft Office for Mac Standard 2011. Book I, Chapter 2 explains how to put your presentation into SkyDrive or SharePoint 2010. All collaborators must have permission to read and write files to the SkyDrive or SharePoint 2010 folder in which the presentation is located.

Start sharing

Each collaborator takes the steps described in the following sections to open the presentation that has been stored on the SkyDrive or SharePoint server.

Opening a presentation stored on SkyDrive

Each collaborator opens the presentation file using a Web browser that opens the URL of the stored document. The URL can be sent to collaborators directly from SkyDrive by choosing Share⇨Send a Link in SkyDrive, as shown in Figure 8-6.

Figure 8-6: Sending the link.

Recent documents on SkyDrive

Coauthoring Demo	Edit in browser	Share ▾	More ▾
basic	Jim From Buffalo	Edit permissions	
Dashboard Template	Glenna Shaw	Send a link	

If a collaborator uses different methods to open the file to be shared on SkyDrive, other collaborators may not be allowed to open the file and will receive a message saying that the file is locked for editing.

When a collaborator opens the presentation in the Web browser, the collaborator clicks Open in PowerPoint. After clicking OK to a message explaining your computer needs to have a compatible Office program, the presentation opens in Microsoft PowerPoint 2011 (on a Mac) or PowerPoint 2010 (on a PC). The download process can take a while, even with a fast Internet connection. After your presentation has finished downloading, it opens in Normal view, ready for editing.

Opening a presentation stored on a SharePoint server

Collaborators need to know the URL of the file to be shared. This can be obtained by navigating to the stored presentation using a Web browser.

Each collaborator does the following to start the sharing session:

1. **Copy the URL of the file on the SharePoint Server.**

2. **In PowerPoint, choose File⇨Open URL.**

   An Open URL field displays.

3. **Paste the URL of the PowerPoint file and then click OK.**

   The presentation opens in Normal view, ready for editing.

After you've opened a presentation from the server, you can quickly open it again by choosing it in the recently used file list in the File menu or in the recent documents list in the PowerPoint Presentation Gallery.

Editing together

Working together, collaborators can be fairly independent, or they can be in constant communication with each other via Messenger, Communicator, or iChat. PowerPoint behaves normally and its interface is as responsive as it is when not coauthoring. You can switch views, change the content of slides and slide notes. You can work with media, transitions, and animations. You can even work with masters.

Detecting coauthors

While collaborating, the status bar at the bottom-left of the window indicates how many people are collaborating and whether any collaborators have saved updates (changes) to the server, as shown in Figure 8-7 (top). Clicking the coauthor's button displays a list of coauthors. Clicking the name of a coauthor displays the presence indicator for that author.

Book IV
Chapter 8

Printing, Sharing, and Coauthoring Presentations

Click to see all co-authors.

Figure 8-7:
Checking for
authors and
updates.

Click the icon on the Slides
pane to see who edited the
slide.

When a new coauthor joins the collaboration, his or her name flashes briefly at the coauthor's button and the number of authors changes.

In addition to the status bar indicators, while in Normal view, the Slides pane displays the badge you see in Figure 8-7 to the left of the slide preview. If you click the badge, you see who else is editing that particular slide. The badge appears only on slides that were changed by a coauthor, and those changes have not yet been synchronized to your computer.

Synchronizing

PowerPoint's Save feature activates the synchronization process. Any coauthor can send changes to the server and at the same time incorporate other coauthor changes as follows:

✦ **Click the Save button on the Standard toolbar.** The Save button has little arrows on it while in coauthoring mode, as shown in the margin.

✦ **Press ⌘-S.**

✦ **Click the Updates Available button** located at the bottom-left of the window (refer to the top portion of Figure 8-7). Choose either of the following:

  • *Save:* Saves and synchronizes with the server.

  • *Save and Review:* Saves, synchronizes with the server, and activates the Compare Changes dialog and feature described earlier in this chapter and shown in Figure 8-6.

You don't have to worry about editing the same slide as another coauthor. If more than one coauthor edits the same slide, PowerPoint's Compare Changes feature will automatically activate so you can accept or reject changes.

Every time you synchronize a presentation that was changed by a coauthor, PowerPoint displays a dialog explaining that changes were incorporated into the server copy of the presentation. By all means, select the check box in the dialog so you don't have to see it every time!

Ending a session

The best way to end a coauthoring session is for each coauthor to save and resolve any conflicts before closing the presentation so that no one has updates waiting. The presentation file is stored on SkyDrive or SharePoint, and of course, any coauthor can save a copy locally on his or her own computer if desired.

If a session terminates abnormally (for example, if a network problem develops and your computer could not synchronize changes you made with the server), that's covered, too. A small application called Upload Center runs in the background but shows itself if there's a problem, as shown in Figure 8-8. Upload Center gives you an opportunity to try saving to the server again by clicking OK, or to cancel the attempt to synchronize your changes.

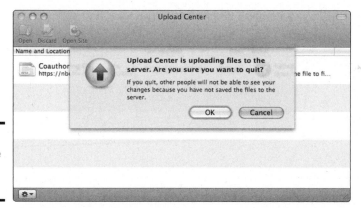

Figure 8-8:
Taking care
of interrup-
tions.

Book V

Outlook 2011

The 5th Wave   By Rich Tennant

"My spam filter checks the recipient address, http links, and any writing that panders to postmodern English romanticism with conceits to 20th-century graphic narrative."

Contents at a Glance

Chapter 1: Upgrading to Microsoft Outlook

In This Chapter

✔ Receiving a warm welcome

✔ Discovering your Identity

✔ Upgrading from Entourage and Apple Mail

✔ Upgrading from Gmail, Yahoo!, and Hotmail

✔ Importing contacts from a text file

✔ Adding Email, Exchange, and Directory accounts

✔ Keeping track of your Identities

*O*utlook 2011 is a milestone in the history of Microsoft Office on the Mac. Of course, all Microsoft Office for Mac products are designed and built only on Macs, but Outlook 2011 is the first completely *Cocoa* Office application in the Office suite. For you, making Outlook in Apple's Cocoa framework means Outlook has a distinctive Mac feel, and you can feel good that it is made with purely Mac ingredients. Delicious!

Outlook is the productivity application within Office 2011 that provides e-mail, calendar, contact manager, task, and notes taking tools to help you stay organized. Integration with Messenger and Communicator enables you to be aware of the presence of your colleagues and associates. Outlook is the premier Microsoft Exchange client on the Mac. And if all those terms sound bewildering, don't worry because we explain them all in this minibook.

Most people already have an e-mail account (or maybe several), and in this chapter, we help you get your e-mail account(s) working in Outlook. And if you get a new e-mail account, we show you how to make that one work, too.

Outlook is not available in the Home and Student edition of Microsoft Office. If you have the Home and Student edition, we recommend using Apple Mail, with Address Book and iCal, continue using Microsoft Entourage if you have it already. To upgrade Home and Student to Home and Office, open Microsoft Word. From Word's menu bar, choose Word⇨Purchase Options. Choose either Enter Your Product Key if you already purchased an upgrade key from a vendor, or choose Purchase a Product Key On Line to purchase an upgrade key, and then return to this screen to enter it.

Getting to Know Microsoft Outlook for Mac

The New in Office 2011 icon could go next to every paragraph in this entire minibook for Outlook 2011. But we're sure you would get tired of seeing it, so we just use it to alert you to specific features that are brand-new in Outlook for Mac. Microsoft Outlook for Mac replaces Microsoft Entourage and continues forward with these features:

✦ **E-mail:** Supports IMAP, POP, and Exchange protocols. Protocols are just a way in which e-mail is handled by the mail server, and unless you're an administrator, you won't ever need to know how these work!

Internet service providers usually offer two different kinds of service: POP and IMAP. At one time, POP was the dominant method, but IMAP is what we recommend now if you have a choice. Here's a brief explanation of the difference:

• *IMAP:* Configured to keep your mail inbox on the provider's server. You can create subfolders on the server to store mail in folders, such as read mail, deleted messages, junk mail, or any folder you want. The advantage of IMAP is that you can connect to the server from various devices. Your message list appears the same from any device, such as your iPod or cellphone, your computer at work, or your laptop. Your e-mail account has the same messages available, regardless of what device you use, no matter where you connect.

• *POP:* Usually configured to download e-mail messages to your local computer and delete them from the server right away. This option is fine if you have only one computer and one location. Although you can set POP to leave the messages on the server, in general, you run the risk of accidentally deleting a wanted message.

✦ **Calendars:** Supports W3C standard calendar protocol and Microsoft Exchange calendar protocol. These are again various ways in which calendars are configured.

✦ **Contacts:** Supports W3C standard vCard protocol and Microsoft Exchange calendar protocol. If you don't want to get too much into this protocol stuff, just be happy that Outlook handles so many of them!

✦ **Tasks:** A built-in task manager with calendar tie-in.

✦ **Notes:** A built-in notes manager.

SkyDrive and SharePoint integration replaces the Entourage Project Center.

Opening Outlook for the First Time

The very first time you open Outlook, you're greeted with the beautiful welcome screen.

You can see Outlook's six major new features immediately by clicking the What's New button in the welcome screen and reading a brief description of each new feature you see in Figure 1-1. We cover details about all of these features in this minibook. Other options from the Welcome screen are as follows:

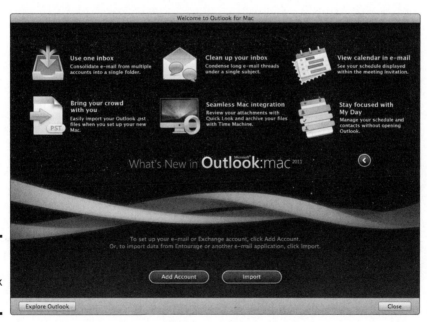

Figure 1-1:
Greetings
from Outlook
2011.

✦ **Explore Outlook:** Click this button to visit the Microsoft Outlook 2011 Web site in your default Web browser.

✦ **Add Account:** Click this button if you aren't upgrading from Entourage, Outlook, or another e-mail program. This option is for starting off completely fresh. Add Account opens the Accounts dialog, discussed later in this chapter, in the "Adding an e-mail account" section.

✦ **Import:** This is the same as choosing File➪Import from the menu bar while Outlook is running. Choose this option to import any of the following into Outlook:

• Outlook data file from Windows or the really old Outlook for Mac. (Yes, a decade or so ago Microsoft abandoned Outlook on the Mac to create Entourage, and now it has come back around to Outlook — call it a full circle.)

• Entourage information from an Entourage archive file or Entourage.

• Information, such as contacts, from another application.

• Contacts or messages from a text file.

• Add holidays to your Outlook calendar. (See Chapter 4 of this minibook.)

✦ **Close:** Closes the welcome screen and runs Outlook.

• If your computer had Entourage 2004 or Entourage 2008 on it, Outlook automatically upgrades your Identity and then runs Outlook. See the section "Upgrading from Microsoft Entourage 2008 or 2004," later in this chapter.

• If your computer didn't have Entourage 2004 or 2008 Identities to upgrade, Outlook simply runs with an empty Identity when you choose this option.

Usually, you get to see the welcome screen only once, but if you want to see it again, choose Help➪Welcome to Outlook from the menu bar.

Learning Your Identity

Outlook has a special folder within the Mac OS X Finder called Office 2011 Identities. (See Figure 1-2.) You can locate it for yourself here:

```
/Users/Username/Documents/Microsoft User Data/
```

Just like it sounds, this special folder contains everything about your Outlook activities. Inside this folder, Outlook stores one folder for each individual Identity. The name of the folder is the name of the Identity. Each Identity folder stores your e-mail, account information, calendar events, tasks, and notes in a database for each Identity. You may also see a `MeContact.plist` file, which you should not disturb.

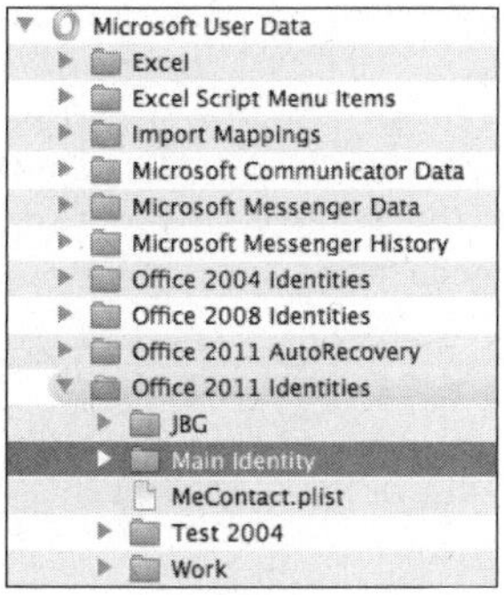

Figure 1-2:
Locating
Outlook
Identities.

```
▼ ◯ Microsoft User Data
  ▶ 📁 Excel
  ▶ 📁 Excel Script Menu Items
  ▶ 📁 Import Mappings
  ▶ 📁 Microsoft Communicator Data
  ▶ 📁 Microsoft Messenger Data
  ▶ 📁 Microsoft Messenger History
  ▶ 📁 Office 2004 Identities
  ▶ 📁 Office 2008 Identities
  ▶ 📁 Office 2011 AutoRecovery
  ▼ 📁 Office 2011 Identities
    ▶ 📁 JBG
    ▶ 📁 Main Identity
      📄 MeContact.plist
  ▶ 📁 Test 2004
  ▶ 📁 Work
```

For Outlook 2011, the structure of an Identity folder is completely new. Outlook now treats each item within an Identity as a discreet file. Each e-mail, calendar event, or task is stored as its own file. This means Time Machine backups for your Identity can take a fraction of a second instead of several minutes or longer as it sometimes did in Entourage. Spotlight searching is much improved as a beneficial side effect.

By default, Outlook makes an Identity for you called *Main Identity,* which stores your first e-mail account's information. It's a good idea to learn where your Identity folder is located, if for no other reason so that you know not to delete or move it. Use Mac OS X Finder application (on your Dock) to navigate your file system. Finder's icon appears in the left margin.

It's possible to have more than one Identity. Figure 1-2 shows that we have four Identities stored in Documents\Microsoft User Data\Office 2011 Identities. Our four Outlook Identities are called JBG, Main Identity, Test 2004, and Home.

Keep in mind that when you upgrade or add an e-mail account, calendar, task, or note, the information is stored within an Identity.

Sticking with standards

The Word Wide Web Consortium (`www.w3c.org`) is an international body that publishes standards so that software engineers can design applications that share compatible files on a variety of platforms. The specifications are an alphabet soup including XML (eXtensible Markup Language), HTML (HyperText Markup Language) used in Web browsers, and HTML e-mail. There are standard file formats for calendar events and contacts (vCards).

Office 2011 is designed to be compatible with applications that adhere to W3C standards. Sending and receiving HTML mail in Outlook should work just fine with other up-to-date standards-based e-mail applications. Sending and receiving contacts and calendar events using Outlook should work with other applications that adhere to W3C standards, such as Gmail, Sunbird, and Thunderbird on Windows, Macintosh, and Linux.

These scenarios illustrate times when having more than one Identity is desirable:

✦ **Separation of work and private life e-mail accounts:** Your work may require you to have an IMAP account, a Gmail account, and an Exchange account, but you want to keep your personal e-mail accounts, contacts, tasks, and notes from mixing in with your business activities. Use one Identity for work and another for your private life.

✦ **Keeping jobs independent:** Perhaps you work two or more jobs and don't want to intermingle mail, calendars, and so on. Making an Identity for each job can help you keep your jobs from getting crossed.

✦ **Organization support:** If you take care of the e-mail for a club or organization, make a separate Identity to keep that mail segregated.

✦ **Special event:** If you manage a special event, such as a conference, webinar, or colloquium, starting a new Identity and e-mail account for the event is the perfect way to manage things.

Upgrading from Entourage 2008 or 2004

Note: If you started with Office 2011 and don't have an older version of Entourage installed, you can skip this section.

Upgrading from Entourage 2008 or 2004 is simple. After you install Office 2011, when you close the welcome screen, Outlook automatically upgrades your Entourage Identity into a new 2011 Identity. Your old Entourage Identity remains on your drive unchanged.

Later, when you're satisfied that Outlook brought forward everything you need from your old Identity, you can save your old Entourage Identity for posterity or trash it. Your old Identity can be found in Documents\ Microsoft User Data folder\Office 2008 (or 2004) Identities. (Refer to Figure 1-2.) Identities can be large, so when you're satisfied that your Identity is working fine in Outlook, deleting your old Identity can free a considerable amount of disc space. Here are some fine details about upgrading from Entourage 2008 or Entourage 2004:

✦ Categories, calendars, calendar events, tasks, and notes are all supported in Outlook and will be carried forward.

✦ Outlook upgrades only one Identity automatically. If you have more than one Identity, see the later section, "Manually upgrading an Entourage Identity."

✦ If you have any Project Center documents, they're left undisturbed. If your project documents are not already in shared locations and you need to share them, consider moving your documents to SkyDrive, SharePoint, Mac OS X sharing, or Windows shared folders.

✦ Project Center projects will be lost because Entourage Project Center is not supported in Outlook.

✦ Outlook does not support Entourage's link feature. Links that were in Entourage will be abandoned when upgrading.

If you're using a version of Entourage older than 2004 or 2008, Outlook may not be able to import your Entourage Identity. To find out which version of Entourage you have, choose Entourage⇨About Entourage. Before installing Office 2011, in Entourage choose File⇨Export to save your Identity as an Entourage Archive file (.rge). See Entourage help for details about how to do this. In Entourage, choose Tools⇨Accounts and gather all the account information. You'll need to re-create your accounts in Outlook. After installing Office 2011, open Microsoft Outlook. Follow these steps to import your Identity into Outlook from the .rge file using a wizard-like series of setup dialogs:

1. **In Outlook, choose File⇨Import from the menu bar.**

The Begin Import dialog displays.

2. **Select the Entourage Information from an Archive or Earlier Version option and then click the right-arrow button at the lower-right corner of the dialog.**

The Choose an Application dialog displays.

3. **Select the Entourage Archive (.rge) option and click the right-arrow button at the lower-right corner of the dialog.**

The Import file browser displays.

4. **Navigate to the saved Entourage archive `.rge` file and click the Import button.**

   Outlook imports your Identity. If it seems like nothing is happening and the progress bar got all the way to the end, just keep waiting. Eventually you see the Done button.

5. **Click Done.**

   Your Identity has been successfully imported.

6. **In Outlook, choose Tools⇨Accounts from the menu bar.**

   Enter account information to restore your accounts, as described later in this chapter, in the "Managing Accounts in an Identity" section.

Switching from Windows Outlook to Mac Outlook

Microsoft makes it easy to switch to Outlook for Mac. As we mention earlier in this chapter, Outlook 2011 is the first Outlook version to take advantage of the new Outlook Identity format. Before starting this process, we recommend that you make a note of the account settings in Outlook for Windows. In Outlook 2010 for Windows, choose File⇨Info⇨Account Settings.

If you're using a version of Outlook for Windows older than Outlook 2010, check Outlook Help for instructions for making an Outlook data file (`.pst`).

Saving an Outlook data file

You can migrate your Windows Outlook Identity by making an Outlook data file (`.pst`) in Outlook for Windows and then importing the `.pst` file into Outlook 2011 for Mac. Here's how to save your Outlook data file in Outlook 2010 for Windows.

1. **In Outlook 2010 for Windows, choose File⇨Options⇨Advanced⇨Export and then click the Export button.**

   The Import and Export wizard displays. If you don't see the wizard, try minimizing the visible window, because the wizard may display behind the current window.

2. **Select Export to a File and then click the Next button.**

   The Create a File of Type dialog displays.

3. **Select Outlook Data File (.pst) and then click the Next button.**

   The Select a Folder to Export From dialog displays with the proper folder selected and the Include Subfolders check box selected.

4. **Click the Next button.**

   The Save Exported File As dialog displays.

Book V
Chapter 1

Upgrading to
Microsoft Outlook

5. **Give your file a name (be sure to use .pst as the file extension) and then click the Browse button to choose a file location. Note its location and then click the Finish button.**

   Outlook asks whether you want to give your file a password.

6. **Leave the Password fields blank and then click OK.**

   If you click the Cancel button, Outlook not only cancels adding a password, it cancels making your (.pst) file, and you'll have to start over in frustration (as we did).

Outlook prepares the data file, which you should copy or move to your Mac using a method of your choice. (DVD, USB drive, SkyDrive, and SharePoint are but four of many possible transfer methods.)

Importing an Outlook for Windows data file

To import your saved .pst file in Outlook for Mac, follow these steps:

1. **In Outlook 2011 for Mac, choose File⇨Import from the menu bar.**

   The Begin Import dialog displays.

2. **Select Outlook Data File (.pst) and then click the right-arrow button at the lower-right corner of the dialog.**

   The Choose a File Type dialog displays.

3. **Select Outlook for Windows Data File (.pst) and then click the right arrow.**

   The Import file browser displays.

4. **Navigate to the Outlook data file and click the Import button.**

   Outlook imports your Identity. If it seems like nothing is happening and the progress bar got all the way to the end, just keep waiting. Eventually you see the Done button.

5. **Click Done.**

   Your Identity has been successfully imported.

6. **In Outlook 2011 for Mac, choose Tools⇨Accounts from the menu bar.**

   Enter account information to restore your accounts, as shown later in this chapter, in the "Managing Accounts in an Identity" section.

Are you one of the hold-outs on System 9 (or 8.6 even!) still using the old Outlook for Mac? Then hold out no more! Get yourself a nice Intel processor-based Mac and you can upgrade to new Outlook 2011. Before you do, in your old computer's Outlook, choose File⇨Export to start a wizard that will let you save your Outlook Identity as an Outlook for Mac (.olm) data file. Move or copy the .olm data file to your new Mac and then follow the steps outlined in the previous steps. In Step 2, choose Outlook Data File for Mac .olm instead of .pst. The rest of the steps remain the same.

Upgrading from Apple Mail

You may hesitate to upgrade to Outlook if you love Apple Mail. However, we encourage you to try out Outlook. You can easily switch back to Apple Mail if you decide you prefer it.

Upgrading to Outlook is quick and easy. If your Apple Mail is using Microsoft Exchange, skip to the steps in the "Adding an Exchange account" section, later in this chapter. For non-Exchange accounts, you upgrade to Outlook in three stages. The first stage in the upgrade is to copy your e-mail messages, accounts, rules, and signatures from Apple Mail to Outlook:

1. **If Apple Mail is open, close it.**

Check Apple Mail's Dock icon to make sure there's no indicator.

2. **In Outlook, choose File⇨Import from the menu bar.**

The Begin Import dialog displays.

3. **Select Information from Another Application and then click the right-arrow button at the lower-right corner of the dialog.**

The Choose an Application dialog displays.

4. **Select Apple Mail and then click the right-arrow button.**

The Import Items dialog displays.

5. **Accept the default (all check boxes selected) and then click the right-arrow button.**

Outlook imports the selected items.

6. **Click Finish.**

Because Apple Mail is not integrated with iCal, the second stage imports Apple iCal calendar events and to-do entries. Outlook understands W3C standard calendar events in the .ics file format, as does Apple Mail, so you can import calendar events as follows:

1. **In Apple iCal, choose File⇨Export.**

   A Save As dialog displays.

2. **Name your exported file, choose a location that you can easily remember, and then click the Export button.**

   Your calendar and events are ready to be imported into Outlook.

3. **In Outlook, press ⌘-2 to display the Outlook Calendar.**

4. **Drag the file you exported from iCal into the Outlook Calendar.**

   Your calendar events are now incorporated into your Outlook calendar.

The final stage copies your Apple Address Book entries into Outlook. We take advantage of the fact that both Apple Address Book and Outlook use W3C standard vCard files for sharing contacts:

1. **In Apple Address Book, select all contacts that you want to bring to Outlook's Contact manager.**

2. **Drag the selected contacts to the desktop.**

   The single vCard file that appears contains the selected contacts.

3. **In Outlook, press ⌘-3 to display Outlook Contacts.**

4. **Drag the vCard into the list of Outlook contacts.**

   If you had groups in Apple Address book, the group members are given the same category and are not put into an Outlook group.

Upgrading from Gmail or Yahoo! Mail

When you upgrade using IMAP with Gmail or Yahoo! mail, your mail is synchronized between Outlook and the Web. For example, when you delete an e-mail in Outlook, it's deleted simultaneously on the Web, and vice-versa.

Before you can use IMAP with these Web services, you must change the settings on the Web to allow IMAP connections to your Web service. Use the Help feature in Gmail and Yahoo! mail and search for the term *IMAP*. Then follow the instructions to allow your account to accept IMAP connections.

Also search the Web service Help for *export*. These services can export your contacts in Comma Separated Values (.csv) file format, which Outlook can import into your Outlook address book. Contacts between Outlook and the Web can't be synchronized.

The next step is to add your Gmail or Yahoo! account to Outlook. See the "Adding an e-mail account" section, later in this chapter. After you have added your account, in Outlook choose File➪Import from the menu bar to import the contacts from the .csv you saved from the Web. See the later section, "Importing Contacts from a Text File," for directions.

Upgrading from Hotmail

The default configuration that Outlook provides for Hotmail is a POP account. We prefer to use IMAP with Hotmail. To use IMAP with Hotmail, we found a wonderful application called mBox Mail for Mac. It's $19.99 USD and works beautifully with Outlook 2011! (No, we don't get a cut of the price.) Here's where to get it:

http://fluentfactory.com/mboxmail-for-mac

See the later section, "Adding an e-mail account," for instructions on how to add your Hotmail account to Outlook.

Search Hotmail Help for instructions on how to export your contacts in the Comma Separated Values (.csv) file format, which Outlook can import into your Outlook address book, as explained in the next section. Contacts between Outlook and the Web can't be synchronized.

Importing Contacts from a Text File

As we mention earlier in this chapter, sometimes you need to make a .csv file of your contacts in a different e-mail program so that you can bring your contacts into Outlook. Outlook also supports -delimited text file formats such as tab (.txt), comma (.csv), and MBOX file formats, which you can use if your old e-mail program is capable of saving in these formats. Importing Contacts is straightforward using a short series of dialogs:

1. **In Outlook, choose File➪Import from the menu bar.**

   The Begin Import dialog displays.

2. **Select Contacts or Messages from a Text File and then click the right-arrow button at the lower-right corner of the dialog.**

   The Choose a File Type dialog displays.

3. **Depending on the file type you need to import, choose either**

   - Import Contacts from a Tab- or Comma-Delimited Text File.
   - Import Messages from an MBOX-Format Text File.

4. **Click the right-arrow in the lower-right corner of the dialog to display the Import Text File dialog file browser.**

5. **Click the Import button.**

   Outlook displays the Import Contacts dialog shown in Figure 1-3.

6. **Choose the field names from your old e-mail programs to equate them with Outlook's fields using the Import Contacts dialog. This maps the old e-mail program's field names to Outlook's field names.**

7. **Click Import and then, in the next dialog, click Finish.**

   Your contacts from the old e-mail program are now in your Outlook Contacts list.

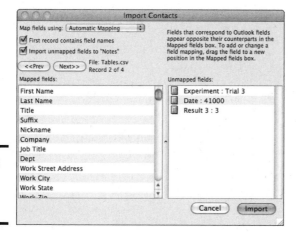

Figure 1-3:
Mapping
imported
fields.

Managing Accounts in an Identity

Earlier in this chapter, we mention that the Welcome screen has an Add Account button. If you click the button, you start with an empty Identity and add the first e-mail account to the Identity. If you already have an e-mail account within an Identity, you can add more accounts, one at a time. You don't have to stick with one kind of e-mail account, either. You could have an IMAP account, an Exchange account, and a POP account all in the same Identity.

You manage accounts within an Identity using the Account dialog. To activate the Account dialog shown in Figure 1-4, click Add Account on the welcome screen; or, in Outlook, choose Tools⇨Accounts from the menu bar.

Set Default Account

The Account dialog lists your Identity's accounts along the left. When you choose an account, the account's settings display on the right. You can make the selected account the default account for the Identity by clicking the Set Default Account button. To add a new account, click the plus (+) sign, and to remove the selected account, click the minus (–) sign. When you click the plus sign, you discover there are three kinds of accounts:

✦ **E-mail:** These are POP and IMAP accounts. (See "Getting to Know Microsoft Outlook for Mac," earlier in this chapter.)

✦ **Exchange:** An account that is hosted on a Microsoft Exchange Server.

✦ **Directory:** This is a lookup service using a protocol called LDAP (Lightweight Directory Assistance Protocol). Large organizations often offer LDAP service either internally or to the entire Internet.

Adding an e-mail account

You may be pleasantly surprised by how easy it is to add an e-mail account to an Outlook Identity. Microsoft has gathered the settings for a large number of popular e-mail providers so that in many cases, all you have to do is enter your e-mail address and password, and Outlook takes care of the rest.

Of course, before you begin, you should obtain your e-mail address, password, and account settings from your Internet service provider. Here's how to add a new e-mail account to an Identity:

1. **In Outlook, choose Tools⇨Accounts from the menu bar.**

The Account dialog displays. (Refer to Figure 1-4.)

2. **Click the plus (+) sign in the lower-left corner. Choose E-Mail from the pop-up menu.**

An import form displays.

3. **Enter the e-mail address and password for your e-mail account and then click OK. (See Figure 1-5.)**

As soon as you enter your e-mail address, additional form fields appear, asking you to supply appropriate settings information provided by your Internet service provider. If Outlook knows the settings, they will be filled in for you and the Configure Automatically check box will remain selected.

4. **If Outlook didn't automatically fill in the account settings, fill them in manually.**

5. **Click the Add Account button to add your e-mail account to the accounts list in the Account dialog.**

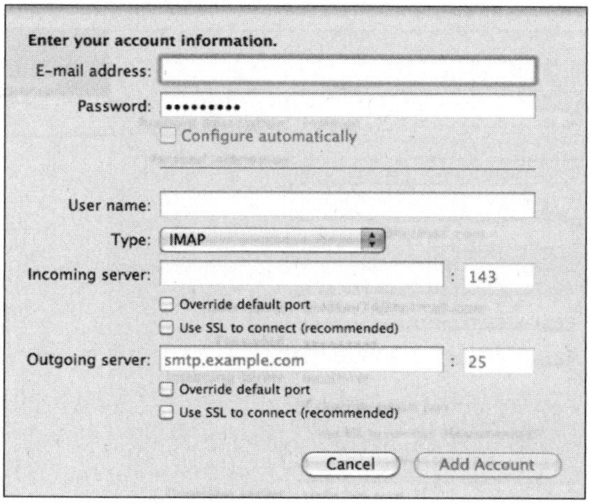

Figure 1-5:
Entering
e-mail
account
settings.

Enter your account information.

E-mail address: [   ]

Password: ••••••••

☐ Configure automatically

User name: [   ]

Type: IMAP �

Incoming server: [   ] : 143

☐ Override default port
☐ Use SSL to connect (recommended)

Outgoing server: smtp.example.com : 25

☐ Override default port
☐ Use SSL to connect (recommended)

(Cancel) (Add Account)

Adding an Exchange account

Adding an Exchange account is easy to do:

1. **In Outlook, choose Tools⇨Accounts from the menu bar.**

   The Account dialog displays. (Refer to Figure 1-4.)

2. **Click the plus (+) sign in the lower-left corner. Choose Exchange from the pop-up menu.**

   An import form displays.

3. **Enter your e-mail address, username, and password in the aptly named text boxes. (See Figure 1-6.)**

4. **From the Method pop-up menu, choose User Name and Password.**

   In most cases, entering these three pieces of information and choosing User Name and Password is all you need to do — Outlook does the rest.

   If you need to use Kerberos to connect to Exchange, click the Method pop-up button and choose Kerberos. Kerberos is an authentication protocol — don't worry too much about this unless your system or the server administrator asks you to opt for this option.

5. **Click the Add Account button.**

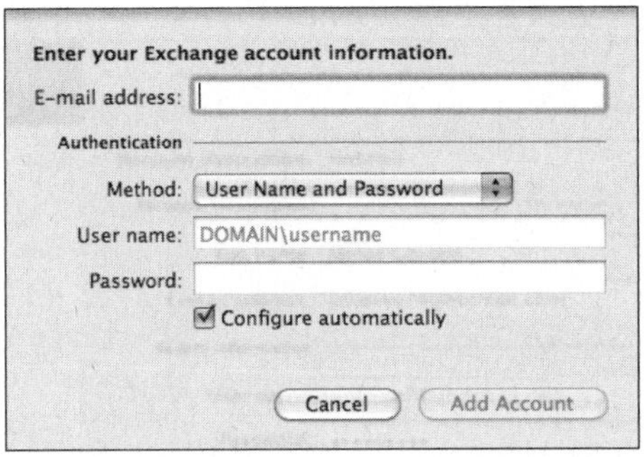

Figure 1-6:
Entering
Exchange
account
settings.

Enter your Exchange account information.
E-mail address: |

Authentication

Method: [User Name and Password ◆]
User name: [DOMAIN\username]
Password: [   ]
   ☑ Configure automatically

(Cancel) (Add Account)

Immediately after connecting, Outlook synchronizes itself with the Exchange server bringing in all your mail, contacts, calendars, tasks, and notes. We were impressed by how fast synchronization took place with our Exchange server.

Adding a directory account

A *directory* is a list of contacts provided in standard LDAP format, typically for a large organization or entity. If you add a directory account to Outlook, the contacts will be automatically available as you type e-mail addresses, and you will be able to search the directory to find individuals. You will need to obtain the LDAP directory settings from the server administrator prior to attempting to add the server to your Outlook accounts. To add an account, take these steps:

1. **In Outlook, choose Tools➪Accounts from the menu bar.**

   The Account dialog displays.

2. **Click the plus (+) sign in the lower-left corner. Choose Directory Service from the pop-up menu.**

   An import form displays.

3. **Enter the name of the LDAP server and then click Add Account.**

   The account is added to the list of accounts in the Account dialog, and the account settings display on the right.

4. **(Optional) Click the Advanced button.**

   Advanced settings display, as shown in Figure 1-7. Adjust settings as required for the LDAP server. In the Search Base field, typically you enter something like **c=US** for a United States Server and **o=*Organization's name*.**

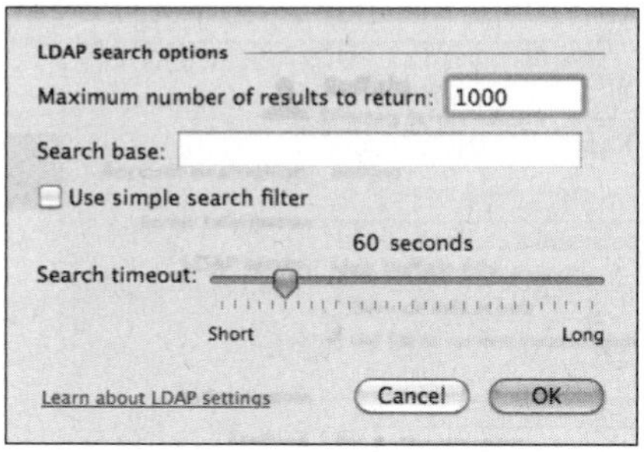

Figure 1-7:
Entering
advanced
LDAP
settings.

LDAP search options

Maximum number of results to return: 1000

Search base:

☐ Use simple search filter

60 seconds

Search timeout: ―――――――――――――――――――

Short   Long

Learn about LDAP settings   (Cancel) (OK)

Managing Identities

At the beginning of this chapter, we introduce the concept of an Identity. In Figure 1-2, we show where your Identities are stored on your Mac. Now we explain how to take care of your Outlook Identities. The default Outlook Identity is called Main Identity. Outlook gives you some tools to help you manage your Identities.

Running Microsoft Database Utility

Microsoft Database Utility, shown in Figure 1-8, is your Identity-managing toolbox.

You must quit Outlook before you can run the Database Utility. To run the Utility, *hold the Option key down as you open Outlook.* Microsoft Database Utility enables you to do the following:

+ **Create a new Identity.** Click the plus (+) sign in the lower-left corner of the Utility window, and then type a name for a new, empty Identity.

+ **Delete the selected Identity.** Select an Identity from the list and then click the minus (–) sign in the lower-left corner to move the selected Identity's folder from the Office 2011 Identities folder to the Trash.

+ **Set the default Identity.** Select an Identity from the list and click the Set as Default button to make it the Identity that Outlook uses when it opens.

+ **Rebuild an Identity.** Select an Identity from the list and then click the Rebuild button to build a new Identity of the same name from the contents of the selected Identity. The old Identity is renamed as Backed Up with the date and time it was rebuilt, as shown in Figure 1-8. After enough time has passed that you're satisfied that the rebuilt Identity is functioning properly, use the Database Utility to delete the backed up file.

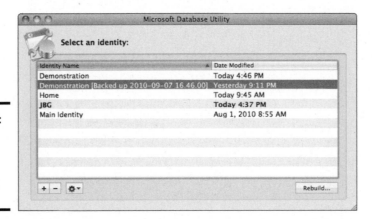

Figure 1-8: Running Outlook's Microsoft Database Utility.

Manually upgrading an Entourage Identity

If you had more than one Identity in Entourage 2008 or 2004 you can manually upgrade them to Outlook 2008. Take these steps to upgrade one of your old Identities. You can update one Identity at a time:

1. Quit Outlook (pressing ⌘-Q quits any application).

2. Run the Microsoft Database Utility as described in the preceding section.

3. In the Database Utility, click the plus (+) sign, and a new name is added to the Identity Name list. Type a name for your new Identity.

4. Set the newly added Identity as the default Identity.

5. Click the red Close button to close the Microsoft Database Utility.

6. Open Outlook.

Outlook will open and run with an empty Identity.

7. Choose File⇨Import from the menu bar.

This starts a series of dialogs. The Begin Import dialog displays.

8. Select Entourage Information from an Archive or Earlier Version and then click the right arrow at the lower-right corner of the dialog.

The Choose an Application dialog displays.

9. Select either Entourage 2004 or Entourage 2008 as appropriate and then click the right arrow.

The Import Items dialog displays with all check boxes selected.

10. Accept the default and click the right arrow.

The Select an Identity dialog displays.

11. Select the Identity you want to upgrade and then click the right arrow.

The default is to display Entourage Identities. You can click the Browse button if your Identities aren't stored in the default location.

12. Outlook upgrades your Identity and then opens so that you can use it.

If you're prompted about allowing items to be updated in your Keychain, choose Always Allow.

Rebuild your freshly imported Identity before using it. (See the previous section, "Running Microsoft Database Utility.")

Switching Identities

Only one Identity at a time can display in Outlook. To switch Identities, take these steps:

1. **Quit Outlook (pressing ⌘-Q quits any application).**
2. **Run the Microsoft Database Utility as described earlier in this chapter.**
3. **Change the default Outlook Identity.**
4. **Click the red close window button in the upper-left corner of the Utility window to quit the Database Utility.**
5. **Start Outlook.**

You can make the Outlook dialog shown in Figure 1-9 display automatically whenever you open Outlook. To make the dialog available:

1. **Quit Outlook (pressing ⌘-Q quits any application).**
2. **In Finder, open your Microsoft Office 2011 Identities folder.**
3. **Change the name of the folder of your default Outlook Identity.**
4. **Start Outlook.**
5. **Select the Show This List When Opening Outlook check box.**

Be sure to select the Show This List When Opening Outlook check box. It's a handy tool for switching Identities instead of using the Database Utility. You can then choose the Identity you want to use and click OK without having to open the Database Utility.

Figure 1-9:
Outlook's
Identity
chooser
dialog.

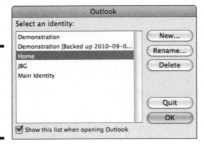

Chapter 2: Using Common Outlook Tools

In This Chapter

✔ Operating in Outlook's default view

✔ Discovering the menu bar

✔ Using and customizing the toolbar

✔ Finding your way around the Ribbon

✔ Switching views

No matter which productivity tool you choose in Outlook, certain aspects of the interface remain the same. In this chapter, we show you the elements of Outlook's interface you can expect to find in all five of Outlook's views.

Opening in Outlook's Default Mail View

When you open Outlook, the default view is Mail. You can always switch to Mail by using the keyboard shortcut ⌘-1, by choosing View➪Go To➪Mail from the menu bar, or by clicking the Mail button at the lower-left corner of the Outlook window. (See Figure 2-1.)

In Chapter 3 of this minibook, we cover using the tools within the Mail view. In this chapter, we focus on the overall Outlook interface.

Standard toolbar

Menu bar

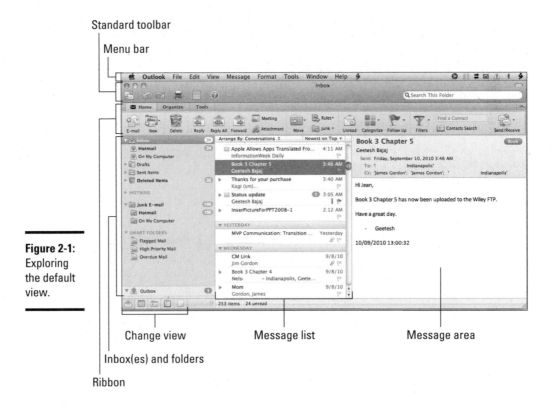

Figure 2-1:
Exploring
the default
view.

Change view

Message list

Message area

Inbox(es) and folders

Ribbon

Moving Around the Menu Bar

Mac users can relax — the menu bar, shown in Figure 2-2, remains an integral part of the Outlook interface. Outlook for Mac, even though it's brand new, sports the traditional menu bar. You can use keyboard navigation with the Outlook menu bar. The Outlook menu bar shows keyboard shortcuts, changes in context as you use Outlook, has the commands found in the Ribbon and toolbars, and works in all views in Outlook. It's the real deal! Well, almost — you can't customize the menu in Outlook like you can in Word, Excel, and PowerPoint as described in Book I, Chapter 2.

To find out what all those keyboard shortcut symbols mean, choose Help➪Outlook Help. In the search field, type **keyboard shortcuts** and then press Return. The topic *Outlook Keyboard Shortcuts* is a good one to start with. Click disclosure triangles in the help topic for more information.

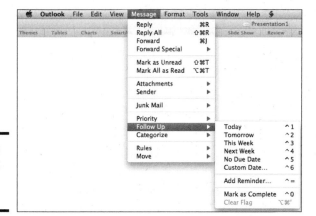

Figure 2-2:
Peeking at
the Follow
Up menu.

The Follow Up feature shown in Figure 2-2 is available not only in Outlook, but also in Word, PowerPoint, and Excel. Use Follow Up to set an Outlook reminder for a selected item.

Tailoring the Toolbar for Quick Access

Just beneath the menu bar is the Standard toolbar. The Standard toolbar in Office for Mac serves the same purpose as the Quick Access Toolbar in Office for Windows — it offers quick access to common tools. The Standard toolbar on the Mac is context sensitive. You can customize the Standard toolbar, as shown in Figure 2-3.

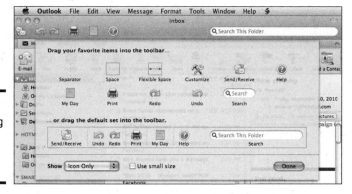

Figure 2-3:
Customizing
Outlook's
Standard
toolbar.

To display the toolbar customization options, choose View⇨Customize Toolbar from the menu bar. You can customize the Standard toolbar as follows:

✦ **To add commands,** drag individual commands from the top portion to the toolbar or drag the complete default set of tools to the toolbar.

✦ **To remove a command,** drag it from the toolbar and then let go. As the command disappears, it will go poof!

✦ **To show a command,** choose one of these options from the Show pop-up menu:

• *Icon and Text:* Toolbar buttons display icon and description.

• *Icon Only:* Toolbar buttons display their icons only.

• *Text Only:* Toolbar buttons display description only.

✦ **To use small icons,** select the Use Small Size check box. (This option may not work until the first update is installed.)

In Outlook, you can open individual items in their own windows. For example, you can open an e-mail message in its own window, or a contact in its own window. You can customize the toolbar options for each different kind of window that you see by choosing View⇨Customize Toolbar from the menu while viewing a window. You see a different set of options for each kind of window. The customization options available in a calendar window are different from the options in a message window, for instance.

The little oval button in the upper-right corner of each window shows and hides the toolbar. If you thought you lost your toolbar, click this button to get it back!

Ringing in the Ribbon

The Ribbon is sandwiched between the Standard toolbar and the work area represented by the various Outlook views. Like menus and toolbars, the Ribbon is context aware, displaying commands that are appropriate for the view or window that's open. The Outlook Ribbon has three tabs:

✦ **Home:** Displays the tools you are most likely to use in the Outlook view you're using.

✦ **Organize:** This tab has additional tools that let you fine-tune actions in the current view to keep you at your most productive.

✦ **Tools:** The Tools tab is a little gold mine of tools you can use to enhance your activities.

On the Ribbon, way off to the right, in the bar that contains the Home, Organize, and Tools tabs, is a little toggle button (shown in the margin). Clicking this button shows or hides the Ribbon. Clicking a Ribbon tab button more than once also shows or hides the Ribbon. In Outlook, you can't customize the Ribbon or change the order of its tabs.

Changing Views

In the lower-left corner of the major view windows are five buttons (shown in Figure 2-4), one for each of the different views in Outlook. These are the same views you have when choosing View➪Go To and choosing a view, or pressing the corresponding ⌘-key shortcut:

View	Keyboard Shortcut
Mail	⌘-1
Calendar	⌘-2
Contacts	⌘-3
Tasks	⌘-4
Notes	⌘-5

Figure 2-4:
Choosing a
view.

Mail   Contacts   Notes

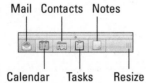

Calendar   Tasks   Resize

If the view buttons are too small for your taste, you can drag the small dot centered above the icons up. The View buttons resize, as shown in Figure 2-5.

Drag the dot up for larger icons.

Figure 2-5:
Displaying
larger view
buttons.

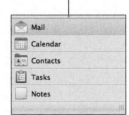

Watching Your Status

The status bar is the white band along the bottom of the menu to the right of the View buttons. (Refer to Figure 2-1.) Keep your eye on this portion of the window to see statistics about your working environment and progress bars for actions taking place. If your computer is connected to a Microsoft Exchange server, the name of the account displays near the right end of the status bar. The bottom-right corner of the status bar is a drag handle that lets you resize the entire window.

Chapter 3: Mastering Mail

In This Chapter

✔ Setting your viewing environment

✔ Arranging and ordering message lists

✔ Changing Outlook's preferences

✔ Reviewing the Ribbon

✔ Reading and writing e-mail

✔ Searching and Smart Folders

✔ Clobbering junk mail

✔ Automating Outlook with rules and schedules

*F*or many, e-mail is old-hat. Perhaps you have several e-mail accounts. You read your mail, reply to whatever is important, just ignore some mail, move whatever you want to folders, and probably delete the rest! Pretty simple. Outlook lets you do all of that with its standard default settings.

But if you want to do more, Outlook is up to the challenge. You can categorize and even automate your e-mail as it comes in. Outlook can send and receive high-quality HTML e-mail, and is the engine that dispatches Mail Merge documents made in Microsoft Word. Outlook can also help you keep spam out of your hair. You can even work with your Outlook calendar right in an e-mail message.

In Chapter 1 of this minibook, we describe what an Identity is and how to manage your Identity. Everything we talk about in this chapter happens within a single Outlook Identity.

In this chapter, we show you how a typical, active e-mail account looks if you had chosen an upgrade option (see Chapter 1 of this minibook) or if you have already configured an account. We believe most users will upgrade, so instead of showing an empty account, we show an active account with Outlook's default view settings. If you open Outlook without having any e-mail accounts, you would see fewer mailboxes, the message list would be empty, and you would see a single Welcome to Outlook message.

Working in Mail View

As we show at the beginning of Chapter 2 of this minibook, when you open Outlook, the program is in Mail view. While Outlook is running, you can always see how many unread e-mail messages you have by glancing at Outlook's dock icon and looking for the number bubble. Even when you press ⌘-Tab to switch applications, you see the bubble, as shown in Figure 3-1. Outlook also tells you how many unread messages you have in a folder or Inbox in the folder pane. (Look ahead to Figure 3-2.)

Figure 3-1:
Unread
messages.

Viewing the default Mail view

Outlook 2011 introduces two new concepts to viewing your mail. The default view, shown in Figure 3-2, has both of these features turned on:

✦ **Grouped Folders:** Look closely at Figure 3-2 and notice the organization of the folders. In this new arrangement, immediately beneath the Inbox you find On My Computer. If you have more than one account in your Identity, folders with similar names are grouped together. Compare this arrangement of folder groupings with Figure 3-3, where folders are not grouped.

✦ **Arranged by Conversations:** Figure 3-2 also shows that messages are arranged by threaded conversations, meaning that all the messages regarding the same subject are grouped together. The conversation thread in Figure 3-2 is lightly shaded, and one of the messages in the conversation has been selected.

Figure 3-2:
Outlook's
default Mail
view.

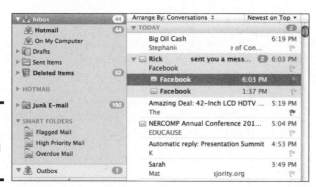

The default view setting is for message bodies to be displayed to the right of the list of messages, with the newest message threads shown at the top of the message list, which lies between the folder list and the message body. The subject of the message displays in bold if there are unread messages in the conversation. Messages that have been read are displayed in normal (not bold) font.

Given the number of requests for threaded messages Microsoft received over the years, it's not surprising that they decided to make Conversation the default arrangement. If you find you don't like Conversation view, we explain how to set things to the old way.

Switching to folder/subfolder arrangement

To use the traditional folder/subfolder arrangement for your folder list, you have only one setting to change. Choose Outlook⇨Preferences from the menu bar. In the Preferences dialog, find the Personal Settings group and click General. In the Folder List group, deselect the check box labeled Group Similar Folders, such as Inboxes, from Different Accounts. Your folder list will now look more like the arrangement shown in Figure 3-3. In particular, notice that folders under the On My Computer heading (meaning they're not on the server, but saved locally on your Mac) are now segregated from the Inbox in traditional folders with subfolders.

Figure 3-3:
Arranging the traditional way.

▼ HOTMAIL		Arrange By: Date Received ‡	Newest on Top ▼
INBOX	6	**Indezine**	9/7/10
Drafts		Indezine News for Jim	
Sent Messages		▼ LAST WEEK	1
Deleted Messages	25	**Kagi (sm)**	9/5/10
Junk	182	**Thanks for your purchase**	
Addins		Kagi (sm)	9/5/10
Book		Thanks for your purchase	
MVP hotmail		Kagi (sm)	9/2/10
Office Live		Thanks for your purchase	
OneCare		Kagi (sm)	9/2/10
Receipts		Thanks for your purchase	
Saved		Kagi (sm)	9/2/10
VBA		Thanks for your purchase *	
		Kagi (sm)	9/1/10
▼ ON MY COMPUTER		Thanks for your purchase	
Inbox		Jim Gordon	9/1/10
Drafts		FW: Turning Technologies' Requeste...	
Sent Items		Kagi (sm)	8/31/10
Deleted Items		Thanks for your purchase	
Junk E-mail		Kagi (sm)	8/30/10
		Thanks for your purchase	
▼ SMART FOLDERS		Kagi (sm)	8/30/10
Flagged Mail		Thanks for your purchase	
High Priority Mail		▼ 2 WEEKS AGO	3
Overdue Mail		Facebook	8/29/10
		Biff Buffalo invited you to the event "...	

Choosing a different message arrangement

Outlook doesn't force you to use the new Conversation arrangement of messages in the message list. The Arrange By label at the top of the message list is also a pop-up menu button. Click it to display a pop-up menu, where you can choose from a wide variety of message arrangements. You can display the same menu by choosing View➪Arrange By from the menu bar.

The Date Received label at the top of the message list is also a pop-up menu. Click it to reverse the order in which messages are displayed.

Even if you don't choose to arrange by conversation, you can still see which messages are in a conversation. When you select a message in the message list, other messages that are in the same conversation are shaded to make it easy to spot them, as shown in Figure 3-3. This is an exceptionally nice touch!

Making a custom message arrangement

When you examine the list of possible arrangements in the Arrange By pop-up menu, you can choose Custom Arrangements➪Edit Custom Arrangements to display the Custom Arrangements: Mail dialog, shown in Figure 3-4, which will be empty until you make a custom arrangement.

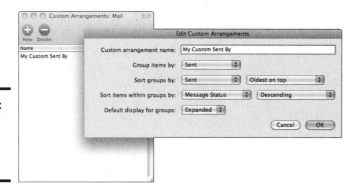

Figure 3-4:
Making a
custom
arrange-
ment.

To make your first custom arrangement, click the New button in the Custom Arrangements: Mail dialog to display the Edit Custom Arrangements dialog, also shown in Figure 3-4. You have thousands of possible arrangement combinations from which to choose. Give your custom arrangement a name, choose options from the pop-up menus and then click OK to add your Custom Arrangement to the list of Custom Arrangements: Mail. To edit a custom arrangement, double-click its name. To delete a custom arrangement, select it in the list and then click the Delete button.

Customizing the Reading Pane

After you select your Inbox in the folder list (on the left side of the window), choose View⇨Reading Pane from the menu bar and then choose one of the following three preview pane arrangements:

✦ **On Right:** This is Outlook's initial arrangement. When the Reading pane is on the right, message subjects appear in a column in the middle. If you select a message subject, the body of your message appears in the Reading pane to the right of the list of message subjects.

✦ **Below List:** This layout option moves the Reading pane to a position below the list of message subjects. When you click a message subject, the message body appears below the list of message subjects.

✦ **Hidden:** This option hides the Reading pane so that the list of message subjects fills a larger area. To read a message, double-click a message subject or right-click on a message and choose Open Message from the contextual menu to open the message in its own window.

Finding and Setting Mail Preferences

Outlook offers hundreds of ways to customize the way messages are presented, processed, and replied to. You can access these settings in the Outlook Preferences dialog, shown in Figure 3-5, which you open by choosing Outlook⇨Preferences from the menu bar.

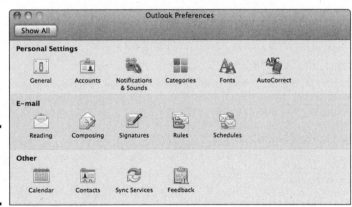

Figure 3-5:
The Outlook
Preferences
dialog.

The settings that affect mail are found in Personal Settings group as well as the E-Mail group in the Outlook Preferences dialog. The settings are well described within the Preferences panel, but we want to make sure you know about these settings in particular:

+ **General:** Click the General icon in the Outlook Preferences dialog to find the Make Default button, which makes Outlook the default application on your computer for e-mail, contacts, and calendars.

+ **Accounts:** Click Accounts in the Outlook Preferences dialog to display the Account dialog. (Alternatively, you can access the dialog by choosing Tools➪Accounts from the menu bar.) Be sure to click the Advanced button in the Account dialog (discussed in Chapter 1 in this minibook) and choose the Folders tab, as shown in Figure 3-6. There are folder automation options to make using e-mail more productive.

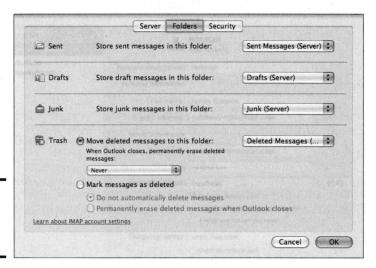

Figure 3-6:
Adjusting folder options.

+ **Notifications & Sounds:** Click Notifications & Sounds in the Outlook Preferences dialog to adjust what kinds of sounds and visual notifications Outlook generates as you work with mail.

+ **Categories:** Click Categories in the Outlook Preferences dialog to classify just about everything in Outlook. You can apply categories manually or with rules; you can organize and search by categories. Managing your categories is simple. To add a new category, click the plus (+) sign, as shown in Figure 3-7. Give your new category a name and choose a color from the pop-up menu.

To delete a category, select it from the list of categories and then click the minus (–) sign. Deleting a category deletes the colored labels and also affects any rules using the deleted category. An object that was categorized is not deleted when you delete its category.

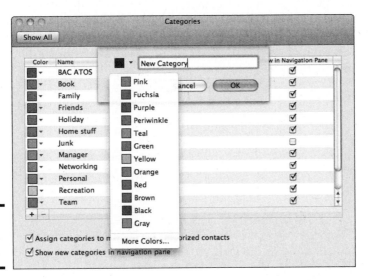

Figure 3-7:
Managing
categories.

✦ **Fonts:** Click Fonts in the Outlook Preferences dialog to choose default fonts for composing HTML and plain text messages. The font you choose for HTML mail affects how your message displays on both your Mac and the recipient's computer. The font you choose for plain text affects how the message displays in Outlook on your Mac but has no effect on your message's appearance on the recipient's computer.

✦ **AutoCorrect:** Click AutoCorrect in the Outlook Preferences dialog to edit AutoCorrect and AutoFormat options for text, as well as bullets and numbering. If you don't want Outlook to automatically format hyperlinks, that setting is here.

✦ **Reading:** Click Reading in the Outlook Preferences dialog to change some of the default settings. Of course, you're free to choose the settings that work best for you:

• *Mark as Read:* We changed the setting to zero seconds for Mark Items as Read after Being Previewed for *X* Seconds. (Two seconds is the default.)

- *Conversations:* We liked the default settings — we especially like Highlight Messages from the Same Conversation.

- *IMAP:* We deselected the Hide IMAP Messages Marked for Deletion check box. Out of sight means out of mind. Hidden deleted messages pile up until you remember to Purge Deleted Messages. Also, you go crazy looking for hidden deleted messages, because they don't go to the Deleted Messages folder by default. (Refer to Figure 3-6.)

- *Security:* We strongly recommend you keep the default setting of Never. Spammers and ne'er-do-wells can spy on you easily otherwise.

✦ **Composing:** Click Composing in the Outlook Preferences dialog to change what kind of formatting is applied to messages you reply to. Experiment with the settings to see which arrangement you like best.

✦ **Signatures:** Click Signatures in the Outlook Preferences dialog to add a signature. (See Figure 3-8.) To add a signature, click the plus (+) sign. To delete a signature, select it in the list and then click the minus (–) sign.

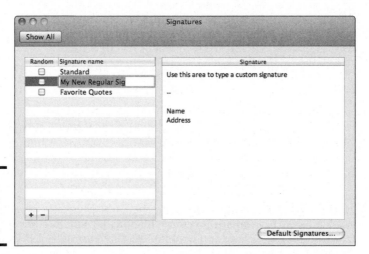

Figure 3-8:
Managing
mail
signatures.

You can choose which signature will be used for each account within an Identity by clicking the Default Signatures button. You can then select which signature to assign to an account, as shown in Figure 3-9. If you have more than one e-mail account in your Identity, Outlook keeps track of which signature will be used when sending or replying to messages. If you want, you can make a large collection of signatures and then choose the Random option to include the signatures selected to be included at random.

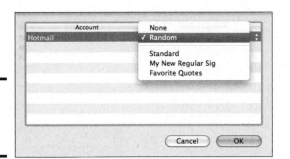

Figure 3-9:
Choosing
a default
signature.

✦ **Rules:** Click Rules in the Outlook Preferences dialog to set rules. Alternatively, choose Tools⇨Rules from the menu bar. For more about rules, see the "Automating with Rules" section, later in this chapter.

✦ **Schedules:** Click Schedules in the Outlook Preferences dialog to tell Outlook to perform operations you specify at predetermined times. See the later section, "Keeping on Schedule," for more information.

Reconnoitering the Ribbon

We've always wanted to use the word *reconnoitering* because it sounds fun, and by gosh we finally found a good use for it! We highlight features on each of the three tabs in Mail view: Home, Organize, and Tools. When you open an individual item in its own window, such as a message, you find additional Ribbon tabs. Those tabs are discussed in the topics for each feature.

Going to the Home tab

The Home tab of the Ribbon, shown in Figure 3-10, is where you spend most of your time when working with e-mail. It has most of the commands you need. Of course, you can always use the menu bar at the top where you may find additional options, or you may find it quicker to right-click and use contextual menus. You're free to choose whichever interface tools you prefer. The buttons on the Home tab of the Ribbon do the following:

Figure 3-10:
The Home
tab in Mail
view.

+ **E-Mail:** Opens a new mail message dialog.

+ **New:** Displays a pop-up menu from which you can choose to make a new e-mail message, meeting, appointment, contact, contact group, task, or note.

+ **Delete:** Deletes the select message. In an IMAP account, the default behavior is to mark the message for deletion and then hide the message.

+ **Reply:** When a message is selected, displays a mail message pre-addressed to the sender of the selected message, with the body of the original message included and indented.

+ **Reply All:** Same as Reply, but all recipients in the To and CC fields in the original message are replied to.

+ **Forward:** Opens a mail message with the contents of the selected message. Fill in recipients in the To field and then click Send to send the message.

+ **Meeting:** Opens a dialog that lets you schedule a meeting, complete with the ability to add a customized meeting invitation to send to invitees, and the ability to use the Scheduling Assistant to help you check for available times in your calendar.

+ **Attachment:** Opens a new mail message with the contents of the selected message attached so that you can send it as-is to recipients you specify. You can include a new message body of your own without disturbing the contents of the original message.

+ **Move:** Select one or more messages in the list and then click this button to display a browser that lets you choose a folder in your folder list. The selected messages will be moved to the folder you choose.

+ **Rules:** Displays a pop-up menu that lets you apply existing rules or display the Rules dialog discussed later in this chapter.

+ **Junk:** Select one or more messages in the message list and then click this to display a menu with the following options:

  • *Mark as Junk:* Changes the category of selected messages to Junk.

  • *Block Sender:* Adds the sender's e-mail address to the list of blocked senders in Tools⇨Junk E-Mail Protection⇨Blocked Senders.

  • *Mark as Not Junk:* Only displays if three or more messages are selected, or if you change the state of a selected message previously classified as junk to not junk.

+ **Unread:** Changes the state of a read message to unread. The button may change to Read so you can change the state of a message from unread to read.

+ **Categorize:** Using the pop-up menu, you can apply a category to selected messages, display a dialog to add or edit categories (refer to Figure 3-7), and clear categories from selected messages.

+ **Follow-Up:** Click the triangle next to the flag to display a pop-up menu that lets you set a reminder for the selected item. Clicking the flag itself sets a reminder for today with the selected item.

+ **Filters:** Click the triangle on the right of this button to display a pop-up menu from which you can choose a variety of filters or clear all filters.

+ **Find a Contact:** Type a contact's name and then press Return or Enter to display the results of your contact search in the Contacts Search.

+ **Contacts Search:** Displays the Contacts Search dialog. If you have an LDAP directory account and/or an Exchange account in this identity, you can choose which contact directory to search.

+ **Send/Receive:** Click this button to tell Outlook to check with the mail server and update the message list and send messages that are queued in the Outbox. Click the small triangle on the right side of the button to display a pop-up menu that includes the all-important Purge Deleted Items for an IMAP account. Also, you can right-click an IMAP folder and choose Purge Deleted Items from the pop-up menu.

By default, Outlook hides deleted messages in an IMAP account. Just because you can't see them, that doesn't mean they're gone. You have to purge deleted items from an IMAP folder to permanently delete the messages from the server.

Getting organized on the Organize tab

Outlook grants exceptional capability to organize your mail. (Note that the Permissions and Properties options will be grayed out on the Organize tab unless you're using a Microsoft Exchange account.) The Organize tab of the Ribbon in Mail view, as shown in Figure 3-11, presents key organization tools:

Figure 3-11: The Organize tab in Mail view.

✦ **New Folder:** Choose an account, or a folder within an account, and then click this button to add a new folder or subfolder.

✦ **Conversations:** Click to change the arrangement of messages in the message list to Conversations or toggle to the date received arrangement.

✦ **Arrange By:** Displays a pop-up menu allowing you to choose options for displaying your message subjects.

✦ **Reading Pane:** Choose Right, Below, or Hidden, as described in the "Customizing the Reading Pane" section, earlier in this chapter.

✦ **All Read:** Marks all messages in your message list or folder as Read.

✦ **Rules:** Displays a pop-up menu from which you can apply or edit Rules. See the "Automating with Rules" section, later in this chapter.

✦ **Delete All:** Deletes all messages in your message list.

✦ **Permissions:** For an Exchange account, displays the Folder Properties dialog on the Permissions tab, as shown in Figure 3-12. This dialog allows you to share your folders in your Exchange account. Click Add User to search for other Exchange users to share with, and add those users to the list of approved users in the dialog. To remove a user from the approved users list, select the user's name in the user list and then click the Remove button.

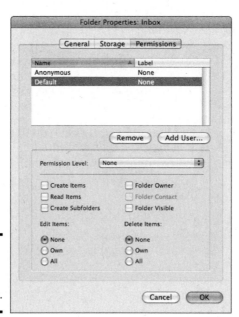

Figure 3-12:
Setting
Exchange
permissions.

✦ **Properties:** For an Exchange account, displays the Folder Properties dialog on the General tab, where there's an option to empty the cache. Read the warning in the dialog before using this feature.

✦ **Sync:** Clicking this button causes the selected folder to be synchronized with the IMAP or Exchange server.

Tackling the Tools tab

The Tools tab of the Ribbon in Mail view, shown in Figure 3-13, gives you unprecedented control over your account:

Figure 3-13: Using the Tools tab in Mail view.

✦ **My Day:** Click to display the My Day mini-application. See Chapter 4 of this minibook, where we discuss calendars.

✦ **Out of Office:** For Exchange accounts only, click to display the Out of Office Assistant dialog, shown in Figure 3-14. Set rules for handling internal and external out of office messages in this dialog.

✦ **Public Folders:** For Exchange accounts only, click to display a folder browser that lets you subscribe to public folders that you have been given permission to use.

✦ **Import:** Displays the Import dialog described in Chapter 1 of this minibook.

✦ **Export:** Displays the Export dialog, where you can choose to save your contacts in a tab-delimited .txt file, or save an Outlook archive (for backing up or moving to another computer) as an .olm file.

✦ **Sync Services:** You can choose to sync your Outlook contacts with Apple Address book and MobileMe. It's likely that additional sync services will be made available in an update by the time you read this.

✦ **Schedules:** Displays a pop-up menu, where you can choose Empty Deleted Items Folder, Send and Receive All, or Send All.

✦ **Mailing Lists:** Displays the Mailing List Manager, where advanced users can set rules to automatically move messages from one folder to another, and even run an AppleScript from Outlook. The options in this dialog are beyond the scope of this book.

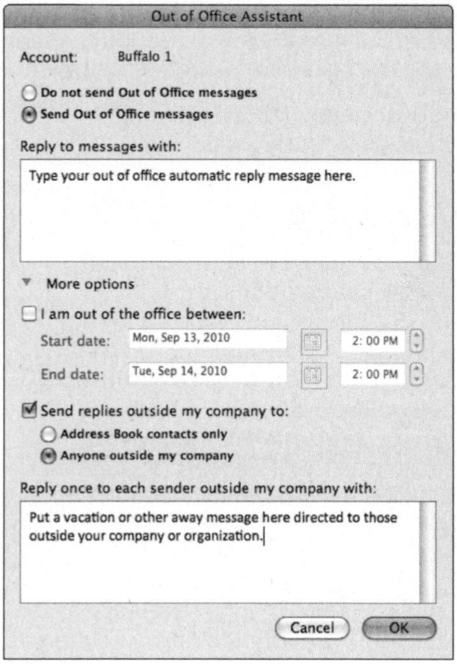

Figure 3-14:
Setting a
vacation
reminder.

✦ **Progress:** Displays a small dialog showing progress bars of any activity between Outlook and servers it's exchanging information with.

✦ **Errors:** Displays a dialog describing errors Outlook encountered. This information may be useful in diagnosing connection and set up problems.

✦ **Online/Offline mode:** This button toggles Outlook to Offline mode, where it remembers your actions. You can work in Offline mode when you're reading and replying to mail, checking or adding calendar events, and so on. When you're connected to the Internet, you can switch back to Online mode, and Outlook synchronizes everything for you automatically.

Reading Mail

Double-click a message subject in the message list to open the message in its own window, as shown in Figure 3-15. This window comes with a mini Message Ribbon that has many of the controls of the Home tab of the Ribbon. The Message window has some handy features of its own.

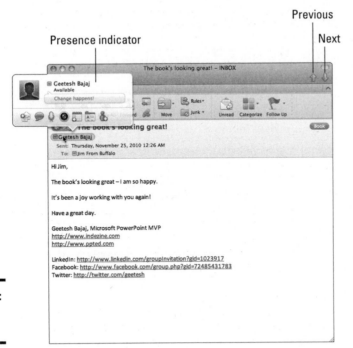

Presence indicator

Previous

Next

Figure 3-15:
Reading a
message.

In Figure 3-15, you see the Presence indicator that displays if you mouse
over the green dot adjoining the name of someone who is in your address
book and is online in MSN Messenger or in Communicator. The tools on
the Message tab of the Ribbon work the same as those on the Home tab
of the main Ribbon. Presence indicators are explained in detail in Book I,
Chapter 10. Here are a few other interesting features you might want to
try while reading a message:

✦ **Speech:** Select message text and then right-click. From the contextual
   menu, choose Speech➪Start Speaking to listen to the words. Choose
   Speech➪Stop Speaking from the same menu to stop speaking.

✦ **Search:** Right-click a word or term in a message and then from the
   resulting pop-up menu choose one of the following:

   • *Search in Spotlight:* Find using Spotlight in Mac OS X.

   • *Search in Google:* We wonder why Google is the option here instead
     of Bing.

   • *Look Up in Dictionary:* Looks up the selection in the Mac OS X
     Dictionary application.

✦ **Hyperlink:** Click a hyperlink to open it in your default Web browser. Right-click a hyperlink to display a pop-up menu that lets you copy the link.

✦ **Attachment:** If you receive a message with one or more attachments, they will be listed just above the message area.

  • *Preview:* Select an attachment and press the spacebar to preview it. You don't even have to open the attachment to preview common attachment types such as Office files, PDFs, and pictures.

  • *Save:* Right-click an attachment to display a Save-As dialog so that you can save the attachment.

Right-click a message subject in the message list to reveal a contextual menu with all sorts of handy options. This is the menu where you can find View Source, which displays a window showing the complete message header.

There's a great new feature for working with invitations right inside a message. For that feature, please see Chapter 4 in this minibook, which is about the Calendar.

You don't have to return to the message list to read additional messages. Clicking the Previous and Next message buttons (shown in Figure 3-15) allows you to stay in the message window while going through your messages.

If you switch to other applications while Outlook is running, when mail is received, a notification appears for a moment, as shown in the margin. The notification offers three options:

✦ **X:** Closes the notification without taking any other actions.

✦ **Delete:** Deletes or marks the message for deletion.

✦ **Clicking the message subject:** Opens the message in Outlook.

To turn this notification off, choose Outlook➪Preferences➪ Notifications and Sounds from the menu bar. In the Message Arrival section, deselect the check box labeled For New Messages Display an Alert on My Desktop.

Composing a Message

You can compose e-mail messages in Microsoft Office in several different ways. In the following sections, we discuss various ways you can make and send an e-mail message.

Perhaps the easiest way to start a new mail message is to click the E-Mail button on the Home tab of the Outlook Ribbon or by pressing ⌘-N. The window shown in Figure 3-16 opens. Outlook displays an empty message-body area. Figure 3-16 shows the Message tab of the Ribbon in the new message window.

To compose a message, enter one or more contacts or e-mail addresses in the To field and, if desired, the Cc or Bcc field. Enter the subject of your message in the Subject field. Then click in the body area and type your message. If you want, you can format the text just as if you were using a word processor. When you're ready to send the message, click the Send button.

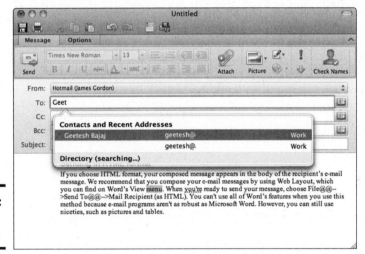

Figure 3-16:
Composing
a message.

There are some specific features we want to draw to your attention:

✦ **Insert Hyperlink:** Select some text in your message and then click this button. Type or paste a URL to make a live hyperlink in your message. Alternatively, you can drag or paste a URL directly into your message and then press Return to activate the link, although long links are not attractive and can be damaged by some e-mail systems. Be sure to use the entire link, including the `http://` part.

✦ **From:** If you have more than one e-mail account in your Identity, this is a pop-up menu that lets you choose which e-mail account and account settings (which mail server, for example) will be used to send your message.

✦ **Directory:** If you've added an LDAP directory to your Identity's accounts, the results of the LDAP search will be available for you to choose from when you begin typing a name in an address field. If you didn't configure an LDAP account, Directory doesn't display. (For more on LDAP, check out Chapter 1 of this minibook.)

✦ **Cc (carbon copy):** Every contact added to the CC block will receive your message, and each recipient can see the name and address of all the To and CC recipients.

✦ **Bcc (blind carbon copy):** Every contact added to the BCC block will receive your message. Recipients added to BCC will not be visible to other recipients. The default is to not display this field. Click the Options tab of the Ribbon and then click the Bcc button to change this setting.

✦ **Check Names:** Makes sure the e-mail addresses are valid before sending.

Figure 3-17 shows the Options tab of the Ribbon in the New Message window. This tab has many useful tools:

Figure 3-17:
Choosing
more
Options.

Creating e-mail in Microsoft Word

Some people are most comfortable using Microsoft Word when they write. You can use Word to create your e-mail messages so that you can use the tools and interface you're familiar with, or perhaps you have templates that you want to use. We can think of three ways to send mail from Microsoft Word. In all cases, Outlook actually sends the mail.

If you choose to share your Word document in HTML format, your composed message appears in the body of the recipient's e-mail message. We recommend that you compose your HTML e-mail messages by using Web Layout view;

in Word, choose View⇨Web Layout from the menu bar. When you're ready to send your message, choose File⇨Share⇨E-Mail as HTML from the menu bar.

If you prefer to use all of Word's features, use any view in Word and then you choose File⇨Share⇨E-Mail as Attachment. If the document you are working on was opened from a SkyDrive or SharePoint location, you can choose File⇨Share⇨E-Mail as Link, which opens a new e-mail message containing a link to your document.

✦ **Format:** Choose HTML to send messages with text formatting and embedded pictures, movies, and sounds. It is the default for Outlook. Choose Plain Text if you anticipate sending messages to recipients with bandwidth limitations. Formatting and embedding are not supported in Plain Text messages.

✦ **Background Color:** You can choose a color for the background of an HTML format message.

✦ **Background Picture:** You can choose a picture for the background of a message in HTML format.

✦ **Permissions:** Displays the Permissions dialog for Exchange account users only. Refer to Figure 3-12.

✦ **Security:** See the section "Understanding Digital Certificates," later in this chapter.

✦ **Scrapbook:** Displays the Scrapbook. See Book I, Chapter 3.

✦ **Reference:** Displays the Reference Tools palette. See Book I, Chapter 3.

✦ **Spelling:** Run spell check on your message.

✦ **Show/Hide button:** Toggle whether or not the Ribbon is visible.

Searching and Smart Folders

There's a secret Ribbon in Outlook. When you're using Mail view and click in the Search field, the Search Ribbon shown in Figure 3-18 wakes up. Enter search criteria and then press Return or Enter to display the search results. Click the Advanced button to turn on additional search filters, or click combinations of buttons on the Search tab of the Ribbon to activate filters and limit or expand your search. In the advanced search, use the pop-up menus to choose criteria to apply to your search. The plus (+) and minus (–) buttons add and remove criteria in the search filter.

If you want to save your search to re-use it later, click the Save button on the Search tab of the Ribbon. A new item is added to the Smart Folders categories of the Folders list. Before clicking elsewhere, type a name for your saved search. You can't rename a Smart Folder. To delete or edit a Smart Folder, right-click its name to display a contextual menu.

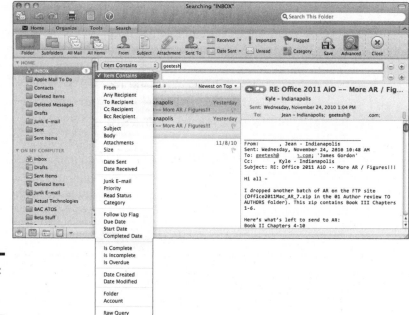

Figure 3-18:
Searching
mail.

Understanding Digital Certificates

Perhaps you've seen a signature (scanned from a letter or other paper) inserted into a Microsoft Word document or an Outlook e-mail message. Or maybe you're accustomed to putting scanned signatures into documents as an indication of authenticity or for any other reason. This is a Bad Idea — it's incredibly easy for anyone to reuse that signature in a forged document. All it takes to get that signature is to right-click and choose Save as Picture, capture a screen shot, or take a picture with a camera. You'd have a very hard time refuting the authenticity of a forged document with your signature on it if you relied on this method for authentication. Please don't use pictures of signatures. Period.

Can you find a free or inexpensive easy way to digitally sign documents? The answer is, "No!" You can use a cumbersome, somewhat expensive way — by purchasing real digital signing

certificates from certificate-issuing authorities, such as Thawte and VeriSign. Plan to spend about $20 each year for each computer you use. It works best when both the sender and receiver have his or her own certificate. A digital signing certificate is the only way to be assured of a sender's authenticity and generate a solid accountability record that he or she actually sent documents.

Using digital certificates takes training and set up time. They usually cost too much for casual communication, but you may find them worth the inconvenience for legal, FBI, CIA, NSA, military, security, and law enforcement communications, as well as communications in which you need privacy, such as with HIPAA–compliant medical communications. Outlook fully supports real digital certificates, but the mechanics of using them aren't within the scope of this book.

Clobbering Junk Mail

We hate junk mail. So does Outlook. Outlook fights junk mail in two ways. First, there's a built-in set of rules and filters that's updated periodically when you update Office. Choose Tools⇨Junk E-Mail Protection⇨Level from the menu bar to set how aggressive you want Outlook to be with your Junk Mail. Choose Tools⇨Accounts⇨Advanced⇨Folders from the menu bar to choose where Outlook should put your junk mail. The second way is to use the Block Sender feature. You add e-mail addresses to the Tools⇨Junk E-Mail Protection⇨Blocked Senders list. Our list has more than 200 and is growing. Adding to this list helps Outlook learn who the bad guys are.

Automating with Rules

Among the most powerful features of Outlook is the ability to automatically apply rules to incoming and outbound e-mail messages. A *rule* is an instruction you make that Outlook follows to automate a procedure. You can apply rules simply, but you have plenty of power to create complex sets of rules if you want them. To get started, choose Tools⇨Rules from the menu bar, or click the Rules button on any Ribbon tab with a Rules button. The Rules dialog opens, which is where Outlook stores the rules that you make. (See Figure 3-19.)

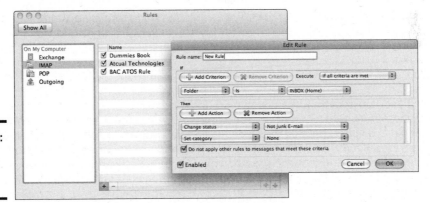

Figure 3-19:
Choosing
more
options.

To add a new rule, click the (+) plus sign in the Rules dialog to display the Edit Rules dialog, also shown in Figure 3-19. Give your new rule a name and set its parameters from the millions of possible combinations using the pop-up menus in the dialog. Click the OK button when you're done setting up your rule.

To remove a rule from the list, select its name and then click the minus (–) sign in the Rules dialog. To edit a rule, double-click its name in the list of rules. Rules are applied first at the top of each list and then in sequence while you go down the list. You can change the order in which the rules are applied by selecting a rule and then clicking the up- or down-arrow buttons located toward the right end of the Rules toolbar.

Keeping on Schedule

Outlook does tasks all by itself, such as performing send- and receive-mail operations, every so often. These operations are done on schedules that you can control. Choose Outlook⇨Preferences⇨E-Mail⇨Schedules from the menu bar to display the Schedules dialog, shown in Figure 3-20.

Figure 3-20:
Scheduling routine tasks.

To add a new schedule, click the (+) plus sign in the Schedules dialog to display the Edit Schedule dialog, also shown in Figure 3-20. Give your new schedule a name and set its parameters from the millions of possible combinations using pop-up menus in the dialog. Click the OK button when you're done setting up your schedule. To edit a schedule, double-click its name in the list of schedules. You can set a schedule to run an AppleScript, as shown in Figure 3-20, which lets you trigger virtually any automation process on a schedule.

To remove a schedule from the list, select its name, and then click the minus (–) sign in the Schedules dialog.

Chapter 4: Crafting Your Calendar

In This Chapter

✔ Peeking at the Calendar interface

✔ Adding holidays to your calendar

✔ Making appointments and meetings

✔ Responding to invitations

✔ Managing invitation responses

✔ Organizing and searching your calendar

✔ Printing your calendar

Clocks and calendars are amazingly intricate timekeepers that have a significant (if often overlooked) place in our daily lives. Fortunately, Outlook makes it easy for you to keep yourself on time and organized. Even if you travel, Outlook can keep your appointments straight while you go from one time zone to another. Do you live in a Daylight Saving Time area? No problem; let Outlook take care of those small details!

Using Outlook Calendar is a quick, easy, and logical endeavor. You can sync your Outlook Calendar with your mobile devices. In fact, after you incorporate using your Outlook Calendar into your everyday activities, you may wonder how you got along without it.

Taking a Look at the Calendar Interface

When you choose View⇨Go To⇨Calendar from the menu bar, click the Calendar button, or press ⌘-2, your calendar displays, ready for you to start filling it. You can view your calendar by Day, Week, Work-Week, and Month. We clicked the Month button on the Home tab of the Ribbon to see Month view, as shown in Figure 4-1.

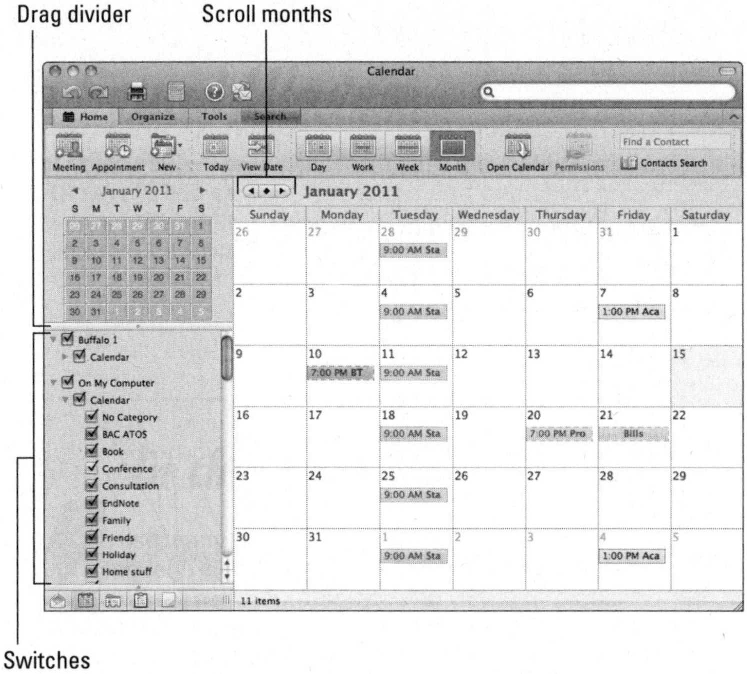

Drag divider   Scroll months

Figure 4-1:
Getting an
overview
of Outlook
Calendar.

Switches

When working with calendar views, you can modify the way the interface looks considerably by choosing View⇨List from the menu bar or by pressing ⌘-Control-0 (zero) to toggle List view on or off.

Dragging the dividing line right and left between the calendar inset and the calendar view area resizes the inset calendar width. Dragging the divider beneath the inset calendar resizes the inset calendar height.

When working in your calendar, select and deselect the check boxes in the area we labeled *Switches* in Figure 4-1. These switches let you choose precisely which items to display in the calendar. If you have more than one account in your Identity, you must put a check mark by each account's calendar in the list to display its calendar's information. You choose which categories to display in the calendar by turning individual categories on and off. If Outlook seems to have forgotten your calendar events, look at the switches — you may have to reselect them.

Going on Holiday

Outlook can put common holidays into your calendar. Outlook's Import Wizard-like series of dialogs comes to your aid. Follow these steps:

1. **Choose File⇨Import from the menu bar.**

   Step 1 of the Import Wizard opens.

2. **Select the Holidays option.**

3. **Click the right arrow at the bottom of the dialog to advance to the next step.**

4. **Choose one or more countries or religions to add their holidays to the Calendar.**

5. **Click the right arrow to continue.**

6. **Click OK on the confirmation message and click the Finish button to exit the wizard.**

After completing these steps, each holiday has a calendar event. You can open a calendar event to set reminders and change other settings.

One of the benefits of having friends and relatives in different countries is that you get to celebrate more holidays!

Adding Meetings and Appointments

Outlook has two kinds of events that you can add to your calendar:

✦ **Appointment:** An event that doesn't involve other people or scheduling of rooms and/or resources.

✦ **Meeting:** An event that involves more than one person. Scheduling a room or other resource may be involved.

Say that you have an event that you need to add to your calendar. Take the following steps to add this event:

1. **(Optional) Click the View Date button on the Home tab of the Ribbon.**

If your event is going to occur in a future month, click the scroll buttons to quickly advance to the month and then choose a date from the pop-up calendar, shown in Figure 4-2. Alternatively, you can use the calendar inset under the Ribbon, also shown in Figure 4-2.

Figure 4-2:
Picking an
event date.

2. **Click Meeting or Appointment on the Home tab.**

• *Click Meeting* on the Home tab of the Ribbon to open a new Meeting event, as shown in Figure 4-3.

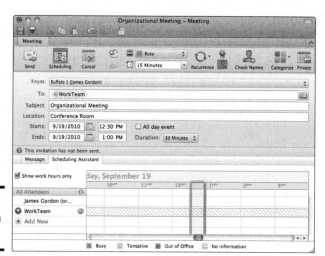

Figure 4-3:
Setting up a
meeting.

- *Click Appointment* on the Home tab of the Ribbon or press ⌘-N to open a new Appointment event, shown in Figure 4-4.

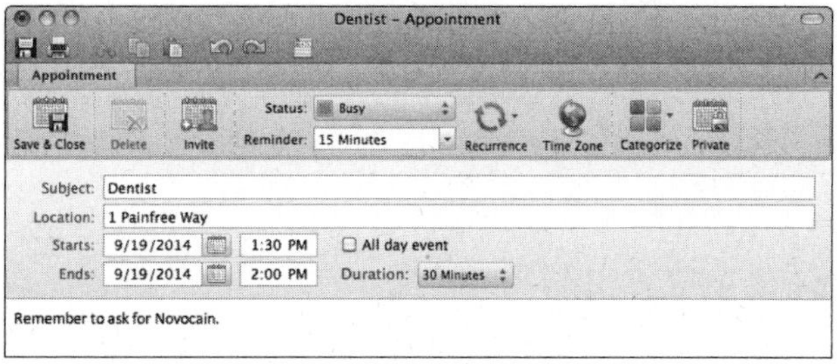

Figure 4-4: Setting up an appointment.

3. **Fill in the Subject, Location, Starts, and Ends fields. Select a length from the Duration pop-up menu. (Optional: Select the All Day Event check box for events that run the entire day.)**

4. **(Optional) When working with Meetings and Appointments, use these additional options as needed:**

   - *From:* If you have more than one account in your Identity, this is a pop-up menu that lets you choose which account to use.

   - *Message area:* Type a message to accompany the invitation.

   - *Private:* Flags the meeting invitation as private. When sharing in Exchange, other users can see the date and time but nothing more about an event made private.

   - *Time Zone:* Display the Time Zone tool. Choose a time zone for the meeting location from the pop-up menu.

   - *Categorize:* Assign a Category to the event.

   - *Recurrence:* Choose from a pop-up menu or design your own custom recurrence schedule by choosing Custom.

   - *Scheduling Assistant:* For Exchange users only, you can click the plus (+) sign to add invitees to the list and see invitee free/busy times to help you choose a time that has the fewest or least important conflicts. When using Scheduling Assistant, you will probably want to resize the window larger.

5. **Click Send (for a meeting) or Save & Close (for an appointment).**

   The appointment or meeting dialog will close, and invitees will receive an e-mail message in standard calendar format.

To edit your event, reopen the event's window by double-clicking the event in the Outlook Calendar.

When you select an event in your Outlook Calendar, the Ribbon displays a purple tab called Meeting or Appointment. Click the purple tab to display on the Ribbon options that are appropriate for working with your event.

Receiving Invitations

When you receive an invitation in Outlook Mail, you open it the same way that you open any other e-mail message. Double-click an invitation to open it in its own window, as shown in Figure 4-5. Good manners suggest that you respond to invitations promptly. You can respond with the click of a button to accept, tentatively accept, or decline invitations, as shown in Figure 4-5. When you accept or tentatively accept an invitation, it's added to your calendar. Declining does not add the event to your calendar. You have these invitation response options for accept, tentatively accept, or decline:

+ **Respond with Comments:** Opens a new window where you can include a message along with your decision notification.

+ **Respond without Comments:** Lets the inviting party know your choice without further ado.

+ **Do Not Send a Response:** If you accept or tentatively accept, this option adds the event to your calendar but does not let the inviting party know you accepted their invitation.

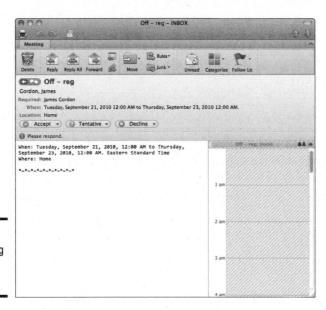

Figure 4-5:
Responding
to an
invitation.

Outlook can process calendar requests from any standards-based calendar application, including Microsoft Entourage, Microsoft Exchange, open-source Sunbird, Oracle, and Google Calendar.

Receiving Acceptances and Rejections

When the event organizer receives an acceptance or rejection notice, Outlook places a notification in the Scheduling Assistant of the invitee's response. In this example, we accepted the invitation. As shown in Figure 4-6, the Scheduling Assistant displays a list of the attendees and their responses.

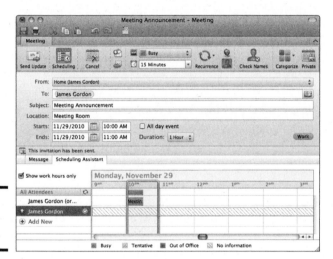

Figure 4-6:
Reviewing responses.

The Scheduling Assistant has some extra control, so if you're the event organizer, you can use this control in case someone changes their mind — and tells you without using an Accept or Reject Calendar message. People often accept an invitation over the phone, or even in the office corridor! You need to input that acceptance into Outlook. Just click the response indicator (see Figure 4-6) from an attendee (even if they haven't yet responded), and manually change the response. The response indicators are actually buttons, even though they may not look like buttons. (See Figure 4-7.)

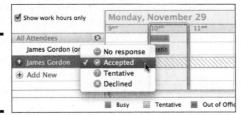

Figure 4-7:
Changing
a response
manually.

Organizing Your Calendars

While working in Calendar view, you can click the Organize tab of the Ribbon to display the options shown in Figure 4-8. Here are some tips for working with tools we have not already described:

Figure 4-8:
The
Calendar's
Organize
tab.

✦ **New Calendar:** You can have as many independent calendars as you want in Outlook. To add a new calendar, just click the New Calendar button. The trick: Know that you have to look in the left pane of the calendar window and click its check box to activate it, as shown in Figure 4-9. To give your calendar a name, click the words *Untitled Folder* and then type a new name. To delete a calendar, right-click its name and choose Delete from the pop-up menu.

✦ **Scale:** In any view except Month, drag the Scale slider left and right to increase or decrease the space between the lines in the view. This is a fun control to use.

✦ **Open Calendar:** For Exchange users, click Open Calendar to display the Open Other User's Folder dialog, shown in Figure 4-10. Type the name of an Exchange user or click Browse to find the user, and then choose an option from the Type pop-up menu: Calendar, Address Book, or Inbox to open the other user's shared folder.

Figure 4-9:
Adding a
calendar.

Figure 4-10:
Browsing
Exchange
Calendars.

The Tools tab of the Ribbon has tools that were already covered in Chapters 2 and 3 of this minibook.

Searching and Using Smart Folders

After you have several years' worth of Calendar events under your belt, finding specific events might be a challenge. Your events likely accumulate, and at times, you might want to quickly search through all your Calendar events to find some particular piece of information.

When Outlook is in Calendar view and you click in the Search field, the Search Ribbon shown in Figure 4-11 displays. Enter search criteria and then press Return or Enter to display the search results. Click the Advanced button to turn on additional search filters, or click combinations of buttons on the Search tab of the Ribbon to activate filters and limit or expand your search. In the advanced search, use the pop-up menus to choose criteria to apply to your search. The plus (+) and minus (–) buttons add and remove criteria in the search filter.

If you want to save your search to re-use it later, click the Save button on the Search tab of the Ribbon. A new item is added to the Smart Folders categories of the Folders list. Before clicking elsewhere, type a name for your saved search. You can't rename a Smart Folder. To delete or edit a Smart Folder, right-click its name to display a contextual menu.

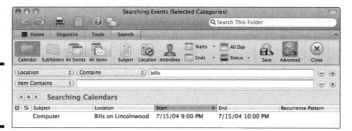

Figure 4-11:
Searching
calendars.

You can get an Exchange account pretty easily. In fact, you or your organization can obtain hosted online Exchange services. A wide variety of hosted options are available at www.microsoft.com/online/exchange-hosted-services.aspx.

Free Exchange for education

For education institutions, at the time of this writing, Microsoft has expanded its offering of no-charge exchange hosting via its Live@ edu program in a head-to-head challenge to Google Gmail. If you're an administrator in K–12 or higher education, compare the features of these and other in-the-cloud hosted services before switching from your current setup. Consider whether Microsoft and/or Google reserve the right to scan user content within their servers for the purpose of targeting ads either directly or indirectly, such as through DoubleClick or other partners. How secure is the cloud against private and government spying and prying, both foreign and domestic? You have a lot to consider. Here's the Web address for Live@edu: http://my.liveatedu.com.

Printing Your Calendar

When you choose a Print option, such as choosing File➪Print or clicking the Print button on the Standard toolbar, while in Calendar view, you're presented with special calendar options in the Print dialog as shown in Figure 4-12.

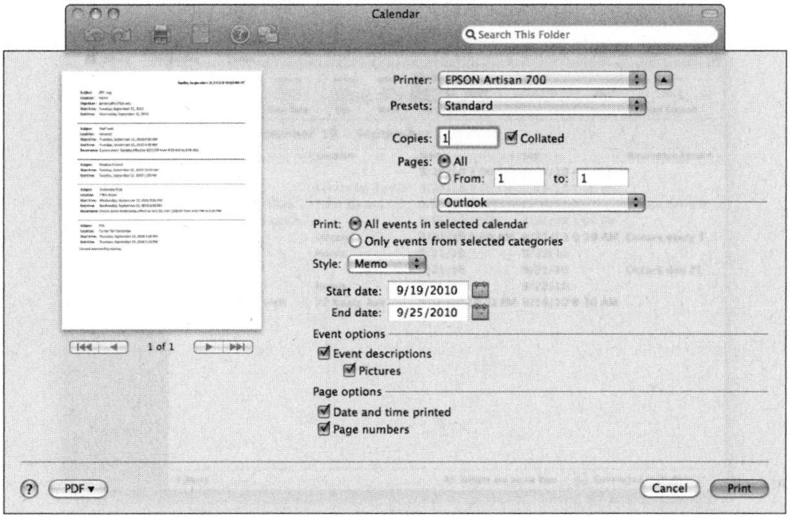

Figure 4-12:
Customizing
calendar
printouts.

Chapter 5: Keeping Up with Contacts

In This Chapter

✔ **Looking over the contacts**

✔ **Creating the Me contact**

✔ **Printing and managing contacts**

✔ **Searching contacts**

✔ **Making a group of contacts**

✔ **Exporting and deleting contacts**

*O*utlook Contacts is the place for personal information about people and businesses, especially the kind of private information about contacts that doesn't appear on their Facebook, LinkedIn, or MySpace pages, such as phone numbers and what you gave them on their birthday. You can search for contacts in corporate directories as well as within your own Contacts database. You can print your contacts as personal directories, and you can choose Outlook Contacts as the source for mail merge in Microsoft Word.

Perusing the Contacts Interface

To get to your Outlook Contacts, just click the Contacts button at the lower left of the Outlook window, choose View➪Go To➪Contacts from the menu bar, or press ⌘-3 while you're using any Outlook view. The Contacts layout is shown in Figure 5-1, showing the Home tab of the Ribbon, with the View option to show contact information beneath the list of contacts.

Figure 5-1:
Viewing
and editing
contacts.

Meeting Yourself

The first time you open Contacts, only one contact appears in your contacts list. As it turns out, that particular contact is very special. Only one contact can be what Outlook calls the Me contact. You can think of the Me contact as the owner of all the other contacts and groups of contacts.

Filling in the information for the Me contact is a great way to get started building your contact list. The Me contact is lightly shaded in the Contacts list. You can display the Me contact at any time by choosing Me on the Organize tab of the Contacts Ribbon.

The Me contact is edited as you would any other contact. Your Me contact opens on an almost empty General tab. You need to go through each of the information tabs and fill in the blanks with your own information. (You can skip the Certificates tab until someone sends you a digitally signed message. We don't cover it because it's outside the scope of this book.)

After you fill in your own contact information for the Me contact, start adding contacts. Here are the two most common ways:

✦ **Add a contact from a mail message.** Select a mail message in Outlook Mail and choose Message⇨Sender⇨Add to Contacts from the menu bar.

✦ **Add a contact while using the Contacts.** Click the Contact or click New⇨Contact on the Home tab of the Ribbon in Contacts.

A dialog appears with the General tab selected. Fill in the name, phone number(s), e-mail address(es), home address, and other personal details about the contact, as shown in Figure 5-2. The title of the dialog will be the name of your contact. If you have more information about a contact, click the Organization, Details, Notes, or Certificates tabs to add those details.

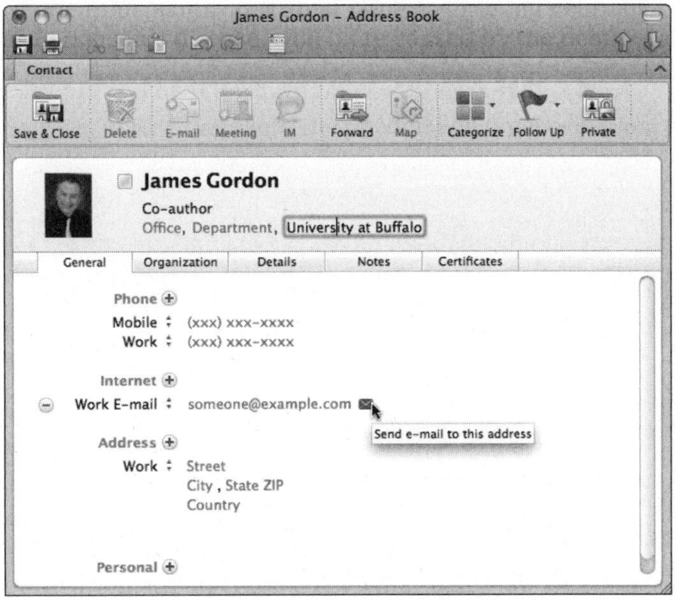

Figure 5-2:
Editing a
contact.

If you have Microsoft Messenger or Microsoft Communicator service running, when a contact is available for chat, the IM (Instant Message) button on the Home tab of the Ribbon becomes available.

Right-click a contact in the contacts list to open a contextual menu that contains many useful options, such as Categorize or Forward as vCard.

If you need directions to a contact's house or office, select the contact in a contact list and then click the Map button on the Home tab of the Ribbon to display a map of the address listed for the contact. (Of course, you need to have the address completely filled in for your contact for this to work!) Typically the map opens in Bing Maps. The Map button also appears on the Contact tab of the Ribbon when a contact is open in its own window.

Printing Contacts

When you click the Print button on the Standard toolbar or choose File⇨Print from the menu bar, you display the full Print dialog with special Print options available, as shown in Figure 5-3.

In the Print dialog, choose which contacts to print and then choose either Address Book or Phone Book style. The large number of custom styles that were supported by Entourage are not supported in Outlook.

Choose Contact and Options and Page Options by selecting and deselecting check boxes. Choose a name format and an alphabetizing order from the pop-up menus. As in every Print dialog, click the Print button to use your printer, or PDF to use one of the PDF options.

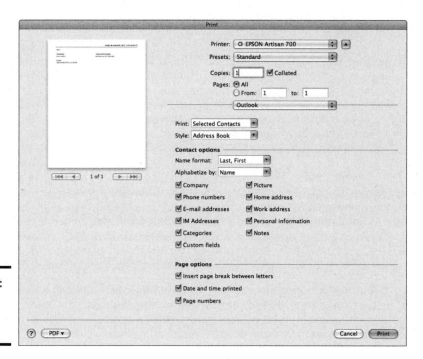

Figure 5-3:
Printing
your
contacts.

Making Contacts Folders

Outlook supports multiple contacts lists. You turn individual folders on and off in the folder list (Microsoft calls this the Navigation pane) at the left side of the Contacts window. Right-click in the pane to add folders, or use the New Folder buttons on the Organize tab of the Ribbon. Although this feature is in Outlook, we think assigning categories to individual contacts and assigning contacts to groups is a better way to organize your contacts.

You can turn the display of Categories on and off by selecting their check boxes. To delete a folder, right-click it and choose Delete from the contextual menu.

Finding Contacts

You can search your contacts list in a variety of ways:

✦ **Folder Search:** Select a folder in the folder list on the left and then enter a keyword in the Search This Folder field. (Refer to Figure 5-1.) This displays the Search tab of the Ribbon, shown in Figure 5-4. Click the Advanced button or search criteria buttons to refine your search. To save this search as a Smart Folder, click the Save button found on the Search tab of the Ribbon.

Figure 5-4:
Searching
a Contact
folder.

✦ **Contacts Search:** Depending how wide your window is, click the Find Contact button or the Contacts Search button in the Home tab of the Ribbon. (Refer to Figure 5-1.) The Contacts Search dialog appears, as shown in Figure 5-5.

TIP

If you've configured an LDAP account (see Chapter 1 of this minibook), you find it listed in the right side pop-up menu, as shown in Figure 5-5.

Figure 5-5:
Searching a Contact folder.

Grouping Contacts

You can easily create groups of contacts. If you create a group, you can send a message to the entire group by entering the name of the group when addressing an e-mail or invitation, instead of having to add people to an address block individually. Follow these steps to create a group of contacts:

1. **Open Outlook Contacts and click the Contact Group button on the Home tab of the Ribbon.**

The group dialog displays, as shown in Figure 5-6.

2. **Type a name for your group in the group name field.**

The default text is Untitled Group, which is displayed in edit mode ready for you to change by typing as long as you don't click away from the input field after Step 1. As with most other fields in Outlook, you can click the group's name field to change it at any time.

TIP

3. **(Optional) Select the Use Bcc to Hide Member Information check box.**

It's good etiquette to hide member information so that when you send messages to the group, private e-mail addresses are not displayed to everyone in the group, and so that private addresses can't be forwarded to non-group members.

Figure 5-6:
Making a
contact
group.

4. **Add members to your group in any of the following ways:**

   • *Double-click and type* names and e-mail addresses in the member list.

   • *Drag contacts* from Outlook contact lists, folders, and search results into the message list.

   • *Click the green Add button* on the Group tab of the Ribbon.

5. **When you're done adding contacts to your new group, click the Save & Close button on the Groups tab.**

Exporting Contacts

Choose File➪Export from the menu bar to open the Export dialog. In the Export dialog (see Figure 5-7), click the right-arrow button to open a Save dialog. Choose a location and then click the Save button to save your contacts as a delimited .txt file, which is a file that Excel, Outlook, and other mail applications can open.

Additionally, you can export individual contacts as vCard files by dragging them from any contacts list into Finder into an e-mail message. Click the Forward button on the Ribbon to attach a contact as a standard vCard to an e-mail message. A vCard is a file that is constructed to conform to w3c. org Web standards so that you can share contacts with standards complaint contact management software such as Outlook for Mac and Windows, Apple Mail, and Thunderbird.

Outlook for Mac doesn't support export to Outlook for Windows via `.pst` files. Outlook for Windows doesn't support import of Outlook for Mac (`.olm`) files. It's possible that soon, Outlook for Windows may be able to import the new Outlook file format already being used by Outlook for Mac. Meanwhile, you'll have to export text files as intermediaries between Outlook for Mac and Outlook for Windows.

Figure 5-7:
Exporting
contacts as
a .txt file.

Deleting a Contact

Sadly, at times, you must delete a contact. To delete an existing contact, simply select the contact in the contacts list and then click the Delete button on the toolbar or press the Delete key.

Chapter 6: Keeping Track of Your Day

In This Chapter

✔ Following up on things

✔ Remembering your tasks

✔ Managing reminders

✔ Moving through your day with My Day

Keeping your daily life in order involves the kind of organization that is designed into Outlook 2011. All the Office applications such as Word, Excel, and PowerPoint can key into the features we discuss in this chapter. Instead of wondering whether things are going as planned, you can find out exactly how your day is going. You can get things done your way because you prioritize them. In the end, you probably find your days more satisfying because you know you did your best to fulfill your own desires.

In this chapter, we deal with the tools that help you get through your day. We start with using the Reminders feature; then we discuss making tasks, to-do lists, and notes; and finally, we describe how all this great Office organization comes together in the My Day feature.

Flagging for Follow Up

Follow Up

You can set reminders in Word, Excel, Outlook, and PowerPoint. You use the Flag for Follow Up feature to set reminders about all kinds of different things. Follow Up is an option on the menus and on the Ribbon in these applications. Outlook is the application that takes care of reminding you, regardless of which application was used to set the reminder.

A *reminder* is a little window that appears on your screen when the event trigger you set for it is met, as shown in Figure 6-1. For example, if you have an 11:00 a.m. meeting and you want to be reminded 30 minutes ahead of time, you can set up 10:30 a.m. as the event trigger for sending you a reminder.

To set a reminder in Outlook, click the small triangle to the right of the Red flag on the Home tab and other Ribbon tabs in the Outlook Interface to display a variety of methods to add a reminder. You can also open a calendar event and set a reminder by clicking the Reminder pop-up menu in the event's Ribbon.

The Office Reminders dialog displays at the time you set. It has two buttons: Snooze and Dismiss, as shown in Figure 6-1. The message in the Office Reminders dialog changes while time passes. You don't have to have Outlook open when it's time for the reminder to appear.

Figure 6-1:
Viewing
and editing
contacts.

+ **Snooze:** If you want to hide the reminder for about ten minutes, click the Snooze button. When the reminder reappears, you can snooze again. In fact, you get unlimited snoozes! You're not obligated to use the default Snooze time length. If you hold your mouse button down on the Snooze button for a couple seconds, a pop-up menu of Snooze options appears.

+ **Dismiss:** When you click the Dismiss button, the reminder goes away permanently. If you have a lot of pending reminders and want to dismiss them all at the same time, click and hold the Dismiss button and choose Dismiss All from the pop-up menu that appears.

Touring Your Tasks

Whether it's for yourself or someone else, you can use Outlook to track tasks. To display the Task view, choose View➪Go to➪Tasks from the menu bar, press ⌘-4, or click the Tasks button in the lower-left corner of the Outlook window. The Tasks view, shown in Figure 6-2, includes list-filtering buttons on the Home tab of the Ribbon. If your interface doesn't look like what you see in Figure 6-2, remember that you need to first add tasks to see them.

Filtering, searching, the tasks list, and creating new custom views work the same way for tasks as they do for calendars, which we discuss in Chapter 5 of this minibook. Tasks can be sorted by clicking the name of a column displayed at the top of the list of Tasks in the Tasks pane. Click the column name a second time to reverse the sort order.

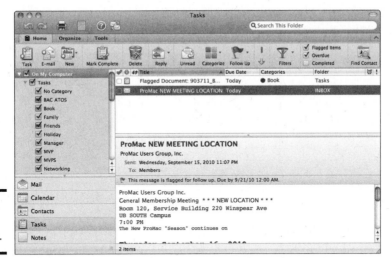

Figure 6-2:
Scoping
Tasks view.

The Tasks interface has a dual personality. In the folder list's On My Computer category, two options result in different sets of items appearing:

✦ **Tasks:** When you select Tasks, tasks that you created in Outlook by using the Tasks application appear.

✦ **To Do List:** You can have as many folders as you want in the Navigation pane. The To Do folder comes built-in.

When you're using the Tasks application, be sure to select both Tasks and To Do List in the Navigation pane so that you don't accidentally overlook something.

Making a new task

When you click the Task button on the toolbar within the Tasks application, you open a new, untitled Task window, as shown in Figure 6-3. You can also create new tasks from My Day, which we cover in the section "Making Your Day with My Day," later in this chapter.

To create a task in the Task window, type a name for your task. Click to the right of the field labels to display a pop-up calendar from which to choose dates for Due, Start, and Reminder. (See Figure 6-3.) Alternatively, click into the Due, Start, and Reminder fields and type or use the spinner controls. You can type, paste, or drag text into the empty space under the gray header.

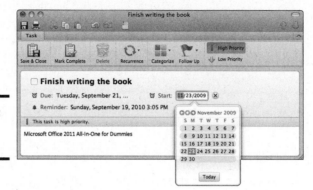

Figure 6-3:
Making a
new task.

Printing tasks

You might want to print out a list of tasks to take with you as you go about your day's activities. The Print dialog, like this dialog in other Outlook applications, offers special choices for printing tasks, as shown in Figure 6-4.

To print out a list of your tasks, while viewing Tasks choose File⇔Print, click the Print button on the Standard toolbar, or press ⌘-P to display the Print dialog shown in Figure 6-4. Choose which tasks to print from the Print pop-up menu and then choose either Menu or Table style from the Style pop-up menu. Select and deselect Task options and Page options as desired.

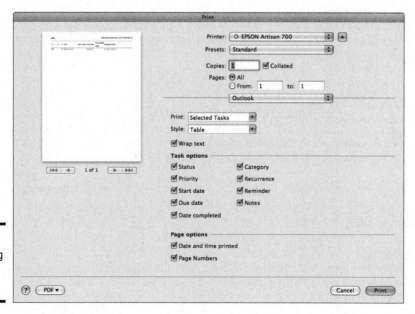

Figure 6-4:
Customizing
Task print
options.

Making a Note for Future Reference

When the thought pops into your head, "I should make a note of that," click the Notes button in the lower-left corner of the Outlook window, press ⌘-5, or choose View➪Go To➪Notes from the menu bar to display the Notes list, as shown in Figure 6-5. The Notes feature fills the need to make a quick note that gets added to your list of notes. Think of notes as a sticky notes equivalent within Outlook.

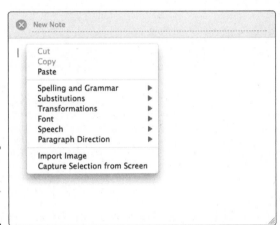

Figure 6-5:
Keeping track of your notes.

Notes view has a consistent look and feel with the other Outlook applications we discuss throughout this minibook. Filtering, searching, sorting the notes list, and creating new custom views work the same way for notes as they do for calendars, which we discuss in Chapter 5 of this minibook.

Making a note on the spot

When you click the Note button on the Home tab of the Ribbon in Notes view, or if you choose File➪New➪Note from the menu bar, a New Note window appears, as shown in Figure 6-6. The New Note window is pretty bare — it's meant to just hold a few lines of text. Start typing your note.

You can also add nontext content to your note by right-clicking the note and choosing Import Image to open a file-browsing dialog.

If you want to include a screen shot in your note, before you type anything in the note, right-click and choose Capture Selection from Screen. Drag diagonally over the screen to pop a screen capture directly into your note.

To save a note, click the X at the upper-left corner of the note and then click the Save button.

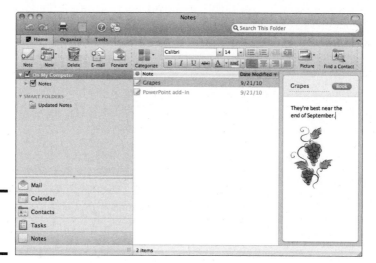

Printing notes

You might want to print a note or all of your notes. To print out a note or all your notes, while viewing Notes choose File⇨Print, click the Print button on the Standard toolbar, or press ⌘-P to display the Print dialog shown in Figure 6-7. Choose whether to print the selected note or all notes from the Print pop-up menu and then select or deselect Note options and Page options as desired.

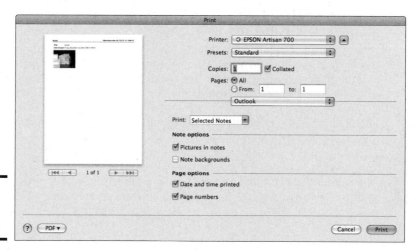

Making Your Day with My Day

My Day is a Mac-only feature of Office. The idea behind My Day is to give you a forward-looking window into the immediate future. The My Day window can float on top of your other application windows. You can also use My Day to create new tasks.

Looking at My Day

To view your My Day, click the Open My Day button on Outlook's Standard toolbar. The My Day interface, as shown in Figure 6-8, is unique. The top half of the interface shows upcoming events from your Outlook Calendar. While time passes during the day, the day's events automatically drop off from the top, and upcoming events appear at the bottom. The lower half of the My Day window shows tasks from your Outlook Tasks list. You can reorder your tasks by dragging them up and down in the tasks list while you go through your day.

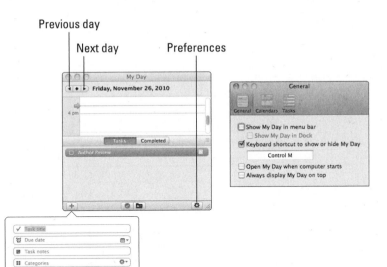

Figure 6-8:
Getting
through My
Day.

Creating a new task

If you want to create a new task, you can do it right from within My Day. Just click the New Task button to expand the hidden sheet, where you can type the name of your task. When you press the Return key, your new task appears in the Tasks portion of My Day, and a new task is added to your Outlook tasks list.

Setting My Day preferences

Click the My Day Preferences button to expose the preferences. You can pick and choose which Outlook content items you want included in your My Day display. Choose from items listed on each of these three buttons: General, Calendar, and Tasks.

Index

le & Macs

d For Dummies
‐0-470-58027-1

one For Dummies,
Edition
‐0-470-87870-5

cBook For Dummies, 3rd
tion
‐0-470-76918-8

c OS X Snow Leopard For
mmies
‐0-470-43543-4

siness

okkeeping For Dummies
‐0-7645-9848-7

Interviews
Dummies,
Edition
‐0-470-17748-8

sumes For Dummies,
Edition
‐0-470-08037-5

rting an
line Business
Dummies,
Edition
‐0-470-60210-2

ck Investing
Dummies,
Edition
‐0-470-40114-9

ccessful
ne Management
Dummies
‐0-470-29034-7

Computer Hardware

BlackBerry
For Dummies,
4th Edition
978-0-470-60700-8

Computers For Seniors
For Dummies,
2nd Edition
978-0-470-53483-0

PCs For Dummies,
Windows
7 Edition
978-0-470-46542-4

Laptops For Dummies,
4th Edition
978-0-470-57829-2

Cooking & Entertaining

Cooking Basics
For Dummies,
3rd Edition
978-0-7645-7206-7

Wine For Dummies,
4th Edition
978-0-470-04579-4

Diet & Nutrition

Dieting For Dummies,
2nd Edition
978-0-7645-4149-0

Nutrition For Dummies,
4th Edition
978-0-471-79868-2

Weight Training
For Dummies,
3rd Edition
978-0-471-76845-6

Digital Photography

Digital SLR Cameras &
Photography For Dummies,
3rd Edition
978-0-470-46606-3

Photoshop Elements 8
For Dummies
978-0-470-52967-6

Gardening

Gardening Basics
For Dummies
978-0-470-03749-2

Organic Gardening
For Dummies,
2nd Edition
978-0-470-43067-5

Green/Sustainable

Raising Chickens
For Dummies
978-0-470-46544-8

Green Cleaning
For Dummies
978-0-470-39106-8

Health

Diabetes For Dummies,
3rd Edition
978-0-470-27086-8

Food Allergies
For Dummies
978-0-470-09584-3

Living Gluten-Free
For Dummies,
2nd Edition
978-0-470-58589-4

Hobbies/General

Chess For Dummies,
2nd Edition
978-0-7645-8404-6

Drawing
Cartoons & Comics
For Dummies
978-0-470-42683-8

Knitting For Dummies,
2nd Edition
978-0-470-28747-7

Organizing
For Dummies
978-0-7645-5300-4

Su Doku For Dummies
978-0-470-01892-7

Home Improvement

Home Maintenance
For Dummies,
2nd Edition
978-0-470-43063-7

Home Theater
For Dummies,
3rd Edition
978-0-470-41189-6

Living the
Country Lifestyle
All-in-One
For Dummies
978-0-470-43061-3

Solar Power Your Home
For Dummies,
2nd Edition
978-0-470-59678-4

Internet

Blogging For Dummies,
3rd Edition
978-0-470-61996-4

eBay For Dummies,
6th Edition
978-0-470-49741-8

Facebook For Dummies,
3rd Edition
978-0-470-87804-0

Web Marketing
For Dummies,
2nd Edition
978-0-470-37181-7

WordPress
For Dummies,
3rd Edition
978-0-470-59274-8

Language & Foreign Language

French For Dummies
978-0-7645-5193-2

Italian Phrases
For Dummies
978-0-7645-7203-6

Spanish For Dummies,
2nd Edition
978-0-470-87855-2

Spanish
For Dummies,
Audio Set
978-0-470-09585-0

Math & Science

Algebra I
For Dummies,
2nd Edition
978-0-470-55964-2

Biology For Dummies,
2nd Edition
978-0-470-59875-7

Calculus For Dummies
978-0-7645-2498-1

Chemistry For Dummies
978-0-7645-5430-8

Microsoft Office

Excel 2010 For Dummies
978-0-470-48953-6

Office 2010 All-in-One
For Dummies
978-0-470-49748-7

Office 2010 For Dummies,
Book + DVD Bundle
978-0-470-62698-6

Word 2010 For Dummies
978-0-470-48772-3

Music

Guitar For Dummies,
2nd Edition
978-0-7645-9904-0

iPod & iTunes For
Dummies, 8th Edition
978-0-470-87871-2

Piano Exercises
For Dummies
978-0-470-38765-8

Parenting & Education

Parenting For Dummies,
2nd Edition
978-0-7645-5418-6

Type 1 Diabetes
For Dummies
978-0-470-17811-9

Pets

Cats For Dummies,
2nd Edition
978-0-7645-5275-5

Dog Training For Dummies,
3rd Edition
978-0-470-60029-0

Puppies For Dummies,
2nd Edition
978-0-470-03717-1

Religion & Inspiration

The Bible For Dummies
978-0-7645-5296-0

Catholicism For Dummies
978-0-7645-5391-2

Women in the Bible
For Dummies
978-0-7645-8475-6

Self-Help & Relationship

Anger Management
For Dummies
978-0-470-03715-7

Overcoming Anxiety
For Dummies,
2nd Edition
978-0-470-57441-6

Sports

Baseball
For Dummies,
3rd Edition
978-0-7645-7537-2

Basketball
For Dummies,
2nd Edition
978-0-7645-5248-9

Golf For Dummies,
3rd Edition
978-0-471-76871-5

Web Development

Web Design
All-in-One
For Dummies
978-0-470-41796-6

Web Sites
Do-It-Yourself
For Dummies,
2nd Edition
978-0-470-56520-9

Windows 7

Windows 7
For Dummies
978-0-470-49743-2

Windows 7
For Dummies,
Book + DVD Bundle
978-0-470-52398-8

Windows 7 All-in-One
For Dummies
978-0-470-48763-1

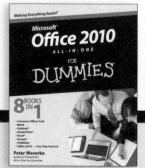

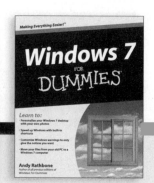

Available wherever books are sold. For more information or to order direct: U.S. customers visit www.dummies.com or call 1-877-762-2
U.K. customers visit www.wileyeurope.com or call (0) 1243 843291. Canadian customers visit www.wiley.ca or call 1-800-567-4797.

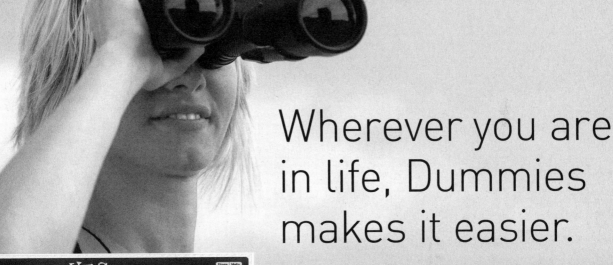

Dummies products make life easier!

DIY • Consumer Electronics • Crafts • Software • Cookware • Hobbies • Videos • Music • Games • and More!

For more information, go to **Dummies.com®** and search the store by category.

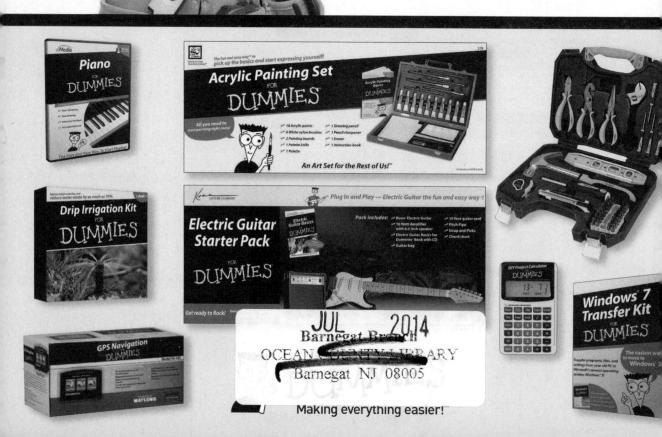

Making everything easier!™